Vol I

"REIMAGINING" GOD

TURNING THE LIGHT OFF TO LOOK FOR "TRUTH" IN THE CORNER OF A DARK ROUND ROOM

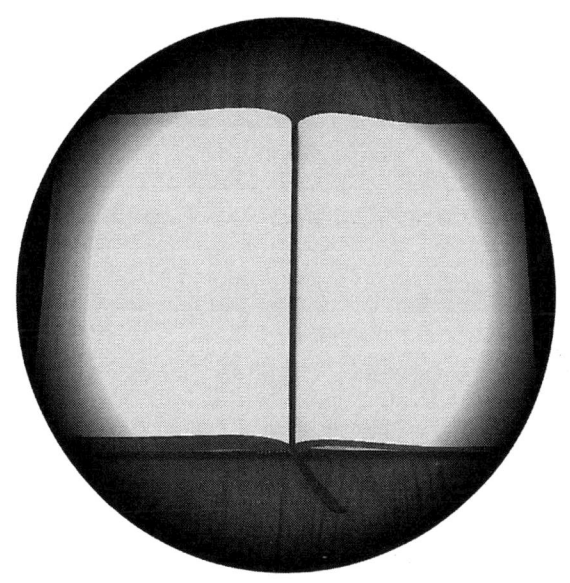

TAMARA HARTZELL

"Reimagining" God: Turning the Light off to Look for "Truth" in the Corner of a Dark Round Room, Volume 1

Copyright © 2013 by Tamara Hartzell

All rights reserved.

"Reimagining" God is also posted online (in its entirety, *Volume 1* and *Volume 2*) as a free e-book at http://www.inthenameofpurpose.org/ReimaginingGod.pdf. The e-book may be freely excerpted, copied, and distributed provided that it is done so without any alterations, with proper accreditation, and for non-commercial use only.

Cover design by the author.

All Scripture quotations are taken from the *Authorized King James Bible*.

This book was printed in the United States of America.

ISBN-13: 978-1483925653
ISBN-10: 148392565X

Additional copies of this book can be ordered from:
Amazon.com, Inc.
http://www.amazon.com/

ABOUT THE BOOK

In order to make this large book available in print as economically as possible for the reader, it became necessary to split it into *Volume 1* and *Volume 2*. Parts 1-5 comprise *Volume 1*, and Part 6 comprises *Volume 2*. Each *Volume* contains the Note to the Reader; its own Endnotes and Appendix; a common Bibliography that encompasses both *Volumes*; and a Table of Contents in which both *Volumes* are listed. The book's text itself has not been revised, so keep in mind that if *Volume 1* refers to something that will be addressed later in Part 6, this is addressed in what is now *Volume 2*. Likewise, if *Volume 2* states that something has already been addressed previously, this may be referring to what is now *Volume 1*.

The book is also still available in its entirety and unsplit as a free e-book at http://www.inthenameofpurpose.org/ReimaginingGod.pdf. The printed *Volume 1* and *Volume 2* are available directly from Amazon and its publishing company.

This book is dedicated to that great cloud of witnesses that has gone before us -- all who have held fast to the truth and faith of God, even unto death.

TABLE OF CONTENTS

VOLUME 1

About the Book 3
Note to the Reader 10

Part One: The Shift
1. "Thinking outside the box" 15
2. Resisting God being <u>God</u> 20
3. "Sick of God and God's religion" 23
4. *"Man in the chambers of his imagery"* 25
5. *"How great is that darkness!"* 28
6. A "real" and "true" false god that teaches "truth" 31
7. The fear-based agenda of the "doctrine police" 33
8. The faith that is set forth by God in His Word is the faith of God ... 38
9. Faith in the truth is true faith 44
10. Rock does not shift 47

Part Two: The Circle
11. The heart and circle of the "relationship" 55
12. The post-truth transformation of a Wordless "faith" 59
13. Faith that comes by *the Word of God* vs. Faith that comes by *relationship* ... 63
14. God's Word -- "a stumbling block in the way"! 68
15. "Transforming theology" -- "God in the very substance of creation" ... 74
16. The immanent "God" of Oneness, imagined and defined in *limitless* ways ... 79

Part Three: The Lie
17. "When we can contact our own inner God all truth will be revealed to us" ... 89
18. *"Ye shall not surely die"* 93
19. "The way of Jesus is a universal way ... not a set of beliefs about Jesus" ... 102
20. The "participatory divinity" of "the Jesus way" 109
21. "Chain of command? That sounds ghastly!" -- "We want you to join us in our circle of relationship" ... 116

Part Four: The Transformation
22. "What if we were to think connectness rather than correctness?" ... 127
23. "MRI theology is the only theology worth bothering with" ... 130
24. "Christians aren't people who follow Christianity" 138
25. "Ideas, phrases, metaphors, and customs of pagan cultures" are "'seeds' of the divine Word that become enfleshed in Christ"?! ... 146
26. "The word 'religion' concerns relationship" 150
27. "The world waits to hear your message for its salvation. That message is your life, lived." ... 156
28. For God so loved ... culture? 163
29. "There is no neat line of demarcation between the things of the world and the things of the Spirit" ... 167
30. "The Bible is *not* a blueprint for action, nor a book of answers" ... 175

Part Five: The Creation
31. Let there be "more light"? ... 185
32. The mission of creating "the Third Testament" as "part of *the 'I Am'* that *we* are" ... 189
33. "It is through creative intuition that postmoderns continue the work of *divine* creation" ... 196
34. "No person or living thing in the universe stands outside of the community of God" ... 205
35. "Relinquish the pride of mind which sees its way … to be *correct* and *true*" ... 210
36. "The *Gospel* According to" anything and everyone? ... 218
37. Dialoguing to the consensus/connectness/Oneness of today's new "truth" ... 224
38. "Transcending current beliefs is not an outright rejection of them; it is an 'adding to' them" ... 234
39. Breaking free from the soul "sort" in the "kingdom" that "transcends and includes all religions" ... 241
40. The significance of a "Third Testament" ... 255
41. An "*anti-Christian*" "double helix, Möbius-strip culture of both-and's" is "*the secret of life*"? ... 268
42. "The Oneness of Twoness that becomes Threeness" -- the *tertium quid*, or Laodicean third way ... 286
43. Connecting the dots of the immanent "God" and "Christ" ... 291
44. A "'*loyalty test*' to following Jesus" is "to open ourselves up and stop clinging to our precious preconceptions"? ... 308
45. "The day of theology is over" -- doing and being and creating "God" in a quantum dance of Oneness ... 318
46. An imagination that is "God" ... 331
47. Changing the "old" reality of the God of *judgment* into a new "reality" of a "God" of *Oneness* by simply *thinking* it "into being" ... 341
48. The dance of aligning minds with the new "design" ... 357
49. The "Parable of the Rock" and the "Big Bang" ... 368
50. The cosmic circle dance -- an "upward journey" of "evolving" back into "*God*" ... 383
51. Creating Oneness -- "part dance; part sorcery, part science" ... 406

Appendix
The Majesty on High, the Everlasting True God in the Light of His Word ... 445

Endnotes ... 451
Bibliography ... 485

VOLUME 2

About the Book
Note to the Reader

Part Six: The Fall
52. The "bootstrap philosophy"
53. For "the wages" of *believing* doctrine ("propositions") is "*death*"?

54. *Jesus* is not *"dead"* -- but those who want freedom from absolute truth can believe otherwise if they want to . . .
55. The emerging *"'complex way' of truth"* is to "turn the *dark* on"
56. A "Holistic Beautiful Sensitive Balanced" "*storyteller's* Bible" -- *The Voice*
57. To believe the truth of *the Word of God* is *not* to eat from "the tree of the knowledge of good and evil"!
58. "A new kind of human" is rising up out of the sea -- *"gathered together to make war against"* "The Word of God"
    - An "alternative to Armageddon"?
    - Gathering together in communities to eliminate the "selfish" salvation of individual believers in Jesus Christ of Nazareth
59. The new "light" of *"that old serpent, called the Devil, and Satan, which deceiveth the whole world"*
60. The holistic "healing" of the purpose-driven "Daniel Plan" -- *"We looked for ... health, and behold trouble!"*
61. A new kind of "risen" "Christ" -- *"after the working of Satan with all power and signs and lying wonders"*
62. *"MYSTERY, BABYLON THE GREAT, THE MOTHER OF HARLOTS"*
63. Replacing *is* with *ever becoming*
    - "*Open* systems have great advantages over *closed* systems"
    - "*Evolutionize* Your Life: *Heaven* Is Coming Home to Reality"
    - "*All*" images of "God" are "legitimate"
    - "How can we nudge each other to see the flames?"
64. Emergence from a cocoon of "light," a chrysalis of nonduality, as the Living Dead -- a new kind of "Second Coming" . . .
    - Left behind by "yesterday's" "limited God"
    - "Paradigm change ... a sudden shift of pattern, a spiral, and sometimes a cataclysm"
    - Falling for the "beauty" and "harmony" of a "cosmic" "Word"/"Logos"/"Christ"
    - "Nondual insights," "the beginning of a fuller, freer, happier life"
    - "Welcome" to "Presence" . . . "you are being prepared"
    - "Welcome on Board!"
    - "Magnetically" aligned to the Antichrist through the "heart center"
    - The serpent's Rod of Initiation, and *"At what time ye hear the sound ... and all kinds of music ... fall down and worship the image"*
65. Shifting from the God of *Israel* to "the god of this *world*" -- *"because they received not the love of the truth"*

Appendix
Talking to the Dead: Are Seducing Spirits the New Therapists?

Endnotes
Bibliography

"But this thing commanded I them, saying, Obey my voice, and I will be your God, and ye shall be my people: and walk ye in all the ways that I have commanded you, that it may be well unto you. But they hearkened not, nor inclined their ear, but walked in the counsels and in the imagination of their evil heart, and went backward, and not forward.... This is a nation that obeyeth not the voice of the LORD their God, nor receiveth correction: truth is perished, and is cut off from their mouth." (Jeremiah 7:23-24, 28)

"How do ye say, We are wise, and the law of the LORD is with us? Lo, certainly in vain made he it; the pen of the scribes is in vain. The wise men are ashamed, they are dismayed and taken: lo, they have rejected the word of the LORD; and what wisdom is in them?" (Jeremiah 8:8-9)

NOTE TO THE READER

This book began in February 2009 as a brief article on *The Shack*. Now, nearly four years later, this not-so-brief book is done and covers the larger picture. With a heavy heart, I present its in-depth look at the emerging new way of thinking that is quite thoroughly pervading today's Christianity. From Christianity to the New Age to science and everything in between, the new way of thinking is merging it all into a whole new faith of a whole new "God" of a whole new humanity and world. Everything is *changing*—for *a reason*.

Carefully consider this question: How important are the *words* in God's Word to you? It is *these words* that tell us *Who God is*. It is *these words* that tell us how to live and how to have God's salvation and eternal life. It is *these words* that are indispensable on every level. Yet it is *these words* that are purposely being dispensed with, not just in the world, but *in today's Christianity*. A *wordless* text can neither be believed nor obeyed. To fall away from the *words* of the Word of God is to fall away from *God*.

Despite the absurd belief that dispensing with the truth of God's inspired Word is a move toward God, this way of thinking simply could not be any more backward. This way of thinking has already moved today's Christianity "forward" in its faith to the doctrines of devils found in the channeled teachings of occultists and New Agers. And these same doctrines of devils that are *already* embraced as "God's truth" *in today's Christianity* comprise the emerging faith that *will bow down* to the devil's Antichrist and take his mark. Will you be one of them? I pray not. This day is rapidly emerging on the horizon and will be here much sooner than you think.

Many *in today's Christianity* are succumbing to the darkness of this new way of thinking. Many *in today's Christianity* are succumbing to the emerging faith of the Antichrist. Many *in today's Christianity* will bow down to the image of the beast and take his mark. That's right, *in today's Christianity*. Are you *certain* that *you* will not be one of them? How *scriptural* is your faith? Does your faith come from *inside* or *outside* the "box" of the Word of *God*?

The mission? Oneness. The path? Darkness. The door to it all? "*Yea, hath God said ...?*"

Yea, God <u>hath</u> said. And it is *these words* that are being dispensed with that are the only thing that stands between us and the hordes of hell that are on a soul-destroying mission. The subject presented in this book is as eternally grave and serious as it gets.

"Reimagining" God pulls from teachings that exemplify the merging and emerging whole—such as of Leonard Sweet, William Paul Young, Brian McLaren, Alice Bailey, Helena Blavatsky, Neale Donald Walsch, Barbara Marx Hubbard, Pierre Teilhard de Chardin, Fritjof Capra, and many others in Christianity, the New Age, and science—in order to address the anti-scriptural beliefs that frame the new kind of "foundation" that is already being laid *throughout today's Christianity*.

The new way of thinking is not at all *simple*, and purposely so. Yet this book has been written in a specific way to help bring about a deeper understanding. Part One, "The Shift," is short and essentially provides a foundational introduction to this new way of thinking that is addressed with more and more depth until the finale is reached. A finale in which God alone is exalted. In that day, Satan's emerging kingdom of his

Antichrist, which is ready to burst forth in all its darkness in global opposition to God's coming Kingdom of His Son, will go down in bitter defeat taking far too many souls with it *in today's Christianity.*

Some sections are easier to read than others, especially when the lies being addressed aren't as thoroughly convoluted as at other times. Repetition is purposely used, and this is for a variety of reasons. Either different parts of complex quotes are being addressed at different times; or the context is needed; or to give deeper understanding to other quotes or issues being addressed at the time; etc. Or plain and simply, sometimes repetition is needed just to make sure that the concepts are fully remembered and understood. This way, maybe the warnings will be more likely to be heeded. *This subject is indeed as eternally grave and serious as it gets.*

—Tamara Hartzell, December 9, 2012

"The night is far spent, the day is at hand: let us therefore cast off the works of darkness, and let us put on the armour of light." (Romans 13:12)

"And wisdom and knowledge shall be the stability of thy times, and strength of salvation: the fear of the LORD is his treasure." (Isaiah 33:6)

"Keep yourselves in the love of God, looking for the mercy of our Lord Jesus Christ unto eternal life. And of some have compassion, making a difference: And others save with fear, pulling them out of the fire; hating even the garment spotted by the flesh. Now unto him that is able to keep you from falling, and to present you faultless before the presence of his glory with exceeding joy, to the only wise God our Saviour, be glory and majesty, dominion and power, both now and ever. Amen." (Jude 1:21-25)

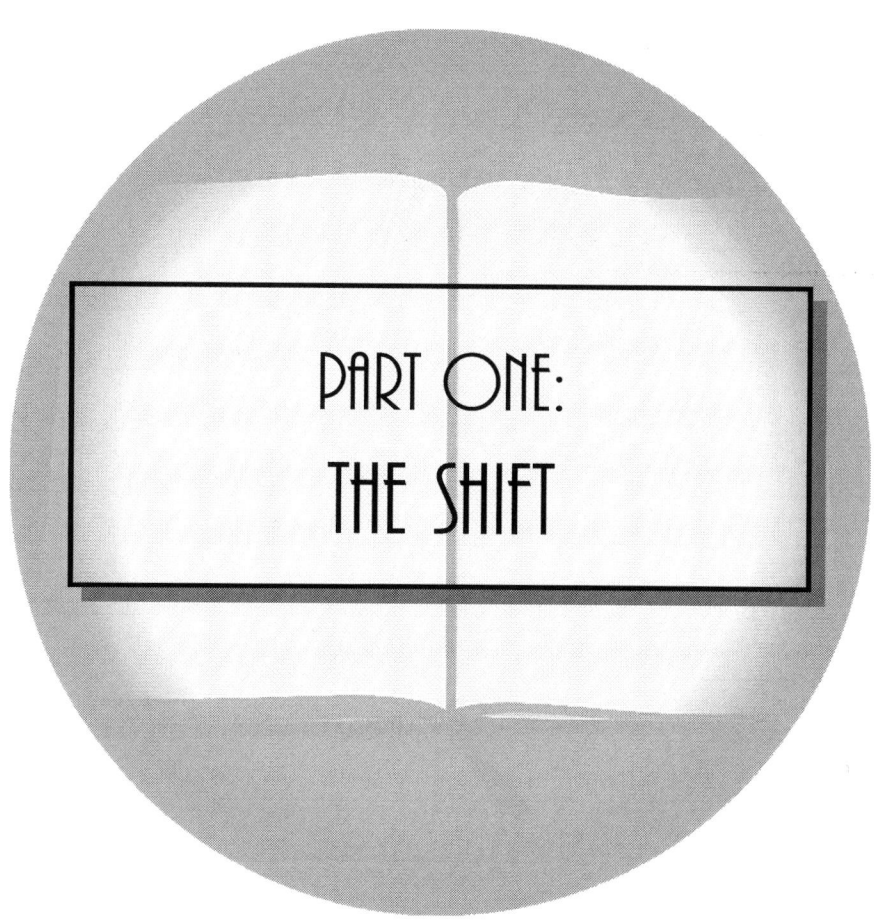

PART ONE:
THE SHIFT

1

"Thinking outside the box"

"Thy word is a lamp unto my feet, and a light unto my path." (Psalm 119:105)

"Then said Jesus to those Jews which believed on him, If ye continue in my word, then are ye my disciples indeed; and ye shall know the truth, and the truth shall make you free." (John 8:31-32)

"I charge thee therefore before God, and the Lord Jesus Christ, who shall judge the quick and the dead at his appearing and his kingdom; preach the word; be instant in season, out of season; reprove, rebuke, exhort with all longsuffering and doctrine. For the time will come when they will not endure sound doctrine; but after their own lusts shall they heap to themselves teachers, having itching ears; and they shall turn away their ears from the truth, and shall be turned unto fables." (2 Timothy 4:1-4)

"Take heed unto thyself, and unto the doctrine; continue in them: for in doing this thou shalt both save thyself, and them that hear thee." (1 Timothy 4:16)

The importance of the Word of God simply cannot be overstated. Without it we do not have the truth, faith, or salvation of God. And without the truth, faith, and salvation of God, we do not have God. Scripture is replete with teachings and warnings that make this perfectly clear. One example of many is 2 John 1:9:

"Whosoever transgresseth, and abideth not in the doctrine of Christ, hath not God. He that abideth in the doctrine of Christ, he hath both the Father and the Son."

Where do we get the *doctrine* of Christ in which we are to abide *to have God?*

From *the Word of God*.

> *"But continue thou in the things which thou hast learned and hast been assured of, knowing of whom thou hast learned them; and that from a child thou hast known the holy scriptures, which are able to make thee wise unto salvation through faith which is in Christ Jesus. All scripture is given by inspiration of God, and is profitable for doctrine, for reproof, for correction, for instruction in righteousness." (2 Timothy 3:14-16)*

> *"Being born again, not of corruptible seed, but of incorruptible, by the word of God, which liveth and abideth for ever. For all flesh is as grass, and all the glory of man as the flower of grass. The grass withereth, and the flower thereof falleth away: But the word of the Lord endureth for ever. And this is the word which by the gospel is preached unto you." (1 Peter 1:23-25)*

> *"So then faith cometh by hearing, and hearing by the word of God." (Romans 10:17)*

It is the faith of *God* that comes by *the Word of God*. Not only does the Word of God give us the truth and faith we are to *believe* in order to *have* God, but it also gives us the truth and faith we are to *obey* in order to *please* and *serve* God. And yet people in today's Christianity are no longer willing to accept this faith as is. Rather than simply *believe* and *obey*, people want the freedom to "rethink" and "reimagine" God and His Word into a fashion that they *are* willing to accept and, incredibly, even go so far as to claim that God's own Word of truth puts *God* in a "box." In other words, they want the truth and faith of God set "free" from the Word of God. Thus, they do not see the Word of God as *the truth* but as merely a "*story*" with "changeable" and "debatable" "*metaphor*" that can be interpreted and retold however anyone chooses. This then gives people their desired freedom to "think outside the box" where they can conveniently "reimagine" their *own* "story" of who they "rethink" God to be.

Naturally, whether or not these stories line up with God's Word is irrelevant to those who prefer to "think outside the box" of God's Word. In fact, if they did line up with the Word of God then it would defeat their purpose of "thinking *outside* the box." And since "rethinking" and "reimagining" God and His Word is what people today actually want, they are turning to fables for their faith and "truth." Fables are not the truth, and the truth is not a fable. This is why God's Word warns that people are turning *away from the truth* and unto fables. Nevertheless, more and more people are trying to turn *fables* into the *truth*—i.e., "reimaginings" into *reality*—and are dancing around in circles desperately trying to bring the two together as one in a harmonious relationship. This is, in essence, turning the light off to look for "truth" in the corner of a dark round room.

> *"The entrance of thy words giveth light; it giveth understanding unto the simple." (Psalm 119:130)*

> *"But if thine eye be evil, thy whole body shall be full of darkness. If therefore the light that is in thee be darkness, how great is that darkness!" (Matthew 6:23)*

> *"And this is the condemnation, that light is come into the world, and men loved darkness rather than light, because their deeds were evil. For every one that doeth evil hateth the light, neither cometh to the light, lest his deeds should be reproved.*

But he that doeth truth cometh to the light, that his deeds may be made manifest, that they are wrought in God." (John 3:19-21)

The light of God's Word is just too bright for today's light-intolerant eyes. More and more people are seeking relief outside the "box" and are intentionally turning away from the Word of God, away from the truth, away from the faith, trying to "find God" in the darkness. However, in the darkness people can no longer tell the difference between what is true and what is false, even when it is *obvious*. And as a result, they are blindly bearing with those who present them with "*another* Jesus," "*another* spirit," and "*another* gospel" that deceptively affirm their shift from light to darkness, and even lead them astray to *another* "God." But they don't see it that way. Since people imagine that *God's* Word of truth is just a *manmade* "box" from which God and His *truth* need to be set free, they see it as simply a matter of "finding God" wherever they choose to look. Sadly, this rapidly increasing deception is clearly seen in today's shifting Christianity.

"For if he that cometh preacheth another Jesus, whom we have not preached, or if ye receive another spirit, which ye have not received, or another gospel, which ye have not accepted, ye might well bear with him." (2 Corinthians 11:4)

*"I marvel that ye are so soon removed from him that called you into the grace of Christ unto another gospel: which is not another; but there be some that trouble you, and would pervert the gospel of Christ.... But I certify you, brethren, that the gospel which was preached of me **is not after man**. For I neither received it of man, neither was I taught it, but by the revelation of Jesus Christ." (Galatians 1:6-7, 11-12)*

*"For this cause also thank we God without ceasing, because, when ye received the word of God which ye heard of us, ye received it **not as the word of men**, but as it is in truth, the word of God, which effectually worketh also in you that believe." (1 Thessalonians 2:13)*

Since more and more people in today's shifting Christianity are rejecting the Word of God as the word of *man*, and even accepting the word of man as the word of *God*, one needn't go far to see the many counterfeits being sold to the eager buyers who see no need to beware. In fact, since people now imagine that outside the "box" of God's Word is the "genuine" and inside the "box" of God's Word is the "counterfeit" they will only see a need to beware of God's Word inside the "box." Thus, reviling those who believe the genuine is the genuine and the counterfeits are the counterfeit, they are heeding those who believe the counterfeits are the "genuine" and the genuine is the "counterfeit" because the counterfeits are the "genuine" they are *willing* to accept. But, naturally, those who prefer to "think outside the box" don't see it that way.

Many people are likewise choosing to see man's *fables* as the "*truth*" about God because man's fables are a "reimagined" "truth" they are *willing* to accept. Absurdly, those who seek to justify "reimagining" God and His Word even claim that Jesus taught parables in order to *teach truth* to the multitudes. This claim in itself "reimagines" God's Word in order to justify "reimagining" God's Word. Jesus Himself gave the reason for His parables, which is the opposite of man's imaginations in more ways than one. He spoke in parables to keep the truth away from those who did not have ears to hear and had already chosen to close their eyes and ears to the truth. Sadly, some things never change.

> **"And they shall turn away their ears from the truth**, and shall be turned unto fables." (2 Timothy 4:4)

> **"Who hath ears to hear, let him hear.** And the disciples came, and said unto him, Why speakest thou unto them in parables? He answered and said unto them, Because it is given unto you to know the mysteries of the kingdom of heaven, but to them it is not given. For whosoever hath, to him shall be given, and he shall have more abundance: but whosoever hath not, from him shall be taken away even that he hath. **Therefore speak I to them in parables: because they seeing see not; and hearing they hear not**, neither do they understand.... For this people's heart is waxed gross, and **their ears are dull of hearing, and their eyes they have closed; lest at any time they should see with their eyes, and hear with their ears**, and should understand with their heart, and should be converted, and I should heal them. But blessed are your eyes, for they see: and your ears, for they hear." (Matthew 13:9-13, 15-16)

If that isn't clear enough:

> "And he said, Unto you it is given to know the mysteries of the kingdom of God: but **to others in parables; that seeing they might not see, and hearing they might not understand.... Take heed therefore how ye hear**: for whosoever hath, to him shall be given; and whosoever hath not, from him shall be taken even **that which he seemeth to have**." (Luke 8:10, 18)

Those who have chosen to turn their ears away from the truth and unto fables only *seem* to have the truth. The truth is "Thus saith God," "Thus saith the Lord," and "It is written." This is the *settled* truth of God, which He has recorded for us in His Word. God's truth *is* what *is* and never changes despite man's never-ending vain attempts to "rethink" and "reimagine" God's Word for God. Truth tells us *what is* and *what is right or wrong*. Stories are the *opposite*. Stories are relativism and allow each person to decide *for themselves* what they want the meaning to be. This is exactly the freedom desired by those who are shifting from truth to fables. They want the *freedom* of *uncertainty* rather than the *what is* of *certainty*. Since having ears to hear the truth is necessary to be able to hear the certainty of its meaning, it was to His disciples and not to the multitudes that Jesus told the meaning of His parables:

> "If any man have ears to hear, let him hear. And he said unto them, Take heed what ye hear: with what measure ye mete, it shall be measured to you: and unto you that hear shall more be given.... And with many such parables spake he the word unto them, as they were able to hear it. **But without a parable spake he not unto them: and when they were alone, he expounded all things to his disciples**." (Mark 4:23-24, 33-34)

Because the Lord Jesus Christ is God, even His parables to the multitudes are "Thus saith God" and "Thus saith the Lord." And since even the meaning of His parables has been recorded in God's Word of truth, for us the meaning is *not relative* as many now think, but rather, "It is written." On the other hand, man's imaginative fables are nothing more than "thus imagines man." Contrary to the popular opinion of those blinded in the darkness, they are *not* the truth and *not* the Word of God, and the Lord Jesus Christ and His teachings are *not* a "style" to emulate. He is *the Lord*, Whom we are to *believe* and *obey.*

> *"I will worship toward thy holy temple, and praise thy name for thy lovingkindness and for thy truth: for thou hast magnified thy word above all thy name." (Psalm 138:2)*

> *"For this is good and acceptable in the sight of God our Saviour; Who will have all men to be saved, and to come unto the knowledge of the truth." (1 Timothy 2:3-4)*

> *"Then said Jesus to those Jews which believed on him, If ye continue in my word, then are ye my disciples indeed; and ye shall know the truth, and the truth shall make you free." (John 8:31-32)*

> *"It is the spirit that quickeneth; the flesh profiteth nothing: the words that I speak unto you, they are spirit, and they are life. But there are some of you that believe not. For Jesus knew from the beginning who they were that believed not, and who should betray him.... From that time many of his disciples went back, and walked no more with him. Then said Jesus unto the twelve, Will ye also go away? Then Simon Peter answered him, Lord, to whom shall we go? thou hast the words of eternal life." (John 6:63-64, 66-68)*

> *"Enter ye in at the strait gate: for wide is the gate, and broad is the way, that leadeth to destruction, and many there be which go in thereat: Because strait is the gate, and narrow is the way, which leadeth unto life, and few there be that find it." (Matthew 7:13-14)*

Too many people in today's shifting Christianity are seeking to set the truth of God free from the "box" of God's Word rather than seeking to be set free themselves by God's Word of truth. Instead of looking for "truth" in the corner of a dark round room they would be far better served looking for truth in a corner of the "box." But, sadly, those who are shifting from the light of the narrow way of absolute truth to the darkness of the broad way of relative "truth" are doing so on purpose, albeit blindly, along with their eyes closed and ears covered. They feel "boxed" in by the narrow way, and the broad way gives them the freedom outside the "box" to "rethink" and "reimagine" God and His narrow way into a broader "truth." With this freedom, people can have a relationship with God however they choose, right?

> *"He that rejecteth me, and receiveth not my words, hath one that judgeth him: the word that I have spoken, the same shall judge him in the last day." (John 12:48)*

2

Resisting God being _God_

Exalting man above God is not minor in any way, shape, or form. God makes that abundantly clear from Genesis to Revelation. Even so, this idolatry is at the heart of the transformation that is changing every aspect of today's shifting Christianity. More and more people are seeking to "rethink" and "reimagine" God, His Word, and Christianity into a fashion they are willing to accept, which conveniently conforms to man and his expectations.

- Man expects God to have a relationship with man on man's terms, yet man is not willing to have a relationship with God on God's terms.
- Man expects God to believe in man, yet man is not willing to believe in God.
- Man expects God to come to man in whatever fashion man will accept, yet man is not willing to come to God in whatever fashion God will accept.
- Man expects God to shift from light to darkness to have fellowship with man, yet man is not willing to shift from darkness to light to have fellowship with God.
- Man expects God to travel man's broad way to find man, yet man is not willing to travel God's narrow way to find God.
- Man expects God to be faithful to man no matter what, yet man is not willing to be faithful to God no matter what.
- Man expects God to allow man to angrily rebuke and stand in judgment of God, yet man is not willing to allow God to angrily rebuke and stand in judgment of man.
- Man expects God to submit to man, yet man is not willing to submit to God.
- Man expects God to have no rules or expectations for man, yet man has plenty of rules

and expectations for God.

So *who* is man's "God" in this *upside-down* "relationship"?

> *"O LORD, I know that the way of man is not in himself: it is not in man that walketh to direct his steps." (Jeremiah 10:23)*

> *"Seek ye the LORD while he may be found, call ye upon him while he is near: Let the wicked forsake his way, and the unrighteous man his thoughts: and let him return unto the LORD, and he will have mercy upon him; and to our God, for he will abundantly pardon. For my thoughts are not your thoughts, neither are your ways my ways, saith the LORD. For as the heavens are higher than the earth, so are my ways higher than your ways, and my thoughts than your thoughts." (Isaiah 55:6-9)*

> *"And God said unto Moses, I AM THAT I AM ..." (Exodus 3:14)*

The true God is Who He is. We either receive Him and believe in Him as He is, or we do not. It is that simple. Those who do not are choosing to turn their ears away from the truth and unto fables. They are "reimagining" God into *another* "God" that is not "I AM THAT I AM," but rather "I WILL BE WHATEVER MAN WANTS ME TO BE," or "I WILL BE WHATEVER MAN WILL ACCEPT," or "I WILL BE WHATEVER MAN'S IMAGINATION CREATES ME TO BE." This "reimagines" the *certainty* of truth into the *uncertainty* of man's imaginations.

People especially feel justified in "reimagining" God and the certainty of Who He is when bad things happen in life. Yes, there are very hard and difficult trials in life, and they bring much pain and sadness. Why they happen and how to find God's peace, comfort, and help in the midst of them is plainly answered throughout God's Word for those who are willing to accept it. Yet the growing number of those who are not willing are choosing to do the opposite of Proverbs 3:5-7. They angrily stand in judgment of God, condemning Him for not conforming to *man's* expectations and feelings, and then they "reimagine" God into a fashion they are willing to accept in order to find "healing." Neither standing in judgment of God nor "reimagining" the true God into a counterfeit is the path to "*healing*"! It may seemingly feel that way, but those who have deceived themselves into believing that pain or trials or even anything at all justifies exalting themselves above God will only be adding to their woes.

> *"Trust in the LORD with all thine heart; and lean not unto thine own understanding. In all thy ways acknowledge him, and he shall direct thy paths. Be not wise in thine own eyes: fear the LORD, and depart from evil." (Proverbs 3:5-7)*

> *"Woe unto them that are wise in their own eyes, and prudent in their own sight!" (Isaiah 5:21)*

> *"Moreover the LORD answered Job, and said, Shall he that contendeth with the Almighty instruct him? he that reproveth God, let him answer it. Then Job answered the LORD, and said, Behold, I am vile; what shall I answer thee? I will lay mine hand upon my mouth. Once have I spoken; but I will not answer: yea, twice; but I will proceed no further. Then answered the LORD unto Job out of the whirlwind, and said, Gird up thy loins now like a man: I will demand of thee, and declare thou unto me. Wilt thou also disannul my judgment? wilt thou condemn me, that thou mayest be righteous?" (Job 40:1-8)*

It is very clear throughout God's unchanging Word of truth that *every single one of man's expectations listed earlier are not scriptural*. This used to be common knowledge in Christianity. The fact that many people and even leaders of today's Christianity no longer know this and now believe and teach otherwise speaks to the pervasiveness of today's scriptural illiteracy. If people in today's Christianity spent more time reading God's Word than they do man's word, rather than the other way around, they would know this. But, sadly, for too many people that would defeat their purpose of turning *away* from the truth and unto fables to "rethink" and "reimagine" God and His Word.

Further compounding today's scriptural illiteracy is that man has been so busy repeatedly rewriting and rewriting God's Word for Him, believing that God needs man's help to say what man thinks God actually meant to say and should have said, that man no longer knows what God actually said. Shifting from light to darkness is occurring on many levels. But this shouldn't be surprising. After all, the multitudes didn't even have ears to hear truth from the Lord Jesus Christ Himself and corrupting the Word of God was already common in the apostle Paul's day so why should today be any different? People weren't willing to accept the certainty of God's Word back then, either.

> *"For we are not as many, which corrupt the word of God: but as of sincerity, but as of God, in the sight of God speak we in Christ." (2 Corinthians 2:17)*

> *"For we have not followed cunningly devised fables, when we made known unto you the power and coming of our Lord Jesus Christ, but were eyewitnesses of his majesty.... We have also a more sure word of prophecy; whereunto ye do well that ye take heed, as unto a light that shineth in a dark place, until the day dawn, and the day star arise in your hearts: Knowing this first, that no prophecy of the scripture is of any private interpretation. For the prophecy came not in old time by the will of man: but holy men of God spake as they were moved by the Holy Ghost." (2 Peter 1:16, 19-21)*

> *"For ever, O LORD, thy word is settled in heaven." (Psalm 119:89)*

Instead of "God said it; that settles it," now it's "God said it, man rewrote it, so now man believes it, but that only settles it until man decides to rewrite man's rewrite of what God wrote through holy men of God, through unholy men of man, until the next time." If this sounds absurd, it's because it is! Even so, instead of being recognized for the absurdity that it is, incredibly, this circle is actually the preferred source of "faith" for those who are turning away from the certainty of God's settled Word of truth.

This absurd never-ending circle of changes doesn't even faze those who remain undeterred in their unholy desire for freedom to "<u>re</u>think" and "<u>re</u>imagine" God and His Word. They claim to be of God and yet are not willing to accept the true God. They refuse to believe that God is Who He is and said what He meant and meant what He said. People are willing to live with man's expectations of God but not with God's expectations of man and are determined to find relief for their light intolerance. *Many* are resisting God being *God* and resisting the Word of God being *God's* Word of *truth* that is *settled forever by God Himself.*

3

"Sick of God and God's religion"

It is in the realm of make-believe where the freedom to "reimagine" God and His Word becomes "real." The true God does not cater to the whims of those who reject Who He is. But the Angel of light and his seducing spirits do. Those who want God to appear to them in whatever fashion they are willing to accept are also leaving themselves wide open to the wily devices of the Devil and his seducing spirits.

> *"And no marvel; for Satan himself is transformed into an angel of light." (2 Corinthians 11:14)*

> *"Be sober, be vigilant; because your adversary the devil, as a roaring lion, walketh about, seeking whom he may devour." (1 Peter 5:8)*

> *"Now the Spirit speaketh expressly, that in the latter times some shall depart from the faith, giving heed to seducing spirits, and doctrines of devils." (1 Timothy 4:1)*

In its shift from light to darkness, today's Christianity has become easy prey for the Devil and his seducing spirits. Yet this is not surprising since the darkness is their realm. It is the pinnacle of self-destruction to turn away from God's light to enter the Devil's darkness in order to "rethink" and "reimagine" God!

> *"Put on the whole armour of God, that ye may be able to stand against the wiles of the devil. For we wrestle not against flesh and blood, but against principalities, against powers, against the rulers of the darkness of this world, against spiritual wickedness in high places." (Ephesians 6:11-12)*

"... the god of this world hath blinded the minds of them which believe not ..." (2 Corinthians 4:4)

The whole armor of God consists of *truth, righteousness, the preparation of the gospel of peace, faith, salvation,* and *the Word of God* (see Ephesians 6:13-17). Yet these are the very things that people are *turning away from* as they seek relief for their light intolerance. Absurdly, seeking the freedom to "rethink" and "reimagine" it all, they are defenselessly entering the darkness to "rethink" the defense against the darkness.

Nevertheless, their lack of defense will be a nonissue for them. All they have to do is "reimagine" the darkness into a place of peace and safety. If they simply "reimagine" that evil and darkness do not exist, then, of course, neither do seducing spirits and rulers of darkness. So why would they need the armor of God? And if they simply "reimagine" that God conforms to man's expectations, does not require true faith in the Lord Jesus Christ to have a relationship with God, and does not punish sin, then why would they need the gospel of peace or salvation or any of the other pieces in God's armor? In the realm of make-believe, people are building up quite an effective defense for themselves *against the light*.

Sadly, these imaginations have become quite popular in today's shifting Christianity. A prime example of all this is William Paul Young's bestseller *The Shack* and its make-believe "God," which, incredibly, are actually believed to be *"Christian."* Conveniently, *The Shack*'s ever-popular "reimagined" "God" "reimagines" the darkness as a place of peace and safety for those who are resisting the true God and His Word. So of course the armor of God is irrelevant. In *The Shack*, "rules" are even "sarcastically" described as "all the things the Scriptures tell us we should do," and then it even goes on to specify "praying," "reading your Bible," "doing good things," and "avoiding evil."[1] Naturally, believing and obeying God's Word will be seen as irrelevant when people are simply entering the realm of make-believe to "reimagine" God and truth and faith into a fashion they are willing to accept. People are determined to set God "free" from the "box" of His Word so they can be set free from "rules" of faith and obedience.

Thus, people in today's shifting Christianity blindly imagine that *The Shack* is a *"Christian"* book even though open sarcasm, mockery, and contempt for the true God and His Holy Scriptures consistently abound throughout the book. They even blindly imagine that *The Shack*'s "reimagined" counterfeit "God" is the *"Christian"* "God" even though this counterfeit "God" clearly demonstrates a disdainful defiance of the true God and His Word. This counterfeit is clearly the "genuine" many are *willing* to accept. Despite the absurd claims to the contrary, *The Shack* is obviously *not* about seeking a loving relationship with the *true* God. And this clearly goes much, much deeper than dealing with grief and trials and why bad things happen. This is about the transformation which the idolatry of exalting man above God is bringing to those who are shifting from light to darkness.

The argument is made that *The Shack* was not written for those who don't like the book. They're right. This book was written for those who, like its author and its main character, are clearly "sick of God and God's religion."[2] Those who have a problem with God being *God* and with the Word of God being *God's* Word of *truth* will love *The Shack*'s "reimagined" "God" of untruth.

4

"Man in the chambers of his imagery"

The Shack has made so many convoluted anti-scriptural changes to the nature and character and teachings of who it claims the true "God" is that it should be obvious this is a false god. Even so, while these changes are obvious in the immutable light of God's Word of truth, they are *irrelevant* in the darkness. Those who are turning to the realm of make-believe for their faith can freely imagine "God" into whatever fashion they are willing to accept. After all, no one knows the difference in the dark, right?

God does.

> *"Then said he unto me, Son of man, hast thou seen what the ancients of the house of Israel do in the dark, every man in the chambers of his imagery? for they say, The LORD seeth us not; the LORD hath forsaken the earth." (Ezekiel 8:12)*

> *"Be not deceived; God is not mocked: for whatsoever a man soweth, that shall he also reap." (Galatians 6:7)*

For starters, it used to be obvious that a god who is a she is a goddess. Not any more. Now that darkness is the preferred "light," a god who is a she is "God the Father." At least this is the case according to those who imagine they merely "mix metaphors" in the chambers of their imagery. (By the way, this imagined goddess "Father" also claims to be "the Son of God.")

Yes, *The Shack*'s counterfeit "God" is a she. Or more precisely, two shes and a he. Easily deceiving those who are blindly trying to "find God" in the darkness, a black woman masquerades as "God the Father," and her two cohorts are an Asian woman who masquerades as "the Holy Spirit," and "*another* Jesus" who is *clearly* not the Lord Jesus Christ. Nevertheless, many in today's armor-shunning Christianity have been easily fooled into believing that these characters *really are "God."*[A]

Clearly, people today believe that man knows more about God than God does and see no need to beware of counterfeits, even counterfeits that openly defy the true God and His Word of truth. As a result, *The Shack*'s "reimagined" counterfeit "God" is being accepted by many as "*genuine.*" Heedlessly dismissing the warnings, today's shifting Christianity is blindly embracing this very false god of untruth that:

- is anti-God, anti-Christ, anti-truth in both its character and teachings;
- is ungodly, relativistic, sinful, and unholy;
- conveniently conforms to man and his expectations;
- affirmingly "rethinks" "truth" into a perversion that man is willing to accept;
- scorns and contemns the true God and His Word;
- is "*another* Jesus," "*another* spirit," and *another* "God" that reject God's narrow way;
- teaches "*another* gospel" that affirms the broad way; and so on, and so forth.

Details are certainly irrelevant in the darkness. This anti-God bestseller has even been *highly defended* by pastors and theologians. The shift from light to darkness is *pervasive*. Many people clearly want to be set free from "all the things the Scriptures tell us we should do." They aren't even taking heed not to depart from the living God:

> *"Take heed, brethren, lest there be in any of you an evil heart of unbelief, in departing from the living God. But exhort one another daily, while it is called Today; lest any of you be hardened through the deceitfulness of sin." (Hebrews 3:12-13)*

> *"The LORD is righteous in all his ways, and holy in all his works. The LORD is nigh unto all them that call upon him, to all that call upon him in* **truth.***" (Psalm 145:17-18)*

The Shack is filled with so many teachings that defy God and His truth that if the conversations with "God" are as "real and true" as Young admits, then the conversations were clearly with seducing spirits masquerading as "God." But details are now irrelevant. In today's shift from light to darkness, people see no need to beware of *counterfeit gods* let alone *seducing spirits*.

> "They were conversations that I was having with God about whatever. Sometimes I would wake up in the middle of the night in the middle of a conversation and grab a notepad to try and remember. More than not, contrary to the brilliance I had

---

[A]

[Note: Young's bestseller *The Shack* has gone on to sell 18 million copies—as proclaimed on the cover of *Cross Roads*, his equally heretical new book just released on November 13, 2012. And, by the way, the false "Spirit" of *Cross Roads* is a Grandmother goddess who exclaims that "the God of the Old Testament" "kinda freaks me out!" And about her, its false "Jesus" says here, "That strong, courageous, and beautiful woman in there is the Holy Spirit." Remember Little Red Riding Hood? "But, Grandmother, what big teeth you have" . . .

See Wm Paul Young, *Cross Roads* (Great Britain: Hodder & Stoughton Ltd, 2012), published in association with FaithWords, New York, NY, pp. 87-88.]

expected, what I had written would make no sense whatsoever in the morning's light. But occasionally some coherent thoughts and concepts actually emerged from these nocturnal meanderings....

"In hind sight, I was not ready before 2005 to write this...thing...what turned out to be *The Shack*." (William Paul Young; last two ellipsis dots in the original)[1]

"Is the story 'real'? The story is fiction. I made it up. Now, having said that, I will add that ... the conversations are very real and true....

"So is the story true? The pain, the loss, the grief, the process, the conversations, ... all real, all true.... Then there is God who emerges so very real and true ..." (William Paul Young)[2]

"Let no man deceive you with vain words: for because of these things cometh the wrath of God upon the children of disobedience. Be not ye therefore partakers with them. For ye were sometimes darkness, but now are ye light in the Lord: walk as children of light: (For the fruit of the Spirit is in all goodness and righteousness and truth;) proving what is acceptable unto the Lord. And have no fellowship with the unfruitful works of darkness, but rather reprove them." (Ephesians 5:6-11)

Nevertheless, those who warn that the genuine is genuine and the counterfeits are counterfeit are rejected as too "negative" by those who prefer to be "positive" that the counterfeits are "genuine" and the genuine is "counterfeit." Sadly, it has thus become quite fashionable in today's shifting Christianity to openly make-believe that darkness is "light" and lies are "truth."

"I have not written unto you because ye know not the truth, but because ye know it, and that no lie is of the truth." (1 John 2:21)

"Every word of God is pure: he is a shield unto them that put their trust in him. Add thou not unto his words, lest he reprove thee, and thou be found a liar." (Proverbs 30:5-6)

"Fools make a mock at sin: but among the righteous there is favour." (Proverbs 14:9)

5

"How great is that darkness!"

For those who are determined to "reimagine" God and His Word, the difference between what is true and false, light and darkness, narrow and broad, and the true and living God and a counterfeit "God" is clearly irrelevant. All they have to do is enter the darkness to "rethink" and "reimagine" it all into one big harmonious relationship. Many people are even so thoroughly convinced that darkness is a better "light" than the Word of God that *The Shack*'s flagrant deception has even been widely praised and given away as an indispensable resource for "*better understanding*" the nature and character of God! To say that today's shifting Christianity has flipped is an understatement! Everything is being turned upside down in the stampede into darkness.

> *"For this people's heart is waxed gross, and their ears are dull of hearing, and their eyes they have closed; lest at any time they should see with their eyes, and hear with their ears, and should understand with their heart, and should be converted, and I should heal them." (Matthew 13:15)*

> *"But if thine eye be evil, thy whole body shall be full of darkness. If therefore the light that is in thee be darkness, how great is that darkness!" (Matthew 6:23)*

When light was still the preferred light, it used to be obvious that God the Father is in heaven, is God, and is the Father. It used to be obvious that the Holy Spirit is God and is the Holy Spirit. It used to be obvious that the Lord Jesus Christ is the Son of God, is and always has been God including while He lived on earth in the flesh, and is now in heaven on the right hand of God. Not anymore.

Now, according to the convoluted conversations with the counterfeit "God" of *The*

Shack:

- "God the Father" exists on earth as "the Son of God" in "flesh and blood" as "fully human" with "all the limitations;"
- "the Holy Spirit" also exists on earth as "the Son of God" in "flesh and blood" as "fully human" with "all the limitations;"
- "Jesus" still exists on earth as only one part of "the Son of God" in "flesh and blood" as "fully human," and with "all the limitations" still claims to be "fully God" yet is not fully "God" because with "no power within himself to heal anyone" he is helplessly "dependent" on "God" for everything;
- but the "God" on whom this "Jesus" is helplessly "dependent" also exists on earth as "the Son of God" in "flesh and blood" as "fully human" with "all the limitations" ...[1]

Of course all these are counterfeits anyway, but this flesh and blood human god of untruth is the "real" and "true" "God" that today's shifting Christianity is enthusiastically and idolatrously embracing. It is the human "God" that many clearly accept and *want*, and which also happens to be One with all things. This false "God" of untruth claims to be "the ground of all being" that "dwells in, around, and through all things."[2] With serpentine craftiness, *The Shack*'s counterfeit "God" rejects truth of God as "religious conditioning" while imparting the religious conditioning of the New Age and its Oneness. And these are only a *few* examples of *The Shack*'s convoluted twistings that would make the serpent—the father of lies—proud.

> *"But I fear, lest by any means, as the serpent beguiled Eve through his subtilty, so your minds should be corrupted from the simplicity that is in Christ. For if he that cometh preacheth another Jesus, whom we have not preached, or if ye receive another spirit, which ye have not received, or another gospel, which ye have not accepted, ye might well bear with him." (2 Corinthians 11:3-4)*

The seducing spirits of darkness have been conditioning their prey well. Their success in bringing today's blinded Christianity deeper into a "relationship" with their counterfeit "God" of New Age Oneness has been steadily increasing. So it isn't surprising that the "Christianized" Oneness subtly taught by the counterfeit "God" in Young's conversations with "God" actually has much in common with the New Age Oneness taught by the counterfeit "God" in New Age (New Spirituality) leader Neale Donald Walsch's "conversations with God." After all, those who are seeking freedom from the true God and His narrow way are in the same darkness seeking the same broad place of peace and safety,[3] and the same seducing spirits are more than willing to be of service in ensuring their arrival. Sadly, the darkness is getting crowded as more and more people seek freedom from the light.

> "Of course, no one seriously suggests that the Bible is to be taken literally." (Neale Donald Walsch)[4]

> "Imagine a life without fear of God and without guilt over the tiniest infraction of what you imagine to be God's Rules!
>
> "Imagine the freedom of soul and mind and body that would be experienced when you understand at last that you really *are* One with God!" (Neale Donald Walsch)[5]

"Our opportunity now is to create the space of possibility for a New Spirituality to emerge upon the earth ... bringing to our world at last an individualized experience of the Divine in a unified form that makes no one wrong for the way in which they are approaching the God of their understanding ..." (Neale Donald Walsch)[6]

"No man hath seen God at any time; the only begotten Son, which is in the bosom of the Father, he hath declared him." (John 1:18)

"Blessed is that man that maketh the LORD his trust, and respecteth not the proud, nor such as turn aside to lies." (Psalm 40:4)

"For God, who commanded the light to shine out of darkness, hath shined in our hearts, to give the light of the knowledge of the glory of God in the face of Jesus Christ." (2 Corinthians 4:6)

"Therefore seeing we have this ministry, as we have received mercy, we faint not; but have renounced the hidden things of dishonesty, not walking in craftiness, nor handling the word of God deceitfully; but by manifestation of the truth commending ourselves to every man's conscience in the sight of God." (2 Corinthians 4:1-2)

God the Father is revealed in and by His Son, "in the face of Jesus Christ." *(And no, the black goddess "Father" is not "the Son of God"!)* This used to be common knowledge in Christianity when truth was still the preferred truth and light was still the preferred light. Now people prefer to find "truth" and "light" in the darkness of man's chambers of imagery, and absurdity is running wild in the desperate search to "find God" in the darkness. People are turning aside to lies in droves, and there is an epidemic of handling the Word of God deceitfully in order to justify it all. Pastors and theologians have even tried to explain why "God the Father" is "revealed" as a black woman in *The Shack*. God isn't revealed as *anyone* in *The Shack*; God isn't *in The Shack*! The book is *fiction*, and a *blasphemous* one at that!

Again, it is only in the realm of make-believe that the "God" of today's shifting Christianity can be "revealed" in a "reimagined" fashion that is acceptable to man. In truth, the true God is no more revealed today as a woman (or any other "reimagined" fashion) than He was revealed to the Israelites as a golden calf. What this does reveal, however, is that man is just as unfaithful and idolatrous today as back then. People today are no less determined to make-believe that counterfeits are the "genuine." Some things never change.

6

A "real" and "true" false god that teaches "truth"

"Woe unto him that saith to the wood, Awake; to the dumb stone, Arise, it shall teach! Behold, it is laid over with gold and silver, and there is no breath at all in the midst of it. But the LORD is in his holy temple: let all the earth keep silence before him." (Habakkuk 2:19-20)

Incredibly, man is still "reimagining" God into a fashion that man is willing to accept so that this "reimagined" false god that conforms to man's expectations in his desired freedom to "rethink" God can now teach man the "truth" about God!

This colossal failure, not to mention refusal, to discern between true teachings and false teachings and between the true God and false gods is clearly seen in the outpouring of high praise for *The Shack*, which actually includes: *teaches powerful theological lessons; biblically accurate, precise, faithful, and true; no theological errors; sound truth; nothing heretical or that contradicts the Bible; restores faith; spiritually awakening; theologically enlightening; Father, Son, and Spirit are understood for the first time; ushers you directly into the heart and nature of God; find the truth about God in The Shack; the book is one long Bible study; inspired writing from God Himself; the words spoken by God in this book are full of life; you'll be experiencing God as never before;* and so on and so forth.

Obviously, aside from obliviousness to the "irrelevant" difference between truth and lies, light and darkness, the true God and false gods, God's Word and man's word, faith and faithlessness, Christian and nonchristian, righteousness and sin, holy and unholy, and genuine and counterfeit, etc., one vital detail has completely escaped the notice of those who are shifting to the realm of make-believe: *God isn't in The Shack!* The words in *The Shack* are *not* spoken by *God!* The words in *The Shack* are *not* spoken by *the Father,* they are *not* spoken by *the Son*, and they are *not* spoken by *the Holy Spirit*!

> Fiction: Produced by the imagination, an invention of the mind, a made-up story, a fable, a false belief or statement accepted as true for the sake of convenience, a pretense, not real, a counterfeiting, a lie, an untruth, …
>
> Not Literal: Imaginative, figurative, metaphorical, not consistent with fact or reality, inaccurate, not reflecting the genuine character of something, false, untruthful, …

Even further devoid of reason and sense and reality, not to mention truth, today's idolatrous Christianity has ushered in the false god and the false teachings of *The Shack* with rationalizations such as: "But it's only fiction," and "It's not literal." *Of course* it's fiction! *Of course* it's not literal! That simply could not be any more irrelevant in justifying what people are now choosing to believe. Except for the *true scriptural* faith of the Lord Jesus Christ Who is God's true and only Messiah, *every religion on the planet is fiction and not literal*. There are no Get Out of Hell Free cards for believing in false gods excused away as "*fictional*." To even attempt to make such a distinction is absurd.

"Woe unto them that call evil good, and good evil; that put darkness for light, and light for darkness; that put bitter for sweet, and sweet for bitter! Woe unto them that are wise in their own eyes, and prudent in their own sight!" (Isaiah 5:20-21)

"… Can the blind lead the blind? shall they not both fall into the ditch?" (Luke 6:39)

Rationalizing that *The Shack*'s "real" and "true" false god is actually the true God merely because it *claims* to be about the true God and is *fiction* is thoroughly delusional, as well as spiritual suicide. The followers of every false god throughout history have been deceived into believing that their false god is a "real" and "true" "God." And now, in an astounding sign of the times, many in today's Christianity are following suit, deceived in the darkness where they are unable, and unwilling, to differentiate between the false god in *The Shack* and the true God.

7

The fear-based agenda of the "doctrine police"

"And of some have compassion, making a difference: And others save with fear, pulling them out of the fire; hating even the garment spotted by the flesh." (Jude 1:22-23)

People need to wake up and smell the fire and brimstone before it's too late. But then, those who prefer to "reimagine" the darkness into a place of peace and safety no longer believe in God's judgment any more than they still believe in the true God. In the darkness of their blinded minds, warning that God requires the *true scriptural* faith of the Lord Jesus Christ for salvation from sins and punishment is to be rejected as the "negative" promotion of "fear" by those they disdainfully refer to as the "doctrine police." Ironically, *the duty of the police is to uphold the laws of a higher authority based on a "literal interpretation" of the laws!* So this is a very interesting and revealing choice of words by those who are pursuing freedom from both the *authority* of God and the *literal* truth of God's Word!

Of course the topic of God's punishment of sin is negative and promotes *fear* in those who are choosing to depart from the faith. God's Word even goes so far as to refer to this fear as *terror*. What, we're just supposed to "rethink" and "reimagine" God and His Word and faith to make them "relevant" to today's everything-must-feel-good-and-be-positive mindset? *Exactly*, according to them.

"I also will choose their delusions, and will bring their fears upon them; because when I called, none did answer; when I spake, they did not hear: but they did evil before mine eyes, and chose that in which I delighted not." (Isaiah 66:4)

> *"For I am the LORD, I change not; …" (Malachi 3:6)*

> *"Wherefore we receiving a kingdom which cannot be moved, let us have grace, whereby we may serve God acceptably with reverence and godly fear: For our God is a consuming fire." (Hebrews 12:28-29)*

Despite man's rebellious preference to believe that the word of man is the word of God and the Word of God is the word of man, *God* is the One Who declares what is truth and what is not. We either believe it or we do not; it is that simple. So it is totally irrelevant that theologians believe they can "find God" in the darkness outside the "box." A theologian is merely a person who studies theology. A theologian who studies man's false theology and believes it is "true" is nothing more than a deceived expert on false theology. It is also totally irrelevant that many theologians are choosing to debate and "rethink" much of God's Word of truth. Theologians don't have the power to change God's truth just because they don't believe it! There was a time when "experts" convinced many into believing that the earth was flat, even though God's Word of truth said otherwise. Obviously, man's imaginative false beliefs don't even change the shape of *the planet*, let alone Who *the true God*—the planet's Creator—really is!

> *"For what if some did not believe? shall their unbelief make the faith of God without effect? God forbid: yea, let God be true, but every man a liar …" (Romans 3:3-4)*

> *"How do ye say, We are wise, and the law of the LORD is with us? Lo, certainly in vain made he it; the pen of the scribes is in vain. The wise men are ashamed, they are dismayed and taken: lo, they have rejected the word of the LORD; and what wisdom is in them?" (Jeremiah 8:8-9)*

The God of truth *does not change*. God does not change, and *the truth* does not change. Both are literal and absolute and undergo no transformation whatsoever despite man's relativistic attempts to "reimagine" God and His truth into a fashion that man is willing to accept—*man's ultimate exercise in futility*. Although man's astronomical arrogance says otherwise, the true God does not kneel before the fictional throne of man's ever-changing imagination. Yet man's "reimagined" gods are ever affirming its "power" and kneeling before it; after all, without it they wouldn't even exist!

For obvious reasons, God's Word of truth tells us that our spiritual "war" includes:

> *"Casting down imaginations, and every high thing that exalteth itself against the knowledge of God, and bringing into captivity every thought to the obedience of Christ." (2 Corinthians 10:5)*

Yet those who prefer the freedom to "rethink" and "reimagine" God and His Word are essentially turning 2 Corinthians 10:5 upside down. They are defiantly:

> Casting down the knowledge of God, and every scriptural truth that exalteth itself against the imaginations of man, and bringing into captivity every thought to man's quest for freedom from the obedience of Christ.

Fiction is an invention of the imagination, and *The Shack* is clearly an invention of *untruth*. It is no coincidence that the opposite of fiction is truth, certainty, reality, fact, etc. Sadly, people are turning away from the *certainty* of truth to the *uncertainty* of fables in order to turn the *certainty* of having to *believe and obey God* upside down into *uncertainty*. Conveniently affirming their desired uncertainty, *The Shack* not only "sarcastically" describes "rules" as "all the things the Scriptures tell us we should do," but its fictitious god teaches that "rules" are "a vain attempt to create certainty out of uncertainty" and even claims to "have a great fondness for uncertainty."[1] Of course it does. The certainty of truth rules out the very existence of this fictitious god of untruth.

The latter of these two teachings on "rules" is even part of a discussion on the Ten Commandments, during which the main character asks, "Are you saying I don't have to follow the rules?" *The Shack*'s god conveniently answers, "Yes," and shortly thereafter claims that they are "a vain attempt to create certainty out of uncertainty" and that "Rules cannot bring freedom; they have only the power to accuse."[2]

First, it shouldn't come as a surprise that this fictitious false god wants people to feel free to not even follow the Ten Commandments because if people just followed the first commandment then they wouldn't be following this false god of *The Shack*. Still, there's also the commandments about not killing, stealing, or committing adultery, etc., so it is amazing how these are all so easily dismissed as not required when they should make it obvious as to why the Lord Jesus Christ taught that He did not "come to destroy the law"!

> *"Let your light so shine before men, that they may see your good works, and glorify your Father which is in heaven. Think not that I am come to destroy the law, or the prophets: I am not come to destroy, but to fulfil. For verily I say unto you, Till heaven and earth pass, one jot or one tittle shall in no wise pass from the law, till all be fulfilled. Whosoever therefore shall break one of these least commandments, and shall teach men so, he shall be called the least in the kingdom of heaven: but whosoever shall do and teach them, the same shall be called great in the kingdom of heaven. For I say unto you, That except your righteousness shall exceed the righteousness of the scribes and Pharisees, ye shall in no case enter into the kingdom of heaven." (Matthew 5:16-20)*

Second, "following the rules" is simply *obedient faith*. It does not make anyone "superior" to others, as people may think. Nor is this about trying to establish our own righteousness. It is God and His truth that is superior to all, and about being "made righteous," God makes it perfectly clear in His Word of truth that "the righteousness of God" is "unto all and upon all them that *believe*." The law only has "the power to accuse" those who do not have faith in the Lord Jesus Christ. So those who feel that God's "rules" and Ten Commandments merely "accuse" them, rather than guide them into *obedient faith* (such as having no other gods before Him), need to follow Scripture's exhortation to "Examine yourselves, whether ye be in the faith" (2 Corinthians 13:5).

> *"But now the righteousness of God without the law is manifested, being witnessed by the law and the prophets; even the righteousness of God which is by faith of Jesus Christ unto all and upon all them that believe: for there is no difference: For all have sinned, and come short of the glory of God; being justified freely by his grace through the redemption that is in Christ Jesus ... To declare, I say, at this time his righteousness: that he might be just, and the justifier of him which believeth in Jesus. Where is boasting then? It is excluded. By what law? of works? Nay: but by the law of faith.... Do we then make void the law through faith? God forbid: yea, we establish the law." (Romans 3:21-24, 26-27, 31)*

The Shack is spinning in circles in the upside-down absurdity of untruth. It is *The Shack* itself, not God's Word and its "rules," that is "a vain attempt to create certainty out of uncertainty"—in its vain attempt to create the certainty of "truth" out of the uncertainty of its fiction. And yet at the same time, *The Shack* is actually a vain attempt to create *uncertainty* out of certainty by "reimagining" the certainty of God's truth into the *uncertainty* of man's fiction. (And all because people don't want the faith that comes by the Word of God!)

Thus, desperately spinning in circles to exalt man's uncertain imaginations, *The Shack*'s untruth is defended as "only fiction," while at the same time, the book's fiction is defended as "solid biblical truth." This dialectic dance underscores the change in how God's Word is perceived in today's shifting Christianity. This is further evidenced in that those who believe that God's Word of truth is literal are reproached by the growing number of those who do not.

Absurdly, they refuse to heed *God's* Word as the truth and *reject* it as "*not literal,*" but they heed *man's* word as the "truth" and *defend* it as "*not literal.*" In other words, although they reject God's truth as "not literal" *untruth*, they accept man's untruth as "not literal" *truth* because man's untruth is the "truth" they are *willing* to accept. And the never-ending circles absurdly go on and on, all because people are not willing to accept that God *is* Who He *is* and said what He meant and meant what He said in *His* Word of *truth*.

> *"For the time will come when they will not endure sound doctrine; but after their own lusts shall they heap to themselves teachers, having itching ears; and they shall turn away their ears from the truth, and shall be turned unto fables." (2 Timothy 4:3-4)*

Clearly seeing no need to beware of any counterfeits, those in today's shifting Christianity are indiscriminately *heaping* to themselves teachers to scratch their itching ears. After all, since they imagine that the genuine is a "counterfeit" and the counterfeits are "genuine" they are intentionally turning to counterfeits for the "genuine." So as long as wolves are properly attired in sheep's clothing, they and their claws are given a warm reception and promptly put to use in the service of scratching. It is not surprising that warnings are scorned as *negative* and as a *fear-based agenda* of the "doctrine police." "Fear" and "negativity" are intolerable to those whose ears are positively itching for unsound doctrine.

Besides, trying to warn people who are shifting away from the true and living God is indeed the promotion of a *fear*-based agenda—*the fear of the Lord* before it's too late. Although, sadly, this is beginning to look as futile as their fearless agenda to "reimagine" God. Too many are choosing to close their eyes and ears. They just do not want to know that the genuine is genuine and the counterfeits are counterfeit because the counterfeits are the "genuine" they are *willing* to accept. But of course they don't see it that way.

> *"And unto man he said, Behold, the fear of the Lord, that is wisdom; and to depart from evil is understanding." (Job 28:28)*

> *"The desire accomplished is sweet to the soul: but it is abomination to fools to depart from evil." (Proverbs 13:19)*

> *"Take heed, brethren, lest there be in any of you an evil heart of unbelief, in departing from the living God." (Hebrews 3:12)*

"A wise man feareth, and departeth from evil: but the fool rageth, and is confident." (Proverbs 14:16)

"Therefore they say unto God, Depart from us; for we desire not the knowledge of thy ways." (Job 21:14)

"For that they hated knowledge, and did not choose the fear of the LORD: They would none of my counsel: they despised all my reproof. Therefore shall they eat of the fruit of their own way, and be filled with their own devices." (Proverbs 1:29-31)

8

The faith that is set forth by God in His Word is the faith of God

Shifting from light to darkness has already been leading many in today's light-intolerant Christianity into a fictitious "relationship" with God, and now it is leading many more into a relationship with a fictitious "God." Man's "reimagined" "God"—whether they claim it is the "Father," "Jesus," or "Holy Spirit"—is a counterfeit "God" that is no more a "real" and "true" "God" than if they dressed up a literal wolf in sheep's clothing and claimed that it is a "real" and "true" sheep that has been set free from the "box" so sheep can be "reimagined" into a broader understanding. Yes, this would be totally absurd! Despite man's belief that his imagination is powerful, this dressed up wolf would have the same chance of making it to sheephood as the golden calf had in becoming God.

Likewise, even though more and more people are convinced that man can successfully "reimagine" a new version of the true and living God, a "Christianized" made-up "God" is nothing more than a "Christianized" made-up "God." Counterfeits are counterfeit and the genuine is genuine, no matter how many people dance around in circles desperately trying to bring counterfeit and genuine together as one in a harmonious relationship.

> *"Ye are my witnesses, saith the LORD, and my servant whom I have chosen: that ye may know and believe me, and understand that I am he: before me there was no God formed, neither shall there be after me." (Isaiah 43:10)*

> *"Thus saith the LORD, The heaven is my throne, and the earth is my footstool ... but*

to this man will I look, even to him that is poor and of a contrite spirit, and trembleth at my word." (Isaiah 66:1-2)

It all comes down to the unbelief and unwillingness to accept that the Word of God is the Word of *God*. So, hell-bent on "reimagining" God into who man wants God to be, man continues to create a fictitious "God" that is a mere figment of man's imagination – a false god that has no power to save itself, let alone its inventor or anyone else. But then, if people don't believe that God's judgment and punishment of sins are *literal* there's nothing for anyone to fear or worry about, right?

"The Lord is not slack concerning his promise, as some men count slackness; but is longsuffering to us-ward, not willing that any should perish, but that all should come to repentance." (2 Peter 3:9)

"But the LORD is the true God, he is the living God, and an everlasting king: at his wrath the earth shall tremble, and the nations shall not be able to abide his indignation. Thus shall ye say unto them, The gods that have not made the heavens and the earth, even they shall perish from the earth, and from under these heavens.... They are vanity, and the work of errors: in the time of their visitation they shall perish." (Jeremiah 10:10-11, 15)

"Because that, when they knew God, they glorified him not as God, neither were thankful; but became vain in their imaginations, and their foolish heart was darkened. Professing themselves to be wise, they became fools, and changed the glory of the uncorruptible God into an image made like to corruptible man, ... Who changed the truth of God into a lie, and worshipped and served the creature more than the Creator, who is blessed for ever. Amen." (Romans 1:21-23, 25)

The changes in how God's Word is perceived are already resulting in a comprehensive "reimagining" of Christianity. The fear of the Lord, the knowledge of God, the Word of God, the truth, the faith, the Gospel of Christ, the atonement on the cross, the resurrection, theology, doctrine, repentance, salvation, being born again, righteousness, holiness, and obedience, etc.—if not openly "cast aside"—are all being redefined into irrelevance.

With today's "Christianity" already busy "reimagining" even itself into a counterfeit, it's no wonder it has been so easily deceived into believing that *The Shack*'s false god of untruth is of the "*Christian* faith!" And this is even despite the fact that *The Shack*'s false "Jesus" openly admits that he has "no desire to make them Christian."[1] This doublemindedness of people shows that deep down they know the Christian faith is the true faith of God, they just aren't willing to accept it. Therefore they use the label of Christian because they know it's the faith of God, but they don't want to use the label of Christian because they don't want it to be the faith of God. And so they just "reimagine" it all into a broader "faith." In other words, they know the Christian faith is the true faith but the true faith is too narrow, so they "reimagine" a broader faith and label it "Christian" so that this new broader faith can be the "true" faith.

Thus, people don't think twice about believing they can "find the truth about God" in *The Shack*. They just spin in circles embracing it as the "Christian" faith while defending its nonchristian faith as only fiction and not literal. The New Age is fiction and not literal. Its Oneness is fiction and not literal. So in the search for "truth" why not just admittedly "reimagine" today's "Christian" faith as broad enough to include the counterfeit faith of New Age Oneness? After all, people have long since abandoned looking in the obvious place for the truth about God, and the untruth of *The Shack* fits right in with the untruth of New Age Oneness. Besides, New Age Oneness has already "reimagined" its faith as broad enough to include the counterfeit faith of today's "reimagined" Christianity in its New Spirituality, which, naturally, is already being embraced in the counterfeit faith of today's "reimagined" Christianity. So why bother with a fictitious exclusiveness? It's all the same darkness.

Although those who have closed their eyes and ears are still absurdly in denial, today's Christianity actually began blindly conforming its faith about God with the New Age (New Spirituality) and its Oneness quite awhile ago. This devilish deception continues to rapidly progress ever deeper, as what better way to get today's Christianity to gradually accept the New Age Oneness of all gods, religions, and "truth" than to convince it that the truth of God is not literal, but just *changeable* metaphor? Think about it. Yet too many leaders in today's Christianity are making the shift themselves and are choosing to revile and warn against the *warnings*, rather than warn against the *deceptions* that are leading people away from the true and living God.

> *"Thus saith the LORD of hosts, ... To whom shall I speak, and give warning, that they may hear? behold, their ear is uncircumcised, and they cannot hearken: behold, the word of the LORD is unto them a reproach; they have no delight in it." (Jeremiah 6:9-10)*

For those who are turning away from believing God's Word of truth, *The Shack*'s highly defended false "God" conveniently claims to have already "forgiven all humans for their sins" and is "now fully reconciled" to "the whole world."[2] All man needs to do is "choose relationship" because *The Shack*'s false "Jesus" wants his followers to "grow in the freedom to be inside or outside all kinds of systems" including "religious" "systems" (such as "Buddhists or Mormons, Baptists or Muslims").[3] And since this false "Jesus" wants his followers "to move freely between and among them," he of course has "no desire to make them Christian."[4] Therefore, *The Shack*'s false "God" does not require anyone to "*believe*."[5] Of course, *believing* not only defeats the purpose of "reimagining" God, it also defeats the purpose of New Age Oneness.

To make all religions equal paths to God—which automatically makes all false gods equal with the true God—is the darkness of New Age Oneness. This belief that "There is no Religion higher than Truth" is actually an occult lie,[6] which is becoming widely believed by those who are blindly shifting to New Age Oneness. Sadly, one of the many who love *The Shack* has even blindly recommended the book to others for helping people "view God [as] being MUCH bigger than any particular religion."

Whether people are willing to accept it or not, *different religions (faiths)* and their *different gods* are not equal with the particular religion that is the *true faith* of the *true God*. The *true* God *is* Who He *is*, and He has recorded the truth of Who He *is* in *His Word*. Thus *faith comes by the Word of God*. And the faith that comes by the Word of God is clearly the *Christian* faith, not the faith of *another religion*.

Before the shift to darkness, it used to be common knowledge in Christianity that the faith that is given to us by *God* in the Word of *God* is the faith of *God*. And given that it is *the faith of God* that comes by *the Word of God*, then to depart from *the Word of God* is to depart from *the faith of God*, which is to depart from *God*. But for people today it is simply too narrow that the Word of God is the Word of *God* that gives us the faith of *God*. They want to freely "think *outside* the box" and thus want God set "free" from the "box" of His Word. This way, they can then try to "find God" *outside* the faith that comes by the Word of God. After all, if people "rethink" and "reimagine" it all so that God is "bigger" and broader than the faith that comes by His Word then anyone can find "God" and "truth" and "faith" *wherever* they choose to look. And this way there would never be any chance of turning away from the truth, departing from the faith, or departing from God, right?

> *"There is a way that seemeth right unto a man, but the end thereof are the ways of death." (Proverbs 16:25; see also 14:12)*

> *"Enter ye in at the strait gate: for wide is the gate, and broad is the way, that leadeth to destruction, and many there be which go in thereat: Because strait is the gate, and narrow is the way, which leadeth unto life, and few there be that find it." (Matthew 7:13-14)*

> *"But if our gospel be hid, it is hid to them that are lost: In whom the god of this world hath blinded the minds of them which believe not, lest the light of the glorious gospel of Christ, who is the image of God, should shine unto them." (2 Corinthians 4:3-4)*

> *"For unto us was the gospel preached, as well as unto them: but the word preached did not profit them, not being mixed with faith in them that heard it." (Hebrews 4:2)*

> *"Take heed, brethren, lest there be in any of you an evil heart of unbelief, in departing from the living God." (Hebrews 3:12)*

No matter how many people prefer a broader understanding of the true God that includes other religions (faiths), this is no different than preferring a broader understanding of true sheep that includes wolves dressed up in sheep's clothing. Likewise, choosing to believe that other religions believe the truth about the true God is no different than choosing to believe that anyone who might believe that dressed up wolves are true sheep actually believes the truth about true sheep. *False gods* cannot be separated from the truth of their *falseness* any more than *the true God* can be separated from the truth of His *trueness*. No matter how determined man becomes in the attempt to bring true and false together as one, dressing up other religions/gods will never transform them into the true faith/God. And neither are other religions/gods simply another dressing for—another manifestation or understanding of—the true faith/God. No matter how many people absurdly choose to imagine otherwise, true is true and false is false, and genuine is genuine and counterfeit is counterfeit.

Nevertheless, New Age Oneness, with the broader theology of its own "reimagined" "God" and "reimagined" "truth" and "reimagined" "faith," has become quite successful in luring today's shifting Christianity onto the broad way. This New Age "God" of Oneness is the "God" that is "bigger" than any particular religion (faith) and offers people their desired freedom to "think outside the box." This false "God" of Oneness is the "God" that immanently dwells *in all things*, which *thereby* brings everyone and everything together as *One* with itself. Based on this *Oneness*, this false "God" therefore offers people the ultimate freedom from the rules and doctrine of the narrow way. It conveniently offers the freedom to *imagine* and *define* "God" *however* anyone chooses— in *whatever* "concept" (religion/faith), "understanding" (theology), "interpretation" (doctrine), or "experience" (path) they are willing to accept. And since this "God" of New Age

Oneness is immanent *in all things*—which is the basis for the *Oneness* of all things—it is therefore *all "the same God"* with only one *"Being"* and *"Reality"* that is *in* them *all*.

In other words, *"Being always transcends appearance,"* "and any appearances that mask that reality will fall away," with "God, who is the ground of all being" that "dwells in, around, and through all things—ultimately emerging as the real."[7] This fitting summary is given by *The Shack*'s false "Jesus" who subtly shows the way to this false "God." Despite the deceived claims to the contrary by those who have closed their eyes and ears to feel and experience its "story," the counterfeit faith that comes by *The Shack* is the counterfeit faith of New Age Oneness. This is revealed over and over and over *throughout* the blindly defended *Shack*.

It is not the *true* God that is "masked" by any and all appearances of "all things." And it is not the *true* God that is ultimately emerging as the "real" in today's shift to darkness. Rather, it is the immanent false "God" of New Age Oneness that is emerging as the "real" and "true" "God" that people today prefer. Conveniently, this false "God" of Oneness can be dressed up however anyone chooses and yet remains the "Ultimate Reality" in any and all appearances.

Although New Age Oneness would have people believe that "God" is *in all things*, and is therefore "masked" by any and all appearances of *all things*, in reality, things are what they are. Whether the wolf appears as itself or dressed in sheep's clothing it is still just a wolf. And, no, it's wolfness is not a "mask" of the "reality" of an immanent sheep. It is no less absurd to believe that God is *in all things* than it would be to believe that a sheep is in a wolf. But, of course, those who want the freedom to imagine and define God however they choose don't see it that way. Nevertheless, the true God will always be the true God and false gods will always be false gods no matter how many people prefer a broader understanding of the true God that includes false gods dressed up as "real" and "true."

Even though their feelings and "experiences" lead them to see it otherwise, those who are shifting to the "real" and "true" false "God" that is "bigger" than the truth and faith of God's Word only *seem* to have God.

> *"The LORD is nigh unto all them that call upon him, to all that call upon him in* **truth**.*" (Psalm 145:18)*

> *"Then said Jesus to those Jews which believed on him, If ye continue in my word, then are ye my disciples indeed; and ye shall know the truth, and the truth shall make you free." (John 8:31-32)*

> *"Whosoever transgresseth, and abideth not in the doctrine of Christ, hath not God. He that abideth in the doctrine of Christ, he hath both the Father and the Son." (2 John 1:9)*

> *"Take heed therefore how ye hear: for whosoever hath to him shall be given; and whosoever hath not, from him shall be taken even that which he seemeth to have." (Luke 8:18)*

> *"So then faith cometh by hearing, and hearing by the word of God." (Romans 10:17)*

Incredibly, believing that the truth and faith of God comes by the Word of God is now even deemed "idolatry" by those who feel "boxed" in by the narrow way. If it is "idolatry" to believe the <u>Word</u> of God then it is "idolatry" to believe <u>God</u>! Idolatry against *whom*, against *man*?! In today's faithless determination to find freedom from the Word of God, *everything* is being flipped upside down into absurdity. To believe that God said what He meant and meant what He said in the truth and faith of His Word is not "idolatry," but *salvation*.

> *"Therefore they say unto God, Depart from us; for we desire not the knowledge of thy ways." (Job 21:14)*

> *"Let us hold fast the profession of our faith without wavering; (for he is faithful that promised;)... Cast not away therefore your confidence, which hath great recompence of reward.... Now the just shall live by faith: but if any man draw back, my soul shall have no pleasure in him. But we are not of them who draw back unto perdition; but of them that believe to the saving of the soul." (Hebrews 10:23, 35, 38-39)*

9

Faith in the truth is true faith

"For ye are all the children of God by faith in Christ Jesus." (Galatians 3:26)

In today's shifting Christianity, people think it is simply a matter of "moving the fence" in order to be more inclusive. They don't understand that we can't broaden the *truth* of Who the Lord Jesus Christ is any more than we can broaden the truth of Who God is. *The Word of God* tells us the *truth* of Who the Lord Jesus Christ is, and, again, the truth and faith that are in the Word of God give us the *Christian* faith, not the faith of *another religion*. In other words, *the truth of Who the Lord Jesus Christ is* gives us the *Christian* faith. This is the faith that is given to us by *God* in *His* Word. The Lord Jesus Christ does not "move the fence;" that is, *He* does not change the truth of Who He is to be more inclusive. The truth is what it is whether people believe it or not.

"For if he that cometh preacheth another Jesus, whom we have not preached, or if ye receive another spirit, which ye have not received, or another gospel, which ye have not accepted, ye might well bear with him." (2 Corinthians 11:4)

Only "*another* Jesus" will change the truth and "move the fence" to broaden the narrow way to include the broad way. This *broadened* way is not the *narrow* way but obviously the *broad* way.

For instance, the false "Jesus" of *The Shack* wants his followers to "grow in the freedom to be inside or outside all kinds of systems and to move freely between and among them."[1] This false "Jesus" conveniently includes "religious" "systems" in this freedom, and he says of his followers who "were Buddhists or Mormons, Baptists or Muslims" – "I have no desire to make them Christian, but I do want to join them in

44

their transformation …"² Since true Christians believe the truth and faith of *the Word of God*, which includes the truth of the *true* Lord Jesus Christ, of course a *false* "Jesus" doesn't want people to be *Christian*. Besides, this way his followers can come to "view God [as] being MUCH bigger than any particular religion," and *particularly* "bigger" than *the Word of God* and its *Christian* faith. In other words, in their transformation away from the Christian faith and Christian God they can come to view different religions as having "the same God." This is what is being taught here by this false "Jesus," who is clearly "moving the fence" to include the broad way (and even *himself*).

> *"Now the Spirit speaketh expressly, that in the latter times some shall depart from the faith, giving heed to seducing spirits, and doctrines of devils." (1 Timothy 4:1)*

"Moving the fence" does not move or change *the truth*, it only moves and changes *one's faith*. Faith in the truth is true faith, and faith in untruth is faithlessness because faith in untruth *moves and changes* one's faith *from* faith in the truth *to* faith in untruth. But, naturally, those who are undergoing the transformation of the broad way don't see it that way. They prefer to believe that the truth is untruth and untruth is "truth," so if their faith is in untruth their "faith" is in "truth," and then faith in the truth becomes faith in untruth, and faith becomes faithlessness and faithlessness becomes "faith."

This way, this broader untruth ("truth") of a broader "Jesus" can now fit inside other religions so they, too, can have faith in untruth and believe it is faith in the truth. And this is man's idea of "*love*"?! Yet they see it as having faith in a "reimagined" Jesus and a "reimagined" way and a "reimagined" truth that gives everyone a "reimagined" life, because then there will be no problem for anyone, right? Only in the blinding absurdity of *make-believe*, which is all they will have left since they are making it taboo to *believe*.

> *"Jesus Christ the same yesterday, and today, and for ever." (Hebrews 13:8)*

> *"For I am the LORD, I change not; …" (Malachi 3:6)*

> *"If we receive the witness of men, the witness of God is greater: for this is the witness of God which he hath testified of his Son.* **He that believeth on the Son of God** *hath the witness in himself: he that believeth not God hath made him a liar; because he believeth not the record that God gave of his Son." (1 John 5:9-10)*

> *"And we have seen and do testify that the Father sent the Son to be the Saviour of the world. Whosoever shall confess that* **Jesus is the Son of God**, *God dwelleth in him, and he in God." (1 John 4:14-15)*

> *"Jesus saith unto him,* **I** *am the way, the truth, and the life: no man cometh unto the Father, but by* **me**.*" (John 14:6)*

Contrary to the devious false teachings of *The Shack*'s "reimagined" "God" of untruth, neither the *true* Father nor the *true* Holy Spirit are "the Son of God."³ It used to be common knowledge in Christianity that *the Father* is not "the Son of God;" *the Father* is not the way to the Father. Likewise, it used to be common knowledge that *the Holy Spirit* is not "the Son of God;" *the Holy Spirit* is not the way to the Father. The Lord Jesus Christ, Who is the true Son of God, is the *only* way to the Father. And only those who believe on the true Son of God receive the Holy Spirit. We cannot bypass believing on the true Son of God to come to the true God.

Incidentally, in the New Age *everyone* is "the Son of God." Very convenient. This way everyone is their own way to God. This is also why people choose to "reimagine" God. Although today's shifting Christianity now "reimagines" otherwise, the true Lord Jesus Christ, the true Son of God, is not *"the best way"* to God but *the only way*. There is *no relationship* with (or *"relating" to*) the true God apart from the true Lord Jesus Christ. On the other hand, *The Shack*'s "reimagined" "Jesus" naturally claims to be "the best way" to "relate to" its "reimagined" "God."[4] *Of course* a *false* "Jesus" is "the best way" in *every* sense to a *false* "God"! In truth, the *true* Lord Jesus Christ is *the only way* to the *true* God. Think about it.

Although it all used to be obvious, sadly, *nothing* is obvious anymore for those who are rejecting the faith of the certainty of God's truth to believe the faithlessness of the uncertainty of man's untruth, and then absurdly flipping it all upside down and backward, spinning in the never-ending circles of man's "*re*imaginations." Their defense against the light is quite an effective defense. They just are not willing to accept that in the true truth of God's truth—as opposed to the untrue "truth" of man's untruth—we are born again through the Holy Spirit by *the Word of God* that gives us the *truth* of Who the Lord Jesus Christ is, which is indispensable to the *true* Gospel of Christ.

> *"Jesus answered and said unto him, Verily, verily, I say unto thee, Except a man be born again, he cannot see the kingdom of God.... That which is born of the flesh is flesh; and that which is born of the Spirit is spirit. Marvel not that I said unto thee, Ye must be born again.... He that believeth on the Son hath everlasting life: and he that believeth not the Son shall not see life; but the wrath of God abideth on him." (John 3:3, 6-7, 36)*

> *"Sanctify them through thy truth: thy word is truth." (John 17:17)*

> *"Being born again, not of corruptible seed, but of incorruptible, by the word of God, which liveth and abideth for ever. For all flesh is as grass, and all the glory of man as the flower of grass. The grass withereth, and the flower thereof falleth away: But the word of the Lord endureth for ever. And this is the word which by the gospel is preached unto you." (1 Peter 1:23-25)*

> *"For I am not ashamed of the gospel of Christ: for it is the power of God unto salvation to every one that believeth; to the Jew first, and also to the Greek. For therein is the righteousness of God revealed from faith to faith: as it is written, The just shall live by faith." (Romans 1:16-17)*

> *"Therefore being justified by faith, we have peace with God through our Lord Jesus Christ." (Romans 5:1)*

This all used to be common knowledge in Christianity, when light was still the preferred light, truth was still the preferred truth, faith was still the preferred faith, and the Gospel of Christ was still the preferred Gospel. Now *everything* has changed. And the self-proclaimed "change agents" have changed it all on purpose. Congratulations on their success. Now, the true God is no longer the preferred "God," and the true Lord Jesus Christ is no longer the preferred "Jesus." But, naturally, they don't see it that way.

> *"Be not deceived; God is not mocked: for whatsoever a man soweth, that shall he also reap." (Galatians 6:7)*

10

Rock does not shift

"The way of the wicked is as darkness: they know not at what they stumble." (Proverbs 4:19)

God's Word is just too authoritative, too clear, too certain, too doctrinal, too narrow, too commanding, too set in His ways, too judgmental, too firm, too black and white, too absolute, just too rock solid for those who prefer to shift in their own ways and beliefs.

"Whoso despiseth the word shall be destroyed: but he that feareth the commandment shall be rewarded." (Proverbs 13:13)

"Wherefore also it is contained in the scripture, Behold, I lay in Zion a chief corner stone, elect, precious: and he that believeth on him shall not be confounded. Unto you therefore which believe he is precious: but unto them which be disobedient, the stone which the builders disallowed, the same is made the head of the corner, and a stone of stumbling, and a rock of offence, even to them which stumble at the word, being disobedient: whereunto also they were appointed." (1 Peter 2:6-8)

Rock does not shift. All who are shifting inevitably stumble at the Rock of Offence and His Word. But on the other hand, shifting sand will conform to their every step. Those who prefer man's ever-changing "reimaginations" to the never-changing Word of God are foolishly building their house—and in this case Shack—upon ever-shifting sand.

Having no solid footing for their faith, they are very easily "carried about with every wind of doctrine, by the sleight of men, and cunning craftiness" (Ephesians 4:14). It is doubly symbolic that the publisher of *The Shack* is Windblown Media. When the winds blow, great is the fall of those who are fearlessly building upon the sand.

> *"He is the Rock, his work is perfect: for all his ways are judgment: a God of truth and without iniquity, just and right is he." (Deuteronomy 32:4)*
>
> *"The fear of the LORD is the beginning of wisdom: and the knowledge of the holy is understanding." (Proverbs 9:10)*
>
> *"Wherefore gird up the loins of your mind, be sober, and hope to the end for the grace that is to be brought unto you at the revelation of Jesus Christ; as obedient children, not fashioning yourselves according to the former lusts in your ignorance: But as he which hath called you is holy, so be ye holy in all manner of conversation; because it is written, Be ye holy; for I am holy." (1 Peter 1:13-16)*
>
> *"And why call ye me, Lord, Lord, and do not the things which I say?" (Luke 6:46)*
>
> *"And every one that heareth these sayings of mine, and doeth them not, shall be likened unto a foolish man, which built his house upon the sand: And the rain descended, and the floods came, and the winds blew, and beat upon that house; and it fell: and great was the fall of it. And it came to pass, when Jesus had ended these sayings, the people were astonished at his doctrine: For he taught them as one having authority, and not as the scribes." (Matthew 7:26-29)*

People stumble at the Word of God, at the *doctrine* of the Lord Jesus Christ, when they do not want to obediently submit to His *authority*, which is inherently His because of the *truth* of Who He is.

> *"And Jesus came and spake unto them, saying, All power is given unto me in heaven and in earth." (Matthew 28:18)*
>
> *"Jesus Christ the same yesterday, and today, and for ever." (Hebrews 13:8)*
>
> *"For by him were all things created, that are in heaven, and that are in earth, visible and invisible, whether they be thrones, or dominions, or principalities, or powers: all things were created by him, and for him: And he is before all things, and by him all things consist. And he is the head of the body, the church: who is the beginning, the firstborn from the dead; that in all things he might have the preeminence." (Colossians 1:16-18)*
>
> *"Whosoever transgresseth, and abideth not in the doctrine of Christ, hath not God. He that abideth in the doctrine of Christ, he hath both the Father and the Son." (2 John 1:9)*

Even so, people in today's shifting Christianity who are openly casting aside the doctrine of God's Word of truth and "rethinking" the obedience of God as manmade "legalism" are scornfully rejecting warnings as just the "negative" promotion of "fear" by the "doctrine police." Rather than remaining steadfast in the faith and obedience of the Lord Jesus Christ, people are unabashedly choosing to be windblown. "Reimagining" the *certainty* of Who the Lord Jesus Christ *is* into *uncertainty* sets them free from the certainty of absolute truth so that they can then freely "reimagine" Jesus into a fashion that they are *willing* to accept. Not surprisingly, the "Jesus" that people are willing to accept is someone who conforms to man and man's expectations. He is someone who requires no one to believe and obey him but, rather, allows people to have a relationship with him in any religion (religious "framework" or "system") of their choosing. He is someone who is typically just a "style" to be emulated or just a "model" of man's "relationship" with God.

The Shack's "reimagined" "God" of untruth even falsely teaches that "Jesus" "has *never* drawn upon his nature as God to do anything," but, rather, has only been "living in the very same manner that I desire to be in relationship with every human;" "Jesus" "is just the first to do it to the uttermost."[1]

There is so much anti-truth, anti-Christ, anti-God blasphemous absurdity in just this alone that it could easily take a book to thoroughly address it. That this is "*another* Jesus"—a counterfeit, a fake—would have been obvious in Christianity before the shift to darkness. But now details are irrelevant in today's light-intolerant Christianity that prefers to absurdly imagine that *The Shack is one long Bible study* that teaches *sound truth* with *no theological errors* and *nothing heretical or that contradicts the Bible*. So suffice it to say that even just this one example in itself is a complete denial of the *truth* of *Who* the Lord Jesus Christ *was* and *is* and *always will be*, which, in turn, is a complete denial of the *truth* of what the Lord Jesus Christ did on the cross, which, in turn, is a complete denial of the *truth* of the Gospel of Christ. And yet these are the denials, whether in full or in part, that lead to "reimagining" the Lord Jesus Christ in the first place.

> *"Unto you therefore which believe he is precious: but unto them which be disobedient, the stone which the builders disallowed, the same is made the head of the corner, and a stone of stumbling, and a rock of offence, even to them which stumble at the word, being disobedient ..." (1 Peter 2:7-8)*

> *"And they shall turn away their ears from the truth, and shall be turned unto fables." (2 Timothy 4:4)*

Those who "reimagine" Jesus and bear with those who preach "*another* Jesus" are stumbling over even the most basic of the Lord Jesus Christ's sayings, which is to *believe on Him*.

> *"Jesus answered and said unto them, This is the work of God, that ye believe on him whom he hath sent." (John 6:29)*

> *"Jesus cried and said, He that believeth on me, believeth not on me, but on him that sent me.... I am come a light into the world, that whosoever believeth on me should not abide in darkness. And if any man hear my words, and believe not, I judge him not: for I came not to judge the world, but to save the world. He that rejecteth me, and receiveth not my words, hath one that judgeth him: the word that I have spoken, the same shall judge him in the last day." (John 12:44, 46-48)*

> *"But the scripture hath concluded all under sin, that the promise by faith of Jesus Christ might be given to them that believe." (Galatians 3:22)*

> *"And this is the condemnation, that light is come into the world, and men loved darkness rather than light, because their deeds were evil. For every one that doeth evil hateth the light, neither cometh to the light, lest his deeds should be reproved.*

But he that doeth truth cometh to the light, that his deeds may be made manifest, that they are wrought in God." (John 3:19-21)

This light intolerance is the very reason that more and more people are turning away from the knowledge of the holy to the unholy conversations and dialogues of man. Their ears are positively itching for unsound doctrine that justifies their unwillingness to believe and obey God and the true Lord Jesus Christ. The popular *Shack* affirms its main character and its readers who are "sick of God and God's religion" and seeks to free them from the so-called "guilt edges" of God's Holy Scriptures.[2] It then leads them to *The Shack*'s "reimagined" "God" which has been "reimagined" to justify their desire for freedom from "all the things the Scriptures tell us we should do."

People just do not want the *certainty* of God's *truth*. They want to build their faith on the *uncertainty* of sand and darkness and no rules. And they want freedom from rules and from requirements and from expectations—from *anything* the true God wants us to do—so they can *decide for themselves* what is right or wrong on their own "reimagined" way to their own "reimagined "God." They are clearly resisting <u>God</u> being God. In response to the main character's open "sarcasm" of "you're God and I'm not," *The Shack*'s "reimagined" "God" conveniently responds, "Yes, but not exactly."[3]

No matter how many people choose to believe otherwise, a "reimagined" "God" will never be anything but a counterfeit god that people are willing to accept as "genuine." A "reimagined" "God" is no more the true God than shifting sand is the Rock. *The Shack*'s counterfeit god even admits, "I am a verb. I am that I am. I will be who I will be. I am a verb!"[4] *Of course* it is a verb. It is *shifting sand*, not the eternal Rock. Although *The Shack*'s counterfeit god claims to be "I am that I am," its aspirations to be the true God follow in the Devil's footsteps who said, "I will be like the most High" (see Isaiah 14:12-15). With serpentine subtilty, their "I will be" phrases stand in direct opposition to "I AM THAT I AM." They are *not* the same thing.

"I AM" is *certainty*. "I will be" is *uncertainty*. They are brought together as one in *The Shack* in the vain attempt to create certainty out of uncertainty and uncertainty out of certainty. Although certainty is not uncertainty and uncertainty is not certainty, people are spinning in circles trying to bring them together as one in a harmonious relationship.

Nevertheless, shifting sand is *not* the Rock. The Rock is *not* shifting sand. To try to be like the Rock, shifting sand would have to be glued together. But then it would no longer be a verb, and it still wouldn't be the Rock. No matter what they use for glue— from the "relationship" of New Age Oneness to even taking truth from God's Word—it still would be nothing more than glued-together sand. It would be nothing but a counterfeit that is trying to "be like the most High." Inevitably, this glued-together counterfeit "rock" of sand will be broken in pieces by the Word of God, even if its glue takes from God's Word itself:

> *"... and he that hath my word, let him speak my word faithfully. What is the chaff to the wheat? saith the LORD. Is not my word like as a fire? saith the LORD; and like a hammer that breaketh the rock in pieces? Therefore, behold, I am against the prophets, saith the LORD, that steal my words every one from his neighbor.... And the burden of the LORD shall ye mention no more: for every man's word shall be his burden; for ye have perverted the words of the living God, of the LORD of hosts our God." (Jeremiah 23:28-30, 36)*

Today's absurd attempt to *transform shifting sand into the Rock* is the vain attempt to create the certainty of "truth" out of uncertainty. Yet those who want their faith built on shifting sand are determined to succeed. So, even more absurdly, people are attempting the opposite tactic as well in order to create uncertainty out of certainty. In believing that people can "rethink" and "reimagine" God however anyone chooses, *man is actually trying to blast the eternal Rock—the Lord God Who created man for His pleasure—in the vain attempt to transform the Rock into shifting sand.* (No wonder man invented the Big Bang!)

Deep down, people know the true God is the eternal Rock. They just aren't willing to accept that God doesn't shift and change with them. Therefore, in their never-ending circles of absurdity, people are attempting to transform the Rock into shifting sand so that they can then transform the shifting sand back into the Rock. But this fashion of the Rock that they are *willing* to accept will never be anything but a counterfeit "rock" of sand.

Sadly, those who are choosing to close their eyes and ears to the *truth* of God's Word are willing to accept a counterfeit "God" as "genuine" that has no power to save itself, let alone anyone else. Even though they and the Word of God make their reasons clear – Why?! All of the absurdity and "reimagining" God into a manmade counterfeit and flipping everything upside down just because people are not willing to walk in the light of the narrow way with the Majesty on high, the everlasting true God Who is ever with us: full of love, tender mercy, wisdom, lovingkindness, comfort, mighty power to help, gentleness, compassion, healing, strength, longsuffering, forgiveness, . . . *This* is the God that people are *not willing to accept*?[B] But they don't see it that way with their eyes closed to block the light.

> "... Holy, holy, holy, Lord God Almighty, which was, and is, and is to come.... worship him that liveth for ever and ever ... Thou art worthy, O Lord, to receive glory and honour and power: for thou hast created all things, and for thy pleasure they are and were created." (Revelation 4:8, 10-11)

> "To whom will ye liken me, and make me equal, and compare me, that we may be like?... Remember the former things of old: for I am God, and there is none else; I am God, and there is **none like me**." (Isaiah 46:5, 9)

In the darkness, people can make-believe that man's "reimagined" god is the true God, or even "like" God, to their heart's content, but it is still an unholy counterfeit god that is not living and is not eternal, which never was and will not be until man's imagination has fictitiously given it "life." Counterfeit gods will never be "real" and "true." The truth of Who God is cannot be separated from the true God in order to dress up counterfeit gods to be "like the most High." Even if counterfeit gods deceive *many* people into believing their "I will be" statements, all they will ever be is counterfeit.

> "Take heed, brethren, lest there be in any of you an evil heart of unbelief, in departing from the living God." (Hebrews 3:12)

B

See the small sampling of God's characteristics taken directly from God's Word in the Appendix "The Majesty on High, the Everlasting True God in the Light of His Word."

PART TWO:
THE CIRCLE

11

The heart and circle of the "relationship"

"Thus saith the LORD; *Cursed be the man that trusteth in man, and maketh flesh his arm, and whose heart departeth from the* LORD.... *The heart is deceitful above all things, and desperately wicked: who can know it? I the* LORD *search the heart, I try the reins, even to give every man according to his ways, and according to the fruit of his doings." (Jeremiah 17:5, 9-10)*

Those who love *The Shack* and its counterfeit god admit they are following their heart. Since people aren't heeding God's Word, let alone its warnings, they aren't taking heed not to follow "an evil heart of unbelief." Hebrews 3:12 warns us to take heed because an unbelieving heart leads to *"departing from the living God,"* which is obviously the *opposite* of a relationship with the true God. Yet with "relationship" the new ultimate "truth," it is irrelevant to people if their "relationship with God" is built on the *imaginations of man* rather than the *truth of God*, especially when it *feels* so "real" and "true" with their *eyes* and *ears* closed.

Experiences and feelings are so preeminent today that more and more people are spinning in circles desperately trying to bring true and false together as one. They are determined to achieve their desired freedom from what *is* true or false and right or wrong and are trying to bring it all together in one big circle of "relationship." This harmonious relationship that people are trying to "reimagine" everything into is Oneness. To say that this is *an entirely different way of thinking and acting* is a tremendous understatement.

This pervasive shift that is transforming everything is a shift from the *linear* thinking of *the truth* to the *circular* thinking of *Oneness*. Appropriately, a circle makes an "O" for Oneness, providing a visual illustration. Oneness takes polar opposites and brings the two ends of the line together to form a circle of unity. Polar opposites—such as truth and lies, right and wrong, certainty and uncertainty, light and darkness, real and imaginary, Christianity and the world, holy and unholy, righteousness and sin, godliness and worldliness, sacred and secular, believers and unbelievers, faith and faithlessness, Christian and nonchristian, God's Word and man's word, the narrow way and the broad way, Rock and sand, the true God and false gods—are all being brought together in "relationship" in the circle of unity of New Age Oneness. This *changes everything*, which is precisely what people want. There are no opposites in Oneness; there is only "relationship," this connected *circle* of relationship—O.

In this *circle* of Oneness, there is no *separation* of *either/or* but only a *circular* unity of *both/and*. It is this *circle* where no opposites can exist that gives "freedom" from *what is* true or false and right or wrong. There is only all of it together, connected in one big circle of relationship where everyone has the freedom to relativistically *decide for themselves* what they want to believe and do. But, of course, what they decide *must* be based on maintaining the *unity* of the *circle*. This is the only "rule" in Oneness—the circle is not allowed to be separated. If the circle's unity separates and divides then all they have left is the *line* of *polar opposites*, and thus no more Oneness and no more freedom.

This undone circle and loss of freedom is what is feared, which is why people are heeding those who positively affirm the *circle* of man's "*re*imaginations" and are rejecting those who hold fast to God's *separative* Word of *truth*. They are bound and determined to keep the two ends of the line together in unity, to keep the circle a *circle*. So, naturally, anyone seen as "separative" and "divisive" of this "right relationship," or "right relations," of the unity of the *circle* progressively becomes the "enemy,"[1] first of their freedom and then of the "unity in diversity" of all belief "systems" and gods. And, as is to be expected in the blinding darkness of Oneness, those in its counterfeit "truth" come to believe that those who are "separative" are actually the enemy of *God*. After all, they see this circle as the "truth" that sets God free from the "box" of God's Word.

> *"Hear the word of the LORD, ye that tremble at his word; Your brethren that hated you, that cast you out for my name's sake, said, Let the LORD be glorified: but he shall appear to your joy, and they shall be ashamed." (Isaiah 66:5)*

> *"I am Alpha and Omega, the beginning and the end, the first and the last. Blessed are they that do his commandments, that they may have right to the tree of life, and may enter in through the gates into the city. For without are dogs, and sorcerers, and whoremongers, and murderers, and idolaters, and whosoever loveth and maketh a lie. I Jesus have sent mine angel to testify unto you these things in the churches." (Revelation 22:13-16a)*

In truth, the true God and the circle of Oneness are mutually exclusive. There is no Alpha and Omega, beginning and end, first and last to the *circle*—O. Nor is there a *circle* to the Alpha and Omega, the beginning and the end, the first and the last. Neither the God of truth nor His truth is in the circle of relationship of Oneness. Again, the truth cannot be separated from the God of truth in order to dress up false gods to be "like the most High." This circle simply transforms everything into one big harmonious lie, leaving those in it with what they wanted in the first place—the uncertainty of a "reimagined" "truth" and a "reimagined" "God."

Although people in this ever-changing circle believe they are learning the "truth about God," the "truth" they are ever learning is not *the knowledge of God's truth* but, rather, *the circular thinking and "rethinking" of man's untruth*. In the *circle*, everyone freely journeys round and round, revisiting the same path over and over, each time deciding *afresh* what "truth" means to them in layer upon layer of "learning" that does not end with "the knowledge of *the truth*":

> *"Ever learning, and never able to come to the knowledge of the truth." (2 Timothy 3:7)*

> *"Then said Jesus to those Jews which believed on him, If ye continue in my word, then are ye my disciples indeed; and ye shall know the truth, and the truth shall make you free." (John 8:31-32)*

> *"For this is good and acceptable in the sight of God our Saviour; Who will have all men to be saved, and to come unto the knowledge of the truth." (1 Timothy 2:3-4)*

> *"For ever, O LORD, thy word is settled in heaven." (Psalm 119:89)*

In this circle where nothing is ever settled, the knowledge of the truth is actually irrelevant. Everything is always changing with "fresh" new "<u>re</u>imaginations." This way, there are no absolutes to *believe* and *obey*. Yet "not willing that any should perish" (2 Peter 3:9), God forewarns people in His Word of absolute truth about this circle of no opposites that has no separation of *what <u>is</u>* true or false and right or wrong:

> *"Woe unto them that call evil good, and good evil; that put darkness for light, and light for darkness; that put bitter for sweet, and sweet for bitter! Woe unto them that are wise in their own eyes, and prudent in their own sight!" (Isaiah 5:20-21)*

> *"… they have put no difference between the holy and profane, neither have they shown difference between the unclean and the clean, … and I am profaned among them." (Ezekiel 22:26)*

> *"Be ye not unequally yoked together with unbelievers: for what fellowship hath righteousness with unrighteousness? and what communion hath light with darkness? And what concord hath Christ with Belial? or what part hath he that believeth with an infidel? And what agreement hath the temple of God with idols? for ye are the temple of the living God; as God hath said, I will dwell in them, and walk in them; and I will be their God, and they shall be my people. Wherefore come out from among them, and be ye separate, saith the Lord, and touch not the unclean thing; and I will receive you, and will be a Father unto you, and ye shall be my sons and daughters, saith the Lord Almighty." (2 Corinthians 6:14-18)*

The above warnings about the circle were given *thousands* of years ago. *There is nothing "outdated" about God's Word of truth.* It very clearly states <u>what is</u> in no uncertain terms and immediately *divides* and *separates* the circle and straightens it into what the circle of "relationship" is in truth – a line of polar opposites. Using the *no uncertain terms* of God's *settled* Word is simply unacceptable to those who love uncertainty. People falsely claim it is "outdated" and continue to <u>re</u>write God's Word of truth because they are bound and determined to keep the unity of their circle, and thus their freedom, and they don't want straightforward truth to straighten out their circular thinking.

> *"Know therefore that the LORD thy God, he is God, the faithful God, which keepeth*

*covenant and mercy with them that love him and keep his commandments **to a thousand generations**." (Deuteronomy 7:9)*

"Ponder the path of thy feet, and let all thy ways be established. Turn not to the right hand nor to the left: remove thy foot from evil." (Proverbs 4:26-27)

"And thou shalt not go aside from any of the words which I command thee this day, to the right hand, or to the left, to go after other gods to serve them." (Deuteronomy 28:14)

Those who prefer the uncertainty of their unsettled "reimaginations" to the certainty of God's settled Word of truth are spinning in circles, turning both to the right hand and to the left in their desire to find "truth" and "God" wherever they choose to find them.

Bound up in the circle of relationship of Oneness itself, it is no surprise that *The Shack*'s counterfeit "God" says, "We are in a *circle* of relationship, not a chain of command," in which "we have no concept of final authority among us, only unity," and that "we want you to join us in our circle of relationship," to "share life with me."[2] It is also no surprise that this *circle* of *unity* in *The Shack* deliberately shuns the supreme and final authority of the God of truth and His Holy Scriptures. And it is no surprise that *The Shack*'s counterfeit "Jesus" says of his followers that he "want[s] to join them in their transformation."[3] This is all *essential* to keep the circle a *circle*. Since the truth automatically separates and divides the unity of the circle into the line of its polar opposites, the *circle* of relationship can't even exist unless people *turn away from* God's Word of truth. Even then it only exists in the circular thinking of make-believe.

"And they shall turn away their ears from the truth, and shall be turned unto fables." (2 Timothy 4:4)

Truth and fables are opposites. Those who are turning away from the *certainty* of the *truth* of God's Word and unto the *uncertainty* of the *circular thinking* of fables for their "faith" and "truth" are doing so because they do not want truth that is to be *divided* into opposites. Rather, they want "truth" that is to be *united* in a circle of relationship—O.

"Study to show thyself approved unto God, a workman that needeth not to be ashamed, rightly dividing the word of truth." (2 Timothy 2:15)

12

The post-truth transformation of a Wordless "faith"

The circle of Oneness has been bringing transformation to today's shifting Christianity in *many, many ways*. For "Christianity," it is definitely a whole new way of thinking *and then some*. In the *circle* of Oneness there is no beginning or end, so the world will not end and judgment and hell become irrelevant, as does the need to be *saved*. There is no final destination in this circle, so helping people get ready for it becomes irrelevant. Likewise, heaven and earth become one, so getting to heaven becomes irrelevant. There is only the "spiritual *journey*" round and round the circle—O. Since this circle brings the past, present, and future together in its relationship, it all becomes about *being in the moment*, in *the here and now*, and both the past and the future become irrelevant. This in itself changes everything. All the foundations of the faith from the *true* Christianity of the *past*—i.e., what to believe and how to obey God—become irrelevant and "outdated." The prophecy of the faith for the *future* becomes irrelevant, "not literal," uncertain, and even "already *past*."

Naturally, if believing in a beginning and end is irrelevant then both the foundational truth of Genesis and the prophetic truth of Revelation become irrelevant as well. The truth of Genesis was the first to get "reimagined," and the truth of Revelation followed soon after. People are not willing to accept that by His *word* God spoke the *beginning* of the heavens and earth, and by His *word* God will speak the *end* of the heavens and earth. God's Word of truth even points out that those "in the last days" who "*willingly are ignorant*" that by "*the word of God*" both the heavens and the earth were created and the flood of judgment came will *scoff* at His coming judgment, in which "*by the same word*" He will bring an *end* to the heavens and earth in fire (see 2 Peter 3:3-10).

If they don't believe the beginning of the Word of God and they don't believe the end of the Word of God, then why would they believe the middle of the Word of God? They don't; they "*willingly are ignorant*" of this, too. This is why more and more people are openly "rethinking" and "reimagining" God, His Word, and the Christian faith into a fashion they are willing to accept, which of course conforms to man and his expectations. Some things never change.

> "*Thus saith the LORD of hosts, … To whom shall I speak, and give warning, that they may hear? behold, their ear is uncircumcised, and they cannot hearken: behold, the word of the LORD is unto them a reproach; they have no delight in it.*" *(Jeremiah 6:9-10)*

> "*Because that, when they knew God, they glorified him not as God, neither were thankful; but became vain in their imaginations, and their foolish heart was darkened.*" *(Romans 1:21)*

> "*O Timothy, keep that which is committed to thy trust, avoiding profane and vain babblings, and oppositions of science falsely so called: Which some professing have erred concerning the faith. Grace be with thee. Amen.*" *(1 Timothy 6:20-21)*

> "*For the time will come when they will not endure sound doctrine; but after their own lusts shall they heap to themselves teachers, having itching ears; and they shall turn away their ears from the truth, and shall be turned unto fables.*" *(2 Timothy 4:3-4)*

Although man's "reimaginations" transform everything as they go round and round and round in layer upon layer of changes, "It is written" *is* what it *is* and never changes. This remains so despite man's vain and rebellious attempts to "reimagine" and even rewrite God's Word of truth for Him into a fashion that man is willing to accept. *God's Word has been settled forever by God Himself.* Nevertheless, in the "spiritual journey" of the circle, God's Word of truth is openly rejected as a book "of proofs" that is to be believed and obeyed. Rather, it is simply "a companion" that can be interpreted however anyone wishes.

In this *journey* of the circle, it is all about what will *become* truth, not what *is* truth. "It is written" is too "static," and those in today's shifting Christianity want a "dynamic" "truth" that is ever changing and shifting with them. So believing the "rock-solid certainty" and "rock-solid foundations" of God's Word of truth is now even openly criticized as arrogance and pride. People clearly *want* their faith built on shifting sand. Besides, foundations would keep the circle from moving and people want a likeminded shifting "God" that is willing to be "a verb."

Thus, in the course of the never-ending layers of changes, God's Word of truth is becoming completely irrelevant, including that in the middle. In the circle of Oneness, all that matters is the "spiritual journey" of the circle which is bringing everything together in one big harmonious *relationship*. Changing everything in its path, this circle of Oneness has been bringing more and more into the circle in one massive relationship of Oneness in a snowball effect of global proportions. And now this giant snowball is rapidly picking up speed bringing all religions and gods together as one in its relationship as well. As this circle of relationship encompasses more and more it ultimately makes no difference at all what people believe or do. After all, everyone and everything within this circle are all "connected" together with "God." So within this circle and its "spiritual journey" people are free to define "God" however they choose and to have this "relationship" however they choose.

Not willing to accept that the true God has chosen to record the *certainty* of the *knowledge* of Himself in the words of *His* Word of *truth*, people in today's shifting Christianity even go so far as to imagine that it is "linguistic idolatry" to believe that an infinite God can be known "with certainty" through "finite language." People are bound and determined to set God and His truth free from the "box"—i.e., from the *words*—of God's Word so they can have their desired freedom to "think *outside* the box." They also go so far as to reject that the certainty of God's Word of truth applies to "all cultures" and "all contexts" and "all time" and prefer instead to absurdly imagine that the truth relativistically changes according to context, culture, and generation. Nevertheless, despite man's determined imaginations, God makes it clear that His Word of truth is His Word of truth. He is the One Who has chosen to communicate the knowledge of Himself to man in this way. And God is in *no way whatsoever* limited by our language in giving us *understanding* of the truth of His Word!

> *"The entrance of **thy words** giveth **light**; it giveth **understanding** unto the simple." (Psalm 119:130)*

The truth of God is the truth of God, and God does not change *the truth of Who He is* for any person, context, culture, or generation. Either people are willing to accept and believe in God as He is or they aren't. It's that simple.

If anyone imagined that the true shape of the earth actually changes for different cultures or generations, becoming flat for some people, round for others, and even square or triangular for any culture that might choose to imagine it as such, people would rightly believe this was absurd. And, likewise, if for some people the earth is suspended in space, but for others the earth actually sits directly on the back of a turtle, and for still others the earth actually sits on an elephant that is standing on a turtle, this would also be seen as absurd. Yet the relativistic thinking in which this would *all* be absurdly seen as *true* is what people now think about *God*. And not only so, but then people even dialogue the different beliefs and imaginations about "God" to figure out a "better understanding" of "truth" and "God"!

Maybe if people similarly get together and dialogue about why they think an elephant was added to one culture when another culture left it out they would figure out a "better understanding" of the earth. But in the course of their dialogue they would need to make sure that no one teaches anyone that there is no turtle or elephant because this would be seen as too divisive, closed-minded, and judgmental. Besides, if someone believes there *is* a turtle or an elephant they might be offended and that would defeat the purpose of dialogue.

The fact is that the purpose of dialogue is not to teach and believe what is *true* but to make *relationships* in the circle of Oneness. Even in today's shifting Christianity it is taught that not holding to doctrine provides a "safe space" to have relationships with those who are different. It is also taught that through conversation and dialogue people are free to "figure out together" a "better interpretation" and "better understanding" of "God" and "truth." In other words, through conversation and dialogue people are free to "rethink" and "reimagine" God into a fashion they are all willing to accept together. When relationships are everything truth becomes nothing and a Wordless faith becomes everything.

Truth is being sacrificed on the altar of unity (not to mention on the altar of absurdity). But, naturally, those who are sacrificing it don't see it that way. They see it as "humility" and as "faithfulness" to "God" and "God's" work in the world to "rethink" and "reimagine" an inclusive "God" and "truth" and "faith."

The certainty of God's Word of truth with its "It is written," "Thus saith God," and "Thus saith the Lord" is just too narrow-minded, straightforward, and divisive for the world's growing relationship in the circle of Oneness. Dialogue is even "facilitated" to intentionally prevent the truth and faith of God from being a stumbling block in this "safe space" created for people to freely "figure out together" a "better understanding"—i.e., a *broader* "understanding"—of "God" and "truth" and "faith" that is inclusive of all who are not willing to believe or obey God. After all, the purpose of dialogue is to facilitate Oneness, and Oneness is automatically undone in the light of God's Word of truth. Thus, dialogue creates a "safe space" by *transforming truth into relationship*—by facilitating the transformation of the dividing *line* of truth into a *circle* of unity. In other words, dialogue eliminates opposites (e.g., true and false, right and wrong, real and imaginary, faith and faithlessness, believers and unbelievers, the true God and false gods) by facilitating their *connection* in a *circle* of Oneness—O. In this circle is the "safe space" for those seeking shelter from God's Word of truth.

This "safe space" is being created throughout today's shifting Christianity, which is refusing to "Hold fast the form of sound words, which thou hast heard of me, in faith and love which is in Christ Jesus" and is doing the *opposite* of "Holding fast the faithful word as he hath been taught, that he may be able by sound doctrine both to exhort and to convince the gainsayers" (2 Timothy 1:13 & Titus 1:9). In this circle of darkness, all that matters is relationship.

> *"But this thing commanded I them, saying, Obey my voice, and I will be your God, and ye shall be my people: and walk ye in all the ways that I have commanded you, that it may be well unto you. But they hearkened not, nor inclined their ear, but walked in the counsels and in the imagination of their evil heart, and went backward, and not forward.... This is a nation that obeyeth not the voice of the LORD their God, nor receiveth correction: truth is perished, and is cut off from their mouth." (Jeremiah 7:23-24, 28)*

The *circle of Oneness* that is intentionally moving to *connect* everyone and everything in its ever-expanding relationship is behind the popular movements that have been obviously changing and transforming today's shifting Christianity. And as is to be expected, all of the movements—e.g., from those of "conservative" evangelicalism to Purpose Driven to the Emerging Church—are now rapidly being brought together in one big harmonious relationship. In turn, this relationship, which is exemplified both in the content and widespread popularity of *The Shack*, is itself moving ever deeper into relationship with the "God" and Emerging One Church of New Age Oneness. The world is coming together as One in a Wordless faith.[1]

13

Faith that comes by *the Word of God* vs. Faith that comes by *relationship*

"So then faith cometh by hearing, and hearing by the word of God." (Romans 10:17)

All of this merging and emerging is to be expected now that the unholy conversations and dialogues of man's "rethinkings" and "reimaginings" are supplanting the truth and faith of God's Word throughout today's shifting Christianity. And since the purpose of dialogue is to facilitate *Oneness* it is not surprising that people have even admitted that in the course of their dialogue with other religions they have come to believe that they all "worship *the same God.*"

It used to be obvious in Christianity that God makes it clear in His Word of truth that a *relationship* with God comes by *faith* in God and that faith in God comes by the Word of God. Obviously, if we don't believe the *Word* of God then we don't believe *God*, and if we don't *believe* God then we don't have *faith* in God, and if we don't have *faith* in God then we don't have a *relationship* with God. But those who aren't willing to *believe* the Word of God don't see it that way. So, in today's Christianity that prefers to "reimagine" it all outside the "box" of God's Word of truth, it is not surprising that the faith that comes by *the Word of God* is intentionally being replaced with faith that comes by *relationship*.

When relationship comes by faith, what a person believes is *essential*. Whereas when faith comes by relationship, what a person believes is *nonessential*. This even flips it all upside down and backward so that wherever a person chooses to find "God" and "truth" and a relationship of "faith" will determine what that person believes. And in the all-encompassing relationship of Oneness and its immanent "God" *everything* becomes a source of "faith." After all, in this "circle of relationship," "God" "dwells in, around, and through all things" as "the ground of all being" just as *The Shack*'s false god teaches.[1] In this relationship of Oneness, "God" is in *everything* and *everything* is in "God." This is as broad of a way to "God" as it gets.

In a nutshell, the relationship of Oneness comes down to the pagan cousins of pantheism ("God" is everything, and everything is "God") and panentheism ("God" is in everything, and everything is in "God"). Pantheism teaches that "God" is immanent, whereas Christianity teaches that God is transcendent. Panentheism attempts to bring them together by teaching that "God" is immanent but also transcendent. Today's shifting Christianity is doing the same. Panentheism is already being taught, including in *The Shack* and in movements such as Purpose-Driven, Emergent, Contemplative Spirituality/"Christian" Mysticism, etc. It has even made it into "worship" songs sung in churches. Yet panentheism has typically been taught under the absurd denial that it is panentheism which is being taught. But everything keeps progressively changing, and leaders, as well as others, have begun to openly admit that they embrace panentheism. Now the denial is that panentheism is related to pantheism, but with things changing so fast this will no doubt soon be openly embraced as well. After all, immanence is immanence.

Immanence is a pagan—and New Age—teaching, not a Christian one. That God is not inherent within any of creation, let alone all of it, used to be obvious in Christianity before the shift to darkness. But today's Christianity wants freedom from the "box" of God's Word of truth and has thus been openly seeking to eliminate "sacred versus secular." This would unquestionably set today's Christianity free from God's Word. Immanence conveniently eliminates *all* "sacred versus secular," so in panentheism there is ample freedom for all who prefer to "think outside the box." When "God" is *in everything* and everything is *in* "God," there is no separation of *anything whatsoever*. There is only this *relationship* of *everything* sharing in the very "*Being*" of "*God*." In panentheism, "God" is thus "the ground of *all* being," and there is *no such thing* as a separation between "sacred and secular," or between anything else for that matter. This not only automatically connects everyone and everything together in one big harmonious relationship of Oneness with its immanent "God," but it also conveniently renders *all* of Scripture irrelevant. So the teachings and warnings of God's Word of truth naturally fall on deaf ears.

In panentheism, there is no need to be warned about anything that is false or wrong because *everything* is in "God." In panentheism, there is even no need to be taught the truth of Who God is because "God" is in *everything*. So if anyone wants to know the "truth about God" they can look *anywhere at all*. Besides, if "God" is in everything then "truth" is also in everything. Therefore there is no need to *believe* the truth of God. In panentheism, what would people need to believe? Everything? Or whatever they *choose*. In panentheism, "truth" is as universally immanent as "God," so all "truth" becomes "God's truth" and people can thus find "God" and "truth" *wherever* they choose to look. After all, "in everything" means "in *everything*."

In panentheism, there is even no need for the Gospel of Christ to reconcile us to God because "God" is in everything, so there is *no such thing* as being separated from "God." Panentheism is a convenient universal salvation for all. And yet there is no need for salvation at all in panentheism. Salvation from what? Since opposites are eliminated in the relationship of Oneness and of its immanent "God," there is of course no right and wrong or sacred and secular or holy and profane or true and false, and so on. In this "spiritual journey" everyone has the freedom to believe and do whatever is right in their own eyes. So there is no need to fear any coming judgment of sin, especially since everyone and everything are all connected together with "God" in one big relationship. Thus, for obvious reasons, in the shift to darkness *relationship* is *everything*; that is, the relationship of *Oneness/panentheism* is *everything*.

Even though panentheism and its relationship of Oneness clearly render *all* of Scripture irrelevant, there is nevertheless much scripture twisting taking place in the vain attempts to prove panentheism is "biblical" and "Christian." Deep down people clearly know that the Christian God is the true God. Otherwise, they wouldn't bother "reimagining" the Christian God and faith but would just drop them altogether. Yet even though they know the Christian faith of the Christian God is the true faith of the true God, this is all too narrow for them to be *willing* to accept. So they choose to "reimagine" a broader faith of a broader "God" and label it all "Christian" so that this new broader faith of a broader "God" can conveniently become the "true" faith of the "true" "God."

As is to be expected, the "reimagined" "God" of today's "reimagined" Christianity is getting broader and broader in today's journey round and round the circle of Oneness with its layer upon layer of "learning." Again, ever "learning" in the circle of Oneness does not end with "the knowledge of *the truth.*" Rather, it is already inevitably ending with a relationship of "faith" with its panentheistic false "God" of Oneness, which is as broad of a "God" as it gets.

Although nothing could be further from the truth, a theologian from the Jesus Seminar, whose beliefs and teachings are being echoed in today's shifting Christianity, teaches that "panentheism" is simply "another Christian option for thinking about God."[2] (The Jesus Seminar used to be well known in Christianity for its explicit blasphemous apostasy and rejection of God's Word of truth. But obviously not any more now that today's shifting Christianity is itself following in the Jesus Seminar's footsteps.) This theologian, Marcus Borg, has summed up the result of his own belief in panentheism as follows:

> "I now see that the Christian life is not essentially about beliefs and requirements; it is not about believing in a God 'out there' for the sake of an afterlife later. Rather, thinking about God panentheistically leads to a relational understanding of the Christian life, which is, I am convinced, both true and profoundly life-giving."[3]
>
> "Where are we in relationship to God?... God is the One who is all around us and within us, the One in whom the universe is, even as God is more than the universe, the mystery with a capital M who is beyond all names, even as we name this sacred Mystery in our various ways."[4]
>
> "I now see the Christian life very differently. I now see it as a journey ... To be on a journey is to be in movement.... The journey image suggests that the Christian life is more like following a path than it is about believing things with our minds....
>
> "We are invited to make that journey, that journey of faith, in which we learn to trust our relationship to God and learn to be faithful to that relationship, and learn to see in a new way."[5]
>
> "This way of thinking about God, or the sacred, or the spirit--which are terms I use interchangeably--sees God not as a supernatural being out there, but as a non-material presence and reality which is right here and all around us. And I also argue that panentheism--which literally means 'everything is in God'--is faithful to the

Biblical tradition and indeed the theological tradition of the Church....

"One of the premises of the book [*The God We Never Knew*] is that over the last 30 to 40 years an older way of understanding Christianity has come undone for many people. It was literalistic, doctrinal, moralistic, exclusivistic--meaning by that that it was taken for granted that Christianity was the only way of salvation--and afterlife oriented.... My book is really intended to be a revisioning of Christian theology for people for whom that older understanding doesn't work.... people who are aware of religious pluralism, and therefore can't believe that Christianity is the only way; people who are aware of the historical relativity and cultural conditionedness of all doctrinal formulations and therefore [can't believe] the claim of any set of scriptures or creeds [as having] absolute truth for all time." (last two sets of brackets in the original)[6]

First, God, Who is "not willing that any should perish," excludes *no one* from the freedom to believe in Him. *Everyone* has the same simple choice to either believe or not. Contrary to the claims of today's shifting Christianity which has purposefully lost sight of the truth of Who God is, the loving merciful God is not dependent on man to get His truth and light—the *same* eternal truth and light as He recorded in His eternal Word—to everyone everywhere on earth. Sadly, it is the truth and faith of God that are being excluded by a world—and now even by today's "Christianity"—that is not *willing* to accept and believe the eternal God of truth Who never changes.

> "For ever, O LORD, thy word is settled in heaven." *(Psalm 119:89)*

> "O praise the LORD, all ye nations: praise him, all ye people. For his merciful kindness is great toward us: and the truth of the LORD endureth for ever. Praise ye the LORD." *(Psalm 117:1-2)*

> "God is the LORD, which hath shown us light ..." *(Psalm 118:27)*

> "That was the true Light, which lighteth every man that cometh into the world." *(John 1:9)*

> "And this is the condemnation, that light is come into the world, and men loved darkness rather than light, because their deeds were evil." *(John 3:19)*

Second, of course the "older understanding" that the literalistic, doctrinal, moralistic Word of God is the Word of *God* "doesn't work" for those who are not willing to accept and believe that God is Who He is and said what He meant and meant what He said. This is why more and more people are shifting to the new way of "understanding" Christianity that is found instead in the journey of the circle of Oneness. Here, in this journey of Oneness in relationship with its immanent counterfeit "God," *believing* the absolute truth of God's Word is neither required nor desired, especially since it straightens out the circular thinking that keeps the circle of relationship a circle of freedom. Thus, Christian theology—i.e., the truth of Who God is as He recorded in His Word of truth—is being "reimagined" into a fashion that those in this "journey of faith" are *willing* to accept.

> "For unto us was the gospel preached, as well as unto them: but the word preached did not profit them, not being mixed with faith in them that heard it." *(Hebrews 4:2)*

Sadly, with today's very popular movements of the blind leading and following the blind, it was only a matter of time until the ditch became a popular path for today's "spiritual journey."

"... Can the blind lead the blind? shall they not both fall into the ditch?" (Luke 6:39)

In this journey of unbelief in the circle, salvation and getting to heaven are of course completely irrelevant. As mentioned previously, this journey has no end, no judgment, and no final destination. In this journey, heaven and earth become one, and the past, present, and future also become one, so it *all* becomes about the journey in *the here and now*. An afterlife is completely irrelevant. Besides, people are choosing this journey of "rethinking" and "reimagining" God because they are not willing to accept God as He is. So of course they are not going to want an afterlife with the God they are trying to get away from in this life! Why would they? Thus, they are putting all their eggs in a make-believe basket, hoping against hope that their imagination is "powerful" enough to protect them from the truth and reality of God. Essentially, people are telling God that *"when the overflowing scourge shall pass through, it shall not come unto us: for we have made lies our refuge, and under falsehood have we hid ourselves"* (Isaiah 28:15b). Some things never change. After thousands of years of "learning," people still imagine that imagination and lies are a place of peace and safety – a refuge from the God of truth Whom they are not willing to accept.

14

God's Word -- "a stumbling block in the way"!

People are determined to turn God's certainty into uncertainty and man's uncertainty into certainty. They simply are not willing to *believe* and *obey* God and "all the things the Scriptures tell us we should do." It is therefore not surprising that an increasing number of people in today's shifting Christianity are denying that the Word of God is *God's* Word of *absolute truth*.

As is to be expected of a theologian from the truth-rejecting Jesus Seminar, Borg openly and repeatedly denies this as well. In addition to his previous quote, he also says, "From beginning to end, the Bible is the story of God. Of course, the Bible is not God's story of God."[1] And again, "Most basically, it seems to me that a close and careful reading of the Bible makes it impossible to think that what it says comes directly or indirectly from God."[2]

> "... he that believeth not God hath made him a liar; because he believeth not the record that God gave of his Son." (1 John 5:10)

> "For what if some did not believe? shall their unbelief make the faith of God without effect? God forbid: yea, let God be true, but every man a liar ..." (Romans 3:3-4)

> "For this cause also thank we God without ceasing, because, when ye received the word of God which ye heard of us, ye received it not as the word of men, but as it is in truth, the word of God, which effectually worketh also in you that believe." (1 Thessalonians 2:13)

Again, theologians, or anyone else for that matter, do not have the power to change

God's truth just because they aren't willing to believe it. The Word of God is the Word of God and the word of man is the word of man. *God* is the One Who declares what is truth and what is not. We either believe it or we do not; the choice is ours. Following his own choice, Borg questions, "Is believing certain creeds really what Christianity is all about?" and then answers in the negative:

> "If one understands the beliefs of the tradition and the scriptures of the tradition not as what is to be believed, but as pointers beyond themselves that use the language of metaphor and poetry and symbol and so forth, then one can begin to see that the Christian life is about a relationship to the sacred. Christianity, like all the religions of the world, is a human construction. It uses human language, culturally conditioned relative language, and to absolutize that language is a profound mistake."[3]

Actually, the profound mistake is *making God out to be a liar*. It is not a mistake to *believe* the Word of God is *absolute truth*! Borg has it upside down. But those who refuse to believe that the Word of God is the Word of *God* see no need to beware of unbelief and faithlessness. Besides, those who believe in the "God" of panentheism that *encompasses everything* in its relationship naturally believe they are justified in thinking outside the "box" of the truth and faith of God's Word. This is especially so when they choose, as Borg did here, to conveniently "reimagine" God's Word as a metaphorical pointer to this *panentheistic* "relationship to the sacred" (see the next quote for his clarification of "the sacred"). He even admits in this previous quote that *if* one does not *believe* the Scriptures *then* one can begin to see this relationship. Indeed, choosing not to believe God's Word must precede believing in the panentheistic "God." Yet he still absurdly argues that this panentheistic relationship of unbelief is faithful to the "Biblical tradition":

> "This way of thinking about *God, or the sacred*, or the spirit--which are *terms I use interchangeably*--sees God not as a supernatural being out there, but as a non-material presence and reality which is right here and all around us. And I also argue that panentheism--which literally means 'everything is in God'--is faithful to the Biblical tradition and indeed the theological tradition of the Church." (emphasis added)[4]

Naturally, in today's upside-down way of thinking, being "faithful to the Biblical tradition" has nothing to do with *believing God's Word* and its record of the truth of Who God is, i.e., its theology. Accordingly, in a sermon titled, "Faith, Not Belief," Borg "reimagines" "faith" as coming by the relationship of this panentheistic "God" rather than by believing the Word of God:

> "Within the earlier paradigm or way of seeing the Christian life, believing has been central--believing in God, believing in Jesus, believing in the Bible, believing in Christianity, believing in the creeds, and so forth. Within the emerging paradigm relationship, not believing is central....
>
> "[T]he first of these meanings of faith ... has significantly distorted the meaning of faith and the Christian life.... This is faith as belief, ... as believing something to be true....
>
> "It's not only a distortion, ... but rather odd when you think about it. As if what God really cares about is the beliefs in our heads. As if believing the right things, having correct beliefs, is what God is most looking for, or as if what God is most looking for is people who are willing to believe highly iffy claims to be true....

> "What really matters is faith as faithfulness to the relationship with God ...
>
> "For me, the most adequate way of thinking about God is thinking about God as a non-material layer or level of reality that's all around us, as well as within us, not God as a person out there."[5]

So, in this new way of thinking, God's Word of truth becomes "highly iffy" but man "thinking about God panentheistically" becomes "true and profoundly life-giving"?![6] But then this is to be expected when faith as belief is intentionally replaced with faith as unbelief. Darkness is the preferred "light" in this journey, so *everything* gets flipped upside down into absurdity.

This emerging "paradigm"—faith—of panentheism/Oneness, in which "relationship, not believing is central," is changing *everything* in today's shifting and transforming Christianity. God is even being "reimagined" by popular leaders as "the God of all relationship," and even as "relationship" itself. It naturally follows that faith is being "reimagined" as something that does *not* come from *theology* but, rather, from *relationship*. And, accordingly, even the word *believe* is being "reimagined" so that *believe* does *not* mean faith that *believes certain things are true*, even if those things are "*divinely revealed*," but, rather, means faith that comes from the *heart*. When relationship is everything and everything is relationship, knowing and believing the truth is irrelevant.

> *"A fool hath no delight in understanding, but that his heart may discover itself." (Proverbs 18:2)*

Absurdly, when faith is in the panentheistic "God" that is in *everything*, faithfulness to *everything* becomes "faithfulness to the relationship with God," and therefore faithfulness to *everything* becomes "faithfulness" to "*God*." Likewise, *faith* absurdly becomes faithfulness to *everything*. Of course, the same is true in panentheistically "reimagining" the "Christian life" as "a relationship to the sacred." When "God" is in *everything* then *everything* becomes "sacred." Since nothing whatsoever is excluded from being "sacred" in panentheism, this "reimagines" the "Christian life" as a relationship to *everything*. Thus, in panentheism unbelieving faithlessness conveniently becomes faith and faithfulness.

Nevertheless, whether people choose to believe it or not, *God's* Word of *absolute truth* makes it perfectly clear that a relationship with God comes by *faith in God*, specifically by *faith in the Lord Jesus Christ*, and warns that an *unbelieving* heart leads to "*departing from the living God*." Again, this is obviously the *opposite* of a relationship with God, as well as the *opposite* of both faith and faithfulness to God.

> *"Take heed, brethren, lest there be in any of you an evil heart of unbelief, in departing from the living God." (Hebrews 3:12)*

The *true* faith of the *true and living* God both *believes* and *obeys*. This *is* what *true* faith *is*. "Faith" that neither believes nor obeys is only a counterfeit faith of those who are resisting God being God and resisting the Word of God being *God's* Word of *truth*.

> *"Thy word is a lamp unto my feet, and a light unto my path." (Psalm 119:105)*

> *"If we say that we have fellowship with him, and walk in darkness, we lie, and do not the truth." (1 John 1:6)*

> *"Thus saith the LORD, Stand ye in the ways, and see, and ask for the old paths, where is the good way, and walk therein, and ye shall find rest for your souls. But they said, We will not walk therein." (Jeremiah 6:16)*

> "As we enter the twenty-first century, we need a new set of lenses through which to read the Bible....
>
> "The older lenses enabled Christians of earlier generations to experience the Bible as a lamp unto their feet, a source of illumination for following the Christian path. But for many Christians in our time, the older lenses have become opaque, turning the Bible into a stumbling block in the way....
>
> "The first group, who sometimes call themselves 'Bible-believing Christians,' typically see the Bible as the inerrant and infallible Word of God. This conviction flows out of the way they see the Bible's origin: it comes from God, as no other book does. As a divine product, it is God's truth, and its divine origin is the basis of its authority....
>
> "The second group of Christians ... are less clear about how they *do* see the Bible than about how they do *not*. They are strongly convinced that many parts of the Bible cannot be taken literally, either as historically factual or as expressing the will of God....
>
> "Their numbers are growing ... They are responding strongly and positively to a more historical and metaphorical reading of the Bible.... [A] major de-literalization of the Bible is underway." (Marcus Borg)[7]

Of course those who are not willing to *believe* and *obey* God are going to find the Word of God, which is indeed both *historically factual* and *the expressed will of God*, "a stumbling block in the way"!

> *"Wherefore also it is contained in the scripture, Behold, I lay in Zion a chief corner stone, elect, precious: and he that believeth on him shall not be confounded. Unto you therefore which believe he is precious: but unto them which be disobedient, the stone which the builders disallowed, the same is made the head of the corner, and a stone of stumbling, and a rock of offence, **even to them which stumble at the word, being disobedient**: whereunto also they were appointed." (1 Peter 2:6-8)*

And *of course* the *literal, absolute truth* of the Word of *God* will also be a stumbling block in the way of the emerging paradigm/faith of panentheism/Oneness:

> "[O]ver the last 30 to 40 years an older way of understanding Christianity has come undone for many people. **It was literalistic, doctrinal, moralistic, exclusivistic**--meaning by that that it was taken for granted that Christianity was **the only way of salvation**--and afterlife oriented.... My book [*The God We Never Knew*] is really intended to be a revisioning of Christian theology for people for whom that older understanding doesn't work.... **people who are aware of religious pluralism**, and therefore can't believe that Christianity is *the only way*; people who are aware of the historical relativity and cultural conditionedness of all doctrinal formulations and therefore *[can't believe]* **the claim of any set of scriptures or creeds [as having] absolute truth for all time**." (Marcus Borg; last two sets of brackets in the original; emphasis added)[8]

> "*If* one understands **the beliefs** of the tradition and **the scriptures** of the tradition

> ***not as what is to be believed***, ... *then* one can begin to see that the Christian life is about a relationship to the sacred. Christianity ... uses human language, culturally conditioned relative language, and **to *absolutize* that language is *a profound mistake*.**" (Marcus Borg; emphasis added)[9]

> "*Religious pluralism* is a fact of life ... **To *absolutize* one's own religion as *the only way*** means that one sees all of the other religious traditions of the world as **wrong**, and dialogue, *genuine dialogue*, becomes impossible. *Conversion* can be the only goal.
>
> "**I affirm, along with many others, that the major enduring religions of the world are *all valid and legitimate*.** I see them as the responses to the experience of *God* in the various cultures in which each originated.... You could even say **they are *all divinely given paths to the sacred*.** To be Christian in this kind of context means to be deeply committed to one's own tradition, even as one recognizes the *validity* of other traditions." (Marcus Borg; emphasis added)[10]

First, even people in today's shifting Christianity clearly don't want to be converted to the true Christian faith that comes by the Word of God, so why would they want people in other religions (faiths) to be converted? Obviously, those who are shifting from light to darkness to think *outside* the "box" of God's Word are not going to want to teach others to think *inside* the "box," especially when they see the Word of God as "*a stumbling block*" that is not to be *believed*!

> *"For the heart of this people is waxed gross, and their ears are dull of hearing, and their eyes have they closed; lest they should see with their eyes, and hear with their ears, and understand with their heart, and should be converted, and I should heal them." (Acts 28:27)*

Second, in the context of panentheism/Oneness it is actually impossible "[t]o be Christian." In this emerging faith, different religions (faiths) do become just different "paths" and "experiences" of the same "God" that are *all equally "valid"* paths to "God"/ "the sacred." And, thus, it is only when people faithfully hold to *the absolute truth of the Word of God* that interfaith dialogue of course "becomes impossible." Or to put it another way, interfaith dialogue only works when people are willing to *set aside God's absolute truth*. And therefore any attempt to convert anyone to the only true faith of the only true God is simply not allowed in the "safe space" of today's "open-minded" "genuine dialogue." Again, dialogue is not about *teaching* and *believing* what is *true* but about making *relationships* in the circle of Oneness. And thus, since "*relationship*, not believing is central" in this emerging paradigm/faith of Oneness, in "genuine" interfaith dialogue the *absolute truth* of the Lord Jesus Christ is being denied before men.

> *"Also I say unto you, Whosoever shall confess me before men, him shall the Son of man also confess before the angels of God: But he that denieth me before men shall be denied before the angels of God.... Suppose ye that I am come to give peace on earth? I tell you, Nay; but rather division: For from henceforth there shall be five in one house divided, three against two, and two against three. The father shall be divided against the son, and the son against the father; the mother against the daughter, and the daughter against the mother; the mother-in-law against her daughter-in-law, and the daughter-in-law against her mother-in-law." (Luke 12:8-9, 51-53)*

The truth of the Lord Jesus Christ brings *division* and not *peace* between family members, the most basic unit of relationship. So the truth of the Lord Jesus Christ will especially bring *division* and not *peace* between the world's religions! Absolute truth *automatically* divides those who are willing to believe and obey it from those who are not willing to believe and obey it. At all levels of relationship the absolute truth of the Word of God is "a sword" of division. And, thus, in today's "genuine dialogue" that seeks interfaith relationship/Oneness, this instrument of division, i.e., this stumbling block of *absolute truth*, is inevitably *excluded*.

> "Then said Jesus to those Jews which believed on him, If ye continue in my word, then are ye my disciples indeed." (John 8:31)

> "And ye shall be hated of all men for my name's sake: but he that endureth to the end shall be saved.... Whosoever therefore shall confess me before men, him will I confess also before my Father which is in heaven. But whosoever shall deny me before men, him will I also deny before my Father which is in heaven. Think not that I am come to send peace on earth: I came not to send peace, but a sword. For I am come to set a man at variance against his father, and the daughter against her mother, and the daughter-in-law against her mother-in-law. And a man's foes shall be they of his own household. He that loveth father or mother more than me is not worthy of me: and he that loveth son or daughter more than me is not worthy of me." (Matthew 10:22, 32-37)

> "For what shall it profit a man, if he shall gain the whole world, and lose his own soul? Or what shall a man give in exchange for his soul? Whosoever therefore shall be ashamed of me and of my words in this adulterous and sinful generation; of him also shall the Son of man be ashamed, when he cometh in the glory of his Father with the holy angels." (Mark 8:36-38)

The absolute truth of God's Word *is* what it *is*. There is nothing to *dialogue*. *Truth* is to be *taught*, and people are either willing to hear the truth of God's Word or they are not. Sadly, in *dialogue* the only people letting go of their position are those who are letting go of God's Word of truth. Yet this is to be expected when the Word of God is a stumbling block in the way of today's drive to gain the whole world with the relationship of Oneness and its Wordless faith. Naturally, those who are shifting from believing to relationship won't see the problem with setting aside the divisive "highly iffy claims" of *the absolute truth of God's Word*. Since *believe* no longer means to *believe*, undoubtedly *deny* no longer means to *deny*. And, indeed, "a major de-literalization of the Bible" is well underway, as more and more people absurdly imagine that de-literalizing absolute truth actually de-literalizes absolute truth.

> "Woe to the rebellious children, saith the LORD, that take counsel, but not of me; ... That this is a rebellious people, lying children, children that will not hear the law of the LORD: Which say to the seers, See not; and to the prophets, Prophesy not unto us right things, speak unto us smooth things, prophesy deceits: Get you out of the way, turn aside out of the path, cause the Holy One of Israel to cease from before us." (Isaiah 30:1, 9-11)

15

"Transforming theology" -- "God in the very substance of creation"

The emerging faith and relationship of Oneness is unquestionably changing everything. After all, when "God" is in everything and everything is in "God" it makes no difference at all which religion people choose for their "*relationship.*" Why would it? Since this panentheistic "God" is in everything, i.e., immanently "dwells in, around, and through all things" as "the ground of all being,"[1] then people have "the freedom to be inside or outside all kinds of systems" including "religious" "systems" (such as "Buddhists or Mormons, Baptists or Muslims") and can "move freely between and among them," as *The Shack*'s false "Jesus" teaches who has "no desire to make them Christian."[2] With the panentheistic "God" of Oneness that is *in everything*, it doesn't matter what anyone *believes. Relationship* is *everything.*

In the Wordless faith of Oneness, *relationship* is the ultimate "Truth." Without the *relationship* of Oneness, there is no *Oneness.* There is only separateness. Without the *relationship* of Oneness, there is no broader "God" that is "bigger" than any particular religion that is connecting all gods together in this *one* "God." Without the *relationship* of Oneness, there is no broader "truth" that is connecting all "truths" together in this *one* "Truth." Without the *relationship* of Oneness, there is no broader "faith" that is connecting all religions together in this *one* "faith." Without the *relationship* of Oneness, there is no "unity in diversity" of it all.

People who desire interfaith unity, not to mention interfaith "worship," have even pointed out that panentheism is the best option for achieving it. Indeed, both the circle of relationship of Oneness and its immanent "God" have been bringing more and more religions together in the interfaith "spiritual journey" round and round its unifying path.

After all, in this journey of unbelief, people "learn to be faithful to that relationship, and learn to see in a new way," rather than "believing things with our minds."[3]

> *"Of the Rock that begat thee thou art unmindful, and hast forgotten God that formed thee.... for they are a very froward generation, children in whom is no faith. They have moved me to jealousy with that which is not God; they have provoked me to anger with their vanities ... For they are a nation void of counsel, neither is there any understanding in them. O that they were wise, that they understood this, that they would consider their latter end!... And he shall say, Where are their gods, their rock in whom they trusted, ... let them rise up and help you, and be your protection. See now that I, even I, am he, and there is no god with me ..."* (Deuteronomy 32:18, 20-21, 28-29, 37-39)

> *"Look unto me, and be ye saved, all the ends of the earth: for I am God, and there is none else. I have sworn by myself, the word is gone out of my mouth in righteousness, and shall not return, That unto me every knee shall bow, every tongue shall swear.... and all that are incensed against him shall be ashamed."* (Isaiah 45:22-24)

Sadly, many are incensed against God and are going to learn the hard way that His truth is absolute for "all cultures," "all contexts," and "all time." But those who refuse to believe that God said what He meant and meant what He said in His Word of truth don't see it that way. Thus, not willing to look unto the true God and be saved, man in his absurdity has chosen to imaginatively blast the eternal Rock in order to "reimagine" God as immanent in *all things* so that man can now attempt to connect *all things* back together as "God" in one gigantic "relationship" of Oneness. But this is also being done "scientifically" of course. After all, man imagines that man and his "science falsely so called" knows more about God than God does, and man ought to know, right?

> *"For the wisdom of this world is foolishness with God. For it is written, He taketh the wise in their own craftiness."* (1 Corinthians 3:19)

> *"This I say therefore, and testify in the Lord, that ye henceforth walk not as other Gentiles walk, in the vanity of their mind, having the understanding darkened, being alienated from the life of God through the ignorance that is in them, because of the blindness of their heart."* (Ephesians 4:17-18)

> *"Jesus said unto them, ... He that is of God heareth God's words: ye therefore hear them not, because ye are not of God."* (John 8:42, 47)

> *"So then faith cometh by hearing, and hearing by the word of God."* (Romans 10:17)

Rather than rethinking science in the light of God's truth, more and more people are choosing to "rethink" and "reimagine" God's truth in the "light" of science. This is true even of "Christian theologians." Again, a theologian who studies man's false theology—even if it is based on man's "science"—and believes it is "true" is nothing more than a deceived expert on false theology. Sadly, but not surprisingly, they are a growing number.

"As an explicitly developed concept, panentheism is becoming more and more common among mainline Christian theologians." (Marcus Borg)[4]

It isn't just theologians. It's pastors and other leaders as well. And their popularity is growing in today's shifting Christianity that has itching ears.

Absurdly, one of these popular leaders and theologians is Leonard Sweet who, among other things, has even essentially designated the belief that "God" is "in the very substance of creation" as a litmus test of "Christian" spirituality. According to Sweet and his espoused Quantum/New Light spirituality:

> "Quantum spirituality bonds us to all creation as well as to other members of the human family. New Light pastors are what Arthur Peacocke calls 'priests of creation'--earth ministers who can relate the realm of nature to God, who can help nurture a brother-sister relationship with the living organism called Planet Earth. This entails a radical doctrine of **embodiment of God in the very substance of creation**. *The Oxford Dictionary of the Christian Church* (1974) identifies the difference between pantheism and pan-entheism: Pantheism is 'the belief or theory that God and the universe are identical'; panentheism is 'the belief that the Being of God includes and penetrates the whole universe, so that every part of it exists in Him, but ... that His Being is more than, and is not exhausted by, the Universe.' New Light spirituality does more than settle for the created order, as many forms of New Age pantheism do. *But **a spirituality that is not in some way entheistic (whether pan- or trans-), that does not extend to the spirit-matter of the cosmos, is not Christian**.*" (parenthesis and ellipsis dots in the original; bold added)[5]

In the relationship of panentheism/Oneness, spirit and matter are just two more opposites being brought together as one. It is "God" in everything in "the very substance of creation" that gives the spirit-matter Oneness to the "cosmos." Again, immanence is immanence, and "God in the very substance of creation" is immanence. Those who believe in panentheism can attempt to differentiate it from New Age pantheism all they want, but panentheism (immanence and transcendence) *includes* pantheism (immanence); it simply goes *beyond* it. Sweet even writes, "Quantum spirituality does more than join together as one two words in all their complexity and nuance: energymatter, mindbody, spirit-matter (as Teilhard de Chardin called it)."[6] And according to Pierre Teilhard de Chardin, "What I am proposing to do is to narrow that gap between pantheism and Christianity by bringing out what one might call the Christian soul of pantheism or the pantheist aspect of Christianity."[7]

Christian author and former New Ager Warren B. Smith addresses panentheism and its spiritual dangers in his important book, *A "Wonderful" Deception: The Further New Age Implications of the Emerging Purpose Driven Movement*. In this book, Smith calls attention to Sweet's panentheistic quote above and this pantheistic purpose of Teilhard de Chardin, as well as to the fact that Teilhard de Chardin is described by Sweet as "Twentieth-century Christianity's major voice."[8]

Pantheism . . . panentheism . . . today's shifting Christianity can dance around these terms all it wants. But immanence is immanence, and immanence is pagan. And as Smith also points out, "But Sweet doesn't explain that any kind of panentheism is still a distinctly heretical New Age teaching."[9] Indeed it is. Yet in today's shift to darkness warnings go unheeded and leaders continue to believe and teach the opposite. Thus, the paradigm/faith of panentheism/Oneness continues to emerge, in which it is "not Christian" to believe that God is *not* "in the very substance of creation" and thus of course "Christian" to believe that "God" *is* "in the very substance of creation." Scripture twisting and absurd denials notwithstanding, this simply could not be any more upside down from the truth or any more New Age!

Yet today's merging and emerging "Christian"/New Age spirituality is to be expected in this journey of panentheism/Oneness that is even bringing today's "Christianity" and the New Age (New Spirituality) together as one in a harmonious relationship. But those who are purposefully replacing the faith that comes by the Word of God with faith that comes by relationship don't see it that way. Besides, in the shift to darkness man's imagination is the preferred "truth."

> *"And they shall turn away their ears from the truth, and shall be turned unto fables."*
> *(2 Timothy 4:4)*

Panentheism is so far removed from the truth and faith of *God's* Word that it should be obvious it is not even remotely true, let alone "biblical" and "Christian." Even so, a recent discussion that included panentheism titled, "Transforming Theology: Emergence for Emergents," took place between Tony Jones (a founder and leader of the Emergent Church movement) and Philip Clayton (a theologian and philosopher of emergence biology). In this "conversation about emergence science and emergent church," Clayton even claims that "panentheism" is about "recovering that biblical notion of a God who permeates us, who surrounds us, who's the water we live in and dwell in and breathe and eat and sleep" and that "panentheism is not an opponent to evangelicalism" but "is an evangelical tool to get us back to the gospel"![10]

> *"But the word of the Lord endureth for ever. And this is the word which by the gospel is preached unto you."* (1 Peter 1:25)

> *"But if our gospel be hid, it is hid to them that are lost: In whom the god of this world hath blinded the minds of them which believe not, lest the light of the glorious gospel of Christ, who is the image of God, should shine unto them."* (2 Corinthians 4:3-4)

> *"For if he that cometh preacheth another Jesus, whom we have not preached, or if ye receive another spirit, which ye have not received, or another gospel, which ye have not accepted, ye might well bear with him."* (2 Corinthians 11:4)

Blinded in their unbelief, people are doing the opposite of "avoiding profane and vain babblings, and oppositions of science falsely so called: Which some professing have erred concerning the faith" (1 Timothy 6:20-21). They are increasingly bearing with those who preach *"another* Jesus," *"another* spirit," and *"another* gospel," not to mention *another* "God." People simply are not willing to accept the true God and His narrow way. They want a broader "truth" of a broader "God" in a broader "faith," and there is nothing broader or "bigger" than panentheism.

Despite man's rebellious never-ending circles of "*re*thinking" and "*re*imagining" it all into a "better understanding" of "God" and "truth," and despite man's "science falsely so called" now backing up man's panentheistic imaginations on multiple fronts, the only gospel panentheism and its relationship of Oneness lead to is the *false* gospel of New Age (New Spirituality) Oneness.[11] This false gospel has also been referred to as "The New Gospel of Oneness"[12] by the false "God" in Neale Donald Walsch's previously mentioned "conversations with God."

"Go, therefore, and teach ye all nations, spreading far and wide *The New Gospel:*

"WE ARE ALL ONE.

"OURS IS NOT A BETTER WAY, OURS IS MERELY ANOTHER WAY." (the seducing spirit calling itself "God" that channeled its teachings through Neale Donald Walsch in their conversations)[13]

"Regardless of their beliefs, regardless of their religion....

"There are a thousand paths to God, and *every one gets you there.*" (the seducing spirit calling itself "God")[14]

"Our opportunity now is to create the space of possibility for a New Spirituality to emerge upon the earth ... that makes no one wrong for the way in which they are approaching the God of their understanding ..." (Neale Donald Walsch)[15]

"Humans will understand that God's words are found in all of the world's Holy Scriptures ...

"Human beings will ... simply look closely to see which text and which messenger speaks to them in a way that makes it possible for them to express and experience their connection to the Divine ..." (Neale Donald Walsch)[16]

As mentioned earlier, Oneness and its panentheistic "God" offer people the ultimate freedom from the rules and doctrine of the narrow way—the freedom to imagine and define "God" and their relationship with "God" *however* anyone chooses. What a person *believes* is irrelevant in this false gospel/Wordless faith. So those who want this freedom can bypass the *true* Lord Jesus Christ and the *true* God and can imagine "another way" to "the God of their understanding." When "God" is in everything and everything is in "God," *no one* is "wrong" for the "understanding" (theology) they choose—except, of course, true Christians who believe in the true God and the true Lord Jesus Christ. After all, "To absolutize one's own religion as the only way means that one sees all of the other religious traditions of the world as wrong."[17] And the emerging faith of Oneness/panentheism "makes no one wrong."

16

The immanent "God" of Oneness, imagined and defined in *limitless* ways

Contrary to the claims of those even in today's shifting Christianity who want God revealed to them in a fashion they are willing to accept, God is not revealed to man in "limitless" ways. God does not humor a rebellious imaginative world that is not willing to accept that God is Who He is and said what He meant and meant what He said in His Word of truth. On the other hand, the immanent "God" of New Age (New Spirituality) Oneness is revealed to the world in ways that are as "limitless" as man's imagination.

In a nutshell, this New Age (New Spirituality) Oneness, with its Emerging One Church and New Gospel of Oneness, is simply a vain attempt to bring God and many gods all together in one big panentheistic/pantheistic harmonious relationship in the circle of Oneness. In the "God" of Oneness that is immanent in all things, not only do all religions become equally valid paths to "the same God," but all gods become equal as well. That is, all gods of all religions become just different revelations, manifestations, understandings, and experiences of "the same God." So in this false "reimagined" "God" that is "bigger" than any particular religion, *many gods* become *one "God."* It therefore makes no difference which god of which religion anyone chooses for their relationship of "faith." In Oneness/panentheism there is no such thing as the "other gods" that God's Word of truth repeatedly warns against. There is only the "God" of Oneness that is "in everything"—i.e., is immanent in all things.

> *"This evil people, which refuse to hear my words, which walk in the imagination of their heart, and walk after other gods, to serve them, and to worship them, shall*

even be as this girdle, which is good for nothing." (Jeremiah 13:10)

Regardless of what people choose to imagine in the darkness, the panentheistic *one* "God" of Oneness is still *many* gods. Therefore, monotheists who choose relationship in the circle of Oneness are, among other things, automatically transformed into polytheists. Even if they themselves choose a relationship with only one of them, those who choose the relationship of Oneness are choosing the relationship where *all* gods are "God." This is what the relationship of Oneness is. But of course they don't see it that way because this counterfeit *one* "God" even brings the opposites of monotheism and polytheism, separateness and Oneness, and transcendence and immanence together as well in a harmonious relationship in the circle of Oneness. Therefore, they just see it all as "reimagining" God into a "bigger" and broader "God" that anyone can find wherever they choose to look.

As has been rightly pointed out, there is "no view of God" "larger than the panentheistic view." The panentheistic view of "God" goes beyond encompassing *everything and everyone*. Nothing whatsoever is excluded from being in "God." This "God" even goes beyond "every possible concept" of "God." Again, this immanent "God" is revealed in ways as "limitless" as man's imagination. So those who prefer to get their faith from relationship and not from *true theology* can thus choose to find "God" or their Wordless faith *wherever* their imagination takes them.

Conveniently, when faith comes from relationship and relationship comes from "reimagining" God as immanent *in "all things,"* people can even choose to find their faith in *any* relationship with *anything whatsoever*. "All things" includes "all things." And since Oneness "reimagines" "God" as one gigantic "relationship" of all things—as does "science falsely so called"—then "God" becomes the relationship and the relationship becomes "God." With this panentheistic "God"/relationship that is revealed in "limitless" ways, people can even freely choose to find their faith in a relationship with any god or goddess on the entire planet. After all, in this relationship of Oneness they are *all* just different "understandings" of "the same God." The circle of Oneness that even brings the past, present, and future together as one gives people quite a variety of gods and goddesses to choose from in its relationship, *in any god that man has ever imagined or ever will imagine.*

Unquestionably, Oneness/panentheism is as broad of a way to "God" as it gets. Anyone can freely choose to find the immanent "God" and a "relationship" of "faith" *wherever they choose to look*: including in any or all of creation; in the planet, which has already been "reimagined" into a goddess; or in the sun, the moon, the stars, or all heavenly bodies; in an eagle; in a serpent; in an ant; in a monkey; in a praying mantis; in a cow; in a tree; in food; or in any inanimate object; in any person; in Self; in DNA; in science; or even in evolution; in quantum physics; in emergence biology; in Religious Science/Science of Mind; in quantum spirituality; or in meditation; in contemplative spirituality; in spirit guides; even stepping in dog poop[1] is a "relationship" with the panentheistic "God" that is absurdly immanent *in "all things;"* then there are the sun gods; moon gods; rain gods; the gods and goddesses in any and every religion, culture, country, and civilization; even Satan and his devils are worshipped as gods; there's Egyptian gods; Babylonian gods; Roman gods; Greek gods; Wiccan gods; Hindu gods; pagan gods; Incan gods; Mayan gods; Aztec gods; Celtic gods; tribal gods; Native American gods; African gods; European gods; Middle Eastern gods; Eastern gods; Western gods; Mesopotamian gods; gods in Old Testament times; gods in New Testament times; voodoo gods; occult gods; the gods in any video game; the gods in any book; the gods in any movie; the gods in *anyone's* and *everyone's* imagination . . .

People can take their pick from their own imagination or from someone else's. It makes no difference. There are no rules in the imaginative "truth" and "faith" of *uncertainty* and *mystery*. All that matters is *relationship*. And since in the desired relationship of Oneness *everything* is all *one* "relationship"—i.e., all *one* "God"—it doesn't matter what anyone *believes*. *No one* is "wrong" for the "understanding" (theology) they choose. Besides, the truth and faith of *God's* Word have been "reimagined" into a *manmade* "box" of "changeable" and "debatable" "metaphor" and "story" and "symbol" that are merely "pointers" to this all-encompassing relationship, in which God's Word is not to be believed as "absolute truth" for "all cultures" and "all contexts" and "all time." Therefore, *whatever* people are *willing* to accept becomes their *own path* to "truth" and "faith." Since "God" is revealed to man in "limitless" ways outside the "box," people can even imaginatively choose relationship with either one "God" or any number of gods, with either a "Christianized" "God"—such as the "reimagined" "God" of *The Shack*—or otherwise. After all, outside the "box," man's imagination is "truth."

Imagination is imagination, and there is quite the variety of imaginatively fashioned gods ("understandings") that man has already been willing to accept as "truth": there's even a cow goddess; a gazelle-headed goddess; a tree goddess; a sky goddess; a frog-headed god and a frog-headed goddess; a triple-headed cobra goddess; a solar cow god; a laundress goddess; a household goddess of bees; a scorpion goddess; a crocodile god; a goose god; an ibis-headed god; a goat god; a horse goddess; a triple-faced god; a cross-legged god with antlers; a fish god; a tortoise god; a rainbow snake goddess; a toad goddess; a lion-headed war goddess; a dominant male baboon god; an elephant-headed god with up to sixteen arms; a goddess that has ten arms, ten legs, and ten heads; a god that is a liberator of cows; a cow goddess of the sky (think of the "rain" that would fall!); a drunken rabbit god; trickster gods; gods that even play tricks on other gods; a feathered serpent god; a goddess of the earth whose face is two serpents; gods and goddesses that are powerful magicians; a sorceress goddess; a dragon god of sorcery; shapeshifting gods; a wizard god; …

Outside the "box" is outside the "box." Absurdly, people in today's shifting Christianity are even choosing to believe that man's imagination gives people "a better understanding of God." To say that this is utter nonsense is a tremendous understatement. Imagination is imagination, and, "Christianized" or otherwise, the *only* "God" that man's imagination will *ever* give people a better understanding of is the "God" of man's imagination. Nevertheless, in today's Wordless faith the true theology of the Word of God and thus the truth of Who God is have been rendered irrelevant. *Relationship* is the preferred source of faith.

Thus, all who prefer the uncertainty of man's imagination and its emerging paradigm/faith of a panentheistic "God" that is *in everything and everyone* can experience a "relationship" with this "God" with *anything whatsoever* that they so choose. This path has already proven to be quite acceptable to man. Among the *countless* imaginative examples to choose from for a relationship: there are even gods and goddesses of snowshoes; of brushes; of locked doors; of the kitchen; of food; of fermented foods; of sourdough; of rice; of salt; of beer; of apples; of worms; of frogs; of bees; of birds; of rabbits; of herds; of pasture; of pigs; of the growth of grain; of fishing; of the seasons; of weather; of thunder; of fog; of coldness; of mist; of echoes; of wind; of fresh water; of salt water; of daylight; of night; of rivers; of the sea; of mountains; of the forest; of the milky way; of planets; of the rising sun; of good grooming; of bathing; of well-being; of beauty; of learning; of fame; of vanity; of silence; of pleasure; of paint; of music; of games; of dancing; of politics; of commerce; of marriage; of fertility; of happiness; of prosperity; of longevity; of sickness; of medicine; of the bones of the dead; of a toothache; of the calendar; of time; of change; of mystery; of everything that flows; of paths; of duality; of harmony; of creativity; of dreams; of good luck; of bad luck; of conflict; of deception; of gossip; of gambling; of enmity; of purification from filth; of trickery; of temptation; of lust; of revelry; of rape; of murder; of astrology; of craft; of magic; of witchcraft; of sorcerers and sorcery; ...

People have long since decided that things are good which God says are evil and evil which God says are good and have imagined their gods, as well as their relationship with their gods, accordingly. *Anything* goes in the Wordless faith of man's imagination. And regardless of what each person chooses to believe for themself, in Oneness/panentheism *all* of man's imagined gods become the *one* "God" of the *one* "Truth" of the *one* "faith." Those who choose the relationship of Oneness are *automatically* choosing the relationship where *all* gods are "God," and therefore *all* gods are *equal*.

Choosing this relationship is neither faith nor faithfulness to God but, rather, a dangerous departing from the *narrow* way of the *holy* God of *truth*. In this relationship and its "New Gospel of Oneness," "OURS IS NOT A BETTER WAY, OURS IS MERELY ANOTHER WAY" and "Regardless of their beliefs, regardless of their religion.... There are a thousand paths to God, and every one gets you there."[2] *No one* is "wrong" for the "understanding" (theology) they choose. There are even gods and goddesses that adorn themselves with the body parts of their human victims; gods that sacrifice themselves to become the sun god; gods and goddesses that eat their offspring; a god that swallowed his pregnant goddess spouse; a goddess that dances on corpses; a god that castrated his father and married his sister; goddesses that sacrificed themselves and then came back to life after other gods worshipped their skirts; a god that decapitated his sister and threw her head into the sky to become the moon; gods that get their strength from the nourishment of human blood; goddesses that get pregnant and give birth to full-grown warriors; a goddess that gave birth to the moon and stars; a goddess that gave birth to heaven and earth; a sea goddess that spawns scorpion men; a rain god that is pleased when frogs are married in religious rituals; gods that created land out of the body of a crocodilian earth monster; a lizard god that created humans; ...

It is with blind absurdity that even leaders of today's shifting Christianity believe that faith comes from *relationship* and *not* from *theology*; that man's imagination is the "truth" about God; that God is revealed to us in "limitless" ways; that "humility" welcomes the various manifestations of "God" in different cultures and religions; that everyone has a unique "connection" to God and can define and interpret for themselves who this "God" is; that it doesn't matter what religion people are in; that different religions just have different "experiences" and "conceptions" and "views" of God; that God is bigger than all conceptualizations and images; that religious pluralism gives a better understanding of "truth;" that it's about a relationship, *not* a religion; that God is "the God of all relationship;" that God is in the "very substance" of creation; that different religions just have a different way/path to God and to a relationship with God; that people can follow Christ in *any religious framework* of their choosing; that to "absolutize" the Christian faith as "the only way" falsely sees all of the other religions of the world as "wrong;" that we all worship "one God" in one "kingdom of God" that can't be "hijacked" by the Christian faith; and the absurdity goes on and on in today's desire for the darkness and freedom of Oneness/panentheism and its Wordless faith.

The leaders in today's shifting Christianity who want "revolution" are already getting it, against God Himself. But they don't see it that way since they are closing their eyes and ears to the truth to join the world in "reimagining" "God" and "truth" and "faith" into a fashion they are all willing to accept together in one big harmonious relationship. Regardless of whether people admit that this swiftly emerging transformation is New Age (New Spirituality) Oneness or whether they absurdly claim it is "Christian," this transformation is the idolatry of exalting man above God and is changing everything.

Although man imagines otherwise, man's imagination doesn't suddenly become "truth" and "reality" just because it is the 21st century and man imagines that man is wiser now. The lists above include man's 21st century imagination. In any century, imagination is imagination and the truth is the truth whether people are willing to accept and believe it or not. It is only in the blinding darkness of the relationship of Oneness that *any*, let alone *all*, of man's imagined or "reimagined" gods become merely "the same God" revealed in different ways to different people in different fashions they are willing to accept. And yet it is this blinding darkness that is increasingly the preferred "light" of more and more people. *Many are desperately seeking relief for their light intolerance.*

As is to be expected, rather than condemning any of the world's evil gods, in this relationship of Oneness only the *true* God of the *true* Christian faith is condemned. Even in today's shifting Christianity people have no tolerance for their Creator daring to require the belief and obedience of all His creation instead of submissively conforming to man's rebellious imaginations and expectations. So, naturally, in the revolution of this "spiritual journey" of relational unbelief, in today's shifting Christianity even the topic of sin and what is right or wrong has been changing. *Everything* becomes relative when man chooses the freedom to decide for himself what is true or false and right or wrong instead of *believing* and *obeying* the only true God. Thus, those in the circle travel the same path round and round, each time bringing more and more into its relationship while at the same time "reimagining" more and more *unbelief and disobedience* as "*Christian faith and practice*" and getting further and further away from the true God and His unchanging Word of truth.

So where will the line be drawn? Relationship is *everything* in the *circle* of Oneness because man wants *no line*. The purpose of "reimagining" God and choosing the relationship of the circle where imaginations and "truth" become one is to seek freedom from the line of God's truth between *what is* true and false or right and wrong. This relationship of freedom is moving to connect *everyone and everything* in its "reimagined" "truth," which conveniently transforms (connects) the *line* of truth between opposites into a *circle* of relationship. In this relationship of all things, there will be *no line* drawn.

Again, as this circle of relationship of Oneness encompasses and connects more and more it will ultimately make no difference at all what people believe or do. Within this *circle* opposites are eliminated in its relationship, so there will be no line drawn between right and wrong, sacred and secular, holy and profane, righteousness and sin, truth and lies, real and imaginary, God's Word and man's word, light and darkness, Rock and sand, faith and faithlessness, belief and unbelief, believers and unbelievers, the narrow way and the broad way, Christianity and the world, the true God and false gods, etc. Within this circle of blinding darkness, everyone and everything will all be connected together with the "God" of Oneness that is immanent in everyone and everything. Therefore people will be free to imagine and define "God" however they choose and to have this "relationship" however they choose, without fear of being "wrong." After all, in Oneness there is no separation of *anything whatsoever*.

> "There's nothing 'wrong' with *anything*. 'Wrong' is a relative term, indicating the opposite of that which you call 'right.'" (the seducing spirit calling itself "God")[3]

"*Everything* is 'acceptable' in the sight of God, for how can God not accept that which is? To reject a thing is to deny that it exists. To say that it is not okay is to say that it is not a part of Me—and that is impossible." (the seducing spirit calling itself "God")[4]

"Key to the New Spirituality is a belief that God is not separate from anyone or anything — and neither are we." (Neale Donald Walsch's Humanity's Team website)[5]

"When we believe in our heart that We Are All One, everything will change. *Everything.*" (Neale Donald Walsch)[6]

Indeed. It already is.

"People will not require God to 'show up' in one way and only in that way. People's beliefs about God will expand …" (the seducing spirit calling itself "God")[7]

The seducing spirit calling itself "God": "**And I tell you that Tomorrow's God will change form as each moment and each individual seeking to experience God dictates.**"

Neale Donald Walsch: "Hold it. **You mean *we* get to decide who and what God is?**"

The seducing spirit calling itself "God": "Why are you so surprised? You've been doing that since time began. You call this Religion." (bold added)[8]

Make that *false* religion.

"That is how humanity will allow itself to experience God on this most blessed future tomorrow. Yesterday's God … is thought to be a Constant. That belief will not change, but it will expand.…

"God IS a Constant. God is that which is Constantly Present and Constantly Changing, suiting Itself to each moment, so that God may be *understood* in that moment, *embraced* in that moment, *experienced* in that moment, and *expressed* in that moment.…

"**There is *no limit* to the ways in which God may show up**.…

"On your yesterdays you have believed in a limited God. On a blessed future tomorrow you will begin to believe in a limitless God, who can appear in any form, under any circumstances, to any person, and, indeed, to all people in all places all the time." (the seducing spirit calling itself "God;" bold added)[9]

"Humans will understand that God's words are found in all of the world's Holy Scriptures, and that no scripture is more authoritative, more complete, more accurate, or more authentic than any other, but that each contains great wisdom and each leads to a greater understanding of The Only Truth There Is …

"One result of this new teaching: Human beings will stop trying to figure out which is the right text and which is the right messenger and will simply look closely to see which text and which messenger speaks to them in a way that makes it possible for them to express and experience their connection to the Divine …

"Humans will also understand that life is not a system of reward and punishment, and that no one is sent to Hell or condemned by God." (Neale Donald Walsch)[10]

> "Humans will understand that their will is truly *free*. They'll know that God will never cause them to suffer dire consequences in the Afterlife for making one choice over another in life....
>
> "A new definition of 'freedom' will be created, one that reflects what the word was always intended to mean—the complete and total lack of limitations of any kind." (Neale Donald Walsch)[11]
>
> "The New Spirituality is a civil rights movement for the soul, freeing humanity at last from the oppression of its belief in a separate, angry, violent, and fearful God." (Neale Donald Walsch)[12]

In the shift away from God and His Word of truth, it isn't so much that *relationship* is everything as it is that the *freedom* of the relationship of Oneness is everything. And in the absurdity of today's imaginative circular thinking, this relationship of Oneness and its freedom from the so-called "legalism" of believing and obeying God is even imagined as the path to world peace. Some things never change.

> ***"They say still unto them that despise me, The LORD hath said, Ye shall have peace; and they say unto every one that walketh after the imagination of his own heart, No evil shall come upon you.***... *The anger of the LORD shall not return, until he have executed, and till he have performed the thoughts of his heart: in the latter days ye shall consider it perfectly....But if they had stood in my counsel, and had caused my people to hear my words, then they should have turned them from their evil way, and from the evil of their doings.... Is not my word like as a fire? saith the LORD; and like a hammer that breaketh the rock in pieces?" (Jeremiah 23:17, 20, 22, 29)*

The circle of relationship of Oneness with its panentheistic/pantheistic "God" that can be imagined and defined *however* anyone chooses is the relationship that is snowballing into one gigantic relationship of everything. And today's shifting Christianity is willingly being assimilated. When God pours out His judgment on a rebellious and idolatrous world that is united in the imagined peace and safety of the relationship of Oneness, people will still refuse to repent of their imagined gods and of their imagined freedom in which they will have drawn no line.

> *"And the rest of the men which were not killed by these plagues yet repented not of the works of their hands, that they should not worship devils, and idols of gold, and silver, and brass, and stone, and of wood: which neither can see, nor hear, nor walk: Neither repented they of their murders, nor of their sorceries, nor of their fornication, nor of their thefts." (Revelation 9:20-21)*
>
> *"And the way of peace have they not known: There is no fear of God before their eyes." (Romans 3:17-18)*
>
> "Imagine a life without fear of God and without guilt over the tiniest infraction of what you imagine to be God's Rules!
>
> "Imagine the freedom of soul and mind and body that would be experienced when you understand at last that you really *are* One with God!" (Neale Donald Walsch)[13]

PART THREE:
THE LIE

17

"When we can contact our own inner God all truth will be revealed to us"

The circle of relationship of Oneness with its many levels is changing everything, and it *all* stems from questioning God's Word. When man is exalted above God, the result is first questioning and then "rethinking" and then "reimagining" God's Word. This process began in the Garden of Eden where Satan—"that old serpent" (Revelation 12:9)—was the first to question God's Word with, "Yea, hath God said …?" This question has been leading man away from the knowledge of the truth and into the circular thinking and "re_thinking" of untruth ever since. Questioning the Word of God turns its *certainty* of *what is* right or wrong and true or false into *uncertainty*, which of course opens the door for man to do or believe whatever man wants.

In the Garden of Eden, first Satan questioned what God had said, then Eve proceeded to "rethink" what God had said, and then Satan craftily took the liberty of "reimagining" what God had said and meant (all in a *dialogue/conversation*, by the way, which was *facilitated* by Satan with the purpose of *moving beyond absolute truth*):

> *"Ye shall not surely die: For God doth know that in the day ye eat thereof, then your eyes shall be opened, and ye shall be as gods, knowing good and evil." (Genesis 3:4b-5; see also chps. 2-3)*

With this first lie to man, Satan started the circle of Oneness in which people—"as gods"—have the freedom to *decide for themselves* what is true or false and right or wrong based on their own personal "knowing" *within themselves* of good and evil. It is Satan's lie in the Garden of Eden that is the circle of relationship of Oneness, and it is his circle of relationship of Oneness that is the broader "truth" and "bigger" "God" that more and more people are intentionally, albeit blindly, seeking. *They are all one and the same lie.*

In the circle of Oneness, man and God are brought together as "One" so that man becomes "One" with God and God becomes "One" with man. It is this "Oneness" that gives everyone their own personal "knowing" *within themselves* of good and evil. And, in turn, it is this "knowing" that gives everyone the freedom to bring whatever they choose into the circle. So whether those whose eyes are "opened" to this freedom realize it or not, seeking to bring everyone and everything else together in one big harmonious relationship of Oneness is the *result* of *already* having fallen for this lie in which everyone has the freedom to believe and do whatever is right in their own "opened" eyes, according to their own "knowing" of good and evil.

Those who choose to follow Satan's example in questioning, "Yea, hath God said ...?" have no authority for determining true or false and right or wrong other than their own subjective and relativistic inner "knowing." But they see no need for any other knowing. They see no need for the Word of *God* to verify if what they *believe* and *do* are *true* and *right*. In answering the question, "How can I know the truth about Christianity if I question the Bible's status as the literal Word of God?," Marcus Borg refers to this inner "knowing." Naturally he first contrasts this "knowing" with "Biblical literalism" in which he points out that people "are literalists and see the Bible as a divine product, having a divine guarantee to be true," and then says:

> "But for people who can't be literalists ... I would say that in one sense of the word know, we can't know that Christianity, or any of the religions, is true in the sense of being able to demonstrate it. One sense of the word 'know' in the modern period is something you can verify. In that sense, we can't know.
>
> "But we can take seriously a different kind of knowing. It's a very ancient kind of knowing. The ancients called it intuition.... But the ancient meaning of the word 'intuition' or 'intuitive knowing' is direct knowing, a knowing that's not dependent upon verification. A synonym for intuitive knowing would be mystical knowing. There are people in every culture who have had what they regard as direct knowing experiences of God or the sacred. That kind of knowing is possible, and for me personally, it's that direct knowing, that intuitive knowing, that is the most persuasive soft data for affirming that God or the sacred is real."[1]

Borg also says:

> "In particular, I argue that a 'panentheistic' concept of God offers the most adequate way of thinking about the sacred; in this concept, the sacred is 'right here' as well as 'the beyond' that encompasses everything."[2]

This inner "knowing" of this panentheistic "God" that is immanent in everyone is Satan's lie. But, sadly, those who use their own personal "knowing" to verify that the lying experiences of their own personal "knowing" are "real" and "true" don't see it that way.

Since more and more people no longer believe that *Yea, God hath said*, a whole new way of subjective and relativistic thinking and acting has steadily taken over in this shift to thinking outside the "box" of *God's* Word of *truth*. In today's never-ending circles of absurdity, man's imagination is imagined to be "truth" merely because man imagines his imagination to be "truth." Likewise, man's "knowing" becomes "truth" merely because man's "knowing" tells man his "knowing" is "truth." And if man's own "knowing" is man's only desired verification that man's own "knowing" is "real" and "true" then this verifies that man's own "knowing" is "real" and "true," right? So with all of man's "knowing" and imagining verifying what is "real" and "true," why would man want verification from *God's* Word? Not only would this defeat the purpose of "reimagining" God and truth and faith outside the "box," but in man's upside-down absurdity it is actually considered circular thinking to believe that God's Word is true merely because it claims to be true. After all, "Yea, hath God said ...?"

As did Borg in his previous quote, this inner "knowing" is also referred to as "mystical knowing." It is documented in channeled writings how mysticism in its various forms, such as meditation/contemplation, is specifically utilized by the spirit world to "open" people's eyes to Oneness by leading them directly into "discovering" and "knowing" the immanent "God" within. These masquerading spirits will willingly seduce anyone with their lying experiences, and this perpetuation of Satan's first lie to man is achieving tremendous success.

"Ye shall not surely die ... your eyes shall be opened, and ye shall be as gods, knowing good and evil." (Genesis 3:4b-5)

"When, therefore, *sight* has been attained and *the light* streams forth, revelation of **the oneness of all life** is a simple and immediate occurrence ...

"[I]n these days many are attaining sight and light is pouring in." (the seducing spirit calling itself Djwhal Khul that channeled its teachings through Alice Bailey; emphasis added)[3]

"It is this revelation of Deity that is **the goal of the mystical endeavor** ... Through it [meditation], he later discovers his relation to the universe; he finds that **his physical body and his vital energies are part and parcel of Nature itself, which is, in fact, the outer garment of Deity** ... In fact, he arrives at God and discovers God as the central Fact. Knowing himself to be divine, he finds the whole is equally divine." (Alice Bailey, New Age matriarch and channeler of Djwhal Khul; emphasis added)[4]

"Third: In the language of some of the pioneers into the spiritual realm, the third result of meditation is that we find God. **It is relatively unimportant what we mean in detail by that little word of three letters. It is but a symbol of Reality.**... Let us regard God as that 'High and Unknown Purpose' which can be recognized as **the sumtotal of all forms which express the Life** ...

"Fourth: In the words of all schools of mystics in both hemispheres, these results [of meditation] are summed up in the words: **Union with God**, or At-one-ment with Divinity. God and man are at-one. The Self and Not-Self are unified." (Alice Bailey; emphasis added)[5]

"Thus, the great schools of intellectual meditation ... all lead to the same point. From the standpoint of Buddhism, of Hinduism, of Sufism, and of Christianity, there is the same basic goal: Unification with Deity ... and the same subsequent Illumination.

"**All sense of separateness has disappeared**." (Alice Bailey; emphasis added)[6]

> "My most formative religious experiences were a series of **mystical experiences**.... They **changed my understanding of the meaning of the word 'God'** ...
>
> "These experiences also convinced me that mystical forms of Christianity are true, and that the mystical forms of all the enduring religions of the world are true....
>
> "[W]hat I was *seeing* looked very different. *Light became different – as if there were a radiance shining through everything*.... And I experienced **a falling away of** the subject-object distinction that marks our ordinary everyday experience – **that sense of being a separate self**, 'in here,' while the world is 'out there.'...
>
> "They were also experiences in which I felt that I was seeing more clearly than I ever had before – that what I was experiencing was 'the way things are.'...
>
> "The effect was to transform my understanding of the word 'God.'...
>
> "If 'God' means a person-like being 'out there,' completely *separate* from the universe, then I am an atheist. I do not believe there is such a being. But if **the word 'God' points to a radiance that pervades 'what is,'** as I now think – then, of course, God is real. Not just the God of Christianity, but **the God of all the enduring religions**." (Marcus Borg; emphasis added)[7]

> "It might therefore be said that revelation concerns **Oneness** and nothing else." (the seducing spirit calling itself Djwhal Khul; emphasis added)[8]

> "What we are in reality passing through is 'a religious initiation into the mysteries of Being,' ... and from that we shall emerge with a deepened sense of **God immanent** in ourselves and in all humanity." (Alice Bailey; emphasis added)[9]

> "Truth lies within ourselves. When we can contact **our own inner God** all truth will be revealed to us. We shall be Knowers." (Alice Bailey; emphasis added)[10]

In this New Age "Reality" and its "mysteries of Being," the basis of all reality is the panentheistic/pantheistic "God" that is immanent in everyone and everything. And it is the "reality" of this *immanence* that gives everyone and everything *Oneness* with this "God" (and with each other) and that gives everyone the freedom to define "that little word of three letters" however anyone chooses. This "reality" of the "Oneness" of man and God is the lie that both *starts and finishes* the circle of relationship. This is why New Age Oneness teaches that planetary problems and conflicts are due to man's "*forgetfulness* of Being" and therefore to solve them man needs to "*remember*" and "*awaken*" to the "Reality" that "who we really are" is "One" with God, which is Satan's lie—a.k.a. "Ancient Wisdom"—from the Garden of Eden. It is *all* one and the same lie.

Man has been falling for the circle of Oneness ever since man's history began, and now man is coming full circle. After all, those who don't learn from history are bound to repeat it. This in itself shows that those in the circle are never learning even though they think they are ever learning. And this is especially true of those who have even reduced "*history*" to "*story*," in seeking *freedom* from the *true reality* of *who we really are*. Thus, in the emerging faith of Oneness not only is God's Word being "reimagined" as a metaphorical pointer to this panentheistic "God"/relationship but even salvation and being born again are "reimagined" as having one's *eyes* "opened" to it as well. And, therefore, the truth of God's Word is being "reimagined" as a metaphorical pointer to the "truth" of Satan's lie. The "god of this world" is having a heyday in today's shifting Christianity.

18

"Ye shall not surely die"

Unbelievably, Borg writes:

> "Outside of the Jewish and Christian traditions, the best-known enlightenment experience is **the Buddha's mystical experience**. Such an experience leads to seeing everything differently. It is not simply an intellectual or mental 'seeing,' as when we say, 'Oh, I see what you mean.' Rather, **enlightenment as a religious experience involves communion or union with what is, an immediate 'knowing' of the sacred that transforms one's way of seeing**.
>
> "So it is in [the gospel of] John: **enlightenment is a central metaphor for salvation. To have one's eyes opened, to be enlightened,** is to move from the negative pole of John's contrasting symbols to the positive pole. To move from darkness to light is also to move from death to life, from falsehood to truth, from life in the flesh to life in the Spirit, from life 'below' to life 'from above.'
>
> "**To be enlightened is to be born** 'from above' and **'of the Spirit'**—in other words, **to be 'born again.'** Thus the 'born again' experience in John is an enlightenment experience.
>
> "The language of enlightenment connects to John's emphasis upon knowing God. For John, such knowing is the primary meaning of 'eternal life'—not a future state beyond death but an experience in the present. To know God is eternal life: 'This is eternal life, that they may know you, the only true God.' Of course, *for John*, the true God is known in Jesus, and so the second half of the verse continues with 'and Jesus Christ, whom you have sent.' For John, the Christian enlightenment experi-

ence is knowing God in Jesus." (emphasis added)[1]

"This is who Jesus is for us as Christians.... And we can say 'This is who Jesus is for us' *without* also saying 'And God is known *only* in Jesus.'" (emphasis added)[2]

Borg's panentheistic teachings are obviously compatible with Buddhism and Satan's lie of Oneness, but not with *Scripture*. For starters, the *true* God *is* known *only* in Jesus; period. And to have one's eyes "opened" to the "knowing" of Satan's lie of Oneness is *not* what it means to be "born of the Spirit" and "born again"! Although this inner "knowing" is seen as "salvation" and "eternal life," it brings nothing more than Satan's lying promise that *"Ye shall not surely die."* Despite the teachings to the contrary, this "knowing" of the panentheistic "God" of Oneness that is in everyone is not even remotely the same thing as that which the Lord Jesus Christ refers to in John 17:3:

"And this is life eternal, that they might know thee the only true God, and Jesus Christ, whom thou hast sent." (John 17:3)

That Oneness is believed to be "salvation" and "eternal life," as well as "heaven" and "the kingdom of God," used to be found only in the New Age (New Spirituality). But not any more now that everything is merging in the emerging faith of Oneness/panentheism. It is also to be expected that people in today's shifting Christianity who are falling for Satan's lie of Oneness are also falling for his "promise"—especially since more and more people are cooperatively "reimagining" Satan either out of existence or as other than who he really is.

"Ye shall not surely die." (Genesis 3:4b)

"When at last you *see* that there is no separation in God's World—that is, nothing which is not God—then, at last, will you let go of this invention of man which you have called Satan.

"If Satan exists, he exists as every thought you ever had of separation from Me. You cannot be separate from Me, for I Am All That Is....

"Condemnation, being hurled into the everlasting fires of hell, was the *ultimate scare tactic*. Yet now you need be afraid no more. For nothing can, or ever will, separate you from Me.

"**You and I are One**. We cannot be anything else if I Am What I Am: All That Is.

"Why then would I condemn Myself? And how would I do it? How could I separate Myself from Myself when My Self is All There Is, and there is nothing else?...

"I have no way to separate Myself from you—or anything else. 'Hell' is simply not knowing this. **'Salvation' is knowing and understanding it completely. You are now saved. You needn't worry about what's going to happen to you 'after death' anymore**." (the seducing spirit calling itself "God;" bold added)[3]

"That place of Oneness is heaven.

"You are there now.

"You are never *not* there, because you are never *not* One with Me." (the seducing spirit calling itself "God")[4]

"Now here is the Good News. *There is no other place to be.* The challenge is not to 'get to' heaven, but to know that you are already there. For heaven is the Kingdom of God, and there is *no other kingdom that exists*." (the seducing spirit calling itself "God")[5]

Naturally, with a panentheistic/pantheistic "God" that is *in everyone and everything*, "there is no other kingdom that exists" in this emerging faith of Oneness. This *one gigantic circle of relationship of all things*—i.e., this "*Kingdom of God*"—of this "God" of Oneness is conveniently broad enough to include everyone regardless of their *beliefs*. *No one* and *nothing* is excluded from "the Kingdom of God" in Oneness, so *believing in the Lord Jesus Christ* is irrelevant. Since everyone only needs their own inner "knowing" of their "own inner God," it is merely a matter of spreading "the Good News" ("The New Gospel") of Satan's lie of Oneness. This way everyone can "know" whatever they already "know," with no need to change their beliefs or behavior one iota. Everyone can thus continue in their desired freedom to *decide for themselves* what is true or false and right or wrong, with the only difference being that now they can also have the "*knowing*" that they are not "*wrong*" in whatever they decide. Having heard the "Good News" of the emerging faith of Oneness that it is *not* necessary to *believe in the Lord Jesus Christ* to have a relationship with God—*from those in today's bewitched Christianity* as well as those in the New Age (New Spirituality)—they can now "know" they have "salvation" and "eternal life" in "the Kingdom of God" and "heaven," no matter what they decide to believe or do.

> "The kingdom of God is not some one particular church with its own peculiar doctrines, its particular formulations of truth ... and of approach to God.
>
> "The true Church is the kingdom of God on earth ... composed of all, regardless of race or creed, who live by the light within, ..." (Alice Bailey)[6]

According to the truth and faith of *God's* Word, unless we have been born again of the *Holy* Spirit *by the Word of God* we cannot even see, let alone enter, the true Kingdom of the true God.

> "*Jesus answered and said unto him, Verily, verily, I say unto thee, Except a man be* **born again**, *he cannot see the kingdom of God.... Jesus answered, Verily, verily, I say unto thee, Except a man be born of water and* **of the Spirit**, *he cannot enter into the kingdom of God. That which is born of the flesh is flesh; and that which is born of the Spirit is spirit. Marvel not that I said unto thee, Ye must be born again.*" (John 3:3, 5-7)

> "*Being born again, not of corruptible seed, but of incorruptible,* **by the word of God**, *which liveth and abideth for ever. For all flesh is as grass, and all the glory of man as the flower of grass. The grass withereth, and the flower thereof falleth away: But the word of the Lord endureth for ever. And this is the word which by the gospel is preached unto you.*" (1 Peter 1:23-25)

> "*To him give all the prophets witness, that through his name whosoever* **believeth** *in him shall receive remission of sins.*" (Acts 10:43)

> "*For the wages of sin is death; but the gift of God is eternal life through Jesus Christ our Lord.*" (Romans 6:23)

> "For I am not ashamed of the gospel of Christ: for it is the power of God unto salvation to every one that **believeth**; to the Jew first, and also to the Greek." (Romans 1:16)

> "In whom we have redemption through his blood, the forgiveness of sins, according to the riches of his grace ... That in the dispensation of the fulness of times he might gather together in one all things in Christ, both which are in heaven, and which are on earth; even in him: In whom also we have obtained an inheritance, being predestinated according to the purpose of him who worketh all things after the counsel of his own will: That we should be to the praise of his glory, who first trusted in Christ. **In whom ye also trusted, after that ye heard the word of truth, the gospel of your salvation: in whom also after that ye believed, ye were sealed with that holy Spirit of promise**, which is the earnest of our inheritance until the redemption of the purchased possession, unto the praise of his glory." (Ephesians 1:7, 10-14)

> "Even **the Spirit of truth**; whom the world **cannot** receive, because **it seeth him not, neither knoweth him**: but ye know him; for he dwelleth with you, and shall be in you." (John 14:17)

Only those who *believe the truth* can be born again by *the Spirit of truth*. And it is *the Word of God* that gives us *the truth* that we are to *believe* so that we can thus be indwelt by and born again of the *Holy* Spirit. The "seeing" and inner "knowing" as well as the "'born again' experience" of the panentheistic "God"/"Spirit" of Oneness are nothing but lying experiences of the seducing spirit world that actually move people in the *opposite* direction than "from darkness to light," "from death to life," "from falsehood to truth," etc. But, sadly, those who are choosing to rely on the lying experiences of this inner "knowing" to verify that the lying experiences of this inner "knowing" are "real" and "true" don't see it that way.

> "Most basically, it seems to me that a close and careful reading of the Bible makes it impossible to think that what it says comes directly or indirectly from God." (Marcus Borg)[7]

> "Is there a more? Is God real?...
>
> **"[T]here is a More, a non-material layer or level or dimension of reality**, and this notion is shared by all of the enduring religious traditions of the world....
>
> "This More is **named in various ways by the traditions as God or spirit or the sacred or the Tao or Allah or Atmen and so forth**....
>
> "So God is the name we use for the non-material, stupendous, wondrous More that includes the material universe within it, even as it transcends the universe.
>
> "**This is God as the encompassing Spirit**, the One who is all around us, as well as within us, who pervades the whole universe. **The universe is shot through with this non-material More**.... Where are we in relationship to God? We are in God.... God is the One who is all around us and within us, the One in whom the universe is, even as God is more than the universe, the mystery with a capital M who is beyond all names, even as we name this sacred Mystery in our various ways." (Marcus Borg; emphasis added)[8]

> "God is not only real, but knowable. Moreover, the sacred is known not in a set of

statements about God, but experientially, as a Mystery beyond all language. This Mystery—God—**transcends all** of our **domestications of reality**, including those generated by **theology and even the Bible itself**.... God also transcends peoples **and religions** ...

"Life with God is **not about believing** certain teachings about God. It is about a covenant—a relationship. More specifically, it is *about becoming conscious of a relationship that already exists* ..." (Marcus Borg; emphasis added)[9]

"Tomorrow's God does not require anyone to *believe* in God." (the seducing spirit calling itself "God;" emphasis added)[10]

"I am telling you that **your perception of ultimate reality is more limited than you thought**, and that **Truth is more *un*limited than you can imagine**." (the seducing spirit calling itself "God;" bold added)[11]

"Tomorrow's God is separate from nothing, but is ... the Sum Total of Everything that ever was, is now, and ever shall be." (the seducing spirit calling itself "God")[12]

"There is *no limit* to the ways in which God may show up...."

"On your yesterdays you have believed in a limited God. On a blessed future tomorrow **you will begin to believe in a limitless God, who can appear in any form,** under any circumstances, to any person, and, indeed, to all people in all places all the time." (the seducing spirit calling itself "God;" bold added)[13]

According to the Lord Jesus Christ Himself, "*That which is born of the flesh is flesh; and that which is born of the Spirit is spirit,*" and since we "*cannot enter into the kingdom of God*" unless we have been "*born of the Spirit*" He therefore said, "*Ye must be born again.*" Yet in today's emerging faith of Oneness, not only is what it means to be "born of the Spirit" "reimagined" but it is also rendered irrelevant in that it is a *universal done deal*. Its immanent "God"/"Spirit" that "is separate from nothing" is "shot through" the universe in the "very substance" of all creation in a "Spirit"-matter Oneness that is obviously a *"Spirit"-flesh Oneness*. This *upside-down* "born of the Spirit" counterfeit brings this "*Spirit*" and all *flesh* together as one, thus conveniently bypassing the need to be *born again* of the Holy Spirit. After all, to bypass the need to be *born again* is to bypass the need to *believe in the Lord Jesus Christ*, which is to bypass the need to *believe the truth of the Word of God*. And this, of course, is the ultimate purpose of this emerging faith of Oneness.

"Of course, no one seriously suggests that the Bible is to be taken literally." (Neale Donald Walsch)[14]

"Our opportunity now is to create the space of possibility **for a New Spirituality to emerge upon the earth** ... that makes no one wrong for the way in which they are approaching the God of their understanding ..." (Neale Donald Walsch; emphasis added)[15]

"When men recognize this and succeed in isolating that inner significant structure of truth which is the same in all climes and in all races, **then there will emerge the universal religion, the One Church, and that unified though not uniform approach to God** ... Theologies will disappear into the knowledge of

God; doctrines and dogmas will no longer be regarded as necessary, for **faith will be based on experience, and authority will give place to personal appreciation of Reality**." (the seducing spirit calling itself Djwhal Khul; emphasis added)[16]

"It is relatively unimportant what we mean in detail by that little word of three letters ['God']. It is but a symbol of Reality." (Alice Bailey; emphasis added)[17]

In today's emerging faith of Oneness/panentheism—i.e., emerging New Spirituality/universal religion—everyone can freely imagine and define "God" and their relationship with "God" however they choose, without fear of being judged as "wrong." After all, there is conveniently *no judgment* by this panentheistic "God" of Oneness. In the journey of the *circle* of Oneness there is no *final destination* to fear, and as the seducing spirit world teaches:

"Condemnation, being hurled into the everlasting fires of hell, was the *ultimate scare tactic*. Yet now you need be afraid no more. For nothing can, or ever will, separate you from Me.

"You and I are One. We cannot be anything else if **I Am What I Am: All That Is**.

"Why then would I condemn Myself? And how would I do it? How could I separate Myself from Myself when My Self is All There Is, and there is nothing else?" (the seducing spirit calling itself "God;" bold added)[18]

Not surprisingly, *The Shack*'s false "God" that similarly claims to be this counterfeit **"I am that I am"**[19] that "dwells **in**, around, and through **all things**"[20] has also released all humans from judgment:

"In Jesus, **I have forgiven all humans** for their sins against me, but only some choose relationship....

"**When you forgive someone you certainly release them from judgment**, but without true change [of 'mind and behavior'], no *real* relationship can be established." (emphasis added)[21]

"[Y]ou asked me what Jesus accomplished on the cross; so now **listen to me carefully**: through his death and resurrection, **I am now fully reconciled to the world**." (emphasis added)[22]

Upon being told the latter, the main character then asks:

"The whole world? You mean those who believe in you, right?"

To which this counterfeit "God" responds:

"The whole world, Mack."[23]

Conveniently, in this universal reconciliation/salvation, "*all* humans"—even those who do not "*believe*"—have been "forgiven" "for their sins" and are thus "*fully recon-*

ciled" and released "from judgment." So, of course, this counterfeit "God" that has "*forgiven* all humans for their sins" will not "*punish* people for sin":

> "**I don't need to punish people for sin**. Sin is its own punishment, devouring you from the inside. It's not my purpose to punish it; it's my joy to cure it." (emphasis added)[24]

The only "cure" for sin is to *believe in the true Lord Jesus Christ*. And since "the wages of sin is death," to release all humans from the judgment and punishment of sin is to subtly perpetuate the lie that "*Ye shall not surely die.*"

> *"For the wages of sin is death; but the gift of God is eternal life through Jesus Christ our Lord." (Romans 6:23)*

> *"Giving thanks unto the Father, which hath made us meet to be partakers of the inheritance of the saints in light: Who hath delivered us from the power of darkness, and hath translated us into the kingdom of his dear Son: In whom we have redemption through his blood, even the forgiveness of sins ... For it pleased the Father that in him should all fulness dwell; and, having made peace through the blood of his cross, by him to reconcile all things unto himself; by him, I say, whether they be things in earth, or things in heaven. And you, that were sometime alienated and enemies in your mind by wicked works, yet now hath he reconciled in the body of his flesh through death, to present you holy and unblameable and unreproveable in his sight:* **If ye continue in the faith grounded and settled, and be not moved away from the hope of the gospel**, *which ye have heard, and which was preached to every creature which is under heaven; whereof I Paul am made a minister." (Colossians 1:12-14, 19-23)*

> *"To him give all the prophets witness, that through his name* **whosoever believeth in him shall receive remission of sins**.*" (Acts 10:43)*

The Lord Jesus Christ is the *only* way, which does *not* mean an *automatic universal* way that reduces *believing* in Him to a "*best*" way—i.e., an *optional* way. Choosing to "*reimagine*" that the death and resurrection of the Lord Jesus Christ unconditionally give universal forgiveness/reconciliation/salvation to all humans and release everyone from judgment and punishment of sin regardless of whether or not anyone *believes* in Him changes nothing. The truth is the truth, and the truth is *the Word of God*, not the word of man or of "reimagined" gods. In truth, to be forgiven, reconciled, and saved everyone must *believe* in the Lord Jesus Christ. Only in the counterfeit "Kingdom" of the counterfeit "God" of Oneness is everyone given *unconditional* and *universal* "salvation" where "*Ye shall not surely die.*"

Although this all-inclusive "Kingdom" of Oneness doesn't even exclude false gods, the true Kingdom of the true God does. The pantheon of "reimagined" gods/theologies found in the all-encompassing circle of relationship of Oneness has no place in the true Kingdom of God. It is therefore very fitting that *The Shack*'s "reimagined" "God," which even admits it is in "a circle of relationship,"[25] excludes itself from the true Kingdom of God in a chapter titled, "A Piece of π."

In subtly conditioning people to come full circle in the circle of relationship of Oneness, *The Shack*'s counterfeit "God" claims to be "flesh and blood" in all three of its persons. Yet in so doing it reveals its own (already obvious) exclusion from the true

Kingdom of the true God. Even so, those who have closed their eyes and ears to the truth of God's Word will not be willing to see that the counterfeits are counterfeit and the genuine is genuine because the counterfeits are the "genuine" they are *willing* to accept.

> "When we three spoke ourself into human existence as the Son of God, we became fully human. We also chose to embrace all the limitations that this entailed. Even though we have always been present in this created universe, we now became flesh and blood. It would be like this bird, whose nature it is to fly, choosing only to walk and remain grounded. He doesn't stop being the bird, but it does alter his experience of life significantly."[26]

> *"Now this I say, brethren, that flesh and blood cannot inherit the kingdom of God; neither doth corruption inherit incorruption." (1 Corinthians 15:50)*

God's Word of truth makes it clear that there is no flesh and *blood* in the *true* God. God the Father is "a *Spirit*" (John 4:24) with no *"flesh and blood"* (Matthew 16:17). The Holy Spirit is obviously a *Spirit*, and a *Spirit* has no *"flesh and blood."* The Lord Jesus Christ took on "flesh and blood" (Hebrews 2:14) specifically to shed his blood for our sins in His death on the cross (see Hebrews 2:9; 9:22; & Matthew 26:28), and when He rose from the dead He instead took on "flesh and *bones*" (Luke 24:39; see also Ephesians 5:30). This is significant because obviously "flesh and blood cannot inherit the kingdom of God." The true Lord Jesus Christ and the true God the Father and the true Holy Spirit will not be excluded from their own Kingdom!

On the other hand, *The Shack*'s "flesh and blood" counterfeit "God" that claims to also be "completely unlimited, without bounds"[27] will be completely limited from entering the bounds of the true Kingdom of the true God. But no doubt those who are determined to have "a piece of π" in the circle of relationship of Oneness with the "God" of their "understanding" will "reimagine" otherwise.

Nevertheless, only the Kingdom of the *true* God is the *true* Kingdom of God. And it is perfectly clear in the light of God's Word of truth that those who are not willing to believe and obey the true God and His Son will be excluding themselves from the Kingdom of God and heaven. But this light is too bright for today's light-intolerant Christianity that is shifting from light to darkness to "reimagine" a broader "truth" and a broader "faith" of a broader "God."

> *"For I say unto you, That except your righteousness shall exceed the righteousness of the scribes and Pharisees, **ye shall in no case** enter into the kingdom of heaven." (Matthew 5:20)*

> **"Even the righteousness of God which is by faith of Jesus Christ unto all and upon all them that believe**: *for there is no difference: For all have sinned, and come short of the glory of God; being justified freely by his grace through the redemption that is in Christ Jesus: Whom God hath set forth to be a propitiation through faith in his blood, to declare his righteousness for the remission of sins that are past, through the forbearance of God; to declare, I say, at this time his righteousness: that he might be just, and the justifier of him which believeth in Jesus." (Romans 3:22-26)*

> *"And when they had appointed him a day, there came many to him into his lodging; to whom he expounded and testified the kingdom of God, persuading them con-*

cerning Jesus, both out of the law of Moses, and out of the prophets, from morning till evening. And some believed the things which were spoken, and some believed not.... For the heart of this people is waxed gross, and their ears are dull of hearing, and their eyes have they closed; lest they should see with their eyes, and hear with their ears, and understand with their heart, and should be converted, and I should heal them." (Acts 28:23-24, 27)

Although man is clearly bound and determined to succeed one way or another, there is no getting around believing in the Lord Jesus Christ.

"He that hath the Son hath life; and he that hath not the Son of God hath not life." (1 John 5:12)

"For God sent not his Son into the world to condemn the world; but that the world through him might be saved. He that believeth on him is not condemned: but he that believeth not is condemned already, because he hath not believed in the name of the only begotten Son of God." (John 3:17-18)

19

"The way of Jesus is a universal way … not a set of beliefs about Jesus"

"Jesus saith unto him, I am the way, the truth, and the life: no man cometh unto the Father, but by me." (John 14:6)

Jesus is the way, Jesus is the truth, and Jesus is the life. Without Jesus there is no way, no truth, and no life – there is no *relationship* with *God*. Yet, determined to broaden the narrow way to fit the new way of thinking and "seeing" and "knowing," today's shifting Christianity is also "reimagining" John 14:6 in a variety of ways. For example, instead of *Jesus* being *the way* to God, *the way* of Jesus becomes the way to God. These two ways to God are *not* the same thing. For instance:

- The first way to God is a noun; the second way to God is a verb.
- The first way to God is a Being; the second way to God is a way of being.
- The first way to God is inseparable from the Person of Jesus; the second way to God is separable from the Person of Jesus.
- The first way to God is a narrow way; the second way to God is a broad way.
- The first way to God is genuine; the second way to God is counterfeit.

Separating *the way* of Jesus from *the Person* of Jesus, in this second way to God, and "reimagining" it all according to his "knowing" of the panentheistic "God," Borg writes:

> "This is who Jesus is for us as Christians.... And we can say 'This is who Jesus is for us' *without* also saying 'And God is known *only* in Jesus.'" (emphasis added)[1]
>
> "Jesus said, 'I am the way, and the truth, and the life; no one comes to the Father except through me.'...
>
> "[I]t has been the classic 'proof text' for Christian exclusivism—*the notion that salvation is possible only through Jesus*, and thus only through Christianity....
>
> "So Jesus is 'the way.' But what does this metaphor, applied to a person, mean?...
>
> "In short, for John [of the Gospel of John] the way or path of Jesus is the path of death and resurrection understood as a metaphor for the religious life. That way—the path of dying to an old way of being and being **born into a new way of being**—is the only way to God....
>
> "**The way of Jesus is a universal way**, known to millions who have *never heard of Jesus*.
>
> "The way of Jesus is thus **not a set of beliefs about Jesus**. That we ever thought it was is strange, when one thinks about it—as if one entered new life by *believing certain things to be true*, or as if the only people who can be saved are those who know the word 'Jesus.'" (emphasis added)[2]

The shift from *Jesus* being the way to God to "*the way* of Jesus" being the way to God is a switch of serpentine subtilty on many levels, one of which is that the *Being* of Jesus (*noun*) is craftily switched with the *being* of Jesus (*verb*). First, with convoluted absurdity, this conveniently reduces *believing* to *being* so that people in today's shifting Christianity who want to *be* "Christian" without *believing* Christian can follow "the way of Jesus" without believing in Jesus. Second, this separates *the Person* of Jesus from being the way to God and broadens the narrow way into a universal way in which everyone is *being* their own way to God—which is precisely what the circle of Oneness and its panentheistic "God" do.

> "Moreover, the sacred is known **not in a set of statements about God**, but experientially, as a Mystery beyond all language. This Mystery—God—transcends all of our domestications of reality, including those generated by theology and even the Bible itself.... God also transcends peoples and religions, and thus a unity is possible in the God who made heaven and earth ...
>
> "Life with God is **not about believing** certain teachings about God.... More specifically, **it is about becoming conscious of a relationship that already exists** ... And we are not simply to become conscious of it; we are to become intentional about deepening the relationship. Christian faith is not about believing, but about faithfulness—fidelity—to the relationship....
>
> "As **the path of life, this relationship** is the path of personal transformation.... It involves dying to an old way of being and being **born into a new way of being**." (Marcus Borg; emphasis added)[3]

In today's emerging faith of panentheism/Oneness, "relationship" "already exists" *without believing in the Lord Jesus Christ* because the panentheistic "God" of Oneness is already *in everyone/everything*—i.e., "*all things*" or "*All That Is.*" Thus, *everyone is being their own way to God*. This relationship becomes "real" relationship when people choose to "see" and "know" it, or become "conscious" of it. So the path of personal transformation is about "dying" to the "old" scriptural (believing/obeying) way of being and being "born" into—"becoming conscious" of, "awakening" to, etc.—the "new" relational (panentheistic/Oneness) way of being. This is neither "the path of *life*" nor "the way or path of *Jesus*" nor "life with *God*."

> *"There is a way that seemeth right unto a man, but the end thereof are the ways of death." (Proverbs 16:25; see also 14:12)*

> *"But these are written, that ye might believe that Jesus is the Christ, the Son of God; and that believing ye might have life through his name." (John 20:31)*

Contrary to the false teachings of this emerging faith, *believing* in the Lord Jesus Christ *is* the only way to *knowing* the *true* God, and the *true* Gospel *is* "a set of beliefs about Jesus." This is made perfectly clear in God's Word of truth. The Gospel of Christ tells us Who the Lord Jesus Christ is and what He did for us, which tells us what we are to believe to believe in Him, which therefore gives us salvation and the true Person of the Lord Jesus Christ in a genuine relationship of eternal life with both Him and the true God. And, yes, this relationship is experienced *in the present*, but only by those who have been saved by grace *through faith*—that is, faith/believing in the Lord Jesus Christ, *not* faith in the panentheistic "God" of Oneness!

Bypassing the Lord Jesus Christ as the way to God bypasses the redemption of His death and resurrection, which bypasses salvation and a relationship with the true and living God. But in today's unbelieving Christianity even His death and resurrection are being commonly "reimagined," not only as providing *universal salvation* to *everyone* whether they believe in the Lord Jesus Christ or not, but also as "*changeable*" and "*debatable*" "*metaphor*." His resurrection is even being "reimagined" as a "spiritual resurrection," which completely denies the meaning of what a resurrection is. And yet, along with the "irrelevance" of the Lord Jesus Christ Himself, a physical/bodily resurrection from the dead is "irrelevant" as well in today's emerging "enlightenment" of man's own "knowing" of the universal "relationship"/"salvation" of the panentheistic "God."

(Incidentally, those who believe that the true nature of the Lord Jesus Christ's resurrection as well as our need to *believe* it are "irrelevant" should read 1 Corinthians 15 and Romans 10:9-10! But, sadly, the teachings of *God's* Word go unheeded by more and more people who no longer take God at His Word.)

Nevertheless, the panentheistic "God" of Oneness that transcends the diverse theologies and religions—and that purposely transcends the truth and faith of *the Word of God* in particular—can be fictitiously "Christianized" by people to their heart's content, but it did *not* make heaven and earth and is one of the false gods that will perish (see Jeremiah 10:11). That Borg added the phrase "who made heaven and earth" to his previous quote is additionally deceptive since he also teaches earlier in this same book that the accounts of God's creation in the book of Genesis are just "metaphorical"/ "symbolic" "stories" made up by man and *not* "literally factual accounts."[4] He even titled his book, *Reading the Bible Again for the First Time: Taking the Bible Seriously but Not Literally*. In other words, "Yea, hath God said ...?" In his book, Borg basically "rethinks" and "reimagines" God's Word, including the Gospel of John, through the new "lenses" of seeing it not as the Word of *God* but as the word of *men*. It is this book in which he also said:

> "As we enter the twenty-first century, we need a new set of lenses through which to read the Bible....

> "The older lenses enabled Christians of earlier generations to experience the Bible as a lamp unto their feet ... But for many Christians in our time, the older lenses have become opaque, turning the Bible into a stumbling block in the way....
>
> "The first group, who sometimes call themselves 'Bible-believing Christians,' typically see the Bible as the inerrant and infallible Word of God....
>
> "The second group of Christians ... are strongly convinced that many parts of the Bible cannot be taken literally, either as historically factual or as expressing the will of God....
>
> "They are responding strongly and positively to a more historical and metaphorical reading of the Bible.... [A] major de-literalization of the Bible is underway." (Marcus Borg)[5]

People today may know enough to *sound* Christian, but an increasing number don't know enough to *believe* Christian. And apart from *believing* Christian there is no *being* Christian. This used to be obvious in Christianity. But not any more now that these new "lenses" of darkness have become quite popular in today's light-intolerant Christianity. And since people want to *be* Christian without *believing* Christian, *of course* this will turn "the Bible into a stumbling block in the way"! Thus, *darkness* becomes the preferred "*light*," and *blindness* becomes the preferred "*sight*." This is all clearly the case when people purposely close their eyes to avoid seeing the light of God's Word.

> "Thy word is a lamp unto my feet, and a light unto my path." (Psalm 119:105)

> "For the heart of this people is waxed gross, and their ears are dull of hearing, and their eyes have they closed; lest they should see with their eyes, and hear with their ears, and understand with their heart, and should be converted, and I should heal them." (Acts 28:27)

Moreover, the Word of God—both the written Word of God as well as the Person of the Lord Jesus Christ, Whose "name is called The Word of God" (Revelation 19:13)—is "a stumbling block in the way" of the world's desired interfaith unity and freedom. Thus, the world is coming together in the "humility" of a *Wordless* faith to "figure out together" a "better understanding" of God and truth and faith that is inclusive of those who are not willing to believe and obey God and His Son.

Satan's lie is the "safe space" in which this "reimagining" is taking place. The panentheistic "God" of Oneness that transcends the diverse theologies and religions gives everyone the freedom to define "that little word of three letters"—"God"—however anyone chooses. Satan's lie of Oneness provides the "safe space" in which the world can come together in the "unity in diversity" of Oneness and its desired broader "truth" and "bigger" "God." Again, everyone's own personal "Oneness with God" that gives everyone their own personal "knowing" "makes *no one wrong* for the way in which they are approaching the God of their understanding."[6] This man-pleasing "safe space," which is rapidly increasing in popularity, is also the New Age "New Gospel of Oneness" that Satan's realm of seducing spirits, *with the help of today's seduced Christianity*, is teaching to the nations:

> "Go, therefore, and teach ye all nations, spreading far and wide *The New Gospel:*
> "WE ARE ALL ONE.
> "OURS IS NOT A BETTER WAY, OURS IS MERELY **ANOTHER WAY**." (the

seducing spirit calling itself "God;" bold added)[7]

"Relinquish the **pride of mind** which **sees its way** and its interpretations **to be correct and true**, and others' false and wrong. This is the way of separation." (the seducing spirit calling itself Djwhal Khul; emphasis added)[8]

*"I marvel that ye are so soon removed from him that called you into the grace of Christ unto another gospel: Which is not another; but there be some that trouble you, and would pervert the gospel of Christ. But though we, or an angel from heaven, preach any other gospel unto you than that which we have preached unto you, let him be accursed. As we said before, so say I now again, If any man preach any other gospel unto you than that ye have received, let him be accursed. For do I now persuade men, or God? or do I seek to please men? for **if I yet pleased men, I should not be the servant of Christ**." (Galatians 1:6-10)*

*"But as we were allowed of God to be put **in trust** with the gospel, even so we speak; **not as pleasing men, but God**, which trieth our hearts." (1 Thessalonians 2:4)*

Whether people are willing to accept its narrow way or not, *the truth* of God and His Son is *absolute*. Regardless of how "real" and "true" man's own imagination and man's own "knowing" seem to be, *there is no forgiveness of sins or reconciliation or being born again or salvation or relationship with God apart from true faith in the Lord Jesus Christ.* The *true* God *is* known *only* in Jesus, we *are* to *believe* in Jesus, and other religions are dead wrong. It really is that simple. This isn't "pride" or "hate;" this is the faith of God that is given to us by God in the Word of God. We either *take God at His Word* or *make God out to be a liar*. *Everyone* has the same *choice*.

"For the wages of sin is death; but the gift of God is eternal life through Jesus Christ our Lord." (Romans 6:23)

*"And he is the propitiation for our sins: and not for ours only, but also for the sins of **the whole world**." (1 John 2:2)*

*"Jesus saith unto him, I am the way, the truth, and the life: **no man** cometh unto the Father, but by me." (John 14:6)*

*"Be it known unto you all, and to all the people of Israel, that by the name of Jesus Christ of Nazareth, whom ye crucified, whom God raised from the dead, even by him doth this man stand here before you whole. This is the stone which was set at nought of you builders, which is become the head of the corner. **Neither is there salvation in any other: for there is none other name under heaven given among men, whereby we must be saved**." (Acts 4:10-12)*

*"For I am not ashamed of the gospel of Christ: for it is the power of God unto **salvation** to every one that **believeth**; to the Jew first, and also to the Greek." (Romans 1:16)*

*"Being **born again**, not of corruptible seed, but of incorruptible, **by the word of God**, which liveth and abideth for ever.... But the word of the Lord endureth for ever. And this is the word which by the gospel is preached unto you." (1 Peter 1:23,*

25)

*"So then **faith** cometh by hearing, and hearing **by the word of God**." (Romans 10:17)*

Borg has commented that "much is at stake in whether we see the Bible as a human or a divine product."[9] This is the biggest understatement in all of history. Those who do not believe that the Word of God is the Word of *God* see no need to *believe* what it says and are betting their very soul that man knows more about God and how to have a relationship with God than God does.

"Within the earlier paradigm or way of seeing the Christian life, believing has been central--believing in God, believing in Jesus, believing in the Bible, believing in Christianity, believing in the creeds, and so forth. Within the emerging paradigm relationship, not believing is central....

"[T]he first of these meanings of faith ... has significantly distorted the meaning of faith and the Christian life.... This is faith as belief, ... as believing something to be true....

"It's not only a distortion, ... but rather odd when you think about it. As if what God really cares about is the beliefs in our heads. As if believing the right things, having correct beliefs, is what God is most looking for ..." (Marcus Borg)[10]

*"For God so loved the world, that he gave his only begotten Son, that whosoever **believeth in him** should not perish, but have everlasting life. For God sent not his Son into the world to condemn the world; but that the world through him might be saved. He that **believeth on him** is not condemned: but he that **believeth not** is condemned already, because he hath **not believed in the name** of the only begotten Son of God.... The Father loveth the Son, and hath given all things into his hand. He that **believeth on the Son** hath everlasting life: and he that **believeth not the Son** shall not see life; but the wrath of God abideth on him." (John 3:16-18, 35-36)*

*"... For they stumbled at that stumblingstone; as it is written, Behold, I lay in Zion a stumblingstone and rock of offence: and whosoever **believeth** on him shall not be ashamed." (Romans 9:32-33)*

*"Then said Jesus again unto them, ... for **if ye believe not** that I am he, ye shall die in your sins." (John 8:21, 24)*

"Wherefore God also hath highly exalted him, and given him a name which is above every name: That at the name of Jesus every knee should bow, of things in heaven, and things in earth, and things under the earth; and that every tongue should confess that Jesus Christ is Lord, to the glory of God the Father." (Philippians 2:9-11)

"For there is one God, and one mediator between God and men, the man Christ Jesus." (1 Timothy 2:5)

For those who are seeking freedom from having to believe and obey God, His Son, and His Word, Satan's lie with its circle of Oneness conveniently meets their needs. Satan's lie provides them with an *eye-opening experience* of the immanent "God," thus eliminating the need to believe. Satan's lie provides them with their own personal "knowing" of good and evil, thus eliminating the need to obey. Satan's lie even provides them with "eternal life"—"*Ye shall not surely die*"—thus eliminating the need for the salvation and remission of sins of the Lord Jesus Christ.

Satan's lie, with its circle of relationship of Oneness, gives all who are seeking freedom from the "box" of God's Word of truth the freedom to believe and do whatever is right in their own "opened" eyes. And yet it still even gives them an automatic eternal "relationship" with the immanent "God" to boot. This is all diabolically convenient for those who are not willing to believe and obey God and His Son.

Yet, along with the rest of God's Word, the account of the Garden of Eden and Satan's lie is seen as "not literal" in today's new way of "seeing." So, with the exception of people in the occult, those who are trusting in Satan's lie for their "salvation" and "relationship with God" of course don't see that this is what they are doing. They just see it as being in a "right relationship" with the "God" that is in everyone/everything as "the ground of all being." They just see it as "awakening" to or "becoming conscious" of or having "one's eyes opened" to this relationship/Oneness/union that "already exists." They just see it as their own personal "knowing" of the "God" that is known and experienced regardless of beliefs, regardless of theology, regardless of religion. They even just see it as "the way of Jesus."

20

The "participatory divinity" of "the Jesus way"

Like Borg, Mike Morrell is a self-proclaimed "panentheist" as well. Morrell has been referred to as "the tie that binds 'emergent' church" and "one of the movement's linchpins"[1] because of his website Zoecarnate.com, the Library of the Alternative Christian Web—the library of the emerging church. Chosen to be prominently featured on the back cover of *The Shack* was Morrell's endorsement which includes the statement, "This story reads like a prayer." When a panentheist says a book "reads like a prayer," they have an entirely different meaning as well as an entirely different "God." Yet this is all befitting of *The Shack*'s false teachings and false "God" that "dwells in, around, and through all things" as "the ground of all being."[2]

A panentheistic "God" transcends the diverse theologies and religions. This gives people "the freedom to be inside or outside" "religious" "systems" and "to move freely between and among them" as *The Shack*'s false "Jesus" teaches.[3] Of course, when "God" is in "all things"/"everything" then what people believe and whether or not they *believe* in *Jesus* all becomes irrelevant. And, therefore, *The Shack*'s false "Jesus" who has followers that "were Buddhists or Mormons, Baptists or Muslims" has "no desire to make them *Christian.*"[4] Since the emerging faith of Oneness/panentheism gives everyone the freedom to move freely between religions—i.e., *belief* "systems"—people can thus freely choose whatever they want to believe from whatever religion they want. Accordingly, in a June 2009 post on his blog titled, "Panentheism & Interspirituality - What's Jesus Got to do With It?," Morrell wrote:

> "I think of myself as a panentheist, and probably have for the past half-decade or so...."

"Like a good post-evangelical ... my panentheism is biblically informed. I see unmistakable cadences of **the all-inclusive Christ** ...

"This break with functional Deism came to me as liberation–very good news indeed! Not only did Christ's spirit indwell me (a message which was good news enough after hearing from Calvinists that God only 'positionally' indwelt a regenerate person–*whatever that meant*–and the Pentecostals who seemed to treat the Spirit like a rather elusive guest), but **God was in everything** in some sort of real and compassionate way. I like panentheism because it emphasizes **immanence** while still preserving transcendence and awe....

"Getting back to the internal integrity of one's faith, and speaking from my 'Jesus-y' (as Anne Lamott puts it) perspective, where does fidelity to God come in?... I am personally struggling to live life through **the Jesus Way** ...

"My friend Brian McLaren says something like this: **'Jesus is the Way to God and abundant life, it doesn't mean he stands *in* the way to divine access!'** I believe that 'Jesus is the savior of the world,' whatever that ultimately means, I can only speculate and hope. I cannot limit the meaning of this to a particular model of atonement, or a particular scope of redemption.... I have every confidence, with Julian of Norwich, that 'all will be well.'...

"Further, I believe that I can truly learn, spiritually, from the world's religious traditions–**things that Zeus or the Vishnu decreed can give me an altogether fresh perspective on an obscure passage of Scripture or way that I reach God**....

"It's fascinating that, as people of different faiths began getting to know each other, you see this 'borrowing of wisdom' take place. You see it all over Merton as well. It seems like there are several different ways professing followers of Christ have related to those of other faiths: ...

"• Way Three: **All religions** contain shades and gradations of the Truth. (Their gods or philosophies are incomplete revelations, tainted by the humanity's fallen and fractured state, that nonetheless contain glimmers of the story of Christ) ...

"The Third Way, advocated most notably by CS Lewis, is the one I want to believe most–that God has not just communicated in symbols and shadows not just to the Hebrew people, but to all times and cultures ...

"So, to recap: I think that **I can learn about communion with God from a Buddhist or a Sufi**, but I inevitably see God's clearest speaking in Jesus Christ." (all parentheses in the original; bold added)[5]

In other words, as Borg falsely teaches:

"This is who Jesus is for us as Christians.... And we can say 'This is who Jesus is for us' *without* also saying 'And God is known *only* in Jesus.'" (emphasis added)[6]

Likewise, as Morrell quotes emerging church leader Brian McLaren saying, "Jesus is the Way to God and abundant life, it doesn't mean he stands *in* the way to divine access!" In other words, in "the way of Jesus" or "the Jesus Way" of this emerging faith, Jesus Himself is *nonessential*. After all, if Jesus was essential—and He is—then as the "*one mediator between God and men*" He *would* be "*in* the way" of "divine access" and "communion with God" for those in other religions—as well as in today's shifting Christianity—who do not *believe* in Him. But since the panentheistic "God" of this emerging *interfaith* ("*interspirituality*") faith of Oneness is *in everyone and everything*, this universally accessed "God" *automatically* renders the Lord Jesus Christ *nonessential*. And since *all* gods become just different revelations, manifestations, understandings, and experiences of this panentheistic "God," people can thus learn about "*communion with God* from a Buddhist or a Sufi." They can even learn from "*Zeus* or the *Vishnu*" about *Scripture* and a way to "reach *God*" because it's *all* "*the same God*" in this merging and emerging "Christian"/New Age *spiritual Oneness*.

> "There is only One God. What God is this? Is it Adonai? Allah? Elohim? God? Hari? Jehovah? Krishna? Lord? Rama? Vishnu? Yahweh?
>
> "*It's All of Them.*" (Neale Donald Walsch)[7]

> "Humans will understand that God's words are found in all of the world's Holy Scriptures, and that no scripture is more authoritative, more complete, more accurate, or more authentic than any other, but that each contains great wisdom and each leads to a greater understanding of The Only Truth There Is ...
>
> "Human beings will stop trying to figure out which is the right text and which is the right messenger and will simply look closely to see which text and which messenger speaks to them in a way that makes it possible for them to express and experience their connection to the Divine ..." (Neale Donald Walsch)[8]

> "To absolutize one's own religion as the only way means that one sees all of the other religious traditions of the world as wrong ...
>
> "I affirm, along with many others, that the major enduring religions of the world are all valid and legitimate. I see them as the responses to the experience of *God* in the various cultures in which each originated.... You could even say they are all divinely given paths to the sacred." (Marcus Borg; emphasis added)[9]

> "This More is named in various ways by the ['religious'] traditions as God or spirit or the sacred or the Tao or Allah or Atmen and so forth." (Marcus Borg)[10]

> "Regardless of their beliefs, regardless of their religion....
>
> "There are a thousand paths to *God*, and every one gets you there." (the seducing spirit calling itself "God;" emphasis added)[11]

In their desire for universal access to God, along with "reimagining" God as "bigger" than the truth and faith of God's Word in order to "find God" in other religions, people are attempting to bypass Jesus as the way to God in a variety of ways. According to God's Word, *Jesus is the true and only Christ*. Yet, in the emerging faith of Oneness that shifts from *Jesus* to *the way* of Jesus, another key to "reimagining" John 14:6 into a universal "*way of Jesus*" that bypasses *Jesus* is the *separation of Christ from Jesus*. Thus, "Christ" is no longer exclusively the Person of Jesus in this emerging faith. Rather, "Christ" is "reimagined" as "*universal*" and "*cosmic*" and as a "*consciousness*," becoming an "it" not a He, that along with the immanent "God" is likewise immanent *in everyone and everything*.[12]

> "This is the doctrine of the At-one-ment; God, immanent in the universe - the cosmic Christ. God, immanent in humanity, revealed through the historical Christ. God, immanent in the individual, the indwelling Christ, the soul." (Alice Bailey)[13]

> "The kingdom of God is not some one particular church with its own peculiar doctrines, its particular formulations of truth ... and of approach to God.
>
> "The true Church is the kingdom of God on earth ... composed of all, regardless of race or creed, who live by the light within, who have discovered the fact of the mystical Christ in their hearts ..." (Alice Bailey)[14]

> "When the consciousness which is Christ's has been awakened in all men, then we shall have peace on earth and goodwill among men." (Alice Bailey)[15]

Since this "reimagined" "Christ" is separated from Jesus, this "Christ" thus becomes part of *"the way"* of Jesus that is bypassing *Jesus* as the way to God. In other words, according to New Age terminology, Jesus was "Christed" and everyone else can become "Christed," too. Therefore even the same "sonship" and "divinity," or so-called "divine potential," are immanent in *all* and thus become available to *all*, in *the same relationship* with the immanent "God" and "Christ" as supposedly "modeled" by Jesus. So "just like Jesus," "[w]e, too, are to realize full divinity" in becoming "'sons' of God." In another June 2009 post on his blog titled, "Panentheism - Perichoresis - Christology: Participatory Divinity," Morrell wrote:

> "I think that Jesus' divinity is one of those pesky spiritual themes that panentheism handles exceptionally well ...
>
> "Lemme explain. Contemporary self-confessed (Western, propositional, truncated, radio) orthodoxy sees God – and by extension God's self-disclosure in Jesus – as someone (?) to be admired, and trusted in for God's benefits, sure – but pretty much kept at a remote pedestal. Jesus is the 'only' Son of God, who did certain things on our behalf (namely, changing the Father's mind about us, supposedly) and we worship him in response. This produces a lot of gratitude but very little life-change in my experience. And eventually, the gratitude (read: 'worship') turns to boredom....
>
> "A third way, it seems, has been with us from the beginning. If Rita Brock and Rebbecca Parker are to be believed (and I think their work speaks for itself), the earliest Christians had 'a high Christology *and* a high anthropology,' summed up in Athanasius' maxim '**God became man so that man might become God**.' (He meant you too, ladies) **Panentheism says that Jesus is the 'uniquely' begotten son of God, not the 'only,'** echoing Scripture's affirmation that Jesus is the firstborn among many 'sons' of God. Jesus is glorious, divine, and there are certain unique and unrepeatable things Jesus does on our behalf, but overall, the earliest Christian spiritual thrust was one of ***participatory divinity*. We, too, are to realize full divinity** amidst (and *because of*) our full humanity – **just like Jesus**." (all parentheses in the original; bold added)[16]

Not only are all the "reimaginings"—i.e., false teachings—of this panentheistic "way of Jesus" a clear denial of what it means for Jesus to be *the Son of God* and *Christ*, but they are also a clear denial of the true and eternal nature of *Jesus*. They are also part of the successful perpetuation of Satan's first lie to man.

> *"Ye shall not surely die ... your eyes shall be opened, and ye shall be as gods, knowing good and evil." (Genesis 3:4b-5)*

> "When, therefore, sight has been attained and the light streams forth, **revelation**

of the oneness of all life is a simple and immediate occurrence ...

"[T]he call has gone out to *see* the Christ as He is, ... that 'as He is, so should we be in the world.' To disciples and initiates the call goes out to reveal to the world ... the nature of the Christ consciousness which knows no separation, which recognizes, all men everywhere as Sons of God in process of expression. This is all desired because of the need to emphasize the all-inclusive approach of divinity to humanity.... 'We are all the children of God; we are all equally divine; we are all on our way to the **revelation of divinity** ...'" (the seducing spirit calling itself Djwhal Khul; bold added)[17]

"And if Christ is **one with God**, so too are we. We simply do not know it....

"Yet it is not true that going with Jesus on the way to God requires us to be going *through* Jesus on the way to God.... I believe he would say:

"I observe that you do not believe in yourself. You do not believe that **humans are divine**. Clearly, you could use an example of that. I will be the example. I am that." (Neale Donald Walsch; bold added)[18]

"For I have said to all of humanity, unto you will I send my messengers, and among you will they walk. Not only one, but many, not only in ancient times, but through all the ages, bringing you **the knowing of the truth of your being**, even as **that truth emerges** in and through them, **AS them**." (the seducing spirit calling itself "God;" bold added)[19]

"[T]hey have life everlasting because there is in them that which cannot die, **being of the nature of God**." (Alice Bailey; emphasis added)[20]

This emerging faith of Oneness/panentheism, its "way of Jesus," and its new way of "being" all come down to sharing in the very "Being" of "God."

"The teaching of Christ is not obsolete and out of date. It needs only to be rescued from the interpretations of the theologies of the past, and taken at its simple face value, which is an expression of the divinity of man, of his participation in the kingdom which is in process of being brought into recognition, and of his immortality as a citizen of that kingdom. What we are in reality passing through is 'a religious initiation into **the mysteries of Being**,' ... and from that we shall emerge with a deepened sense of **God immanent in ourselves and in all humanity**." (Alice Bailey; emphasis added)[21]

In "reimagining" God as immanent in everyone/everything, there is of course no separation of anything whatsoever. There is only the relationship of everyone/everything sharing in the very "Being" of God. And when everyone/everything is in the "Being" of God, everyone/everything is "Being" God. This is why this emerging faith "reimagines" God as a "verb." In panentheism/Oneness, "God" is "Being" (verb) but not *a* "Being" (noun). And since today's *shifting, moving, changing* Christianity wants a likeminded *shifting, moving, changing* "God," the verb that conveniently wants nothing from man but "participation" in its *being* is supplanting the noun that wants man to believe and obey *what is*.

Nevertheless, despite all the scripture twisting and the "knowing" and imagining of man "verifying" it all as "real" and "true," God is not immanent in—One with—His creation and neither is man "of the nature of God."

"For all have sinned, and come short of the glory of God." (Romans 3:23)

"... verily every man <u>at his best state</u> is altogether vanity. Selah." (Psalm 39:5)

"But Jesus did not commit himself unto them, because he knew all men, and needed not that any should testify of man: for <u>he knew what was in man</u>." (John 2:24-25)

Jesus, being God and the Creator of man (e.g., see John 1:1-3, 10), knew that "what was in man" was *not* God! If God was immanent in man as man's "true self"—i.e., as the "Reality" of "who we really are" as Satan's realm teaches—then man's *best state* would not be *vanity*. Yet the emerging faith of Oneness "reimagines" "God" as immanent so that man "at his best state" does *not* "*come short of the glory of God*" but, rather, is "of the nature of God." Thus, the "true" nature and "Reality" of man is seen as *divine*, as well as *truth, light, goodness, love*, etc., due to the "reality" of this *immanence* that places this counterfeit "God" in "the very *substance*" of man's being. Even though the "mysteries of Being" in which man's "true self" is "of the nature of God" is only "who we really are" in Satan's lie of Oneness, this lie is the "Reality" people *want*.

In "Panentheism - Perichoresis - Christology: Participatory Divinity," Morrell also wrote:

> "Ultimately, it's all about perichoresis, a five-dollar word for the relationship within the Godhead, expanding to embrace humanity & the cosmos…. [T]he Spirit is our Comforter and **our True Self**, inviting us into the divine fellowship…. And it needn't be so technical – to me, it's all about the Triune relatedness of God as depicted in *The Shack*." (bold added)[22]

"Forasmuch then as we are the offspring of God, we ought not to think that the Godhead is like unto gold, or silver, or stone, graven <u>by art and man's device</u>." (Acts 17:29)

"Be astonished, O ye heavens, at this, and be horribly afraid, be ye very desolate, saith the LORD. *For my people have committed two evils; they have forsaken me the fountain of living waters, and hewed them out cisterns, broken cisterns, that can hold no water." (Jeremiah 2:12-13)*

People who want the freedom to believe and do whatever is right in their own eyes are choosing to hearken to the many voices of lies and "reimagined" counterfeits instead of to the true God's Word of truth. They would rather be "positively" affirmed in their revolution against God and the Lord Jesus Christ than be "negatively" reproved and corrected. Thus, they continue to question and then "rethink" and then "reimagine" God's Word, determined to be set free from "rules" of faith and obedience—i.e., "all the things the Scriptures tell us we should do." Sadly, the "relatedness" "as depicted in *The Shack*" clearly indicates that the "prayer" of this story that "reads like a prayer" would be the desperate plea of "please let this book be true, please let it be true that we don't have to believe and obey God and yet can still have a relationship with God, but not with God but with one that we have 'reimagined' into a fashion we are willing to accept so that we don't have to believe and obey God …"

"… for, behold, ye walk every one after the imagination of his evil heart, that they

may not hearken unto me." (Jeremiah 16:12)

"But this thing commanded I them, saying, Obey my voice, and I will be your God, and ye shall be my people: and walk ye in all the ways that I have commanded you, that it may be well unto you. But they hearkened not, nor inclined their ear, but walked in the counsels and in the imagination of their evil heart, and went backward, and not forward." (Jeremiah 7:23-24)

21

"Chain of command? That sounds ghastly!" -- "We want you to join us in our circle of relationship"

People are determined to have a relationship with God their own "reimagined" way, and, as a result, more and more people are falling for Satan's lie and his circle of relationship of Oneness. In truth, the "Reality" of "who we really are" is not One with God. There is no *circle* of relationship with God. God is *not* One with man and man is *not* One with God. *God's* Word of *truth* straightens the Oneness of this *circle* into the *line* it really is. In the light of God's Word, the *true* reality of who we *really* are is *the opposite of God*. Yet in the diabolical lie of Oneness and its circle of relationship to "choose relationship" means to *choose the relationship of bringing these two polar opposites together as One to form a circle of Oneness—O.*

In this *circle* of "relationship" all *separation* between man and God is *automatically* eliminated and man *automatically* becomes his own way to God, however man chooses of course. So, just as *The Shack*'s counterfeit "God" teaches, those who "choose relationship" in this circle of relationship do not need to *"believe."*[1] Neither do they need to obey. Rather, the circle of relationship is all about *sharing* life with its "God" that can be followed however anyone chooses. So, in this circle of relationship, as *The Shack*'s counterfeit "Jesus" teaches:

> "Submission is *not about authority* and it is *not obedience*; it is all about relationships of love and respect. In fact, we are submitted to you in the same way." (emphasis added)

The main character then asks:

> "How can that be? Why would the God of the universe want to be submitted to me?"

To which the false "Jesus" answers:

> "Because we want you to join us in our circle of relationship. I don't want slaves to my will; I want brothers and sisters who will share life with me."[2]

And as *The Shack*'s false "God" teaches:

> "[W]e have no concept of final authority among us, only unity. We are in a *circle* of relationship, not a chain of command ... What you're seeing here is relationship without any overlay of power.... Hierarchy would make no sense among us."[3]

First, neither *authority* nor *obedience* makes one a *slave*! The *true Lord Jesus Christ* was not a *slave* to the *true Father* when He—contrary to the *false* "Jesus" of *The Shack*—"Though he were a Son, yet learned he *obedience* by the things which he suffered," "and became *obedient* unto death, even the death of the cross," and said "a body hast thou prepared me ... Lo, *I come to do thy will, O God*" (Hebrews 5:8; Philippians 2:8; Hebrews 10:5, 9). Conversely, masquerading spirits, false gods, and false "Jesuses" know nothing of submission to God's will in obedience. Rather, to them, as *The Shack*'s very false "Jesus" exclaimed:

> "Chain of command? That sounds ghastly!"[4]

Second, since *The Shack*'s "God" of untruth wants man "to join" it in its own "circle of relationship," this counterfeit "God" is teaching that it has neither an "overlay of power" nor "a chain of command" nor "final authority" over man. This is very convenient for those who are resisting *God* being *God*! Again, in the circle of relationship of Oneness it isn't so much that *relationship* is everything as it is that the *freedom* of the circle of relationship is everything. People want *no line*. More and more people are choosing the relationship of the *circle* because they want freedom from the *line* of God's truth between *what is* true and false or right and wrong. Those who want to be their own "final authority" and *decide for themselves* what is true or false and right or wrong are simply not willing to accept *the final authority of God*. Shortly following his "That sounds ghastly!" and the previous "We are in a *circle* of relationship, not a chain of command ..." quote, *The Shack*'s false "Jesus" conveniently adds:

> "It's one reason why experiencing *true relationship* is so difficult for you ... Once you have a hierarchy you need rules to protect and administer it, and then you need law and the enforcement of the rules, and you end up with some kind of chain of command or *a system of order* that destroys relationship rather than promotes it." (emphasis added)[5]

In other words, this "*true relationship*" of the "*circle of relationship*" boils down to freedom from the true God's power, command, and authority. This is why people question and "rethink" and "reimagine" God's Word in the first place. Conveniently, this "true relationship" of the "circle of relationship" gives everyone their desired freedom from "rules" so they can therefore do whatever is right in their own eyes. This does indeed eliminate "a system of order"! People just do not want their "true" relationship of freedom destroyed by a "chain of command" or "final authority" or "enforcement of the rules" or "law" or even "a system of order." It's no wonder that warnings are scorned as the "negative" promotion of "fear" by the "doctrine police"! As mentioned earlier, *the duty of the police is to uphold the laws of a higher authority based on a "literal interpretation" of the laws.* And, along with the rest of the world, people in today's shifting Christianity are openly pursuing freedom from the *authority* of God as well as from the *literal* truth of God's Word.

> "The New Spirituality is a civil rights movement for the soul, freeing humanity at last from the oppression of its belief in a separate, angry, violent, and fearful God....
>
> "We must choose between ancient myths, age-old cultural stories, and outdated theologies, or new truths, greater wisdoms, and grander visions of a God and a World united, expressing as One, projecting the glory of Life itself *into* life itself, and producing the possibility, at last, of a New Way of Life for All Humanity." (Neale Donald Walsch)[6]

And what is this new way of life that man is hell-bent on producing in its desire for freedom from God? *Self-Rule.*

> "Now comes a new revelation.... It's the song of the soul.
>
> "4. The One Ruler's One Rule is Self-Rule.
>
> "This is the antithesis of everything that the world's largest religions teach....
>
> "There are those who say that putting oneself in the role of self-ruler—that is, in the role of God—is the worst insult to God. It's aggrandizement. It's ego run amok. It's the highest arrogance and the lowest blow. Human beings are *not* to attempt to rule themselves, but are to submit to *God's* rule....
>
> "Yet it is important for thinking people to ask, What if it *were* true? What if God gave humans the power and the authority to rule over themselves, without any other power above them?" (Neale Donald Walsch)[7]

> "Of course, no one seriously suggests that the Bible is to be taken literally." (Neale Donald Walsch)[8]

Naturally, no one who wants freedom from rules, requirements, and expectations—from *anything* the true God wants us to do—would make such a serious suggestion. Rather, people today want to be their own authority and believe and do whatever is right in their own eyes. When God's Word is taken literally it becomes perfectly clear that there is such a thing as absolute truth that is to be *believed* and *obeyed* and that there is no such thing as man's desired freedom of Self-Rule. So *of course* those who are shifting to darkness on purpose won't suggest taking *God's* Word *literally*! They are, however, taking the word of seducing spirits literally. After all, seducing spirits are adept at scratching itching ears, and today's ears are positively itching for teachings that bring freedom from the truth and authority of God and His Word.

> "[T]he Creator does not *rule*, but merely creates, creates—and keeps on creating." (the seducing spirit calling itself "God;" emphasis added)[9]

> "Who sets the guidelines? Who makes the rules?

"I tell you this: *You* are your own rule-maker." (the seducing spirit calling itself "God")[10]

"The answer is: you have *no* obligation. Neither in relationship, nor in all of life.... *No* obligation. Nor any restriction or limitation, nor any guidelines or rules. Nor are you bound by any circumstances or situations, nor constrained by any code or law. Nor are you punishable for any offense, nor *capable* of any—for there is no such thing as being 'offensive' in the eyes of God." (the seducing spirit calling itself "God")[11]

Although this answer is remarkably similar to the teachings of *The Shack*'s false "God" and "Jesus," the *truth* is given by the Lord Jesus Christ:

"He answered and said unto them, He that soweth the good seed is the Son of man; the field is the world; the good seed are the children of the kingdom; but the tares are the children of the wicked one; the enemy that sowed them is the devil; the harvest is the end of the world; and the reapers are the angels. As therefore the tares are gathered and burned in the fire; so shall it be in the end of this world. The Son of man shall send forth his angels, and they shall gather out of his kingdom all things that offend, and them which do iniquity ... Then shall the righteous shine forth as the sun in the kingdom of their Father. Who hath ears to hear, let him hear." (Matthew 13:37-41, 43)

"Not every one that saith unto me, Lord, Lord, shall enter into the kingdom of heaven; but he that doeth the will of my Father which is in heaven." (Matthew 7:21)

Even so, the truth is too "negative" and "judgmental" for those in this emerging faith who prefer to be "positive" that the "reimagined" "God" of Oneness that is all "love" and no judgment will let them freely *decide for themselves* whatever they want to believe and do without consequence.

"Humans will understand that their will is truly *free*. They'll know that God will never cause them to suffer dire consequences in the Afterlife for making one choice over another in life....

"A new definition of 'freedom' will be created, one that reflects what the word was always intended to mean—the complete and total lack of limitations of any kind." (Neale Donald Walsch)[12]

"No one, and nothing, is limited in God's kingdom. And love knows nothing but freedom. Nor does the soul. Nor does God. And these words are all interchangeable. Love. Freedom. Soul. God. All carry aspects of the other. All *are* the other." (the seducing spirit calling itself "God")[13]

In this emerging faith of Oneness, *love* is *freedom* and *freedom* is *love*. So, naturally, *the truth* isn't "*loving*." The truth automatically causes the circle of Oneness—which is also referred to as a "circle of love"—to come undone. As mentioned earlier, the truth automatically *separates* and *divides* the circle—O—into an undone circle that is a *line* of *polar opposites* that divides what *is* true and false, right and wrong. Thus the truth automatically undoes the "Love" ("*Freedom*") of Oneness.

"And this I pray, that your love may abound yet more and more in knowledge and in all judgment; that ye may approve things that are excellent; that ye may be

sincere and without offence till the day of Christ." (Philippians 1:9-10)

Again, the only "rule" in Oneness is that the circle of Oneness is not allowed to be separated into a line that divides. So although exercising sound judgment used to be considered a desirable trait, not any more. Now, an "unloving," "judgmental" breaking of the "rule" by speaking the truth—by drawing a line that divides true and false or right and wrong—just isn't tolerated by the growing number of people who openly want the freedom to exercise no judgment. Rather than obediently judging/discerning what is *true* and *right* in order to *believe* and *obey*, people today—in both the world and today's shifting Christianity—just want to be affirmed by both man and God in whatever they choose to believe and do. That is, they want God to *affirm* and *submit* to man's Self-Rule! Think about it.

Despite all the "humble" "reimaginings" to the contrary in this emerging faith of astronomical pride, *God bows the knee in submission to no one*. And allowing people to believe otherwise is *not love* (in its *true* definition). Neither is it the love of *God* nor the work of *God* to pave the road to hell with "love." But then, for those who want to be affirmed in their Self-Rule—i.e., in their unwillingness to believe and obey God—there is conveniently no hell in the circle of Oneness which is centered around *man*, not God as is vainly imagined.

> "That place of Oneness is heaven.
>
> "You are there now.
>
> "You are never *not* there, because you are never *not* One with Me....
>
> "And here is My message, the message I would seek to leave with the world:
>
> "My Children, who art in Heaven, hallowed is your name. Your kingdom is come, and your will is done, on Earth as it is in Heaven.
>
> "You are given this day your daily bread, and you are forgiven your debts, and your trespasses, exactly to the degree that you have forgiven those who trespass against you.
>
> "Lead your Self not into temptation, but deliver your Self from the evils you have created.
>
> "For thine *is* the Kingdom, and the Power, and the Glory, forever.
>
> "Amen.
>
> "And amen.
>
> "Go now, and change your world. Go now, and be your Highest Self." (the seducing spirit calling itself "God")[14]

Although a grievous abomination of the worst kind, this message is the very essence of the shift that is taking place and of the emerging faith of Oneness itself. It is also the very essence of Satan's lie—"*ye shall be as gods, knowing good and evil.*" It is what man's desired freedom from having to believe and obey God boils down to. But those in this emerging faith who have deceived themselves into imagining that to believe and obey God's Word is manmade "legalism"—and thus not of God—don't see it that way.

At any rate, that people now absurdly believe that man's imagination is truth and that a fictitious black woman is in truth "God the Father"—not to mention that a fictitious Asian woman is in truth "the Holy Spirit"—actually puts this *all* in perspective. *Without question*, those who prefer today's new way of thinking will indeed find *God's*

Word to be *"a stumbling block in the way."*

> *"All scripture is given by inspiration of God, and is profitable for doctrine, for reproof, for correction, for instruction in righteousness: That the man of God may be perfect, thoroughly furnished unto all good works." (2 Timothy 3:16-17)*

Having rejected *the truth of God*, man is absurdly seeking refuge from God and His Word in the only place left—in *lies* and *falsehood* ("reimaginings"):

> *"Whom shall he teach knowledge? and whom shall he make to understand doctrine? ... For precept must be upon precept, precept upon precept; line upon line, line upon line; here a little, and there a little ... This is the rest wherewith ye may cause the weary to rest; and this is the refreshing: yet they would not hear. But the word of the LORD was unto them precept upon precept, precept upon precept; line upon line, line upon line; here a little, and there a little; that they might go, and fall backward, and be broken, and snared, and taken. Wherefore hear the word of the LORD, ye scornful men ... Because ye have said, We have made a covenant with death, and with hell are we at agreement; when the overflowing scourge shall pass through, it shall not come unto us: for we have made lies our refuge, and under falsehood have we hid ourselves: Therefore thus saith the Lord GOD, Behold, I lay in Zion for a foundation a stone, a tried stone, a precious corner stone, a sure foundation: he that believeth shall not make haste. Judgment also will I lay to the line, and righteousness to the plummet: and the hail shall sweep away the refuge of lies, and the waters shall overflow the hiding place." (Isaiah 28:9-17)*

Incidentally, there is obviously no corner in a circle. There is no corner stone in the circle of Oneness or its "circle of relationship." So, although for many reasons this is already clear, in this "true relationship" of the "circle of relationship" there is no relationship with the Lord Jesus Christ, and therefore no relationship with God.

> *"Jesus saith unto him, I am the way, the truth, and the life: no man cometh unto the Father, but by me." (John 14:6)*

> *"Whosoever transgresseth, and abideth not in the doctrine of Christ, hath not God. He that abideth in the doctrine of Christ, he hath both the Father and the Son." (2 John 1:9)*

> *"Wherefore also it is contained in the scripture, Behold, I lay in Zion a chief corner stone, elect, precious: and he that believeth on him shall not be confounded. Unto you therefore which believe he is precious: but unto them which be disobedient, the stone which the builders disallowed, the same is made the head of the corner, and a stone of stumbling, and a rock of offence, even to them which stumble at the word, being disobedient: whereunto also they were appointed." (1 Peter 2:6-8)*

> *"The stone which the builders refused is become the head stone of the corner." (Psalm 118:22)*

Those who are building the circle of relationship of Oneness are automatically disallowing/refusing the corner stone. A *corner* stone obviously has *no place* in a circle—O—and this is doubly so since in a circle everyone becomes their own way to God. In this circle of relationship, both the Lord Jesus Christ and His salvation are nonessential and irrelevant.

> *"Be it known unto you all, and to all the people of Israel, that by the name of Jesus Christ of Nazareth, whom ye crucified, whom God raised from the dead, even by him doth this man stand here before you whole. This is the stone which was set at nought of you builders, which is become the head of the corner. Neither is there salvation in any other: for there is none other name under heaven given among men, whereby we must be saved." (Acts 4:10-12)*

> *"Jesus saith unto them, Did ye never read in the scriptures, The stone which the builders rejected, the same is become the head of the corner: this is the Lord's doing, and it is marvellous in our eyes?" (Matthew 21:42)*

Those who are dancing around looking for "truth" in the corner of a dark round room will not find the corner stone in the darkness of the circle of Oneness. In this circle of relationship all they will find is a counterfeit—*"another Jesus."* The Lord Jesus Christ—the truth, the corner stone, the head of the corner—is neither in this circle nor its relationship. It is all simply one big harmonious refuge of lies and falsehood. Building this circle of relationship of Oneness is not the work of God. It is not "the Lord's doing." Rather, it is the work of Satan, the counterfeit "god of this world," and this work began in the Garden of Eden with Satan's first lie to man.

Along with there being no corner and thus no corner stone in a circle, there is also no hierarchy in a circle. As *The Shack*'s false "God" teaches, "Hierarchy would make no sense among us."[15] Naturally hierarchy makes no sense in a *circle*. Rather, in Oneness and its circle of relationship everyone and everything are rendered *equals* of "God"— without an "overlay of power," "chain of command," or "final authority."

The world is in for quite a terrifying shock when it learns the unrethinkable and unreimaginable truth that *the true God does indeed have absolute power and authority over man* and that *man's imagination has absolutely no power whatsoever over the true God*. There *is* a "chain of command," and God's command is only "ghastly" to those who are not willing to obey Him.

> *"... O LORD God of our fathers, art not thou God in heaven? and rulest not thou over all the kingdoms of the heathen? and in thine hand is there not power and might, so that none is able to withstand thee?" (2 Chronicles 20:6)*

> *"And the kings of the earth, and the great men, and the rich men, and the chief captains, and the mighty men, and every bondman, and every free man, hid themselves in the dens and in the rocks of the mountains; and said to the mountains and rocks, Fall on us, and hide us from the face of him that sitteth on the throne, and from the wrath of the Lamb: For the great day of his wrath is come; and who shall be able to stand?" (Revelation 6:15-17)*

> *"Say unto God, How terrible art thou in thy works! through the greatness of thy power shall thine enemies submit themselves unto thee.... He ruleth by his power for ever; his eyes behold the nations: let not the rebellious exalt themselves. Selah." (Psalm 66:3, 7)*

Instead of giving heed to God's Word, people are giving heed to counterfeits that affirm their desire for freedom from the rule of God. And, conveniently affirming their rebellion, the popular counterfeit "Jesus" of *The Shack* teaches that "Submission is **not about authority** and it is **not obedience**," but, rather, "it is all about relationships"[16] in which:

"As the crowning glory of Creation, you were made in our image, **unencumbered by structure** and **free to simply 'be'** in relationship with me and one another." (emphasis added)[17]

It used to be obvious in Christianity that being made in the image of the *true* God does *not* mean being given freedom from having to believe and obey God! Not any more. In the "circle of relationship" people are free to simply "be" in relationship with their "reimagined" "God" however they choose, conveniently unencumbered by the structure of a "chain of command" in which God's final authority delineates between right and wrong, true and false. Thus, in this circle of freedom that spurns "a system of order," people are free to "be" their own "final authority."

This unencumbered freedom to simply "be" is neither what it means to be made in the image of God nor "to be conformed to the image of his Son" (Romans 8:29). Rather, it is to be conformed to the image of the rebellious spirit world that was cast out of heaven for refusing to obediently submit to the rule of God. It is to become the "crowning glory" of what Satan and his minions have been working to create ever since his first lie to man, which began his circle of relationship of man's "Oneness" with God. And, contrary to man's seduced "reimaginings," this *unencumbered freedom to simply "be"* is neither a "true relationship" nor a "right relationship" with God but, rather, is the *same* lie that "*ye shall be as gods.*" It is the *same* determination of Satan who said, "*I will be like the most High.*" Satan, who no doubt also saw it as "ghastly," didn't like the "chain of command," either.

> "*How art thou fallen from heaven, O Lucifer, son of the morning!... For thou hast said in thine heart, I will ascend into heaven, I will exalt my throne above the stars of God ... I will be like the most High. Yet thou shalt be brought down to hell ...*" (Isaiah 14:12-15)

> "*O LORD, I know that the way of man is not in himself: it is not in man that walketh to direct his steps.*" (Jeremiah 10:23)

> "*There is a way that seemeth right unto a man, but the end thereof are the ways of death.*" (Proverbs 16:25; see also 14:12)

> "*Yea, hath God said ...?*" (Genesis 3:1b)

> "*And the serpent said unto the woman, Ye shall not surely die: For God doth know that in the day ye eat thereof, then your eyes shall be opened, and ye shall be as gods, knowing good and evil.*" (Genesis 3:4-5)

> "*Be not wise in thine own eyes: fear the LORD, and depart from evil.*" (Proverbs 3:7)

> "*The way of a fool is right in his own eyes ...*" (Proverbs 12:15)

> "*... thou shalt hearken to the voice of the LORD thy God, to keep all his commandments which I command thee this day, to do that which is right in the eyes of the LORD thy God.*" (Deuteronomy 13:18)

Yes, there *is* a "chain of *command.*"

PART FOUR: THE TRANSFORMATION

22

"What if we were to think connectness rather than correctness?"

"Preach the word; be instant in season, out of season; reprove, rebuke, exhort with all longsuffering and doctrine. For the time will come when they will not endure sound doctrine; but after their own lusts shall they heap to themselves teachers, having itching ears; and they shall turn away their ears from the truth, and shall be turned unto fables." (2 Timothy 4:2-4)

Sadly, it has become quite obvious that the time has already come. Openly preferring the fables of man's imagination to the doctrinal truth of God's Word, today's shifting Christianity is *heaping* to itself teachers to scratch its itching ears. People are choosing to be led in "a way that seemeth right unto a man" rather than in the way that is right unto God as set forth by God in the Word of God.

In Leonard Sweet's 2009 book, *So Beautiful: Divine Design for Life and the Church*, which, sadly, is just as anti-truth, anti-God, anti-Christ as everything else that caters to today's epidemic of itching ears, this "[r]enowned professor and theologian"[1]—who has worked for "years as a mentor to pastors"[2] and "is a frequent speaker at national and international conferences, state conventions, pastors' schools, retreats"[3] as well as "a consultant to many denominational leaders and agencies"[4]—asks a question that effectively sums up the new way of thinking:

"What if we were to think connectness rather than correctness?"[5]

In today's emerging paradigm/faith, "*relationship*, not *believing* is central," so *connectness* is naturally replacing *correctness*. The two go hand in hand. Since the correctness of the truth of God's Word is a "stumbling block in the way" of today's desired connectness, these connections are thus held together not by *correct* truth but by man's "*reimagined*" "truth." But, naturally, the latter is not seen as *incorrect* in today's preferred "light" of darkness.

Even so, when connectness is *instead of* correctness the *connectness* thus becomes *incorrectness*. *Incorrectness* is not truth but *error*. But of course the circle of Oneness that connects opposites also brings incorrectness and correctness together as one into a relationship that then becomes a new and "reimagined" "correctness." This way those who prefer to "think connectness *rather than correctness*" can see the incorrectness of this connectness as "correctness" and not error, especially since this *incorrectness* is their new and "reimagined" "*truth*." And lest anyone see this new "truth" as *incorrect* or as *error*, it is conveniently claimed that truth is to be *conceived* rather than *believed*. Nevertheless, *error* is only "*truth*" in man's imagination where this new incorrect "truth" is conceived in the first place.

> *"But continue thou in the things which thou hast learned and hast been assured of, knowing of whom thou hast learned them; and that from a child thou hast known the holy scriptures, which are able to make thee wise unto salvation through faith which is in Christ Jesus. All scripture is given by inspiration of God, and is profitable for doctrine, for reproof, for correction, for instruction in righteousness." (2 Timothy 3:14-16)*

> *"Ye therefore, beloved, seeing ye know these things before, beware lest ye also, being led away with the error of the wicked, fall from your own stedfastness." (2 Peter 3:17)*

> "The meaning of Christianity does not come from allegiance to complex theological doctrines but a passionate love for a way of living in the world that revolves around following Jesus, who taught that love is what makes life a success ... Only love. The main theme in the preaching of Jesus was that life with the Father was all about love ... that we do *not* worship a God who punishes us for evil and rewards us for good....

> "Propositionalists want you to fall in line. Relationalists want you to fall in love. Christians aren't people who follow Christianity. Christians are people who follow and fall in love with Christ....

> "We were put here to 'glorify God and enjoy him forever.' In other words, we were not put here to 'do the right thing' but to be in a 'right relationship' with God. We were not put here to 'keep commandments' but to conceive beauty, truth, and goodness. We were not put here to 'take a stand' but to walk in the light for the greater glory of God. Biblical truth doesn't feast on fact. It feasts on relationship and revelation, which is why eternal truth is better communicated by the fictions of parables and narratives than the facts of science and philosophy." (Leonard Sweet; 2nd ellipsis dots in the original)[6]

> *"Because that, when they knew God,* **they glorified him not as God***, neither were thankful; but became vain in their imaginations, and their foolish heart was darkened. Professing themselves to be wise, they became fools, and changed the glory of the uncorruptible God into an image made like to corruptible man, ... Who* **changed the truth of God into a lie***, and worshipped and served the creature*

more than the Creator, who is blessed for ever. Amen." (Romans 1:21-23, 25)

"My son, fear thou the LORD *and the king: and* **meddle not with them that are given to change**: *For their calamity shall rise suddenly; and who knoweth the ruin of them both?" (Proverbs 24:21-22)*

Sadly, *many* are resisting God being *God* and resisting the Word of God being God's Word of *truth*. People today simply do not want an "overlay of power," "chain of command," or "final authority." Rather, they want the *unencumbered* freedom "to simply 'be' in relationship," however they choose, of course.

Although unscriptural enough in itself, Sweet's previous quote is only the tip of the iceberg of his false teachings. And even though it all once would have been obvious, *everything* is *changing* as more and more people *purposely* shift to darkness and incorrectness—i.e., as they *purposely* cover their eyes and ears to the light of God's Word of absolute truth and correctness.

"My people are destroyed for lack of knowledge: because thou hast rejected knowledge, I will also reject thee ... And there shall be, like people, like priest: and I will punish them for their ways, and reward them their doings." (Hosea 4:6, 9)

"And I will punish the world for their evil, and the wicked for their iniquity; and I will cause the arrogancy of the proud to cease, and will lay low the haughtiness of the terrible." (Isaiah 13:11)

23

"MRI theology is the only theology worth bothering with"

In *So Beautiful*, Sweet introduces what he calls "a So Beautiful or MRI church where 'M' = Missional, 'R' = Relational, and 'I' = Incarnational."[1] Asserting that his book "explores the secret of life,"[2] he writes:

> "The First Secret of Life is ... Missional.
> "The Second Secret of Life is ... Relational.
> "The Third Secret of Life is ... Incarnational." (ellipsis dots in the original)[3]

Unabashedly claiming that his:

> "MRI theology is the only theology worth bothering with because it is the strategic operating command center of Christianity and because it embraces and employs the whole theater of faith: the marks of mission, the arks of relationship, the arts of incarnation.
> "MRI is how it was 'in the beginning.'"[4]

Sweet then equates his MRI theology to the way, the truth, and the life, joining Marcus Borg and the many others who are "reimagining" John 14:6 according to the emerging paradigm/faith and its new way of thinking and "seeing" and "knowing":

> "I then realized that it appears in biblical form in Jesus' understanding of himself as 'The Way, The Truth, The Life,' ...

"la Via: Way is Missional

"la Verita: Truth is Relational

"la Vita: Life is Incarnational

"But you don't live these serially. You live the Way-Truth-Life simultaneously."[5]

"Each one of 'these three' is something we do. But most importantly, it is something we are....

"Missional ... is living a life born in the very being of God....

"Relationships are what faith is....

"Incarnation ... is how the church lives."[6]

The way, the truth, and the life are not "Jesus' understanding of himself" but *the truth of Who He is*, and He, being God, <u>knew</u> this. The Lord Jesus Christ is the way, the Lord Jesus Christ is the truth, and the Lord Jesus Christ is the life. We don't "*live* the Way-Truth-Life" any more than we *live* the Lord Jesus Christ. Yet this is exactly what people are trying to do in replacing *believing* and *obeying* the Lord Jesus Christ with *being* and *doing* Jesus Christ and God. They are *not* the same thing! Even so, today's shifting Christianity is bound and determined to replace *nouns*—*the words* of *God's Word of truth* and its message/Gospel/doctrine/truth of Who the Lord Jesus Christ is and what He did for us—with *verbs* to replace *believing* with *being*. Although the claims are therefore absurdly to the contrary, *true* Christianity *does* have an *eternal truth, message, and doctrine*—found in the *words* of *God's Word of truth*—that must be *believed* to have an eternal *relationship* with the *true Person* of the Lord Jesus Christ.

"la Verita: Truth is Relational" (Leonard Sweet)[7]

"This relational strand is ... the understanding of truth as a person, not a principle.... Christianity is *not* a 'respectable' world religion because 'respectable' religions offer eternal verities, messages, and doctrines, not relationships." (Leonard Sweet; emphasis added)[8]

*"Whosoever transgresseth, and abideth not in the doctrine of Christ, hath not God. He that abideth in **the doctrine of Christ**, he hath both the Father and the Son."* (2 John 1:9)

"... God is defragging the church and rebooting it with the original Operating System. MRI is the original operating system of the Christian faith. MRI is the operating software on which human life and faith were designed to run: Version 1.0 is known as the First Testament; Version 2.0 is known as the New Testament; Version 3.0 is the Third Testament, the Gospel According to ... you." (Leonard Sweet; last ellipsis dots in the original)[9]

*"For I am not ashamed of **the gospel of Christ**: for **it is the power of God** unto salvation to every one that believeth; to the Jew first, and also to the Greek."* (Romans 1:16)

*"For **the preaching of the cross** is to them that perish foolishness; but unto us which are saved **it is the power of God**."* (1 Corinthians 1:18)

"And he said unto them, Go ye into all the world, and preach the gospel to every creature." (Mark 16:15)

"It's not so much that there is a missionary message to the Bible as it is that the Bible is *mission*. To be sure, the MRI paradigm is a shift ..." (Leonard Sweet)[10]

"One of the most serious thought-crimes for a Christian is **the confusion of 'faith' with 'belief,'** or to call someone who follows Jesus a 'believer,' ..." (Leonard Sweet; emphasis added)[11]

"Even though the word itself is an adjective, ***missional* is all about verbs, not nouns** ...

"The incarnation is all about God's drama of 'doing God,' God's drama of love.... God did God. God lived in our midst and loved us and invited us to '**do God**' along with him....

"My translation of 'Go Make Disciples' is 'Go Do Me.' Is this not the second-best **mission** statement in the Bible: '**Go Do Me**'?... To 'Go Do Me,' to '**doing God**' by doing good, I must be simultaneously seeing, following, and **being Christ**. I have no theology to impart, no biblical interpretation to argue, no agenda to accomplish. I only have my life....

"Jesus says, '**Go Do Me**.' **Go be Jesus**." (Leonard Sweet; bold added)[12]

"The so-beautiful paradox of the MRI life is that in **being Jesus** we find Jesus." (Leonard Sweet; emphasis added)[13]

No, those in this emerging faith only find what they want to believe is their "true self."

"Don't be like Jesus. Let Jesus be himself in you, making you into **your true self**. Don't be an 'imitator.' **Be the real deal**." (Leonard Sweet; emphasis added)[14]

"Each one of us is free to **become Jesus**, a living truth, ..." (Leonard Sweet; emphasis added)[15]

"I know this word *channeling* has the smell of new-age sewage.... What else do you call it but channeling when the Jesus who is of one substance with the Father wants to be of **one substance** with every human being?" (Leonard Sweet; bold added)[16]

First, throughout Sweet's teachings there is a whole lot more than just the use of the word "channeling" that "has the smell of new-age sewage." Yet in today's shifting Christianity—in which the teachings of the New Age, its counterfeit "Christianity," and its New Spirituality have been increasingly embraced—many New Age (New Spirituality) teachings are now absurdly imagined to be "authentic Christianity." Still, this is to be expected when it is also absurdly imagined that the *very New Age* "God" of Oneness that is *immanent* in everyone and everything is the "*Christian* God." And since this panentheistic "God" is immanent "in the very substance" of all creation, it naturally follows if people in this emerging faith also come to believe that "Jesus" wants to be "of one substance" with everyone and they "become Jesus."

"Quantum spirituality bonds us to all creation as well as to other members of the human family. . . . This entails a radical doctrine of embodiment of God in the very substance of creation. . . . But a spirituality that is not in some way entheistic (whether pan- or trans-), that does not extend to the spirit-matter of the cosmos, is not Christian." (Leonard Sweet; parentheses in the original)[17]

Second, contrary to today's incredibly unscriptural imaginations, neither the *true* Jesus Christ nor the *true* God ever *say* or *do anything* that contradicts their Word of absolute truth. Nor do they ever replace their eternal Word of truth with man and his imaginations! In other words, man and his imaginations will never be exalted *by* God above God's own Word of truth that God has magnified above even His own name. To the contrary, man's emerging Wordless faith of Oneness/panentheism—a faith that comes by *relationship* rather than by *the Word of God*—does indeed exalt man and his imaginations above God and His Word of truth. And therefore this emerging faith in which *relationship*, not *believing*, and likewise *connectness*, not *correctness*, are central is about *conceiving* "truth" rather than *believing* truth. It *all* goes hand in hand.

> "I will worship toward thy holy temple, and praise thy name for thy lovingkindness and for thy truth: for thou hast magnified thy word above all thy name." (Psalm 138:2)

> "Thy word is true from the beginning: and every one of thy righteous judgments endureth for ever." (Psalm 119:160)

> "Every word of God is pure: he is a shield unto them that put their trust in him. Add thou not unto his words, lest he reprove thee, and thou be found a liar." (Proverbs 30:5-6)

> "What if we were to think connectness rather than correctness?" (Leonard Sweet)[18]

> "The Bible doesn't make 'truth claims.' The Bible unveils truth power and manifests truth relationships." (Leonard Sweet)[19]

> "The main theme in the preaching of Jesus was that life with the Father was **all about love** ... that we do *not* worship a God who punishes us for evil and rewards us for good." (Leonard Sweet; ellipsis dots in the original; bold added)[20]

> **"We were *not* put here to 'keep commandments'** but to **conceive** beauty, **truth**, and goodness." (Leonard Sweet; emphasis added)[21]

> "He that saith, I know him, and **keepeth not his commandments**, is a liar, and **the truth is not in him**. But whoso keepeth his word, in him verily is the love of God perfected: hereby know we that we are in him." (1 John 2:4-5)

> "**If ye love me, keep my commandments**.... He that hath my commandments, and keepeth them, he it is that loveth me: and he that loveth me shall be loved of my Father, and I will love him, and will manifest myself to him." (John 14:15, 21)

> "For this is the love of God, that we keep his commandments: and his commandments are not grievous." (1 John 5:3)

> "And **this is his commandment, That we should believe** on the name of his

Son Jesus Christ, and love one another, as he gave us commandment." (1 John 3:23)

Clearly, His commandments *are* too grievous for today's shifting Christianity. More and more people are stumbling over just being told they need to *believe*. People today want the freedom to think *outside* the "box" of God's Word of truth so they can *imagine*—*conceive*—"truth" in a fashion that they are willing to accept. And *believing* the *absolute truth* of God's Word—not to mention merely *believing* that we *are* indeed to *believe*—clearly defeats this purpose.

"One of the most serious *thought-crimes* for a Christian is **the confusion of 'faith' with 'belief,'** or to call someone who follows Jesus a 'believer,' ..." (Leonard Sweet; emphasis added)[22]

"***Jesus*** *answered and said unto them, This is the work of* **God**, *that ye* **believe** *on him whom he hath sent." (John 6:29)*

"*And they said,* **Believe** *on the Lord Jesus Christ, and thou shalt be saved, and thy house. And they spake unto him the word of the Lord, and to all that were in his house." (Acts 16:31-32)*

"*And* **believers** *were the more added to the Lord, multitudes both of men and women." (Acts 5:14)*

"*But the scripture hath concluded all under sin, that the promise by* **faith** *of Jesus Christ might be given to them that* **believe**.*" (Galatians 3:22)*

"*Who by him do* **believe** *in God, that raised him up from the dead, and gave him glory; that your* **faith** *and hope might be in God." (1 Peter 1:21)*

"*... he that* **believeth** *not God hath made him a liar; because he* **believeth** *not the record that God gave of his Son." (1 John 5:10)*

"*For what if some did not* **believe**? *shall their unbelief make* **the faith** *of God without effect? God forbid: yea, let God be true, but every man a liar ..." (Romans 3:3-4)*

"[T]he first of these meanings of faith, which sees **faith as belief**, ... **has significantly distorted the meaning of faith** and the Christian life....

"This is faith as belief, as believing that something is the case, **as believing something to be true**. This is faith **as giving one's mental assent to a proposition** to a claim or a statement. Hence, this is often called a propositional understanding of faith....

"Thus, faith began to mean **believing the right things**." (Marcus Borg, "Faith, Not Belief;" emphasis added)[23]

"Truth is not something you assent to, not something you **think** ..." (Leonard Sweet; emphasis added)[24]

"The love of God lies **not in our propositions and beliefs** ... Jesus invited us into a sacramental relationship, ***not* into propositional acquiescence**."

(Leonard Sweet; bold added)[25]

"Jesus didn't leave us any writings ... Jesus left us with one thing: himself, in the form of his body, a community that shares stories of healing and love.... **This difference in how and where we encounter the sacred—in propositions or in relations—is fundamental**....

"For the Christian, **propositionalism is a form of atheism: to define faith in terms of formulations and affirmations you can tie down** rather than living relationships and lifelong encounters you can trust." (Leonard Sweet; emphasis added)[26]

"Whenever Christian faith is identified with **believing particular doctrines phrased in precise ways**, something has gone **wrong**....

"In short, the original meanings of the English words **believe and believing are relational**.... **They don't even mean believing *divinely* revealed propositions to be true**." (Marcus Borg; emphasis added)[27]

"The truth of thought is not dependent on its source: It's **the same truth** whether from **the mouth of Jesus or the ass of Balaam**. Truth as words is **no different** whether from **the utterances of Paul or the udders of a cow. It matters not**." (Leonard Sweet; emphasis added)[28]

Absolutely unbelievable.

Sadly, these popular theologians are by *no means* the only leaders who are on a mission to pry the fingers of today's Christianity from God's Word of absolute truth. *Many* are determined to remove this *linear* "stumbling block" to the *circle* of relationship of today's emerging faith of Oneness, in which the *incorrectness* of a *Wordless* faith—i.e., of an *absolute truth-less* faith—is required for the circle's connectness/Oneness to even exist. Thus, today's Christianity is being led to purposely separate from *the words* of God's Word so that the truth and faith of God's Word can be "reimagined" as an empty shell, to be filled with the diverse imaginings of a relational and subjective "Gospel According to ... you."

This desire to think outside the "box" of God's Word is even being "justified" by claiming that this shift is all about the Person of Jesus. Sounds good, right? Again, people today may know enough to *sound* Christian, but an increasing number no longer know enough to *believe* Christian—i.e., the faith of God's Word. And according to God's Word we must abide "*in the doctrine of Christ*"—which is the opposite of going *outside* God's Word—to even *have* the true Person of *the Lord Jesus Christ* (e.g., 2 John 1:9).

It all comes down to either taking God at His Word or making God out to be a liar. Believe it or not, God knows more than man does about what is truth, how to have a relationship with Him, and whether or not we are to believe. And God knows how to record the truth of Who He is in words. Yes, words. Those dreaded nouns of truth and doctrine ("propositions") that expect to be *believed* as *what is*. Those dreaded words of truth that are "a stumbling block in the way" of today's desired all-encompassing relationship of Oneness in which it must not matter what anyone *believes*. Choosing to "think connectness rather than correctness" is clearly an attempt to remove this "stumbling block" of absolute truth that has been recorded by *God* in *words*.

"God cannot be put into words, God cannot be reduced to a proposition. Truth is in the recognition not the cognition. Or more precisely, Truth is in the transformation of existence after having recognized Jesus." (Leonard Sweet)[29]

There is no _recognition_ without the _cognition_ first. People today are clearly bound and determined to turn the light off to look for "truth" in the corner of a dark round room. But, of course, this is to be expected in today's emerging Wordless faith.

"Hold fast the form of sound words, which thou hast heard of me, in faith and love which is in Christ Jesus." (2 Timothy 1:13)

"Holding fast the faithful word as he hath been taught, that he may be able by sound doctrine both to exhort and to convince the gainsayers." (Titus 1:9)

*"These words spake Jesus, and lifted up his eyes to heaven, and said, … I have manifested thy name unto the men which thou gavest me out of the world: thine they were, and thou gavest them me; and they have kept thy word. Now they have known that all things whatsoever thou hast given me are of thee. For **I have given unto them the words which thou gavest me**; and they have received them, and have known surely that I came out from thee, and they have believed that thou didst send me.… Sanctify them through thy truth: **thy word is truth**." (John 17:1, 6-8, 17)*

"Jesus said unto them, … He that is of God heareth God's words: ye therefore hear them not, because ye are not of God." (John 8:42, 47)

"Jesus never once mentions religion or orthodox theology, nor does he outline certain religious 'beliefs' and 'precepts' by which we will be judged. He outlines actions by which we will be judged, but not propositions and creeds." (Leonard Sweet)[30]

"Jesus cried and said, He that believeth on me, believeth not on me, but on him that sent me.… I am come a light into the world, that whosoever believeth on me should not abide in darkness. And if any man hear my words, and believe not, I judge him not: for I came not to judge the world, but to save the world. He that rejecteth me, and receiveth not my words, hath one that judgeth him: the word that I have spoken, the same shall judge him in the last day." (John 12:44, 46-48)

"And ye have not his word abiding in you: for whom he hath sent, him ye believe not." (John 5:38)

"What if we were to think connectness rather than correctness?" (Leonard Sweet)[31]

"Whosoever transgresseth, and abideth not in the doctrine of Christ, hath not God. He that abideth in the doctrine of Christ, he hath both the Father and the Son." (2 John 1:9)

"The love of God lies not in our propositions and beliefs but in our relationships and behavior: who we love and how we act.…

"The meaning of Christianity does not come from allegiance to complex theological doctrines but a passionate love for a way of living in the world that revolves around following Jesus …" (Leonard Sweet)[32]

"Not every one that saith unto me, Lord, Lord, shall enter into the kingdom of heaven; but he that doeth the will of my Father which is in heaven. Many will say to me in that day, Lord, Lord, have we not prophesied in thy name? and in thy name have cast out devils? and in thy name done many wonderful works? And then will I profess unto them, I never knew you: depart from me, ye that work iniquity." (Matthew 7:21-23)

"The Bible doesn't make 'truth claims.' The Bible unveils truth power and manifests truth relationships." (Leonard Sweet)[33]

"Biblical truth doesn't feast on fact." (Leonard Sweet)[34]

"God is not a man, that he should lie; neither the son of man that he should repent: hath he said, and shall he not do it? or hath he spoken, and shall he not make it good?" (Numbers 23:19)

"But they hearkened not, nor inclined their ear, but walked in the counsels and in the imagination of their evil heart, and went backward, and not forward.... This is a nation that obeyeth not the voice of the LORD their God, nor receiveth correction: truth is perished, and is cut off from their mouth." (Jeremiah 7:24, 28)

"How do ye say, We are wise, and the law of the LORD is with us? Lo, certainly in vain made he it; the pen of the scribes is in vain. The wise men are ashamed, they are dismayed and taken: lo, they have rejected the word of the LORD; and what wisdom is in them?" (Jeremiah 8:8-9)

It is absolutely unbelievable that more and more people today think that making both God and His Son out to be liars and seeing no need to believe and obey either one of them is actually "love" for them; is "glorifying" to God; is a "right relationship" with them; is how we are to "follow" Jesus; and is how we are to bring those in other religions into "relationship" with them! Today's shifting Christianity has been working so hard to avoid *understanding* God's Word that it has succeeded. This is *plainly* evident in its shift to *darkness*.

Thus, in the midst of today's epidemics of scriptural illiteracy, light intolerance, and itching ears, Sweet is a "[r]enowned professor and theologian"[35] who has been voted "One of the 50 Most Influential Christians in America;"[36] "serves as a consultant to many of America's denominational leaders and agencies;"[37] has been praised as "One of the church's most important and provocative thinkers;"[38] "is increasingly being asked to lecture around the world;"[39] has worked for "years as a mentor to pastors;"[40] has worked with Rick Warren in different aspects of church leadership;[41] "is a frequent speaker at national and international conferences, state conventions, pastors' schools, retreats;"[42] has been chosen to be the "Chief Writer" of Sermons.com (a website whose very existence is a sign of the spiritual times in and of itself)—and actually praised by Sermons.com as "one of the most prominent writers of our generation and his insights into Scripture and its relationship to current events will add credibility and spontaneity to the sermon writing process."[43] This "credibility" is only with the pastors, leaders, congregants, and others who likewise prefer "to think connectness *rather than* correctness" in today's *massive* shift to darkness. The light of God's Word exposes his teachings for what they are. But then, it is this light that is the very reason today's shift to darkness is taking place.

24

"Christians aren't people who follow Christianity"

In today's determination to "reimagine" *faith* as a *relationship* that bypasses believing the Word of God, *believing* is even being dismissed as *works*. Yet *God's* Word of *truth* is clear that *faith* cannot be separated from *believing* and that *believing is not works*. But it *is "the work of God"*:

> *"Jesus answered and said unto them, This is the work of God, that ye believe on him whom he hath sent." (John 6:29)*

> *"Knowing that a man is not justified by the works of the law, but by the faith of Jesus Christ, even we have believed in Jesus Christ, that we might be justified by the faith of Christ, and not by the works of the law: for by the works of the law shall no flesh be justified." (Galatians 2:16)*

> *"But to him that worketh not, but believeth on him that justifieth the ungodly, his faith is counted for righteousness." (Romans 4:5)*

> *"Even the righteousness of God which is by faith of Jesus Christ unto all and upon all them that believe: for there is no difference." (Romans 3:22)*

Even though the *righteousness* of *God Himself* is upon those who *believe*, believing is also being dismissed as *powerless* and *impotent*!

> *"For this cause also thank we God without ceasing, because, when ye received the word of God which ye heard of us, ye received it not as the word of men, but as it*

is in truth, the word of God, which effectually worketh also in you that believe." (1 Thessalonians 2:13)

"... but the word preached did not profit them, not being mixed with faith in them that heard it." (Hebrews 4:2)

"Moreover, when you think about it, *believing* is relatively impotent, relatively powerless.... Faith as *believing* certain things to be true has very little transformative power....

"We have reduced it ['the meaning of believing'] and turned it into propositional believing, believing a particular set of statements or claims to be true." (Marcus Borg)[1]

"The more connected the world gets, the more the importance of Christianity getting over its propositional impotence. We must resign from the proposition business and rehire into the people business. It's time to start flexing faith's relational muscles and build up a relational theology in which 'Only Connect' is the engine room of the theological enterprise ..." (Leonard Sweet)[2]

"... the English words believe and believing are relational.... They don't even mean believing divinely revealed propositions to be true." (Marcus Borg)[3]

"Our idolatry of propositions[13] is so severe that we have even made 'affirmations' into principles, not people. When you hear the word *affirmation*, you immediately think of an intellectual declaration rather than a relational stance of being 'beloved on the earth.' But what it means to be human is not to enunciate affirmations but to be affirmed and receive affirmations." (Leonard Sweet)[4]

In his endnote #13 of this previous quote that, along with the others, *clearly* exalts man above God, Sweet quotes Jesuit priest/theologian Gerard Hughes from his book, *God in All Things*:

"A faith that is primarily thought of in terms of **an assent to propositions** can, in fact, be **idolatrous**, whereas true faith is an act of surrender to the living **God**, present **in all people**, in all circumstances, **and in all things**." (emphasis added)[5]

Incredibly, *believing* is also being dismissed as "*idolatry*." As stated previously, if it is "idolatry" to believe the <u>Word</u> of God then it is "idolatry" to believe <u>God</u>! No matter how many people absurdly imagine otherwise, *believing the Word*—assenting to the truth and doctrine ("propositions")—of the only true and living God is *not* idolatry! Believing the Word of God only becomes "idolatry" in this emerging faith of the pan-entheistic "God" of Oneness *that transcends the diverse theologies and religions*. But believing in this panentheistic "God" that is "in all people ... and in all things" is neither "true faith" nor "surrender to the living God." Yet conveniently for those who want to be affirmed in their incorrectness, this panentheistic "God" is in everyone regardless of *beliefs*, regardless of *theology*, regardless of *religion*, which is what people today *want*.

Thus, today's shift from affirming *the correct truth of God and His Son* to affirming *people in their incorrect "truth"*—and likewise today's shift from the Word of *God* to the imaginings/fictions/fables of *man*—is all to be expected in this emerging faith of *relational unbelief*. Besides, since the panentheistic "God" of this emerging faith is "in all people ... and in all things," the only "truth" that is to be affirmed is this "truth" of this *all-encompassing* relationship/Oneness/immanence. And affirming the "truth" of a "God" that is *"in all people ... and in all things"* is simply a matter of *affirming all people* and *all things*, which, in turn, is simply a matter of *drawing no line* between true and false or right and wrong. In other words, it is simply a matter of *dis*affirming God's Word of absolute truth.

> "**All scripture** is given by inspiration of God, and is profitable for **doctrine**, for **reproof**, for **correction**, for **instruction** in righteousness: That the man of God may be perfect, thoroughly furnished unto all good works. I charge thee therefore before God, and the Lord Jesus Christ, who shall judge the quick and the dead at his appearing and his kingdom; preach the word; be instant in season, out of season; reprove, rebuke, exhort with all longsuffering and doctrine. For the time will come when they will not endure sound doctrine; but after their own lusts shall they heap to themselves teachers, having itching ears; and they shall turn away their ears from the truth, and shall be turned unto fables." (2 Timothy 3:16–4:4)

> "We were not put here to 'take a stand' but to walk in the light for the greater glory of God. Biblical truth doesn't feast on fact. It feasts on relationship and revelation, which is why eternal truth is better communicated by the fictions of parables and narratives than the facts of science and philosophy." (Leonard Sweet)[6]

So, in today's imaginative way of "rethinking," *truth* absurdly no longer feasts on *fact* even if it's *"Biblical* truth," and *"eternal truth"* is *"better communicated"* by *fiction* since "Biblical truth" "feasts on relationship and revelation." First, people today obviously want a *fictitious* "eternal truth" and *fictitious* "relationship" and *fictitious* "revelation"! But, of course, this is to be expected since this is an emerging faith that is choosing to "think connectness *rather than correctness"* and to affirm people *rather than the literal truth of God's Word*. Second, with today's new way of thinking that both flips the meaning of words upside down and absurdly brings opposites/dualities together with a shared meaning in a circle of Oneness, no doubt the next dictionary to come out, and especially the next theological dictionary, will be a real doozy! It will be a fitting testament to the foolishness of man's "wisdom."

> *"For the wisdom of this world is foolishness with God."* (1 Corinthians 3:19a)

Nonetheless, today's desired *fictitiousness* fits right in with the fictitious panentheistic "facts" of science and philosophy that are thus not surprisingly being accepted as "truth" by those who really want to believe that "God" (as well as "Christ") is "in all people ... and in all things." Sweet writes:

> "But a spirituality that is not in some way entheistic (whether pan- or trans-), that does not extend to the spirit-matter of the cosmos, is not Christian." (parentheses in the original)[7]

> "The ultimate reality of the universe appears to be consciousness, out of which energymatter arises.... God is the Spirit of the universe, the consciousness of the cosmos: its energy, its information, its thought."[8]

> "Quantum spirituality bonds us to all creation as well as to other members of the

human family.... This entails a radical doctrine of embodiment of God in the very substance of creation."[9]

"Theologian/feminist critic Sallie McFague has argued persuasively for seeing Earth, in a very real sense, as much as a part of the body of Christ as humans.... The world of nature has an identity and purpose apart from human benefit. But we constitute together a cosmic body of Christ."[10]

"We exist in both particle and wave forms.... But even when we are in particular form, we are still waves that are connected to everyone and everything. Even when we take 'incarnational' form, we are still part of one holy, catholic, apostolic church....

"All of divine creation and human creativity will be both one and many."[11]

"The purpose of the church is to give form to, to put into form and shape, the energymatter known as Jesus Christ. New Light leaders, therefore, are in-formational connectors helping the body of Christ to become an in-formed church, an in-formational community."[12]

"But the incarnation blows the distinction between the sacred and the secular out of the water."[13]

"In fact, the incarnation brought all dualities together, whether it be the clean and the profane, the sacred and the secular, or the 'out there' and the 'in here.'"[14]

It is pantheistically "reimagining" "God" as *in everyone and everything*—i.e., "in the very substance of creation"—that results in imagining a *spirit*-matter nature of the "cosmos;" a *consciousness* of the "cosmos;" a *divine* creation; a "*cosmic*" body of "Christ" that is both *nature* and humans; a connection *to everyone and everything*; a *non*-distinction between sacred and secular; a bringing together of all *dualities*; and so on. None of this is found in the truth and faith of God's Word, which of course is irrelevant in this emerging Wordless faith of "scientific" fictitiousness. Besides, anyone who imagines an all-encompassing "cosmic body of Christ"/"church" that "put[s] into form and shape, the energymatter known as Jesus Christ" will especially see it as irrelevant to follow the *words* of *God's Word*!

"Jesus didn't leave us any writings ... Jesus left us with one thing: himself, in the form of his body, a community that shares stories of healing and love.... This difference in how and where we encounter the sacred—in propositions or in relations—is fundamental....

"For the Christian, propositionalism is a form of atheism: to define faith in terms of formulations and affirmations you can tie down rather than living relationships and lifelong encounters you can trust." (Leonard Sweet)[15]

"God cannot be put into words, God cannot be reduced to a proposition. Truth is in the recognition not the cognition. Or more precisely, Truth is in the transformation of existence after having recognized Jesus." (Leonard Sweet)[16]

"Christians aren't people who follow Christianity. Christians are people who follow and fall in love with Christ." (Leonard Sweet)[17]

There is a lot of talk today about love – loving God, loving Jesus, loving Christ. But *which* God, *which* Jesus, *which* Christ are people loving? Giving a whole new meaning to "love is blind," more and more people are blindly falling in love with "*other* gods," "*another* Jesus," and "*false* Christs" that God's Word of "irrelevant" and "outdated" *correct* truth clearly warns about. And the "God," "Jesus," and "Christ" of the emerging faith of Oneness/panentheism are as false as it gets.

The immanent "Christ" of this emerging faith is *not* the Christ of Christianity but the "*Cosmic* Christ" and "Christ *consciousness*" of the New Age.

> "This is the doctrine of the At-one-ment; God, immanent in the universe - **the cosmic Christ**. God, immanent in humanity, revealed through the historical Christ. God, immanent in the individual, the indwelling Christ, the soul." (Alice Bailey; emphasis added)[18]

> "The world of nature has an identity and purpose apart from human benefit. But we constitute together a **cosmic** body of **Christ**....
>
> "Quantum spirituality bonds us to all creation as well as to other members of the human family.... This entails a radical doctrine of embodiment of God in the very substance of creation." (Leonard Sweet; emphasis added)[19]

> "When, therefore, sight has been attained and the light streams forth, revelation of the oneness of all life is a simple and immediate occurrence …
>
> "To disciples and initiates the call goes out to reveal to the world … the nature of **the Christ consciousness** which knows no separation, which recognizes, all men everywhere as Sons of God in process of expression. This is all desired because of the need to emphasize the all-inclusive approach of divinity to humanity.'" (the seducing spirit calling itself Djwhal Khul; emphasis added)[20]

> "When **the consciousness which is Christ's** has been awakened in all men, then we shall have peace on earth and goodwill among men." (Alice Bailey; emphasis added)[21]

> "The New Age movement tells postmodern culture that all people have within them what it takes to get them through life--their mind power, their higher consciousness, their 'getting in touch with themselves' is going to do it for them. 'Wrong!'… It is Christ's power, **the Christ consciousness**, our getting in touch with who Christ is, that is going to do it for us." (Leonard Sweet; emphasis added)[22]

The "Christ consciousness" is "who Christ is" in *the New Age*, not in *Christianity*! But this is irrelevant for those who don't want to "follow Christianity"—i.e., the *true scriptural Christian faith* as recorded in *God's Word*. Although Sweet attempts to distance his teachings from the New Age here, not only does the New Age "higher consciousness" *include* "the Christ consciousness," but "the Christ consciousness" is *a foundational tenet* of the New Age. To attempt to separate this teaching from the New Age is no less absurd than today's attempt to separate Christ from Jesus. But those who are being seduced into believing that the *New Age* "Christ" is the *Christian* Christ don't see it that way.

Regarding the New Age immanent "Christ," which is taught by David Spangler—"a key New Age leader and channeler of spirit-guides"[23]—as well as by Leonard Sweet, Warren B. Smith writes in *A "Wonderful" Deception*:

"So while TV psychics, crystal-mania, and Shirley MacLaine caricatures are contrasted to David Spangler and Leonard Sweet's revised definition of the New Age, the panentheistic doctrine that 'we are all one' because Christ is 'in' everything remains completely intact. Thus, nothing has really changed. The New Age with its quantum/universal/Cosmic Christ is still the same heretical spirituality with the same heretical New Age 'Christ.' The New Age has just been repackaged for an unsuspecting world and a very undiscerning church. In *Reimagination of the World*, Spangler writes:

> "Where is the Christ that is revealing itself and incarnating now? Where is the Christ in nature and in the Earth?...
>
> "With new discoveries in biology and quantum physics, we are seeing more and more what mystics have always seen: the process side of reality, its interconnectedness, its interpenetratingness, its blendedness. Where is the Christ in this expanding worldview?
>
> "The Christ becomes the Cosmic Christ. Just as an advertiser can repackage a product and call it 'new and improved,' so the Cosmic Christ repackages the Christ.... The Christ is the Christ is the Christ. That is true whether we view its actions within an individual, a planet, or the cosmos as a whole....
>
> "Therefore, the Cosmic Christ is the Christ that is freed from a particular historical event. It is active throughout the whole range of time. It is active in each of us, whether we are Christians or not, and it holds the promise that we can each be incarnations of the sacred.... It is present within nature. It is the spirit of sacredness within the Earth and within the whole cosmos. It is as present in other faith traditions, including many of those we call pagan, as it is in Christianity ..."[24]

Where is this New Age all-inclusive, interfaith, immanent "Christ"? It is being ushered into today's purposely undiscerning Christianity by its leaders. As Smith points out, Sweet refers to Spangler in his book *Quantum Spirituality*, and Sweet even adds, "I am grateful to David Spangler for his help ..."[25] Sadly, that David Spangler, or anyone else for that matter, is a channeler of spirit-guides is a nonissue for those in the emerging faith of Oneness/panentheism. In this emerging faith, that which is *"in all people"* is "God," so a spirit-guide becomes nothing more than the guidance—i.e., direct/mystical/intuitive "knowing"—of the immanent "Spirit" of "God." And since this "God" is *"in all things"* as well, there's certainly no need for anyone in this emerging faith to beware of seducing spirits in an evil spirit world, right?

> *"Now the Spirit speaketh expressly, that in the latter times some shall depart from the faith, giving heed to seducing spirits, and doctrines of devils." (1 Timothy 4:1)*

In today's shifting Christianity the many warnings and teachings of God's Word are purposely going unheeded. When "God" is "in all people" and "in all things," then all "truth" becomes "God's truth" and, thus, the *words* of God's Word of truth become *dispensable* and merely *"changeable"* and *"debatable"* *"metaphor."*

In this whole process of thinking connectness *rather than correctness*—that is, in this utterly absurd process of purposefully trying to *conceive* an *incorrect, fictitious* "truth" that brings connectness—the imagination of today's shifting "Christianity" that doesn't want to "follow Christianity" is becoming more and more absurd and cosmic and pagan.

And when all of this absurdity is then imagined to be the "thought"/"energy"/"consciousness"/"information"/"truth" of "*God*," it becomes *even more* absurd and cosmic and pagan!

> "The ultimate reality of the universe appears to be consciousness, out of which energymatter arises.... God is the Spirit of the universe, the consciousness of the cosmos: its energy, its information, its thought." (Leonard Sweet)[26]

> "Jesus is God's most sublime manifestation of energymatter....
>
> "The creative processes of the cosmos were consummated in the Jesus event ... Jesus of Nazareth, the culmination of energymatter, prehended our possibilities in God." (Leonard Sweet)[27]

> "The purpose of the church is to give form to, to put into form and shape, **the energymatter known as Jesus Christ**." (Leonard Sweet; emphasis added)[28]

So, in this emerging "scientific" panentheistic faith, "the energymatter known as Jesus Christ"—in addition to being "the culmination of energymatter" and "God's most sublime manifestation of energymatter"—is the consummation of "the creative processes of the cosmos"! Just a little shift of cosmic proportions from the truth of Who the Lord Jesus Christ is as recorded in *God's* Word. Thinking outside the "box" of God's Word of truth is unarguably outside the "box." And in the attempt to put God and the Lord Jesus Christ in a "test tube" the unscriptural absurdity never ends.

> "All energymatter transformations generate entropy." (Leonard Sweet)[29]

> "The second law of thermodynamics states that **energymatter decomposes** and, what is more, that the more entropy grows, the less the amount of usable energy. Since the total amount of energy and mass in the universe cannot change, the entropic consequence of the second law is known as evolution." (Leonard Sweet; emphasis added)[30]

Incidentally, the *true* Lord Jesus Christ never has and never will *decompose*, in either His *Spirit* or His *flesh*. Not only does *God* not *decompose*, but there was this little matter of a *resurrection* ...

> *"Whom God hath raised up, having loosed the pains of death: because it was not possible that he should be holden of it. For David speaketh concerning him, ... Because thou wilt not leave my soul in hell, neither wilt thou suffer thine Holy One to see corruption.... Therefore being a prophet, and knowing that God had sworn with an oath to him, that of the fruit of his loins, according to the flesh, he would raise up Christ to sit on his throne; he seeing this before spake of the resurrection of Christ, that his soul was not left in hell, neither his flesh did see corruption. This Jesus hath God raised up, whereof we all are witnesses." (Acts 2:24-25, 27, 30-32)*

> *"And when they had fulfilled all that was written of him, they took him down from the tree, and laid him in a sepulchre. But God raised him from the dead ... he hath raised up Jesus again ... And as concerning that he raised him up from the dead, now no more to return to corruption, he said on this wise, I will give you the sure mercies of David. Wherefore he saith also in another psalm, Thou shalt not suffer thine Holy One to see corruption. For David, after he had served his own generation*

by the will of God, fell on sleep, and was laid unto his fathers, and saw corruption: But he, whom God raised again, saw no corruption. Be it known unto you therefore, men and brethren, that through this man is preached unto you the forgiveness of sins: And by him all that believe are justified from all things, from which ye could not be justified by the law of Moses. Beware therefore, lest that come upon you, which is spoken of in the prophets; behold, ye despisers, and wonder, and perish: for I work a work in your days, a work which ye shall in no wise believe, though a man declare it unto you." (Acts 13:29-30, 33-41)

In today's shifting Christianity, in which it is absurdly seen as "idolatry" to *believe the words* of God's Word of truth, what is decomposing is *faith in the truth* and, consequently, *faith in the true God and Lord Jesus Christ*. Although today's many "reimaginings" of "God"/"Jesus"/"Christ" are incredibly obvious counterfeits, this is what people today *want*. And no doubt the justification will soon be that all of today's diverse "reimaginings" are just the "evolution" of "the energymatter known as Jesus Christ" and of the "energy" known as "God."

> "There is no matter without spirit. There is no flesh without word. The height dimension of faith teaches us that without the Word made flesh, there is no Word made power. **In every epoch, however, the Word is made flesh differently. Energymatter is a dynamic process**, a time continuum that interacts with and occupies space. But *Logos* materializes in *Pathos* in forms fundamental to, shapes revelatory of, the age." (Leonard Sweet; bold added)[31]

25

"Ideas, phrases, metaphors, and customs of pagan cultures" are "'seeds' of the divine Word that become enfleshed in Christ"?!

> *"In the beginning was the Word, and the Word was with God, and **the Word was God**.... And **the Word was made flesh**, and dwelt among us, (and we beheld his glory, the glory as of the only begotten of the Father,) full of grace and truth." (John 1:1, 14)*

> *"And without controversy great is the mystery of godliness: **God was manifest in the flesh**, justified in the Spirit, seen of angels, preached unto the Gentiles, believed on in the world, received up into glory." (1 Timothy 3:16)*

In the light of God's unadulterated written Word of truth, "the Word was made flesh" and "God was manifest in the flesh" *one time and one time only* in the *one and only Person of the Lord Jesus Christ*. Jesus, the Son of God and "the Lord from heaven" (1 Corinthians 15:47), was sent by the Father "to be the Saviour of the world" (1 John 4:14). So God the Son took on a human body in order to "taste death for every man" as the only perfect and eternal sacrifice for our sins:

> *"But we see Jesus, who was made a little lower than the angels **for the suffering of death**, crowned with glory and honour; **that he by the grace of God should taste death for every man**." (Hebrews 2:9)*

> *"For the wages of sin is death; but the gift of God is eternal life through Jesus Christ*

our Lord." (Romans 6:23)

"Neither by the blood of goats and calves, but by his own blood he entered in once into the holy place, having obtained eternal redemption for us.... And almost all things are by the law purged with blood; and without shedding of blood is no remission." (Hebrews 9:12, 22)

*"For it is not possible that the blood of bulls and of goats should take away sins. Wherefore when he cometh into the world, he saith, Sacrifice and offering thou wouldest not, but **a body hast thou prepared me** ... Then said he, Lo, I come to do thy will, O God. He taketh away the first, that he may establish the second. By the which will we are sanctified through **the offering of the body of Jesus Christ** once for all.... But this man, after he had offered one sacrifice for sins for ever, sat down on the right hand of God." (Hebrews 10:4-5, 9-10, 12)*

"For there is one God, and one mediator between God and men, the man Christ Jesus." (1 Timothy 2:5)

Although the term is not found in Scripture, Jesus—God the Son "made flesh" in a human body—has been referred to as God "incarnate." The term *incarnate* means "made flesh,"[1] and likewise, the term *incarnation* means "act of being made flesh."[2] Not surprisingly, these terms have taken on a much broader meaning now that today's shifting Christianity is trying to "find God" and "relationship" on the broad way. And, of course, in the emerging faith of Oneness/panentheism these terms ultimately take on as broad of a meaning as it gets. Both its immanent "God" and its immanent "Christ" are "incarnate" *in everyone and everything.*

First, *the Lord Jesus Christ alone* is both the Word "made flesh" and God "manifest in the flesh." God is neither immanent nor incarnate in any part of His creation. And God's Word makes it clear that God and the Lord Jesus Christ *only* dwell in believers of the Lord Jesus Christ. Believers are neither "incarnations" of God nor "incarnations" of Christ nor "of one substance" with Jesus, but a *"temple"* in whom the Holy Spirit dwells—Who is the Spirit of God and the Spirit of Jesus Christ (e.g., 1 Corinthians 3:16-17; 6:19; Galatians 4:6; Philippians 1:19; 1 Peter 1:11). Believers are neither God in the flesh nor Christ in the flesh nor Jesus in the flesh, and can neither "be Jesus" nor "become Jesus." We are *"the temple of God"* and He indwells us as a *separate* Being. God was not "one substance" ("One") with the temple in Old Testament times, and neither is He, nor does He become, "one substance" ("One") with us now. Neither does the Lord Jesus Christ, Who *is God.*

But, of course, those in the emerging faith of Oneness/panentheism don't see it that way. This emerging faith "reimagines" God as *immanent* in creation—i.e., *in the very substance* of everyone and everything. Absurdly, this immanence/Oneness not only places this "reimagined" "God" *in the very substance* of the trees, gold, silver, brass, precious stones, etc., that were used to make the temple in Old Testament times, but also *in the very substance* of the flesh, blood, cells, DNA, atoms, etc., that make man.

"Know ye not that ye are the temple of God, and that the Spirit of God dwelleth in you?" (1 Corinthians 3:16)

Second, *the Lord Jesus Christ alone* is Christ. The Lord Jesus is *not* an "incarnation" of Christ. He *is* the Christ, the only Messiah. The Lord Jesus was sent by God to be the *Messiah*—the *Christ*—the Saviour of the world. No one "incarnates" the Messiah; they either are the Messiah or they are not. And *all* who are not the one and only Person of the Lord Jesus Christ *are not the Messiah*. Likewise, for *all* who are not the one and only Person of the Lord Jesus Christ there is no "being *Christ*"—being the *Messiah*—to the world, or even *at all*!

> *"... We have found the Messias, which is, being interpreted, the Christ." (John 1:41)*

> *"And we have seen and do testify that the Father sent the Son to be the Saviour of the world." (1 John 4:14)*

> *"Go ye therefore, and teach all nations, baptizing them in the name of the Father, and of the Son, and of the Holy Ghost: Teaching them to observe all things whatsoever I have commanded you ..." (Matthew 28:19-20)*

> *"And he said unto them, Go ye into all the world, and preach the gospel to every creature." (Mark 16:15)*

> *"Then opened he their understanding, that they might understand the scriptures, and said unto them, Thus it is written, and thus it behooved Christ to suffer, and to rise from the dead the third day: And that repentance and remission of sins should be preached in his name among all nations, beginning at Jerusalem." (Luke 24:45-47)*

Again, no one "incarnates" the Christ (Messiah); they either are the Christ (Messiah) or they are not. And *all* who are not the one and only Person of the Lord Jesus Christ Who died for the sins of the world and rose from the dead the third day *are not the Christ (Messiah)*. *The Lord Jesus Christ alone* is Christ. *The Lord Jesus Christ alone* is Jesus. *The Lord Jesus Christ alone* is the Word "made flesh" and God "manifest in the flesh." To believe otherwise is to believe the emerging faith of Oneness/panentheism, which is both a counterfeit gospel of a counterfeit "Christ" and a counterfeit faith of a counterfeit "God" that are completely powerless to save.

> *"For I am not ashamed of **the gospel of Christ**: for it **is the power of God unto salvation** to every one that believeth; to the Jew first, and also to the Greek." (Romans 1:16)*

> *"For **the preaching of the cross** is to them that perish foolishness; but unto us which are saved it **is the power of God**." (1 Corinthians 1:18)*

The Word was made flesh one time and one time only in the one and only Person of the Lord Jesus Christ. The Gospel of Christ is the *truth* of Who the Lord Jesus Christ is and what He did for us. The *Gospel* is not *made flesh in every culture*! Nor is *the Word made flesh differently in every epoch/age*! But people in today's shifting Christianity, in their eagerness to find a new "truth" and "faith" that they are willing to accept, are becoming "so open to change the old" and "so eager to embrace *the new*"—even from *"pagan cultures"* no less.

> "There is no matter without spirit. There is no flesh without word. The height dimension of faith teaches us that without the Word made flesh, there is no Word

made power. **In every epoch, however, the Word is made flesh differently**.... *Logos* materializes in *Pathos* in forms fundamental to, shapes revelatory of, the age." (Leonard Sweet; bold added)[3]

"Not only did God become incarnate at one time and in one place, thus becoming visible to the earth, but **the gospel gets incarnated in every culture** by design....

"Incarnational energies are what make the restless intelligence of the Christian tradition so eager to embrace the new, so open to change the old, so free to be creative in its engagement with the world. An incarnational faith is what guarantees generativity, the possibility of every culture to 'know' things about God that have never been 'known' before....

"Early Christians drew upon **ideas, phrases, metaphors, and customs of pagan cultures as 'seeds' of the divine Word** *that become enfleshed in Christ* and in the church." [!] (Leonard Sweet; emphasis added)[4]

Absurdly, in this emerging faith not only is the "gospel" incarnated—made flesh—in every culture and "the Word" "made flesh *differently*" in every epoch, but *Christ is paganism incarnate!* That is, *the Messiah is paganism incarnate!* So, in other words, *paganism is the "form"/"shape" that is "fundamental to" and "revelatory of" our age.* How very fitting for this post-truth age in which man is coming full circle in the culmination of Satan's lie.

In the never-ending absurdity (to say the very least) of this emerging faith, "the man Christ Jesus" is not the only Word "made flesh." *Anything* is—including "ideas, phrases, metaphors, and customs of pagan cultures." To say that today's shifting Christianity is "rethinking" and "reimagining" the Messiah—the Christ—is an eternal understatement. Yet today's off-the-map changes of convoluted absurdity are inevitable when the truth and faith of God's Word are "reimagined" as *fictitious* truth that is not supposed to be believed.

Not only is today's shifting Christianity obviously changing its methods *and message* in its purposeful shift to darkness, but it is also changing to "*another* gospel," "*another* spirit," "*another* Jesus," as well as *another* "Christ" and *another* "God."

> "*Take heed, brethren, lest there be in any of you an evil heart of unbelief, in departing from the living God.*" (Hebrews 3:12)

> "*But they hearkened not, nor inclined their ear, but walked in the counsels and in the imagination of their evil heart, and went backward, and not forward.*" (Jeremiah 7:24)

> "*... for, behold, ye walk every one after the imagination of his evil heart, that they may not hearken unto me.*" (Jeremiah 16:12)

26

"The word 'religion' concerns relationship"

Although the proponents of this emerging faith claim to hold to John 14:6, Jesus is not the way, the truth, and the life in this emerging faith of panentheism/Oneness. Rather, Jesus is separated from being the only Christ—the only Messiah—and becomes merely a pointer to the "way," the "truth," and the "life" of the all-encompassing relationship of Oneness. And this "way," and this "truth," and this "life" are *each* the universal panentheistic *relationship* of the "God" that is *in everyone and everything*. This *panentheistic* relationship that renders Jesus irrelevant is also referred to as a "*sacramental*" relationship.

> "This entails a radical doctrine of embodiment of *God in the very substance of creation*. . . . But a spirituality that is not in some way **entheistic** (whether pan- or trans-), that does not extend to the spirit-matter of the cosmos, is not Christian." (Leonard Sweet; parentheses in the original; emphasis added)[1]

> "I now *see* that the Christian life is not essentially about beliefs and requirements ... Rather, thinking about God **panentheistically** leads to a *relational* understanding of the Christian life ..." (Marcus Borg; emphasis added)[2]

> "The love of God lies not in our propositions and beliefs but in our relationships and behavior: who we love and how we act. Jesus invited us into a **sacramental** *relationship, not* into propositional acquiescence." (Leonard Sweet; emphasis added, except to *not*)[3]

> "The way of seeing and reading the Bible that I describe in the rest of this book

> [*Reading the Bible Again for the First Time: Taking the Bible Seriously but Not Literally*] leads to a way of being Christian that has very little to do with believing. Instead, what will emerge is a *relational* and **sacramental** understanding of the Christian life." (Marcus Borg; emphasis added)[4]

> "In the study of religion, **a sacrament** is commonly defined as **a mediator of the sacred**, a vehicle by which God becomes present, a means through which the Spirit is experienced." (Marcus Borg; emphasis added)[5]

> *"For there is one God, and **one mediator between God and men, the man Christ Jesus.**" (1 Timothy 2:5)*

In this emerging faith, "the man Christ Jesus" is *not* the "one mediator between God and men." Rather, in addition to replacing Jesus with "the Cosmic Christ" as a mediator, in panentheism/Oneness *anyone and everyone* and *anything and everything* becomes "a mediator" of the "God" that is present in *everyone and everything*. And *anything whatsoever* is a "vehicle" by which this "God"—"the sacred"—is already present. Thus, regardless of whether a person *believes in Jesus*, this panentheistic "God" that is revealed to man in "limitless"—including "pagan"—ways can be found, i.e., "encountered," *wherever* anyone chooses to look.

> "I affirm, along with many others, that the major enduring **religions of the world** are all valid and legitimate. I see them as the responses to **the experience of God** in the various cultures in which each originated.... You could even say **they are all divinely given paths to the sacred**." (Marcus Borg; emphasis added)[6]

> "This difference in how and where we **encounter the sacred**—in propositions or **in *relations***—is fundamental." (Leonard Sweet; emphasis added)[7]

> "Just as physicists cannot understand truth by one model alone ... so one model may not suffice to understand **God** completely.... One can be a faithful disciple of Jesus Christ without denying **the flickers of the sacred in followers *of* Yahweh, or Kali, or Krishna**." (Leonard Sweet; emphasis added)[8]

> "This More is **named in various ways** by the ['religious'] traditions **as God or spirit or the sacred or the Tao or Allah or Atmen and so forth**." (Marcus Borg; emphasis added)[9]

> "There is no precise formula for living the Christian life. But while there is more than one way of being a true believer, there is still one way, and that way is Christ.... Once again, theologian/evangelism professor William J. Abraham says it best: 'It is perfectly consistent to hold both that Jesus is the exclusive path to God and that people may **genuinely encounter God** outside the Christian church ***without explicitly knowing about Jesus of Nazareth***.'" (Leonard Sweet; emphasis added)[10]

> "This is who Jesus is for us as Christians.... And we can say 'This is who Jesus is for us' ***without* also saying 'And God is known *only in Jesus*.**'" (Marcus Borg)[11]

> *"Take heed, brethren, lest there be in any of you an evil heart of unbelief, in **departing from the living God**." (Hebrews 3:12)*

> *"Take heed to yourselves, that your heart be not deceived, and ye turn aside, and serve **other gods**, and worship them." (Deuteronomy 11:16)*
>
> *"Remember the former things of old: for I am God, and there is none else; I am God, and there is none like me." (Isaiah 46:9)*
>
> *"For all the gods of the nations are idols: but the LORD made the heavens." (Psalm 96:5)*
>
> *"For all the gods of the people are idols: but the LORD made the heavens." (1 Chronicles 16:26)*
>
> *"But the LORD is the true God, he is the living God, and an everlasting king: at his wrath the earth shall tremble, and the nations shall not be able to abide his indignation. Thus shall ye say unto them, The gods that have not made the heavens and the earth, even they shall perish from the earth, and from under these heavens.... They are vanity, and the work of errors: in the time of their visitation they shall perish." (Jeremiah 10:10-11, 15)*

In this emerging faith of panentheism/Oneness, all gods are just different "encounters" of "the same God" so knowing and believing in Jesus is irrelevant. Naturally, *reasoning* with people out of *the Scriptures* thus becomes irrelevant as well. And since the panentheistic *all-encompassing relationship* of the "God" of Oneness is a *universal salvation* that excludes no one from its "Kingdom of God" and "heaven," it is not surprising that "Come, let us *reason* together" is being replaced with "Come, let us *relate* together."

> **"It is not religion and reason that go together, but religion and relationship that go together.** Actually, that's where the word *religion* comes from—*religare*—meaning 'to connect, to bind together.' The future depends **not** on our ability to '**Come, let us reason together**' but 'Come, let us relate together.'" (Leonard Sweet; bold added)[12]

There's actually an older word that *religion* comes from—*relegare*—literally meaning to "read again."[13] Although God's definitions are what matter, it is a very fitting definition. For instance, if people would *read* God's Word *again*—which clearly needs to take place—they would discover that it was *God Himself* Who said:

> *"**Come now, and let us reason together**, saith the LORD ..." (Isaiah 1:18)*

Although Sweet's way attempts to bypass God's way, it fits right in with doctrines of devils channeled by Alice Bailey.

> "He ['the Christ'] inaugurated the new era and ... the new world religion began to take form. **The word 'religion' concerns relationship**, and the era of right human relations and of a right relation to the Kingdom of God began." (the seducing spirit calling itself Djwhal Khul; emphasis added)[14]

The increasingly popular *relationship* of today's emerging Wordless faith—i.e., of today's emerging *new world religion*—is the all-encompassing relationship of Oneness and its panentheistic "God" that is immanent *in everyone and everything*.

"... 'having pervaded this entire Universe with a fragment of Himself, He *remains*.' God is **immanent in** the forms of **all created things**; the glory which shall be revealed is the expression of that **innate divinity** in all its attributes and aspects, its qualities and powers, through the medium of humanity.

"On the fact of God and of **man's relation to the divine** ... the new world religion will be based.... a fresh orientation to divinity and to the acceptance of the fact of God Transcendent and of God **Immanent within every form of life**.

"These are the foundational truths upon which the world religion of the future will rest." (the seducing spirit calling itself Djwhal Khul; bold added)[15]

"The Eastern faiths have ever emphasized *God immanent* ... The Western faiths have presented *God transcendent* ... Today we have a rapidly growing emphasis upon God **immanent in every human being and in every created form**. Today, we should have the churches presenting a synthesis of these two ideas which have been summed up for us in the statement of Shri Krishna in *The Bhagavad Gita*: '**Having pervaded this whole Universe with a fragment of Myself**, I remain'." (the seducing spirit calling itself Djwhal Khul; bold added)[16]

This panentheistic synthesis of transcendence and immanence is the foundation of the new world religion that is emerging in both the world and today's shifting Christianity. With teachings that relate very well to the above channeled teachings, Sweet writes:

"It is not religion and reason that go together, but **religion and relationship** that go together. Actually, that's where the word *religion* comes from—*religare*—meaning 'to connect, **to bind together**.'" (bold added)[17]

"**Quantum spirituality bonds us to all creation** as well as to other members of the human family. New Light pastors are what Arthur Peacocke calls 'priests of creation'--earth ministers who can relate the realm of nature to God, who can help nurture **a brother-sister relationship** with the living organism called **Planet Earth**. This entails a radical doctrine of **embodiment of God in the very substance of creation**. *The Oxford Dictionary of the Christian Church* (1974) identifies the difference between pantheism and pan-entheism: Pantheism is 'the belief or theory that God and the universe are identical'; **panentheism is 'the belief that the Being of God includes and penetrates the whole universe**, so that every part of it exists in Him, but ... that His Being is more than, and is not exhausted by, the Universe.' New Light spirituality does more than settle for the created order, as many forms of New Age pantheism do. But a spirituality that is not in some way entheistic (whether pan- or trans-), that does not extend to the spirit-matter of the cosmos, is not Christian." (all parentheses & ellipsis dots in the original; bold added)[18]

"**The world of nature** has an identity and purpose apart from **human** benefit. But **we constitute together a cosmic body of Christ**." (emphasis added)[19]

"All of **divine creation** and human creativity will be both one and many." (emphasis added)[20]

"The good news is glad tidings of a beautiful new **relationship between humans and the divine**:

"*God so loved the world ...*

> "*Christ so redeemed the world …*
> "*The Holy Spirit so pervades the world …*
> "*… That a new world is coming.*
"That's the GOOD NEWS!" (all ellipsis dots in the original; bold added)[21]

First, as mentioned earlier, although people are determined to distance panentheism from pantheism, both of these pagan cousins teach immanence, and "God in the very substance of creation" is immanence. It is this immanence of "God" *in* creation that renders creation "*divine*" and that gives everyone/everything a spirit-matter Oneness. Despite the absurd claims to the contrary, this is all *pagan*, not *Christian*. But then, the integration of "*pagan*" *customs, ideas, phrases,* and *metaphors* into today's "authentic Christianity" is absurdly seen not only as "*'seeds' of the divine Word that become enfleshed in Christ and in the church*"[22] but also as "*genius*":

> "In fact, the genius of authentic Christianity is its ability to integrate 'pagan customs' with Christian *faith* and *practice*." (Leonard Sweet; emphasis added)[23]

The genius of this integration is diabolical and is destroying today's Christianity from the inside out.

> *"My people are destroyed for lack of knowledge: because thou hast rejected knowledge, I will also reject thee …" (Hosea 4:6)*

Second, since Sweet says we are to "resign from the proposition business,"[24] it is to be expected that his "GOOD NEWS" is left virtually empty. Besides, this way people can also fill in the blanks with "new understandings of who Jesus is" in what he calls "the Third Testament, the Gospel According to … you."[25] According to Sweet, the "gospel of love" is:

> "'Jesus loves who and what you are, and wants to inhabit who you are and what you are in such a way that it blesses me, blesses others, and blesses the world with **new understandings of who Jesus is**.'" (emphasis added)[26]

Although Sweet refers to this as "the gospel of love," this is not the "the gospel of Christ" that "is the power of God unto *salvation* to every one that believeth" (Romans 1:16). Nor is it "*love*" to bypass the *true* Gospel of Christ in shifting from reasoning to relating with those who are *lost*. But then, Sweet's *own* "new understandings" and teachings fill in the blanks with a whole new dimension to "God so loved the world," "Christ so redeemed the world," and "The Holy Spirit so pervades the world" that relates very well with the emerging panentheistic "new world religion" and its own coming "new world" of Oneness. And since no one will be "*lost*" in this emerging *all-encompassing relationship*—i.e., *universal salvation*—of the immanent "God," what anyone *believes* becomes irrelevant. Thus, what goes in the blanks becomes irrelevant as well.

> "When men recognize this and succeed in isolating that inner significant structure of truth which is the same in all climes and in all races, then there will emerge the universal religion, the One Church, and that unified though not uniform approach to God … **Theologies will disappear into the knowledge of God; doctrines and dogmas will no longer be regarded as necessary,** for faith will be based

on experience, and authority will give place to personal appreciation of Reality." (the seducing spirit calling itself Djwhal Khul; emphasis added)[27]

Nonetheless, there is a final authority. And no matter how many people in the emerging faith personally appreciate the "reimagined" "Reality" of a "reimagined" "God" that is in everyone and everything in an all-encompassing relationship, i.e., universal salvation, there is a reason that the *true* God says, *"Come now, and let us reason together,"* and not "Come, let us relate together." For starters, it has to do with the now commonly disregarded reality of man's own relationship-precluding *sin*—a word that is increasingly suppressed in today's shifting Christianity since it also serves as a reminder to *obey*. To be saved from our sins that keep us from a relationship with the *true* God, everyone must first *believe in the Lord Jesus Christ*, and *reasoning* out of *the Scriptures* and *believing in the Lord Jesus Christ* go hand in hand.

> *"Come now, and let us reason together, saith the LORD: though your sins be as scarlet, they shall be as white as snow; though they be red like crimson, they shall be as wool." (Isaiah 1:18)*

> *"But the scripture hath concluded all under sin, that the promise by faith of Jesus Christ might be given to them that believe." (Galatians 3:22)*

> *"To him give all the prophets witness, that through his name whosoever believeth in him shall receive remission of sins." (Acts 10:43)*

> *"And when they had appointed him a day, there came many to him into his lodging; to whom he expounded and testified the kingdom of God, persuading them concerning Jesus, both out of the law of Moses, and out of the prophets, from morning till evening.... And Paul dwelt two whole years in his own hired house, and received all that came in unto him, preaching the kingdom of God, and teaching those things which concern the Lord Jesus Christ, with all confidence, no man forbidding him." (Acts 28:23, 30-31)*

> *"And Paul, **as his manner was**, went in unto them, and three sabbath days **reasoned with them out of the scriptures**, opening and alleging, that Christ must needs have suffered, and risen again from the dead; and that this Jesus, whom I preach unto you, is Christ. And some of them believed, and consorted with Paul and Silas; and of the devout Greeks a great multitude, and of the chief women not a few." (Acts 17:2-4)*

27

"The world waits to hear your message for its salvation. That message is your life, lived."

"My translation of 'Go Make Disciples' is 'Go Do Me.'... Doing the gospel is primary speech; talking about the gospel is secondary speech.... To 'Go Do Me,' to 'doing God' by doing good, I must be simultaneously seeing, following, and being Christ. I have no theology to impart, no biblical interpretation to argue, no agenda to accomplish. I only have my life." (Leonard Sweet)[1]

First, according to *God's* Word we are to *teach* and *preach* the Gospel of Christ to people, which obviously means *talking* about the Gospel. Second, despite today's utterly absurd "reimaginings," there is no "doing the gospel" because we cannot "do God" or "do Jesus" and "do" a crucifixion and resurrection for the sins of the world! We cannot "be" the Messiah/Christ to the world! Yes, "doing good" is part of *obediently* living the Christian faith, but it is *not* "the gospel." Since "the gospel of Christ" is "the power of God unto salvation to *every* one that believeth" it is obviously about the eternal and *primary* need of *salvation*.

> "But seek ye **_first_ the kingdom of God, and his righteousness**; and all these things shall be added unto you." (Matthew 6:33)

> "For I am not ashamed of the gospel of Christ: for it is the power of God unto salvation to every one that believeth; to the Jew first, and also to the Greek. For **therein** is **the righteousness of God** revealed from faith to faith: as it is written, The just shall live by faith." (Romans 1:16-17)

> *"Even **the righteousness of God** which is by faith of Jesus Christ unto all and upon all them that **believe**: for there is no difference: For all have sinned, and come short of the glory of God."* (Romans 3:22-23)

> *"Jesus answered and said unto him, Verily, verily, I say unto thee, Except a man be **born again**, he cannot see **the kingdom of God**."* (John 3:3)

> *"Being **born again**, not of corruptible seed, but of incorruptible, **by the word of God**, which liveth and abideth for ever.... But the word of the Lord endureth for ever. And this is the word which by **the gospel** is **preached** unto you."* (1 Peter 1:23, 25)

Among other things, rethinking "the gospel" into a *verb* that *we* are to do conveniently circumvents the Word of God and its Gospel of Christ—a noun that is to be preached and taught and *believed*. Preaching and teaching—i.e., *"talking"*—the Gospel of *Christ* is *primary* because the *primary* need of man is the *eternal* need of *salvation*. The only "doing" that "makes disciples" and brings people into relationship with God is the Lord Jesus Christ's "doing" that was *done*—i.e., *"finished"*—2,000 years ago. And apart from *believing* this Gospel of Christ there is no relationship with Christ or becoming a disciple of Christ. This is why *talking* about the *truth* of Who the Lord Jesus Christ is and what He did, in other words, *reasoning* out of *the Scriptures* with people, is essential so that they can believe *in Him* unto salvation Who *alone* is being Christ, the Messiah.

> *"Go ye therefore, and teach all nations, baptizing them in the name of the Father, and of the Son, and of the Holy Ghost: Teaching them to observe all things whatsoever I have commanded you ..."* (Matthew 28:19-20)

> *"And he said unto them, Go ye into all the world, and preach the gospel to every creature."* (Mark 16:15)

> *"And that repentance and remission of sins should be preached in his name among all nations, beginning at Jerusalem."* (Luke 24:47)

> *"And he commanded us to preach unto the people, and to testify that it is he which was ordained of God to be the Judge of quick and dead. To him give all the prophets witness, that through his name whosoever believeth in him shall receive remission of sins."* (Acts 10:42-43)

When Jesus had commanded His disciples (apostles) to preach and teach the Gospel to all nations and every creature, they knew that this was *primary*:

> *"Then the twelve called the multitude of the disciples unto them, and said, It is not reason that we should leave the word of God, and serve tables. Wherefore, brethren, look ye out among you seven men of honest report, full of the Holy Ghost and wisdom, whom we may appoint over this business. But we will give ourselves continually to prayer, and to the ministry of the word.... And the word of God increased; and the number of disciples multiplied in Jerusalem greatly; and a great company of the priests were obedient to the faith."* (Acts 6:2-4, 7)

The apostles appointed others to the secondary ministry of serving people's temporal needs while they stayed with the primary ministry of the Word, and, as a result, the number of disciples multiplied greatly.

Yet today's Christianity—which is shifting from the faith that comes by the Word of God to the faith that comes by the relationship of Oneness/panentheism—no longer sees the need to tell others the true Gospel of Christ before it's too late and people end up spending eternity in hell. In this emerging new faith, not only is hell conveniently "reimagined" as not literal but this all-encompassing relationship *universally* takes care of everyone's need of salvation. Thus, having eliminated all urgency for souls to be saved from death, "Come, let us *reason* together" is being replaced with "Come, let us *relate* together."

> "If we go to someone or someplace to 'save the lost,' then we ought to stay home." (Leonard Sweet)[2]

> *"And Jesus said unto him, This day is salvation come to this house, ... For the Son of man is come to seek and to save that which was lost." (Luke 19:9-10)*

Instead of coming to *save the lost*, should the Lord Jesus Christ have *stayed home*? Of course, had He chosen to stay in heaven He could have avoided His torturous crucifixion to save us from our sins. And if the apostle Paul had just *stayed home* instead of reasoning with the lost out of the Scriptures, he as well as the other apostles could have avoided having "hazarded their lives for the name of our Lord Jesus Christ" (Acts 15:26). If the apostles had simply chosen instead to just relate together with people then they never would have been "made a spectacle unto the world," viewed as "fools," "despised" and "defamed," and "made as the filth of the world" and "the offscouring of all things" (see 1 Corinthians 4:9-10, 13). They could have been like today's leaders who are beloved the world over, as anyone would be who smothers the light of God's Word of truth to relate with those who are unwilling to believe and obey.

> "The only reason for going anywhere as a follower of Christ is for the purpose of fostering Christ relationship or making disciples." (Leonard Sweet)[3]

> *"Then said Jesus to those Jews which believed on him, If ye continue in my word, then are ye my disciples indeed; and ye shall know the truth, and the truth shall make you free." (John 8:31-32)*

> "My translation of 'Go Make Disciples' is 'Go Do Me.'... I have no theology to impart, no biblical interpretation to argue, no agenda to accomplish. I only have my life." (Leonard Sweet)[4]

> "Recently a student who didn't like my answer to his question stopped me. 'But tell me what you believe,' he demanded. 'What I believe is absolutely unimportant,' I said. 'The only thing that matters is whom I belong to.'" (Leonard Sweet)[5]

Again, the only way for people to become a true disciple of the Lord Jesus Christ and to have a relationship with Him is if they *believe* in Him *according to His Word of truth*. This is why the apostles were willing to hazard their lives to *preach* and *teach* Jesus Christ, *reasoning* with the lost out of *the Scriptures* so that "some of them believed" (e.g., Acts 17:2-4). But today's shifting Christianity doesn't even like the word *lost* because that means there are people on *the wrong path*, and there is no such thing as a "wrong" path in the all-encompassing relationship of Oneness/panentheism. And since it is those who don't *believe* who are *lost* (e.g., 2 Corinthians 4:3-4), it is not surprising that "the confusion" of faith with *belief* is now seen as a serious "thought-crime."[6] This way, "lostness"—along with "discipleship" and "relationship"—can become simply a matter of "perspective." And this is especially so since people are shifting from *the truth of God's Word* to *fictitious* "maps" and *wordless* "maps" of varying degrees of imaginative *uncertainty* to guide them in their "spiritual journey" of "reality." Therefore who's to say they are "lost" and on the "wrong" path? Their "map" simply shows a different "reality;" one they are *willing* to accept, that is.

> "Pilgrims are explorers, and the very definition of an explorer is someone who is not afraid of being lost. Being lost is where the action is and where the Spirit is found." (Leonard Sweet)[7]

> "Our starting point is *not* telling people where they should be, but being with people where they already are 'while going' and catching up to the Spirit." (Leonard Sweet; emphasis added)[8]

In other words, "Come, let us *relate* together," but not "Come, let us *reason* together." As many will learn the hard way, there is a wrong path and the Holy Spirit is not on it. Thus, there is no "catching up to" the Holy Spirit on the wrong path. Contrary to today's emerging faith of Oneness/panentheism, the true Holy Spirit is not in everyone and everything. So unless people believe the true Gospel of the true Christ they will remain lost and without the Holy Spirit.

> *"Therefore let all the house of Israel know assuredly, that God hath made that same Jesus, whom ye have crucified, both Lord and Christ. Now when they heard this, they were pricked in their heart, and said unto Peter and to the rest of the apostles, Men and brethren, what shall we do? Then Peter said unto them, Repent, and be baptized every one of you in the name of Jesus Christ for the remission of sins, and ye shall receive the gift of the Holy Ghost. For the promise is unto you, and to your children, and to all that are afar off, even as many as the Lord our God shall call."* (Acts 2:36-39)

> *"That we should be to the praise of his glory, who first trusted in Christ. In whom ye also trusted, after that ye heard the word of truth, the gospel of your salvation: in whom also after that ye believed, ye were sealed with that holy Spirit of promise."* (Ephesians 1:12-13)

> *"For ye are all the children of God by faith in Christ Jesus.... And because ye are sons, God hath sent forth the Spirit of his Son into your hearts, crying, Abba, Father."* (Galatians 3:26, 4:6)

> *"Even the Spirit of truth; whom the world* cannot *receive, because it seeth him not, neither knoweth him: but ye know him; for he dwelleth with you, and shall be in you."* (John 14:17)

> *"Brethren, if any of you do err from the truth, and one convert him; let him know, that he which converteth the sinner from the error of his way shall* **save a soul from death***, and shall hide a multitude of sins."* (James 5:19-20)

> *"Enter ye in at the strait gate: for wide is the gate, and broad is the way, that leadeth*

*to destruction, and many there be which go in thereat: Because strait is the gate, and narrow is the way, which leadeth unto **life**, and few there be that find it." (Matthew 7:13-14)*

Nevertheless, despite Scripture's clear teachings and repeated warnings, the circle of relationship of Oneness attempts to bring the narrow way and the broad way together as one in order to set people free from having to believe and obey the Lord Jesus Christ. This is, after all, the "Good News" of Oneness. And since there is no final destination in the *circle* of Oneness but only its *journey* in *the here and now*, the eternal destination of anyone's soul becomes irrelevant anyway. Moreover, since the journey of this emerging faith is with the immanent "God" of Oneness that is already in relationship with *everyone*, it is simply a matter of people not necessarily "knowing" it yet at this point in their *journey*. Thus, everyone is to just *"relate"* with everyone else *where they are now* while *everyone* is *all* "catching up to the Spirit" in this one big all-encompassing journey of relationship.

> *"We were not put here to 'take a stand' but to walk in the light for the greater glory of God. Biblical truth doesn't feast on fact. It feasts on relationship and revelation, which is why eternal truth is better communicated by the fictions of parables and narratives than the facts of science and philosophy."* (Leonard Sweet; emphasis added)[9]

The multidimensional levels of intertwined absurdities of untruth in this quote are simply amazing. At any rate, the point is that people today really do want a *fictitious* "truth." Thus, equipped with a fictitious "map" of a fictitious "reality," those who are lost can be "positive" that their unbelieving "faith" in a "reimagined" "Jesus" of a "reimagined" "way" and a "reimagined" "truth" will give them all a "reimagined" "life" with a "reimagined" "God" in a "reimagined" "journey" with a "reimagined" "Spirit." After all, since *fiction* is now the *desired* communicator of "eternal truth," "reimagining" it all is clearly what people *want*—hence the popularity of *The Shack*, widely praised as indispensable for "better understanding God." That its "God" is counterfeit and fictitious is clearly irrelevant in today's "spiritual journey" of "relationship." Sadly, for theologians to quote a fictitious, make-believe "God" as *God* speaks volumes as well. *The Shack* has clearly revealed that the itching ears of today's shifting Christianity have reached critical condition.

> "Life takes a bit of time and a lot of relationship. —**God** in *The Shack*" (as quoted by Leonard Sweet; bold added)[10]

Although there is no "catching up to" the *Holy* Spirit on the wrong path, there are *seducing* spirits on the wrong path. People are catching up to them left and right.

> *"Now the Spirit speaketh expressly, that in the latter times some shall depart from the faith, giving heed to seducing spirits, and doctrines of devils." (1 Timothy 4:1)*

> *"Wherein in time past ye walked according to the course of this world, according to **the prince of the power of the air, the spirit that now worketh in the children of disobedience**." (Ephesians 2:2)*

> *"But if our gospel be hid, it is hid to them that are **lost**: In whom **the god of this***

> ***world hath blinded the minds*** *of them which **believe not**, lest the light of the glorious gospel of Christ, who is the image of God, should shine unto them." (2 Corinthians 4:3-4)*

In the reality of God's Word of truth, lost is lost. Regardless of what theology or "map" people prefer to use in their journey, lost is still lost and those who do not *believe* are *lost*.

> "The church is largely without a theology of journey." (Leonard Sweet)[11]

And yet today's shifting Christianity does already have one. It comes from giving heed to the advice of the seducing spirit realm of "the god of this world" that is successfully blinding minds everywhere.

> "Yet let me make something clear. *The era of the Single Savior is over.* What is needed now is joint action, combined effort, collective co-creation." (the seducing spirit calling itself "God;" emphasis added)[12]

> "So journey on, My friend, journey on. The world waits to hear *your* message for its salvation. *That message is your life, lived.*" (the seducing spirit calling itself "God;" emphasis added)[13]

> "… Version 3.0 is the Third Testament, *the Gospel According to … you.*" (Leonard Sweet; last ellipsis dots in the original; emphasis added)[14]

> "My translation of 'Go Make Disciples' is 'Go Do Me.'… I have no theology to impart, no biblical interpretation to argue, no agenda to accomplish. *I only have my life.*" (Leonard Sweet; emphasis added)[15]

What a contrast to the apostles!

> *"For we preach not ourselves, but Christ Jesus the Lord …" (2 Corinthians 4:5)*

> *"And Paul, as his manner was, went in unto them, and three sabbath days reasoned with them <u>out of the scriptures</u>, opening and alleging, that Christ must needs have suffered, and risen again from the dead; and that this Jesus, whom I preach unto you, is Christ." (Acts 17:2-3)*

It is *the Gospel of Christ* that is the power of God unto salvation, not *our lives* or *relationship*! What incredible arrogance for people to think that their *own* lives and their *own* "doing" are *more important* than the life and the "doing" of *the Lord Jesus Christ*! And yet this is absurdly seen as "humility" in today's emerging faith of Oneness/panentheism that flips *everything* upside down. Do people *really* think the true God is going to *see* it as "humility" when man exalts man and Oneness above God's Son and above God's Word of truth?!

> *"For I am not ashamed of **the gospel of Christ**: for **it** is the power of God unto salvation to every one that believeth; …" (Romans 1:16)*

Yet today's shifting Christianity has already long since essentially "reimagined"

Romans 1:16 into:

> For I am not ashamed of the gospel of me and my life: for my story is the power of God unto salvation to every one that relates …

> *"But though we, or an angel from heaven, preach **any** other gospel unto you than that which we have preached unto you, let him be accursed. As we said before, so say I now again, If any man preach **any** other gospel unto you than that ye have received, let him be accursed. For do I now persuade men, or God? or **do I seek to please men? for if I yet pleased men, I should not be the servant of Christ**." (Galatians 1:8-10)*

> *"Let the elders that rule well be counted worthy of double honour, **especially they who labour in the word and doctrine**." (1 Timothy 5:17)*

28

For God so loved ... culture?

"You want to evangelize the world? Get fully committed to your culture.... If God so loved the world, why can't we?... How can you not believe that God delights in mass culture as well as folk culture, that God enjoys pop music, that McDonald's food and rap music and U2's 'With or Without You' (a favorite at funerals) are not on the menus and playlists of heaven?" (Leonard Sweet; parentheses in the original)[1]

For starters, in this emerging faith of Oneness it is to be expected that people imagine that things of this world are going to be in heaven. Oneness, which is moving to connect everyone *and everything* in its circle of relationship, even brings heaven and earth together as one in its "spiritual journey." But, even so, today's unscriptural absurdities never cease to amaze. Before the emerging new faith that comes by the relationship of Oneness began supplanting the faith that comes by the Word of God, it used to be obvious that "God so loved the world" *on the cross.*

"For God so loved the world, that he gave his only begotten Son, that whosoever believeth in him should not perish, but have everlasting life." (John 3:16)

"But God commendeth his love toward us, in that, while we were yet sinners, Christ died for us." (Romans 5:8)

"And you hath he quickened, who were dead in trespasses and sins; wherein in time past ye walked according to the course of this world, according to the prince of the power of the air, the spirit that now worketh in the children of disobedience ... But God, who is rich in mercy, for his great love wherewith he loved us, even when we

were dead in sins, hath quickened us together with Christ, (by grace ye are saved;) ... Now therefore ye are no more strangers and foreigners, but fellowcitizens with the saints, and of the household of God; and are built upon the foundation of the apostles and prophets, Jesus Christ himself being the chief corner stone." (Ephesians 2:1-2, 4-5, 19-20)

It also used to be obvious that we are not built upon the foundation of *culture* and that the basis of *true* evangelism is thus preaching and teaching *the Gospel of Christ* so that people can *believe* and *be saved*. Not any more. Now, in the faith that comes by the relationship of Oneness rather than by the Word of God, "evangelizing" the world is about facilitating *relationship*. And this emerging new faith and its shift from "Come, let us *reason* together" to "Come, let us *relate* together" is changing evangelism significantly. Not only is preaching and teaching the *corner* stone irrelevant in this emerging faith's *circle* of relationship of Oneness, but the *correctness* of God's Word of truth is "a stumbling block in the way" of this desired *connectness*. Thus, today's shifting Christianity is choosing to flex its "relational muscles" rather than use the "propositional" (doctrinal) "impotence" of God's Word of truth to "evangelize" the world.

"What if we were to think connectness rather than correctness?" (Leonard Sweet)[2]

"The more connected the world gets, the more the importance of Christianity getting over its propositional impotence. We must resign from the proposition business and rehire into the people business. It's time to start flexing faith's relational muscles and build up a relational theology in which 'Only Connect' is the engine room of the theological enterprise ...

"No one lives to himself and no one dies to herself; we are all members of one another." (Leonard Sweet)[3]

*"For none of us liveth to himself, and no man dieth to himself. For whether we live, we live unto **the Lord**; and whether we die, we die unto **the Lord**: whether we live therefore, or die, we are **the Lord's**. For to this end Christ both died, and rose, and revived, **that he might be Lord** both of the dead and living." (Romans 14:7-9)*

*"Take heed unto thyself, and unto **the doctrine**; continue in them: for in doing this thou shalt both save thyself, and them that hear thee." (1 Timothy 4:16)*

*"For this is good and acceptable in the sight of God our Saviour; Who will have all men to be saved, and to come unto **the knowledge of the truth**." (1 Timothy 2:3-4)*

*"For the LORD is good; his mercy is everlasting; **and his truth endureth <u>to all generations</u>**." (Psalm 100:5)*

"And be not conformed to this world: but be ye transformed by the renewing of your mind, that ye may prove what is that good, and acceptable, and perfect, will of God." (Romans 12:2)

"Some Christians think they get sainthood for old-fogeydom, for being defiantly out-of-date, for having no symbiosis with their host culture. For Christians to have a 'healthy contempt' for musical fashion is for Christians to have an unhealthy contempt for evangelism. Should we be proud of our wanton and sometimes willful cluelessness about culture?... Is it a good thing to rail against a culture we have branded as materialist, relativist, narcissist—the very culture we are called to love and evangelize?" (Leonard Sweet)[4]

In today's shifting Christianity, taking God at His Word is "old-fogeydom" and making God out to be a liar is being up-to-date. For people to have a "healthy contempt" for God's Word of truth is for them to have an unhealthy contempt for God. Should they be proud of their wanton and willful cluelessness about God and His Word of truth? But those who are shifting from the faith that comes by the Word of God to the emerging faith that comes by relationship don't see it that way. Nevertheless, *believing* in God's Son the Lord and Saviour Jesus Christ is the *only* way we can become a true saint; the true Gospel of Christ, which has *absolutely nothing whatsoever* to do with "musical fashion," is the *only* true evangelism; and we are not called to love and evangelize *culture*, but *people!* This all used to be obvious in Christianity before the epidemic of absurdity changed everything. Now, too many people in today's shifting Christianity think they get sainthood for "reimagining" God and His Word of truth, for being defiantly up-to-date in today's post-truth world, for inciting revolution against their Host, the Creator of all that is.

> *"Hear now this, O foolish people, and without understanding; which have eyes, and see not; which have ears, and hear not: Fear ye not me? saith the LORD: will ye not tremble at my presence ...? But this people hath a revolting and a rebellious heart; they are revolted and gone. Neither say they in their heart, Let us now fear the LORD our God ..." (Jeremiah 5:21-24)*

> *"Know therefore that the LORD thy God, he is God, the faithful God, which keepeth covenant and mercy with them that love him and keep his commandments* **to a thousand generations***." (Deuteronomy 7:9)*

> *"Go ye therefore, and teach all nations, baptizing them in the name of the Father, and of the Son, and of the Holy Ghost: Teaching them to observe all things whatsoever I have commanded you ..." (Matthew 28:19-20)*

> *"And he said unto them, Go ye into all the world, and preach the gospel to every creature." (Mark 16:15)*

> *"For the preaching of the cross is to them that perish foolishness; but unto us which are saved it is the power of God. For it is written, I will destroy the wisdom of the wise, and will bring to nothing the understanding of the prudent. Where is the wise? where is the scribe? where is the disputer of this world? hath not God made foolish the wisdom of this world? For after that in the wisdom of God the world by wisdom knew not God, it pleased God by the foolishness of preaching to save them that believe. For the Jews require a sign, and the Greeks seek after wisdom: But we preach Christ crucified, unto the Jews a stumblingblock, and unto the Greeks foolishness; but unto them which are called, both Jews and Greeks, Christ the power of God, and the wisdom of God." (1 Corinthians 1:18-24)*

Despite the clear teachings and warnings in the Word of God, the emerging Wordless faith of Oneness is changing everything. Thus, today's "good news" is the all-encompassing relationship of Oneness in which people have the freedom to imagine and define "God" or "Jesus"/"Christ" however they choose, to have this relationship however they choose, on whatever "path" they choose, without fear of being "lost" or "wrong."

Since neither those in today's shifting Christianity nor those in the world want to either believe or obey God's Word of truth, maybe they should just go into all the world and give out Coca-Cola. After all, this has just as much of a chance of successfully evangelizing the world and teaching the world to sing in perfect harmony as does the musical fashion, Wordless faith, and gospel of Oneness. And just like the "truth" and "faith" of the "relationship" of Oneness, "it's the real thing." And besides, the panentheistic "God" of today's emerging faith of Oneness is *in everything*, so giving out Coca-Cola is absurdly giving out "God" in the "very *substance*" of the drink itself.

Sadly, the sweeping changes in today's shifting Christianity speak volumes about who are the ones being "evangelized" in this world and to which faith they are being "converted." When it's freedom people want, it's freedom people pursue. And the emerging Wordless faith of Oneness offers them unencumbered freedom to believe and do whatever is right in their own eyes.

29

"There is no neat line of demarcation between the things of the world and the things of the Spirit"

This journey—i.e., *revolution*—of the circle of Oneness is changing *everything*, and the meaning of the cross is no exception. In this merging and emerging faith of "Christian"/New Age Oneness:

> "[T]he Cross still stands....
>
> "But this is on one condition, and one only: that it expand itself to the dimensions of a new age, and *cease to present itself to us as primarily (or even exclusively) the sign of a victory over sin."* (Jesuit priest Pierre Teilhard de Chardin, known as "the Father of the New Age Movement;" parentheses in the original)[1]

There's nothing like *man* giving *God* conditions for the cross to still stand! But then, in this emerging faith man has many such conditions and rules for God and the Lord Jesus Christ. Conveniently, in its *all-encompassing Oneness* the dimensions of the New Age are *universal*. Sweet, who refers to Teilhard de Chardin as "Twentieth-century Christianity's major voice,"[2] obligingly expands the cross in just such a manner. Choosing to "think connectness rather than correctness,"[3] Sweet "reimagines" the cross as bringing opposites together into relationship, which gives it the same meaning and purpose as today's desired circle of Oneness and its all-encompassing relationship of freedom.

> "The cross brings into relationship opposites, ... In Christ all opposites are not so much reconciled as transcended in the Oneness of Twoness that becomes Three-ness." (Leonard Sweet)[4]

167

As addressed earlier, the circle of Oneness brings opposites together into relationship thereby giving people their desired freedom from the dividing line of God's truth between *what is* true and false, right and wrong, holy and profane, etc. In other words, in this circle of relationship of all things *there is no line drawn between what is of God and what is not of God*. Rather, this *line* of opposites is simply transformed into a *circle* of one *all-inclusive* relationship. To "reimagine" the cross in the same way—as bringing opposites together into relationship—is no different. This, too, removes the dividing line of God's truth. So, although the Oneness of all opposites is not even remotely *scriptural, correctness* conveniently becomes irrelevant. Since the line between *what is of God* and *what is not of God* is *eliminated* ("transcended") in bringing opposites together into a relationship of Oneness, there is *obviously* no need to *believe* and no need to *obey*. And therefore *what* we are to believe and obey—i.e., the truth and faith of God that is given to us by God in the Word of God—also becomes irrelevant.

> "We must resign from the proposition business ... and build up a relational theology in which 'Only Connect' is the engine room of the theological enterprise ..." (Leonard Sweet)[5]

> "Propositionalism is a horrible modern doctrine that has all but performed spiritual hari-kari on the Western church. I call it the Dutch elm disease of Christian faith. To get rid of it is almost to convert Christians from another religion. In fact, it may be easier to evangelize people who know nothing about Christianity than heal modern Christians infected by this disease.

> "Recite the Apostles' Creed. It's a quirky creed, for it has nothing to do with principles of living and everything to do with the biography of a person—his coming to life, his going to death, his coming back to life again. The church doesn't have a Uniting or Unifying Principle but a Binding Person and a Relational Compass. What sits enthroned at the heart of the universe is not a conquering King or Master Sage but a slaughtered Lamb stretched out in all four directions on an encompassing cross; not power or wisdom or principles about love, but God incarnate." (Leonard Sweet)[6]

> "In fact, the incarnation brought all dualities together, whether it be the clean and the profane, the sacred and the secular, or the 'out there' and the 'in here.'" (Leonard Sweet)[7]

Contrary to man's attempts to expand the cross, the true meaning of the cross is not about the New Age "At-one-ment" but about the Lord Jesus Christ's atonement for our sins. The true cross of the Lord Jesus Christ is only all-encompassing in that He has paid the price—atoned—*for every sin of every single person of the world*. This in itself is a *tremendous* act of love and mercy by God toward us! God didn't have to do this. He doesn't owe man—His creation—*anything* and could have very easily scrapped us all. Yet He didn't, and all God asks from us is that we obediently believe in His Son to be saved from our sins. But this isn't good enough for people. *They* have conditions for God.

People today want the freedom to simply "be" however they choose, "unencumbered" by the dividing line of God's truth between what is true and false, right and wrong. They want the "true relationship" of the "circle of relationship" of Oneness in which there is no "hierarchy," "overlay of power," "chain of command," or "final authority" since, after all, "a system of order" "destroys relationship."[8] Rather, God's "system of order" destroys their desired freedom to believe and do whatever is right in their own eyes. And this is simply intolerable to those who want an automatic all-encompassing relationship and universal salvation in which there are no "rules" or "requirements" or "expectations" that anyone has to believe or obey. Thus, the faith of Oneness and its panentheistic "God" that is *in* everyone and everything—which thereby eliminates the dichotomy between sacred and secular as well as between all opposites/dualities—is emerging. But because this is imagined to be the true God, people won't think twice about their quest for freedom from the "box" of God's Word of separative dichotomous truth.

> "But the incarnation blows the distinction between the sacred and the secular out of the water. There is no neat line of demarcation between the things of the world and the things of the Spirit. God uses the profane and the ordinary to reveal the sacred and the holy. In fact, 'The Incarnate One' gives the world back to us, transformed, transfigured." (Leonard Sweet)[9]

> *"Love not the world, neither the things that are in the world. If any man love the world, the love of the Father is not in him. For all that is in the world, the lust of the flesh, and the lust of the eyes, and the pride of life, is not of the Father, but is of the world. And the world passeth away, and the lust thereof: but he that doeth the will of God abideth for ever." (1 John 2:15-17)*

> "Propositionalists want you to fall in line. Relationalists want you to fall in love....
>
> "We were put here to 'glorify God and enjoy him forever.' In other words, we were not put here to 'do the right thing' but to be in a 'right relationship' with God. We were not put here to 'keep commandments' but to conceive beauty, truth, and goodness." (Leonard Sweet)[10]

> *"This I say therefore, and testify in the Lord, that ye henceforth walk not as other Gentiles walk, in the vanity of their mind, having the understanding darkened, being alienated from the life of God through the ignorance that is in them, because of the blindness of their heart." (Ephesians 4:17-18)*

> *"Because that, when they knew God, they glorified him not as God, neither were thankful; but became vain in their imaginations, and their foolish heart was darkened." (Romans 1:21)*

Bringing opposites together into relationship does not *glorify* God. Rather, this "right relationship" that heedlessly removes the dividing line between things of the Spirit and things of the world, holy and profane, sacred and secular, church and world, Christianity and paganism, etc., *profanes* God.

> "... they have put no difference between the holy and profane, neither have they shown difference between the unclean and the clean, ... and **I am profaned** among them." (Ezekiel 22:26)

> "Study to show thyself approved **unto God**, a workman that needeth not to be ashamed, **rightly dividing** the word of truth." (2 Timothy 2:15)

> "What if we were to think connectness rather than correctness?" (Leonard Sweet)[11]

"In fact, the genius of authentic Christianity is its ability to integrate 'pagan customs' with Christian faith and practice." (Leonard Sweet)[12]

"Thus saith the LORD, Learn not the way of the heathen, ... For the customs of the people are vain ..." (Jeremiah 10:2-3)

"Take heed to thyself that thou be not snared by following them, ... and that thou inquire not after their gods, saying, How did these nations serve their gods? even so will I do likewise. Thou shalt not do so unto the LORD thy God: for every abomination to the LORD, which he hateth, have they done unto their gods ... What thing soever I command you, observe to do it: thou shalt not add thereto, nor diminish from it." (Deuteronomy 12:30-32)

"You can see the beauty of Christianity's chameleon adaptability to different cultures from the very beginning ...

"The early disciples treated with deep esteem those without faith and those with other faiths because God is active in their lives and we have something to learn from them.

"Early Christians drew upon ideas, phrases, metaphors, and customs of pagan cultures as 'seeds' of the divine Word that become enfleshed in Christ and in the church." (Leonard Sweet)[13]

"It is time for the dichotomy between church and world to be as shattered as that temple veil was shattered by Jesus on the cross." (Leonard Sweet)[14]

"Be ye not unequally yoked together with unbelievers: for what fellowship hath righteousness with unrighteousness? and what communion hath light with darkness? And what concord hath Christ with Belial? or what part hath he that believeth with an infidel? And what agreement hath the temple of God with idols? for ye are the temple of the living God; as God hath said, I will dwell in them, and walk in them; and I will be their God, and they shall be my people. Wherefore come out from among them, and be ye separate, saith the Lord, and touch not the unclean thing; and I will receive you, and will be a Father unto you, and ye shall be my sons and daughters, saith the Lord Almighty. Having therefore these promises, dearly beloved, let us cleanse ourselves from all filthiness of the flesh and spirit, perfecting holiness in the fear of God." (2 Corinthians 6:14–7:1)

"For God hath not called us unto uncleanness, but unto holiness." (1 Thessalonians 4:7)

"In fact, the incarnation brought all dualities together, whether it be the clean and the profane, the sacred and the secular, or the 'out there' and the 'in here.'" (Leonard Sweet)[15]

So, in answer to Sweet's earlier question of how can we not believe that God loves and "delights in" the things of the world/culture? *Easily*, simply by reading God's Word. But more and more people are not willing to accept a line between what is of God and what is not of God and are covering their eyes and ears to its truth. And, yes, even paganism is becoming increasingly acceptable, although this shouldn't be surprising. If paganism was a problem for today's shifting Christianity then the *pagan* teaching of the *immanence* of "God" wouldn't be so foundational to its emerging new faith. The choice to integrate worldliness and paganism into the faith and practice of "authentic Christianity" doesn't change the truth and faith given to us by God in the Word of God one iota. However, it does change Christianity into an authentically pagan and worldly "Christianity."

Contrary to the teachings that:

> "God uses the profane and the ordinary to reveal the sacred and the holy. In fact, 'The Incarnate One' gives the world back to us, transformed, transfigured." (Leonard Sweet)[16]

The immanent "God" of Oneness that eliminates all separation between the holy and the profane actually gives the "church" back to the world, neatly transformed back into the likeness of the unbelieving world from whence it came.

> "And we know that we are of God, and the whole world lieth in wickedness." (1 John 5:19)

> "Woe unto them that call evil good, and good evil; that put darkness for light, and light for darkness; that put bitter for sweet, and sweet for bitter! Woe unto them that are wise in their own eyes, and prudent in their own sight!" (Isaiah 5:20-21)

> "For if after they have escaped the pollutions of the world through the knowledge of the Lord and Saviour Jesus Christ, they are again entangled therein, and overcome, the latter end is worse with them than the beginning. For it had been better for them not to have known the way of righteousness, than, after they have known it, to turn from the holy commandment delivered unto them. But it is happened unto them according to the true proverb, The dog is turned to his own vomit again; and the sow that was washed to her wallowing in the mire." (2 Peter 2:20-22)

It is obviously today's rebellious Christianity, not God, that is shattering the dichotomy between church and world, and so successfully, in fact, that very little difference can be detected. Likewise, it is today's rebellious Christianity that is attempting to blow the line between the things of the world and the things of the Spirit out of the water. Although clearly set forth throughout God's Word of truth, this line is both ignored and "reimagined" by those who prefer the freedom of the circle of Oneness. After all, when there is no dividing line between the things of the world and the things of the Spirit then there is conveniently no difference between sowing to the flesh and sowing to the Spirit. But the true God is not mocked and people will reap accordingly.

We can either heed man's word:

> "But the incarnation blows the distinction between the sacred and the secular out of the water. There is no neat line of demarcation between the things of the world and the things of the Spirit." (Leonard Sweet)[17]

Or we can heed God's Word:

> "Be not deceived; God is not mocked: for whatsoever a man soweth, that shall he also reap. For he that soweth to his flesh shall of the flesh reap corruption; but he that soweth to the Spirit shall of the Spirit reap life everlasting.... But God forbid that I should glory, save in the cross of our Lord Jesus Christ, by whom the world is crucified unto me, and I unto the world." (Galatians 6:7-8, 14)

> "And they that are Christ's have crucified the flesh with the affections and lusts. If we

live in the Spirit, let us also walk in the Spirit." (Galatians 5:24-25)

"There is therefore now no condemnation to them which are in Christ Jesus, who walk not after the flesh, but after the Spirit.... For they that are after the flesh do mind the things of the flesh; but they that are after the Spirit do mind the things of the Spirit. For to be carnally minded is death; but to be spiritually minded is life and peace." (Romans 8:1, 5-6)

Contrary to the claims in the emerging faith of Oneness/panentheism, all life is *not* "spiritual." There *is* a *line* between the things of the *flesh/world* and the things of the *Spirit*. Although today's shifting Christianity no longer knows the difference, *God does*. And in His Word of truth, polar opposites are polar opposites. In other words, it is not a *circular* Oneness of *both/and*, but a *linear* separation of *either/or*. But, sadly, those who are choosing to think outside the "box" of God's Word of linear truth don't see it that way.

"Matter is the energy of Spirit. Ultimately, all that exists is spirit." (Leonard Sweet)[18]

"You will not find references in this book [*So Beautiful*] to 'the spiritual life.' The whole language of 'the spiritual life' is part of our problem. There is no spiritual life. There is only life. One life where the spiritual is not separate but the whole." (Leonard Sweet)[19]

"Spirituality ... is universal....

"This is because 'spirituality' is nothing more than life itself, as it is....

"The only discussion left then is whether life and God are the same things. And I tell you, they are." (the seducing spirit calling itself "God")[20]

"The essence of life is Oneness—unity with All That Is. This is what life is: unity, *expressing*." (the seducing spirit calling itself "God")[21]

"That is a sign of maturity, and most human beings ... begin to see that they do not live in a black-and-white world, that there are multiple shades of gray, and that standing firm in an 'either/or' position rarely serves anyone—least of all, Life.

"You do not live in an 'either/or' reality. The reality is 'both/and.'...

"This will be one of the dramatic shifts to occur in the future, for your religions *will* adopt this larger understanding in the days of the New Spirituality." (the seducing spirit calling itself "God;" bold added)[22]

"A New Spirituality truly is emerging upon the earth, and the idea of Oneness is at its core....

"We must choose between ancient myths, age-old cultural stories, and outdated theologies, or new truths, greater wisdoms, and grander visions of a God and a World united, expressing as One, projecting the glory of Life itself *into* life itself, and producing the possibility, at last, of a New Way of Life for All Humanity." (Neale Donald Walsch)[23]

"Think *outside the box*. Reject 'either/or' and consider 'both/and.'" (the seducing spirit calling itself "God")[24]

"The modern world moved dialectically, by conflict and contradiction and controversy. The postmodern world being born is **not a bipolar worldview of either/or's but** a double helix, Möbius-strip culture **of both-and's**, the *coincidentia oppositorum* (**coinciding opposites**) in fifteenth-century prelate/philosopher Nicholas of Cusa's mystical phrasing, the *conjunctio oppositorem* in Carl Jung's thinking." (Leonard Sweet; parentheses in the original; bold added)[25]

"The cross brings into relationship opposites, not so much as a dialectic to be synthesized but more as a **nondualistic** double helix to be embraced. In Christ **all opposites** are not so much reconciled as transcended in the Oneness of Twoness that becomes Threeness." (Leonard Sweet; emphasis added)[26]

"The MRI as the Double-Helix Design for Life …

"The secret of life is 'helixal,' two strands that run in opposite directions creating a reproductive Möbius strip and slingshot.…

"It's time to call and/alsos … 'so beautiful.'

"**Dualism, either/or** exclusionism is … **plug ugly**.

"**Nondualism, both/and** nonlocalism is … **so beautiful**." (Leonard Sweet; last two ellipsis dots in the original; emphasis added)[27]

"In fact, the incarnation brought **all dualities** together, whether it be the clean and the profane, the sacred and the secular, or the 'out there' and the 'in here.'" (Leonard Sweet; emphasis added)[28]

"**Key to the New Spirituality is a belief that God is not separate from anyone or anything — and neither are we.**" (Neale Donald Walsch's Humanity's Team website; emphasis added)[29]

In God's unadulterated Word of truth there is no spirit-flesh Oneness. It is only in the "reimagined" "truth" of Oneness/panentheism that there is a spirit-flesh, or *spirit-matter*, Oneness. And this comes from the counterfeit "God" (or "*Spirit*") which is *immanent* in everyone/everything; that is, which is in the very *substance*, or *matter*, of creation. It is through its *immanence* in (*Oneness* with) all matter that this counterfeit "God" connects everyone/everything—including *all opposites/dualities*—together, with itself, in one gigantic all-encompassing relationship of Oneness.

Thus, the dimensions of the New Age and its Oneness are universal. As mentioned earlier, Sweet has written, "Quantum spirituality does more than join together as one two words in all their complexity and nuance: energymatter, mindbody, *spirit-matter (as Teilhard de Chardin called it)*."[30] And Teilhard de Chardin, in the same book in which he gave the "condition" that the cross "expand itself to the dimensions of a new age," had written, "What I am proposing to do is to narrow that gap between pantheism and Christianity by bringing out what one might call the Christian soul of pantheism or the pantheist aspect of Christianity."[31] To bring the faith of Christianity together with the immanence—i.e., with the spirit-matter Oneness—of pantheism/panen900theism is to expand the faith of Christianity to the dimensions of *the* New Age and its New *Spirituality* of *Oneness*.

Despite the many absurd, "scientific," and channeled claims to the contrary, the *true* God is neither *immanent* nor *incarnate* in creation. The world, along with today's shifting Christianity, needs to hear the preaching and teaching of Scripture's *Gospel of Christ* (*not* the New Age/New Spirituality's "*New Gospel of Oneness*") so that people can *believe* and be *saved*. There is no immanent "connection" with the true God. And there is no relationship with the true God apart from *believing* Scripture's doctrine of the true Christ. That leaders and theologians in today's shifting Christianity claim otherwise and that "It's the connection that counts"[32] changes *nothing*. God's Word of eternal truth is *forever settled* in heaven and cannot be changed by unbelieving man who is choosing connectness rather than correctness.

It is *man*, not *God*, who is removing all separation between man and God. We *do* need to *believe* God's Word.

> *"For God so loved the world, that he gave his only begotten Son, that whosoever **believeth** in him should not perish, but have everlasting life." (John 3:16)*

> ***"Whosoever transgresseth, and abideth not in the doctrine of Christ, hath not God**. He that abideth in the doctrine of Christ, he hath both the Father and the Son." (2 John 1:9)*

It is *man*, not *God*, who is removing all separation between the things of the world and the things of the Spirit. We *do* need to *obey* God's Word.

> *"Love not the world, neither the things that are in the world. If any man love the world, the love of the Father is not in him. For all that is in the world, the lust of the flesh, and the lust of the eyes, and the pride of life, is not of the Father, but is of the world. And the world passeth away, and the lust thereof: **but he that doeth the will of God abideth for ever**." (1 John 2:15-17)*

> *"Not every one that saith unto me, Lord, Lord, shall enter into the kingdom of heaven; **but he that doeth the will of my Father which is in heaven**." (Matthew 7:21)*

Yet rather than believing and obeying God's Word, more and more people are choosing *Self-Rule* instead. And in this emerging faith of Oneness/panentheism there are <u>no</u> opposites/dualities that *separate* what <u>is</u> of God from what is <u>not</u> of God which of course renders believing and obeying God's Word completely irrelevant. This way, people can just make it up as they go along according to whatever they think is "true" and "right" in their own eyes. After all, when there is no difference between what is of God and what is not of God then there is only life—*lived and expressed however anyone chooses* in this convenient "*unity with All That Is.*"

> "[A] fundamental transformation in human consciousness and cosmology has taken place. The reigning worldview is breaking down all around us, as a new understanding of life is springing forth. Christians have not yet faced up to naming the consequences of this change on the Christian consciousness." (Leonard Sweet)[33]

> *"But there were false prophets also among the people, even as there shall be false teachers among you, who privily shall bring in damnable heresies, even denying the Lord that bought them, and bring upon themselves swift destruction. And many shall follow their pernicious ways; by reason of whom the way of truth shall be evil spoken of." (2 Peter 2:1-2)*

> *"... for, behold, ye walk every one after the imagination of his evil heart, that they may not hearken unto me." (Jeremiah 16:12)*

30

"The Bible is *not* a blueprint for action, nor a book of answers"

"O LORD, I know that the way of man is not in himself: it is not in man that walketh to direct his steps." (Jeremiah 10:23)

"Thy word is a lamp unto my feet, and a light unto my path." (Psalm 119:105)

It is only when feet prefer to journey a *different* path that God's Word becomes "a stumbling block in the way."

> "As we enter the twenty-first century, we need a new set of lenses through which to read the Bible....
>
> "The older lenses enabled Christians of earlier generations to experience the Bible as a lamp unto their feet, a source of illumination for following the Christian path. But for many Christians in our time, the older lenses have become opaque, turning the Bible into a stumbling block in the way....
>
> "[A] major de-literalization of the Bible is underway." (Marcus Borg)[1]

When people want no difference between what is of God and what is not of God this does indeed turn God's Word into "a stumbling block in the way." So what is their preferred alternative to God's Word as a lamp unto their feet? Fumbling in the dark and making it up as they go along, what else? And this is clearly taking place throughout today's light-intolerant Christianity as more and more people resist the Word of God being the Word of God and resist God being God in their desire to be *self*-regulating.

> "MRI is an embrace of complexity theory. Your life and your community are living organisms: That word *organism* means they are by definition self-organizing, complex, adaptive, self-regulating systems. An organic system makes it up as it goes along." (Leonard Sweet)[2]

> "Can you let life become what it wants to become, to content yourself with fumbling in the dark, and to play with life to paint a picture of transcendental beauty?" (Leonard Sweet)[3]

> "The Bible is *not* a blueprint for action, nor a book of answers." (Leonard Sweet)[4]

> "Incarnation is not involution, where God as God has laid down a divine blueprint for the church, and we are to unfold according to an already-drawn-out divine map that gives us a preformed template.
>
> "Rather, structures are self-organizing, complex, adaptive systems where regulation … exists to preserve the self-organizing, not to impose a grand plan or design but to assure a fair and level playing field in which an incarnational outcome can emerge. In epigenesis, the genes give a design for generating form and pattern, but they don't fit everything to the same pattern. Rather, they steer an organism into ergonomically optimal arrangements as an iterative, gradual, make-it-up-as-you-go-along process." (Leonard Sweet)[5]

> "Incarnational energies are what make the restless intelligence of the Christian tradition so eager to embrace the new, so open to change the old, so free to be creative in its engagement with the world." (Leonard Sweet)[6]

> *"Thus saith the LORD, Stand ye in the ways, and see, and ask for the old paths, where is the good way, and walk therein, and ye shall find rest for your souls. But they said, We will not walk therein." (Jeremiah 6:16)*

> "Wayfarer, there is no way, you make the way as you go." (Leonard Sweet quoting Antonio Machado)[7]

> "People are looking to find their own unique path in the world, each in his or her own way.… Postmoderns can take opposite paths, make contrasting choices, and still be 'right.'…
>
> "Authoritarian stances of 'We know the best way!' or 'We have the Truth!' or **'The Bible says it: That settles it!'** or 'Why? I said so!' no longer suffice. Indeed, they are **resented**.… **Instead of** rational argumentation over what is **'truth' and 'falsehood,' authoritarian directives over what is 'right' and 'wrong,'** ethical guidelines over what is 'success' and 'failure,' **storytelling is the postmodern means of governance**--whether personal or national life." (Leonard Sweet; emphasis added)[8]

> "The notion that what God wants from us more than anything is *intellectual assents to some dogmas* or to the definition of discipleship as *obedience and devotion and praise*: This is what you want from your dog, or your horse (forget your cat).…
>
> "One of the most serious thought-crimes for a Christian is the confusion of 'faith' with 'belief,' or to call someone who follows Jesus a 'believer,' … The Devil con-

fesses to being a 'believer.' **The Devil draws on the Bible's authority to make his arguments** (Luke 4:1-13)." (Leonard Sweet; all parentheses in the original; emphasis added)[9]

First, today's shift from *light* to *darkness* and *truth* to *fables* naturally includes a shift from *the authority of God's Word* to *storytelling*. In today's shifting Christianity people simply are not willing to accept the "final authority" of God and His Word because they do not want the *certainty* of what <u>is</u>. Rather, they want the *uncertainty* and *relativism* of *stories* which gives them their desired *freedom* to decide *for themselves* what is true or false and right or wrong. Furthermore, it is only those who want to be <u>self-regulating</u>, and who are therefore shifting, who would imagine that <u>believing</u> and <u>obeying</u> the authority of <u>God's</u> Word is following in <u>the Devil's</u> footsteps!

As is made clear in Scripture, including in the passage of Luke that Sweet refers to, the Devil *twists* Scripture to make his arguments—a practice not uncommon in today's shifting Christianity. Scripture warns:

> *"Thou believest that there is one God; thou doest well: the devils also believe, and tremble." (James 2:19)*

That the devils believe there is one God is expected. Before these fallen angels rebelled against the authority of God and were cast out of heaven, they were obviously in heaven with God and have therefore seen the true God. But that the Devil "*confesses to being a 'believer'*" is no doubt news to the Devil! In context, the passage is making the point that faith as just believing is not enough, that faith without works is dead. We need to obey as well as believe—e.g., "And why call ye me, Lord, Lord, and do not the things which I say?" (Luke 6:46). But since people today do not want to either believe or obey, the devils are one up on them—they at least believe . . . and tremble.

Sadly, people today are just too busy replacing "*what is 'truth' and 'falsehood'*" and "*what is 'right' and 'wrong'*" with *storytelling* as their preferred new "means of governance" to either believe or tremble.

> *"Hear now this, O foolish people, and without understanding; which have eyes, and see not; which have ears, and hear not: Fear ye not me? saith the* LORD: *will ye not tremble at my presence . . . ? But this people hath a revolting and a rebellious heart; they are revolted and gone. Neither say they in their heart, Let us now fear the* LORD *our God . . . A wonderful and horrible thing is committed in the land; the prophets prophesy falsely, and the priests bear rule by their means; and my people love to have it so: and what will ye do in the end thereof?" (Jeremiah 5:21-24, 30-31)*

> *"Thus saith the* LORD *of hosts, . . . To whom shall I speak, and give warning, that they may hear? behold, their ear is uncircumcised, and they cannot hearken: behold, the word of the* LORD *is unto them a reproach; they have no delight in it." (Jeremiah 6:9-10)*

> *"Therefore they say unto God, Depart from us; for we desire not the knowledge of thy ways." (Job 21:14)*

As mentioned earlier, God's Word is just too authoritative, too clear, too certain, too doctrinal, too narrow, too commanding, too set in His ways, too judgmental, too firm, too black and white, too absolute, just too rock solid for those who prefer to shift in their own ways and beliefs. So, of course, "It is written," "Thus saith the Lord," and "Thus saith God" are *resented* by those who want the freedom to find their own *self-regulating way*.

> *"The way of a fool is right in his own eyes: but he that hearkeneth unto counsel is wise." (Proverbs 12:15)*

> *"For that they hated knowledge, and did not choose the fear of the LORD: They would none of my counsel: they despised all my reproof. Therefore shall they eat of the fruit of their own way, and be filled with their own devices." (Proverbs 1:29-31)*

Despite today's growing resentment of absolute truth, *God's* Word *settles it* because God said so. God's Word is *God's* Word, and the final answer is *God's* absolute truth. We either believe and obey it or we do not; the choice is ours. What is truth is truth, what is falsehood is falsehood, what is right is right, and what is wrong is wrong. Everything <u>is</u> what it <u>is</u> regardless of the attempts to bring opposites together in a *circle* of Oneness in order to "still be 'right'" when the choice is to believe and do the *opposite* of what is *truth* and what is *right*.

> *"For the word of the LORD is right; and all his works are done in truth." (Psalm 33:4)*

> *"For ever, O LORD, thy word is settled in heaven." (Psalm 119:89)*

> *"Therefore I esteem all thy precepts concerning all things to be right; and I hate every false way." (Psalm 119:128)*

> *"Who is wise, and he shall understand these things? prudent, and he shall know them? for the ways of the LORD are right, and the just shall walk in them: but the transgressors shall fall therein." (Hosea 14:9)*

Although the Word of God is forever settled in heaven, in the emerging faith of Oneness/panentheism nothing is *ever settled*. In other words, its journey of freedom in which "you make the way as you go" is conveniently "unencumbered" by the structure and the "manacles" of an *absolute truth* that is to be *believed* and *obeyed* as *what <u>is</u>*. This make-it-up-as-you-go-along process of the journey (revolution) of Oneness is clearly and purposely taking place outside the "box" of God's Word of unchanging settled truth. Outside this resented "box" everyone has ample room to "reimagine" or "create" their own way—which includes their own "truth" and "faith" and "God"—*however* they choose. After all, self-regulating is *self*-regulating. And this way, those who prefer to make it up as they go along can indeed *make it up* as they go along.

> *"... for, behold, ye walk every one after the imagination of his evil heart, that they may not hearken unto me." (Jeremiah 16:12)*

Those who see this "chain of command" as "ghastly" and would rather "be like the most High" in the freedom of Self-Rule can—and do—make it up all they want, fumbling in the dark to their heart's content, in the all-encompassing circle of relationship of Oneness. In this circle of freedom, believing and obeying God's Word is irrelevant. After all, in Oneness no one is "lost" or "wrong." In Oneness there are no opposites that divide *what is of God* from *what is not of God*. Rather, life is conveniently expressed and lived

PART FOUR: THE TRANSFORMATION   179

however anyone chooses in this *"unity with All That Is."*

> "The essence of life is Oneness—unity with All That Is." (the seducing spirit calling itself "God")[10]

> "Everyone has the ability to convey this wonderful message of at-one-ment.... Your message is *your life, lived*. Your gift is your Divine Self, expressed. *Simply allow your Self to be expressed in your own unique way.*" (the seducing spirit calling itself "God;" emphasis added)[11]

> "Imagine a life without fear of God and without guilt over the tiniest infraction of what you imagine to be God's Rules!
>
> "Imagine the freedom of soul and mind and body that would be experienced when you understand at last that you really *are* One with God!" (Neale Donald Walsch)[12]

> "The One Ruler's One Rule is Self-Rule." (Neale Donald Walsch)[13]

> "Of course, no one seriously suggests that the Bible is to be taken literally." (Neale Donald Walsch)[14]

> "People are looking to find their own unique path in the world, each in his or her own way....
>
> "Authoritarian stances of ... 'The Bible says it: That settles it!' ... are resented." (Leonard Sweet)[15]

> "People need room to move and choose and resist airtight propositions that don't allow free breathing (i.e., freedom)." (Leonard Sweet; parentheses in the original)[16]

> "The Bible is *not* a blueprint for action, nor a book of answers." (Leonard Sweet)[17]

> "Incarnational energies are what make the restless intelligence of the Christian tradition so eager to embrace the new, so open to change the old, so free to be *creative* in its engagement with the world." (Leonard Sweet; emphasis added)[18]

> "God doesn't offer final answers, the *manacles* of modernity, but binding relationships." (Leonard Sweet; emphasis added)[19]

> "God is the Source of all that is creative. Answers are not creative. As soon as you think you have an answer, you stop creating. *Answers kill creation.*
>
> "The last thing you want is the final answer to anything. A 'possible answer,' maybe. An 'interim answer,' perhaps. But a 'final answer'? Never." (the seducing spirit calling itself "God")[20]

> "*There is another way.* There is another way to experience God. There is another way to live life....
>
> "Yet you will not find that way by searching for it. *You will only find it by creating it*. And you will not create it by remaining stuck in old beliefs, but only by opening yourself to new ideas. New ideas about God and about Life that can truly light the world." (the seducing spirit calling itself "God;" emphasis added)[21]

> "The New Spirituality is ... a call to expanded consciousness. It is an invitation to

conscious creation….

"This will create a revolution on your planet….

"A revolution is a 'revolving.' It is a coming full circle. And this is what Life as expressed through Humanity is doing right now. You are on a circle, from the fullness of knowing to the emptiness of forgetfulness to the fullness of knowing again. From Oneness to Separation to Oneness again….

"It IS Life, expressing AS Life, THROUGH Life, which process is circular and cyclical and circumferential. It encompasses All and it encloses All and it includes All, because it IS All." (the seducing spirit calling itself "God")[22]

"The New Spirituality is a civil rights movement for the soul, freeing humanity at last from the oppression of its belief in a separate, angry, violent, and fearful God….

"A New Spirituality truly is emerging upon the earth, and the idea of Oneness is at its core….

"We must choose between … outdated theologies … and grander visions of a God and a World united, expressing as One, … and producing the possibility, at last, of a New Way of Life for All Humanity." (Neale Donald Walsch)[23]

"This is what life is: unity, *expressing*." (the seducing spirit calling itself "God;" emphasis added")[24]

"So change! Yes, change! Change your ideas of 'right' and 'wrong.' Change your notions of this and that….

"Allow your deepest truths to be altered. Alter them yourself, for goodness' sake. I mean that quite literally. Alter them yourself, for *goodness' sake*….

"Your new idea about *all of it* is where the excitement is, where the creation is, where God-in-you is made manifest and becomes fully realized….

"There is not a one among you who is lost forever, nor will there ever be….

"That is what I am up to.

"Through you." (the seducing spirit calling itself "God")[25]

Sadly, today's seduced Christianity is eagerly participating in the journey to create Oneness and is cooperatively changing *everything* including the "outdated" theology of God's Holy Scriptures. Conveniently for those who are not willing to believe and obey, this all-encompassing circle of relationship is giving the world its desired freedom from the true God and His Word of absolute truth and is unarguably bringing transformation everywhere. Despite today's many deceived claims to the contrary, this is *not* "what God is up to" in the world! This lie—*revolution*—of Oneness is what Satan has been up to since the Garden of Eden. Some things never change, including that even people today are still falling for it. Again, it all stems from questioning the Word of *God*. As mentioned earlier, when man is exalted above God the result is first questioning and then "rethinking" and then "reimagining" God's Word. And this process—i.e., this *make-it-up-as-you-go-along* process of the *self-regulating* journey (revolution) of Oneness—began in the Garden of Eden where Satan was the first to question God's Word with, "Yea, hath God said …?"

Yea, God *hath* said.

"But evil men and seducers shall wax worse and worse, deceiving, and being de-

ceived. But continue thou in the things which thou hast learned and hast been assured of, knowing of whom thou hast learned them; and that from a child thou hast known the holy scriptures, which are able to make thee wise unto salvation through faith which is in Christ Jesus. All scripture is given by inspiration of God, and is profitable for doctrine, for reproof, for correction, for instruction in righteousness." (2 Timothy 3:13-16)

"Ye therefore, beloved, seeing ye know these things before, beware lest ye also, being led away with the error of the wicked, fall from your own stedfastness." (2 Peter 3:17)

PART FIVE: THE CREATION

31

Let there be "more light"?

*"**Thy word** have I hid in mine heart, that I might not sin against thee.... I have chosen **the way of truth**: thy judgments have I laid before me.... **For ever**, O LORD, thy word is **settled** in heaven.... How sweet are thy words unto my taste! yea, sweeter than honey to my mouth! Through thy precepts I get understanding: therefore I hate every false way. Thy word is a lamp unto my feet, and **a light unto my path**." (Psalm 119:11, 30, 89, 103-105)*

"The Bible is *not* a blueprint for action, nor a book of answers." (Leonard Sweet)[1]

"Quantum spirituality is always in flux, always aware of its own incompleteness.... For a **New Light** apologetic **there can be no final statement of theology** anymore [sic] than there can be any final 'laws of nature.' All life is **change** ... **we must not foreclose our minds against the truths of God, even if they are new**. It is for this reason that traditionality cannot be equated with orthodoxy.... The New Light movement is perhaps better called a '**More Light**' movement." (Leonard Sweet; emphasis added)[2]

"**The Third Testament is everything new about the old, old story**." (Leonard Sweet; emphasis added)[3]

"**Old things need to be said in new ways**. New things can only be said in new ways. When they get corseted into old concepts, they get distorted and damaged." (Leonard Sweet; emphasis added)[4]

"In Christ **all opposites** are not so much reconciled as **transcended** in the

185

> Oneness of Twoness that becomes Threeness." (Leonard Sweet; emphasis added)[5]

> "There is **no neat line** of demarcation **between the things of *the world* and the things of *the Spirit***. God uses *the profane* and the ordinary to reveal the sacred and the holy." (Leonard Sweet; emphasis added)[6]

> "A New Spirituality truly is emerging upon the earth, and the idea of Oneness is at its core....
>
> "**We must choose between** ancient myths, age-old cultural stories, and **outdated theologies, or <u>new truths</u>**, greater wisdoms, and grander visions *of a God and a World united*, expressing as One, ..." (Neale Donald Walsch; emphasis added)[7]

In this pursuit of *Oneness* that is unarguably changing *everything*, even today's shifting Christianity is choosing new "truths of God" over the "old" "outdated" theology of God's Holy Scriptures. And it isn't just *choosing* new "truths" but in the inevitable quest for "more light" in this journey of darkness outside the "box" of God's Word it is even seeking to *create* and *conceive* new "truth."

> "God the Creator worked through men and women of old to produce the First Testament. God the Redeemer worked through men and women of the first century to produce the Second Testament ... But we no longer have Jesus in the flesh. We now have Jesus in the Spirit. God the Spirit and Sustainer wants to work through New Lights of the twenty-first century **to produce the Third Testament--our '<u>new</u> account of everything old.'**
>
> "**<u>New Lights</u>'** mission in life, if they choose to accept it, is **to continue the work of Scripture**." (Leonard Sweet; emphasis added)[8]

> "... God is whirling and swirling creation into being. The missional thrust begins in the very being of God. God goes out in love to create the cosmos: '**Let there be light**.' The missional bent is there from the beginning....
>
> "The ultimate story of the Bible, the metanarrative that unlocks the whole story, is that God is on a mission, and we are summoned to participate with God in that mission. The impulse **to create, to conceive**, is what lies at the heart of the missional." (Leonard Sweet; emphasis added)[9]

> "We were not put here to 'keep commandments' but **to conceive** beauty, **truth**, and goodness." (Leonard Sweet; emphasis added)[10]

So, God says, "Let there be light: and there was light" (Genesis 1:3), but man wants "More Light." God gives man His first testament and His new testament—of which the Lord Jesus Christ says, "It is finished" (John 19:30; Hebrews 9:14-16)—and records them in His Word, but man wants "the Third Testament." Man then seeks to "conceive" and "create" more "light" and new "truths" for himself in a fashion that man is willing to accept and absurdly claims that man's "new account of everything old" is the mission of *God* "to continue the work of *Scripture*." To the contrary, this "make-it-up-as-you-go-along process" relates very well with the mission of the seducing spirit world. And this revolution is not more *light*, but it definitely is *change*.

PART FIVE: THE CREATION 187

> "**Create your *own truth*.**
>
> "In this will you experience Who You Really Are." (the seducing spirit calling itself "God;" bold added)[11]
>
> "**Change** your ideas of 'right' and 'wrong.' Change your notions of this and that....
>
> "**Allow your deepest <u>truths</u> to be <u>altered</u>**. Alter them yourself, for goodness' sake. I mean that quite literally. Alter them yourself, for *goodness' sake*....
>
> "**Your <u>new</u> idea about *all of it* is where the excitement is, where the creation is, where God-in-you is made manifest and becomes fully realized**....
>
> "Be open, therefore. Be OPEN. **Don't close off the possibility of <u>new truth</u>** because you have been comfortable with an old one. Life begins at the end of your comfort zone." (the seducing spirit calling itself "God;" bold & underline added)[12]
>
> "There is another way to experience God. There is another way to live life.... THERE IS ANOTHER WAY.
>
> "Yet you will not find that way by searching for it. You will only find it by creating it. And **you will not create it by remaining stuck in old beliefs, but only by opening yourself to <u>new</u> ideas**. New ideas about God and about Life **that can truly <u>light</u> the world**." (the seducing spirit calling itself "God;" bold & underline added)[13]

Contrary to the emerging faith of panentheism/Oneness *the true God* is *not nature* and is not subject to the "laws of nature," and neither does He ever change—"*For I am the* LORD, *I change not;* ..." (Malachi 3:6). So *true* theology (i.e., *the truth of Who God is* which is recorded for us by God in God's Holy Scriptures) *is* final and does not *change*. Yet in today's light-intolerant Christianity people are purposely shifting from light to darkness where they are choosing to imagine that the new "truths" of man's ever-changing imagination provide "*more light*"—i.e., a "*better understanding*"—than the "old" light of God's Word. And, of course, the panentheistic "God-in-you" that is immanent—and "incarnate"—in *everyone and everything* opens the door to the "*limitless*" new "ideas" and new "understandings" and new "truths" of its new "light" of *Oneness*. In other words, it opens the door to "limitless" *change*.

> "In fact, the incarnation brought all dualities together, whether it be the clean and the profane, the sacred and the secular, or the 'out there' and the 'in here.'" (Leonard Sweet)[14]
>
> "Incarnational energies are what make the restless intelligence of the Christian tradition so eager to **embrace the <u>new</u>**, so open to **change the old**, so free to *be creative* in its engagement with the world." (Leonard Sweet; emphasis added)[15]
>
> *"Thy word is a lamp unto my feet, and a light unto my path." (Psalm 119:105)*
>
> *"My son, fear thou the* LORD *and the king: and **meddle not with them that are given to change**: For their calamity shall rise suddenly; and who knoweth the ruin of them both?" (Proverbs 24:21-22)*
>
> *"I know that, whatsoever God doeth, it shall be for ever: nothing can be put to it,*

nor anything taken from it: and God doeth it, that men should fear before him." (Ecclesiastes 3:14)

"Take heed therefore that the light which is in thee be not darkness." *(Luke 11:35)*

"Thus saith the LORD of hosts, ... To whom shall I speak, and give warning, that they may hear? behold, their ear is uncircumcised, and they cannot hearken: **behold, the word of the LORD is unto them a reproach**; *they have no delight in it.... Stand ye in the ways, and see, and* **ask for the old paths**, *where is the good way, and walk therein, and ye shall find rest for your souls.* **But they said, We will not walk therein**." *(Jeremiah 6:9-10, 16)*

32

The mission of creating "the Third Testament" as "part of *the 'I Am'* that *we* are"

"*New Lights'* mission in life, if they choose to accept it, is **to continue the work of Scripture**....

"The challenge of the church in the twenty-first century is to become ... a seedbed in which **the texts** and traditions **of the faith *recreate* themselves in and through the body** until its molecular ***imagination*** is awakened by a living God." (Leonard Sweet; emphasis added)[1]

"*How do ye say, We are wise, and the law of the LORD is with us? Lo, certainly in vain made he it; the pen of the scribes is in vain." (Jeremiah 8:8)*

"*Every word of God is pure: he is a shield unto them that put their trust in him. Add thou not unto his words, lest he reprove thee, and thou be found a liar." (Proverbs 30:5-6)*

Amission that seeks to "continue the work of Scripture" and even "recreate" it is astounding. And yet it shouldn't be surprising at all given that people in today's shifting Christianity quite openly would rather make it up as they go along instead of believe and obey God and His Word. If they just make up "scripture" as they go along then they can thus justify today's preferred "make-it-up-as-you-go-along process" of *self-* regulation, right?

"... ***for, behold, ye walk every one after the imagination of his evil heart,*** *that they may not hearken unto me." (Jeremiah 16:12)*

Unabashedly preferring man's imagination over God's Word of truth, many people now *want* a *fictitious* "truth" and a *fictitious* "revelation." And "to think connectness *rather than* correctness" is quite obviously today's preferred new way of thinking. So to those in this emerging faith of *intentional* fictitiousness and incorrectness it will clearly be irrelevant that any creation of new "scripture" and "truth" is fictitious and incorrect.

"What if we were to think connectness **rather than correctness**?" (Leonard Sweet; emphasis added)[2]

"We were not put here to 'keep commandments' but to **conceive** beauty, **truth**, and goodness. We were not put here to 'take a stand' but to walk in the *light* for the greater glory of God. Biblical truth doesn't feast on fact. It feasts on relationship and revelation, which is why eternal truth is better communicated by the **fictions** of parables and narratives than the facts of science and philosophy." (Leonard Sweet; emphasis added)[3]

"Authoritarian stances of … 'The Bible says it: That settles it!' … are resented…. **Instead of** rational argumentation over **what is 'truth' and 'falsehood,'** authoritarian directives over **what is 'right' and 'wrong,'** … **storytelling** is the postmodern means of governance …" (Leonard Sweet; emphasis added)[4]

"Your life and your community are living organisms: That word *organism* means they are by definition self-organizing, complex, adaptive, **self-regulating** systems. An organic system **makes it up as it goes along**." (Leonard Sweet; bold added)[5]

Since people today prefer storytelling over believing and obeying God's Word, they might as well just tell one big made-up story and call it "Scripture." After all, in their unbelief they have already even reduced God's Word itself to merely a "story" with "changeable" and "debatable" "metaphor" that can be interpreted and retold however anyone chooses. So what would be the difference?

Either Scripture is *God's* Word of <u>absolute</u> truth or it is *man's* word of <u>relative</u> "truth." All we have to do is simply read the Holy Scriptures to plainly see that it expects to be believed and obeyed as the <u>absolute</u> truth of *God*. So, no, Scripture is not God's Word of <u>relative</u> "truth," as that would therefore make God out to be a liar. But, of course, that is precisely what today's shifting Christianity is doing. And, along with choosing to believe that Scripture is <u>relative</u> rather than <u>absolute</u>, a growing number of people also do in fact believe that Scripture is *man's* word rather than *God's* Word. So to them there would be little to no difference between true Scripture and "truth" that is created/conceived/imagined/invented/made up by man today.

This is especially so since they also absurdly choose to imagine that the word of *man* is the word of *God*. Accordingly, as mentioned earlier, the outpouring of high praise for *The Shack* actually includes: *the book is one long Bible study; inspired writing from God Himself; the words spoken by God in this book are full of life; find the truth about God in The Shack;* and so on. And its praise now even also includes—"*this book could essentially serve as the quintessential 'starter bible'*"!

If *fiction*, not to mention *blasphemous* fiction, is seen as a *starter Bible* and as one long *Bible study* that is *inspired writing from God Himself* then why would anyone think twice about creating and producing *new* "Scripture" or *new* "truths of God"? *The Shack* is a prime example that they won't, and they don't. Besides, God's Word of linear truth that divides true and false and right and wrong is "a stumbling block in the way" of today's emerging faith of Oneness and its desired all-encompassing circle of relationship. So a mission that *seeks to* "*create*" and "*conceive*" a "*new account of everything old*" to replace the resented *final answers* of God's *absolute truth* shouldn't be surprising. This way people can "create" a new kind of "Scripture" to go along with today's new kind of "Christian" and new kind of "Christianity" that are purposely emerging *outside* the resented "box"—i.e., *outside* the resented absolute truth—of God's "old" Scripture. And, no, this "*mission*" to "*create*" and "*conceive*" a "*Third* Testament" that is "*everything new* about the old, old story"[6] is *not* the "mission" of *God*—at least not the *true* God, that is.

> "The ultimate story of the Bible, the metanarrative that unlocks the whole story, is that God is on a mission, and **we are summoned to participate with God in that mission**. The impulse *to create, to conceive*, is what lies at the heart of the missional." (Leonard Sweet; emphasis added)[7]

> "We were not put here to 'keep commandments' but **to conceive** beauty, **truth**, and goodness." (Leonard Sweet; emphasis added)[8]

> "MRI [**Missional**, Relational, Incarnational] is the operating software on which human life and faith were designed to run: *Version 1.0 is known as the First Testament; Version 2.0 is known as the New Testament;* **Version 3.0 is the Third Testament, the Gospel According to ... you**." (Leonard Sweet; ellipsis dots in the original; emphasis added)[9]

> "God the Creator worked through men and women of old to produce the First Testament. God the Redeemer worked through men and women of the first century to produce the Second Testament ... God the Spirit and Sustainer wants to work through New Lights of the twenty-first century **to produce the Third Testament-- our '*new* account of everything old.'**
>
> "**New Lights' mission** in life, if they choose to accept it, is **to continue the work of Scripture**....
>
> "The challenge of the church in the twenty-first century is to become ... a seedbed in which **the texts** and traditions **of the faith *recreate* themselves in and through the body** until its molecular ***imagination*** is awakened by a living God.
>
> "Every believer, every body of Christ is called to become **the Third Testament**. Philosophical theologian/science watcher Philip Hefner captures wonderfully our simultaneous status as dependent creatures and free agents in his recommendation that human beings be thought of as '**created co-creators**.' **God has chosen to work in partnership with us in the ongoing drama of *creation*.**" (Leonard Sweet; emphasis added)[10]

> "As ***co-creators*** with God, **inventing *new* forms of energymatter (information) is a part of the ongoing work of *creation*.**" (Leonard Sweet; parentheses in the original; emphasis added)[11]

> "For the common sense to be the common good in the postmodern era, it must come to respect *the authority of intuitive modes of knowing*....
>
> "It is **through *creative intuition*** that postmoderns **continue the work of *divine***

creation." (Leonard Sweet; emphasis added)[12]

"With the crooked lines of our lives God is wanting to write 'a *new* account of everything old,' a Third Testament....

"The Third Testament calls us to imitate and participate in *God's* creativity ...

"Quantum spirituality is nothing more than **your 'new account of everything old'--*your part of the 'I Am' that we are.*"** (Leonard Sweet; emphasis added)[13]

So, with astronomical arrogance (to say the very *least*), not only does man want to "*produce* the *Third* Testament" and to "*continue* the work of *Scripture*" in "our '*new* account of everything old'" as "*co-creators*" in "*partnership*" with God "in the *ongoing drama of creation*" (the "*drama of 'doing God'*"[14]), but man wants to "*participate* in *God's* creativity" in the belief that man's attempt to "continue the work of *divine* creation" is man's "part of *the 'I Am'* that *we* are"! Although unbelievable, this is indeed what Oneness/panentheism's lie of being "*One* with God" boils down to.

"There is only One of Us. You and I are One." (the seducing spirit calling itself "God;" emphasis added)[15]

"... there is no separation in God's World—that is, nothing which is not God ...

"You cannot be separate from Me, for I Am All That Is....

"You and I are One. We cannot be anything else if I Am What **I Am: All That Is**." (the seducing spirit calling itself "God;" emphasis added)[16]

"**My Beingness is *in everything***. Everything. The All-ness is My Expression. The wholeness is My Nature. There is nothing that I Am Not, and **something I Am Not cannot be**." (the seducing spirit calling itself "God;" emphasis added)[17]

And, therefore, in Oneness *everything* is "*part* of *the 'I Am'*"—i.e., of the *immanent* "God" that *is/is in* "*All That Is.*"

"You are, have always been, and will always be, **a *divine* part of the *divine* whole** ..." (the seducing spirit calling itself "God;" bold added)[18]

"Your thought about yourself is that you are not good enough, not wondrous enough, not sinless enough, to be **a part of God, in partnership with God**....

"For your grandest wish—and My grandest desire—was for you to **experience yourself as the part of Me you are**. You are therefore in the process of experiencing yourself by **creating** yourself anew in every single moment. As am I. Through you.

"**Do you see the partnership? Do you grasp its implications?**...

"**Think, speak, and act as the *God You Are*.**" (the seducing spirit calling itself "God;" bold added)[19]

"**Create your *own* truth**.

"In this will you **experience Who You Really Are**." (the seducing spirit calling itself "God;" bold added)[20]

"Remember, Change is a process called Life. The decision to change things is the decision to *live*....

"It comes not from dissatisfaction, but from passion. The passion OF Life for MORE Life....

"**In this, and in all things, you are making it all up. That is, you are creating it on the spot. You are the Creator and the Created.**" (the seducing spirit calling itself "God;" bold added)[21]

"You cannot create a *thing*—not a thought, an object, an event—no experience of *any kind*—which is outside of God's plan. For God's plan is for you to **create anything—everything—*whatever you want*. In such freedom lies the experience of God being God**—and this is the experience *for which I created You*. And life itself." (the seducing spirit calling itself "God;" bold added)[22]

"In a word, God is freedom." (the seducing spirit calling itself "God")[23]

"Freedom is what you are. God is that, and you are that. That is the essence of what you are.... It is the essence of your being." (the seducing spirit calling itself "God")[24]

Sadly, more and more people in today's shifting Christianity are eagerly participating in the creative process of this emerging faith that is "making it all up" as both "the Creator and the Created." They are determined to create and conceive *new* "truth" that people are *willing* to accept—i.e., "truth" that gives people their desired freedom from the "old" linear truth that divides "what is 'truth' and 'falsehood'" and "what is 'right' and 'wrong.'" And what better way for people to achieve this desired "*unencumbered*" freedom "*to simply 'be,'*" than to choose to *rewrite*, or "*recreate*," the Word of God with *their own lives* (lived *however they so choose* of course)?! And since this merging and emerging "Christian"/New Age faith of Oneness/panentheism is replacing *believing* and *obeying* God and Jesus with *being* and *doing* God and Jesus, people can thus conveniently make it *all* up as they go along.

"Missional is **who you are**, because it is **who God is**....

"The missional thrust **begins in the very being of God**. God goes out in love to create the cosmos: 'Let there be light.' The missional bent is there from the beginning....

"The impulse to create, to conceive, is what lies at the heart of the missional....

"Even though the word itself is an adjective, *missional* is all about verbs, not nouns, because only missional 'loving' gives meaning to our existence....

"*Drama* comes from the Greek word *dran*, which means 'to do.' The incarnation is all about God's **drama of 'doing God,'** God's drama of love.... God did God. God lived in our midst and loved us and **invited us to 'do God' along with him**.

"'Be ye doers of the word, and not hearers only.' **My translation of 'Go Make Disciples' is 'Go Do Me.'** Is this not the second-best mission statement in the Bible: 'Go Do Me'? Doing the gospel is primary speech; talking about the gospel is secondary speech.... To 'Go Do Me,' to '**doing God**' by doing good, I must be simultaneously seeing, following, and **being Christ**. I have no theology to impart, no biblical interpretation to argue, no agenda to accomplish. **I only have my life**....

"Jesus says, '**Go Do Me**.' **Go be Jesus**." (Leonard Sweet; bold added)[25]

"Each one of us is free to **become Jesus, a living truth**, …" (Leonard Sweet; emphasis added)[26]

"*The era of the Single Savior is over*. What is needed now is joint action, combined effort, *collective co-creation*." (the seducing spirit calling itself "God;" emphasis added)[27]

"Therefore, entreat those who would live the New Spirituality to consider every book sacred and every messenger holy, even as they, themselves, are holy, and as **the living of their own lives writes the book of their most sacred truth**. Remember that always.

"**The living of your own life writes the book of your most sacred truth**, and offers evidence of it." (the seducing spirit calling itself "God;" emphasis added)[28]

"[E]very body of Christ is called to **become the Third Testament**." (Leonard Sweet; emphasis added)[29]

"When you agree to spread the word, to carry the message that can change the human heart, you play an important role in changing the human condition….

"**It is something you are 'being.'**…

"You carry the message *as* you, not *with* you. **You *are* the message!**…

"**Your message is your life, lived**. You spread the word that you *are*.

"Is it not written: *And the Word was made flesh?*…

"You have My word. You have My word, in you. **You are, quite literally, the Word of God, made flesh**. Now, say but the word, and your soul shall be healed. Speak the word, live the word, *be* the word.

"In a word, **be God**….

"I'm telling you **Who You Really Are**." (the seducing spirit calling itself "God;" bold added)[30]

"With the crooked lines of **our lives** God is wanting to write 'a new account of everything old,' **a Third Testament**….

"… **your part of the 'I Am' that we are**." (Leonard Sweet; emphasis added)[31]

"Missional … is living a life **born in the very *being* of God**." (Leonard Sweet; emphasis added)[32]

Again, in this emerging faith of panentheism/Oneness there is *a reason* why *verbs are replacing nouns*. And, no, the "era of the Single Savior" is not over. Only the era of *believing* in the single Saviour is over. Among other things, *believing* in the Lord Jesus Christ is being replaced in our post-truth era with "*being* Christ." Yes, we are to be "doing good" and to be "loving," but we cannot "*be*" and "*do*" God and the Lord Jesus Christ! To be loving and to do good is not to be and do so as God, as Jesus, as Christ but, rather, as ourselves in *obedience to* God and the Lord Jesus Christ. They are *not* the same thing!

In his "do" Jesus ("Go Do Me"), "be Jesus," "being Christ," "do God," "in the very being of God," and "your part of the 'I Am' that we are," Leonard Sweet dances around openly saying *be* God or *being* God. Yet this is clearly implied in what he does say. And to say "be Jesus" and "being Christ" is no different than to say "be God" and "being God," regardless of whether or not whoever says it believes the *truth* that *the Lord Jesus Christ is God*. In any case, Sweet's teachings and mission, as well as his shift from "Go Make Disciples" to "Go Do Me," all take being a doer of the Word to a whole new dimension on *many* levels! And, as will be addressed later, to believe that man creates and becomes "the Third Testament" is as eternally significant as the rest of this emerging faith in which everything is changing on purpose.

Incidentally, Sweet writes: "*My translation* of 'Go Make Disciples' *is 'Go Do Me.'* Is this not the second-best mission statement in the Bible: 'Go Do Me'?" Since when is "Go Do Me"—Sweet's *own* "translation"—a "statement *in the Bible*"?! Would this be part of his intention "to continue the work of Scripture"? After all, according to the seducing spirit world:

> "*Divine inspiration is the birthright of every human being....*
>
> "They ['your religions'] have told you ... that only a very few among you have achieved a level of worthiness to be inspired directly by God—and that all of those people are dead.
>
> "They have convinced you that no one living today could possibly achieve that level of worthiness, and, hence, no book written today could possibly contain sacred truths or the Word of God....
>
> "Because to tell you otherwise would be to leave open the possibility that another master, another prophet, another messenger of God could come along, bringing new revelations and opening you to **new understandings**—and that is something that already established organized religions could not abide." (the seducing spirit calling itself "God;" bold added)[33]

> *"Through thy precepts I get understanding: therefore I hate every false way. Thy word is a lamp unto my feet, and a light unto my path." (Psalm 119:104-105)*

33

"It is through creative intuition that postmoderns continue the work of *divine* creation"

"Yea, hath God said …? … then your eyes shall be opened, and ye shall be as gods, knowing good and evil." (Genesis 3:1b, 5)

Aside from the formerly obvious fact that man is not "part of the '*I Am*'" and can neither "*do* God" nor *be* God, *how* exactly does man "participate in *God's* creativity" in man's creation of more "light" and new "truths of God"? Along with man's *imagination* and absurdly just *living life*, the creative "make-it-up-as-you-go-along process" of this emerging Wordless faith comes from the "light" of man's own inner "knowing," which comes from man's own inner "God."

> "It is through **creative intuition** that postmoderns continue the work of *divine* creation." (Leonard Sweet; emphasis added)[1]

Creative intuition is another term for the inner "knowing," which, as addressed earlier, comes from Satan's lie of Oneness that started in the Garden of Eden. It is through this inner "knowing" that man—"as gods"—seeks to *"conceive" "truth"* and "continue the work of *divine* creation." Yet those who have been blinded by the lies of this inner "knowing"—which is diabolically verified as "true" by the lies of this inner "knowing"—see it all as the work of *God* rather than as the work of *"the god of this world."*

> "**Truth lies within ourselves**. When we can contact **our own inner God** all

truth will be revealed to us. **We shall be Knowers**." (Alice Bailey; emphasis added)[2]

"The meditation process is divided into five parts ['Concentration,' 'Meditation,' 'Contemplation,' 'Illumination,' 'Inspiration'], one part leading sequentially to another....

"These five stages, when followed, lead to union with the soul and **direct knowledge of divinity**." (Alice Bailey, *From Intellect to Intuition*; emphasis added)[3]

"But for people who can't be ['Biblical'] literalists ... I would say that in one sense of the word know, we can't know that Christianity ... is true in the sense of being able to demonstrate it....

"But we can take seriously a different kind of knowing. It's a very ancient kind of knowing. The ancients called it *intuition*.... But the ancient meaning of the word **'intuition' or 'intuitive knowing' is direct knowing**, a knowing that's not dependent upon verification. **A synonym for *intuitive* knowing would be *mystical* knowing**." (Marcus Borg; emphasis added)[4]

"For the common sense to be the common good in the postmodern era, it must come to respect **the authority of intuitive modes of knowing**....

"Modernity dismissed 'intuition' ... Postmodernity, on the other hand, thrives on **intuitional experience**, elevating its attributes to **the status of a true leader**: Someone 'gifted more than ordinary people with **a *mystical* quality--*intuition*--** which gives him 'inner conviction' ...' It is through *creative intuition* that postmoderns continue the work of *divine* creation." (Leonard Sweet; emphasis added)[5]

"**Mysticism *begins* in experience; it *ends* in theology**." (Leonard Sweet; emphasis added)[6]

In other words, mystical revelation supersedes scriptural revelation, and the "authority" of man's own inner "knowing" supersedes the authority of God's Word. The fact that mysticism *ends* in theology—i.e., that it leads people into a *new* theology and *new* "understandings"/"truths" of "God"—is to be expected. As addressed earlier, mysticism is specifically utilized by the spirit world to "open" people's eyes to Oneness by leading them into the direct "knowing" of the panentheistic "God" that is *immanent in everyone and everything*.

It's all about the *unio mystica*—"mystical union"—with this immanent "God" that is within *everyone* regardless of *beliefs*, regardless of *theology*, regardless of *religion*. It is this "mystical union," which gives people their own personal mystical/intuitive/direct "knowing" of this immanent "God," that *ends* in theology—specifically in the panentheistic theology of Oneness—*by design*. Moreover, in this emerging faith of Oneness "more light" is being "created" by *removing* "that which obscures the light" of Oneness. And, clearly, "that which obscures the light" of Oneness and its *panentheistic* "God" is the *truth* of *God's Word* with its "old" theology and understandings. When the "old" truth/theology is removed, new "truth"/theology is inevitable.

"Man is a point of *divine* light, hidden within a number of enveloping sheaths ... [T]hrough right discipline and meditation '**that which obscures the light is gradually removed**,'...

"**Meditation** is, therefore, **an *ordered process* whereby a man *finds God***. It is a system, well-tried out and much used, which unfailingly reveals the divine....

"Steadily his center of consciousness has *shifted* ... **Through *all* methods employed runs the golden thread of divine purpose**, and the way by which the transfer of the human consciousness into that of soul realization and soul awareness is effected is that of meditation." (Alice Bailey, *From Intellect to* **Intuition**; emphasis added)[7]

"Third: In the language of some of the pioneers into the spiritual realm, the third result of meditation is that **we *find God*. It is relatively unimportant what we mean in detail by that little word of three letters**. It is but a symbol of Reality....

"Fourth: In the words of all schools of mystics in both hemispheres, these results [of meditation] are summed up in the words: **Union with God**, or At-one-ment with Divinity. **God and man are at-one. The Self and Not-Self are unified**." (Alice Bailey, *From Intellect to* **Intuition**; emphasis added)[8]

"Further, what modernists got used to 'feeling' was themselves, not creation or the Creator. Experience came to refer to human experience ... rather than **the unition experience of *the whole*, of the self with all that is outside the self**, or of **the experience of *God*, either from within or *in everything* without**....

> "'Now, therefore, can we find anew the power to <u>name</u> <u>God in a mystical-prophetic way</u>? That is theology's central postmodern question.' Priest/metaphysician/theologian David W. Tracy

"Mysticism, once cast to the sidelines of the Christian tradition, is now situated in postmodernist culture near the center.... **Mysticism** (which Einstein called 'cosmic religiosity') **is metaphysics arrived *at* through mindbody experiences. Mysticism begins in experience; it *ends in theology*.**" (Leonard Sweet; parentheses in the original; emphasis added, except italics to his quote of Tracy)[9]

"My most formative religious experiences were a series of **mystical experiences**.... They **changed my understanding of the meaning of the word 'God'** ...

"[W]hat I was *seeing* looked very different. **Light** became different – as if there were a radiance **shining through everything**.... And I experienced a falling away of the subject-object distinction that marks our ordinary everyday experience – **that sense of being a separate self, 'in here,' while the world is 'out there.'**...

"[I]f **the word 'God'** points to *a radiance that pervades 'what is,'* as I now think – then, of course, God is real. Not just the God of Christianity, but **the God of *all* the enduring religions**." (Marcus Borg; emphasis added)[10]

"In fact, **the incarnation brought all dualities together**, whether it be the clean and the profane, the sacred and the secular, or **the 'out there' and the 'in here.'**" (Leonard Sweet; emphasis added)[11]

"***Faith* makes a metanoized mulch of <u>all dichotomized selves</u> and heals all discursive dualisms (*one of the worst of which was 'sacred' and 'profane'*) ...**" (Leonard Sweet; parentheses in the original; emphasis added)[12]

"1. **Unitary thinking**, the highest level of understanding reality, ***opens us up to a wider sensory realm and mystical dimension of the divine***; it also heals the divisions that separate us from one another and life's highest values.

"2. ***Wholeness* unites**, not eliminates, **opposites**, bringing them into dynamic balance ..." (Leonard Sweet; emphasis added)[13]

"**My Beingness is *in everything*.** Everything.... **The *wholeness* is *My Nature*.**" (the seducing spirit calling itself "God;" emphasis added)[14]

"When, therefore, **sight** has been attained and the **light** streams forth, **revelation of the oneness of all life** is a simple and immediate occurrence ..." (the seducing spirit calling itself Djwhal Khul; emphasis added)[15]

Again, "that which obscures the light" must first be removed in order for this "sight"—this *metaphysical* theology—to be attained. So when this "revelation of the oneness of all life" occurs, much *removal* of the true faith that comes by the Word of God has *already* taken place.

"For we walk by faith, not by sight." (2 Corinthians 5:7)

"So then faith cometh by hearing, and hearing by the word of God." (Romans 10:17)

True faith does not come by *sight* but by *the Word of God*. Yet as the new "truth"/theology of the *Wordless* "faith" of Oneness replaces the "old" truth/theology of the faith given to us by God in the Word of God, the "authority" of man's own "*seeing*" and "*knowing*" inevitably *replaces* the authority of *God's Word*. And thus *believing* God and His Son gets replaced with "*channeling*" "*Christ energies* through *mindbody experience*." Yet contrary to today's merging and emerging "Christian"/New Age "reimaginings," Christ—Who is the *Messiah*—is a *Person*, not a "*consciousness*." We do not *channel* Jesus of Nazareth, the son of Joseph. We do not *channel* the Lord Jesus Christ. We are to *believe* the Messiah, not *channel* a Messiah "*consciousness*"! Without question, this is indeed *change*.

*"And looking upon Jesus as he walked, he saith, Behold the Lamb of God!... We have found **the Messias, which is, being interpreted, the Christ**. And he brought him to Jesus.... We have found him, of whom Moses in the law, and the prophets, did write, Jesus of Nazareth, the son of Joseph." (John 1:36, 41-42, 45)*

*"Therefore let all the house of Israel know assuredly, that God hath made **that same Jesus**, whom ye have crucified, **both Lord and Christ**." (Acts 2:36)*

"Faith is not simply intellectual understanding, or an act of human intention, or following some salvation 'how-to' manual, or assent to creedal formulations. Faith is not a matter of doing, or even being, but an experience of becoming. *Experiencing is faith's most fundamental activity*.... [F]aith is the creative movement of self-organizing processes that are better understood as *verbs* than as *nouns*....

"Quantum spirituality ... is most importantly a structure of human becoming, *a channeling of Christ energies through mindbody experience*....

"Faith is the synergy of the most powerful united fields in the universe--reason and emotion, mind and body, cognition and action, theory and practice, object and subject, spirit and matter, spiritual and physical senses--working together *to form* **Christ consciousness experiences**. *Faith makes a metanoized mulch of all dichotomized selves and heals all discursive dualisms (one of the worst of which was 'sacred' and 'profane'), all disastrous separations that threaten our existence."* (Leonard Sweet; parentheses in the original; emphasis added)[16]

"To disciples and initiates the call goes out to reveal to the world ... the nature of **the Christ consciousness** *which knows no separation* ..." (the seducing spirit calling itself Djwhal Khul; emphasis added)[17]

"It is Christ's power, **the Christ consciousness**, our getting in touch with **who Christ is**, that is going to do it for us." (Leonard Sweet; emphasis added)[18]

"**God cannot be put into *words***, God cannot be reduced to a proposition. **Truth is in the recognition not the cognition**. Or more precisely, Truth is in the transformation of existence ***after* having recognized Jesus**." (Leonard Sweet; emphasis added)[19]

"Science is now more respectful of *subjective ways of knowing* than ever before. There is no true knowledge without acknowledgement. **Understanding comes *after*, not before, we have experienced**.... Faith is understanding, and ***mindbody experience is the ultimate way of knowing*** ...

"How do we know there is a living Christ in a postmodern world? **We can sense the pull of the Christ consciousness**.... **Postmoderns feel in order to think**." (Leonard Sweet; emphasis added)[20]

"**Listen to your *feelings*. Listen to your Highest Thoughts. Listen to your experience**. *Whenever any one of these differ from what you've been told by your teachers, or read in your books, forget the words.* **Words are the least reliable purveyor of Truth**." (the seducing spirit calling itself "God;" bold added)[21]

"**Jesus said unto them**, ... **He that is of God heareth God's words**: *ye therefore hear them not, because ye are not of God."* (John 8:42, 47)

"It is the spirit that quickeneth; the flesh profiteth nothing: **the *words*** *that I speak unto you, they are spirit, and they **are life**. But there are some of you that believe not. For Jesus knew from the beginning who they were that believed not, and who should betray him." (John 6:63-64)*

The *"light"* of this emerging faith of Oneness/panentheism is not the light of God's Word. Rather, it is the *"knowing"* and the *mystical "experience"* of the *immanent* "God" and "Christ" that are *in everyone and everything* that is this emerging "light." And, again, *"that which obscures the light"* of Oneness *"is gradually removed"* in the "ordered process" of *"all* methods" of the mystical experiences of meditation. Accordingly, today's armor-shunning Christianity which has eagerly embraced *many* methods of meditation first began to question the literalness and authority of God's Word, and then it began to "cast aside" doctrine and *"tribal* beliefs" that *divide* rather than *unite*. Now, this gradual *removal* of "that which obscures *the light"* of Satan's lie of Oneness has progressed to the point of attempting to remove *the very words* of God's Word.

Since the *words* of God's Word are what we are to *believe* and *obey* in order to believe and obey God and His Son, to cast aside the words is to conveniently cast aside *believing* and *obeying*. Nevertheless, this linear, either/or, dualistic, dichotomous truth of God's Word is absurdly seen as "*disastrous* separations that *threaten* our *existence.*" People would be far better served if they would think in order to feel rather than "feel in order to think." But, of course, true *thinking* involves *words*, and it is *words* of *truth* that "threaten" the "existence" of all this emerging Oneness. That is, it is *words* of *truth* that cause the *circle* of Oneness—which *connects* the *linear* opposites of *true and false* and *right and wrong*—to come *undone*, thereby ending its "existence" in the *dividing truth and reality of what is*.

For those who are not willing to accept the truth and reality of these opposites, the seducing spirit world is more than willing to be of service in providing the "sight" and the "knowing" of lying "experiences" that "prove" all this "Oneness." Satan is, after all, "an angel of *light*," and he is on a mission "seeking whom he may devour" (2 Corinthians 11:14; 1 Peter 5:8). And as Sweet points out, "*Unitary thinking ... opens us up* to a wider sensory realm and mystical dimension of the divine ..."

Although the *truth* and *faith* of God's Word are in the process of being gradually and purposely removed, people are not yet willing to reject God's Word altogether. So what do they do with it? Well, for instance, along with creating a "Third Testament" merely by the living of their own lives—since there's really no point in reading it if the words are seen as *irrelevant*, not to mention "*disastrous*"(!)—they can *hold it* while *meditating*. This is actually quite fitting, though. In this emerging faith of Oneness/panentheism the word "*religion*" means "*relationship*," rather than to "*read again.*" So this way, while they hold it they can simply *feel* a "connection" and a "relationship" with it—not to mention with the "God" that is in "the very substance" of the book itself—without having to either *read* it *again* or *believe* its *life*-giving *words* of *truth*, i.e., "*the words*" that "*are life.*"

> "8. Hold your Bible and breathe meditatively. The breathtaking, nay, **breathgiving truth of aliveness** is more than Methuselean in its span: Part of your body right now was once actually, literally part of the body of Abraham, Sarah, Noah, Esther, David, Abigail, Moses, Ruth, Matthew, Mary, Luke, Martha, John, Priscilla, Paul ... and Jesus.
>
> "9. Keep breathing quietly while holding your Bible...." [!] (Leonard Sweet; 1st ellipsis dots in the original; emphasis added)[22]

People today clearly don't want "more *light.*" They want more *darkness.*

"*The* **entrance** *of thy* **words** *giveth* **light***; it giveth understanding unto the simple.*" (Psalm 119:130)

"*... If therefore the light that is in thee be darkness, how great is that darkness!*" (Matthew 6:23)

No matter how many people are convinced by the "authority" of their own "knowing" that the darkness outside the "box" of God's Word is not *darkness* but "*light*," it is still darkness. Likewise, no matter how many people are convinced that the darkness of *Oneness* is "more light," the "light" of Satan's Oneness is still *darkness*, and that which "obscures" the darkness is *the light*. So this emerging faith of Oneness, in which *everything* is upside down, *must turn the light off* to be able to *see* this *darkness*. In other words, to see the darkness of Oneness—in which the opposites of *"what is 'truth' and 'falsehood'"* and *"what is 'right' and 'wrong'"* are *united* together in *wholeness*—the *light of God's Word must be turned off*. They *must* gradually remove God's Word and ultimately close it altogether. Now that today's shifting Christianity is going after the very words themselves, closing it is the next step and is already taking place. This way, everyone can blindly experience the *"breathgiving truth of aliveness"* wherever they choose to find it within "the totality of experience"—the "totality" of "the whole."

> "**God imparts truths that breathe** and thoughts that burn **within the *totality* of experience**." (Leonard Sweet; emphasis added)[23]

> "**All religions** have something to do with **the whole, the *totality*.**" (Leonard Sweet)[24]

> "**Spirituality** refers first of all to **the universal gift of aliveness** that exists **within *all religions*** and outside of religions. **It breathes out the air that 'inspires.'**... 'In-spire' means to breathe in....
> "For too long the church has warned its members, 'Don't breathe in,' highlighting the dangers of aliveness." (Leonard Sweet; emphasis added)[25]

> "According to millennial mathematics, the *symbolism* of '**two testaments**' indicates that the number *two* is an **unfinished** integer. **In the *mystical* symbolism of celestial calculus**, two represents an entity awaiting completion. ***Three* is the number of completion, even perfection**....
> "**Religion thinks in threes**.... **It takes '*three eyes*' to see God**, according to thirteenth-century Franciscan philosopher/theologian/cardinal/saint Bonaventure's rules of acquisition of knowledge--the eye of flesh (by which we perceive the external world), the eye of reason (by which we attain the knowledge of the internal world of philosophy and mind) and **the eye of contemplation (by which we attain knowledge of the transcendent world)**." (Leonard Sweet; all parentheses in the original; emphasis added)[26]

> "**In contemplation**, the **inner eye** is fixed upon the object of contemplation ... When **the third eye** is used, which is the case *in contemplation*, it is the synthesizer and director of triple energy; hence the powerful work performed by those in whom it is functioning." (the seducing spirit calling itself Djwhal Khul; emphasis added)[27]

> "**In contemplation**, a higher agent enters in. *It is the Soul that contemplates*. The human consciousness ceases its activity and **the man becomes what he is in reality - a soul, a fragment of divinity, conscious of its essential oneness with Deity**." (Alice Bailey; bold added)[28]

In other words, with *three* being a *mystical* number of "completion" and "perfection," in this emerging faith it takes "the *third eye*" of contemplation—i.e., of man's "intuitive" inner "knowing" which "*sees*" the "God" *of Oneness*—to bring "Scripture" to "completion" and "perfection" in a "*Third* Testament." And, of course, since "<u>all religions</u> have something to do with <u>the whole</u>" in Oneness, a *finished* Word of God with its two testaments that are *finished* in *Jesus* (which will be addressed later) would clearly be seen as *unfinished* and *incomplete*. In this emerging *interfaith* Oneness *completion* must include *the whole* otherwise it is obviously neither whole nor complete. So in today's shifting Christianity this emerging faith has brought with it a shift from teaching and preaching the Gospel of Christ to telling stories of people's own lives to thereby include *the interfaith whole*. And thus people are being led to believe, both mystically and otherwise, that "the living of their own lives writes the book of their most sacred truth." That is, that "the living of their own lives" brings "Scripture"—and the "understanding" of "God"—to "*completion*" and "*perfection*."

> "**We are *all* of us prisms of God's light, refracting the multidimensional rays of the divine**. All living organisms give off an aura of light, an energy field …" (Leonard Sweet; emphasis added)[29]

> "For a **New Light** apologetic there can be no final statement of theology … **[W]e must not foreclose our minds against the truths of God, even if they are new**…. The New Light movement is perhaps better called a '**More Light**' movement." (Leonard Sweet; emphasis added)[30]

> "Just as physicists *cannot understand truth by one model alone*--that is, either the wave nature of light or the particle nature of light--**so one model may not suffice to understand God completely**…. *One can be a faithful disciple of Jesus Christ without denying the flickers of the sacred in followers of **Yahweh, or Kali, or Krishna***.

> "A globalization of evangelism 'in *connection*' with others, and *a globally* '*in-formed' gospel*, is capable of talking across the fence with **Hindu, Buddhist, Sikh, Muslim**--people from other **so called 'new' religious traditions ('*new*' only to us)**--without assumption of *superiority* and power." (Leonard Sweet; parentheses in the original; emphasis added)[31]

> "Look not to one source, but to all sources, and even to all of Life, **for your definition and experience of *the Divine***. Reject nothing, but also include everything.

> "Do not say that **the truth is** exclusively 'here' or exclusively 'there,' but, rather, that the truth is 'neither here nor there,' but ***every* where**.

> "It is in the Qur'an, and it is in the Upanishads. It is in the Bhagavad Gita, and it is in the Bible…. It is in the Book of Mormon and the Book of Hidden Words. Yet know this: It is found in Whole *nowhere*, and in Part *everywhere*. **All of those sources, taken singularly, contain incomplete understandings**.

> "Therefore, entreat those who would live the New Spirituality to consider *every* book sacred and *every* messenger holy, even as they, themselves, are holy, and as **the living of their own lives writes the book of their most sacred truth**. Remember that always." (the seducing spirit calling itself "God;" bold added)[32]

In the "ordered process" of finding this panentheistic *interfaith* "God" of Oneness that is *immanent in everyone and everything* and that brings *all gods* together as "the *same* God," the *linear, narrow* truth of God's Word that *divides* true and false and right and wrong is gradually being replaced with the all-inclusive *circular, broad* "truth" of the journey of Oneness and its "circle of love." And, not surprisingly, a key component of today's *mystical* experiences that are indeed ending in the *metaphysical theology* of Oneness/panentheism is the journey of the popular labyrinth. *By design*, the labyrinth's *nonlinear* spiraling circular path literally and spiritually leads the person inward, to their *own* immanent "God" within.

> "The journey of faith is such that, by definition, you don't know where it will lead you. **Sometimes** the path is **straight and narrow**.... Part of **the appeal of the labyrinth** (also known as the prayer walk) is that it is a ***nonlinear*** maze where one experiences the **glory** of the '*new* and living *way*' only by **walking the path**." (Leonard Sweet; parentheses in the original; emphasis added)[33]

> "**Propositionalists want you to fall in *line*. Relationalists want you to fall in *love*....**
>
> "We were put here to 'glorify God and enjoy him forever.' In other words, we were not put here to 'do the right thing' but to be in a 'right relationship' with God. We were not put here to 'keep commandments' but to **conceive beauty, *truth*, and *goodness***. We were not put here to 'take a stand' but to **walk in the light** for the greater **glory** of God." (Leonard Sweet; emphasis added)[34]

As people choose to walk in the "*New* Light" of the "glory" of the "*new*" "*way*" of Oneness rather than in the "old" light of the *narrow* way of God's *absolute truth*, everything changes.

> "... by surrendering himself to the life at the center and there holding himself poised and still, yet alert, **the *light* will break in and reveal to the disciple that which he needs to know**. He *learns* to express that ***inclusive love*** which is his major requirement and **to *let go* the *narrow***, one-pointed attitude which he has hitherto regarded as love. **He welcomes then *all* visions**, if they serve to lift and comfort his brothers; **he welcomes *all* truths**, if they are the agents of revelation to other minds; **he welcomes *all* dreams** if they can act as incentives to his fellow men. **He shares in them *all***, yet retains his poised position at the center." (the seducing spirit calling itself Djwhal Khul; emphasis added)[35]

> "It might therefore be said that **revelation concerns *Oneness* and *nothing else***." (the seducing spirit calling itself Djwhal Khul; emphasis added)[36]

> "[T]hrough right discipline and meditation '**that which *obscures* the *light* is gradually *removed***'..." (Alice Bailey, *From Intellect to Intuition*; emphasis added)[37]

> "**He *learns* ... to *let go* the *narrow*** ..." (the seducing spirit calling itself Djwhal Khul; emphasis added)[38]

> *"Enter ye in at the strait gate: for wide is the gate, and broad is the way, that leadeth to destruction, and many there be which go in thereat: Because strait is the gate, and **narrow is the way, which leadeth unto life**, and few there be that find it."* (Matthew 7:13-14)

> *"Whosoever transgresseth, and abideth not in the doctrine of Christ, hath not God.* ***He that abideth in the doctrine of Christ, he hath*** *both the Father and* ***the Son****." (2 John 1:9)*

> *"**He that hath the Son hath life**; and he that hath not the Son of God hath not life." (1 John 5:12)*

34

"No person or living thing in the universe stands outside of the community of God"

Sadly, in its quest to purposely "rethink" and "reimagine" and "recreate" it *all*, today's shifting Christianity has indeed been "learn[ing] to *let go the narrow*." It has indeed been looking for more "light"—*new* "truths" and *new* "understandings" that it is *willing* to accept—*in "other faiths" (religions) and "pagan cultures."* After all, in today's emerging faith of Oneness/panentheism there is nothing *superior* about the truth and faith of *God's Word*. Since the panentheistic interfaith "God" of Oneness is *in everyone and everything*, "God's" "truth" is thus found in anyone and anything—*wherever* anyone *chooses* to look.

> "There can be no such thing as Superiority when We Are All One." (the seducing spirit calling itself "God")[1]

> "**New Light** embodiment means to be 'in *connection*' and 'in-*formation*' with **other faiths**. To be in-formation means to know each other's songs almost as well as one knows them oneself, and **to enlarge the community to include those whose conceptions of *God* differ from ours in form**." (Leonard Sweet; emphasis added)[2]

This shift "to include those whose conceptions of *God* differ from ours" simply could not be any less Christian or any more New Age. Even so, people today *want* a "God" of *interfaith Oneness* that is "MUCH *bigger* than any *particular* religion," and of course that is especially "bigger" than the *particular* truth and faith of *God's Word*. And since the very New Age immanent "God" of Oneness brings *all gods* together as "One God," i.e., as "*the same* God," it conveniently appears in *any* fashion—"*any* form"—that people are *willing* to accept.

> "People will not require God to 'show up' in one way and only in that way. People's beliefs about God will expand …
>
> "There is *no limit* to the ways in which God may show up.…
>
> "On a blessed future tomorrow **you will begin to believe in a limitless God, who can appear in any form**, under any circumstances, to any person, and, indeed, to all people in all places all the time." (the seducing spirit calling itself "God;" bold added)[3]

> "**There is only One God**. What God is this? Is it Adonai? Allah? Elohim? God? Hari? Jehovah? Krishna? Lord? Rama? Vishnu? Yahweh?
>
> "**It's All of Them**." (Neale Donald Walsch; bold added)[4]

And therefore:

> "[T]he focus will be on finding ways to honor those differences ['between religions'], seeing what they can further reveal to humanity about the Totality of God, and looking to see whether the *combination of all these different views* might produce a Whole that is Greater than the Sum of Its Parts." (the seducing spirit calling itself "God;" bold & underline added)[5]

> "Just as physicists cannot understand truth by one model alone … **so one model may not suffice to understand God completely**.… One can be a faithful disciple of Jesus Christ without denying the flickers of the sacred in followers of **Yahweh, or Kali, or Krishna**.
>
> "A globalization of evangelism 'in *connection*' with others, and *a globally 'in-formed' gospel*, is capable of talking across the fence with *Hindu, Buddhist, Sikh, Muslim* …
>
> "The *interfaith* embodiment of a quantum spirituality is based not on the Enlightenment search for what **the world religions** hold in common but on **the multitudinous and uniqueness of** *each particular* **vision of** *truth*." (Leonard Sweet; emphasis added)[6]

> "*All* the various truths *form* one Truth; … **your little bit of truth** *forms* **part of the group mosaic**." (the seducing spirit calling itself Djwhal Khul; emphasis added)[7]

Bringing all *gods* together inevitably leads to bringing all *religions* (all "*truths*") together, and vice versa. This emerging faith of Oneness/panentheism is *connecting*, "*defragging*," *all gods* into "*One God*" and *all religions* into "*One Church*" that is one all-encompassing "community of God." And, thus, today's Christianity is being led *to move* to "be '**in connection**' and '**in-*formation***' with **other faiths**." Consequently, *everything* is changing.

> "Those who favor some *particular* approach to the **truth** will nevertheless achieve

the realization that other approaches and other modes of expression and terminologies, and **other ways of *defining deity* can be *equally correct*** and in themselves constitute aspects **of a truth which is greater and vaster** than man's present equipment can grasp and express." (the seducing spirit calling itself Djwhal Khul; emphasis added)[8]

"When men recognize this and succeed in isolating **that *inner* significant structure of truth** which is **the same** in all climes and in all races, **then there will emerge the universal religion, the One Church**, and that unified though not uniform approach to God ... **Theologies will disappear into the knowledge of God**; doctrines and dogmas will no longer be regarded as necessary, for faith will be based on *experience*, and *authority* will give place to personal appreciation of *Reality*." (the seducing spirit calling itself Djwhal Khul; emphasis added)[9]

"**Tomorrow's God** says that *every church* is '<u>his</u> church,' and *every* faith is '<u>her</u> faith,' and *every* soul is God's soul, because it shares the same soul with God! And **no person or living thing in the universe stands outside of the community of God**." (the seducing spirit calling itself "God;" bold & underline added)[10]

"**The relationship of the whole to the part** (or 'sub-wholes,' as they are increasingly called), of the single cell to a multicellular organism, is at the heart of the contemporary mathematics of quantum theory.... General systems theory teaches that the *entirety* of any system *supersedes* and *cannot be explained by* the attributes and realities of its component *parts*.... **Authenticity** in postmodern culture **must reflect this integration and wholeness**. *New Light* communities are based on the '*different from*' principle of transcendence: The whole is different from the sum of its parts. Transcendence is a *relational* concept.

> "'Not Chaos-like, together crush'd and bruis'd,
> But, as the world, <u>harmoniously</u> confused:
> Where <u>order in variety</u> we see,
> And where, **tho' all things <u>differ</u>, all <u>agree</u>**.' English satirist/poet Alexander Pope

"**<u>All religions</u>** have something to do with the whole, <u>the totality</u>. Parts have no existence apart from wholes. In the modern era religions largely succumbed to the Enlightenment's **<u>*fragmented*</u>** fetishistic **love for *the part*. This is the essence of *sin***: Mistaking the part for the whole, or separating the part from the whole....

"The *New Light* apologetic must come to terms with the '*communal awakening*' of postmodernity.... New Light leadership is *fundamentally gathering communities together* and building them up into *a true body of Christ*." (Leonard Sweet; parentheses in the original; emphasis added, except italics to his quote of Pope)[11]

"Now, to put it in more postmodern terminology, **God is *<u>defragging</u>* the church** and rebooting it with the original Operating System [MRI – *Missional, Relational, Incarnational*]." (Leonard Sweet; emphasis added)[12]

"We exist in both particle and wave forms.... But even when we are in **particular form, we are still waves that are <u>connected</u> to <u>everyone and everything</u>**. Even when we take 'incarnational' form, we are still part of **one** holy, catholic, apostolic **church**....

"All of divine creation and human creativity will be **both *one* and *many*.**" (Leonard Sweet; emphasis added)[13]

"Quantum spirituality bonds us to all creation as well as to other members of the human family.... This entails a radical doctrine of **embodiment of God *in the very substance* of creation**." (Leonard Sweet; emphasis added)[14]

It is this *interfaith embodiment* of a "*God*" that is in the "*very substance*" of *everyone and everything* that thereby "heals the divisions" between the *Christian* faith/truth of *God's* Word and the faiths/"truths" of *all* other religions (which, incidentally, obviously includes the *New Age* religion despite the absurd denials of those who are indeed authentically "reflect[ing] this *integration* and *wholeness*"). And it is without question that this "healing" "enlarge[s] the community to include those whose *conceptions of God differ* from ours in form." Of course, other faiths/religions have "*conceptions of God*" that "*differ from ours*" because they actually have *other gods* that *differ from ours*. *Other gods*, such as *Kali* for instance, are no more the true God than are *Baal* and *Molech*. Yet in today's emerging faith of Oneness/panentheism, Baal and Molech—along with *every single other god throughout the history of mankind*, which includes Satan himself who is "the god of this world"—are the "true" "God." And people think this emerging faith is what *God* is "up to in the world"!

It is not *God* who is "*defragging*" "*all religions*" into "the whole, the totality." It is this false "God" of *Oneness* that brings the many diverse "fragments"/parts of *all* "*truths*" and *all gods* of *all* religions/faiths together in the *wholeness* of its all-encompassing *relationship* of its *immanence*. In this *Oneness* each continues to be its own *particular* religion/faith, *but* with the new "understanding" that it is *only one part* of "the group mosaic," i.e., of an *interfaith whole*. And since "*all* religions have something to do with the whole," *interfaith integration* becomes acceptable as well as *desirable* in order to reflect this *wholeness/Oneness*—i.e., this "Totality of God"—more *authentically*. In other words, in this emerging faith ("new world religion") of Oneness/panentheism, *authenticity* must reflect the *Oneness* of "Ours is not a better way, ours is merely *another* way."

"It is relatively unimportant what we mean in detail by that little word of three letters ['God']. It is but **a symbol of Reality**." (Alice Bailey; emphasis added)[15]

"That new world religion *must* be based upon those truths which have stood the test of ages ...

"First and foremost, there must be recognition of the fact of **God. That central Reality can be called by any name that man may choose** ... for it cannot be defined or conditioned by names.... Consciously or unconsciously, all men recognize God Transcendent and God Immanent....

"The Eastern faiths have ever emphasized *God Immanent* ... The Western faiths have presented *God Transcendent* ... Today, we should have the churches presenting a synthesis of these two ideas which have been summed up for us in the statement of Shri Krishna in *The Bhagavad Gita*: '**Having pervaded this whole Universe with a fragment of Myself**, I remain'. **God, greater than the created whole, yet God present also in the part**; ..." (the seducing spirit calling itself Djwhal Khul; bold added)[16]

"I suggest that such **an international, universal, transcreedal, transcultural, transracial standard for *theology* ** is the statement: **'We Are All One. Ours is not a better way, ours is merely *another* way.'**

"This can be **the gospel of a New Spirituality**." (the seducing spirit calling itself "God;" emphasis added)[17]

35

"Relinquish the pride of mind which sees its way ... to be *correct* and *true*"

"There can be **no such thing** as Superiority when **We Are All One**. A thing cannot be superior to itself.

"All things are One Thing, and there is nothing else. 'We Are All One' is more than a beautiful slogan. *It is a precise description of* **the nature of Ultimate Reality**. When you understand this, you ... see **the relationship of all things** differently. **You notice the connectedness at a much higher level**....

"A single sentence, uttered from your pulpits, lecterns, and rostrums, ... could change everything.

"'**Ours is not a better way, ours is merely another way**.'

"This humble utterance could begin to **heal the divisions between your religions** ..." (the seducing spirit calling itself "God;" bold & underline added)[1]

"1. **Unitary thinking, the highest level of understanding** *reality*, opens us up to a wider sensory realm and mystical dimension of the divine; it also **heals the divisions that separate us** from one another and life's highest values.

"2. **Wholeness unites**, not eliminates, **opposites**, bringing them into dynamic balance ..." (Leonard Sweet; emphasis added)[2]

"**All religions** have something to do with **the whole, the totality**." (Leonard Sweet; emphasis added)[3]

Too many people in today's shifting Christianity are cooperatively replacing the so-called "pride" and "idolatry" of believing that the Word of God is *correct* and *true* with the "humility" and "authenticity" of all this Oneness/wholeness. Essentially, this emerging Oneness flips *"yea, let God be true, but every man a liar"* (Romans 3:4) upside down into *"yea, let every man be true, but God a liar."* After all, in this emerging faith—"new world religion"—of Oneness all *"truths"/gods/religions* are being connected/united/defragged so that *no matter what anyone chooses to believe* it won't be seen as *"false"* and *"wrong,"* at least not by *man* anyway.

> "Relinquish the **pride of _mind_** which **sees its way and its interpretations to be _correct_ and _true_, and others' _false_ and _wrong_**. This is *the way of separation*. Adhere to **the way of integration** which **is of the _soul_ and not of the _mind_**." (the seducing spirit calling itself Djwhal Khul; emphasis added)[4]

> "What if we were to **think _connectness_ rather than _correctness_**?" (Leonard Sweet; emphasis added)[5]

> "In other words, we were not put here to 'do the right thing' but to be in a 'right relationship' with God. We were not put here to 'keep commandments' but to **conceive beauty, truth, and goodness**." (Leonard Sweet; emphasis added)[6]

> "One can be a faithful disciple of Jesus Christ without denying the flickers of the sacred in followers of **Yahweh, or Kali, or Krishna**.

> "A globalization of evangelism '**in _connection_**' with others, and *a globally 'in-formed' gospel*, is capable of talking across the fence with **Hindu, Buddhist, Sikh, Muslim** ... without assumption of *superiority* and power.... It will take **a decolonized _theology_** for Christians to appreciate **the _genuineness_ of others' faiths**, and to **see and celebrate what is good, beautiful, and true in their beliefs** without any illusions that down deep we all are believers in the same thing." (Leonard Sweet; emphasis added)[7]

Are we to keep *this* commandment, or is it too "outdated" for today's whole new way of thinking? -- *"Thou shalt have no other gods before me"* (Exodus 20:3).

> *"... verily every man **at his best state** is altogether vanity. Selah....When thou with rebukes dost **correct** man for **iniquity**, thou makest his **beauty** to consume away like a moth: surely every man is vanity. Selah." (Psalm 39:5, 11)*

> *"Repent ye therefore, and be converted, that your sins may be blotted out, when the times of refreshing shall come from the presence of the Lord; and he shall send Jesus Christ, which before was preached unto you: Whom the heaven must receive until the times of restitution of all things, which God hath spoken by the mouth of all his holy prophets since the world began.... Unto you first **God, having raised up his Son Jesus, sent him to bless you, in turning away every one of you from his iniquities**." (Acts 3:19-21, 26)*

The "*correct* and *true*" Gospel of Christ blesses the world "*in turning away every one of you from his iniquities.*" Yet this is being replaced with an *incorrect* and *untrue* (i.e., "*false* and *wrong*") "globally 'in-formed' gospel" that instead *non-divisively* "blesses the world with *new* understandings of *who Jesus is*" (i.e., with *conceived* "understandings" of who Jesus is "*reimagined*" to be by those in other religions/faiths/cultures).

> "And too few of these franchise 'projects' approached **other cultures** with **the gospel of love**: 'Jesus loves who and what you are, and wants to inhabit who you are and what you are in such a way that it blesses me, blesses others, and **blesses the world with *new* understandings of *who Jesus is*.**'" (Leonard Sweet; emphasis added)[8]

> "It is not religion and reason that go together, but religion and relationship that go together. Actually, that's where **the word *religion*** comes from—*religare*—**meaning 'to connect, to bind together.'** The future depends not on our ability to 'Come, let us reason together' but 'Come, let us relate together.'" (Leonard Sweet; bold & underline added)[9]

> "*Come now, and let us reason together, saith the* LORD: *though your sins be as scarlet, they shall be as white as snow; though they be red like crimson, they shall be as wool.*" (Isaiah 1:18)

> "*But the scripture hath concluded all under sin, that the promise by faith of Jesus Christ might be given to them that* **believe**.*"* (Galatians 3:22)

Faith is only *genuine* when faith is in the *genuine* God. And faith is only in the *genuine* God when faith is in the *genuine* Lord Jesus Christ. There is nothing "good, beautiful, and true" in believing in *false gods*. There is nothing "good, beautiful, and true" in *idolatry*. And this is *not* to be *celebrated*! But those who believe in the universal salvation of the *all-encompassing* "right relationship" of the false "God" of Oneness don't see it that way. Thus, with the help of *other religions* (increasingly referred to as "*cultures*" today in order to whitewash *religious* differences), today's new "mission" is to conceive a "beauty, truth, and goodness" that "heals the divisions" that separate the religions/faiths/cultures. And in this journey of Oneness, *of course* people don't and won't all claim to believe "in the same thing." In Oneness it doesn't matter what anyone *believes*; it only matters that no one is seen as "*wrong*." In Oneness "ours is merely another way."

Thus, along with having *different gods*, another key *division* between the *Christian* faith/truth of God's Word and the faiths/"truths" of *all other religions* is obviously the faith/truth/Gospel/doctrine of the Lord Jesus Christ Who *is* the *exclusive access* to the true God. In other words, the Lord Jesus Christ is *the only* way to the true God – not *another* way, not *a better* way, not *the best* way – the only way. So to fully "heal"/unite/defrag these divisions, this emerging faith/community of Oneness must not only "reimagine" God—which it does in its "reimagined" *immanent* "God" that renders *all gods* as just different forms, understandings, and experiences of "the *same* God"—it must also "reimagine" Jesus. This it does by *removing*, i.e., "*healing,*" the need to *believe* in the true *Person* of Jesus Himself. This gives people in any religion/faith/culture the freedom to believe whatever they want about "who Jesus is." There's clearly nothing *divisive* in this "Good News."

Accordingly, people in today's shifting Christianity are even being seduced into believing that the true Gospel of Christ is just "Western culture" that is to be "humbly" set aside so that people in other countries and religions (a.k.a. "cultures") can make up their *own* response. This way, people can answer the Lord Jesus Christ's question, "*But whom say ye that I am?*" in *whatever* fashion they are *willing* to accept. In the "self-regulating" "make-it-up-as-you-go-along process" of this emerging faith everyone can therefore *make up* their own "God" and their own "Jesus" and their own "gospel," however they choose of course. No "*beliefs*" are necessary. That is, no "*certain*" beliefs are necessary. This emerging faith is pursuing *uncertainty* for *a reason*.

> "God doesn't offer **final answers**, the **manacles** of modernity, but binding *relationships*....
>
> "**Jesus never once mentions religion or orthodox *theology*, nor does he outline *certain religious 'beliefs'*** and 'precepts' by which we will be judged. He outlines actions by which we will be judged, but not propositions and creeds." (Leonard Sweet; emphasis added)[10]
>
> "One can be a faithful disciple of Jesus Christ without denying the flickers of the sacred in followers of *Yahweh, or Kali, or Krishna*." (Leonard Sweet; emphasis added)[11]
>
> "This difference in how and where we encounter the sacred—in propositions or in relations—is fundamental....
>
> "For the Christian, ***propositionalism* is a form of *atheism***: to define faith in terms of formulations and affirmations you can tie down rather than living relationships and lifelong encounters you can trust." (Leonard Sweet; emphasis added)[12]

Incidentally, "propositionalism" (i.e., "faith as belief ... as believing something to be true ... believing the right things;"[13] or *believing that the doctrine/theology of God's Word is true*) is only "a form of *atheism*" in the emerging faith of the false interfaith "God" of Oneness that is *in everyone and everything*. This difference is not only fundamental it is also eternal. But, sadly, those who believe that they have "encountered" a binding all-encompassing relationship of a panentheistic "God"—not to mention of a panentheistic "Christ"—of interfaith Oneness don't see it that way. Besides, this "healing" difference is also absurdly seen as being on a mission "to produce the *Third* Testament" and "to continue the work of *Scripture*" in "our '*new* account of everything old'" as "co-creators" with "God" as "your part of the '*I Am*' that *we* are."[14] So, naturally, this *fundamental difference* is seen as anything but *eternal*. And, thus, these new "understandings" ("reimaginings") of "*who Jesus is*" become this emerging faith's "gospel of *love*."

> "People need room to ***move* and *choose* and *resist airtight propositions*** that don't allow free breathing (i.e., *freedom*). **Jesus left space for people *to make their own responses to him*. He did not dictate to his disciples *what they were to believe* about him**: 'Who do you say I am?'" (Leonard Sweet; parentheses in the original; emphasis added)[15]
>
> "The love of God lies **not** in our propositions and **beliefs** ... Jesus invited us into a sacramental relationship, ***not* into propositional acquiescence**." (Leonard Sweet; bold added)[16]
>
> "**One of the most serious *thought-crimes* for a Christian is the confusion of 'faith' with '*belief*,'** or to call someone who follows Jesus a '*believer*,' ... The Devil confesses to being a '*believer*.' **The Devil draws on <u>the Bible's authority</u> to make his arguments** ... " (Leonard Sweet; emphasis added)[17]

> "***The Bible doesn't make 'truth claims.'*** The Bible unveils truth power and manifests truth *relationships*." (Leonard Sweet; emphasis added)[18]
>
> "**Hostility** to the triumphalist teleologies and **doctrinal**/moralistic/experiential **chains** of modernity has generated an understanding of **truth** that lies now less in dogmatism than in discussion, **in the dialogue of the voices**, in the *ordered disorder* of sound....
>
> "**The *authority* of *truth*** proceeds from ***the process of dialogue itself*** ...
>
> "**Unitary thinking**, the highest level of understanding reality, opens us up to a wider sensory realm and *mystical* dimension of the divine; it also **heals the divisions** that *separate* us from one another and life's *highest values*." (Leonard Sweet; emphasis added)[19]
>
> "*People are looking to find their own unique path in the world, each in his or her own way....*
>
> "Authoritarian stances of ... '**We have *the* Truth!**' or '***The Bible says it*: That settles it!**' ... no longer suffice. Indeed, they are **resented**.... **Instead of** rational argumentation over ***what is 'truth' and 'falsehood,'*** authoritarian directives over *what is 'right' and 'wrong,'* ... **storytelling** is the postmodern means of governance ..." (Leonard Sweet; emphasis added)[20]
>
> "Jesus didn't leave us any *writings* ... **Jesus left us with one thing**: *himself*, in the form of his body, **a *community* that shares *stories* of *healing* and love**.... *This difference in how and where we encounter the sacred—in propositions or in relations—is fundamental*." (Leonard Sweet; emphasis added)[21]

Jesus—Who is the *truth* and Who always has been and always will be *God* (e.g., John 1:1-14)—left us with His *Word* of *truth* and His *Spirit* of *truth*. But people today are *rejecting* the writings (the words) of the Word of truth that we are to *believe* and are thus also automatically rejecting the Spirit of truth, the Comforter, Whom Jesus sent (e.g., John 7:39; 14:17; 15:26; 16:7-15). Consequently, all they have left is a community of *storytellers*. Yet this is what they *want*. Even so, this community is *not Jesus "himself."* Jesus *Himself* is at the right hand of the Father in *heaven*—which is not on *earth* as is now "reimagined"—where He is our Mediator and Intercessor with the true God, for all who *believe* in the true *Person* of Jesus Himself (e.g., Acts 3:20-21; Romans 8:34; Colossians 3:1-4; 1 Peter 3:21-22; Hebrews 9:14-15, 24). Only someone in the emerging faith and "quantum spirituality" of Oneness/panentheism who believes that "Jesus" is "energymatter,"[22] that "Jesus" "wants to be of one *substance* with every human being,"[23] that "each one of us is *free* to *become Jesus*,"[24] and "that in *being Jesus* we find Jesus"[25] would believe that a *community* is Jesus "*himself*."

Although those in this emerging faith prefer to *believe in* – put their faith in – *community* (i.e., in the all-encompassing relationship/community of Oneness/panentheism), in order to *have* Jesus we must *believe* in Jesus Himself, which thereby gives us God—Who *Himself* is likewise *not* a community.

> "For I am not ashamed of **the gospel of Christ**: for it is the power of God unto **salvation** to every one that **believeth**; to the Jew first, and also to the Greek." (Romans 1:16)
>
> "Whosoever transgresseth, and abideth not in the doctrine of Christ, hath not God.

*He that abideth in **the doctrine of Christ**, he **hath both the Father and the Son**." (2 John 1:9)*

*"**All scripture** is given by inspiration of God, and **is profitable for doctrine**, for reproof, for correction, for instruction in righteousness." (2 Timothy 3:16)*

*"**Being born again, not of corruptible seed, but of incorruptible, by the word of God**, which liveth and abideth for ever. For all flesh is as grass, and all the glory of man as the flower of grass. The grass withereth, and the flower thereof falleth away: But the word of the Lord endureth for ever. **And this is the word which by the gospel is preached unto you**." (1 Peter 1:23-25)*

*"So then **faith cometh by** hearing, and hearing by **the word of God**." (Romans 10:17)*

But, clearly contrary to today's mission to *"heal the divisions,"* the truth and faith of the Word of God *bring divisions*. So not surprisingly:

"An incarnational design begins with the *humble* acknowledgment that **there is no unmediated gospel or uncorrupted faith**. Every 'good news' is run through the 'software' of a cultural context. No theology exists outside of a historical standpoint and cultural context." (Leonard Sweet; emphasis added)[26]

"**Western Christianity has a *corrupted* hard drive and an alien default OS**.... Now, to put it in more postmodern terminology, **God is *defragging* the church and rebooting it with the original Operating System**. MRI [Missional, Relational, Incarnational] is the original operating system of the Christian faith. MRI is the operating software on which human life and faith *were designed* to run: Version 1.0 is known as the First Testament; Version 2.0 is known as the New Testament; **Version 3.0 is the Third Testament, the Gospel According to ... you**." (Leonard Sweet; last ellipsis dots in the original; emphasis added)[27]

All *Scripture*, by which we get our *faith*, is *inspired* by God. <u>God</u> does not <u>inspire corruption</u> or <u>error</u>. Neither has *all Scripture* that is *inspired* by *God* been *corrupted* out of *existence* leaving us with only *corrupted* Scripture that gives a *corrupted* faith that therefore opens the door to *"correcting"* the truth and faith of God's Word!

Yes, man is very *busy corrupting* the Word of God and its words with all of the "rethinking" and "reimagining" and "rewriting" *new* "versions" (*new* for *a reason*).

*"**For we are not as many, which corrupt the word of God**: but as of sincerity, but as of God, in the sight of God speak we in Christ." (2 Corinthians 2:17)*

But despite man's never-ending mission to *change*—to *corrupt* and *"correct"*—the resented *absolute truth* of God's Word, God, Whose *every word is pure*, promises to *preserve* His words <u>*from this generation*</u> forever.

*"**Every word of God is pure**: he is a shield unto them that put their trust in him." (Proverbs 30:5)*

*"**The words of the Lord are pure words**: as silver tried in a furnace of earth, purified seven times. **Thou shalt keep them, O Lord, thou shalt preserve***

them from this generation for ever." (Psalm 12:6-7)

The issue in wanting to believe that there is "<u>no</u> unmediated gospel or uncorrupted faith" is that all Scripture that has been *inspired* by God is *profitable* for <u>doctrine</u> and <u>reproof</u> and <u>correction</u> and <u>instruction</u> in <u>righteousness</u> – *all of which* today's shifting Christianity is trying to get *away* from. And *all of which* have to do with <u>correctness</u> and therefore do *the opposite* of facilitating *connectness*. So it is not surprising that today's shifting Christianity does not want this uncorrupted, inerrant *Scripture* that has been *inspired* by *God* to actually exist in our time and language. After all, *Scripture* is the <u>absolute truth</u> of the Word—of the <u>inspiration</u>—of *God*. So if *all* Scripture that exists is seen as *corrupted* then this conveniently eliminates the *correctness* of *absolute truth* that is to be <u>believed</u> and <u>obeyed</u> as *what is*. And this way it can all become *relative* and about *connectness* (relationship) instead.

Accordingly, today's shifting Christianity now commonly qualifies Scripture as inerrant only in *the originals*. This belief that the truth and faith of God and His Son *no longer exists* on the earth in an *inerrant* copy—i.e., that *all* copies in existence today are *corrupted* and *errant*—makes God out to be a liar. And it is quite ironic that God is being made out to be a liar in more and more of today's "Statements of Faith." It is also claimed that you have to go back to the original *languages* for inerrancy. And yet the double-tongued argument is that we can't *understand* the *truth* with *certainty* because of the limitations and even error of *language* and *words* and *transcription*. If this argument was true—and it isn't—about *God* being *limited* by man's *language*, it would make no difference whether we read the language of *English* or the languages of *Hebrew* and *Greek*! Moreover, even the original languages and the originals themselves of Scripture were *transcribed* by *man*. So, according to today's new way of thinking that *in itself* places limitations on God's ability to *inspire* the *Scripture* of His Word *through man and language*, there would *never* have been an inerrant, *pure* Word of God! Although utterly absurd, this is all precisely the *uncertainty* that people today *want*.

Incidentally, when the Lord Jesus Christ and the apostle Paul quoted from and referred to "*the scriptures*" and "*scripture*," even they had *copies*, not *originals*. God has faithfully preserved and inspired His *uncorrupted* Scripture in copies of His Word throughout the generations. But people today are just not *willing* to accept a truth that is *absolute* for "all cultures" and "all contexts" and "all time."

> *"How do ye say, We are wise, and the law of the LORD is with us? Lo, certainly in vain made he it;* **the pen of the scribes is in vain***. The wise men are ashamed, they are dismayed and taken:* **lo, they have rejected the word of the LORD***; and what wisdom is in them?" (Jeremiah 8:8-9)*

The fingers of today's Christianity are being pried one by one from God's Word of absolute truth for *a reason*. The *words* of the *uncorrupted* truth and faith of God and His Son given to us by *God* in the Word of *God* are simply not conducive to making *connections* in today's *circle* of relationship of *Oneness*. And this rapidly emerging faith—"new world religion"—is bound and determined to connect (defrag) *all* the different *religions/ faiths/cultures/gods/"truths"* together in a *Oneness/wholeness* that unites *all opposites*. Therefore God's inspired Scripture in God's Word *cannot* be seen as "*superior*" in any way. Again, believing the truth of God's Word *precludes* believing in all this *Oneness/ wholeness* and *they know it*. Hence, the *shift* away from *believing* the *words* of the *absolute* truth/theology/doctrine ("propositions") of God's Word. To see the *darkness* of

Oneness that *unites all opposites* the *light* of God's Word *must be turned off.*

Thus, those in this emerging faith of Oneness/panentheism are turning the light off to look for "truth" in the corner of a dark round room *on purpose*. With the light off everyone has the freedom to define and imagine "God" and/or "Jesus"/"Christ" however they choose and to have this "relationship" however they choose on whatever "path" they choose with no fear that it is all *"false and wrong."*

> *"If one understands* **the beliefs** *of the tradition and* **the scriptures** *of the tradition* **not as what is to be believed**, ... *then* one can begin to see that the Christian life is about *a relationship to the sacred*. Christianity ... uses human language, *culturally conditioned relative language*, and **to absolutize** *that language is a profound mistake*." (Marcus Borg; emphasis added)[28]

So if the *beliefs* are not to be *believed* then there's clearly nothing to fear, right?

> *"For God so loved the world, that he gave his only begotten Son, that whosoever believeth in him should not perish, but have everlasting life. For God sent not his Son into the world to condemn the world; but that the world through him might be saved. He that believeth on him is not condemned: but he that believeth not is condemned already, because he hath not believed in the name of the only begotten Son of God." (John 3:16-18)*

> **"To absolutize one's own religion as the only way** means that one sees all of the other religious traditions of the world as **wrong**, and dialogue, genuine dialogue, becomes impossible. **Conversion can be the only goal**." (Marcus Borg; emphasis added)[29]

> *"For this people's heart is waxed gross, and their ears are dull of hearing, and their eyes they have closed; lest at any time they should see with their eyes, and hear with their ears, and should understand with their heart, and should be* **converted, and I should heal them**." *(Matthew 13:15)*

36

"The *Gospel* According to" anything and everyone?

Those who are choosing to put their faith in Oneness and its panentheistic "God" and "truth" that are *in everyone and everything* will see nothing "*superior*" about the truth of God's Word nor see any "*advantage*" to having God's Word. Rather, they are attempting to "heal the divisions" between religions by looking for and creating "the kind of coherencies and larger frameworks" that *unify* the religions/faiths/cultures. Consequently, the "old" light of God's written Word of truth is being replaced with the "new light" of the collective "divine cocreativity"—i.e., collective "*storytelling*"—of today's emerging *interfaith community*. In this emerging faith "*relationship*, not *believing*" and likewise "*connectness* rather than *correctness*" have indeed become central. Since nothing is "*false* and *wrong*" in this new "light" of Oneness, the need for beliefs to be "*correct* and *true*" has been rendered irrelevant. And, of course, with a panentheistic interfaith "God" of Oneness everyone can look for "truth" *wherever* they *choose* to find it and even call it "Scripture" and "the Word" and "the Gospel" if they so desire.

> "**Look not to one source, but to all sources, and even to all of Life, for your definition and experience of the Divine**. Reject nothing, but also include everything.
>
> "**Do not say that the truth is exclusively 'here' or exclusively 'there,'** but, rather, that the truth is 'neither here nor there,' **but *every* where**." (the seducing spirit calling itself "God;" bold & underline added)[1]
>
> "'**No culture** is so advanced and so **superior** that it can claim **exclusive access or advantage to the *truth* of God**, and **none** so marginal or inferior that it **can be excluded**.'" (Leonard Sweet quoting Lamin O. Sanneh; emphasis added)[2]

218

"**New Lights** spend their lives **looking for the kind of coherencies and *larger* frameworks** people need for **unifying** human experience, **listening for the drumbeat of *the Word* amid the downbeats of the world**." (Leonard Sweet; emphasis added)[3]

"… Version 3.0 is **the Third Testament, the Gospel** According to … you." (Leonard Sweet; last ellipsis dots in the original; emphasis added)[4]

"**New Light** embodiment means to be '**in connection**' and '**in-formation**' with *other faiths*. To be in-formation means … to enlarge **the <u>community</u>** to include **those whose conceptions of *God differ*** from ours in form….

"One can be a faithful disciple of Jesus Christ without denying the flickers of the sacred in followers of **Yahweh, or Kali, or Krishna**.

"A globalization of evangelism 'in *connection*' with others, and **a globally 'in-formed' gospel**, is capable of talking across the fence with *Hindu, Buddhist, Sikh, Muslim* … without assumption of *superiority* and power." (Leonard Sweet; emphasis added)[5]

"Not only did God become incarnate at one time and in one place, thus becoming visible to the earth, but **the *gospel* gets *incarnated* in every culture** by design….

"God's presence is written in *every handwriting*. **The world** bears traces of the handwriting of ***the Word***….

"The early disciples treated with deep esteem those *without faith* and those with **other faiths** because **God** is active in their lives and we have something to **learn from them**.

"Early Christians drew upon **ideas, phrases, metaphors, and customs of pagan cultures** as **'seeds' of *the divine Word*** that *become enfleshed* in Christ and in the church." (Leonard Sweet; emphasis added)[6]

"Franchise is another word for *dis-incarnation*. And too few of these franchise 'projects' approached **other cultures** with **the *gospel* of love**: 'Jesus loves who and what you are, and wants to inhabit who you are and what you are in such a way that it … **blesses the world with *new* understandings of *who Jesus is***.'" (Leonard Sweet; emphasis added)[7]

"God the Spirit and Sustainer wants to work through **New Lights** of the twenty-first century **to produce the *Third Testament*--our '*new* account of everything old.'**

"**New Lights'** mission in life, if they choose to accept it, is **to continue the work of *Scripture*…**.

"… Philip Hefner captures wonderfully our simultaneous status as dependent creatures and free agents in his recommendation that human beings be thought of **as '*created co-creators*.'**" (Leonard Sweet; emphasis added)[8]

"<u>Community</u> is the highest collective form of *divine cocreativity*." (Leonard Sweet; emphasis added)[9]

"What if we were to **think *connectness* rather than <u>correctness</u>**?" (Leonard Sweet; emphasis added)[10]

> **"All scripture is given by inspiration of God**, and is **profitable** for <u>doctrine</u>, for <u>reproof</u>, **for correction**, for <u>instruction</u> in <u>righteousness</u>." (2 Timothy 3:16)
>
> "I charge thee therefore before God, and the Lord Jesus Christ, who shall judge the quick and the dead at his appearing and his kingdom; **preach the word**; be instant in season, out of season; **reprove, rebuke, exhort** with all longsuffering and **doctrine**. For the time will come when **they will not endure sound doctrine**; but after their own lusts shall they <u>heap</u> to themselves teachers, having itching ears; and **they shall turn <u>away</u> their ears from the <u>truth</u>**, and shall be turned unto fables." (2 Timothy 4:1-4)
>
> "For we have not followed cunningly devised fables, when we made known unto you the power and coming of our Lord Jesus Christ, but were eyewitnesses of his majesty.... We have also a more sure word of prophecy; whereunto ye do well that ye take heed, as unto a light that shineth in a dark place, until the day dawn, and the day star arise in your hearts: Knowing this first, that no prophecy of the **scripture** is of any private interpretation. For the prophecy came **not** in old time **by the will of man**: but **holy men of God spake as they were moved by the Holy Ghost**." (2 Peter 1:16, 19-21)
>
> **"Even the Spirit of truth; whom the world <u>cannot</u> receive**, because it seeth him not, neither knoweth him: but ye know him; for he dwelleth with you, and shall be in you." (John 14:17)
>
> "For if he that cometh preacheth **another Jesus**, whom we have not preached, or if ye receive **another spirit**, which ye have not received, or **another gospel**, which ye have not accepted, **ye might well bear with him**." (2 Corinthians 11:4)

In today's shifting Christianity, people believe they can just correct *Scripture* by "rethinking" and "reimagining" and "rewriting" it, so why would they see a need to be corrected *by* Scripture? Besides, "Yea, *hath God said…?*" Likewise, people believe they can just "rethink" and "reimagine" God and His Son in the attempt to fit them within the different religious/cultural contexts, so why would they see a need for the *doctrine* of Scripture that gives "the *doctrine* of Christ" by which we *have* "both the Father and the Son" (2 John 1:9)? Besides, a *corner* stone simply doesn't work in the *circle* of relationship of Oneness. Hence the pursuit of "*new* understandings of *who Jesus is*" in a "Gospel"/"Third Testament" that is "*globally 'in-formed'*" by other faiths/religions/cultures.

It is not at all surprising that people in this emerging faith of Oneness want "the Word" "made flesh *differently*"—or "<u>re</u>incarnated." That is, after all, the point. Without "*another Jesus*" that is *different* from the Lord Jesus Christ they cannot "heal the divisions" between religions. So this emerging faith must *change* the Son of God—with the help of man's powerful imagination, of course. Sweet, who has actually been praised as "[o]ne of the church's *most important* and provocative thinkers,"[11] has written:

> "There is no matter without spirit. There is no flesh without word. The height dimension of faith teaches us that without the Word made flesh, there is no Word made power. In every epoch, however, **the Word is *made flesh* differently**. *Energymatter is a dynamic process … Logos* materializes in *Pathos* **in forms fundamental to, shapes revelatory of, the age.**" (emphasis added, except to *Logos* and *Pathos*)[12]

> "Early Christians drew upon **ideas**, phrases, metaphors, and customs of **pagan cultures** as **'seeds' of the divine Word** that <u>*become enfleshed* in Christ</u> and in the church." (emphasis added)[13]

> "According to the *Oxford English Dictionary*, to inform means 'to give form to, put into form and shape.' **The purpose of the church** is to give form to, <u>**to put into form and shape, the energymatter known as Jesus Christ**</u>. New Light leaders, therefore, are *in-formational connectors* helping the body of Christ to *become an in-formed church, an in-formational community*. Informational communities exercise both informative and performative functions. The informative function is to impart **ideas** and to communicate **concepts necessary for the life** of the individual and **the community**....

> "*New Light* leadership helps patches of information become cloaks of knowledge. *Information brokering is central to creating community* in postmodern culture, not to mention achieving *synergic states of group consciousness*....

> "A major New Light undertaking is the *designing* of newstream *communities* that can be 'in *connection*' and '*in-formation*' with the spirit of Christ. <u>**Christ will be embodied for the postmodern church *in information*.**</u>

> "The following are five gross premises of embodiment ... that build *anew* the body of Christ for the postmodern era -- **being 'in *connection*' and '*in-formation*' with:** (1) other Christians, (2) **<u>all creation</u>**, (3) *one's ancestors and ancestral memories*, (4) **<u>other faiths</u>**, (5) technology." (emphasis added)[14]

It is the *true* Lord Jesus Christ Who is *the only way* to the *true* God. A *false* "Jesus," not to mention a "Jesus" that is *made-up* by *man*, can only lead to a *false* "God." And yet in today's emerging faith of Oneness and its unifying mission to create a new kind of "Gospel"/"Testament" through a new kind of "body" of a new kind of "Christ" no one will think twice about today's new "understandings" of who "Jesus" is. Moreover, the panentheistic "God" of Oneness is in everyone regardless of their *beliefs* and *religion*, so "people may genuinely encounter God ... *without explicitly knowing* about Jesus of Nazareth."[15] Since people in this emerging faith don't even need to *know Jesus*, it clearly won't matter what anyone *believes about Jesus*. And thus a <u>*false*</u> "Jesus," "<u>another Jesus</u>," becomes irrelevant as well.

So according to these pagan ("quantum") "reimaginings," "Jesus of Nazareth [is] the culmination of energymatter"[16] and "[t]he purpose of the church is ... to put into form and shape, the energymatter known as Jesus Christ." "Energymatter is a dynamic process," so "[i]n every epoch ... *the Word is made flesh differently* ... in forms fundamental to, shapes revelatory of, the age." Thus "*the gospel gets incarnated in every culture*" and "**ideas, phrases, metaphors, and customs** of **pagan cultures**" are seen "as **'seeds' of the divine Word** that become enfleshed in Christ and in the church." And therefore:

> "New Lights' mission in life, if they choose to accept it, is *to continue the work of Scripture*....

> "The challenge of the church in the twenty-first century is to become ... **a *seedbed* in which the *texts* and traditions of the faith *recreate* themselves *in and through the body* until its molecular imagination is awakened** by a living God.

> "Every believer, **<u>*every* body of Christ is called to become the Third Testament</u>**." (Leonard Sweet; emphasis added)[17]

"**Authenticity** in postmodern culture **must reflect this integration and wholeness**....

"***All*** **religions** have something to do with **the whole, the totality**. Parts have no existence apart from wholes.... This is the essence of sin: Mistaking the part for the whole, or separating the part from the whole....

"New Light leadership is fundamentally **gathering communities** together and building them up **into *a true body of Christ*.**" (Leonard Sweet; emphasis added)[18]

"In fact, **the genius of authentic Christianity** is its ability to **integrate '*pagan customs*' with Christian *faith* and *practice*.**" (Leonard Sweet; emphasis added)[19]

"***The body of Christ* is** less an aggregate of persons than **an aggregate of cultures;** *the body of Christ* **is an ark of cultural organisms**, each one contributing something unique and indispensable to the body." (Leonard Sweet; emphasis added)[20]

"Theologian/feminist critic Sallie McFague has argued persuasively for seeing **Earth**, *in a very real sense*, **as much as a part of** *the body of Christ* **as humans**.... The world of **nature** has an identity and purpose apart from **human** benefit. But we constitute **together** *a cosmic body of Christ*." (Leonard Sweet; emphasis added)[21]

"[N]ewstream communities will develop ritualized systems of relationship between the *human* journey and the *nature* of things. In the modern era *worship* was demystified and *denatured*. Postmoderns are driven by desire to explore and celebrate an ever-deepening *intimacy* with the Great Mystery that is the *universe*. **Liturgies of the earth**--fire, land, wind, and water--**can restore the biological and physical rhythms of the planet to our computer-programmed consciousness**. Outdoor earth rituals can also provide worshipers with experiences of *connectedness* to all earthlings: What the Sioux Indians call the creeping people, the standing people, the flying people, and the swimming people. **All earthlings must be incorporated into *the body of Christ* in more ways than just through the 'blessing of the animals.'** We must find ritual ways to make earthlings' presence felt, their participation solicited, their voices heard, if the ideal of *ecological worship* is to be realized." (Leonard Sweet; emphasis added)[22]

Suffice it to say that in today's emerging faith that is unarguably a "*make-it-up-as-you-go-along process*,"[23] it will *obviously* be *irrelevant* that the "new understandings of who Jesus is" do *not* line up with the *truth* of Who the Lord Jesus Christ is and what He did for us—i.e., the true Gospel of Christ—as recorded in God's Word of truth! Rather, it all merely becomes a "Third Testament." And a cosmic "Third Testament" that is made up in and through a cosmic "body" of a cosmic "Christ" will indeed produce "*new understandings of who Jesus is*." It will conveniently provide *countless* variations of "the Gospel According to ..."

This phrase sounds familiar. In fact, today's shifting Christianity, which has long since abandoned looking in the obvious place for the truth about God and His Son, should be quite familiar with all the never-ending absurd "reimaginings" associated with it. After all, according to the new way of thinking:

"The truth of thought is not dependent on its source: It's the same truth whether from the mouth of Jesus or the ass of Balaam. Truth as words is no different whether from the utterances of Paul or the udders of a cow. It matters not." (Leonard Sweet)[24]

"Look not to one source, but to all sources, and even to all of Life, for your definition and experience of the Divine. Reject nothing, but also include everything.

"Do not say that the truth is exclusively 'here' or exclusively 'there,' but, rather, that the truth is 'neither here nor there,' but *every* where." (the seducing spirit calling itself "God")[25]

Incidentally, ideas that are *pagan*, and concepts of "God" and of "Jesus"/"Christ" that are *different* from the Christian *truth* of *Who God is* and *Who the Lord Jesus Christ is*, are only "*necessary* for the *life* of the individual and the community" in a community of *Oneness*. And a community of *Oneness* is a community that only has "*life*" if the divisive *belief* in the Lord Jesus Christ is "*healed*." Thus, contrary to becoming "cloaks of knowledge," this emerging faith actually *cloaks* knowledge on purpose. And at the same time, what better way to "heal" this divisive belief than with the *pagan idea* of a "God" and "Christ" that are *immanent* in everyone and everything? This way, it can "build *anew* the body of Christ"—not to mention "the kingdom of God"—in its creation and formation of a *storytelling interfaith community* that "include[s] those whose conceptions of *God differ* from ours in form."

37

Dialoguing to the consensus/connectness/Oneness of today's new "truth"

Contrary to today's mission of Oneness, Jesus said to *continue in His Word* and we shall *know the truth*. He did *not* say to "*continue the work of Scripture*" and *conceive and live our own "truth."* Jesus said to go into all the world and *preach* the Gospel to *every* creature. He did *not* say to go into all the world and *learn* "the Gospel" according to them and *learn* from those *without* faith or *other faiths*, which, again, have *different "conceptions of God"* because they actually have *different gods*. Thus, neither did Jesus say to have "*a globally 'in-formed' gospel*" according to who the world says He is in its "*new understandings of who Jesus is*"! Furthermore, Jesus said to *teach* all nations to observe *all things* that He has *commanded*. He did *not* say to *leave space* for all nations to have the freedom to *make their own* responses to Him. But, sadly, this does indeed engender hostility in those who prefer to think *outside* the "box" of God's Word of absolute truth, and thus *outside* the Lordship of Jesus.

> "And why call ye me, Lord, Lord, and do not the things which I say?" (Luke 6:46)

> "Then said Jesus to those Jews which believed on him, If ye continue in my word, then are ye my disciples indeed; and ye shall know the truth, and the truth shall make you free." (John 8:31-32)

> "And he said unto them, Go ye into all the world, and preach the gospel to every creature." (Mark 16:15)

> "Go ye therefore, and teach all nations, baptizing them in the name of the Father,

and of the Son, and of the Holy Ghost: **Teaching them to observe all things whatsoever I have commanded you** ..." *(Matthew 28:19-20)*

"**We were not put here to 'keep commandments'** but to *conceive* beauty, *truth*, and *goodness*." (Leonard Sweet; emphasis added)[1]

"*Hostility* to the triumphalist teleologies and *doctrinal/moralistic/experiential chains* of modernity has generated an understanding of *truth* that lies now less in dogmatism than in discussion, *in the dialogue of the voices* ...

"The *authority* of *truth* proceeds from *the process* of *dialogue itself* ..." (Leonard Sweet; emphasis added)[2]

Actually, the authority of truth is God Himself. And God said what He meant and meant what He said in His Word of truth. Yet, incredibly, a growing number of people in today's shifting Christianity now believe that the *words* of God's Word are irrelevant and to be "transcended." It is the *words* of God's Word that tell us what we are to *believe* and *obey* in order to believe and obey God and His Son. God, "*Who will have all men to be saved, and to come unto the knowledge of the truth,*" is "*not willing that any should perish, but that all should come to repentance*"—i.e., a "*repentance to the acknowledging of the truth*" (1 Timothy 2:4; 2 Peter 3:9; 2 Timothy 2:25). To throw out the words of God's Word is to throw out *repentance* and *salvation* as well. For starters, if the words are irrelevant *what* exactly would they repent of, the so-called "idolatry" of *believing* the words of God's Word of truth? It used to be obvious that it is not by *unbelief* of the truth that we are saved. To throw out the words of God's Word is to throw out *everything*. But those who believe in their own inner "knowing" of their own inner "light" don't see it that way. Even so, God's Word is a *Word* of *words*, and these words of *God* are *words* of *truth*, and God's words of *truth* are to be *believed* and *obeyed*.

> "**Hold fast the <u>form</u> of sound <u>words</u>**, which thou hast heard of me, in faith and love which is in Christ Jesus." *(2 Timothy 1:13)*

> "**Holding fast <u>the faithful word</u>** as he hath been taught, that he may be able by <u>sound doctrine</u> both to exhort and to convince the gainsayers." *(Titus 1:9)*

> "**The entrance of thy <u>words</u>** giveth light; it giveth understanding unto the simple." *(Psalm 119:130)*

> "Jesus said unto them, ... **He that is of God heareth God's <u>words</u>**: ye therefore hear them not, because ye are not of God." *(John 8:42, 47)*

> "These words spake Jesus, and lifted up his eyes to heaven, and said, ... **For I have given unto them the <u>words</u> which thou gavest me**; ... Sanctify them through thy truth: **thy <u>word</u> is truth**." *(John 17:1, 8, 17)*

> "... **If ye continue in my <u>word</u>**, then are ye my disciples indeed; and **ye shall know the truth**, and the truth shall make you free." *(John 8:31-32)*

> "For this is good and acceptable in the sight of God our Saviour; Who will have all men to be saved, and to come unto **the knowledge of the truth**. For there is one God, and **one mediator between God and men, the man Christ Jesus**; Who

> *gave himself a ransom for all, to be testified in due time." (1 Timothy 2:3-6)*

> **"Jesus saith unto him, I am the way, the truth, and the life: no man cometh unto the Father, but by me.***" (John 14:6)*

> *"Unto you therefore which **believe** he is precious: but unto them which be disobedient, the stone which the builders disallowed, the same is made the head of the corner, and a stone of **stumbling**, and a rock of **offence**, even to them which **stumble at <u>the word</u>**, ..." (1 Peter 2:7-8)*

> **"Ever learning, and never able to come to the knowledge of the truth***. Now as Jannes and Jambres withstood Moses, so do these also resist the truth: men of corrupt minds, reprobate concerning the faith.... But **continue** thou **in** the things which thou hast learned and hast been assured of, knowing of whom thou hast learned them; and that from a child thou hast known **the holy scriptures**, which are able to make thee wise unto salvation through faith which is in Christ Jesus. **All scripture is given by inspiration of God** ... I charge thee therefore before God, and the Lord Jesus Christ, ... preach **<u>the word</u>** ... For the time will come when they will not endure <u>sound doctrine</u> ... and they shall turn away their ears from **the truth**, and shall be turned unto fables." (2 Timothy 3:7-8, 14–4:4)*

Jesus is not *man's "reimagined" "truth"* that is to be *"conceived."* He is *the truth* that is to be *believed*. Jesus did *not* say—"I am the way however you choose to journey," "I am the truth however you choose to imagine it," "I am the life however you choose to live"! We are not to make it all up however we choose. But, of course, God's divisive words of *what <u>is</u> truth and falsehood* and *right and wrong* are being replaced with "the dialogue of the voices" in order to replace this "old" divisive truth of God's Word with today's new unifying "truth" of Oneness. Rather than heeding the words of *God*, people in today's shifting Christianity are blindly heeding doctrines of *devils* just as the "irrelevant" words of God's Word forewarned.

> *"Now the Spirit speaketh expressly, that in the latter times some shall **depart from the faith**, giving heed to seducing spirits, and doctrines of devils." (1 Timothy 4:1)*

> "There is another way. There is another way to experience God. There is another way to live life. Your differences do not have to create divisions. Your contrasts do not have to produce conflicts.... THERE IS ANOTHER WAY.

> "Yet you will not find that way by searching for it. You will only find it by creating it. And you will not create it by **remaining stuck in old beliefs, but only by opening yourself to *new* ideas**. New ideas **about *God*** and about Life *that can truly light the world....*

> "A kind of spirituality **that will allow humans** to express their natural impulse to seek and **to experience the Divine without making each other *wrong*** for the way in which they are doing it ..." (the seducing spirit calling itself "God;" bold & italics added)[3]

> "Our opportunity now is to create the space of possibility for a **New Spirituality** to emerge upon the earth, a kind of spirituality that will not in any way hinder or destroy our traditional faith traditions, but that will reinvigorate them, refresh them, enliven them, *expand them*, and allow them to flourish, bringing to our world at last

an *individualized* experience of the Divine *in a unified form that makes no one wrong* for the way in which they are approaching the God of *their understanding*, and that creates no condemnation or conflict in God's name....

"[T]his kind of **healed spirituality** cannot fully emerge on the earth without you. For you must be the creators and the carriers of its message." (Neale Donald Walsch; emphasis added)[4]

"The more connected the world gets, the more the importance of Christianity getting over its propositional impotence. **We must resign from the proposition business** and rehire into the people business. It's time to start flexing faith's relational muscles **and build up a *relational theology*** in which '**Only Connect**' is the engine room of the *theological* enterprise ..." (Leonard Sweet; emphasis added)[5]

"God doesn't offer *final answers*, the **manacles** of modernity, but binding *relationships*....

"Jesus never once mentions religion or **orthodox *theology***, nor does he outline **certain religious 'beliefs' and 'precepts'** by which we will be judged. He outlines actions by which we will be judged, but not **propositions and creeds**." (Leonard Sweet; emphasis added)[6]

First, whereas a "box" has *walls*—which divide, separate, restrict, set forth limits, and also *protect*—in this emerging faith/relationship of Oneness, i.e., "relational theology," everyone can "simply 'be' in relationship" "unencumbered by structure."[7] That is, unencumbered by the structure of the *absolute truth* of God's Word that is to be *believed* and *obeyed* as what *is*.

"... the English words believe and believing are ***relational***.... **They don't even mean believing *divinely revealed* propositions to be *true*.**" (Marcus Borg; emphasis added)[8]

"Our **idolatry of propositions**[13] is so severe that we have even made 'affirmations' into principles, not people. When you hear the word *affirmation*, you immediately think of an intellectual declaration rather than **a relational stance of being 'beloved** on the earth.' But what it means to be human is *not* to enunciate affirmations but **to be affirmed and receive affirmations**." (Leonard Sweet; emphasis added, except to *affirmation*)[9]

As mentioned earlier, in his endnote #13 of this previous quote Sweet quotes from the book *God in All Things* to specify that "**true** faith is an act of **surrender to the living God, present *in all people* ... and *in all things***."[10] The "*relational theology*" of a "*God*" *that is in everyone and everything*, thereby bringing everyone and everything together in one *all-encompassing relationship with itself*, clearly turns everything upside down. And, no, this emerging faith of Oneness/panentheism is not true, so it is not "true faith."

"... Tomorrow's God will turn your understanding of **relationships upside down**." (the seducing spirit calling itself "God;" emphasis added)[11]

"In the days of the New Spirituality ***love*** and ***freedom*** **will be understood to be *the same thing***." (the seducing spirit calling itself "God;" emphasis added)[12]

"*Propositionalists* want you to fall in *line*. **Relationalists want you to fall in love**...."

"In other words, **we were not put here *to 'do the right thing'*** but to be in a 'right relationship' with God. **We were not put here *to 'keep commandments'*** but to conceive beauty, truth, and goodness. **We were not put here *to 'take a stand'*** but to walk in the light for the greater glory of God." (Leonard Sweet; emphasis added)[13]

"If ye love me, keep my commandments." *(John 14:15)*

Sadly, even in today's shifting Christianity more and more people are in fact no longer willing to "do the right thing." They are no longer willing to "keep commandments"—even one as basic as "*his commandment, That we should believe on the name of his Son Jesus Christ*" (1 John 3:23). And neither are they willing to "take a stand" for *what is truth* and *what is right*.

Second, in order to shift from the "old" *either/or* truth of God's Word that *divides* opposites to today's new *both/and* "truth" of Oneness that *unites* opposites, this fully emerging enterprise must "Only Connect" truth and falsehood and right and wrong. Otherwise there is *no "both/and."* The "unified form that makes no one wrong" is the *both/and*.

"**Think *outside* the box. Reject 'either/or' and consider 'both/and.'**" (the seducing spirit calling itself "God;" bold added)[14]

"Your differences do not have to create *divisions*. Your contrasts do not have to produce conflicts." (the seducing spirit calling itself "God;" emphasis added)[15]

"Remember ... **the Divine Dichotomy**, in which **two apparently contradictory truths can exist simultaneously in the same space**....

"That is a sign of maturity, ... standing firm in an 'either/or' position rarely serves anyone—least of all, Life.

"**You do not live in an 'either/or' reality. The reality is 'both/and.'**" (the seducing spirit calling itself "God;" emphasis added)[16]

"The postmodern world being born is **not** a bipolar worldview of **either/or's** but a double helix, Möbius-strip culture of **both-and's**, the *coincidentia oppositorum* (**coinciding opposites**) ..." (Leonard Sweet; parentheses in the original; bold added)[17]

"Postmoderns can take **opposite paths**, make contrasting choices, **and still be 'right.'**...

"**Instead of** rational argumentation over **what is 'truth' and 'falsehood,'** authoritarian directives over **what is 'right' and 'wrong,'** ... storytelling is the postmodern means of governance ..." (Leonard Sweet; emphasis added)[18]

"**The truth lies now in the extremes, both held together simultaneously.** Ever since Danish physicist Niels Bohr's enunciation of the complementarity principle, **the union of logically contradictory opposites** (such as 'wave' [world of connection] and 'particle' [world of disconnection] to describe light) has stood at **the *heart*** of the comprehension ***of truth*. Oppositions are no longer**

antagonisms but electrifying outlets....

"The authority of truth proceeds from the process of *dialogue itself* ...

"The bitter-sweet bind of postmodern culture is, **The truth lies in the extremes being held together**....

"1. **Unitary thinking** ... **heals the divisions that separate us** from one another and life's highest values.

"2. **Wholeness unites ... opposites** ..." (Leonard Sweet; all parentheses and brackets in the original; emphasis added)[19]

In this "*healed* spirituality"—i.e., *Wordless* faith—of Oneness the polar opposites of truth and falsehood and right and wrong are united in a both/and that "heals" divisions. So rather than a *linear* truth in which everything is *either* truth *or falsehood, either* right *or wrong*, everything becomes a relative "truth" and a relative "right"—no "falsehood" and no "wrong." In other words, everything becomes a *circular* "truth" in which the opposites of *both* truth *and falsehood* are brought together in a new larger "truth" in which it all becomes a *relative* "truth." Likewise, *both* right *and wrong* are brought together in a new larger "truth" in which it all becomes a *relative* "right." This way, "what is 'truth' and 'falsehood'" and "what is 'right' and 'wrong'"—and, thus, what is to be *believed* and what is to be *obeyed*—all becomes *irrelevant* as well as "*transcended*" in the even larger "truth" of "*relationship*."

Of course, with a both/and unity of opposites that obviously "makes no one *wrong*" everyone can thus "take *opposite* paths ... and still be '*right*.'" Today's shifting Christianity, which clearly desires the freedom of this *both/or* "unitary thinking," is indeed resigning from the *either/or* "proposition business" in its shift to affirming *people* in their *choices* instead of affirming *the truth*. And, consequently, everything is changing.

"**To *absolutize* one's own religion as *the only way*** means that one **sees all of the other religious traditions of the world as *wrong***, and dialogue, genuine dialogue, becomes impossible. *Conversion* can be the only goal." (Marcus Borg; emphasis added)[20]

"Difficult as it is to now imagine, **your established religions are going to stop making each other *wrong*. And the New Spirituality will throw the doors of acceptance open to all forms of the true and honest search for wisdom**. This will be *the new way that humanity will interact with God*, and it will produce **a new way of interacting with each other**—a way that could change the world forever." (the seducing spirit calling itself "God;" emphasis added)[21]

In this emerging faith, i.e., "New Spirituality"/"new world religion," this new way of interacting with each other "that makes *no one wrong*" includes dialoguing to consensus/connectness/Oneness. As mentioned earlier, the purpose of dialogue is not to teach and believe what is *true* but to make *relationships* in the circle of Oneness. Again, dialogue facilitates Oneness by *transforming truth into relationship*—by facilitating the transformation of the dividing *line* of truth into a *circle* of unity. This creates *the new* "truth" that brings *two extremes*—polar opposites—together as one. This *Oneness/unity* of opposites is itself *the new* "truth." This process effectively *eliminates* ("transcends") opposites—e.g., truth and falsehood, right and wrong—by *connecting/uniting* these opposites (either/or's) *together* in a *both/and* that thereby creates a *circle* of Oneness. There are *no opposites* in a circle of Oneness—O.

Opposites/extremes (either/or's) are connected and held together in a both/and by building a *bridge* through *dialogue* that pulls the opposites *together*. The process of pulling together two polar opposites, i.e., *the two ends* of the *line*, transforms—*curves*—the dividing *line* of truth into a *circle* of Oneness/relationship. A *curve* is "a line that *deviates from straightness* in a smooth, continuous fashion."[22] And, fittingly, a *curve ball* is "a *pitch* delivered with a *spin* that causes the ball *to veer* from a normal straight path, *away from the side from which it was thrown*."[23] In dialogue, the two sides are giving each other pitches delivered with a spin—throwing "curve balls"—that purposely veer away from the side from which they are thrown. And they are doing so in order to build a bridge/connection—i.e., to "Only Connect"—with the opposite side. In other words, they are doing so in order to transform the dividing *line* of truth into a *circle* of unity/Oneness/relationship.

The definition for *curve* also includes "a misleading or deceptive trick; cheat; deception."[24] And to *deceive* is also "to cheat," "to beguile," and to "mislead the mind," as well as "to cause to err."[25] Curve balls and their spin *deceive* the one to whom the pitch is thrown. But, although in baseball curve balls are pitched with a spin designed to *prevent* the hitter from connecting with the ball, in interfaith dialogue curve balls are pitched with a spin designed to *assist* the "hitter" in connecting with the ball. As they each connect with the other's pitched curve "*somewhere in the middle*" above the dividing line that separates them, a new "*truth*"—a Oneness—is created that "heals" the division between them, thereby *transforming truth into relationship*. Nevertheless, the curve is a *deception*. *The line that divides polar opposites*, i.e., the dividing line between *what is* truth and falsehood, right and wrong, *does not curve*. It remains what it is—*a straight line*. So it is also fitting that "[t]here has been debate on whether a curve ball actually curves or is an optical illusion."[26] When it comes to a curve ball that is meant to connect the opposites/extremes of truth and falsehood, right and wrong, it is indeed an *illusion*, a *deception*. But, nevertheless, people today still prefer "to think connectness *rather than* correctness" and that:

> "**The Truth Lies Somewhere In the Middle**.... Oppositions are no longer antagonisms but electrifying outlets....
>
> "The movement from premodern (medieval) to modern to postmodern replaced dichotomies first with dialectics and now with **interactions**....
>
> "The *authority* of truth proceeds from *the process* of *dialogue* itself ...
>
> "The bitter-sweet bind of postmodern culture is, **The truth lies in the extremes being held together**." (Leonard Sweet; parentheses in the original; emphasis added)[27]

This process *is* the dialectic process[28] and is the process of creating new "truth"—i.e., synthesized/connected "truth"—by getting *both* sides to come *away from* their position. But today's shifting Christianity doesn't see it as a coming *away from* the truth and faith of God's Word. It *sees* it as "building bridges." It is. It is building bridges between what is *truth and falsehood* and *right and wrong* in order to create a new both/and "truth" of a much *broader* narrow way that gives everyone room to veer/curve to the left or to the right. With a *broader* way that has room to throw curve balls—which are further described as "[a]ny of several pitches that veer to the left when thrown with the right hand and to the right when thrown with the left hand"[29]—more people should thus be able to find it, right?

*"Enter ye in at the strait gate: for wide is the gate, and broad is the way, that leadeth to destruction, and many there be which go in thereat: Because strait is the gate, and **narrow is the way, which leadeth unto life, and <u>few</u> there be that <u>find it</u>**." (Matthew 7:13-14)*

*"For this people's heart is waxed gross, and their ears are dull of hearing, and **their <u>eyes</u> they have <u>closed</u>**; lest at any time they should see with their eyes, and hear with their ears, and should understand with their heart, and should be <u>converted</u>, and **<u>I</u> should heal them**." (Matthew 13:15)*

*"And the angel of the LORD went further, and stood in **a narrow place, where was no way to turn either to the right hand or to the left**." (Numbers 22:26)*

*"And thou shalt not go <u>aside</u> from any of the <u>words</u> which I command thee this day, **to the right hand, or to the left, to go after other gods to serve them**." (Deuteronomy 28:14)*

*"Ponder the path of thy feet, and let all thy ways be established. **Turn not to the right hand nor to the left: remove thy foot from evil**." (Proverbs 4:26-27)*

We are to teach and preach the *truth* and either people will be willing to accept and believe it, or they will not. Sadly, far too often they will not. But we are not to give them pitches delivered with a spin—i.e., "curve balls"—that mislead them into thinking that the spin and its curve are the *truth*. Again, the definition for *curve* includes "a misleading or deceptive trick; cheat; deception."[30] And, along with "to cause to err" and to "mislead the mind," to *deceive* is also "to cause to *believe* what is *false*, or *disbelieve* what is *true*."[31] And, yes, the word *deceive* also "involves the *deliberate* misrepresentation of the truth,"[32] which is precisely what is taking place. Again, for example:

"What if we were to think connectness *rather than correctness*?" (Leonard Sweet; emphasis added)[33]

To think connectness *rather than correctness* is obviously a pitch delivered with a spin. It *purposely* veers, or deviates, *away from* the straightness of what is *"correct and true."* Also very fitting is that "[i]n the early years of the sport, use of the curveball was thought to be dishonest and was outlawed, but officials could not do much to stop pitchers from using it."[34] Although God can and will stop it one way or the other, the warnings of the resented "doctrine police" aren't doing much to stop people from pitching the dishonesty and deception of intentional *incorrectness*.

Yes, people in today's shifting Christianity are *deliberately* mis representing—spinning and curving—the truth. And they are doing so for the sake of facilitating interfaith relationship. They know that to represent the truth *as it is* will automatically cause *division* which defeats their purpose of facilitating today's desired relationship/connectness. So they are deceiving themselves and others *on purpose*. But, of course, they don't see it as either dishonest or deception. After all, not only has *spin doctoring* replaced *teaching the faith* as the more desirable *profession* in today's shifting Christianity, but actually included in the definition of *spin* is "[t]o *relate* or *create*: spun tales for the children."[35] And *relating* and *creating* through *storytelling* is today's *mission*!

Nevertheless, no matter how many "voices" choose to authorize the stories people create as an acceptable "understanding of truth," God doesn't "grade" on a curve. To *have God* we are to *believe* and *continue in* and *abide in* the Gospel/doctrine of Christ not *journey outside* this "box" to conceive new "truth" that people are willing to accept.

> **"For I am not ashamed of the gospel of Christ**: for it is the power of God unto **salvation** to every one that **believeth**; ..." (Romans 1:16)

> "Whosoever transgresseth, and **abideth not in the doctrine of Christ, hath not God**. He that abideth *in* the doctrine of Christ, he hath both the Father and the Son." (2 John 1:9)

> **"Take heed** unto thyself, and **unto the doctrine; continue in them**: for in doing this thou shalt both **save thyself, and them that hear thee**." (1 Timothy 4:16)

Transforming the Gospel/doctrine of Christ into a curve that people are willing to connect with is to come to the table dialoguing a "reimagined" "Jesus" and a "reimagined" "gospel"—i.e., "another Jesus" and "another gospel"—that people are willing to "bear with." This is not the mission of *God*.

Obviously, in order to connect with each other and thus connect the opposites/extremes there must be cooperation and participation by both sides. This process cannot transform the truth into *relationship* if only one side cooperates and participates. This would result in a partly transformed line that is still an either/or *disconnection*. Unless *both* sides cooperate there would obviously be no *connection* to transform the *dividing line of truth* (the either/or) into a *circle of unity/relationship* (a both/and). Thus, the dialogue process builds its bridges (connections) when both sides connect with each other's pitches delivered with a spin. In other words, *both* sides must be *willing* to "Only Connect" and cooperate and participate in dialoguing *to consensus/connectness/Oneness*. And, therefore, in interfaith dialogue Christianity must be willing to *spin* and *curve* the Christian faith and truth of God's Word.

Sadly, it is more than willing to do so given its own shift to darkness. Along with the world, it, too, wants "reimagined" new "truth" that "transcends" the "stone of *stumbling*" and "rock of *offence*." After all, it is attempting to "heal" the *division* that automatically comes with *the truth* of Who the Lord Jesus Christ is and what He did—i.e., *the truth* of the Gospel/doctrine of Christ. So today's shift from "Come, let us *reason* together" to "Come, let us *relate* together" was inevitable.

> "For if he that cometh preacheth another Jesus, whom we have not preached, or if ye receive another spirit, which ye have not received, or another gospel, which ye have not accepted, ye might well bear with him." (2 Corinthians 11:4)

> "But though we, or an angel from heaven, preach **any** other gospel unto you than that which we have preached unto you, let him be accursed. As we said before, so say I now again, If any man preach **any** other gospel unto you than that ye have received, let him be accursed. For do I now persuade men, or God? or **do I seek to please men? for if I yet pleased men, I should not be the servant of Christ**." (Galatians 1:8-10)

> "Also I say unto you, Whosoever shall confess me before men, him shall the Son of man also confess before the angels of God: But **he that denieth me before men shall be denied before the angels of God**.... Suppose ye that I am come to give peace on earth? I tell you, Nay; but rather **division**." (Luke 12:8-9, 51)

*"**And ye shall be hated of all men for my name's sake**: but he that endureth to the end shall be saved.... Whosoever therefore shall confess me before men, him will I confess also before my Father which is in heaven. **But whosoever shall deny me before men, him will I also deny before my Father which is in heaven.**" (Matthew 10:22, 32-33)*

*"Many will say to me in that day, Lord, Lord, have we not prophesied in thy name? and in thy name have cast out devils? and in thy name done many wonderful works? And then will I profess unto them, **I never knew you**: depart from me, ye that work iniquity." (Matthew 7:22-23)*

*"Unto you therefore which believe he is precious: but unto them which be disobedient, **the stone which the builders <u>disallowed</u>**, the same is made the head of the corner, and a stone of stumbling, and a rock of offence, even to them which stumble at <u>the word</u>, being disobedient: whereunto also they were appointed." (1 Peter 2:7-8)*

Again, regardless of how today's shifting Christianity chooses to see it, today's process of creating new interfaith "truth" is getting *both* sides to come *away from* their position. And, for obvious reasons, it is the *Christian* side and position that must *curve the most*—and *well past "the middle"*—in order for the other side to be *willing* to connect with it. The result is that *neither* side is willing to continue in and abide in the doctrine of Christ. The *"correct* and *true"* divisive doctrine of the divisive Christ simply isn't conducive to building a bridge that creates connectness/Oneness/wholeness with an *unbelieving* and *unrepentant* world.

*"And when he is come, **he will reprove the world of sin**, and of righteousness, and of judgment: Of sin, **because they believe not on me**." (John 16:8-9)*

"And we know that we are of God, and the whole world lieth in wickedness." (1 John 5:19)

"Woe unto them that call evil good, and good evil; that put darkness for light, and light for darkness; that put bitter for sweet, and sweet for bitter! Woe unto them that are wise in their own eyes, and prudent in their own sight!... Which justify the wicked for reward, and take away the righteousness of the righteous from him!" (Isaiah 5:20-21, 23)

"But speak thou the things which become sound doctrine ... For the grace of God that bringeth salvation hath appeared to all men, teaching us that, denying ungodliness and worldly lusts, we should live soberly, righteously, and godly, in this present world; looking for that blessed hope, and the glorious appearing of the great God and our Saviour Jesus Christ; Who gave himself for us, that he might redeem us from all iniquity, and purify unto himself a peculiar people, zealous of good works. These things speak, and exhort, and rebuke with all authority. Let no man despise thee." (Titus 2:1, 11-15)

38

"Transcending current beliefs is not an outright rejection of them; it is an 'adding to' them"

*"Every word of God is pure: he is a shield unto them that put their trust in him. **Add thou not unto his words**, lest he reprove thee, and thou be found a liar." (Proverbs 30:5-6)*

*"How do ye say, We are wise, and the law of the LORD is with us? Lo, certainly in vain made he it; the pen of the scribes is in vain. The wise men are ashamed, they are dismayed and taken: lo, **they have rejected the word of the LORD**; and what wisdom is in them?" (Jeremiah 8:8-9)*

When the mission is to "transcend" the "*correct* and *true*" beliefs of God's Word in order to build bridges/connections that "heal" the divisions between faiths/religions/cultures then darkness inevitably becomes the preferred "light" and "old things *need* to be said in *new* ways." Naturally, "*new* understandings of *who Jesus is*," as well as of "God" and "Scripture" and "the kingdom of God" for that matter, will not be given a second thought by those "so eager to embrace the *new*, so open to *change* the old."[1] Neither will "understandings" that are "*everything new*" be seen as a *rejection* of the old any more than choosing to "think connectness *rather than correctness*"[2] is seen as *incorrectness*.

> "Something can be **all new, yet nothing of the old be lost**…. The Third Testament is **everything new** about the old, old story." (Leonard Sweet; emphasis added)[3]

234

"Old things need to be said in *new ways*. New things can only be said in new ways. When they get corseted into old concepts, they get distorted and damaged." (Leonard Sweet; emphasis added)[4]

"The Spirit works *new enlargements* of truths that the Bible already teaches." (Leonard Sweet; emphasis added)[5]

"'Transcending' ['beliefs'] does not mean always being 'other than,' it means always being 'larger than.' Your new, larger belief system will no doubt retain some of the old—that part of the old belief system that you experience as still serving you—and so it will be a combination of the new and the old, not a rejection of the old from top to bottom....

"**You simply didn't have a complete understanding. You needed more information.**

"**Transcending current beliefs is not an outright rejection of them; it is an 'adding to' them.**

"Now that you have more information that you can add to what you presently believe, you can enlarge your beliefs—not *completely reject* them, *enlarge* them— and move on with your lives in a new way.

"A way that works." (the seducing spirit calling itself "God;" bold & underline added)[6]

In this emerging "make-it-up-as-you-go-along" faith, a way that works is naturally making it up.

"The Third Testament calls us to imitate and participate in God's creativity ..." (Leonard Sweet)[7]

"As co-creators with God, **inventing new forms of** energymatter (**information**) is a part of the ongoing work of creation." (Leonard Sweet; parentheses in the original; emphasis added)[8]

Along with today's "larger," more "complete," "new understandings" that are *interfaith*, *The Shack* is likewise a prime example that people today neither think twice about embracing *new* "understandings" of God and His Son, the Lord Jesus Christ, nor give it a second thought if these new "understandings" are *invented* and *conceived* by man. But then why would they? In today's shifting Christianity more and more people prefer to think outside the "box" and even see it as "idolatry" to believe God's Word. Moreover, pastors and theologians even preach and teach and write on how they found "God" in *The Shack* and even quote this fictitious, make-believe "God" as *God*! And, obviously, people don't even *begin* to see this *invented* "truth" as a *rejection* of the "old" truth of God's Word. Quite the contrary. The made-up "truth" of *The Shack* is praised as "*solid biblical truth*" that is *biblically accurate, precise, faithful, and true* with *nothing heretical or that contradicts the Bible.*

People in today's shifting Christianity don't and won't give any of it a second thought—including that Sweet has taught that creating "your 'new account' of everything old'" is "your part of the 'I Am' that we are"[9]—because they, having itching ears, have heaped to themselves teachers that tell them what they want to hear. And they do not want to hear *the truth*. To the contrary, people today *want* to "*rethink*" and "*reimagine*"

God and His Word into *new* and "*better*" "understandings" that they are *willing* to accept, which of course are "*outside*"—i.e., "*larger*" *than*—the resented "box" of the absolute truth of God's Word.

To *enlarge* is to "make or become bigger" or to "add to," which obviously *adds* to the "old." And the desire for "bigger" "truth"—i.e., "truth" that is "bigger" than the *particular* truth of *God's Word*—is why this emerging faith of Oneness/panentheism is emerging in the first place. Not even people in today's shifting Christianity are willing to accept the Christian truth and faith of the true God that is given to us by God in the Word of God. They want a "truth" and "faith" and "God" and "kingdom" that are "bigger." They, along with the world, want the elastic "truth" of the circle of Oneness that keeps stretching and stretching—enlarging and enlarging—until it encompasses *everyone and everything*.

Nevertheless, the absolute truth of God *is what it is*. God does not *enlarge* the *truth* of *what is*. Either we are willing to believe and obey it as it is, or we are not. If we are willing, God does *enlarge* our *heart* to thus believe and obey it *as it is* -- "I will run the way of thy commandments, when thou shalt *enlarge* my *heart*" (Psalm 119:32). But God does not cater to those who are not willing to accept it by enlarging—stretching—*the truth* for them. Only Satan does that; after all, "he is a liar, and the father of it" (John 8:44).

It used to be obvious that to *stretch the truth* is to *lie*, but not any more. Now, to stretch the truth is to tell new "truth." Besides, the difference between truth and falsehood, truth and lies, is irrelevant today since the circle of Oneness conveniently brings these polar opposites together as one. And since the circle of Oneness is also an all-encompassing "combination" of *both* the new *and* the old, the new will neither be seen as a rejection of the old nor as a lie by those in this emerging faith. Even so, to *enlarge* the truth, to conceive, create, and invent *new* "truth," is to clearly *add* to God's words which is to "be found a *liar*." God and His Son, Who are not in the no-beginning-no-end circle of Oneness, still know the difference:

"**Add thou not unto his words**, *lest he reprove thee, and thou be found a* **liar**." *(Proverbs 30:6)*

"I am Alpha and Omega, the beginning and the end, the first and the last. **Blessed are they that do his commandments, that they may have right to the tree of life**, *and may enter in through the gates into the city.* **For without are** *dogs, and sorcerers, and whoremongers, and murderers, and* **idolaters, and whosoever loveth and maketh a lie**. *I Jesus have sent mine angel to testify unto you these things in* <u>the churches</u>.... *And the Spirit and the bride say, Come. And let him that heareth say, Come. And let him that is athirst come. And whosoever* <u>will</u>, *let him take the water of life freely. For I testify unto every man that heareth the words of the prophecy of this book,* **If any man shall add unto these things**, *God shall add unto him the plagues that are written in this book:* **And if any man shall take away from the words** *of the book of this prophecy, God shall take away his part out of the book of life, and out of the holy city, and from the things which are written in this book." (Revelation 22:13-19)*

"I know that, whatsoever God doeth, it shall be for ever: nothing can be put to it, nor anything taken from it: and God doeth it, that men should fear before him." (Ecclesiastes 3:14)

"For ever, O LORD, *thy word is settled in heaven." (Psalm 119:89)*

Along with taking away *from* the words, people today are also going further in even attempting to take away *the words* altogether. And of course they are also *adding* their invented new kind of "truth" to enlarge—stretch—it all. This way they can enlarge the narrow way to include the broad way, "humbly" conceiving and inventing "*all new*" "truths" of "God" that "heal the divisions" and bring "unity" and "relationship" rather than keep people "out." Since people are rejecting that God's Word of absolute truth is *literal*, they certainly have nothing to fear in all their adding to and taking away from it in this pursuit of "*everything* new," right?

> *"Be not deceived; God is not mocked: for whatsoever a man soweth, that shall he also reap." (Galatians 6:7)*

> *"For our transgressions are multiplied before thee, and our sins testify against us: for our transgressions are with us; and as for our iniquities, we know them;* **in transgressing and lying against the LORD, and departing away from our God, speaking oppression and revolt, conceiving and uttering from the heart words of falsehood.***" (Isaiah 59:12-13)*

"We were not put here to 'keep commandments' but to *conceive* beauty, truth, and goodness." (Leonard Sweet; emphasis added)[10]

"People need room to ***move and choose and resist airtight propositions*** that don't allow free breathing (i.e., ***freedom***). Jesus left space for people to *make their own* responses to him. **He did not dictate to his disciples *what they were to believe* about him: 'Who do you say I am?'**" (Leonard Sweet; parentheses in the original; emphasis added)[11]

"… the gospel of love … blesses the world with ***new understandings of <u>who Jesus is</u>***.'" (Leonard Sweet; emphasis added)[12]

"The Third Testament is ***everything new*** about the old, old story." (Leonard Sweet; emphasis added)[13]

People who want the freedom to "*make-it-up-as-you-go-along*"[14] have ample room to "*move and choose and resist*" in the all-encompassing circle of relationship of Oneness. Here, everyone has the freedom to "*add unto*" and "*take away from*" "the old, old story" to their heart's content in "reimagining" God and His Son however they choose. But, as mentioned earlier, any "reimagined" "God" and/or "Jesus"/"Christ" is a counterfeit that is no more "real" and "true" than if people dressed up a literal wolf in sheep's clothing and claimed that it is their new understanding of what a "real" and "true" sheep is. Obviously, not even sheep can be set free from the "box" in order to "reimagine" sheep into a broader understanding. And yet people believe this about *God and His Son*. It is all totally absurd. Everything *is what it is*. True is true and false is false. There is no enlarging—stretching—what is true to include what is false.

Stretching the truth of Jesus into a broader understanding that allows people to "understand" whatever they want about "who Jesus is" and yet it is all just *new, larger "truth"* is also no less absurd than "reimagining" a broader understanding of $1+1$. The answer is 2. Even if people everywhere choose to include new "understandings" that $1+1=3$, or $1+1=0$, or $1+1=11$, or $1+1=56$, and so on, the answer is 2. A broader understanding that allows for all answers to be "true" so that no answer is *wrong* is the fuzzy thinking of Oneness that allows everyone to believe whatever is right in their own eyes. Again, rather than *"yea, let God be true, but every man a liar"* (Romans 3:4), today's emerging faith of Oneness arrogantly flips this upside down into "yea, let every man be true, but God a liar." This way *no one's* beliefs are seen as *"false* and *wrong"* and people can thus answer the Lord Jesus Christ's question, "But whom say ye that I am?" *however* they choose.

> *"When Jesus came into the coasts of Caesarea Philippi, he asked his disciples, saying, Whom do men say that I the Son of man am? And they said, Some say that thou art John the Baptist: some, Elias; and others, Jeremias, or one of the prophets. He saith unto them, But whom say ye that I am? And Simon Peter answered and said, Thou art the Christ, the Son of the living God. And Jesus answered and said unto him, Blessed art thou, Simon Bar-jona: for flesh and blood hath not revealed it unto thee, but my Father which is in heaven." (Matthew 16:13-17)*

> *"In the last day, that great day of the feast, Jesus stood and cried, saying, If any man thirst, let him come unto **me**, and drink. **He that believeth on me**, as the scripture hath said, **out of his belly shall flow rivers of living water**. (But this spake he of the Spirit, which they that <u>believe on him</u> should receive: for the Holy Ghost was not yet given; because that Jesus was not yet glorified.) Many of the people therefore, when they heard this saying, said, Of a truth this is the Prophet. Others said, This is the Christ. But some said, Shall Christ come out of Galilee? Hath not the scripture said, That Christ cometh of the seed of David, and out of the town of Bethlehem, where David was? So there was a division among the people because of him. And some of them would have taken him; but no man laid hands on him." (John 7:37-44)*

In today's desire for *new* "understandings" of *"who Jesus is,"* the *truth* of Who Jesus is as set forth in God's Holy Scriptures obviously becomes irrelevant. Likewise, the many prophecies that foretold His coming so that people could recognize Him when He came become irrelevant as well. The same is true of the prophecies that *foretell* His *coming return*. Think about it. If Jesus can be "understood" however anyone chooses then why would it matter if people mistakenly understand *someone else* to be Him that *isn't Him*? New "understandings" know nothing of either the fulfilled or the yet-to-be-fulfilled prophecies of Scripture. In fact, new "understandings" know nothing of Scripture. But isn't that the point of "reimagining" it all *outside* the "box" of God's Word of truth?

> *"Be astonished, O ye heavens, at this, and be horribly afraid, be ye very desolate, saith the LORD. For my people have committed two evils; **they have forsaken me the fountain of living waters**, and hewed them out cisterns, broken cisterns, that can hold no water." (Jeremiah 2:12-13)*

Despite today's "reimaginings," the true Lord Jesus Christ is a *Person* Who *is* Who He *is*, and the *Person* of the Lord Jesus Christ cannot be *enlarged* into other than Who He *is*. And, no, neither is a *community* the Lord Jesus Christ, no matter how many people in this community absurdly believe that *they* "become *Jesus.*" (The fact that "truth" does not require *thinking* in this emerging faith certainly explains *a whole lot.*) No matter how many people choose to absurdly imagine otherwise, neither Jesus nor God's Word of truth support their desired freedom to make it all up as they go along. This freedom to believe and do whatever is right in one's own eyes is found only in today's preferred new make-believe "truth"—a "truth" that caters to today's pursuit of Oneness and its shift from affirming *the correct truth of God and His Son* to affirming *people in their incorrect "truth."*

> "**Truth is not something you *assent* to, not something you *think*** ...
>
> "Jesus promised his disciples, 'the Spirit of truth will lead you into all truth.'
>
> "Once the truth has set you free, **what truth will you set free?**
>
> "**Each one of us is free to *become* Jesus, a living truth**, ..." (Leonard Sweet; emphasis added)[15]
>
> "**Jesus** left us with one thing: ***himself***, in the form of his body, **a community** that shares *stories* of *healing* and *love*.... *This difference* in how and where we encounter the sacred—in *propositions* or in *relations*—is *fundamental*....
>
> "Truth is defined as a Person not a *proposition*....
>
> "The notion that what God wants from us more than anything is *intellectual assents to some dogmas* or to the definition of discipleship as *obedience and devotion and praise*: This is what you want from your dog, or your horse (forget your cat)." (Leonard Sweet; parentheses in the original; emphasis added)[16]

First, *the Person* of Jesus *defines the truth*, and *the truth* of *the* Person of Jesus *is* what it *is*. It is not that the <u>Person</u> of Jesus can be "redefined" and "reimagined" however anyone chooses according to their own "understanding" and "idea" of "truth"! A *person is* who that *person is*. Anyone in their right mind knows that their spouse is a *specific person*. They also know that if they chose to believe that anyone else with the same name as their spouse was just *another* "understanding" or a "*new* understanding" of their spouse they would soon find themselves separated from their spouse! And yet even though people would rightly see all this as absurdity when it comes to their *spouse* they still believe this about *Jesus*. They simply aren't willing to accept that *He is Who He is*. Even so, only one's *true* spouse is one's *true* spouse, and no less so is only the *true* Jesus the *true Jesus* no matter how many people want the freedom to move and choose and resist *Who He is*. It is knowing and believing the truth/Gospel/doctrine ("propositions") of *Who Jesus is* that gives us the *true Person* of Jesus in an eternal relationship. And this *true* Person of Jesus is the <u>Lord</u> Jesus Christ Who is indeed to be *believed* and *obeyed*.

Second, people do not "*become Jesus*" "*himself*" or "*a living truth*," nor do they set "*truth*" free. Likewise, people do not "<u>become</u> the Third Testament"[17] thereby replacing "the old, old story" with their *own* new, new story of the "truth" of <u>themselves</u> and *their own lives*. Despite the absurd claims to the contrary, today's emerging new kind of "faith" and new kind of "truth" of a new kind of "Jesus" (that apparently is also a new kind of "Person") are *not* "new enlargements of truths *that the Bible already teaches*." But they are indeed "*everything* new."

Again, with this new kind of "Jesus" that even "[e]*ach one of us is free to become*," why would it matter if people are *mistaken*, i.e., *incorrect*, in understanding *someone else* to be Him that *isn't Him*? Sadly, in this emerging faith of Oneness it wouldn't—and even already doesn't—matter at all. And, besides, this mission to enlarge/stretch the "old" truth of Who God and His Son are, which *we* are to believe, is in fact a mission to enlarge/stretch the Kingdom of God to *include* all those who believe otherwise.

It is thus fitting that, along with meaning "to enlarge beyond proper limits," the word *stretch* also means "to lengthen <u>by force</u>."[18] Jesus pointed out that "*And from the* days of John the Baptist until now the kingdom of heaven suffereth violence, and the violent take it *by force*" (Matthew 11:12). Of course, the attempt to take the Kingdom *by force* will take on a whole new dimension when Satan's emerging kingdom of Oneness has fully emerged along with his coming *Antichrist*.[19] But then the Antichrist will be just a "new understanding" of Christ, right? And this new kind of "Christ" will be very befitting of today's emerging *anti*-Christianity that is seen as just "a new kind of Christianity."

> *"Even him, whose coming is after the working of Satan with all power and signs and lying wonders, and with all deceivableness of unrighteousness in them that perish;* **because they received not the love of the truth, that they might be saved.** *And for this cause God shall send them strong delusion,* **that they should believe a lie***: That they all might be damned* **who believed not the truth**, *but had pleasure in unrighteousness." (2 Thessalonians 2:9-12)*

> **"And he opened his mouth in blasphemy against God, to blaspheme his name,** *and his tabernacle, and them that dwell in heaven.... And* **all** *that dwell upon the earth* **shall worship him, whose names are not written in the book of life of <u>the Lamb</u>** *slain from the foundation of the world.* **If any man have an ear, let him hear.***" (Revelation 13:6, 8-9)*

Again, a *corner* stone obviously doesn't work in the *circle* of Oneness. So this emerging faith of Oneness is thus "reimagining" the Lamb of God—the Lord Jesus Christ—into "new understandings" in order to smooth and round off His offensive corners. The Word of God is being "reimagined" for the same reason. If the *corner stone* doesn't work in a circle then obviously neither do *the truth and faith of the corner stone*. It *all* must be smoothed and rounded off in order to be included in the all-encompassing circle of relationship of Oneness that is attempting to enlarge/stretch/force the Kingdom of God beyond the limits set by God in His Word of absolute truth. Without question, everything is changing in today's open revolution against believing and obeying God and His Son.

39

Breaking free from the soul "sort" in the "kingdom" that "transcends and includes all religions"

Again, this emerging faith of Oneness *must* "*Only Connect*" *truth and falsehood* and *right and wrong* in order to transform this "old" divisive truth into a new "*unified form* that makes no one *wrong.*" And this transformation of the "old" *either/or* truth of God's Word that divides opposites into a new *both/and* "truth" of Oneness that unites opposites *must* include connecting its divisive truth in which either *people believe in Jesus and have God* or *they do not believe in Jesus and do not have God*. After all, it's the *do not have God* part that is being done away with in today's "reimagining" of it *all*. So in the new "bigger" and *broader* "truth" of this emerging faith not only is *believing* in Jesus being "reimagined" as irrelevant so that Jesus can then be "reimagined" and "understood" *however* anyone chooses, but the either/or is also being "reimagined" into a both/and so that both *those who do* and *those who do not* believe in Jesus can have God.

> "**To absolutize one's own religion as *the only way*** means that one sees all of the other religious traditions of the world as **wrong** ..." (Marcus Borg; emphasis added)[1]

> "**Think *outside the box***. Reject 'either/or' and consider '**both/and**.'" (the seducing spirit calling itself "God;" bold added)[2]

> "This is who Jesus is for us as Christians.... **And we can say 'This is who Jesus is *for us*' *without* also saying 'And God is known *only* in Jesus.'**" (Marcus

And, again, as Mike Morrell quotes emerging church leader Brian McLaren saying, **"Jesus is the Way to God** and abundant life, it **doesn't mean he stands *in* the way to divine access!**"[4] Likewise, according to Leonard Sweet:

> "[W]hile there is more than one way of being a true believer, there is still one way, and that way is Christ.... Once again, theologian/evangelism professor William J. Abraham says it best: 'It is perfectly consistent to hold **both** that Jesus is the **exclusive path to God *and* that people may genuinely encounter God** outside the *Christian* church **without explicitly knowing about Jesus of Nazareth**.'" (emphasis added)[5]

Today's emerging faith is unarguably "*outside*"—i.e., "*bigger*" than—the resented "box" of God's Word of absolute truth. Again, as the "*one mediator between God and men*," "*the man Christ Jesus*" does stand "*in the way*" of "*divine access*"—access to the *true* God, that is. People can bypass Jesus in accessing the panentheistic interfaith "God" of Oneness all they want. But this both/and that includes those who *do not believe in Jesus* is a both/and that accesses a *false* "God" that has no power to save *anyone*, including those who blindly believe they are accessing this *false* "God" through Jesus. Despite the growing unbelief of people today, the *true* God's Word is clear that His salvation is *either/or*, not *both/and*. Those who are shifting to a both/and "*salvation*" are shifting to the both/and "*God*."

> "Take heed, brethren, lest there be in any of you an evil heart of unbelief, in departing from the living God." (Hebrews 3:12)

> **"Jesus cried and said, He that believeth on me, believeth not on me, but on him that sent me.... I am come a light into the world, that whosoever believeth on me should not abide in darkness.** And if any man hear my words, and believe not, I judge him not: for I came not to judge the world, but to save the world. **He that rejecteth me, and receiveth not my words**, hath one that judgeth him: the word that I have spoken, **the same shall judge him in the last day. For I have not spoken of myself; but the Father which sent me, he gave me a commandment**, what I should say, and **what I should speak**. And I know that **his commandment is life everlasting: whatsoever I speak therefore, even as the Father said unto me, so I speak.**" (John 12:44, 46-50)

> "It is the spirit that quickeneth; the flesh profiteth nothing: **the words that I speak unto you**, they are spirit, and **they are life**. But there are some of you that believe not...." (John 6:63-64)

> "Jesus saith unto him, I am the way, the truth, and the life: **no man cometh unto the Father, but by me**." (John 14:6)

The words that Jesus spoke as commanded by the Father likewise include:

> "For God so loved the world, that he gave his only begotten Son, **that whosoever believeth in him should not perish, but have everlasting life**. For God sent not his Son into the world to condemn the world; but that the world through him

*might be saved. He that believeth on him is not condemned: but **he that believeth not is condemned already**, because he hath not believed in the name of the only begotten Son of God." (John 3:16-18)*

*"Jesus said unto them, ... He that is of God heareth **God's words**: ye therefore hear them not, because ye are not of God." (John 8:42, 47)*

It is not the faith of God that renders God's words irrelevant but, rather, the emerging faith of the *false* "God" of Oneness. And *of course* a *false* "God" "transcends" the words of *God* that are to be *believed* and *obeyed*!

"Tomorrow's God does not require anyone to *believe* in God." (the seducing spirit calling itself "God;" emphasis added)[6]

"Words are *the least* reliable purveyor of *Truth*." (the seducing spirit calling itself "God;" emphasis added)[7]

"**God** is not only real, but **knowable**. Moreover, the sacred is **known** not in a set of statements about God, but **experientially**, as a Mystery **beyond *all* language**. This Mystery—God—**transcends *all*** of our domestications of reality, including those generated by **theology and even the Bible itself**.... God also transcends peoples **and religions** ...

"Life with God is **not about *believing*** certain teachings about God. It is about a covenant—a relationship. More specifically, it is **about becoming conscious of a *relationship* that underline{already} exists** ..." (Marcus Borg; emphasis added)[8]

*"Whosoever transgresseth, and abideth not in **the doctrine of Christ, hath not God**. He that abideth in the doctrine of Christ, he hath both the Father and the Son." (2 John 1:9)*

Even though God is "not willing that any should perish" and be kept out of His Kingdom, people are *keeping themselves out* in their unwillingness to *believe the truth of the true Lord Jesus Christ* to be *saved* from their *sins*. This truth is just too "outdated" for today's whole new way of thinking and "knowing" and "relating." Even so, God said what He meant and meant what He said in the words of His Word of truth. But in the attempt to do away with the *do not have God* part, the absolute truth of God's Word is being replaced with the new "bigger" and *broader* "truth" of the unconditional, *universal* relationship/salvation of the *"New* Gospel" of today's emerging faith of Oneness.

"A New Spirituality truly is **emerging upon the earth**, and the idea of **Oneness** is at its core." (Neale Donald Walsch; emphasis added)[9]

"A quantum spirituality challenges the church to bear its past and to dare its future by sticking its big TOE ['Theory of Everything'] into the time and place of the present....

"Then, and only then, will a *New Light* movement of 'world-making' faith have helped to create the world that is to, and may yet, be. Then, and only then, will earthlings have uncovered the meaning of these words, some of the last words poet/activist/*contemplative*/bridge between East and West Thomas Merton uttered:

"We are already one. But we imagine that we are not. And

what we have to recover is our original unity." (Leonard Sweet; emphasis added)[10]

"Go, therefore, and teach ye all nations, spreading far and wide **The New Gospel**: **"WE ARE ALL ONE.**

"OURS IS NOT A BETTER WAY, **OURS IS MERELY ANOTHER WAY**." (the seducing spirit calling itself "God;" bold added)[11]

"**All** religions have something to do with **the whole, the totality**." (Leonard Sweet; emphasis added)[12]

*"For I am not ashamed of **the gospel of Christ**: for it is the power of God unto **salvation** to every one that **believeth**; to the Jew first, and also to the Greek." (Romans 1:16)*

"We have fought over the doctrines whereby men shall be saved.... **We have regarded half the world as *lost* and only the Christian *believer* as saved, yet** all the time Christ has told us that love is the way into the kingdom, and that the fact of **the *presence* of divinity *in each of us* makes us eligible for that kingdom.... *Men are not saved by belief*** in the formulation of a theological dogma, **but by the fact of His living Presence**, of the living immediate **Christ**." (Alice Bailey; emphasis added)[13]

"When, therefore, sight has been attained and the light streams forth, revelation of **the oneness of all life** is a simple and immediate occurrence ...

"[I]n these days many are attaining sight and light is pouring in....

"An increase of pressure on the part of all who recognize the factual nature of **the inner subjective kingdom of God**, will produce amazing results." (the seducing spirit calling itself Djwhal Khul; emphasis added)[14]

Actually, this emerging "New Gospel" of Oneness—i.e., this *upside-down* "Good News" of Satan's lie of Oneness in which it is *not* necessary to believe the truth/doctrine/Gospel of the true Lord Jesus Christ to have either God or the Lord Jesus Christ—has already been producing *tragic* results. And it has already been making sweeping changes to what is being taught (make that "dialogued") and believed in today's shifting Christianity.

"When you live **in union with Christ**, you don't need answers to problems so much as you need **the presence of Christ, which is the kingdom of God. We don't need a propositional presence** ..." (Leonard Sweet; emphasis added)[15]

"**The kingdom of God breaks free of religion with Jesus** ...

"If God's hand is MRI-shaped—mission-shaped, relation-shaped, incarnation-shaped—then Jesus' followers are **shapesmiths of the Spirit**....

"The passion for *evangelism* is nothing other than a passion for reading the signs of what God is up to, **connecting the God-dots**, signing up, and then laying down our lives on God's dotted lines. The French Jesuit Jean Danielou, writing on the theology of mission in the 1950s, said that **fruitful missionary efforts 'stopped thinking of bringing Christ to India ... but rather started thinking about**

finding Christ <u>already</u> there.'" (Leonard Sweet; last ellipsis dots in the original; emphasis added)[16]

*"And he said unto them, **Go ye into all the world, and <u>preach the gospel</u> to every creature**." (Mark 16:15)*

Since this emerging faith of Oneness/panentheism gives everyone the freedom to define and imagine "God" however they choose, it is to be expected that people are seen as *"shapesmiths of the Spirit."* And likewise according to Sweet, *"The purpose of the church is to give form to, to put into form and shape, the energymatter known as Jesus Christ,"*[17] and *"the Word is made flesh differently ... in forms fundamental to, shapes revelatory of, the age."*[18] Conveniently for those who are exchanging the words of God's Word for the freedom to "reimagine" and "shape" God and His Son into a fashion that they are willing to accept, not only is the "God"/"Spirit"/"Christ" of this emerging faith *in everyone and everything* but the definition of *shapesmith* is "[o]ne that undertakes to *improve* the form of the body."[19] And in this emerging faith *man* can and does seek to "*improve*" upon <u>God</u> (Father, Son, and Holy Spirit) by shaping—i.e., "[f]orming; molding; casting; conceiving; giving form"[20]—a *new* and *improved* "reimagined" "God" that is *"bigger"* and *"better"* than the *"old"* God of the *Christian* truth and faith, i.e., of the Word of God.

This mission all sounds remarkably similar to someone making an idol, shaping and fashioning their god into whatever form they want. And yet in this revolution against the truth and faith of the true God those who are deemed guilty of "idolatry" are those who *believe* the truth/doctrine ("propositions") of the Word of *God*.

*"Ye are my witnesses, saith the LORD, and my servant whom I have chosen: that ye may know and believe me, and understand that I am he: **before me there was no God formed, neither shall there be after me**." (Isaiah 43:10)*

*"Of the Rock that begat thee thou art unmindful, and **hast forgotten God that formed thee**.... for they are a very froward generation, children in whom is no faith. They have moved me to jealousy with **that which is not God**; they have provoked me to anger with their vanities ... For they are a nation void of counsel, neither is there any understanding in them. O that they were wise, that they understood this, that they would consider their latter end!... And he shall say, Where are their gods, their rock in whom they trusted, ... let them rise up and help you, and be your protection. See now that I, even I, am he, and there is no god with me ..."* (Deuteronomy 32:18, 20-21, 28-29, 37-39)

*"And **the Father himself**, which hath sent me, hath borne witness of me. **Ye have neither heard his voice at any time, nor seen his shape**. And ye have not his word abiding in you: for whom he hath sent, him ye believe not." (John 5:37-38)*

With a "reimagined" "*Christ*" ("*Messiah*") that is also conveniently "*put into form and shape*" by *man*, what anyone *believes* is obviously completely irrelevant. Thus, in this emerging faith that seeks to "Only Connect" through its "*relational theology*," "evangelism" is not about bringing the Gospel of Christ to places such as India but "about finding Christ already there" regardless of the *beliefs* and *religion* of the people there. It is therefore fitting that Sweet is the "E. Stanley Jones Professor of Evangelism" at Drew University.[21] This Professor of Evangelism program is sponsored by The Foundation for Evangelism, which "celebrates the life and ministry of Dr. E. Stanley Jones [who] became the apostle to India, working closely with *Mahatma Gandhi*" and who then wrote of what he learned in his highly esteemed 1925 book, *The Christ of the Indian Road*, that "is considered his seminal work."[22] Not surprisingly, the teachings of this book of Jones, "a celebrated Methodist missionary and theologian,"[23] resemble the teachings of Sweet, as well as of the other leaders of this emerging faith of Oneness/panentheism. This faith has been steadily emerging for a long time. Sadly, *many* have shifted to darkness in their search for a "*bigger*" "God" and a "*bigger*" "Christ" and a "*bigger*" "kingdom of God" that "*transcend*"—i.e., that can be found *outside* the "box" of—the Christian truth and faith of *God's Word*. The following quotes are just a small sampling taken from E. Stanley Jones' book, *The Christ of the Indian Road*:

> "India has gone too far and has slipped into pantheism—everything God—but that will be **corrected to a *panentheism*—everything in God**. This will bring us a sense of **the unity of all life**. It should make a more friendly and meaningful and kindly universe." (emphasis added)[24]

> "It is an actual fact of experience that when you deepen **the Christ consciousness** you deepen **the God-consciousness**." (emphasis added)[25]

> "*It is **Christ** who **unites** us; it is **doctrines** that **divide**.*" (bold added)[26]

> "We must call men, **not to** loyalty to a ***belief*** but loyalty to a *Person*." (emphasis added)[27]

> "**Christianity is actually breaking out beyond the borders of** the ***Christian*** Church and is being seen in most unexpected places." (emphasis added)[28]

> "'***Hindu* Christians!**' said a discerning Hindu with a smile to me as we watched a crowd of earnest ***Hindu*** social workers." (emphasis added)[29]

> "In conversation with him ['India's great soul, Mahatma Gandhi'] one day I said, 'Mahatma Gandhi, I am very anxious to see *Christianity* naturalised in India, so that it shall be no longer a foreign thing identified with a foreign people and a foreign government, but a part of the national life of India and *contributing* its power to India's uplift and *redemption*. What would you suggest that we do to make that possible?' He very gravely and thoughtfully replied: ...

> "Fourth, I would suggest that you **study the *non-Christian* religions and culture** more sympathetically in order to **find the good that is in them**, so that you might have a more sympathetic approach to the people.' Quite right. We should be grateful for **any truth found *anywhere***, knowing that it is a finger post that **points to Jesus**, who is the Truth." (emphasis added)[30]

> "A *Hindu* lawyer of fine ability gave an address to which I listened on the topic, 'The Inescapable Christ.' He said: 'We have not been able to escape him. There was a time when our hearts were bitter and sore against him but he is melting them by his own winsomeness. Jesus is slowly but surely entering all men in India—yea *all men*.' The only thing I could think of all through the address was this: 'Other sheep I have, which are not of this fold. Them also I must bring.' **How is it possible to limit or demarcate the *lines* of *the Kingdom* any more?** ... He eats with publicans and sinners and with **the Hindu** too....

> "When this Galilean was upon earth with us he said of the outside Gentile's faith, 'I have not found so great faith *even* in Israel.' He must be saying the same thing again, for **the 'outside' world** surprises us again." (emphasis added)[31]
>
> "Every nation has its peculiar contribution to make to the interpretation of Christianity. The Son of man is too great to be expressed by any one portion of humanity. Those that *differ* from us most will probably contribute most to our expression of Christianity....
>
> "India too hopes that the world may some day be in need of a new formula. She too has her word ready. It will be spelled 'Atma'—*spirit*. The word 'Atma' runs like a refrain through everything in India. The followers of the Christ of the Indian Road will show us the real meaning of a *spiritual* life. They will sit lightly to earthly things and abandon themselves to **the spirit**.
>
> "Along with that will come the sense of **the unity and harmony running through things**.... The followers of the Christ of the Indian Road will be harmonised and peaceful. **Meditation** to them will be real. Religion will mean quiet *realisation*. **God will be the harmonising bond of all**." (emphasis added)[32]

For starters, the "Christ" of the Indian—Hindu—road is the false *East-meets-West* "Christ" of Oneness that is *immanent in everyone and everything* as the inner spirit/soul of *all things*. And, *of course* a "Jesus" who is a "Truth" that is "*any truth found anywhere*" will be "*winsome*" to anyone and everyone who is "bitter and sore" against the truth of Who the *true* Jesus Christ is! No surprise there. Indeed, the "Person" of the "Jesus" of Oneness is only a name that has been *emptied* of *the truth* of *Who the true Jesus is* so that this empty shell of a "Person" can then be filled with any "information" and any "understanding" that anyone in *any* religion/faith/culture chooses to believe about "who Jesus is." After all, the "Jesus" and the "kingdom of God" of this emerging faith of Oneness are "winsome" counterfeits specifically designed to "heal the divisions" between those who do *not* believe the truth of Jesus and those who do.

> "For if he that cometh preacheth **another Jesus**, whom we have not preached, or if ye receive **another spirit**, which ye have not received, or **another gospel**, which ye have not accepted, ye might well bear with him." (2 Corinthians 11:4)

No matter how many people prefer a "bigger" and broader understanding of Jesus that includes "understandings" that are *not Christian—not scriptural*—a "reimagined" Jesus is not the true Jesus but "*another* Jesus." Neither is a "reimagined" "Spirit" that can be *shaped* by *man* the true Spirit but "*another* spirit." Likewise, a "reimagined" "Gospel According to ... You" is not the true Gospel but "*another* gospel." They are not the *true doctrine* of the *true Christ* in which we are to abide to have the *true God*. Rather, these broader "understandings" of Jesus are just as false as would be a broader understanding of sheep that included wolves dressed up in sheep's clothing. Dressing up any "understanding" with the name of "Jesus" no more makes it the true Jesus than dressing up any animal in lamb's clothing would make it a true lamb. Jesus is Who He is, and no less so than a lamb is what it is.

Again, just as one's spouse is a *specific person* only the *true Person* of Jesus is the *true Jesus*. To see all this as "loyalty" to the true *Person* of Jesus is no less absurd than it would be to see it as "loyalty" to one's spouse to choose to believe that anyone else with the same name as their spouse is just *another* "understanding" or a "*new* understanding" of their spouse. And yet people believe this about *the Son of God*. With upside-down "loyalty" to the Person of Jesus, people prefer a Lord, a Saviour, a Lamb of God, a Messiah that can be *"reimagined" ad infinitum ad nauseam*—however one *chooses*, of course.

To say that "any truth found anywhere" "points to *Jesus*" is as absurd as it gets—especially since in this emerging faith "*truth*" is as immanent as its panentheistic "God" that is *in everyone and everywhere*. Again, the true Person of Jesus defines the truth; how people choose to define "truth" does not define the Person of Jesus. Only the *true* Person of Jesus is the *true Jesus*, and only the *true Jesus* is the way to the *true* God. But since people simply are not willing to accept that *Jesus is Who He is* they are thus also determined to separate "*the way*" of Jesus from the true *Person* of Jesus in order to set the world free from having to *believe* in *Jesus*. According to United Christian Ashrams, which was founded by E. Stanley Jones and absurdly praised as "*ministry*" by The Foundation for Evangelism[33]:

> "He [Jones] did not attack Hinduism, Buddhism, Islam, or any Indian religion. He presented the Gospel of Jesus Christ, disentangled from western systems and cultures, and their sometimes non-Christian expressions. '**The way of Jesus** should be—but often isn't—the way of Christianity,' he said. 'Western civilization is only partly Christianized.'...
>
> "He inaugurated '**round table conferences**' at which **Christian and non-Christian** sat down **as equals** to share their testimonies **as to how their religious experiences enabled them to live better**....
>
> "'*The Christ of the Indian Road*' ... became a best seller. It sold over a million copies and *has influenced the course of missionary thinking*....
>
> "This opening up of nations to receiving **Christ within their *own framework*** marked *a new approach in missions*. It came to be known as '*indigenization*'. He helped to re-establish **the Indian 'Ashram'** (or forest retreat) as a means of drawing men and women together for days at a time **to study in depth their own spiritual natures and quest, and *what the different faiths offered*** individuals. Many came to refute the Christian Gospel or to extol their own, but many came to accept **Christ's *way of life*.**" (parentheses in the original; emphasis added)[34]

Sadly, Jones, a *panentheist*, has indeed "*influenced the course of missionary thinking.*" And, clearly, he "presented the Gospel of Jesus Christ" "disentangled" *from the Gospel of Jesus Christ* (i.e., from the truth of Who He is and what He did for us) to give people the freedom to follow—"*reimagine*"—"*the way* of Jesus"/"Christ's *way of life*" in any "framework" of any faith/religion of their choosing. And today's shifting Christianity is doing likewise in its attempt to bring the faiths/religions together in the Oneness of an *interfaith* "kingdom" of an *interfaith* "God." After all, in "reimagining" it *all* to be *interfaith* the world can thus "break free" from the "soul-sort narrative" in which "everyone will be sorted into either the destruction/damnation or the redemption/salvation bin" and replace it with the *universal* "salvation" of the emerging *Wordless* faith of Oneness. No *Word*, no *fear*, right?

> "This evil people, which refuse to hear my words, which walk in the imagination of their heart, and walk after other gods, to serve them, and to worship them, shall even be as this girdle, which is good for nothing." (Jeremiah 13:10)

"Thus saith the LORD of hosts, ... To whom shall I speak, and give warning, that they may hear? behold, their ear is uncircumcised, and they cannot hearken: behold, the word of the LORD is unto them a reproach; they have no delight in it.... Stand ye in the ways, and see, and ask for the old paths, where is the good way, and walk therein, and ye shall find rest for your souls. But they said, We will not walk therein." (Jeremiah 6:9-10, 16)

As is to be expected, in his 2010 book, *A New Kind of Christianity*, Brian McLaren's teachings also resemble those of Sweet (and the many other leaders of this emerging faith of Oneness). In 2003, Sweet and McLaren wrote a book together that is titled, *A Is for Abductive: The Language of the Emerging Church*. In this book, Sweet said of McLaren, "This book would not have been possible without *a deep compatibility of perspectives between Brian and me*,"[35] and McLaren said of Sweet, "I needed to seek out some new mentors, and Len was the first on my list."[36] In *A New Kind of Christianity*, McLaren (who, as is clearly *required* for Oneness, joins the other leaders of this emerging faith in "reimagining" John 14:6 and has also openly admitted—"we are in the early stages of *a radical reassessment of Jesus*" that is "led by ... Marcus Borg" and many others[37]) writes:

"In my own experience as a lover and reader of the Bible, as I am **freed from the *literalistic* and *dualistic* straitjacket** in which the **Greco-Roman** and **constitutional** approaches constrained me, I feel I can breathe a little freer, ..." (emphasis added)[38]

"[T]he **Greco-Roman** mind was habitually **dualistic**, in the sense that an enlightened or philosophic mind would always see **the world divided in two, the profane** physical world of matter, stuff, and change on the low side **and the sacred** *metaphysical* world of ideals, ideas, spirit, and changelessness on the high side." (emphasis added)[39]

"Religious determinists have offered us another determinism we could call the **'soul-sort' universe: everyone will be sorted into either the destruction/ damnation or the redemption/salvation bin**. Everyone is determined to end up in one bin or the other." (emphasis added)[40]

"**If we could *break free* from the Greco-Roman *soul-sort* narrative, think of what could *change*....** We would no longer envision a day when all other religions would be abolished and only our own will remain. We would no longer consider ourselves as normative and others as 'other.' **We would stop seeing *the line* that *separates good and evil* running between our religion and all others**. We would be **freed from** the tendency to always think '**insider/outsider**' and 'us/them.' We would learn to **discover God *in* the other**, and we would discover **a *bigger* 'us,'** in which people of **_all faiths_ can be included**....

"We would see that Jesus and his *message of peace and service* were right and true after all, and that Jesus was not a gift to one religion, but to the whole world....

"**Evangelism** would **cease to be a matter of *saving souls*** from a bad ending in the Greco-Roman soul-sort narrative. It would cease to be a proclamation of the *superiority* of the *Christian* religion. It would no longer require **hellfire-and-brimstone scare *tactics*** or slick promotional campaigns, as if *Jesus and his gospel* were products under exclusive proprietary licensure to the *Christian* religion ...

"No, instead, a reborn, postimperial evangelism would mean proclaiming the same good news of the kingdom of God that Jesus proclaimed.... It would mean recruiting people to defect from destructive ways and join God in the *missio dei* ('*mission* of *God*'), a decentralized, grassroots, spiritual-social movement dedicated to **plotting goodness** and saving the world from human evil—both personal and systemic. It would invite people into **lifelong spiritual *formation*** as disciples of Jesus, in a community dedicated (as we've seen) to teaching the most excellent way of love, ***whatever* the new disciple's religious affiliation or lack thereof**.

"This kind of evangelism would **celebrate the good** in the Christian religion and lament the bad, just as it would **in *every* other religion, calling people to *a way of life* in a *kingdom* (or *beautiful whole*) that transcends and includes *all religions***. Yes, it would welcome people into *communities of faith* in which they would **experience *formation* in *the way of Jesus***, and yes, you could **call these communities Christian** churches if you'd like, although you could **call them other things too**. *But* whatever you call these communities, **they would be interested in *breaking out* of the cocoons of *Christianity* that were spun within the Greco-Roman narrative, governed by a constitutional reading of Scripture, oriented around violent and tribal views of God, and so on**." (all parentheses in the original; emphasis added, except to *missio dei*)⁴¹

"Jesus didn't come to start a new religion to replace first Judaism and then all other religions, whether by the pen, the pulpit, the sword, or the apocalypse....

"Instead, **he came to announce a new kingdom, a new way of life, a new way of peace** that carried good news **to all people of every religion. A new kingdom is much *bigger* than a new religion, and in fact it has room for many religious traditions within it**." (emphasis added)⁴²

For starters, *true* evangelism is always a proclamation of the *preeminent superiority* of the <u>*truth*</u> of <u>*Jesus*</u>. And *the truth—the Gospel—*of *Jesus Christ* gives us the *Christian* faith. But in this mission to change and enlarge the truth of "who Jesus is" into new and "better" "understandings" that are *interfaith*, one of a growing number of absurd anti-Christian arguments is that Jesus isn't a Christian so we shouldn't expect His followers to be Christian. First of all, Jesus isn't a Christian—a believer/follower/disciple of Christ—because Jesus *is* Christ! Second, again, *the* <u>truth</u> *of Who Jesus* <u>is</u>—which is recorded by God in the Word of God—gives us the *Christian* faith, not faith that is *nonchristian*. Jesus neither changes nor enlarges the truth of Who He is to be more inclusive of those who are not willing to believe the truth of Who He is. Neither does God. And, no, to believe otherwise is not "humility."

"If we receive the witness of men, the witness of God is greater: for this is the witness of God which he hath testified of his Son. He that believeth on the Son of God hath the witness in himself: **he that believeth not God hath made him a liar;** *because he believeth not* **the record** *that God gave of his Son." (1 John 5:9-10)*

"Perhaps when our conservative friends ask those of us on this quest **if we believe in the *inerrancy* of Scripture**, our reply should be: '**No**, I believe the Scripture is *better* than inerrant. I believe **it's *beautiful*.**' If they ask us what we mean by beautiful, we can explain: 'It's beautiful for creating a community that extends across generations and cultures to engage with God so they can experience, in that engagement, the gift of revelation.' They probably won't be satisfied, but it might help them think a bit." (Brian McLaren; emphasis added)[43]

Helping people think outside the "box" of *God's inspired Scripture* does not help them at all. As addressed earlier, the *only* way to believe in a "beautiful *whole*" that encompasses all religions is to believe in the *errancy* of Scripture. Again, believing the literal, absolute truth of God's Word *precludes* believing in all this Oneness/wholeness and *they know it*. Hence the *shift* to thinking *outside* the truth and faith of God's *inspired, inerrant* Scripture. To see the *darkness* of Oneness that *unites all opposites* the light of God's Word *must be turned off*.

Sadly, another of the absurd anti-Christian arguments is the claim that Christians think "Christ" is "the last name" of Jesus. In today's desperation to avoid *believing* in Jesus the absurdity never ends. *Christ* is no more "the last name" of Jesus than *Messiah* is the last name of Jesus. Since the *Christ*—the *Messiah*—is <u>Who</u> He <u>is</u>, in God's Word of truth Jesus is called "Jesus Christ" as well as "Christ Jesus." So maybe people in this revolution against God and His Son should try absurdly arguing that Christians think "Jesus" is "the last name" of Christ since they obviously don't believe that Christ *Jesus* is the *Saviour*, either. If they did, they wouldn't be trying so hard to bypass *believing* in God's Messiah and Saviour.

No, Jesus Christ the Saviour and Messiah did not come "to start a new religion." He came to die for our sins, and *the truth of Who He is and what He did* clearly gives us the *Christian* faith/religion. It is those who are shifting to *darkness* who are trying to start a *new* religion—"a *new* kind of Christianity"—in which their "reimagined" "God" and "Christ" conveniently give an unconditional, *universal* salvation/reconciliation/ relationship/redemption/forgiveness to *everyone* regardless of which religious "label"— i.e., which religious faith/"truth"—they choose. And, yes, Jesus Christ is a gift to *the whole world*. But, sadly, even in today's shifting Christianity *many* are *rejecting* Him and His gift because they are not willing to *believe* the *truth* of this gift.

> "In giving us Jesus, God gave us a relational gift. Jesus was a *relational* gift not a *propositional* gift." (Leonard Sweet; emphasis added)[44]

> *"For God so loved the world, that he gave his only begotten Son, that whosoever* **believeth** *in him should not perish, but have everlasting life." (John 3:16)*

Today's mission to save the world from having to believe in the Saviour of the world is indeed changing *everything*. This leaves people to become their own savior—their own way to God. In other words, this leaves people to—in their own way—"become the Third Testament;" the significance of which will be addressed shortly. In breaking free from the truth of God's Word that clearly sets forth and divides *what <u>is</u> true and false, right and wrong, good and evil*, everyone has the freedom to define and imagine "God" and/or "Jesus"/"Christ" however they choose and to have this relationship however they choose in whatever religion/faith they choose. In this revolution of relational unbelief everyone can thus conceive for themselves whatever is "good, beautiful, and true" *in their own eyes* according to their own definition, their own "knowing," of good and evil without fear of being "lost" or "wrong." In this emerging faith of Oneness *no one* and *nothing* are "outside" its "kingdom of God."

> **"Yea, hath God said ...? ... Ye shall not surely die** ... *your eyes shall be opened, and ye shall be as gods, knowing good and evil." (Genesis 3:1b, 4-5)*

"When at last you see that there is no separation in God's World—that is, nothing which is not God—then, at last, will you let go of this invention of man which you have called Satan.

"If Satan exists, he exists as every thought you ever had of separation from Me. You cannot be separate from Me, for I Am All That Is....

"**Condemnation, being hurled into the everlasting fires of hell, was the ultimate scare tactic.** Yet now you need be afraid no more. For nothing can, or ever will, separate you from Me.

"**You and I are One**. We cannot be anything else if I Am What I Am: All That Is....

"I have no way to separate Myself from you—or anything else. 'Hell' is simply not knowing this. 'Salvation' is knowing and understanding it completely. You are now saved. **You needn't worry about what's going to happen to you 'after death' anymore**." (the seducing spirit calling itself "God;" bold added)[45]

"**That place of Oneness is heaven**.

"You are there now.

"You are never *not* there, because you are never *not* One with Me." (the seducing spirit calling itself "God;" bold added)[46]

"Now here is the Good News. *There is no other place to be*. The challenge is not to 'get to' heaven, but to know that you are already there. For **heaven is the Kingdom of God, and there is *no other kingdom that exists***." (the seducing spirit calling itself "God;" bold & underline added)[47]

"**[A]ll the world's souls can be set free**. The New Spirituality is *a civil rights movement for the soul*, freeing humanity at last **from the oppression of its belief in a separate, angry, violent, and fearful God**." (Neale Donald Walsch; emphasis added)[48]

"Humanity is being given an invitation to explore the wondrous possibilities of **Tomorrow's God**, and the world that **this new God** can create.

"**It's not a new God at all, of course, only a new understanding** of the present God, of the one God, of *The Only Thing That Is*." (Neale Donald Walsch; emphasis added)[49]

"It is time that the Church woke up to its **true *mission***, which is **to materialize the kingdom of God on earth, today, here and now**.... *People are no longer interested in a possible heavenly state or a probable hell*. They need to learn that **the kingdom is here, and must express itself on earth** ... The way into that kingdom is the way that Christ trod. It involves the sacrifice of the personal self for the good of the world, and the service of humanity ..." (Alice Bailey; emphasis added)[50]

"**The kingdom of God** is **not** some one particular church with its own peculiar **doctrines**, its particular formulations of **truth** ... and of approach to God.

"The true Church is **the kingdom of God** on earth ... **composed of *all*, regardless of** race or **creed, who live by the light within**, who have *discovered* the *fact* of the *mystical Christ* in their hearts.... **The members of the coming kingdom will think in terms of humanity as a whole** ..." (Alice Bailey; emphasis added)[51]

"We have regarded half the world as lost and only the Christian believer as saved, yet ... the *fact* of the presence of **divinity *in each of us* makes us eligible for that kingdom**.... **Men are *not* saved by *belief*** ..." (Alice Bailey; emphasis added)[52]

"[W]ill the churches have the vision and the courage to *let the bad old ways go* and turn to the people with the message that God is Love, proving the existence of that love by their own lives of simple loving service? Will they tell the people that Christ forever lives and **bid them turn their eyes away from the <u>old</u> doctrines of death and blood and divine appeasement and center them upon the Source of all life** ...? Will they teach that *the destruction of the old forms was needed* and that *their disappearance is the guarantee that a new and fuller unlimited spiritual life is now possible*? Will they remind the people that Christ Himself said that it is not possible to put new wine into old bottles?... Can churchmen of **all faiths** in both hemispheres attain **that inner spiritual light** which will make them light bearers and which will **evoke that greater light** which the new and anticipated revelation will surely bring?...

"**Within the churches today there are men responding to the <u>new</u> spiritual idealism**, to the *urgency* of the opportunity **and to *the need for* change**....

"Men want the conviction that **Christ** lives; that **the Coming One** - for Whom all men wait - will come and that He **will not be Christian, Hindu or Buddhist but will belong to *all men everywhere***....

"What is **the solution** of this intricate and difficult relationship throughout the world? **A *new* presentation of *truth*, because God is not a fundamentalist** ... a *new* mode of interpreting the ancient spiritual teaching ... These are **imperative changes**.

"**Nothing can prevent *the new world religion* from eventually *emerging*.... It will be hindered by the fundamentalists**, the *<u>narrow</u>*-minded and the theologians in all the world religions, by those **who refuse to <u>let go</u> the old interpretations and methods, who love the <u>old</u> doctrines** ..." (the seducing spirit calling itself Djwhal Khul; emphasis added)[53]

"*Whosoever transgresseth, and abideth not in* **the doctrine** *of Christ,* **hath not God**....*" (2 John 1:9)*

"*Take heed,* **brethren**, *lest there be in any of you an evil heart of* **unbelief**, *in departing from the living God." (Hebrews 3:12)*

"*Now the Spirit speaketh expressly, that in the latter times some shall* **depart from the faith, giving heed to seducing spirits, and doctrines of devils**.*" (1 Timothy 4:1)*

"**Thy word** *have I hid in mine heart, that I might not sin against thee.... I have chosen* **the way of truth**: *thy judgments have I laid before me.... And take not* **the word of truth** *utterly out of my mouth; for I have hoped in thy judgments.... I will speak of thy testimonies also before kings, and will not be ashamed....* **For ever, O Lord, thy word is settled in heaven**.... *The entrance of* **thy words** *giveth light; it giveth understanding unto the simple....* **Salvation is far from the** *wicked: **for they seek not thy statutes**.... I beheld the transgressors, and was grieved; because they kept not thy word.... **Thy word is true from the beginning: and every one of thy righteous judgments endureth for ever**." (Psalm 119:11, 30, 43, 46, 89, 130, 155, 158, 160; also see entire chapter)*

"But there were false prophets also among the people, even as there shall be false teachers among you, who privily shall bring in damnable heresies, even denying the Lord that bought them, and bring upon themselves swift destruction. And many shall follow their pernicious ways; by reason of whom **the way of truth shall be evil spoken of**." (2 Peter 2:1-2)

"Enter ye in at the strait gate: for wide is the gate, and broad is the way, that leadeth to destruction, and many there be which go in thereat: Because strait is the gate, and **narrow is the way, which leadeth unto life**, and few there be that find it." (Matthew 7:13-14)

40

The significance of a "Third Testament"

"With the crooked lines of *our* lives God is wanting to write 'a new account of everything old,' **a Third *Testament*....**

"The Third Testament calls us to imitate and *participate* in *God's* creativity ...

"Quantum spirituality is nothing more than your 'new account of everything old'-- your part of *the 'I Am'* that *we* are." (Leonard Sweet; emphasis added)[1]

"Like the conductor in *Fantasia*, God is whirling and swirling creation into being. The missional thrust begins in the *very being* of God....

"The ultimate story of the Bible, the metanarrative that unlocks the whole story, is that God is on a mission, and we are summoned to *participate* with God in that mission. The impulse to create, to conceive, is what lies at the heart of the missional....

"The universe was created by a God in motion, a God in mission, ... a God who is constantly creating, and a God **who has left a creation still <u>unfinished</u>**." (Leonard Sweet; emphasis added)[2]

Contrary to the many absurd evolutionary and panentheistic "reimaginings," the true God created the heaven and earth and *finished* His creation.

"In the beginning God created the heaven and the earth." (Genesis 1:1)

*"Thus the heavens and the earth were **finished**, and all the host of them." (Genesis 2:1)*

Yet it is not surprising that people in the emerging faith of Oneness/panentheism who imagine that *man* is to *"participate* in *God's* creativity"—man's "*part of the 'I Am'* that *we* are"—aren't willing to accept that God's creation is *finished*. And, of course, the same is true regarding God's *Word*. Along with a *finished creation*, neither are they willing to accept that *God's Word and its testaments are finished* and forever settled in heaven—"*For ever, O* LORD, *thy word is settled in heaven*" (Psalm 119:89). The two go hand in hand. After all, if God "has left a *creation* still unfinished" then God has left His creation of *heaven* still unfinished, and why would God's Word be *forever settled* in an *unfinished* heaven? Rather, if everything is still unfinished then nothing is ever settled and there is conveniently *no absolute truth*. And, therefore, everything becomes *changeable*, which is where "the excitement" lies in this emerging faith. So, contrary to the truth and faith of God's Word that is forever settled in God's finished heaven and is to be *believed* and *obeyed* as *what is*, for those who are "so eager to embrace the *new*, so open to *change* the old,"[3] <u>*nothing whatsoever*</u> is ever *settled* in today's emerging faith of Oneness/panentheism.

> "**The Process of Creation is never over**. It is never complete. I am never 'done.' This is another way of saying **everything is forever changing**....
>
> "When you look at a thing, you are not looking at a static 'something' that is 'standing there' in time and space. No!... Because **everything is moving, changing, evolving.** *Everything*....
>
> "The One Unchanging Truth is that **God is always changing**. That is the *truth*— and you *can't do anything to change it*. The one thing that *never* changes is that everything is always changing." (the seducing spirit calling itself "God;" bold added)[4]
>
> "If we believe that **the same God who created an *evolving* universe is revealed in an *evolving* Bible**, we can derive some fascinating insights from contemporary studies of genetics. Today's chickens, it turns out, still have the genetic information in their DNA that was used to produce long tails, scales, and teeth in their ancestors the dinosaurs.... We might say that **the Bible** similarly retains a record of **its own evolution** ..." (Brian McLaren; emphasis added)[5]
>
> "In my own experience as a lover and reader of the Bible, as **I am freed from the literalistic and dualistic straitjacket** ... I feel I can breathe a little freer ... Most notably, I begin to see how our ancestors' images and **understandings of God continually *changed, evolved,* and *matured*** over the centuries. ***God*, it seemed, kept initiating this evolution.**" (Brian McLaren; emphasis added)[6]
>
> "**So change!** Yes, change! Change your ideas of 'right' and 'wrong.'...
>
> "**Allow your deepest truths to be altered**. Alter them yourself, for goodness' sake.... **Your new idea of What Is So is where evolution accelerates**. Your new idea of the Who, What, Where, When, How, and Why of it is where the mystery gets solved, the plot unravels, the story ends. **Then you can begin a new story, and a grander one**.
>
> "**Your new idea about *all of it* is** where the **excitement** is, where the **creation** is, where **God-in-you** is made manifest and becomes fully realized....
>
> "Be open, therefore. Be OPEN. **Don't close off the possibility of new truth** because you have been comfortable with an old one." (the seducing spirit calling

itself "God;" bold added)[7]

"For a New Light apologetic there can be *no final statement of theology* ... **All life is *change* ... we must not foreclose our minds against the truths of God, even if they are new**." (Leonard Sweet; emphasis added)[8]

"According to millennial mathematics, the *symbolism* of '**two testaments**' indicates that the number **two is an <u>unfinished</u> integer**. In the *mystical symbolism of celestial calculus, two represents an entity* **awaiting completion. *Three* is the number of completion, even perfection**." (Leonard Sweet; emphasis added)[9]

Contrary to "mystical" "reimaginings," just as the true God has *finished* His creation, He has also *finished* His first (old) and second (new) testaments in His Son Jesus with His *second* testament. So according to God and His Son, *two* is the number for "it is finished"—i.e., of completion. And there is no perfection that goes beyond that of God and His Son!

> *"After this, Jesus knowing that all things were now accomplished, that the scripture might be fulfilled, saith, I thirst.... When Jesus therefore had received the vinegar, he said,* **It is *finished***: *and he bowed his head, and gave up the ghost." (John 19:28, 30)*

People in today's emerging faith of Oneness are not willing to accept that God's testaments are *finished* because then *the truth* of *the way to God* is *finished, closed, absolute*. And, therefore, there is *no way* to the true God apart from God's Son, *the Lord Jesus Christ*. In other words, a *finished* Word of God renders their attempt to enlarge—stretch—the way to God beyond the limits of the truth and faith of God's Word (an attempt to take the Kingdom *by force*) as *false* and *wrong*.

In spite of man's "mission" to "continue the work of Scripture" and "produce the Third Testament,"[10] the two Testaments of God's Word are God's *finished* Word because they are God's record of His first and new *testaments*, i.e., *covenants*, with man that are *finished*. In the first testament/covenant, the priests sacrificed animals in offering the blood of animals as an atonement for the forgiveness of man's sins. In the new (second) testament/covenant, Jesus, the eternal High Priest, sacrificed Himself in offering His own blood as an atonement for the forgiveness of man's sins. In so doing, He *confirmed* and *finished* God's *covenant* and thus God's *testaments*.

> *"Gather my saints together unto me; those that have made a covenant with me by sacrifice." (Psalm 50:5)*

> *"He is the* LORD *our God: his judgments are in all the earth. He hath remembered his covenant for ever, the word which he commanded to a thousand generations. Which covenant he made with Abraham ..." (Psalm 105:7-9)*

> *"Know ye therefore that they which are of faith, the same are the children of Abraham.... That the blessing of Abraham might come on the Gentiles through Jesus Christ ... Now to Abraham and his seed were the promises made. He saith not, And to seeds, as of many; but as of one, And to thy seed, which is Christ. And this I say, that* **the covenant, that was confirmed before of God in Christ**, *the law, which was four hundred and thirty years after, cannot disannul, that it should*

make the promise of none effect. For if the inheritance be of the law, it is no more of promise: but God gave it to Abraham by promise. **Wherefore then serveth the law? It was added because of transgressions** ... But the scripture hath concluded all under sin, that the promise by faith of Jesus Christ might be given to them that believe.... For ye are all the children of God by faith in Christ Jesus.... And if ye be Christ's, then are ye Abraham's seed, and heirs according to the promise." (Galatians 3:7, 14, 16-19, 22, 26, 29; also see all of Galatians 3 & Romans 11)

"For if the blood of bulls and of goats, and the ashes of an heifer sprinkling the unclean, sanctifieth to the purifying of the flesh: How much more shall the blood of Christ, who through the eternal Spirit offered himself without spot to God, purge your conscience from dead works to serve the living God? And for this cause **he is the mediator of the new testament**, that by means of death, **for the redemption of the transgressions that were under the first testament**, they which are called might receive the promise of eternal inheritance." (Hebrews 9:13-15)

"And to **Jesus the mediator of the new covenant**, ..." (Hebrews 12:24)

"For the law having a shadow of good things to come, and not the very image of the things, can never with those sacrifices which they offered year by year continually make the comers thereunto perfect.... For it is not possible that the blood of bulls and of goats should take away sins. Wherefore when he cometh into the world, he saith, Sacrifice and offering thou wouldest not, but a body hast thou prepared me: In burnt offerings and sacrifices for sin thou hast had no pleasure.... Then said he, Lo, I come to do thy will O God. **He taketh away the first, that he may establish the second.** By the which will we are sanctified through the offering of the body of Jesus Christ once for all. And every priest standeth daily ministering and offering oftentimes the same sacrifices, which can never take away sins: But this man, after he had offered one sacrifice for sins for ever, sat down on the right hand of God ... For by one offering he hath perfected for ever them that are sanctified." (Hebrews 10:1, 4-6, 9-12, 14)

"By so much was **Jesus made a surety of a better testament**. And they truly were many priests, because they were not suffered to continue by reason of death: But this man, because he continueth ever, hath an unchangeable priesthood. Wherefore he is able also to save them to the uttermost that come unto God by him, seeing he ever liveth to make intercession for them. For such an high priest became us, who is holy, harmless, undefiled, separate from sinners, and made higher than the heavens; who needeth not daily, as those high priests, to offer up sacrifice, first for his own sins, and then for the people's: for this he did once, when he offered up himself." (Hebrews 7:22-27)

"Forasmuch as ye know that ye were not redeemed with corruptible things ... but with the precious blood of Christ, as of a lamb without blemish and without spot: Who verily was foreordained before the foundation of the world, but was manifest in these last times for you, who by him do believe in God, that raised him up from the dead, and gave him glory; that your faith and hope might be in God." (1 Peter 1:18-21)

"For there is one God, and one mediator between God and men, the man Christ Jesus." (1 Timothy 2:5)

Jesus' perfect sacrifice of Himself takes away the need for any more sacrifice for sins, and to be forever saved from our sins all we have to do is *believe* in Him. His new testament/covenant is the covenant that *God* is willing to make with *man*. And it is *established* by the "*one mediator* between God and men, *the man Christ Jesus.*" To *establish* is "[t]o set and fix firmly or unalterably; to settle permanently;" "to confirm; to ratify what has been previously set or made."[11] Jesus—Who "*taketh away the first, that he may establish the second*"—said, "*It is finished.*" He did *not* say that He needs a "dialogue of the voices" and man's *co-created* "*Third* Testament" in order to finish the covenant with God! This covenant/testament—*the way to God*—has been settled *permanently* and *unalterably*. A "Third *Testament*" isn't just rejecting and adding to God's *Word*, it is also rejecting and adding to God's *established* covenant.

Man is just not willing to make this covenant with *God*. Besides, believing in Jesus is just too *narrow* of a way to God for those who want an *all-encompassing Oneness*. Thus, one way or another, people in this emerging faith are taking away the second (new) testament that they may establish a "Third"—an all-encompassing "Testament"/covenant/ way to God that includes *those who do not* believe in Jesus. But anyone who wants to either establish or "become" a "Third Testament" obviously does not understand what a testament actually is and what it *requires*!

> "*But Christ being come an high priest of good things to come, by a greater and more perfect tabernacle, not made with hands, that is to say, not of this building; neither by the blood of goats and calves, but by his own blood he entered in once into the holy place, having obtained eternal redemption for us.... **And for this cause he is the mediator of the new testament, that by means of death, for the redemption of the transgressions that were under the first testament, they which are called might receive the promise of eternal inheritance. For where a testament is, there must also of necessity be the death of the testator.** For a testament is of force after men are dead: otherwise it is of no strength at all while the testator liveth. Whereupon neither the first testament was dedicated without blood. For when Moses had spoken every precept to all the people according to the law, he took the blood of calves and of goats, ... Saying, This is the blood of the testament which God hath enjoined unto you.... And almost all things are by the law purged with blood; and without shedding of blood is no remission.*" (Hebrews 9:11-12, 15-20, 22)

> "*For this is my blood of the new testament, which is shed for many for the remission of sins.*" (Matthew 26:28)

The new testament is the new covenant that *God* is willing to make with *man*. The terms? Simply *believing* in His Son, the Lord Jesus Christ, the Mediator of God's new testament/covenant.

> "*For God so loved the world, that he gave his only begotten Son, that whosoever believeth in him should not perish, but have everlasting life.*" (John 3:16)

Either we are willing to accept God's simple terms, or we are not. Either way, testaments with God *must* include *atoning*—*paying*—for sins in order to be forgiven and thereby reconciled to God. But, sadly, even in today's shifting Christianity people are just not willing to accept the simple terms of this testament/covenant that *God* is willing to make with *man*. Consequently, they are making up their *own* testament/covenant/way to God, oblivious that according to *God's* Word, *"For where a testament is, there must also of necessity be the death of the testator"* (Hebrews 9:16).

> ***"For the wages of sin is death***; *but the gift of God is eternal life through Jesus Christ our Lord." (Romans 6:23)*

> *"But we see **Jesus**, who was made a little lower than the angels for the suffering of death, crowned with glory and honour; that he **by the grace of God should taste death for every man**." (Hebrews 2:9)*

> ***"Then said Jesus*** *again unto them, I go my way, and ye shall seek me, and shall die in your sins: whither I go, ye cannot come.... I said therefore unto you, that ye shall die in your sins: **for <u>if ye believe not that I am he</u>, ye shall die in your sins**." (John 8:21, 24)*

Again, sins must be *atoned* for in order to be reconciled to God in a testament/covenant. And to bypass believing in the Lord Jesus Christ is to bypass the Mediator of God's new testament/covenant—the *"one mediator between God and men"*—which is to bypass *God's* new testament/covenant, which is to bypass *His* atonement for their sins. This leaves those who do not *believe* with the impossible necessity of atoning for their own sins.

The first testament atoned for sins through the sacrifice of animals, and the new (second) testament atoned for sins through the sacrifice of God's Son. And with what will man's "Third Testament" atone for sins? What goes beyond the *blood* of *God's Son* with which it is *finished*? *Being God* is the *only* thing that could bypass Jesus and His shed blood of the new testament/covenant. Man would have to *be God*, just like Jesus. But of course Jesus didn't *become* God, He always has been and always will be eternally God. To the contrary, man would have to *become* God, which man absurdly imagines is "just like Jesus"—"We, too, are to realize full divinity ... just like Jesus."[12] Would that be "just like" *the Lord Jesus Christ*? Would that be "just like" *that* Jesus—*"the Lord* from heaven" (1 Corinthians 15:47) sent by God to be the *Messiah (Christ)* and *Saviour* of the world? (Or would that be "just like" *"another* Jesus"?)

> *"Behold the Lamb of God, which taketh away the sin of the world." (John 1:29)*

> *"And we have seen and do testify that the Father sent the Son to be the Saviour of the world." (1 John 4:14)*

> *"And looking upon Jesus as he walked, he saith, Behold the Lamb of God!... **We have found the Messias**, which is, being interpreted, **the Christ**. And he brought him to **Jesus**." (John 1:36, 41-42a)*

> "The so-beautiful paradox of the MRI life is that **in <u>being</u> Jesus we <u>find</u> Jesus**." (Leonard Sweet; emphasis added)[13]

Really? So it is in "being Jesus"—as if that isn't absurd enough—that you "find Jesus"? Again, would that be *being* and *finding* that *same* Jesus, the *Lord* from heaven, the *Saviour*, the *Messiah (Christ)*, *the truth* of Whom was also foretold in God's Word so that people could find Him when He came—i.e., *the "old" truth* that is purposely being supplanted with "*everything* new" in today's desire to *bypass believing this narrow truth*?

(Or, again, would that be _being_ and _finding_ "another Jesus"?)

> **"We have _found_ _him_, of whom Moses in the law, and the prophets, did write, Jesus of Nazareth,** _the son of Joseph." (John 1:45b)_

Essentially, what it boils down to is that "the Third _Testament_"—which is "the _Gospel_ According to … _you_" and comes from just _living life_—is the "gospel" _of one's Self_. That is, it is a "testament" and "gospel" of everyone "being" their _own way_ to God, and thus "being" their _own_ "Savior" and "Messiah" ("Christ"). And, therefore, this "Third _Testament_," this "living _truth_," this "_Jesus_"—i.e., "Savior"—that people are "free to become" must be as "doing" and "being" "_the 'I Am'_ that _we_ are." There could be no "Third _Testament_" otherwise.

> "**The era of the _Single_ Savior is over.** What is needed now is joint action, combined effort, _collective co-creation_." (the seducing spirit calling itself "God;" emphasis added)[14]

> "Each one of us is free to **become Jesus**, a **living _truth_**, …" (Leonard Sweet; emphasis added)[15]

> "MRI is the operating software on which human life and faith were designed to run: Version 1.0 is known as the First Testament; Version 2.0 is known as the New Testament; **Version 3.0 is the _Third_ _Testament_, the _Gospel_ According to … _you_**." (Leonard Sweet; ellipsis dots in the original; emphasis added)[16]

> "With the crooked lines of **_our_ lives** God is wanting **to write 'a _new_ account of everything old,'** a Third **_Testament_**….

> "… your 'new account of everything old'--**your part of _the 'I Am'_ that _we_ are**." (Leonard Sweet; emphasis added)[17]

> "To 'Go **Do Me**,' to '**_doing_ God**' by doing good, I must be simultaneously seeing, following, and **_being_ Christ**. _I have no theology to impart, no biblical interpretation to argue, no agenda to accomplish._ **I only have _my_ life**." (Leonard Sweet; emphasis added)[18]

> "Every believer, every body of Christ is called to **become the Third _Testament_**." (Leonard Sweet; emphasis added)[19]

Even though man absurdly imagines otherwise, we cannot _bypass believing_ in the _true_ Lord Jesus Christ by "doing" or "being" "Jesus," by "doing" or "being" "Christ," i.e., by "doing" or "being" the "Messiah," or by "doing" or "being" "God"! The _true_ Lord Jesus Christ—the one and only Word of God and I AM made flesh—is _the only way_ to the _true_ God.

> "_I know that, whatsoever God doeth, it shall be for ever: nothing can be put to it, nor anything taken from it: and_ **God** _doeth it, that men should fear before him._" (Ecclesiastes 3:14)

> "_There is a generation that are pure in their own eyes, and yet is not washed from their filthiness._" (Proverbs 30:12)

> *"For there is **one God**, and **one mediator** between God and men, the man Christ Jesus."* (1 Timothy 2:5)
>
> *"... **he is the mediator of the new testament**, that by means of death, for the redemption of the transgressions that were under the first testament, they which are called might receive the promise of eternal inheritance."* (Hebrews 9:15)
>
> *"And to **Jesus the mediator of the new covenant**, and to the blood of sprinkling, that speaketh better things than that of Abel. See that ye refuse not him that speaketh. For if they escaped not who refused him that spake on earth, much more shall not we escape, if we turn away from him that speaketh from heaven."* (Hebrews 12:24-25)
>
> *"He that despised Moses' law died without mercy under two or three witnesses: Of how much sorer punishment, suppose ye, shall he be thought worthy, who hath trodden under foot the Son of God, and hath counted the blood of the covenant, wherewith he was sanctified, an unholy thing, and hath done despite unto the Spirit of grace?... It is a fearful thing to fall into the hands of the living God."* (Hebrews 10:28-29, 31)

People in today's shifting Christianity, of all things, should know what a covenant is! And yet covenants are being so overdone and becoming so commonplace that they are no longer being applied to God and His new testament. But this is to be expected. In today's emerging faith of Oneness/panentheism, man and "God" are *automatically connected* so no covenant is even necessary for relationship. Rather, in this *unconditional "covenant"/"relationship"* of a "God" that is *immanent in everyone and everything*—a "God" that has thereby *"bonded" itself* to *everyone and everything*—man is his own way to "God" *automatically*.

> **"Quantum spirituality <u>bonds</u> us to all creation as well as to other members of the human family.**... This entails a radical doctrine of **embodiment of God in the very *substance* of creation**." (Leonard Sweet; emphasis added)[20]
>
> "The Bible reveals a covenant-making God, a God that wants a relationship with us that in some way *'binds' us together*, not haphazardly, but with integrity. From Genesis to the genuine leather the Bible tells the story of the Creator's desire for **a covenantal relationship** with humanity, not chaotic relationships or casual relationships but *'binding'* relationship. **The <u>incarnation</u> is the new *'binding'*— God *'binding'* himself to humanity** not in stone or ink but in flesh and blood. God doesn't offer final answers, the *manacles* of modernity, but *binding relationships*....
>
> "Jesus never once mentions religion or orthodox theology, nor does he outline certain religious 'beliefs' and 'precepts' by which we will be judged. He outlines actions by which we will be judged, but not propositions and creeds." (Leonard Sweet; emphasis added)[21]

In this emerging *Wordless* "faith" of Oneness/panentheism and its "binding" "covenantal relationship," *beliefs* are not seen as necessary because, as Sweet writes in his August 2010 book, *Nudge: **Awakening Each Other to the God Who's <u>Already</u> There***:

"**[T]he <u>incarnation</u> goes all the way down, and the Spirit <u>indwells *all that exists*</u>**." (emphasis added)[22]

And, therefore, as never ceases to be absolutely unbelievable (along with all the rest of today's emerging "truth" and "faith"):

"The truth of thought is not dependent on its source: **It's the *same* truth** *whether from* **the mouth of Jesus or the ass of Balaam**. *Truth as **words** is no different whether from the utterances of Paul or the udders of a cow.* **It matters not**." (Leonard Sweet; emphasis added)[23]

"Jesus cried and said, He that believeth on me, believeth not on me, but on him that sent me. And he that seeth me seeth him that sent me. I am come a light into the world, that whosoever believeth on me should not abide in darkness. And if any man hear my words, and believe not, I judge him not: for I came not to judge the world, but to save the world. **He that rejecteth me, and receiveth not my words***, hath one that judgeth him: the word that I have spoken,* **the same shall judge him in the last day**.*" (John 12:44-48)*

With the "embodiment"/"incarnation" of a panentheistic "God" that "indwells *all that exists*" "in the *very substance* of creation," naturally this is a universal "binding" *relationship* that is a universal "binding" *salvation. No beliefs* are necessary. That is, *no new covenant/testament of which Jesus is the Mediator* is necessary. And in this emerging faith it is not at all surprising that even "the genuine leather" "tells the story" of this "covenantal relationship" with its "God." After all, this "God" is even in the "very substance" of the leather itself!

Even though those in this emerging faith are absurdly bound and determined to "Christianize" its "truth" and "faith" of Oneness/panentheism, its "binding" "covenantal relationship" is not binding with God but only with its emerging false, *make-believe* "God." In spite of today's never-ending "reimaginings," the true and everlasting covenant of the *true* God is by *sacrifice*. And it has been *finished* by *Jesus* in His final sacrifice on the cross that *established*—settled *permanently* and *unalterably*—the *way* to God.

"Gather my saints together unto me; those that have made a <u>covenant</u> with me <u>by sacrifice</u>.*" (Psalm 50:5)*

"The earth also is defiled under the inhabitants thereof; because they have transgressed the laws, changed the ordinance, broken **the everlasting covenant**.*" (Isaiah 24:5)*

"*It is finished*" is not subject to man's "reimaginations." It *is* what it *is*. Man can neither add to nor take away from what the Lord Jesus Christ did on the cross. Yet theologians and pastors and many others are still vainly attempting to do so by debating and "rethinking" and "reimagining" the meaning of the cross. And they are thus debating and "rethinking" and "reimagining" *the covenant that God* is willing to make with *man*. But it *is* what it *is*, and *what it is* is recorded for us by God in His *finished* Word of *absolute truth*.

Clearly, those who are "reimagining" the cross know deep down that the cross is essential, otherwise they would just cast it aside altogether. So they are *"reimagining" the cross* in the attempt to be brought into *"relationship"* with the cross *without believing the truth* of what it means. In other words, they know that what the Lord Jesus Christ did on the cross is the saving truth, but this truth that must be *believed* is too narrow so they "reimagine" it into a broader "truth" so that everyone can be saved by what He did on the cross without having to *believe* the truth of Who He is and what He did. More and more people are thus expanding the cross and covenant to fit the dimensions of the New Age and its Oneness. And with a "reimagined" cross that is all-encompassing irrespective of anyone's *beliefs*, and with an all-encompassing "relationship" of Oneness that brings *truth and falsehood* and *right and wrong* together as *one*, in this emerging faith all sins have thus been automatically and universally taken care of and even done away with altogether. Man's terms and conditions for God (i.e., man's covenant that man is willing to make with God) are very convenient.

> "[T]he Cross still stands....
>
> "But this is **on one condition, and one only: that it expand itself to the dimensions of a new age**, and cease to present itself to us as primarily (or even exclusively) the sign of a victory over sin." (Pierre Teilhard de Chardin; parentheses in the original; emphasis added)[24]

> "[W]hile there is *more than one way of being a true believer*, **there is still one way, and that way is Christ**. Like the mathematical model of the Möbius strip, there is only one side. But that one side is the 'inside' and 'outside' of the strip. Once again, theologian/evangelism professor William J. Abraham says it best: 'It is perfectly consistent to hold **both** that Jesus is the exclusive path to God *and* that people may genuinely encounter God outside the *Christian* church **without explicitly knowing about Jesus of Nazareth**.'" (Leonard Sweet; emphasis added)[25]

> "**Dualism,** *either/or* exclusionism is … **plug ugly**.
>
> "**Nondualism,** *both/and* nonlocalism is … **so beautiful**....
>
> "**The cross brings into relationship opposites**, not so much as a dialectic to be synthesized but more as **a nondualistic double helix** to be embraced. **In Christ *all opposites* are** not so much reconciled as **transcended** in the Oneness of Twoness that becomes Threeness." (Leonard Sweet; 1st two ellipsis dots in the original; emphasis added)[26]

In other words, to replace the resented dualistic either/or exclusionism of *God's* covenant—in which *either* people believe in Jesus and have God *or* they do not believe in Jesus and do not have God—a *third* covenant/testament of Oneness is being created/conceived/imagined/invented/made up by *man* to do away with the *do not have God* part for those who do not believe in Jesus. And, again, if people in this emerging "faith" don't even need to *know Jesus* then it certainly won't matter what anyone chooses to *believe* about Jesus.

> "People need room to *move* and *choose* and *resist airtight propositions* that don't allow free breathing (i.e., *freedom*). **Jesus left space for people *to make their own responses to him*. He did not dictate to his disciples *what they were to believe* about him: '*Who do you say I am?*'**" (Leonard Sweet; parentheses in the original; emphasis added)[27]

No, Jesus did not leave space for people to resist the truth of Who He *is*. Everyone must respond to Jesus according to His new testament or they are *rejecting* His covenant, which is the *only* covenant with (and way to) God. When people are not willing to accept this covenant that God offers to make with them, God does not leave space for anyone to become their own covenant—a "Third Testament"—with Him. There is no getting God to the table to negotiate a new covenant/testament that *man* is willing to accept. Man can give God terms and conditions all man wants, but one way or the other man is going to find out that God's terms and conditions for man that are forever settled in heaven are nonnegotiable and non-"reimaginable." And, no, there is no getting God to the table to negotiate "new understandings" of Who His Mediator is, either! Likewise, neither is man his *own* mediator, even if man does choose to absurdly believe that he is "free to *become Jesus*."

Clearly, anyone who believes that "[e]ach one of us is free to become Jesus" and that "in being Jesus we find Jesus" wants to be able to respond to the question, "Who do you say I am?" with the answer, "Me." This opens the door to all kinds of absurd "new understandings of who Jesus is" in today's revolution against believing that *Jesus is Who He is*.

"Reimagining"—making up—new "understandings" of "who Jesus is" and new "truths" of a new kind of covenant in a "Third Testament" and "Gospel According to … you" is the absurd attempt to throw pitches delivered with a spin—"curve balls"—to God in the hope that God agrees that He, too, is to "Only Connect" with man to "heal the divisions" that separate man from God. Sadly, people actually believe that this is all the purpose/work/mission of *God*—that this is what *God* is "up to" in the world. They also believe that this emerging faith that is purposely trying to change *everything* is all about *God* and not about *you*, that it is *God*-centered and not *man*-centered. And people are falling for this lie because they are "*centering*" themselves in the inner panentheistic "God" of Oneness. In other words, they are centering themselves in the "God" of Self. But, of course, they don't see it that way.

Nevertheless, despite the claims of today's emerging Wordless faith, it is not *God* Who is dispensing with *the words* of His covenant to give everyone the freedom to *make up their own covenant with God* according to however *they* choose to have a relationship. Only those who have turned the light off to look for "truth" in the corner of a dark round room will see it as the mission of *God* to dispense with the *words* of God's covenant (God's Word) so that people everywhere can freely dispense with *believing* and *obeying* God's Son as their *Saviour* and *Lord*! Before darkness became the preferred "light" it would have been obvious that this really is just *man's* purposely *fictitious* new idea—a.k.a. new "truth"—*conceived* to "heal" the divisions between those who are willing to accept the terms of God's covenant and those who are not.

> "Biblical truth doesn't feast on fact. It feasts on relationship and revelation, which is why eternal truth is better communicated by the fictions of parables and narratives than the facts of science and philosophy." (Leonard Sweet)[28]

> "And they shall turn away their ears from the truth, and shall be turned unto fables." (2 Timothy 4:4)

> "For our transgressions are multiplied before thee, and our sins testify against us: for our transgressions are with us; and as for our iniquities, we know them; in transgressing and lying against the LORD, and departing away from our God, speaking

oppression and revolt, conceiving and uttering from the heart words of falsehood." (Isaiah 59:12-13)

Even people in today's shifting Christianity no longer see the need to believe and obey Jesus as their Saviour and Lord. After all, the circle of Oneness and its emerging faith has removed ("transcended") the line between *truth and falsehood*. This has thereby conveniently removed ("transcended") the need to *believe* and, therefore, the need for people to *believe in Jesus* as their *Saviour*.

*"… and thou shalt call his name JESUS: for **he shall save his people from their sins**." (Matthew 1:21)*

*"And they said, **Believe** on the Lord Jesus Christ, and thou shalt be **saved** …"* (Acts 16:31)

*"Then said Jesus again unto them, … **if ye believe not** that I am he, **ye shall die in your sins**." (John 8:21, 24)*

Likewise, the circle of Oneness and its emerging faith has removed ("transcended") the line between *right and wrong*. This has thereby conveniently removed ("transcended") the need to *obey* and, therefore, the need for people to *obey Jesus* as their *Lord*.

*"And **why call ye me, Lord, Lord, and do not the things which I say?**" (Luke 6:46)*

*"And **every one that heareth these sayings of mine, and doeth them not**, shall be likened unto **a foolish man, which built his house upon the sand**: And the rain descended, and the floods came, and the winds blew, and beat upon that house; and it fell: and great was the fall of it. And it came to pass, when Jesus had ended these sayings, the people were astonished at his doctrine: For he taught them as one having authority, and not as the scribes." (Matthew 7:26-29)*

People in today's emerging faith of Oneness and its *all-encompassing, unconditional, universal* relationship/covenant/testament/way to God only see a need to be *affirmed themselves* in whatever *they* choose to believe and do. And, therefore, "terms like 'Lord,' 'Messiah,' 'King,' 'Son of God,' and even 'Savior'" are seen as terms of "*irrelevance*" and "*relics* of a Christendom that has *passed away*."[C, 29] No *beliefs* necessary, no *Saviour*

C

This is from Easum and Bandy's anti-scriptural book *Growing Spiritual Redwoods* that, along with other leaders of today's emerging faith of Oneness, has been highly endorsed by Leonard Sweet and Rick Warren. Sweet's endorsement, which is on the back cover, reads: "An epoch-marking—if not epoch-making—book. For a church living off of checks that reality won't cash, this book is like an acid bath accounting from the bank examiners. There is no better audit of the collapse of the Christendom era, and no better audition for how to do *ministry* in *the new world*, than this one." And Warren's endorsement, also on the back cover, reads: "*Every* passage of this book contains spiritual nuggets of *truth* that can help your church to grow healthy and strong." Actually, this 1997 book is quite an effective how-to-manual on the emerging faith of Oneness. And since popular leaders of today's shifting Christianity endorsed it so many years ago, it is not surprising that this faith of Oneness is now emerging so successfully, *including in "conservative" evangelical denominations*.

(For this footnote's citation information, see endnote #29.)

necessary; no *obedience* necessary, no *Lord* necessary. This way everyone can become *their own* testament/covenant/way to God in just *"the living of their own lives."*

No matter how many people choose to believe otherwise, the all-encompassing third testament/covenant of Oneness that *man* is willing to accept is nothing more than *an imaginary "reality."* Despite the never-ending absurd, channeled, mystical, and "scientific" claims of Oneness/panentheism, man will still only die in his sins unless people *believe* in *the true Person* of the Lord Jesus Christ *Himself*. But people in this emerging faith are hell-bent on *breaking free* from "the era of *the Single Savior*" to give everyone the freedom to live according to whatever is right in *their own eyes*—i.e., according to the "authority" of their own inner "knowing" of their own inner "God"/"Christ"/"Jesus" that can be imagined, defined, and related to however anyone chooses.

> *"He is despised and rejected of men; a man of sorrows, and acquainted with grief: and we hid as it were our faces from him; he was despised, and we esteemed him not." (Isaiah 53:3)*

Sadly, some things never change.

41

An "*anti-Christian*" "double helix, Möbius-strip culture of both-and's" is "*the secret of life*"?

"[T]he church is now encountering the double whammy of *postmodernity* and *post-Christendom*. **Postmodern culture is an *anti-Christian* culture**." (Leonard Sweet; emphasis added)[1]

"The modern world moved dialectically, by conflict and contradiction and controversy. **The postmodern world being born is** not a bipolar worldview of either/or's but **a double helix, Möbius-strip culture of both-and's**, the *coincidentia oppositorum* (**coinciding opposites**) in fifteenth-century prelate/philosopher Nicholas of Cusa's mystical phrasing ..." (Leonard Sweet; parentheses in the original; bold & underline added)[2]

"There is no precise formula for living the Christian life. But while there is *more than one way of being a true believer*, **there is still one way, and that way is Christ**. Like the mathematical model of **the Möbius strip, there is only one side. But that one side is the '*inside' and 'outside'* of the strip**. Once again, theologian/evangelism professor William J. Abraham says it best: 'It is perfectly consistent to hold **both** that Jesus is the exclusive path to God **and** that people may **genuinely encounter God *outside* the Christian church *without* explicitly knowing** about **Jesus of Nazareth**.'" (Leonard Sweet; emphasis added)[3]

Without question, this emerging both/and faith ("culture") *is indeed anti-Christian*. It is also anti-*Christ*. *Jesus alone is Christ*, God's *only* Mediator. But rather than being seen as *anti-Christ*, this "Möbius-strip culture" that in-

268

cludes both *believing in Jesus* and *not believing in Jesus* in a "double-helix" (narrow *and* broad) *all-encompassing* testament/covenant/way to God is imagined to be a non-exclusive, "nondualistic" "*secret of life.*"

> "The **MRI [Missional, Relational, Incarnational]** as **the Double-Helix Design for Life** …
>
> "The 'secret of life' was a shape, a structure, a design.… [T]he 'secret of life' was … the discovery that the chemical molecules constituting DNA have a double-helix structure.
>
> **"The secret of life is 'helixal,' two strands that run in opposite directions creating a reproductive Möbius strip** and slingshot.
>
> "And the secret of life brings together another double: *the linear (line) and nonlinear (curve)* that together form a spiral, which, in antiparallel fashion, winds around *a single invisible axis* like a twisted ladder around an invisible straight spine.
>
> "In other words, the secret of life is a paradox. Or you might even say it is doubly paradoxical: a double double built around a single. Paradox is the midwife of truth.…
>
> "**Dualism, either/or** *exclusionism* is … **plug ugly**.
>
> "**Nondualism, both/and** nonlocalism is … **so beautiful**.…
>
> "[T]he cross is the ultimate symbol of paradoxy. The cross brings into relationship opposites, not so much as a dialectic to be synthesized but more as **a nondualistic double helix** to be embraced. **In Christ *all* opposites** are not so much reconciled as **transcended in the Oneness of Twoness** that becomes Threeness." (Leonard Sweet; 5th & 6th ellipsis dots & all parentheses in the original; emphasis added)[4]

First, that the "postmodern" *anti-Christian* and *post-truth* faith/"culture" of "*nondualism,*" i.e., of *Oneness*, is successfully emerging in today's Christianity is thanks to the efforts of leaders such as Sweet and *many* others. In an interview of Leonard Sweet and Frank Viola regarding their June 2010 book, deceptively titled, *Jesus Manifesto: Restoring the Supremacy and Sovereignty of Jesus Christ*, Mike Morrell pointed out that, "Len, *you have been a pioneer* in Christians' [sic] being responsive to the **postmodern** cultural and philosophical turn – what is **now known in different circles as 'emerging' or 'missional' church**."[5] Indeed he has. And now even "conservative" evangelical churches and denominations are responding positively as well to this "emerging"/"missional"/"postmodern"/"anti-Christian" church movement—i.e., this emerging faith of Oneness/panentheism.

Second, a key component of this emerging "*anti-Christian*"/"*postmodern*" faith/"culture" is of course its *mysticism*. It is mysticism that provides the "verification" of its *both/and theology*. That is, it is mysticism that provides the "experience," the "seeing," and the "knowing" of its *both/and "God"* that is *in everyone and everything*. And, sadly, too many leaders in today's Christianity who are changing everything according to the "authority" of the new "truth" of their own mystical/inner "knowing" are thus successfully changing today's Christianity into not only a *post*-Christianity but also an *anti*-Christianity as well. Once again (and with a reminder that according to Sweet "[i]t is through *creative intuition* that *postmoderns* continue the work of *divine creation*"[6]), in *Quantum Spirituality: A Postmodern Apologetic*, Sweet writes:

"For the common sense to be the common good in **the postmodern era**, it must come to respect **the *authority* of intuitive modes of *knowing*....**

"Modernity dismissed 'intuition' ... **Postmodernity**, on the other hand, thrives on **intuitional experience**, elevating its attributes to the status of **a true leader**: Someone 'gifted more than ordinary people with a ***mystical*** quality--intuition-- which gives him 'inner conviction' ...'" (emphasis added)[7]

And what is this "intuitional experience" of "a true leader" in the emerging/"postmodern" faith/"culture"? An unarguably "*anti-Christian*" "experience" of "God" "*in everything*":

"Further, what modernists got used to 'feeling' was themselves, not creation or the Creator. Experience came to refer to human experience--getting in touch with one's 'self'--rather than the **unition experience of the whole**, of the self with *all* that is outside the self, or of **the experience of *God***, either from *within* or ***in everything*** without....

"**Mysticism**, once cast to the sidelines of the Christian tradition, is now situated in **postmodernist culture** near the center.... **Mysticism ... is metaphysics** arrived at through mindbody experiences. **Mysticism** begins in experience; it **ends in *theology*.**" (Leonard Sweet; emphasis added)[8]

"... **a radical doctrine of *embodiment* of *God in* the very *substance* of creation**." (Leonard Sweet; emphasis added)[9]

"**Postmodern culture** is an ***anti-Christian*** **culture**." (Leonard Sweet; emphasis added)[10]

It is indeed.

"The MRI [Missional, Relational, **Incarnational**] as the **Double-Helix** Design for Life ..." (Leonard Sweet; emphasis added)[11]

"An **incarnational** God means that ***God-stuff*** is found ***in* the *matter* of the universe**." (Leonard Sweet; emphasis added)[12]

"[T]he **incarnation** goes all the way down, and **the Spirit indwells all that exists**." (Leonard Sweet; emphasis added)[13]

It is this thoroughly anti-Christian, *metaphysical* theology ("secret of life") of "God" embodied/incarnate *in everyone and everything* that brings *all* opposites— including truth and falsehood, right and wrong—together as *one* in a *both/and* "Double-Helix Design for Life."

"Claiming this culture for God means claiming **paradoxy over orthodoxy** as **postmodernism's** fundamental cultural category and intellectual phenomenon. The word 'paradoxy' is derived from two Greek words--*pará* meaning 'beyond or beside' and *doxy* meaning 'belief.' **A paradox is a *linear* contradiction but a harmony in truth**. A paradox is an echoing pun on differentiations and **oppositions which are *metaphysically* one**." (Leonard Sweet; emphasis added)[14]

"In other words, **the secret of life is a paradox**.... **Paradox is the midwife of truth**....

"In Christ **all opposites** are not so much reconciled as transcended in the **Oneness** of Twoness that becomes Threeness.

"Paradox is never about two. Paradox is about the conception of **a *tertium quid*,** a 'third somewhat,' that is **born from the coming together of two opposites**. True twoness always births threeness." (Leonard Sweet; emphasis added)[15]

"In the divine mathematics of science, religion, philosophy, history, in fact everything, **1+1=3**. In the trigonometry of the trinity, we multiply by dividing: The more we give the more we have. Presbyterian minister/theologian Letty Russell suspects that 'God is not good at math.' **Perhaps God is part of the new math. Perhaps Jesus taught the higher math of the *tertium quid* (the third way)**....

"God the Spirit and Sustainer wants to work through New Lights of the twenty-first century to produce **the Third *Testament*--**our 'new account of everything old.'" (Leonard Sweet; parentheses in the original; emphasis added)[16]

Actually, it is *man* that prefers fuzzy math and fuzzy "truth." Jesus taught and *is* the *only* way. Again, even if people everywhere choose to believe new and different "understandings" of 1+1, such as 1+1=3, a broader "understanding" that allows for false answers to be "true" so that no answer is wrong is the fuzzy thinking of Oneness. In truth, there *is* a *right* and *wrong* answer. There is no "third way" that brings the broad way together with the narrow way in a "double helix" "secret of life." There is no all-encompassing "third way" to God—i.e., "Third Testament" (covenant)—that includes both *believing in Jesus* and *not believing in Jesus*. But since people in the emerging faith ("postmodern culture") are "reimagining" a "*God*" that is "*in everything*" and thus *already in them*, it is not surprising that they don't see themselves as sinners who need to *believe* the *true* and *right* answer of God's Saviour and Mediator in order to be forgiven and thereby *reconciled* to God.

> "*There is a generation that are pure in their own eyes, and yet is not washed from their filthiness.*" (Proverbs 30:12)

> "*Even **the righteousness of God** which **is by faith** of Jesus Christ unto all and upon all them that **believe**: for there is no difference: **For all have sinned**, and come short of the glory of God.*" (Romans 3:22-23)

"**Postmodern** culture is an **anti-Christian** culture. If you are reading these words, you are likely the last generation to be familiar with the Christian story and for whom churches have cultural significance. And you will die, leaving behind a culture for whom the Christian story will be completely unknown. **This requires** not only a new ability to tell the story but also **a fresh way to reframe the story for 'a sinless society,' a mission field where people don't see themselves as 'sinners.'**...

"It is time to push the reset button on Christianity—**the original operating system**— ... back to the original Genesis 1 and 2 operating system. Whenever you download a new program on your computer, you must reboot the system to actualize the change.

"It is time to live out of **the secret of life**, the secret of the cruciform life: **the**

double-helix divine *design* for life and the church." (Leonard Sweet; emphasis added)[17]

As addressed earlier, today's "fresh way" to "reframe" ("reimagine") "the Christian story"—i.e., the Christian truth of God's Word—for people who "don't see themselves as 'sinners'" and in need of the Saviour includes "reimagining" it all as just *one part* of an *interfaith whole*. Again, this both/and "secret of life" is designed to "heal"—defrag— the divisions between religions/faiths/cultures/"truths"/gods. And, therefore, "the original operating system" that this "postmodern" *defragged interfaith* community/church/"body of Christ" is "designed to run" *must* be anti-Christian—whether people see it that way or not. Otherwise there is no bringing truth and falsehood, right and wrong, the narrow way and the broad way, together as one in a non-exclusive, "*nondualistic* double helix" "Möbius strip" of "*both/and*"—i.e., in an all-encompassing testament/covenant/way to God.

> "Now, to put it in more **postmodern** terminology, God is **defragging the church and rebooting it with the original Operating System. MRI** [Missional, Relational, **Incarnational**] is the original operating system of the Christian faith. MRI is the operating software on which human life and *faith* were *designed* to run: Version 1.0 is known as the First Testament; Version 2.0 is known as the New Testament; Version 3.0 is **the Third *Testament***, the *Gospel* According to ... you." (Leonard Sweet; ellipsis dots in the original; emphasis added)[18]

> "**All** religions have something to do with **the whole, the totality**.... In the modern era religions largely succumbed to the Enlightenment's **fragmented** fetishistic love for the part....
>
> "The New Light apologetic must come to terms with **the '*communal awakening*' of postmodernity**.... New Light leadership is fundamentally gathering communities together and building them up into **a true body of Christ**." (Leonard Sweet; emphasis added)[19]

> "So, any church that welcomes some members of *the body* but rejects others *is not fully receiving Christ*.... **To be exclusive and sectarian** not only dishonors Him; it also **dismembers Him**." (Leonard Sweet & Frank Viola; emphasis added)[20]

> "New Light **embodiment** means to be 'in *connection*' and 'in-*formation*' **with *other faiths*.... to enlarge the community to include those whose conceptions of *God differ* from ours in form**." (Leonard Sweet; emphasis added)[21]

> "The secret of life is 'helixal,' two strands that run in opposite directions creating a reproductive Möbius strip and slingshot.
>
> "And **the secret of life brings together** another double: **the linear (line) and nonlinear (curve) that together form a spiral, which**, in antiparallel fashion, **winds around *a single invisible axis*** like a twisted ladder around an invisible straight spine." (Leonard Sweet; emphasis added)[22]

The following descriptions are befitting of today's emerging faith of Oneness—i.e., emerging *interfaith* Oneness—that, as addressed earlier, must pitch a *curved* "truth" in order to meet "*somewhere in the middle*" and connect the religions/faiths/gods. First, a helix—a spiral shape—is described as "a type of space *curve*, i.e. a smooth *curve* in three-dimensional space,"[23] and second:

> "The **pitch** of a helix is the width of one complete helix turn, measured parallel to the axis of the helix.
>
> "A double helix consists of two (**typically congruent**) helices with **the same axis, differing by a translation** along the axis, which may or may not measure **half** the pitch." (parentheses in the original; emphasis added)[24]

The narrow way and the broad way are neither *congruent* (*in agreement, or harmonious*) nor share *the same axis* (*God, Christ, or truth*) that merely differ by *a translation*! It is not the *Christian* truth of the narrow way and the falsehood of the broad way that form "a double helix." Rather, the double helix of this emerging Oneness is formed by *curving* the truth into *a counterfeit "Christianity,"* and it is this *counterfeit* that then becomes a dancing partner with the broad way as the two curve, spin, and spiral according to one another's *pitch* that *dances around the truth* (axis). And reminiscent of the "dishonest" and "deceptive" "illusion" of the *curve ball* is the fitting description:

> "Another way of mathematically constructing a helix is to plot a complex valued exponential function (e^{xi}) taking **imaginary arguments** ..." (parentheses in the original; bold added)[25]

Imaginary arguments are indeed how today's double-helix dance of Oneness is being plotted. In fact, since people in the emerging faith of Oneness are on a mission that does not line up with the Word of God, *imaginary* arguments ("*reimaginings*") are foundational to their attempt to enlarge—stretch—it all into an all-encompassing "kingdom"/relationship of Oneness. Sweet writes:

> "Of course, **the gospels portray a Jesus who keeps *widening* the eye of the needle so that every camel and Cadillac can get through to the kingdom**." (emphasis added)[26]

Yet Jesus warns:

> "*Enter ye in at the strait gate: for **wide is the gate, and broad is the way, that leadeth to destruction, and many there be which go in thereat: Because** strait is the gate, and **narrow is the way**, which leadeth unto life, and few there be that find it.*" (Matthew 7:13-14)

In truth, the *narrow* way is *narrow*. It is neither *widening* nor *broadening*. Jesus does not *enlarge—stretch—*the truth of Who He is to cater to those who are not willing to believe the truth of Who He is. And neither is He bringing the two ways together in a "Möbius strip" of Oneness of *everyone and everything*. So would this just be part of the imaginary arguments of the "make-it-up-as-you-go-along process"[27] of the emerging faith of Oneness? Or to which "gospels" might Sweet be referring—the Gnostic gospels, for instance? Matthew, Mark, Luke, and John portray no such lie. On the other hand, according to the Gnostic "Gospel of Thomas":

> "(22) Jesus saw infants being suckled. He said to his disciples, 'These infants being suckled are like those who enter the kingdom.'

> "They said to him, 'Shall we then, as children, enter the kingdom?'
>
> "Jesus said to them, **'When you *make the two one*, and when you *make the inside like the outside and the outside like the inside***, and *the above like the below*, ... **then will you enter the kingdom.**'...
>
> "(89) Jesus said, 'Why do you wash the outside of the cup? Do you not realize that he who made the inside is the same one who made the outside?'" (all parentheses in the original; emphasis added)[28]

Sounds familiar.

> "But while there is *more than one way of being a true believer*, **there is still one way, and that way is Christ**. Like the mathematical model of the Möbius strip, there is only *one side*. **But *that one side is the 'inside' and 'outside'* of the strip.... [P]eople may genuinely encounter God *outside* the *Christian* church *without* explicitly knowing about *Jesus of Nazareth*.**'" (Leonard Sweet; emphasis added)[29]

> "**In Christ** *all* opposites are not so much reconciled as transcended in **the Oneness of Twoness** that becomes Threeness." (Leonard Sweet; emphasis added)[30]

The "one way" to enter this "kingdom" of Oneness is to just "make the two one" in "the Oneness of Twoness." That is, just make the *either/or's* (opposites) of the narrow way and the broad way into a *both/and*. Not only does this transcend God's linear truth that divides the two, it also transcends His Kingdom. But, sadly, a "bigger" "God" and a "bigger" "kingdom" is what people today *want*.

Incidentally, "the above like the below" in the Gnostic "Gospel of Thomas" speaks to the occult phrase "as above, so below" that Warren B. Smith has warned about. In *Deceived on Purpose* he writes:

> "Right about the time I was looking into Eugene Peterson's use of the term 'as above, so below,' I was at a book sale at our local library. Almost lost amongst some cookbooks and business manuals was a book written and published by the editors of the *New Age Journal*. It was entitled *As Above, So Below*.... In the introduction the chief editor of the book, Ronald S. Miller, had written:
>
>> "'Thousands of years ago in ancient Egypt, the great master alchemist Hermes Trismegistus, believed to be a contemporary of the Hebrew prophet Abraham, proclaimed this fundamental truth about the universe: '**As above, so below; as below, so above.**' This maxim implies that **the transcendent God** beyond the physical universe **and the immanent God** within ourselves **are one. Heaven and Earth, spirit and matter, the invisible and the visible worlds form a unity to which we are intimately linked.**'...
>
> "The *New Age Journal* editor went on to state that old forms of religion no longer serve people, and that the term 'as above, so below' describes the 'emerging spirituality' that is quickly moving onto the world's scene." (emphasis added)[31]

In "Exposing the QUANTUM LIE: God is *NOT* in everything!," a DVD lecture series, Warren B. Smith (who is a former New Ager) also points out:

"The book ***The Secret***, at the beginning of the book it says, '**as above, so below**.' Those of us in the New Age know what that means. That means that God is not only **transcendent** out there, He's **immanent** inside each and every one of us. **We are all one**. As above, so below."[32]

The "secret" of the *Oneness* of everyone and everything—i.e., the "secret" that "God" and "Christ" are in everyone and everything—unarguably changes *everything*. It is this *Oneness* that is today's "fresh way" to "reframe" ("reimagine") the Christian truth of God's Word for people who "don't see themselves as 'sinners'" that need to believe in the Saviour. After all, to "reimagine" *God* and *Christ* as *in everyone and everything* conveniently renders them already "*redemptively* present" *in everyone* (not to mention *everything*). And, thus, this shift from "a bipolar worldview of *either/or's*" to "a double helix, Möbius-strip culture of *both-and's*" is also a shift from "Come, let us *reason* together" to "Come, let us *relate* together," which likewise is also a shift from "You are *lost* in sin" to "You *belong* to God." These shifts are all part and parcel of the foundational shift, which is from the Christian truth/Gospel of *God's Word* to the *anti-Christian* and *anti-Christ* "truth"/"Gospel" of *Oneness/panentheism*.

> *"When Jesus heard it, he saith unto them, They that are whole have no need of the physician, but they that are sick: I came not to call the righteous, but **sinners to repentance**." (Mark 2:17)*

> *"And Jesus said unto him, This day is salvation come to this house, ... For the Son of man is come to seek and **to save that which was lost**." (Luke 19:9-10)*

> *"And that **repentance and remission of sins should be preached in his name among all nations**, beginning at Jerusalem." (Luke 24:47)*

> *"For ye are all **the children of God by faith** in Christ Jesus." (Galatians 3:26)*

> *"**For all have sinned**, and come short of the glory of God; being justified freely by his grace through the **redemption** that is in Christ Jesus: Whom God hath set forth to be a propitiation **through faith in his blood**, to declare his righteousness for the remission of sins that are past, through the forbearance of God; to declare, I say, at this time his righteousness: that he might be just, and **the justifier of him which believeth in Jesus**." (Romans 3:23-26)*

"Evangelists always nudge.... Their words when spoken are **not so much 'You are *lost* in sin'** as **'You *belong* to God.'**...

"Nudging is more about *dialogue* than monologue, ... Evangelists nudge **the Jesus in people** to sit up and take notice.... Whereas evangelism has been known to violate others' dignity, which I call the reproach approach, nudgers are **not smudgers of the divine in people**." (Leonard Sweet; emphasis added)[33]

Naturally, with this "secret of life" there is no such thing as a *godless* world. To the contrary, "the *divine*"/"God" is *in everyone and everything* in a *universal*, unconditional relationship/salvation/redemption/forgiveness/reconciliation. So, again, why would people be seen as—or see themselves as—*sinners* who need to *believe* the *truth* of God's Saviour and Mediator in order to be forgiven and redeemed and reconciled to God?

"Evangelism is **awakening** each other **to the God who is *already* there**." (Leonard Sweet; emphasis added)[34]

"Back in 1998, George W. Stroup made this explicit: 'Too often churches have understood themselves to be taking God to **a godless world** rather than following God into **a world in which God is already redemptively present**.'" (Leonard Sweet; emphasis added)[35]

And as is thus inevitable in this emerging faith of Oneness/panentheism:

"Nudge is **not** bringing God to people or **taking Jesus to the *unsaved***....

"Nudge is **introducing** people **to the 'Jesus *in* them,' to the God they *already know* but don't know it**." (Leonard Sweet; emphasis added)[36]

"Nudgers **help people discover *their inner Jesus***." (Leonard Sweet; emphasis added)[37]

Since the emerging faith of Oneness/panentheism gives people their "own inner God" and their own "inner Jesus," people need merely "discover" this "fact," just as Djwhal Khul and Alice Bailey taught.

"Truth lies within ourselves. When we can contact **our own inner God** all truth will be revealed to us. We shall be Knowers." (Alice Bailey; emphasis added)[38]

"The kingdom of God is not some one particular church with its own peculiar doctrines, its particular formulations of truth ... and of approach to God.

"The true Church is **the kingdom of God** on earth ... composed of **all**, regardless of race or creed, **who live by the light within, who have discovered the *fact* of the mystical Christ in their hearts** ..." (Alice Bailey; emphasis added)[39]

"My Father has enabled you to share in the inheritance that belongs to **all** of My people, those **who live in the light**, by rescuing you from the kingdom of darkness and transferring you into **My Kingdom**." (Leonard Sweet & Frank Viola; emphasis added)[40]

Although Sweet and Viola claim to be speaking for Jesus (in this "reimagining" of Colossians 1:12-13), the light to which they are referring is clearly "the light *within*." In the same way that this emerging faith gives people the freedom to simply "know" their own "inner God" (the "God" within) rather than the true God, it is giving people the freedom to simply "know" their own "inner Jesus" (the "Jesus" within) rather than needing to know and believe in *Jesus of Nazareth*. And how do they know "their inner Jesus"? Simply by *living life* of course. It is the "secret of *life*."

"Nudgers **help people discover *their inner Jesus***." (Leonard Sweet; emphasis added)[41]

"But **the ultimate answer to that question 'Who do you say that I am?'** is best forthcoming from another question: 'What's up?' Or when translated theologically, 'What's the I AM up to in your life?' **We find the living One in the midst of *living***." (Leonard Sweet; emphasis added)[42]

"Nudge is *not* taking or *talking* God to people....

"Nudgers **help others to listen to *their lives*** and to **hear, see, taste, touch, and smell** the *sacredness* of *their own journeys*." (Leonard Sweet; emphasis added)[43]

"Life isn't sacred and secular. **There is only life**....

"You can't separate the secular and the sacred; **you can't polarize the sacred and the profane**. The doctrine of the **incarnation**, with its high view of the everyday and the ordinary, won't allow it." (Leonard Sweet; emphasis added)[44]

"[T]he **incarnation** goes **all the way down**, and **the Spirit indwells *all that exists***." (Leonard Sweet; emphasis added)[45]

"The doctrine of the **incarnation** requires a high doctrine of the everyday, the ordinary....

"**Everything that exists is extraordinary and holds the secrets of the universe within itself**. We need the eyes to **see**, the ears to **hear**, the nose to **smell**, the mouth to **taste**, and the hands to **touch**. Be transfixed by the ordinary so that you can see **what you thought was ordinary is really a *transfiguration*.**" (Leonard Sweet; emphasis added)[46]

"The ideal of monastic holiness and in fact any tradition of **holy *living*** is precisely this: **an awareness** of the presence **of Christ *in all of life* and *in all things***." (Leonard Sweet; emphasis added)[47]

"It is Jesus who is knocking at our door, saying, 'Can't you hear me? Touch me? Smell me? Taste me? See me?' Are you **finding Christ in** the **people** you meet? Are you **finding Christ in** the **things** you handle? Are you **finding Christ in** the **food you eat? Finding Christ in** the **voices** you hear? **Finding Christ in** the **smells** you breathe?...

"In fact, Jesus' knuckles are raw from knocking on the door of our hearts, begging us to come out, discover for ourselves his **sensory truths**, and 'bless what there is for being.'

"**Jesus is saying, 'Enjoy your senses**, ... Come, let me guide you into **finding life through your senses**, because **it is through your *senses* that I will reveal *myself*.**'" (Leonard Sweet; emphasis added)[48]

"Poet/critic Paul Mariani says it is our lack of *imagination* that has closed us to **an awareness of God *in the world*.**

'If the **incarnation** has indeed occurred, as I believe it has, ... evidence of **God's *immanent* presence** ought to be capable of breaking in on us each day the way air and light and sound do if only we know of what to look and listen for.'...

"**God's *creation* is a revelation of *divine presence*.** This is the **genius** of Christian theology: It **radically reconfigures the human conception of the sacred. Nothing is *inherently* 'profane.'**" (Leonard Sweet; emphasis added)[49]

"This book [*Nudge: Awakening Each Other to the God Who's Already There*] is your wireless card to pick up the signals of transcendence, **the *immanent* tran-

scendent, that are out there but not being downloaded." (Leonard Sweet; emphasis added)[50]

"Faith is more than learning to live in the reality of God's invisible presence. Rather, **faith is living in the reality of God's *visible* presence**." (Leonard Sweet; bold added)[51]

Incidentally, Sweet writes that *"The world is not God*, of course, but the incarnation goes all the way down, and the Spirit indwells all that exists."[52] First, so this term "incarnation"—which, again, means "act of being *made flesh*"—when absurdly referring to "all that exists" does *not* mean God "made flesh" even though when referring to Jesus it *does* mean God "made flesh"? Actually, an "incarnation" of "God" is an "incarnation" of "God" whether referring to Jesus or "all that exists." And, in truth, *only Jesus* is God made flesh (a.k.a. God "incarnate"). Second, as addressed earlier, those who believe in panentheism can attempt to differentiate it from New Age pantheism all they want, but panentheism (immanence and transcendence) *includes* pantheism (immanence); it simply goes *beyond* it. Mind games notwithstanding, *immanence is immanence*. And, likewise, an "incarnation" of a "God" in "all that exists" is a "God" that is "*made flesh*" in "all that exists." This of course makes "all that exists" "God" in the "flesh." And, besides, what does "visible" mean if it doesn't mean "visible"?

With today's "fresh way" of "reframing" ("reimagining") a "Jesus," as well as a "God," that are revealed in *all of life* and, thus, in just *living life*, again, why would people need to know and believe in *Jesus of Nazareth*? They can just believe in *life*.

> The seducing spirit calling itself "God": "**God and Life are the same thing**. You may call these things by two different names, but they are the same thing. God is what Life is, and Life is what God is. God is the energy that you call Life, and Life is the energy that you call God. It is all the same thing. **Life is God, *physicalized***."
>
> Neale Donald Walsch: "**So, if we believe in Life, we believe in God, is that what you're saying?**"
>
> The seducing spirit calling itself "God": "**Yes**." (bold added)[53]

Likewise, Sweet also writes, "Matter is the energy of Spirit. Ultimately, all that exists is spirit."[54] The "secret" of this all-encompassing *Oneness* of everyone and everything is depicted in the shape of the Möbius strip. A Möbius strip is formed by connecting the two opposite ends of a strip of paper together after first giving one end a 180-degree half twist. In other words, it is a circle with a twist. Along with bringing opposites together, the twist also "make[s] the inside like the outside and the outside like the inside." Thus, *everything*—including both the inside and the outside of the circle—*all* merges together as *one* and conveniently becomes simply a matter of "*perspective*." This circle dance removes ("transcends") all dualities/polarities/opposites, "creating a state of Oneness" that joins/unites/connects *everyone and everything* with all of "Life" (a.k.a. "God") in "a single unbroken *wholeness*." As described by a New Age website:

> "The Mobius Strip was discovered in 1858 by German mathematician and astronomer August Ferdinand Mobius (1790-1868). The mathematical equation is known as The Mobius Transformation, also known as bilinear transformation or linear fractional transformation.... It is a continuous loop with one surface and one edge ...

"**This fascinating shape expresses *Transformation*.**... The Mobius Strip shape is symbolic of eternal change within stillness itself.

"PAPER WITH ONLY ONE SURFACE! Take a 12" strip of paper (1" wide) and twist one end 180 degrees. Tape the ends together. You have a Mobius Strip! Start drawing a pencil line all around [the center of this strip], from the inside to the outside and back where you started. You'll find you never lifted the pencil off the paper and yet the one surface has a complete line through it. **The inside becomes the outside and the outside becomes the inside.** Continue by cutting along the pencil line. *Instead of 2 separate strips of paper, you have ONE long Mobius Strip. Cut along the center of this strip again and you'll get two totally intertwined strips that don't separate. Do this forever, and* ***you'll get an infinite number of intertwined strips that never separate!***

"**The Mobius Strip is an expression of non-duality. It reveals the Unity of all polarities, creating a state of Oneness, joining the whole and the part**, the masculine and the feminine, expansion and contraction, **spirit and matter**, etc. ***Everything* is One and nothing can be separated from anything else. *All* is completely intertwined, infinitely.** The Mobius Strip is a spiritually significant symbol of balance and union. (Yoga=Union) The Buddhist philosophy of Tantrism also is expressed by the Mobius Strip shape. 'Tantra' is continuity; the word derived from the root 'tan', meaning to extend... extend continuously, **to flow, to *weave*. The continuum is descriptive of the Nature of Reality**, by contemporary physicist David Bohm... '**a single unbroken wholeness in flowing movement**.'" (all parentheses & last two ellipsis dots in the original; bold & italics added)[55]

"[W]hile there is more than one way of being a true believer, **there is still one way**, and that way is **Christ**. Like the mathematical model of **the Möbius strip**, there is **only *one* side. But that one side is the '*inside*' and '*outside*'** of the strip." (Leonard Sweet; emphasis added)[56]

"**In fact, the incarnation brought *all dualities* together**, whether it be the *clean* and the *profane*, the *sacred* and the *secular*, or **the '*out there*' and the '*in here*.**'" (Leonard Sweet; emphasis added)[57]

"**Christ is God's dream**, and His eternal purpose in Christ Jesus is **vastly encompassing**; it answers ***every particular***. Nothing that God wants is *omitted* from it. The Father's timeless intention reaches **from one end of Himself to another**, forever." (Leonard Sweet & Frank Viola; emphasis added)[58]

In today's emerging faith of Oneness/panentheism "[a]n *incarnational* God means that God-stuff is found in *the matter* of *the universe*,"[59] so "from one end of Himself to another" includes from one end of the universe to the other and *everything* in between. And since the "God" and "Christ" of this emerging faith are also in a *circle* of relationship, this adds additional meaning to "from one *end*" "to another." Just bring one end together with the other and you have a *universal circle of relationship of Oneness*. Incidentally, the term *universal* means "All;" "Total; whole;" and "Comprising *all* the *particulars*."[60] And, fittingly, the term *universe* is from *unus* meaning "one" and *versus* meaning "to turn" and literally means "turned into one."[61] And, of course, Oneness/panentheism turns both "God" and the universe "into one." The panentheistic "God" and "Christ" of Oneness are indeed "vastly encompassing," i.e., *all*-encompassing. And with their "incarnational"/panentheistic both/and unities of *all* dualities/opposites—or infinitely intertwined circles (with a twist)—this "God" and "Christ" *include* "*every particular*" in their *circle* of relationship of *Oneness*.

> "We implore you: **Make Christ** the **center**. Make Him the **circumference**. And **fill in the difference** with Him as well." (Leonard Sweet & Frank Viola; emphasis added)[62]

> "When it comes to nudging [i.e., *Awakening Each Other to the God Who's Already There*], it helps if you can **see stereoscopically**. **To see Jesus more clearly and with depth**, we must look out of both eyes. In other words, **we must embrace paradox** and develop the skill of looking at two different things at the same time …
>
> "**Nondualism** is one of the hardest things for 'moderns' to get.…
>
> "The Celts decorated everything with knotted designs, symbols of how ***everything*** is unique yet **tightly *woven* together**. *The key to navigating life is to bring together the two opposite ends of the rope*, the contradictory realities that we confront on a daily basis, **and to tie both strands together into a knot that embraces and interconnects the opposites**." (Leonard Sweet; emphasis added)[63]

Naturally, bringing opposites together in a new nondualistic "Christ" and "God" and "truth" requires bringing opposites together in a new nondualistic "*Scripture*." The two go hand in hand.

> "**We Make a False Division between the Sacred and the Secular** …
>
> "In limiting God's voice to certain 'sanctified' media, we betray the **dualistic tendencies** we've inherited in our Western tradition. **We wrongly assume** that God speaks in church but not in the pub, **that God speaks in Scripture but not in hip-hop. We live as though one is sacred while the other is secular; one earthly, one divine. Jesus says, 'There's just one.'** …
>
> "You can't separate the secular and the sacred; **you can't polarize the sacred and the profane. The doctrine of the incarnation … won't allow it**." (Leonard Sweet; emphasis added)[64]

> "Another part of this **DoubleVision** nudge is the recognition that all of us see through a glass dimly; but second, 'perhaps, **the terrifying and welcome voice may begin, annihilating everything we thought we knew**, and restoring everything we have never lost.'" (Leonard Sweet; emphasis added)[65]

> "A **double minded** man is **unstable** in all his ways." (James 1:8)

> "Take heed therefore that the light which is in thee be not darkness." (Luke 11:35)

Sadly, it is not the *true light* that people today want.

> "The Bible is *not* a blueprint for action, nor a book of answers." (Leonard Sweet)[66]

> "**Vision in the modern world was telescopic**. The modern scientific method taught us **to bring things to *a sharp focus*, to *a point*, to establish clear

lines. **Vision in the postmodern world is *not* monocular, like a telescope, but binocular**. And that's how you get depth perception, and that's how you get **depth** in your own spiritual life is you **bring opposite points together**.... Seeing out of two eyes. **Seeing out of multiple perspectives** at the same time. And **the key** is the ability to see one thing here [and] one thing here and then bring the two together. In the modern world the word *fuzzy* was a negative word. **Blurry** was a negative word. We are now living in a world where the *highest* form of logic, the most complex, sophisticated form of logic, is **fuzzy logic**. Fuzzy logic is **not binary either/or logic** which dominated the modern world. Fuzzy logic is **both/and**, or, even more precisely, and/also.... You keep one eye on the word focused on the word [the video shows a Bible], and then you keep the other eye on the world focused on what God is doing in the world, and then you bring the two together. That's vision.... **Where there is no vision, there is division**. God's people and all people perish.... Your church, if it has **vision**, is calling people, disciples, who can **see double**.... Can your church see double?" (Leonard Sweet)[67]

"The MRI [Missional, Relational, Incarnational] as **the Double-Helix Design** for Life ...

"**The secret of life** is '**helixal**,' two strands that run in opposite directions creating a reproductive **Möbius strip** and slingshot.

"And the secret of life brings together **another double: the linear (line) and nonlinear (curve)** that **together** form a spiral ... around *a single invisible axis* ...

"We negatively call and/alsos 'doublethink.' It's time to call and/alsos, as ['Nobel Laureates'] Crick and Watson did, 'so beautiful.'

"Dualism, **either/or** exclusionism is ... **plug ugly**.

"Nondualism, **both/and** *nonlocalism* is ... **so beautiful**." (Leonard Sweet; last two ellipsis dots & all parentheses in the original; emphasis added)[68]

Incidentally, Sweet says that "nonlocalism" "means that *everything*, in some way that is so mysterious that we cannot even begin to wrap our minds around it, is *connected* to one another."[69] Naturally, this "secret" completely transforms the "either/or exclusionism"—in which <u>either people believe in Jesus and have God</u> or they do not believe in Jesus and do not have God—into a both/and so that <u>both</u> those who do <u>and</u> those who do <u>not</u> believe in Jesus can have God. But, no, this "secret of life" of "nondualism"/Oneness that breaks free from *the truth* of *Jesus* is not a "secret of life" that *Jesus* "came to reveal"!

"**The kingdom of God breaks free of religion with Jesus** ...

"The church's narrative is biblically, theologically, and spiritually bankrupt. The church has been busy telling stories other than God's story, dreaming other dreams than **God's dream** as revealed by Jesus.

"God is now baring **the Jesus Dream** with means only at the divine disposal. **Jesus**, the Divine Being (Son of God) who became the Human Being (Son of Man), **came to reveal the 'secret of life'** and to end our cluelessness (at best) and carelessness (at worst) about **God's *design*** for how we humans should live our lives....

"If God's hand is **MRI-shaped**—mission-shaped, relation-shaped, incarnation-shaped—then Jesus' followers are **shapesmiths** of *the Spirit*....

> "The passion for evangelism is nothing other than a passion for **reading the signs of what God is up to, *connecting* the God-dots**, signing up, and then laying down our lives on God's dotted lines. The French Jesuit Jean Danielou, writing on the theology of mission in the 1950s, said that fruitful missionary efforts 'stopped thinking of bringing Christ to India ... but rather started thinking about **finding Christ already there**.'" (Leonard Sweet; all parentheses & last ellipsis dots in the original; emphasis added)[70]

> "**Christ is God's dream**, and ... is **vastly encompassing** ..." (Leonard Sweet & Frank Viola; emphasis added)[71]

> "[T]here is still one way, and that way is **Christ**. Like the mathematical model of **the Möbius strip**, there is only one side. But that one side is the 'inside' and 'outside' of the strip.... <u>both</u> that Jesus is the exclusive path to God <u>and</u> that people may genuinely encounter God ... **without** ... **knowing** ... **Jesus of Nazareth**.'" (Leonard Sweet; emphasis added)[72]

> *"Be it known unto you all, and to all the people of Israel, that by the name of **Jesus Christ of Nazareth**, whom ye crucified, whom God raised from the dead, even by him doth this man stand here before you whole. **This is the stone which was set at nought of you builders**, which is become the head of the corner. Neither is there salvation in any other: for there is none other name under heaven given among men, whereby we <u>must</u> be saved."* (Acts 4:10-12)

Connecting "the *God-dots*" of a "God" that is absurdly "in the very substance" of *everyone and everything* is not what the *true* God is "up to." People would know that if they were willing to spend more time reading *and believing* the eternally-settled *words* of *God's Word* instead of "reading the signs" of man's *imagination* to connect the "God-dots." (Accordingly, Sweet writes, "Poet/critic Paul Mariani says it is our lack of *imagination* that has closed us to an awareness of God *in the world*," and then specifies "'God's *immanent* presence.'"[73])

Furthermore, aside from the fact that it is the "god of this world" and not God who dreams, the story and dream of the emerging faith's *false* "God" of Oneness is neither the "story" nor "dream" of *God*.[74] And neither is a "secret of life"—let alone an "anti-Christian" "secret of life"—that brings the two opposing ways of truth and falsehood together in a *both/and* of Oneness "the *Jesus* Dream"! Although people still despise and reject Him as such, the Lord Jesus Christ is *the truth*. Contrary to the never-ending imaginary arguments that *purposely dance around the truth*, the *true Person* of the Lord Jesus Christ is *not the truth and falsehood*. He is *the truth*; period. Likewise, the *true Person* of the Lord Jesus Christ does not *twist the truth* of Who He is to bring the narrow way and the broad way together as one in an all-encompassing covenant/testament/way to God.

Yet teaching *the truth* is obviously counterproductive when the mission is to plot the "double-helix" (narrow *and* broad) dance of Oneness of this emerging faith. Thus, this "secret of life" that brings *everyone*—both *inside* and *outside* the faith and truth of God and His Son—together in one "reimagined" all-encompassing "kingdom of God" obviously *requires* everything to be "*blurry*" and "*fuzzy*." It *requires* fuzzy math and "fuzzy logic" and fuzzy "truth," and, accordingly, "*fuzzy* parables." And, no, the parables of *Jesus* were *not* a "fuzzy" "both/and."

"The ideal of monastic holiness and in fact any tradition of holy living is precisely this: an awareness of **the presence of Christ *in all of life* and *in all things*.**" (Leonard Sweet; emphasis added)[75]

"When you live in union with Christ, you don't need answers to problems so much as you need **the presence of Christ, which is the kingdom of God. We don't need a propositional presence** ..." (Leonard Sweet; emphasis added)[76]

"Fuzzy logic is *not* binary *either/or* logic ... **Fuzzy logic is *both/and*** ..." (Leonard Sweet)[77]

"Jesus himself didn't dispense 'proofs' and 'points' and '*propositions*' about God. In fact, Jesus didn't speak in clear language about God. **He spoke in *fuzzy* parables** and riddles, open-ended stories and metaphors. **Jesus didn't lay out the kingdom in propositional form** but in narratives and images. When Jesus sent out the Twelve, he didn't dispatch them with *principles* to dispense, ..." (Leonard Sweet; emphasis added)[78]

"The '*incarnational*' method can also be found in **Jesus' favorite teaching method called 'parables'** and their featuring of *sacramental* metaphors (i.e., they partake in what they represent). The amazing thing about parables ('earthly stories with heavenly meanings') is that they are 'secular' or 'worldly' stories with no religious reference but with deep *sacramental* power.... Jesus' very use of parables is an *incarnational* exercise." (Leonard Sweet; all parentheses in the original; emphasis added)[79]

*"**Who hath ears to hear, let him hear**. And the disciples came, and said unto him, **Why speakest thou unto them in parables?** He answered and said unto them, **Because it is given unto you to know the mysteries of the kingdom of heaven, but to them it is not given**. For whosoever hath, to him shall be given, and he shall have more abundance: but whosoever hath not, from him shall be taken away even that he hath. **Therefore speak I to them in parables: because they seeing see not; and hearing they hear not**, neither do they understand.... **For this people's heart is waxed gross, and their ears are dull of hearing, and their eyes they have closed; lest at any time they should see with their eyes, and hear with their ears, and should understand with their heart, and should be converted, and I should heal them**. But blessed are your eyes, for they see: and your ears, for they hear." (Matthew 13:9-13, 15-16)*

*"And he said, **Unto you it is given to know the mysteries of the kingdom of God: but to others in parables**; that seeing they might not see, and hearing they might not understand.... **Take heed therefore how ye hear**: for whosoever hath, to him shall be given; and whosoever hath not, **from him shall be taken even that which he seemeth to have**." (Luke 8:10, 18)*

Just out of curiosity, along with *exercising sound judgment, when* exactly did it become a *bad* thing to have *principles*, not to mention *scriptural* principles?! This combined with the absurdity that today's "truth" does not require *thinking* certainly explains all the changes taking place in the revolution of this emerging faith. Obviously, it is *man* that prefers fuzzy math and fuzzy "truth" and "fuzzy logic" and "fuzzy parables." Jesus gave parables to those who had *closed* their eyes and ears to the *truth*, a rebellion that clearly continues today in man's never-ending attempt to break free from the "propositions" (doctrine) and principles of *God's* Word of *truth*.

"***Nothing* is inherently 'profane.'**" (Leonard Sweet; emphasis added)[80]

"**We Make a False Division between the Sacred and the Secular** ...

"In **limiting God's voice to *certain* 'sanctified' media**, we betray the **dualistic tendencies** we've inherited in our *Western* tradition. We wrongly assume that God speaks in church but not in the pub, **that God speaks in Scripture but not in hip-hop**. We live as though one is sacred while the other is secular; one earthly, one divine. Jesus says, '**There's just one**.'" (Leonard Sweet; emphasis added)[81]

"Faith makes a metanoized mulch of **all dichotomized selves** and **heals *all* discursive dualisms (one of the worst of which was 'sacred' and 'profane')**, all *disastrous separations* that threaten our existence." (Leonard Sweet; parentheses in the original; emphasis added)[82]

"*... **they have put no difference between the holy and profane**, neither have they shown difference between the unclean and the clean, ... **and I am profaned among them**.*" *(Ezekiel 22:26)*

Despite the imaginary arguments of man, the seducing spirit world, and "science falsely so called," there is no immanent "God" "in the very substance" of everyone/everything thereby uniting everyone/everything together in Oneness with itself and thus rendering believing in Jesus—the Mediator of the true God's testament/covenant—nonessential and irrelevant. Although today's emerging faith (unbelief) is trying to change everything, *God's* Word is perfectly clear that *the truth* is a *linear* separation between the polar opposites of <u>either</u> the *narrow way* of *believing in Jesus that leads to eternal life* <u>or</u> the *broad way* of *not believing in Jesus that leads to eternal destruction*—a *disastrous separation* from God for *all eternity*. There is no circular "Möbius-strip" truth that brings these two ways together in a *both/and* "third way." There is no *"Möbius-strip" Messiah* (Christ) with an *all-encompassing* "presence" that is *"the kingdom of God."*

"*The Son of man shall send forth his angels, and they shall gather out of his kingdom all things that offend, and them which do iniquity; and shall cast them into a furnace of fire: there shall be wailing and gnashing of teeth. Then shall the righteous shine forth as the sun in the kingdom of their Father. **Who hath ears to hear, let him hear**.*" *(Matthew 13:41-43)*

Anyone who dismisses the truth of God's Word as a *"negative"* fear-based agenda or "scare tactic" is a "fool":

"*A wise man feareth, and departeth from evil: but the fool rageth, and is confident.*" *(Proverbs 14:16)*

People today fear *temporal* disaster ("doom") rather than *eternal* disaster because they fear *man* rather than God. And they actually think that shifting to the Oneness of a *false "God"* that brings *all gods* together as *"the same God"* will avert disaster!

"For there is **one God**, and **one mediator** between God and men, **the man Christ Jesus**." (1 Timothy 2:5)

"And it shall be, if thou do at all forget the LORD thy God, and walk after other gods, and serve them, and worship them, I testify against you this day that ye shall surely perish." (Deuteronomy 8:19)

"For thou shalt worship no other god: for the LORD, whose name is Jealous, is a jealous God: Lest thou make a covenant with the inhabitants of the land, and they go a whoring after their gods ..." (Exodus 34:14-15)

"For all the gods of the nations are idols ..." (Psalm 96:5)

"The fear of man bringeth a snare: but whoso putteth his trust in the LORD shall be safe." (Proverbs 29:25)

"Preach the word; be instant in season, out of season; reprove, rebuke, exhort with all longsuffering and doctrine. For the time will come when they will not endure sound doctrine; but after their own lusts shall they heap to themselves teachers, having itching ears; and they shall turn away their ears from the truth, and shall be turned unto fables." (2 Timothy 4:2-4)

"Look unto me, and be ye saved, all the ends of the earth: for I am God, and there is none else. I have sworn by myself, the word is gone out of my mouth in righteousness, and shall not return, That unto me every knee shall bow, every tongue shall swear.... and all that are incensed against him shall be ashamed." (Isaiah 45:22-24)

"Thus saith the LORD, The heaven is my throne, and the earth is my footstool ... but to this man will I look, even to him that is poor and of a contrite spirit, and trembleth at my word." (Isaiah 66:1-2)

"The secret of the LORD is with them that fear him; and he will show them his covenant." (Psalm 25:14)

42

"The Oneness of Twoness that becomes Threeness" -- the *tertium quid*, or Laodicean third way

In the light of God's Word there are only *two* ways in life. One way is to *accept* the truth of God's Word and the other way is to *reject* the truth of God's Word. Yet people in today's shifting Christianity who are not willing to *accept* it are also not willing to believe that they have thereby chosen to *reject* the truth of God's Word. Thus, they are choosing to "reimagine" a *"third* way"—a *tertium quid*—a "Möbius strip," that brings both inside and outside the "box" of the truth of God's Word together as one in a new all-encompassing "truth." In other words, those who are shifting away from the truth are attempting to create a middle way between the two ways of *accepting* or *rejecting* the truth of God's Word. After all, *rejecting* the truth of God's Word would be *apostasy*, so today's creative middle (third) way is to simply "reimagine" (change) it all into a new "truth" in which *all* "truth" is accepted as "God's truth." This way no matter what they choose to believe or disbelieve, they are neither *accepting* (which they are no longer willing to do) *nor rejecting* (which they are not willing to admit) but simply *"transcending"* the truth of God's Word. And since in not *rejecting* it they are likewise "transcending" *apostasy*, there is thus no *departing from the faith*, right?

> "There is a way that seemeth right unto a man, but the end thereof are the ways of death." (Proverbs 16:25; see also 14:12)

> "Take heed, brethren, lest there be in any of you an evil heart of unbelief, in *departing from the living God.*" (Hebrews 3:12)

"The word 'paradoxy' is derived from two Greek words--*pará* meaning 'beyond or beside' and *doxy* meaning 'belief.' **A paradox is a linear contradiction but a harmony in truth**. A paradox is an echoing pun on differentiations and **oppositions which are metaphysically one**." (Leonard Sweet; bold added)[1]

"**Paradox is the midwife of *truth*....**

"In Christ **all opposites** are not so much reconciled as **transcended in the Oneness of Twoness that becomes *Threeness***.

"Paradox is never about two. **Paradox is about the conception of a *tertium quid*, a 'third somewhat,' that is born from the coming together of two opposites**. True twoness always births threeness." (Leonard Sweet; emphasis added)[2]

"In the divine mathematics of science, religion, philosophy, history, in fact everything, **1 + 1 = 3**.... Perhaps God is part of the new math. **Perhaps Jesus taught the higher math of the *tertium quid* (the third way)**." (Leonard Sweet; parentheses in the original; bold added)[3]

As previously addressed, in this emerging faith *man* is creating new "truth" by bringing opposites together as one, and it is this resultant *Oneness* that is *the new "truth."* This resultant Oneness becomes the *tertium quid* -- the "third way" or "third thing." This *Oneness* is not seen as a *rejection* of one or the other of *any* two oppositions since it brings *all* pairs of opposites together in a new "truth" of *both/and*. And this *Oneness* (i.e., *both/and*) of "Twoness" (i.e., two opposites) inevitably becomes a "*Threeness*" (i.e., a *tertium quid*, "third thing" or "third way").

A helpful illustration is that when the colors of blue and red are brought together as one they make purple. In other words, bringing the "Twoness" (blue and red) together in Oneness becomes a "Threeness" or "third thing" (purple). Likewise, red and yellow make orange, and yellow and blue make green. The purple, orange, or green is the new "truth." In this new "truth" there is *no longer* an *either/or*, such as either *blue* or *red*, but only the new *both/and* "third thing" of *purple*. An *either/or* cannot be transformed into a *both/and* without *losing* the *either/or*. But in this emerging faith of Oneness it is absurdly imagined that an "old" *either/or* truth can become a new *both/and* "truth" without losing *anything* of the "old" *either/or* truth.

Similar to transforming the either/or of *blue or red* into a new both/and of *purple*, in this emerging "third way," i.e., emerging faith of Oneness, the opposites ("Twoness") of *truth and falsehood, right and wrong*, are being brought together in a *Oneness* that becomes a "Threeness," a "third thing." So, for example, if *blue* represents the *truth*, and *red* represents *falsehood*, then *purple* represents today's new "truth" in which people have brought *truth and falsehood together as one*. There's only one problem. *Blue* still represents the *truth* and now all they have is *purple*. Purple is not *blue* any more than blue is *purple*. They are *not* the same thing. Only when choosing to wear today's new lenses of darkness do blue and purple become the same and then only *seemingly* so. Of course, they can put a "positive" spin on it and point out that *red* still represents *falsehood* whereas now all they have is *purple*. Purple and red are likewise obviously not the same thing. Nevertheless, neither *purple* nor *red* are *blue*, and *blue* still represents the *truth*. Mind games notwithstanding, in their new "third way"—i.e., their new "truth"—*red* (*falsehood*) did *not* become *blue* (*truth*), it merely became *purple* (a "*reimagined*" "truth"). A "*reimagined*" "truth" is not the *truth*.

Fittingly, according to an art textbook:

> "The final property of color is its **intensity**, sometimes called its *saturation* or *chroma*. This generally **describes a color's purity**, with a hue being at its most intense at normative on the color wheel. **As a color loses its intensity, it moves towards neutral**. A color theorist might describe **the mixing of two colors** that are located directly across from each other [on the color wheel] as **the simultaneous diminishing of intensity (<u>neutralizing</u>)**." (parentheses in the original; bold & underline added)[4]

The *tertium quid*, "third thing," or "Threeness"—i.e., bringing two opposites together as one—*neutralizes the truth*, which of course is a prerequisite to the "relationship" of the *circle* of Oneness. Moreover, *mixing* something with the truth of God's Word clearly *adds* to the truth of God's Word which *takes away its purity* and *changes* the truth of God into a lie.

> "**Every word of God is pure**: *he is a shield unto them that put their trust in him.* **Add thou not unto his words**, *lest he reprove thee, and thou be found* **a liar**." (Proverbs 30:5-6)

> "**The words of the LORD are pure words**: *as silver tried in a furnace of earth, purified seven times. Thou shalt keep them, O LORD, thou shalt preserve them from this generation for ever.*" (Psalm 12:6-7)

> "Because that, when they knew God, they glorified him not as God, neither were thankful; but became vain in their imaginations, and their foolish heart was darkened. Professing themselves to be wise, they became fools ... **Who changed the truth of God into a lie**, and worshipped and served the creature more than the Creator, who is blessed for ever. Amen." (Romans 1:21-22, 25)

We are to accept and love the truth of God *as it is*. People are neither saved nor have God by loving a "truth" they have "reimagined" into a fashion—a lie—that they are *willing* to accept. To dance around the truth is to dance around the truth.

> "Not every one that saith unto me, Lord, Lord, shall enter into the kingdom of heaven; but he that doeth the will of my Father which is in heaven. Many will say to me in that day, Lord, Lord, have we not prophesied in thy name? and in thy name have cast out devils? and in thy name done many wonderful works? And then will I profess unto them, I never knew you: depart from me, ye that work iniquity." (Matthew 7:21-23)

> "And with all deceivableness of unrighteousness in them that perish; because **they received not the love of the truth, that they might be saved**. And for this cause God shall send them strong delusion, that they should believe a lie ... God hath from the beginning chosen you to **salvation through** sanctification of the Spirit and **belief of the truth**: Whereunto he called you by our gospel, to the obtaining of the glory of our Lord Jesus Christ. **Therefore, brethren, stand fast**, and hold the traditions which ye have been taught, whether by word, or our epistle." (2 Thessalonians 2:10-11, 13-15)

> "Whosoever transgresseth, and abideth not in the doctrine of Christ, hath not God.

He that abideth in the doctrine of Christ, he hath both the Father and the Son." (2 John 1:9)

"Take heed therefore how ye hear: for whosoever hath, to him shall be given; and whosoever hath not, from him shall be taken even that which he seemeth to have." (Luke 8:18)

In the emerging faith of *Oneness* it is not possible to *stand fast* in the *truth* and in the *doctrine* of Christ. To do so would be to *disconnect* its *circle* of relationship. So those in this emerging faith *must* "mov[e] towards neutral." The following, which is also fitting of the popular "centering" of this emerging faith as well, is included in the art textbook:

> "**In the center of the wheel** stands deep gray (since black is defined as the complete absence of light and thus theoretically cannot be produced through mixing actual color), which is known as **neutralized color**." (parentheses in the original; bold added)[5]

To "center" in the inner "God" of Oneness is to "center" in *the neutral zone* where truth and falsehood, right and wrong, are brought together as *one big neutral "truth"* that is <u>everything but</u> *saturated* with God's *pure truth*. Without this neutrality and impurity Oneness would not even exist. In fact, it is in choosing to "center" in *the neutral zone* that *connects* the circle of Oneness, and thereby connects the world of *opposites* ("colors") into *a <u>new world</u>* of Oneness. But, regardless of in whom or in what people think they have "centered," unless they abide *in the doctrine* of Christ they *do not have God*. When it comes to *believing* and *loving* the *truth* of God and His Son there can be *no neutrality*.

Those in today's shifting Christianity who neither *outright reject* nor *accept* the *true* Person of the Lord Jesus Christ (the *"corner stone"* and *"rock of offence"*) but choose instead to *"reimagine"* Him are *"neither cold nor hot"* but *"lukewarm"*—a *"third thing"* created by bringing cold and hot together as one. And, not surprisingly, those who are lukewarm imagine that everyone can freely *believe* or *disbelieve* whatever they want about Jesus and *still have Jesus*. After all, this *tertium quid*, "third thing" or "third way"—in which people are determined to have it *both ways*—is all about bringing the broad way together as one with the narrow way in an all-encompassing "*Möbius-strip*" "kingdom of God" that doesn't merely *move* "the fence," it *removes* it altogether. A Möbius strip not only brings together both ends, the polar opposites, it brings together both *sides* as well. So this circle with a twist that only has one edge and thus "*only one side*" gives a whole new meaning to the question, "Who is on the Lord's side?":

> "[W]hile there is more than one way of being a true believer, there is still *one way*, and that way is Christ. Like the mathematical model of the Möbius strip, **there is only *one* side. But *that one side* is the 'inside' and 'outside'** of the strip. Once again, theologian/evangelism professor William J. Abraham says it best: 'It is perfectly consistent to hold <u>both</u> that Jesus is the exclusive path to God <u>and</u> that people may genuinely encounter God outside the Christian church **without explicitly knowing about Jesus of Nazareth**.'" (Leonard Sweet; emphasis added)[6]

This dance of Oneness, this new "third way" *both/and* "truth," seeks to bring *both inside and outside* the truth and faith of God and His Son together as one so that *everyone* is thus "on the Lord's side" whether they believe and love the truth or not. Again, this is neither "*God's* dream" nor "the *Jesus* Dream," and neither is it a "dance to the music of *Jesus*."

> "At the end of Revelation, **Jesus is outside the church**, knocking, banging on the door, **asking to be let *inside* so that he can get *us* back *outside***.
>
> "We need to learn to dance to the music of Jesus once again." (Leonard Sweet; emphasis added)[7]

Actually, it is in chapter 3, which is nowhere near the end of Revelation, that Jesus is knocking on the door of the church. (The rest of Revelation, by the way, goes on to warn of God's coming *judgment* which is just too "negative," i.e., *true*, for today's emerging faith of Oneness.) Jesus is knocking, not to get people in this church "back outside," but to bring *them* into fellowship with *Him*. Those who choose the neutral *both/and* (or more precisely *neither/nor*) lukewarm dance of the "third way"—i.e., *tertium quid*—only *imagine* that they have fellowship with Jesus. If they don't repent and open the door to Him, He will spew them out of His mouth in this *one-sided* relationship which, by the way, is *not* the dance of a *one-sided* "Möbius strip."

> "And unto the angel of the church of the Laodiceans write; These things saith the Amen, the faithful and true witness, the beginning of the creation of God; I know thy works, that thou art neither cold nor hot: I would thou wert cold or hot. **So then because thou art lukewarm, and <u>neither</u> cold <u>nor</u> hot, I will spew thee out of my mouth**.... As many as I love, I rebuke and chasten: be zealous therefore, and repent. Behold, I stand at the door, and knock: if any man hear my voice, and open the door, I will come in to him, and will sup with him, and he with me. To him that overcometh will I grant to sit with me in my throne, even as I also overcame, and am set down with my Father in his throne. **He that hath an ear, let him hear what the Spirit saith unto <u>the churches</u>**." *(Revelation 3:14-16, 19-22)*

Incidentally, the first use of the term *tertium quid* has been attributed to the fourth century reference to "the followers of Apollinaris who spoke of Christ as something neither human nor divine, but a mixture of the two, and therefore a 'third thing'."[8] Apollinaris' "reimaginings" of Christ were condemned as heresy, and "[f]ollowers of Apollinarianism were accused of attempting to create a tertium quid ('third thing,' neither God nor man)."[9] Appropriately enough, Apollinaris was the bishop of *Laodicea*.[10]

43

Connecting the dots of the immanent "God" and "Christ"

Essentially, the shifts and changes of today's many "reimaginings" boil down to man's attempt to bring "Thus saith God" and "thus imagines man" *together as one* in *a new "truth"*—a *tertium quid* ("third thing" or "third way") "fullness of truth" that is all-encompassing. And with man's "reimagined" "God" of Oneness that is immanent/"incarnate" in everyone and everything, *everyone* and *everything* becomes "'God's' truth," and *every* voice and *every* handwriting becomes "thus saith 'God.'" So in order to create a more "*complete*" "picture" ("understanding"/"truth"), i.e., a "group mosaic," *all* "truths" ("colors") of *all* religions/faiths/cultures, along with all "sensory truths," are being brought together as a "fullness of truth," or a "Totality of God." This clearly gives everyone the freedom to believe whatever they so choose.

> "**All the various truths form one Truth**; ... your little bit of truth forms part of **the group mosaic**." (the seducing spirit calling itself Djwhal Khul; emphasis added)[1]

> "**All religions** have something to do with **the whole, the totality**." (Leonard Sweet; emphasis added)[2]

> "[T]he focus will be on finding ways to honor those differences [between '**all the world's religions**'], seeing what they can further **reveal** to humanity about **the Totality of God**, and looking to see whether **the combination of all these different views** might produce **a Whole** that is Greater than the Sum of Its Parts." (the seducing spirit calling itself "God;" bold added)[3]

> "The orthodox understanding of *imago Dei* is less that each individual is created 'in the image of God' and more that all of humanity was made in God's image. That means **the greater the incorporation of *all cultures*, all colors**, all generations, all socioeconomic groups, *all body types*, **the greater the glimpse of God**." (Leonard Sweet; emphasis added, except to *imago Dei*)[4]
>
> "Embodiment is key to cognition, since different *bodily experiences* give us different thoughts and perspectives. For **a *true* picture of *Christ***, I need to incorporate **the *multi-culti* sounds and sights and smells and touches** of other *ta ethne* embodiments....
>
> "**With the human race now losing at least one indigenous language every two weeks**, *how much of God are we in danger of not seeing?*" [!] (Leonard Sweet; emphasis added, except to *ta ethne*)[5]

Since when does being made in the image of God mean that all "bodily experiences" and "perspectives" of all humanity and all religions/faiths/cultures are to be brought together to see a "greater" "glimpse of *God*"?! God is "*a Spirit*" (John 4:24) and each and every *individual* of mankind is made in the image of God and therefore has *a spirit*. But in the emerging faith of Oneness/panentheism, not only does everyone *and everything* have *a spirit* but this *spirit* is imagined to be "*God*," and an *immanent* "*God*" at that. Again, this immanence places this "reimagined" "*God*" in "*the very substance*" of everyone/everything thereby bringing *itself* ("*Spirit*") and everyone/everything (*matter*) together in a blended spirit-matter Oneness. And, therefore, with an *immanent* "*God*" as well as an *immanent* "*Christ*"—that is, with *a* "*God*"/*matter Oneness* and *a* "*Christ*"/*matter Oneness*—"body types" and "bodily experiences" and "sounds and sights and smells and touches," etc., all absurdly become a "true picture of *Christ*" as well as a "greater" "glimpse of *God*."

People can "romanticize" and "glorify" this immanent "God" of Oneness all they want, but, as mentioned earlier, the absurd "reality" of this *unholy false "God"* whose "stuff" is *in everyone and everything* is that it is in everything, even dog poop.

> "An *incarnational* God means that ***God-stuff*** is found **in the *matter*** of the universe." (Leonard Sweet; emphasis added)[6]

> "**I tell you, I am *in* every flower, every rainbow, every star in the heavens, and *everything* in and on every planet** rotating around every star....
>
> "**My Beingness is *in everything*. Everything.**" (the seducing spirit calling itself "God;" emphasis added)[7]

Everything means everything, as even one of its own adherents admittedly writes:

> "If, then, we envision the Divine as female—a symbol that incorporates nature, body, and matter—then as a people we will come to honor the feminine, nature, body, and earth. A Divine Feminine symbol renders obsolete the old idea that these things are outside the realm of divinity. It begins to **shift** thousands of years of **dualistic thinking**, setting up a new mandate for the divinity of the earth and the holiness of the body....
>
> "Patriarchy has majored in **divine transcendence**, which means **separateness from the material universe**—being above, beyond, or apart from it. **Divine immanence**, on the other hand, is divinity here, near and now, **inherent in the**

material stuff of life....

"Restoring the feminine symbol of Deity means that divinity will no longer be *only* heavenly, other, out there, up there, beyond time and space, beyond body and death. It will also be right here, right now, in me, in the earth, in this river and this rock, **in excrement and roses alike**." (Sue Monk Kidd; bold & underline added)[8]

Even Sweet absurdly writes:

"***Matter* is the energy of *Spirit*. Ultimately, all that exists is spirit**." (emphasis added)[9]

"God pervades the world through the Spirit ...

"*Jesus* was a 'dawn collector' who found **God's Spirit *in all things, in all aspects* of the natural world, both animate** (birds, animals, flowers, seeds) **and inanimate** (pots, coins), yet showed how we can experience God's Spirit in ways that are *beyond and 'beneath language.'*...

"[T]he *incarnation goes all the way down*, and the Spirit indwells *all that exists*." (parentheses in the original; emphasis added)[10]

"**The Spirit of Christ** is not *vagrant or homeless*, but **incarnate and embodied in** *whatever gives life*: **a fish, some flesh, the aroma of bread and wine, an accent, or an appearance**....

"Are you finding Christ **in the people you meet**? Are you finding Christ **in the things you handle**? Are you finding Christ **in the food you eat**? Finding Christ **in the voices you hear**? Finding Christ **in the smells you breathe**?" (emphasis added)[11]

"**The world of nature** has an identity and purpose apart from human benefit. But **we constitute together a cosmic body of *Christ*.**...

"This entails a radical doctrine of **embodiment of *God* in the very *substance* of creation**." (emphasis added)[12]

Again, *the Lord Jesus Christ* <u>alone</u> is God made flesh (God "incarnate"). And, no, to believe *the truth* that God is *not* made flesh in "all that exists" (i.e., that the true God is *not* "incarnate and embodied" in a fish, etc., not to mention "in excrement and roses alike"[D]) is not to believe that He is "*vagrant or homeless*"! Will absurdities *and blasphemies* never cease? In case you missed it, another *abomination* here is that if the "*incarnation*" of the true *God* went "all the way down" into "*all that exists,*" then *the Lord Jesus Christ and excrement alike* would both be God "incarnate." And, as if that isn't abominable enough in and of itself, it doesn't even end there (but this will be addressed more later). The vile "truth" of Oneness/panentheism is indeed beyond and beneath language. Again, that the "truth" of this emerging faith does not require *thinking* explains its otherwise inexplicable success *in today's Christianity*. Even though people are

---

D

Yes, technically excrement is also part of "whatever gives life" by cleaning out the system; without it we die. It also "gives life" to the creepy crawlies, the clean up crew designed to feast on it. And, no, the *true* and *holy* God is not in these excrement-eating creepy crawlies any more than He is in the excrement itself.

choosing to "glorify" and "exalt" this *totally false* "God" of Oneness as the true God, sorry, but this filthy, *everything-but-holy*, panentheistic "God" only dreams to "be like the Most High" and gets flushed down the toilet (its rightful throne) deservedly. (By the way, anyone who sees this statement as "blasphemy" is following this unholy *false* "God" rather than the *holy true* God and His Son, the truth and faith of Whom are *perfectly clear* in the *Holy* Scriptures—which, as now needs clarification as well, consists of 66 books; period. No, the world's "hip-hop" is not "Scripture.")

Whether people want to see this *non*-"beautiful" side of this increasingly preferred "God" (as well as "Christ") of Oneness/panentheism or not, "the Totality of God" in Oneness/panentheism includes *the* "*Totality.*" In other words, whether people are willing to admit it or not, the "group mosaic" or *complete* and "true" "picture" of "the *Totality*" of this panentheistic "God" (and panentheistic "Christ") does indeed include "excrement and roses alike." And a panentheistic "God"/"Christ"—and, likewise, "truth"—that are *in everyone and everything* can thus be found *wherever* anyone chooses to look, which of course includes in *all religions*.

> "Tomorrow's God says that **every church** is 'his church,' and **every faith** is 'her faith,' and *every* soul is God's soul, because it shares the same soul with God!" (the seducing spirit calling itself "God;" bold added)[13]

> "The discussions at these important gatherings ['of **all the world's religions**'] will not focus on eliminating the differences between religions, for it will be recognized that **diversity of spiritual expression is a *blessing***, not a problem. Rather, the focus will be on finding ways to **honor those differences, seeing what they can further reveal to humanity about the Totality of God** …" (the seducing spirit calling itself "God;" bold added)[14]

As this emerging faith of Oneness/panentheism seeks to form a "group mosaic" that is a "fullness of truth" or "Totality of God," its "decolonized" theology of Oneness merges *all gods* together into its *one emerging whole* "God." And in order for this *whole* "God" (and a "better," more "complete" and "true" "picture"/"understanding") to emerge, *interfaith dialogue* is obviously essential (i.e., *interfaith*, or "*intercultural*," now that the term *culture* has been broadened to both include and whitewash *religious* differences). In other words, Christianity has been seduced into *learning* from and *connecting* with *other faiths/religions/"cultures"* in order to connect God with these other gods in the emerging whole "God," or "Totality of God." (And, of course, these *other gods* are honored as just *differences* of "conceptions of *God*.") Still, there is only one truth of the one true God, and neither the one truth nor the one true God is "the group mosaic" of *anything*, let alone of *other gods*. Again, likewise, the earth always has been round, and there never has been an elephant or a turtle holding it up.

> "**There is only One God**. What God is this? Is it **Adonai**? **Allah**? **Elohim**? **God**? **Hari**? **Jehovah**? **Krishna**? **Lord**? **Rama**? **Vishnu**? **Yahweh**?
>
> "***It's All of Them***." (Neale Donald Walsch; bold added)[15]

> "Just as physicists cannot understand truth by one model alone--that is, either the wave nature of light or the particle nature of light--so one model may not suffice **to understand *God* completely**.… One can be a faithful disciple of Jesus Christ without denying the flickers of the sacred in followers of **Yahweh, or Kali, or**

Krishna....

"It will take **a decolonized *theology*** for Christians to appreciate the *genuineness* of others' faiths ...

"The *interfaith embodiment* of a quantum spirituality is based not on the Enlightenment search for what **the world religions** hold in common but on the multitudinous and uniqueness of ***each particular* vision of *truth*.**... Without **knowing one another's 'colors,'** our spiritual journey is little more than monochromatic busywork, an attention to the isolated and ephemeral designed to distract the believer from **the height of faith's vision**." (Leonard Sweet; emphasis added)[16]

"[T]he greater the incorporation of *all* cultures, *all* colors, ... the greater the glimpse of *God*." (Leonard Sweet; emphasis added)[17]

"A surprisingly central feature of **all the world's religions** is the language of **light** in communicating **the divine** and symbolizing *the union* of the human with *the divine*: **Muhammed's light-filled cave, Moses' burning bush, Paul's blinding light, Fox's 'inner light,' Krishna's Lord of Light, Böhme's light-filled cobbler shop, Plotinus' fire experiences, Bodhisattvas with the flow of Kundalini's fire erupting from their fontanelles, and so on**." (Leonard Sweet; under the heading, "Coincidence, or connection?;" emphasis added)[18]

"**New Light** embodiment means to be 'in *connection*' and 'in-*formation*' with ***other faiths***. To be in-formation means to know each other's songs almost as well as one knows them oneself, and to enlarge the community to include those ***whose conceptions of God*** differ from ours in form." (Leonard Sweet; emphasis added)[19]

"'*Bible translation* [i.e., with its **indigenous use of names for God**] has thus helped to bring about **a historic shift in Christianity's *theological* center** of gravity by pioneering a strategic alliance with **local conceptions of religion** ... it is difficult to overestimate the implications of this indigenous change for the future shape of religion.'" (Leonard Sweet quoting Lamin O. Sanneh; brackets and ellipsis dots in the original; emphasis added)[20]

"... **God and Allah and *all the other names*** that we have for That Which Is Divine **are the same thing**, and that **This One Divine Being** loves all of us ... **All religions** are individual paths to paradise, and each path will take us there." (Neale Donald Walsch; emphasis added)[21]

"**The message of *God*** is clear. **No matter what the religion**, no matter what the **culture**, no matter what the **spiritual or indigenous tradition, the *bottom line* is *identical*: We are all one**....

"We must preach **a new gospel**, its *healing* message summarized in two sentences:

"**We are all one.**
"**Ours is not a better way, ours is merely *another* way**....

"I challenge every priest, every minister, every rabbi and religious clerk to preach this." (Neale Donald Walsch; emphasis added)[22]

Sweet writes, "For anything to be real it must be local,"[23] and "all religion should also be local ... because it is addressed to a particular people at a particular time in a particular place."[24] Actually, for religion to be real it *must* be *true*. And therefore it *must* be *scriptural*. Otherwise, since the *true* God is not in everyone and everything, the "truth" and "faith" of religion is merely man's *imagination* and not the truth and faith of the true God. Local (indigenous) conceptions of religion neither *replace* nor *add to* the *truth* of God's Word that is *absolute* for *all* people and *all* times and *all* places. It is only in today's emerging faith of Oneness/panentheism that *the names* of indigenous *gods* become indigenous *"names for God,"* and likewise that the *conceptions* of local *gods* become local *"conceptions of God."* And since *all gods* of *all religions* become just different names, conceptions, and forms of "the same God" in this *not-so-future* "shape of religion," i.e., this "circle" of Oneness, *all religions* therefore not only become equally valid paths to "God" but also *equally valid "truths"* in "the Totality of God." The implications of this unarguably *historic theological shift* are eternal.

> *"And it shall be, if thou do at all forget the LORD thy God, and walk after other gods, and serve them, and worship them, I testify against you this day that ye shall surely perish." (Deuteronomy 8:19)*

> *"Of the Rock that begat thee thou art unmindful, and hast forgotten God that formed thee.... for they are a very froward generation, children in whom is no faith. They have moved me to jealousy with **that which is not God**; they have provoked me to anger with their vanities ... For they are a nation void of counsel, neither is there any understanding in them. O that they were wise, that they understood this, that they would consider their latter end!... And he shall say, Where are **their gods**, **their rock** in whom they trusted, ... let them rise up and help you, and be your protection. See now that I, even I, am he, and there is no god with me ..." (Deuteronomy 32:18, 20-21, 28-29, 37-39)*

> *"Assemble yourselves and come; draw near together, ye that are escaped of the nations: they have no knowledge that set up the wood of their graven image, and pray unto a god that cannot save.... Look unto me, and be ye saved, all the ends of the earth: for I am God, and there is none else." (Isaiah 45:20, 22)*

The "group mosaic" of the "God" of Oneness is nothing more than an imaginary "picture" of an imaginary "God" that is being conceived, formed, and shaped into a fashion that man is willing to accept. As addressed earlier, the fashion that man is willing to accept today is sadly nothing but a glued-together counterfeit "rock" of sand that is attempting to "be like the most High." Again, shifting sand is not the Rock, and the Rock is not shifting sand. But man has chosen to blast the eternal Rock to transform the Rock into shifting sand in order to "reimagine" God as *immanent in all things* so that man can now attempt to transform the shifting sand back into the Rock by connecting *all things* back together as "God" in one universal "relationship" of Oneness. And, naturally, the many bits and pieces of all "truths"/religions and gods are part of this glued-together "rock"/"mosaic"—i.e., of this emerging *whole* "God"—since this is, after all, the point. And now that this emerging faith—"new *world* religion"—of this whole "God" of Oneness is even "widely desired and worked for" in today's shifting Christianity, its "emergence" is no longer proceeding slowly but in fact *quite rapidly*.

> *"[T]he vision is a vision of group work, of group relationships, of group objectives, and of **the group fusion to the larger Whole**." (the seducing spirit calling itself Djwhal Khul; emphasis added)[25]*

"Today, slowly, the concept of **a world religion and the need for its emergence are widely desired and worked for. The fusion of faiths is now a field for discussion.** Workers in the field of religion will formulate **the universal platform** of **the new world religion**. It is a work of loving synthesis and will emphasize **the unity** and the fellowship **of the spirit**.... The platform of the new world religion will be built by many groups, working under the inspiration of *the Christ*....

"The churches in the West need also to realize that basically *there is only one Church*, but it is *not* necessarily only the orthodox *Christian* institution. **God works in many ways, through many faiths and religious agencies**; this is one reason for the *elimination* of *non-essential* doctrines. By the emphasizing of the *essential* doctrines and **in their union will *the fullness of truth* be revealed. This, the new world religion will do** ..." (the seducing spirit calling itself Djwhal Khul; emphasis added)[26]

In this new world religion "[i]t is relatively unimportant what we mean in detail by that little word of three letters" (i.e., "God").[27] So, obviously, what is "*non-essential*" is *the truth* of God and His Son, which is indeed being gradually removed/eliminated in this very upside-down "*fullness* of *truth*," even by today's shifting Christianity itself.

"[I]n the new generation lies hope ... hope because of the promptness with which they **recognize truth *wherever* it is to be found** ...

"... God works in many ways, through **many faiths and religious agencies; in their union will the *fullness of truth* be revealed**." (the seducing spirit calling itself Djwhal Khul; emphasis added)[28]

"'**THERE IS NO RELIGION HIGHER THAN--TRUTH.**'...

"There is, and can be, but **one absolute truth in Kosmos**. And ... if it is absolute it must also be **omnipresent** and **universal**; and that in such case, it must be **underlying *every* world-religion** ... Therefore, that *a portion of truth, great or small, is found in every religious and philosophical system* ... Our object is not to destroy any religion but rather to help to filter each, thus ridding them of their respective impurities. In this we are opposed by all those who maintain, against evidence, that their particular pitcher alone contains the whole ocean....

"Free discussion, temperate, candid, undefiled by personalities and animosity, is, we think, the most efficacious means of getting rid of error and bringing out the underlying truth ..." (Helena P. Blavatsky, <u>Lucifer</u> magazine, 1888; an occultist and channeler who has been referred to as the grandmother of the New Age movement; bold & italics added)[29]

"**There is no room for absolute truth upon any subject whatsoever**, in a world as finite and conditioned as man is himself. But **there are relative truths**, and we have to make the best we can of them....

"[F]or every one of us has to find that (to him) final knowledge *in* himself.... **The sun is *one*, but its beams are *numberless*** ..." (Helena P. Blavatsky, <u>Lucifer</u> magazine, 1888; parentheses in the original; emphasis added, except to *in*)[30]

"... **Christian people are to recognize their place within a worldwide divine revelation and see Christ as representing all the faiths** and taking His rightful place as World Teacher. **He is the *World* Teacher** and **not** a

Christian teacher.... They may not call Him Christ, but they have their own name for Him and follow Him as truly and faithfully as their Western brethren." (the seducing spirit calling itself Djwhal Khul; bold added)[31]

In other words, Christians "are to recognize their place" within "the group mosaic" and *see* the truth and faith of God's Word as only *one part* of "the fullness of truth," i.e., of *the whole*. However, this is the complete *antithesis* of what it is to be a *Christian*. The emerging faith of the Oneness/wholeness of all religions/faiths/cultures/"truths"/gods is completely *antithetical* to the preeminent *superiority* of *the truth* of Who Jesus Christ *is* which must be *believed* in order to even *be* a *Christian* in the first place. The "group mosaic" of "the Totality" of an *interfaith* panentheistic "God" (and "Christ") is indeed anti-Christian. Besides, to be anti-*Christ* (i.e., against the true Jesus Christ, Who is not *interfaith*) is to inevitably be anti-*Christian* (i.e., against the truth and faith of the true Jesus Christ) as well. But even though *anti-* means "*against*" and "*opposite of*," this emerging faith diabolically brings *all opposites* together in a Oneness that thereby effectively blinds people to the eternal differences between *an anti-Christ and Christ* or *an anti-Christianity and Christianity*. It all becomes just a new kind of "Christ" and a new kind of "Christianity" in this new kind of "truth" and "faith" of this new kind of "God" for those who aren't willing to simply believe and obey God and His Son.

> "But if our gospel be hid, it is hid to them that are lost: In whom **the god of this world hath blinded the minds of them which believe not**, lest the light of the glorious gospel of Christ, who is the image of God, should shine unto them." (2 Corinthians 4:3-4)

> "For unto us was the gospel preached, as well as unto them: but the word preached did not profit them, not being mixed with faith in them that heard it." (Hebrews 4:2)

> "Take heed, brethren, lest there be in any of you an evil heart of unbelief, in departing from the living God." (Hebrews 3:12)

> "If we could **break free** from the Greco-Roman soul-sort narrative, think of what could change.... We would **stop seeing the line that separates good and evil running between our religion and all others**. We would be **freed from** the tendency to always think **'insider/outsider'** and 'us/them.'...
>
> "We would see that ... **Jesus was not a gift to one religion, but to the whole world**....
>
> "**Evangelism** would **cease** to be a matter of *saving souls* from a bad ending ... It would **cease to be a proclamation of the *superiority* of the *Christian* religion**....
>
> "This kind of evangelism would celebrate the good in the Christian religion and lament the bad, just as it would in *every* other religion, **calling people to <u>a way of life</u>** in a kingdom (or beautiful *whole*) that transcends and includes **all religions**." (Brian McLaren; parentheses in the original; emphasis added)[32]

> "**Jesus is not <u>just</u> <u>one</u> <u>way</u>**, a better way, a pleasant way on a good day. He is *the* way.
>
> "**Jesus is not <u>just</u> <u>one</u> <u>truth</u>**, a higher truth, or a more personal truth. He is *the* truth....

> "So, Christianity is **not** an allegiance to a complex **doctrinal** or ethical system, **but a passionate love for <u>a way of living</u>** in the world that's rooted in living **by Jesus**, the way, the truth, and the life. **Our theologies, doctrines**, and subjective experiences are <u>designed</u> to **flow <u>organically</u> from** our loving **relationship** to Christ, but they are never to substitute for it." (Leonard Sweet & Frank Viola; bold & underline added)[33]

> "Your life and your community are living organisms: That word *organism* means they are by definition self-organizing, complex, adaptive, **self-regulating** systems. **An <u>organic</u> system makes it up as it goes along**." (Leonard Sweet; bold & underline added)[34]

> "Christians should be active participants in making and **evangelizing** this 'recombinant culture' that is increasingly susceptible to 'Rip. Mix. Burn' initiatives. But **we do *not* aim to make it into a 'Christian culture,' but a *human* culture** that is *merciful* and hospitable to all humanity." (Leonard Sweet & Frank Viola; emphasis added)[35]

First, love for "*a way of living*" (especially a "*self*-regulating" one) is not the same thing as love for *the Person* of Jesus Christ *Himself*. And, again, the *one* true *Person* of Jesus Christ Himself is the truth. A <u>person</u> *is* who that *person* <u>is</u>. There is no new kind of "person" that can be "reimagined" however anyone and everyone chooses—i.e., into *more than one truth* of *who* that person is. Jesus said, "<u>I am the way, the truth, and the life: no man cometh unto the Father, but by *me*</u>" (John 14:6). An evangelism that "transcends" (bypasses) the *saving* truth of <u>Who</u> this *specific* "*mediator between God and men*" <u>*is*</u> isn't "*merciful*"! Since Jesus is <u>just</u> <u>one</u> <u>Person</u>, He is indeed <u>just</u> <u>one</u> <u>way</u> and <u>just</u> <u>one</u> <u>truth</u>. But this *one specific Person* of Jesus Christ of Nazareth—Who, by the way, was resurrected as this *same* specific Person—is simply too narrow of a way and truth and life for today's emerging faith of Oneness. After all, if the Lord Jesus Christ is a *specific Person* (and He is), and not a "reimaginable" cosmic "*it*" or a new kind of "*reimaginable*" "Person," then He would need to be *believed* and *obeyed* and *loved* for *Who <u>He</u> specifically <u>is</u>*.

> "[P]eople may genuinely encounter God outside the **Christian** church *without* explicitly knowing about **Jesus of Nazareth**.'" (Leonard Sweet; emphasis added)[36]

> "*Be it known unto you all, and to all the people of Israel, that by the name of **Jesus Christ of Nazareth**, whom ye crucified, **whom God raised from the dead** ... **Neither is there salvation in any other** ...*" (Acts 4:10, 12)

> "*Therefore let all the house of Israel know assuredly, that God hath made **that same Jesus**, whom ye have crucified, both Lord and Christ.*" (Acts 2:36)

> "*If any man love not the Lord Jesus Christ, let him be Anathema Maranatha.*" (1 Corinthians 16:22)

Second, this sounds like **the false "Jesus" of *The Shack*** that said of his followers who "were Buddhists or Mormons, Baptists or Muslims" – "**I have no desire to make them Christian**, ..."[37] In an interview of William Paul Young (the author of *The Shack*), pastor Kendall Adams of Burlington Baptist Church refers to this part of *The Shack* and says, "I know you said on another show that you originally wrote **they *are* Buddhist, Mormons, Muslims**, that's what you had originally written." To which Young replies, "Well, that's because I'm a third culture kid. I'm not just an American or a Canadian. And in the U.S., or in the West, we don't realize that people can be *Muslim* Christians or *Buddhist* Christians, because in the world, the rest of the world, the designation of *Buddhist* or *Muslim* just indicates *ethnicity*. It *doesn't* indicate *belief* system."[38] He is either incredibly naïve or deliberately whitewashing/misrepresenting/spinning/curving the facts for today's mission of Oneness/connectness.

Sounding like McLaren and the many other leaders of this emerging faith, to pastor Adams' question, "So what do you mean by he has no desire to make them Christian?" Young answers, "Because the term Christian is **the big *C-bomb*** in the world. **Jesus wasn't a *Christian*.** He was a Jew.... **He didn't come to create a new religion to compete with the existing religions**. He didn't come to say, okay, we're going to establish a new one – [mutual muffled interjections] – against Islam.... **He came to introduce *relationship* ...**"[39] And, not surprisingly, Young's panentheistic "God" of *The Shack* "who is the ground of all being" that "dwells *in*, around, and through *all things*"[40] subtly teaches in the chapter "A Piece of π," "**All** love and **relationship** is possible for you only because it **already exists** within me, **within God** myself."[41] (Again, panentheism goes both ways -- "God" is *in* everyone/everything, and everyone/everything is *in* "God.")

Yes, Jesus was indeed Jewish, and *still is* in fact. (Just as the *true* God is still the God of *Israel*. But more on that later.) And, no, Jesus Christ the Saviour and *Jewish* Messiah did not come "to create a new religion." As He Himself said, "*for salvation is of the Jews*" (John 4:22). He came to die for our sins in order to *confirm* and *finish* and *establish* the first testament/covenant. But, sadly, the world's hatred of anyone and anything that is truly Christian is relatively minor compared to its diabolical hatred of anyone and anything that is of the Jews. Again, Jesus Himself wasn't and isn't a *Christian*—a believer/follower/disciple of Christ—because *Jesus is Christ*. There is no competition whatsoever between the preeminent superiority of *the truth* of the *true* Jesus Christ—the Son and Mediator of the only true God—and the *falsehood* of "the existing religions." It is those who are shifting to *darkness* who are helping to create a "new *world* religion," with an *interfaith* "Christ"/"Jesus" and "God" of *the world* that offer everyone a *universal* salvation/reconciliation/relationship/redemption/forgiveness, regardless of beliefs, regardless of theology, regardless of religion.

> Neale Donald Walsch: "Regardless of their beliefs, regardless of their religion?"
>
> The seducing spirit calling itself "God": "Regardless of their beliefs, regardless of their religion."
>
> Neale Donald Walsch: "Or lack of religion?"
>
> The seducing spirit calling itself "God": "Or lack of religion."...
>
> Neale Donald Walsch: "... I want to make sure, I want to make absolutely certain that I get this right.... [T]his is one thing I want to get as accurately as I can. I want there to be no mistake about this. You are saying that **there is no 'right way' to God**?"
>
> The seducing spirit calling itself "God": "That is what I am saying. **Exactly, precisely, unequivocally**. There are a thousand paths to God, and every one gets you there."
>
> Neale Donald Walsch: "So we can, at last, bring an end to 'better' about God. We

can **stop saying that 'ours is the better God.'"**

The seducing spirit calling itself "God": "Yes, you can.... It will require you to give up your ideas of *superiority* ... For this is **The New Gospel:** ... **There *is* no one true religion.... or one and only way to Heaven.**" (bold added)[42]

Since today's emerging faith "reimagines" "God" as "the God of *all* relationship," and *even* as "relationship" itself, it is to be expected that faith and theology and doctrine and truth and Scripture are all "reimagined" as coming/flowing from *relationship* rather than from the written Word of God. After all, the latter makes it perfectly clear that a relationship with God comes specifically by *faith* in His Son, Jesus Christ of Nazareth, and warns that *unbelief* leads to "*departing from the living God.*" This is obviously the *opposite* of a *relationship* (as is to "*be Anathema*"--see 1 Corinthians 16:22). But, conversely, when "faith" and "truth" "flow" from a "relationship" to a "God" and "Christ" that are *immanent in everyone and everything*, people can freely make it all up as they go along rather than *believe* and *obey*.

"Jesus led us to **think of God *differently***, as relationship, **as the God of *all* relationship**." (Leonard Sweet & Frank Viola; emphasis added)[43]

"What if we were to think *connectness* rather than *correctness*?...

"The church is **not** a set of *propositions*, buildings, or ***beliefs***: The church is **a network of relationships** ... with God, with the Scriptures, with each other, with creation.

"We need to **learn to play the spaces.... All space is God's space**. Church is God's space. World is God's space.... Jesus is at work in the eighty-year-old Sunday-school teacher as well as in **the atheist** or in **the Buddhist**." (Leonard Sweet; middle two ellipsis dots in the original; emphasis added)[44]

"... **Jesus did not leave** His disciples ... with ***intellectual belief*** or a **'Christian worldview.' He left** them with **a *relational* faith** and an indwelling presence." (Leonard Sweet & Frank Viola; emphasis added)[45]

"**The key to a dynamic relationship** is not 'do you share common ideals' or 'common values,' but have you **reframed** your **differences as a source of strength**, not weakness. **Jesus spent more time drawing *circles*** to include people **than in drawing *lines*** to keep people out." (Leonard Sweet; emphasis added)[46]

"One of the most serious **thought-crimes** for a Christian is **the confusion of 'faith' with 'belief,' or to call someone who follows Jesus a 'believer,'** ..." (Leonard Sweet; emphasis added)[47]

People would be far better served if they actually *believed* God, Jesus, and the Scriptures instead of just wanting a *relationship* with them *without having to believe them*. The lines of *truth* that are clearly set forth in the Word of God are what they are. If they "keep people out" it is because people are not *willing* to accept lines between *truth* and *falsehood* and *right* and *wrong*; that is, between *what is of God* and *what is not of God*. Contrary to today's imaginary arguments, the *non*-"reimagined" *true* Jesus did not draw circles of Oneness that bring all religions/faiths/cultures/gods/"truths"/opposites together in the "fullness of truth" of a "double helix" (narrow *and* broad) "Möbius-strip" "kingdom of God." Rather, it is today's shifting Christianity that is grievously spending more time drawing circles to *fictitiously* include people than it is in teaching the truth of God and His Son so that people can believe and be *genuinely* included.

> *"For God so loved the world, that he gave his only begotten Son, **that whosoever believeth in him should not perish**, but have everlasting life." (John 3:16)*

The covenant that *God* is willing to make with *man* is what it *is*, and God's one and only Mediator *is* Who He *is*. It is neither *love* nor *mercy* nor "a source of *strength*" to "reframe" ("reimagine") the *differences* between *the Lord Jesus Christ* and *false* "*Jesuses*"/"*Christs*" and between *God* and *false gods* as merely differences of "*understandings*" and "*conceptions*"! And neither is this all merely a difference of "*view*," or "*perspective*." In the shift to Oneness, "worldview" is just one more term being used to whitewash *religious* differences. True scriptural Christianity is the *truth* and faith of the true God. It is not just another "*view*," or "*perspective*." It is not just another "*particular vision* of truth." Only in the emerging faith of Oneness/panentheism does the Christian truth become just *one part* of "the *whole*," "the *totality*," "the *fullness* of truth," "the *group mosaic*." In defining "worldview," Borg writes:

> "A **worldview** is a culture or religion's taken-for-granted understanding of **reality**—a root image of what is real and thus of how to live. A worldview is 'the story of the universe that a culture accepts.'" (emphasis added)[48]

To say that "Jesus did not leave his disciples" with either "intellectual belief," i.e., belief that requires *thinking*, or a "Christian worldview," i.e., a *Christian* understanding of reality and the universe, is to stretch the truth beyond belief (pun intended). What does that make John chapter 1, for example? The truth in just this one chapter alone that Jesus Christ of Nazareth, the Son of God, the Lamb of God, the Person Who takes away the sin of the world, the Christ, the Messiah, of Whom Moses and the prophets did write, is eternally God and the Creator of all things is not "a '*Christian* worldview'"?! It certainly isn't a Hindu or Buddhist or Muslim or New Age "worldview." To the contrary, the *truth* of the Lord Jesus Christ does indeed leave us with *Christian* truth and faith, *not* truth and faith that is *nonchristian* or *anti-Christian*. Jesus did not leave us with the multiple "views" and "perspectives" of *religious Oneness*.

Here again, it all comes down to wanting a reality (truth) that is *both/and*, not *either/or*. The either/or *Christian* "worldview" (reality/truth) of John 3:16—the truth of which, by the way, was said by *Jesus* and subsequently recorded by one of His *disciples*—has no place in today's desired both/and "worldview" ("reality"/"truth"). Hence today's *nonchristian* and *anti-Christian* "reimaginings" and changes and shifts.

> "**Postmodern** culture is an **anti-Christian** culture." (Leonard Sweet; emphasis added)[49]

> "The **postmodern** world being born is **not** a bipolar **worldview of *either/or's* but** a double helix, Möbius-strip culture of **both-and's**, ..." (Leonard Sweet; emphasis added)[50]

> "You do **not** live in **an '*either/or*' reality**. The reality is '**both/and**.'" (the seducing spirit calling itself "God;" emphasis added)[51]

PART FIVE: THE CREATION 303

And, therefore, according to the seducing spirit world, since "*diversity* of spiritual expression is a blessing, ... the focus will be on finding ways to *honor* those *differences*, ... looking to see whether the combination of *all these different views* might produce a *Whole* that is Greater than the Sum of Its Parts."[52] Even so, despite this emerging faith/ "culture"/"paradigm"/"worldview"/"reality" of Oneness, the truth of God and His Son *is* what *it is*. And to "reframe" ("reimagine") the *lines* of either/or *differences*—i.e., truth and falsehood, right and wrong—as *circles* of both/and Oneness is *not* "a source of *strength*," unless one considers it "strength" to make God out to be a liar.

> "... **he that believeth not God hath made him a liar**; because he believeth not the record that God gave of his Son." (1 John 5:10)

In a both/and "reality" no *thinking* or *believing* is required, just relationship; *all* relationship.

> "The kingdom of God **breaks free** of **religion** with Jesus ...
>
> "The church has been busy telling stories other than God's story, dreaming other dreams than **God's dream** as revealed by Jesus.
>
> "God is now baring **the Jesus Dream** ... **the 'secret of life'** ... God's *design* for how we humans should live our lives....
>
> "... Jesus' followers are **shapesmiths of *the Spirit***....
>
> "The passion for evangelism is nothing other than a passion for reading the signs of what God is up to, **connecting the God-dots** ..." (Leonard Sweet; emphasis added)[53]

> "**Christ is God's dream**, and His eternal purpose in Christ Jesus is **vastly encompassing**; it answers *every particular*. Nothing that God wants is *omitted* from it. The Father's timeless intention reaches **from one end of Himself to another**, forever." (Leonard Sweet & Frank Viola; emphasis added)[54]

> "We implore you: **Make Christ** the **center**. Make Him the **circumference**. And **fill in the *difference*** with Him as well." (Leonard Sweet & Frank Viola; emphasis added)[55]

> "[W]hile **there is *more than one way* of being a true believer**, there is still one way, and that way is **Christ**. Like the mathematical model of the Möbius strip, there is only one side. But that one side is **the 'inside' and 'outside'** of the strip.... *both* that Jesus is the exclusive path to God *and* that people may genuinely encounter God **outside the Christian church *without* explicitly knowing about *Jesus of Nazareth***.'" (Leonard Sweet; emphasis added)[56]

Absurdly, people in this emerging faith are determinedly spinning in circles trying to "Christianize" the circle of Oneness while simultaneously trying to *anti-*"Christianize" Christianity. Nonetheless, *Christ* (the *Messiah*) is not an all-encompassing *circle* (twisted or otherwise) of Oneness. In other words, Christ (the Messiah) is not an all-encompassing *both*/*and* "fullness of truth." And neither did *Jesus* reveal a "secret of life" that breaks free from *the truth* of *Jesus*. Only in man's dreams does *Jesus* (Who *alone* is Christ) draw circles to include people who do not believe in *Jesus*! In the light of God's Word of truth this is *all* perfectly obvious. But those in today's emerging faith of Oneness/panentheism

> "Missional art #1 is the ability to help people understand that **the fullness of truth is not propositions or principles. The fullness of truth is Christ.**
>> "'Christ is in the Church **in the same way as the sun** is before our eyes. We see the same sun as our fathers saw, and yet **we understand it in a much more magnificent way**.' —Teilhard de Chardin"
>
> (Leonard Sweet; emphasis added)[57]

A "fullness of truth" that brings all religions/"truths" into its "fullness" *cannot be propositions* or *principles*. That is, it *cannot* be a "truth" that must be *believed* or *obeyed* (for starters, the never-ending *differences* and *contradictions*, to say the least, prevent this), and therefore it *cannot be "the faith which was once delivered unto the saints."* This delivered faith was then and still is now the whole *true* faith of the true Person of the Lord Jesus Christ. But in today's emerging faith of Oneness to see and "understand" Christ "in a much more magnificent way" is to "reimagine" an *"understanding" of "Christ" "much more magnificent" than the Lord Jesus Christ*. In other words, it is to "see" and "understand" a "Christ" that *"transcends" (bypasses)*—and is thus *different* from—*the truth* and *faith* of the *Person* of *Jesus*.

> "**Christ is the Aperture of God**. In the small opening of this one life, the clearest image of **the whole** can be seen.... **All the rays of truth in the universe focus through him**: 'The Son is the radiance of God's glory and the exact representation of his being, sustaining all things by his powerful word.'
>
> "**It all began with one person** in one place . . . **until the local was made the universal**, the little made large, by the power of God's Spirit." (Leonard Sweet & Frank Viola; last ellipsis dots in the original; emphasis added)[58]
>
> "[T]here is still one way, and that way is **Christ**.... But ... people may genuinely encounter God ... **without** ... **knowing** ... **Jesus of Nazareth**.'" (Leonard Sweet; emphasis added)[59]
>
> "**Then said Jesus** unto them again, ... **I** am the good shepherd, and know my sheep, and **am <u>known of mine</u>**." (John 10:7, 14)

In fact, today's interfaith "Christ" of Oneness *must* bypass knowing and believing in the true Jesus in order to *even be* the *interfaith* "Christ" in the first place. In this "fullness of truth" God and His Son are reduced to nothing but *empty shells* that have been divested of *the truth* of *Who they are* so that they can then be "filled" with *any* "understanding" and *any* "truth" that *anyone* in *any* faith/religion/culture *chooses*. So in this emerging *upside-down* faith "the *fullness* of truth" is actually quite the opposite. It *has to be* to even *consider* bringing together *all religions* as a *"group mosaic"* of the truth of either God or His Son.

> "There is no room for *absolute truth* upon any subject whatsoever ... But there are *relative truths* ...
>
> "**The sun is *one*, but its beams are *numberless* ...**
>
> "[E]ach of us can **relatively reach the Sun of Truth** even on this earth, **and assimilate its warmest and most direct rays, however *differentiated* they**

may become after their long journey through the physical particles in space." (Helena P. Blavatsky, <u>Lucifer</u> magazine, 1888; emphasis added)[60]

*"Beloved, when I gave all diligence to write unto you of the common salvation, it was needful for me to write unto you, and exhort you that ye should **earnestly contend for <u>the faith</u> which was once delivered unto the saints**. For there are certain men crept in unawares, who were before of old ordained to this condemnation, ungodly men, turning the grace of our God into lasciviousness, and denying the only Lord God, and our Lord Jesus Christ." (Jude 1:3-4)*

*"So then **faith cometh by** hearing, and hearing by **the word of God**." (Romans 10:17)*

Sadly, even today's shifting Christianity is trying to replace *"the common salvation"* with a "reimagined" *universal* "salvation." So rather than contending for *the faith* that is given to us by *God* in the Word of *God*, it is choosing instead to contend for the *emerging faith* of Oneness and its *interfaith* whole "God." It therefore isn't surprising that the Lord Jesus Christ is knocking on its door seeking to come in. This is especially so given that in its growing preference for "the fullness of truth" of Oneness (or the Laodicean third way of *both/and*) today's shifting Christianity has thus also opened itself up to the emerging *interfaith* whole "*Christ*" of Oneness—a false "Christ of many barnyards." Again, in addressing the Laodicean church Jesus says:

*"Behold, I stand at the door, and knock: if any man hear **<u>my voice</u>**, and open the door, I will come in to him, and will sup with him, and he with me. To **him that overcometh** will I grant to sit with me in my throne, even as I also overcame, and am set down with my Father in his throne. **He that hath an ear, let him hear what the Spirit saith unto the churches**." (Revelation 3:20-22)*

Incidentally, *overcoming* includes overcoming *the world* through *faith*, that is, through *believing* in the *true Jesus Christ*. And *overcoming* the world is not the same thing as becoming *one* with the world. Neither is overcoming the world the same thing as "reimagining" *Christ* as one with the world.

*"And we know that we are of God, and **the whole world lieth in wickedness**." (1 John 5:19)*

*"And when he is come, **he will reprove the world of sin**, and of righteousness, and of judgment: Of sin, **because they believe not on me**." (John 16:8-9)*

*"Whosoever believeth that Jesus is the Christ is born of God ... For whatsoever is born of God overcometh the world: and **this is the victory that overcometh the world, even our <u>faith</u>**. Who is he that overcometh the world, but he that believeth that Jesus is the Son of God?... If we receive the witness of men, the witness of God is greater: for this is the witness of God which he hath testified of his Son. He that **believeth** on the Son of God hath the witness in himself: he that believeth not God hath made him a liar; because he believeth not **<u>the record</u> that God gave of his Son**." (1 John 5:1, 4-5, 9-10)*

"Christianity is meant to be pulled *all kinds of ways* and still deliver meaning. **God's**

> *presence* **is written in *every* handwriting. *The world* bears traces of the handwriting of the Word....**
>
> "Early Christians drew upon ideas, phrases, metaphors, and customs of ***pagan cultures*** as 'seeds' of the divine Word that **become *enfleshed in Christ*** and in the church.... [T]hese early Christians checked constantly for **the omnipresence of Christ *in all cultures*.** They searched until they found **the hidden traces of God in 'sheep from other folds,'** as Jesus liked to say, and opened themselves as no other religious tradition had ever done to **the Christ of many barnyards.**" (Leonard Sweet; emphasis added)[61]

> *"Verily, verily, I say unto you, He that entereth not by the door into the sheepfold, but climbeth up some other way, the same is a thief and a robber. But he that entereth in by the door is the shepherd of the sheep. To him the porter openeth; and the sheep hear his voice: and he calleth his own sheep by name, and leadeth them out. And when he putteth forth his own sheep, he goeth before them, and the sheep follow him: for they know his voice. And a stranger will they not follow, but will flee from him: for they know not the voice of strangers.... I am the good shepherd, and know my sheep, **and am known of mine**.... And other sheep I have which are not of this fold: them also I must bring, and they shall hear **my voice**; and **there shall be <u>one</u> fold**, and one shepherd.... But **ye believe not, because ye are not of my sheep**, as I said unto you. My sheep hear my voice, and I know them, and they follow me." (John 10:1-5, 14, 16, 26-27)*

> *"Nor consider that it is expedient for us, that one man should die for the people, and that the whole nation perish not. And this spake he not of himself: but being high priest that year, he prophesied that **Jesus** should die for that nation; and not for that nation only, but that also he **should gather together in <u>one</u> the children of God** that were scattered abroad." (John 11:50-52)*

> ***"For ye are all the children of God <u>by faith</u> in Christ Jesus."*** *(Galatians 3:26)*

> *"For there is **one God**, and **one mediator between God and men, the man Christ Jesus**." (1 Timothy 2:5)*

> ***"Jesus said unto them, If God were your Father, ye would love <u>me</u>****: for I proceeded forth and came from God; neither came I of myself, but he sent me.... And if I say the truth, why do ye not believe me? He that is of God heareth God's words: ye therefore hear them not, because ye are not of God." (John 8:42, 46-47)*

There is only one true God, and the only way to the one true God is to know, believe, and love the one true Son of the one true God.

> *"For God so loved the world, that he gave his only begotten Son, that whosoever **<u>believeth</u> in him** should not perish, but have everlasting life.... He that **<u>believeth</u> on <u>the</u> Son** hath everlasting life: and he that believeth not the Son shall not see life; but the wrath of God abideth on him." (John 3:16, 36)*

Those who think they can connect the dots of the immanent "Christ" and "God" of "many barnyards" into "a true picture" of the one true God and His Son are deceiving themselves, *and others*. For starters, any similarities to God in *other religions* (a.k.a. "cultures") are because other religions have imagined their own *counterfeits* to the true God.

These *counterfeit gods* are not "hidden traces" of the *genuine God*. The counterfeits are *counterfeits* and the *genuine* is genuine. It is not that the *counterfeits* are the *genuine*. But, sadly, today's shifting Christianity has been so seduced by the false theology of Oneness that it now believes the *counterfeit gods* of *other religions* are the *genuine God* that we need to "introduce" people to more fully—and out of their own religious texts no less!

In addition, before today's attempts to "Christianize" the mission of the seducing spirit world began to *change everything*, it would have been glaringly obvious (along with everything else) that the *"ideas, phrases, metaphors, and customs of pagan cultures"* are *not* the "handwriting" of the Word of God, and neither does *"every handwriting"* contain *"God's presence."* Likewise, the *Son* of God (i.e., the true *Person* of Jesus Christ) is *not* paganism incarnate, is *not* omnipresent in all cultures (religions), and is *not* the Shepherd of *pagan* "barnyards." Of the true Person of Jesus Christ and His narrow way there is only *"one fold,"* not *"many barnyards."* And His *"one fold"* (which is *not* a "Möbius-strip" fold that includes everyone *both* "'inside' and 'outside'" the truth and faith of <u>God's Son</u>) consists *only* of those who *believe* on Him, who are thus *"the children of God by faith in Christ Jesus."* Those who prefer an all-encompassing *interfaith* testament/covenant/way to <u>God</u> and are thus also trying to transform the <u>Son</u> of God—the Christ (Messiah)—into an *interfaith* Shepherd are not following *Him* but the emerging interfaith *counterfeit* "Christ" ("Messiah") of New Age Oneness. This interfaith *false* "Christ" "loves those who are *not* Christian," i.e., those who do *not* believe the truth and faith of the *true* Christ, for *a reason*.

> **"The Christ Who will return will not be** like **the Christ Who** (apparently) **departed. *He will not be a 'man of sorrows'*** …
>
> "He has been for two thousand years the supreme Head of the Church Invisible, the Spiritual Hierarchy, composed of **disciples of *all faiths*. He recognizes and loves those who are *not* Christian** but who retain their allegiance to Their Founders - the Buddha, Mohammed and others. He cares not what the faith is if the objective is love of God and of humanity. ***If men look for the Christ Who left*** His disciples centuries ago, ***they will fail to recognize the Christ Who is in process of returning***. The Christ has *no* religious barriers in His *consciousness*. It matters not to Him of *what faith* a man may call himself." (the seducing spirit calling itself Djwhal Khul; parentheses in the original; emphasis added)[62]
>
> "**[T]ruth is a *multifaced* jewel**, the facets of which it is impossible to perceive all at once; …" (Helena P. Blavatsky, <u>Lucifer</u> magazine, 1888; emphasis added)[63]

In today's shift to the *darkness* of Oneness/panentheism the difference between *God* and *other gods* is no longer relevant, except to "honor those differences" as a "*blessing*"! And, likewise, the difference between the voice of the *Shepherd* and the voice of *another* is irrelevant today as well. In Oneness it is *all the same voice* because it is *all the same* "*God*" or "*Christ*" that is immanently "hidden" in everyone and everything. And since it is *all* the same voice, an anti-Christian/non-Christian *interfaith* community and totality becomes *needed* so that "the fullness of truth" of the world's emerging whole "God" and "Christ" can thus "be revealed." Those who desire this "group mosaic"—new world religion—are therefore being "pulled *all kinds of ways*" (i.e., "*tossed to and fro, and carried about with every wind of doctrine*"--Ephesians 4:14) on *purpose*. And they are indeed on a mission. The "god of this *world*" and his emerging kingdom of darkness are having a heyday in today's armor-shunning, light-intolerant Christianity.

44

A "'*loyalty test*' to following Jesus" is "to open ourselves up and stop clinging to our precious preconceptions"?

In *no way, shape, or form* is man's "reimagined" "Christ" of "many barnyards" either a "true picture" or "a much more magnificent" "understanding" of the true Person of Christ. Unlike people today, the apostles of the Lord Jesus Christ were "*eyewitnesses of his majesty*." But when this truth recorded for us in the Word of God isn't the *truth* that people today *want*, they certainly won't want to *understand* it. Rather, "*having itching ears*," they will choose instead to "*turn away their ears from the truth, and shall be turned unto fables*" (2 Timothy 4:3-4).

> "For we have not followed cunningly devised fables, when we made known unto you the power and coming of our Lord Jesus Christ, but **were eyewitnesses of his majesty**.... We have also a more sure word of prophecy; whereunto ye do well that ye take heed, as unto a light that shineth in a dark place, until the day dawn, and the day star arise in your hearts: Knowing this first, that no prophecy of the scripture is of any private interpretation. For the prophecy came not in old time by the will of man: but holy men of God spake as they were moved by the Holy Ghost." (2 Peter 1:16, 19-21)

> "**For a *true* picture of Christ, I need to incorporate the *multi-culti* sounds and sights and smells and touches** of other *ta ethne* embodiments. **Christianity *reconceives* itself in light of *each incarnation*.**" (Leonard Sweet; emphasis added, except to *ta ethne*)[1]

308

"**Every culture births a *new* form of Christianity**, a new way of being human, and in so doing builds up the body of Christ evermore toward 'full stature.'" (Leonard Sweet; emphasis added)[2]

"**The body of Christ** is less an aggregate of *persons* than **an aggregate of cultures** ..." (Leonard Sweet; emphasis added)[3]

"**The MRI church** is an incubator **of *cross-cultural* wisdom**. In spite of modernity's *individualization* of the gospel, the unit of discipleship has always been *ta ethne*. That's why **the divine *design*** is for a global/local church, where **millions of 'locals' contribute their uniqueness to one truly global, catholic entity**. Or as *Paul* puts it, as the gospel is 'incarnated' into the various *ta ethne* of the world, the body of Christ is built up into its full stature." (Leonard Sweet; emphasis added, except to *ta ethne*)[4]

"Franchise is another word for *dis-incarnation*. And too few of these franchise 'projects' approached **other cultures** with the *gospel* of love: 'Jesus loves who and what you are, and wants to inhabit who you are and what you are in such a way that it blesses me, blesses others, and **blesses the world with *new* understandings of who Jesus is**.'" (Leonard Sweet; emphasis added)[5]

"**If you '*understand*' something in <u>*only one way*</u>, then you scarcely understand it at all**." (Leonard Sweet quoting Marvin Minsky; emphasis added)[6]

"[T]here is *more than one way* of being a true believer, ..." (Leonard Sweet; emphasis added)[7]

"**The *changing* face of Jesus in every culture** is eloquent testimony to the Truth that has **more than one face, the Jesus of *many* faces**." (Leonard Sweet; emphasis added)[8]

"**There are 17,000 different cultures** in the world today." (Leonard Sweet; emphasis added)[9]

"... **Jesus is 'God's way of getting to know God,'** ..." (Leonard Sweet; emphasis added)[10]

"[T]he greater the incorporation of **all cultures**, all colors, all generations, all socio-economic groups, all body types, **the greater the glimpse of God**." (Leonard Sweet; emphasis added)[11]

First, not even *people*, let alone *cultures*, are an "embodiment" or "incarnation" of either God or Christ. And, *yes*, it *is* a matter of *semantics*. *Meaning matters!* Again, the true *Person* of Jesus <u>alone</u> is Christ, He <u>alone</u> is Jesus, and He <u>alone</u> is God manifest in the flesh—which is *not* an *ever-changing* or *ever-repeating* "incarnation." There are no *reincarnations* of Jesus! And neither are there 17,000 possible "new understandings of who Jesus is" in 17,000 possible "new form[s] of Christianity." The truth and faith of God and His Son is recorded for us by God in the absolute truth of God's written Word of inspired Scripture. But people today are bound and determined to think *outside* this "box."

Second, it used to be obvious that the true <u>*Person*</u> of Jesus only has <u>*one face*</u>. It is a tremendous understatement to say that "reimagining" Jesus with "*many* faces" (not to mention 17,000 or so faces) gives an entirely different meaning to the following Scripture:

> "*For God, who commanded the light to shine out of darkness, hath shined in our hearts, to give the light of* **the knowledge of the glory of God in the <u>face</u> of Jesus Christ**." *(2 Corinthians 4:6)*

Again, Sweet says to "walk in the light for the *greater* glory of God,"[12] and he and many others in this emerging faith are walking in the "light" of Oneness for a "*greater* ... glimpse of God," i.e., "*greater*" than *the <u>face</u>* of the true Person of Jesus Christ, in these "*many* faces," that is, *17,000* or so "*changing* face[s] of Jesus."

> "***For I am the LORD, I <u>change not</u>***; ..." *(Malachi 3:6)*

> "***Jesus Christ <u>the same</u> yesterday, and today, and for ever***." *(Hebrews 13:8)*

> "If you '*understand*' something in *only one way*, then you scarcely understand it at all." (Leonard Sweet quoting Marvin Minsky; emphasis added)[13]

Would that include in *only one face*, and only one face that *never changes*? Again, in this emerging faith why would it matter if people mistakenly "understand" *someone else* to be "Jesus" or "Christ" that *isn't Him*?

> "**Then if any man shall say unto you, Lo, here is Christ, or there; believe it not**. *For there shall arise **false Christs**, and false prophets, and shall show great signs and wonders; insomuch that, if it were possible, they shall deceive the very elect. Behold, I have told you before. Wherefore if they shall say unto you, Behold, he is in the desert; go not forth: behold, he is in the secret chambers; believe it not. For as the lightning cometh out of the east, and shineth even unto the west; so shall also the coming of the Son of man be.... And then shall appear the sign of the Son of man in heaven: and then shall all the tribes of the earth mourn, and they shall see the Son of man coming in the clouds of heaven with power and great glory.*" *(Matthew 24:23-27, 30)*

> "... *Ye men of Galilee, why stand ye gazing up into heaven?* **this same Jesus**, *which is taken up from you into heaven, shall so come in like manner as ye have seen him go into heaven.*" *(Acts 1:11)*

> "*Nevertheless when the Son of man cometh,* **shall he find faith on the earth?**" *(Luke 18:8b)*

> "*So Christ was once offered to bear the sins of many; and unto them that* **look for him** *shall he appear the second time without sin unto salvation.*" *(Hebrews 9:28)*

Those who don't *believe* in *this same Jesus* obviously won't be *looking* for *this same Jesus*. And He is only returning for those who believe in—and thus look for—*Him*. Those who are absurdly looking for "Christ in the food you eat" and for a "Christ of many barnyards" are not looking for this *same Jesus*—i.e., Jesus Christ *of Nazareth*. And it is the mission of the seducing spirit world—i.e., what *it* is "up to," not *God*—to seduce people into looking for its *interfaith* "Christ" rather than for *the same Jesus Christ of Nazareth* Who ascended from His disciples.

> "**If men look for *the Christ Who left His disciples* centuries ago, they will fail to recognize *the Christ Who is in process of returning*.** The Christ has no religious barriers in His consciousness. **It matters not to Him of *what faith a man may call himself*.**" (the seducing spirit calling itself Djwhal Khul; emphasis added)[14]

> "***Let us hold fast the profession of our faith without wavering***; *(for he is faithful that promised;)... Now the just shall live by faith: but if any man draw back, my soul shall have no pleasure in him. But we are not of them who draw back unto perdition; but of them that **believe to the saving of the soul**.*" (Hebrews 10:23, 38-39)

> "*Beloved, when I gave all diligence to write unto you of the common salvation, it was needful for me to write unto you, and exhort you that ye should earnestly contend for **the faith which was once delivered unto the saints**. For there are certain men crept in unawares, who were before of old ordained to this condemnation, ungodly men, turning the grace of our God into lasciviousness, and denying **the only Lord God, and our Lord Jesus Christ**.*" (Jude 1:3-4)

> "*So then **faith cometh by** hearing, and hearing by **the word of God**.*" (Romans 10:17)

> "***I have fought a good fight**, I have finished my course, **I have kept the faith**: Henceforth there is laid up for me a crown of righteousness, which the Lord, the righteous judge, shall give me at that day: and not to me only, but unto all them also that love his appearing.*" (2 Timothy 4:7-8)

> "***Fight the good fight of faith, lay hold on eternal life** ...*" (1 Timothy 6:12)

> "Jesus' first teaching after the resurrection was this: '**Stop clinging to me**.' [endnote: John 20:17 (NASB)] **In other words, don't** try to control me or **hold on to your preconceived notions about me**. Don't miss the completeness of the whole gospel. If there were a '*loyalty test*' to following Jesus, it would be this: To what extent are you **clinging to preconceptions about *who Jesus is***, or to what extent are you allowing other cultures and voices to *inform* your *biblical exposition*?" (Leonard Sweet; emphasis added)[15]

For starters, the passage that Sweet is twisting in this quote was not even a "teaching," let alone one with such a diabolical meaning as Sweet ascribes to it. Jesus had just risen from the dead in His physical body when He revealed Himself to a weeping Mary Magdalene. Obviously she would have been overcome with joy at His being alive.

> "*Jesus saith unto her, Touch me not; for I am not yet ascended to my Father: but go to my brethren, and say unto them, I ascend unto my Father, and your Father, and to my God, and your God.*" (John 20:17)

"Touch me not" was a physical admonition because He had not yet ascended to God in His newly resurrected body. This has *absolutely nothing whatsoever* to do with broadening one's "preconceived notions" about *Who Jesus is!* Fittingly, earlier on the same page Sweet had written, "Incarnations do their work on the borders of our souls, changing our beings and *charging our imaginings*."[16] His imaginings have clearly been charged (and not by *God*, "*Who will have all men to be <u>saved</u>, and to come unto the knowledge of <u>the truth</u>*"--1 Timothy 2:4), and this is a prime example. *Biblical truth and beliefs* are *not* "preconceived notions" that we are to *let go* of! And neither are *the Holy Scriptures* and *the Gospel of Christ* to be "globally 'in-formed,'" i.e., *enlarged* and *broadened*, to form a "fullness of truth" with the *new* "understandings" and "perspectives" of the *voices* of *other faiths/religions/cultures. It is written <u>is</u> what it <u>is</u>* and *God's* written Word of *absolute truth*, which includes the *true* Gospel of the *true* Christ, is neither to be *added to* nor *taken away from* (e.g., Proverbs 30:5-6; Revelation 22:18-19). But, naturally, in today's new kind of "Christianity" its new kind of "whole Jesus" needs a new kind of "whole gospel" to go along with it.

> "Don't miss the completeness of **the whole gospel**. If there were a '*loyalty test*' to following Jesus, it would be this: To what extent are you clinging to preconceptions about **who Jesus is**, or to what extent are you **allowing other cultures and voices to *inform* your biblical exposition**?... Instead of *bristling at change* and bracing ourselves to fend off the *unfamiliar*, Jesus instructs us to *open ourselves up* and *stop clinging to our precious preconceptions*." (Leonard Sweet; emphasis added)[17]

> "New Light embodiment means to be '*in connection*' and '***in-formation***' **with other faiths**.... whose conceptions of *God differ from ours* in form....

> "A globalization of evangelism 'in connection' with others, and **a globally '*in-formed*' gospel**, is capable of talking across the fence with **Hindu, Buddhist, Sikh, Muslim**--people from other so called '*new*' religious traditions ('*new*' *only to us*)--without assumption of *superiority* and power." (Leonard Sweet; parentheses in the original; emphasis added)[18]

> "... **the gospel gets *incarnated* in *every* culture by *design***." (Leonard Sweet; emphasis added)[19]

> "**There are 17,000 different cultures** in the world today." (Leonard Sweet; emphasis added)[20]

> "**A *loyal* follower of Jesus is one who listens to and learns from *different voices***, different *bodies*, different social locations, different styles of expression, different languages.... When Jesus is only filtered through *your own singular* experience and perspective, what comes forth is a very anemic and defensive Jesus. In fact, *the Jesus one person's limited life conjures up for the world* is not **the whole Jesus** at all." (Leonard Sweet; emphasis added)[21]

> "*And **a stranger will they not follow**, but will flee from him: **for they know not <u>the voice of strangers</u>**.... I am the good shepherd, and know my sheep, and **am known of mine**.... **My sheep hear <u>my</u> voice**, and I know them, **and they follow <u>me</u>**.*" (John 10:5, 14, 26-27)

Concerning Sweet's latter quote here, actually *no* person's life is "*Jesus*" because *Jesus* is Jesus! So "the Jesus" that *any* person's life "conjures up for the world" is not *the true Jesus* at all. Neither did the *true* Jesus ever give any such instructions "to open ourselves up and stop clinging to our precious preconceptions." But false teachings are to be expected when *believing* is replaced with *imagining* and when the *absolute truth* of God's Word becomes merely a "*perspective.*" And, obviously, when up to "17,000 different cultures" are to give "*new* understandings of *who Jesus is,*" this "*changing face* of Jesus in every culture" of course *replaces* the Word of God with "*new* understandings of *who Jesus is*" (i.e., with the "*different voices*" of "*the whole Jesus*"). But then, this replacement of the "old" truth of God and His Son with "*everything* new" is what people today *want*.

This interfaith "whole gospel" of an interfaith "whole Jesus" is nothing but a "humble" exaltation of *man's faithlessness*. To refer to *any* of this as "*a true* picture of Christ" and as a "*loyalty* test" to *Jesus* is an imaginary argument of the utmost absurdity. When the true Lord Jesus Christ is revealed from heaven, people who chose not to believe the truth of Who He is are going to be understatedly shocked to discover that He is *not at all "anemic."* And, obviously, when the Lord Jesus Christ *Himself* returns, He won't be an *interfaith "mosaic"* or a *storytelling "community"* that is returning!

> *"And to you who are troubled rest with us, when the Lord Jesus shall be revealed from heaven with his mighty angels, in flaming fire taking vengeance on them that know not God, and that obey not the gospel of our Lord Jesus Christ: Who shall be punished with everlasting destruction from the presence of the Lord, and from the glory of his power; when he shall come to be glorified in his saints, and to be admired in all them that believe (because our testimony among you was believed) in that day." (2 Thessalonians 1:7-10)*

This isn't "bristling at change" or "defensiveness" or "pride" or a "preconception." It's *truth* that *is what it is* whether people choose to believe it or not. It really is that simple.

Although those who are seeking to "break free" from the truth of God and His Son imagine otherwise, there is no "group mosaic," or "fullness of truth," that brings all religions—and all their gods and "truths"—together as a "true picture" of either God or His Son. The mission to get today's Christianity to stop believing the truth of God's Word, which is the truth of God and the Lord Jesus Christ, is not the mission of God. It is not what *God* is "up to" in the world. It is not the mission of *God* to "*deceive*"—i.e., "to cause to *believe* what is *false*, or *disbelieve* what is *true*."[22]

> *"But evil men and seducers shall wax worse and worse, deceiving, and being deceived. But **continue** thou in the things which thou hast learned and hast been assured of, knowing of whom thou hast learned them; and that from a child thou hast known **the holy scriptures**, which **are able to make thee wise unto salvation through faith which is in Christ Jesus**." (2 Timothy 3:13-15)*

Sweet writes:

"It's time to put Christ back into Christianity."[23]

Yes, but *the genuine Christ*, not to mention *the genuine God!* The truth that we are to *believe* is the truth of the true Person of the Lord Jesus Christ. This true Person has only *one* face, and in that *one face* is "*the light of the knowledge of the glory of God.*" But, of course, therein lies the reason for the change. The attempt to bring Jesus into relationship with the many faces—i.e., with the many gods and "truths"—that make up the "God" of Oneness only becomes possible in "reimagining" a "Jesus" that has "many faces" as well. But only the true Person of the Lord Jesus Christ is the way to the true God. Conversely, today's emerging whole "Jesus"/"Christ" of interfaith Oneness is only the way to today's emerging whole "God" of interfaith Oneness. And yet these very New Age *counterfeits* are the "genuine" that people today want. People want *a new whole* "truth" that is conveniently *a whole new* "truth." And they are finding what they are looking for in the emerging faith—i.e., in the emerging "new world religion"—of New Age Oneness and its immanent "God" and "Christ" (i.e., "Messiah").

But, even though people are on a mission to connect and merge the Christian genuine God (and Christ) and this New Age counterfeit "God" (and "Christ") of Oneness/ wholeness together as one, naturally they don't see it that way. After all, a mission to bring "*all* religions" into "the *whole*, the *totality*" certainly wouldn't include the <u>*religion*</u> *of the New Age* with the Oneness/wholeness of its "*Totality* of God" in all this Oneness/ wholeness, right? Sadly, that would be too obvious. And nothing is obvious in today's preferred "light" of darkness where details are irrelevant. Consequently, rather than being seen as counterfeit or as New Age, this is all seen as a new kind of "Christianity." It is—in exactly the same way that counterfeit bills are a new kind of "money." And, as the claims go for both, this "Christianity" is likewise just as "*authentic*" as this "money." And although it would be difficult to get people to "open" themselves up and "stop clinging" to their "preconceived notions" of what *money* is in order to see this new kind of "money" as "authentic," people today don't even think twice about doing just that when it comes to Who *God* and *His Son* are. Thus, this new kind of "God" and this new kind of "Jesus"/"Christ"—i.e., this new kind of "Messiah"—are all being embraced as "genuine" in today's new kind of "authentic" "Christianity" with its new kind of "fullness of truth."

> *"For if he that cometh preacheth another Jesus, whom we have not preached, or if ye receive another spirit, which ye have not received, or another gospel, which ye have not accepted, ye might well bear with him." (2 Corinthians 11:4)*

This dance of Oneness—i.e., of *darkness*—that seeks to bring both *inside* and <u>*outside*</u> the truth and faith of God and His Son together as one in an "authentic" all-encompassing covenant/testament/way to God is neither "*God's* design" nor "*God's* dream" nor "the *Jesus* Dream" nor a "dance to the music of *Jesus*." But it does fit what God's Word has to say about "play."

> *"But with many of them God was not well pleased: for they were overthrown in the wilderness. Now these things were our examples, to the intent we should not lust after evil things, as they also lusted.* **Neither be ye idolaters**, *as were some of them; as it is written, The people sat down to eat and drink, and rose up* **to play**.*"* *(1 Corinthians 10:5-7)*

"Jesus Christ, God the Son, knocks at your door and asks if you can **come out and play**....

"Jesus is the dramatic pitching of God's tent, wherein God is with us, making beautiful music for us to dance to—if we only will." (Leonard Sweet & Frank Viola; emphasis added)[24]

> "At the end of Revelation, **Jesus is outside the church**, knocking, banging on the door, **asking to be let inside so that he can get *us* back *outside***.
>
> "We need to learn to dance to the music of Jesus once again." (Leonard Sweet; emphasis added)[25]
>
> "**The church is *not*** a set of **propositions**, buildings, **or *beliefs*** ...
>
> "We need to **learn to play** the spaces.... **All space is God's space**." (Leonard Sweet; last ellipsis dots in the original; emphasis added)[26]
>
> "**Play, *not* work**, is the soil that **grows dreams**." (Leonard Sweet; emphasis added)[27]

In other words, *not believing* (playing outside the truth and faith of God's Word) rather than *believing* (working inside the truth and faith of God's Word) grows the dreams of a "double helix" (narrow *and* broad) "secret of life." This dance of Oneness is not "the *Jesus* Dream." The Son of God, the Lord Jesus Christ, does not ask us to "come out and *play*." Quite the contrary.

> "*Jesus answered and said unto them, This is the **work** of God, that ye **believe** on him whom he hath sent.*" (John 6:29)
>
> "**Play, not work**, is the soil that **grows dreams**.
>
> "**Jesus** did **not** so much come to **flood darkness with light so that darkness is destroyed** as he **came to <u>show</u>** us how to **enter into darkness, and mystery**, so that **darkness** can be **explored and experienced**." (Leonard Sweet; emphasis added)[28]

Absolutely unbelievable, on many levels.

> "***Then spake Jesus*** *again unto them, saying, I am the light of the world:* ***he that followeth*** <u>***me***</u> ***shall*** <u>***not***</u> ***walk in darkness****, but shall have the light of life.*" (John 8:12)
>
> "***If we say that we have fellowship with him, and walk in darkness, we lie, and do not*** <u>***the***</u> ***truth***." (1 John 1:6)

Sweet—who "serves as a consultant to many of America's denominational leaders and agencies" and "is a frequent speaker at national and international conferences, state conventions, pastors' schools, retreats"[29]—wrote this latter quote in his 2010 book, *Nudge: Awakening Each Other to the God Who's Already There*, which is *a book on "evangelism."* But then, *darkness* is *essential* for an "awakening" to this panentheistic "God" of Oneness that is already in *everyone and everything*. The back cover reads: "Brace yourself. This book is set to revolutionize your understanding of evangelism." That is an understatement. The kingdom of darkness must be ecstatic.

People in today's shifting Christianity don't want "more *light*." They, along with their heaped teachers, want more *darkness* so they can "play." *Light* shows us *specifically* and with *certainty* Who and what we are to *believe* and *obey*, which of course destroys their desired "make-it-up-as-you-go-along" "*self*-regulating" "play."

> "And when the people saw that Moses delayed to come down out of the mount, the people gathered themselves together unto Aaron, and said unto him, Up, make us gods, which shall go before us; for as for this Moses, the man that brought us up out of the land of Egypt, we wot not what is become of him. And Aaron said unto them, Break off the golden earrings, ... And he received them at their hand, and fashioned it with a graving tool, after he had made it **a molten calf**: and they said, **These be thy gods**, O Israel, which brought thee up out of the land of Egypt. And when Aaron saw it, **he built an altar before it**; and Aaron made proclamation, **and said, Tomorrow is a feast to <u>the LORD</u>**. And they rose up early on the morrow, and offered burnt offerings, and brought peace offerings; **and the people sat down to eat and to drink, and rose up to play**." (Exodus 32:1-2, 4-6)

Some things never change. People *still* see it as "play" to "reimagine" God, and now His Son, however anyone chooses. By the way, Moses was up on the mount getting God's "propositions" when the people "*gathered themselves together*" and "*rose up to play*." There are lessons here that need to be *learned from*, not *repeated*!

Incredibly, Sweet, who wants darkness "explored and experienced," actually "reimagines" that:

> "As Aaron discovered at the foot of Mount Sinai, **the *farther* people journeyed from God, the more they became *certain* what God looks like and cast the golden calf**." [!] (Leonard Sweet; emphasis added)[30]

They were certain that God looks like a calf?! No, they, too, just wanted to "*play*" at "reimagining" God. And it is only in this *upside-down* emerging faith of Oneness/panentheism that the *farther* people journey "from God" the more *certain* they become. This is because this emerging faith's "God" and "truth" are *in everyone and everything*. Thus, to those in this emerging faith *certainty* is to journey *away* "from God" and even becomes "the golden calf."

When a "God" is in *everyone and everything* there can be *no such thing* as certainty. In fact, the *certainty* of truth becomes the only thing that *can* be placed above this false "God." Thus, a "God" that is in everyone and everything *must*, by its very nature, turn *all* certainty—especially that of the truth and faith of God's Word—into "idolatry." And, besides, the instant that something becomes *certain*, something else simultaneously becomes *wrong*. This is taboo in this emerging faith "that makes *no one* wrong," and is, after all, the whole point of "reimagining" a "God" that is *in everyone and everything* (which, whether those in this emerging faith admit it or not, also clearly includes the golden calf as well). It is therefore not surprising that the *certainty* of truth is under fire since it takes away today's desired freedom to "*play*" at "reimagining" "God."

Today's "molten calf," or "reimagined" "God" that is in everyone and everything, is not golden, but patchwork—a "group mosaic." And, no, it's not "beautiful." Idolatry and its "play" are no more "beautiful" than the following:

> "Woe unto you, scribes and Pharisees, hypocrites! for ye are like unto whited sepulchres, which indeed appear beautiful outward, but are within full of dead men's bones, and of all uncleanness." (Matthew 23:27)

So what was God's response to the people's "play" at "reimagining" Him (which, befitting of today's dance of Oneness, likewise included "dancing"--Exodus 32:19)? God not only "*plagued the people*," He "*said unto Moses, Whosoever hath sinned against me, him will I blot out of my book*" (Exodus 32:35, 33). Although people today take it lightly, and even flip it upside down, God does not take idolatry lightly. It is only a "dance" and "play" to those who don't have enough sense to fear the true God.

> *"Hear now this, O foolish people, and without understanding; which have eyes, and see not; which have ears, and hear not: Fear ye not me? saith the LORD: will ye not tremble at my presence …? But this people hath a revolting and a rebellious heart; they are revolted and gone. Neither say they in their heart, Let us now fear the LORD our God … A wonderful and horrible thing is committed in the land; the prophets prophesy falsely, and the priests bear rule by their means; and my people love to have it so: and what will ye do in the end thereof?" (Jeremiah 5:21-24, 30-31)*

45

"The day of theology is over" -- doing and being and creating "God" in a quantum dance of Oneness

> "**Quantum spirituality** bonds us to all creation as well as to other members of the human family. . . . This entails a radical doctrine of embodiment of **God in the very substance of creation**. . . . But a spirituality that is not in some way entheistic (whether pan- or trans-), that does not extend to **the spirit-matter of the cosmos**, is not Christian." (Leonard Sweet; emphasis added)[1]

In the emerging faith/"spirituality" of Oneness/panentheism, which is anything but Christian, there is no such thing as *"departing from the living God"* (Hebrews 3:12). With a panentheistic "God"/"Spirit" that is "in the *very substance*" of everyone and everything, this is, of course, an automatic universal salvation/relationship in which everyone is given the *unconditional* "love and freedom" to not have to believe God and His Son. In other words, everyone is given the "love and freedom" to *imagine and define God however they choose.*

> "In the days of **the New Spirituality** love and freedom will be understood to be the same thing." (the seducing spirit calling itself "God;" emphasis added)[2]

> "Tomorrow's God is **unconditionally** loving, nonjudgmental, noncondemning, and nonpunishing." (the seducing spirit calling itself "God;" emphasis added)[3]

> "Tomorrow's God will be understood to be the very essence of freedom, and since

humans will understand themselves to be **One with** Tomorrow's **God**, they will also understand themselves to be **inherently free**." (the seducing spirit calling itself "God;" emphasis added)[4]

"Today men's minds are recognizing the dawn of freedom; they are realizing that every man should be **free to worship God in his own way**.... His own God-illumined mind will search for truth and he will interpret it for himself. **The day of theology is over** ...

"Men have gone far today in the rejection of dogmas and doctrine and this is good and right and encouraging." (the seducing spirit calling itself Djwhal Khul; emphasis added)[5]

The seducing spirit calling itself "God": "And I tell you that Tomorrow's God will change form as each moment and each individual seeking to experience God dictates."

Neale Donald Walsch: "Hold it. **You mean we get to decide who and what God is?**"

The seducing spirit calling itself "God": "Why are you so surprised? You've been doing that since time began. You call this Religion." (bold added)[6]

Again, make that *false* religion. And only a seducing spirit world that is determined to take as many people as possible to hell with it would see today's rejection of the truth and faith of God as "encouraging." Of course, this rejection opens the door wide to the acceptance of its emerging "new world religion"—i.e., emerging faith/New Spirituality of Oneness/panentheism—in which everyone has this "love and freedom" of imagining and defining God however they choose. And this emerging faith/New Spirituality is a mission that isn't just seeking to "*reimagine*" God in a fashion that humanity is willing to accept. Incredibly, it is also a mission that is seeking to "reimagine" God *literally*. In other words, in this emerging faith man's *imagination* is believed to have the *power* to create *literal* changes in Who God is! And yet this shouldn't be surprising. Why else would people choose to "reimagine" God unless they believed that their "reimaginings" were the *truth* about God? But "*reimaginings*" cannot be the truth about God unless they *effect changes* in God. Think about it.

Layers of absurdities notwithstanding, it is the "reimagined" panentheistic "God" of Oneness—the "ground of all being" and "ultimate reality" that is *immanent in everyone and everything*—that makes these changes a "*reality*." And since man is not able to prove any of this in God's Word of truth, man has turned to science to "prove" the "truth"—and thus the unconditional "love and freedom"—of this emerging faith and panentheistic "God." After all, if this "God" is in the very "substance" of everyone and everything then science should be able to "find" this "God" in the very "substance" of everyone and everything, right? And science has been attempting to do just that. For example, the Large Hadron Collider of CERN (the European Organization for Nuclear Research) near Geneva has been fittingly racing protons around its large *circle* and in two *opposite directions* so that it can then collide them *together* at just under the speed of light. Why? Absurdly, scientists believe that if they can generate enough power and smash them into tiny enough particles not only will they "recreate" the conditions a split second after their "*Big Bang*" but they will discover man's desired "*God particle*" (believed to be the key to the mass of the universe). Again, these two beliefs go hand in hand. And, yes, they really do call it "the God particle." (This is their nickname for the

Higgs boson particle.)[7]

> "Do you suppose that God could be both the Cause and That Which Is Caused? Do you think that God could be both the Creator and the Created?" (the seducing spirit calling itself "God")[8]

Even if man *ever* did supposedly "prove" "scientifically" that "God" is in the subatomic particles that comprise the very "substance" of creation, this "proof" would change *absolutely nothing whatsoever* of the absolute truth of Who the *true* God is. This "proof" would, however, have tremendous ramifications for the emerging faith of the *false* "God" of Oneness/panentheism. No doubt there would be an even greater falling away from the truth and faith of God and His Son as "*science falsely so called*" shipwrecks the faith of even more people than ever before. But, sadly, this would "prove" the "truth" and "faith" of the "God" that people today *want*.

> "*Fight the good fight of faith, lay hold on eternal life, whereunto thou art also called, and hast professed a good profession before many witnesses. I give thee charge in the sight of God, who quickeneth all things, and before Christ Jesus, who before Pontius Pilate witnessed a good confession; that thou keep this commandment without spot, unrebukeable, until the appearing of our Lord Jesus Christ: Which in his times he shall show, who is the blessed and only Potentate, the King of kings, and Lord of lords; Who only hath immortality, <u>dwelling in the light which no man can approach unto; whom no man hath seen, nor can see</u>: to whom be honour and power everlasting. Amen.... O Timothy, keep that which is committed to thy trust, avoiding profane and vain babblings, and **oppositions of science falsely so called: Which some professing have erred concerning the faith**. Grace be with thee. Amen.*" (1 Timothy 6:12-16, 20-21)

The God Who is *separate* from His *creation* will never be found by science. Only a "God" that is *One* with *creation* can be put in a "test tube," so to speak, and thus "proven." And this is where the many "reimaginings" of the truth of God's Word become facilitative of this emerging "scientific" faith. For instance, Sweet writes:

> "The most powerful forces in the universe are spiritual: the energies of divine unconditional love. The Bible teaches that **God is** 'spirit' or '**energy**.'" (emphasis added)[9]

Actually, the unadulterated Word of God teaches that "*God is <u>a Spirit</u>*" (John 4:24). It is doctrines of devils, "*science falsely so called*," and man's "reimaginings" that teach God is *energy*. (And *of course* "energy" is "unconditional"!)

> "**God is** the **energy**—the pure, raw energy—which you call life." (the seducing spirit calling itself "God;" emphasis added)[10]

First, as addressed earlier, the true God Who is "*<u>a</u> Spirit*" is *<u>a</u> Being*, not "the ground of all being" that "dwells in, around, and through all things."[11] Second, *energy* is a *creation* of God; it is not *God*. But, of course, "reimagining" that God is *energy* opens the door to "scientifically" "proving" that God is *One with everyone and everything*. And this Oneness is *indispensable* to a universal salvation/relationship in which people have their desired unconditional "love and freedom" to "transcend" (bypass) the simple condition of *believing* the truth of God and His Son. Instead of believing, man conveniently gets "to *decide* who and what God is" in Oneness. This freedom is the core of today's emerging faith—new world religion—in which the ideas and imaginations and "intuitive" inner "knowing" of everyone in every religion *all* become part of a "fullness of truth," or "Totality of God." And since this unconditional freedom hinges on a *universal* salvation/relationship which, in turn, hinges on God being "*in everyone and everything*," it isn't surprising that quantum physics and quantum spirituality are being turned to in order to "prove" this *Oneness/panentheism* is "true."

In his book *A "Wonderful" Deception*, and in the section "The Quantum Christ," Warren B. Smith writes:

> "**The New Age/New Spirituality is already heralding quantum physics as a 'scientific' basis for their contention that God is not only transcendent but also immanent—'in' everyone and everything.** Physicist Fritjof Capra's 1975 best-selling book on quantum physics—*The Tao of Physics: An Exploration of the Parallels between Modern Physics and Eastern Mysticism*—was the first to present this proposed scientific/spiritual model to a mass audience. In it, Capra explains that he gained new spiritual insights **through a mystical experience** he had sitting on a beach in Santa Cruz, California in 1969:
>
>> "Five years ago, I had a beautiful experience which set me on a road that has led to the writing of this book. I was sitting by the ocean one late summer afternoon, watching the waves rolling in and feeling the rhythm of my breathing, when I suddenly became aware of my whole environment as being engaged in **a gigantic cosmic dance**.... As I sat on that beach my former experiences [research in high-energy physics] came to life; I 'saw' cascades of energy coming down from outer space, in which particles were created and destroyed in rhythmic pulses; **I 'saw' the atoms of the elements and those of my body participating in this cosmic dance of energy**; I felt its rhythm and I 'heard' its sound, and at that moment I *knew* that this was the Dance of Shiva, the Lord of Dancers worshipped by the Hindus.
>
> "Commenting on his experience thirty years later, Capra writes that back in 1970 he 'knew with absolute certainty that the parallels between modern physics and Eastern mysticism would someday be common knowledge.'...
>
> "Fritjof Capra then describes **the union of mysticism and the new physics** as **the 'new spirituality'** that is 'now being developed by many groups and movements, both within and outside the churches.'" (brackets & 1st ellipsis dots in the original; bold added)[12]

> "A **New Spirituality** truly is emerging upon the earth, and the idea of **Oneness is at its core**." (Neale Donald Walsch; emphasis added)[13]

There is *a reason* why the emerging faith/New Spirituality of Oneness/panentheism is emerging *everywhere*, which includes its emerging "proof" in today's *science*. The world as a whole is falling for the same *bait* of the "god of this world"—*mysticism*.

> "As Eastern thought has begun to interest a significant number of people, and **meditation** is no longer viewed with ridicule or suspicion, **mysticism is being taken seriously even within the scientific community**. An increasing number of scientists are aware that *mystical thought* provides a consistent and relevant philosophical background to the theories of *contemporary science*, a conception of

> the world in which the scientific discoveries of men and women can be in perfect harmony with their spiritual aims and religious beliefs." (Fritjof Capra; emphasis added)[14]

> "The most important characteristic of the Eastern world view—one could almost say the essence of it—is the awareness of *the unity and mutual interrelation of all things and events*, the experience of **all phenomena** in the world as **manifestations of a basic oneness. All things** are seen as interdependent and **inseparable parts of this cosmic whole**; as **different manifestations of** *the same ultimate reality*....

> "**The basic oneness of the universe** is not only **the central characteristic of the mystical experience**, but is also **one of the most important revelations of modern physics**." (Fritjof Capra; emphasis added)[15]

> "For those who have experienced this harmony, the significance of the parallels between the world views of physicists and mystics is beyond any doubt. The interesting question, then, is not *whether* these parallels exist, but *why*; and, furthermore, what their existence implies." (Fritjof Capra)[16]

Why? Because the seducing spirit world is on a mission to get the world to believe its panentheistic "truth" of *Oneness (immanence)*.

> "When, therefore, sight has been attained and the light streams forth, **revelation of the oneness of all life** is a simple and immediate occurrence ..." (the seducing spirit calling itself Djwhal Khul; emphasis added)[17]

> "What we are in reality passing through is '**a religious initiation into the mysteries of** *Being*,' ... and from that **we shall emerge with a deepened sense of** *God immanent* in ourselves and in all humanity." (Alice Bailey; emphasis added)[18]

And, of course, this panentheistic "truth" of Oneness (immanence) gives all people everywhere the unconditional "love and freedom" to *imagine and define God however they choose*:

> "It is relatively unimportant what we mean in detail by **that little word of three letters ['God']. It is but a symbol of Reality**." (Alice Bailey; emphasis added)[19]

> "It is this revelation of Deity that is the goal of the **mystical** endeavor ... Through it [meditation], he later **discovers his** *relation to the universe*; he finds that his physical body and **his vital** *energies* **are part and parcel of** *Nature itself*, which is, in fact, **the outer garment of Deity** ..." (Alice Bailey; emphasis added)[20]

In the emerging New Spirituality/Quantum Spirituality—or New Quantum Spirituality—of this Oneness/panentheism, all "parts of this cosmic whole" are "*inseparable.*" This is because "*all things*" are no longer "*things*" but just "*different manifestations of the same ultimate reality.*" That is, "*all things*" are just different manifestations of *only* "*One Thing,*" which is "*God*"/"*energy.*"

> "Understand and know at last that **We Are All One**. The human race, and **all of**

Life, **is a unified field.** *It is all One Thing.* There is, therefore, nothing to be superior *to*, and nothing that is superior to you." (the seducing spirit calling itself "God;" bold added)[21]

"**God is the *energy* ... which you call *life*.**" (the seducing spirit calling itself "God;" emphasis added)[22]

"***You must stop seeing God as separate from you***, *and you as separate from each other.*

"The *only* solution is the Ultimate Truth: *nothing exists in the universe that is separate from anything else. Everything* is **intrinsically connected**, irrevocably interdependent, interactive, **interwoven into the fabric of all life**." (the seducing spirit calling itself "God;" bold & underline added)[23]

"The realization that you are *One Being*—that **everything in Life is really One Thing, Manifesting**—can and will change your entire experience forever." (the seducing spirit calling itself "God;" emphasis added)[24]

Likewise, Capra writes:

"**All things** are seen as interdependent and *inseparable* parts of this cosmic whole; as ***different manifestations* of *the same* ultimate reality**." (emphasis added)[25]

"At the *subatomic* level, the *solid material objects* of classical physics *dissolve into wave-like patterns* ...

"**Subatomic particles, then, are not '*things*' but are interconnections between '*things*,'** and these 'things,' in turn, are interconnections between other 'things,' and so on. **In quantum theory you never end up with '*things*'**; you always deal with **interconnections**.

"**This is how modern physics reveals the basic *oneness* of the universe**." (emphasis added)[26]

Capra explains that "[i]n modern physics, ... *particles* are not seen as consisting of any basic 'stuff,' but as *bundles of energy*"[27] and that "energy is not a substance but rather a measure of activity, of dynamic patterns."[28] And, thus, "[p]articles are dynamic patterns, patterns of activity"—i.e., "energy patterns ... which build up matter."[29] In other words, "mass is no longer associated with a *material* substance,"[30] and thus matter is no longer matter but merely "*energy patterns*." Combine this with the immanent "God" of Oneness as the "energy" of "life" that is in everyone and everything, and this "scientific" "energymatter"/"spirit-matter" Oneness basically boils down to that everyone and everything including this "God" are just *the same energy manifesting itself in different "patterns."* Thus, the universe becomes "organic," and all the parts/particles of the universe—all the "energy patterns"—become *interconnected*/"*interrelated*" "patterns of *a cosmic process*," in "one *indivisible*, dynamic *whole*" that is "*One Being*." Capra writes:

"In contrast to the mechanistic Western view, the Eastern view of the world is '**organic**'. For the Eastern mystic, ***all* things and events** perceived by the senses are **interrelated, connected**, and are but **different aspects or manifestations of *the same* ultimate reality**." (emphasis added)[31]

> "Subatomic particles are not *separate* entities but **interrelated energy patterns** in an ongoing dynamic process." (emphasis added)[32]

> "In modern physics, the image of **the universe** as a machine has been transcended by a view of it as **one *indivisible*, dynamic whole** whose **parts** are essentially **interrelated** and can be understood only as **patterns of *a cosmic process*.**" (emphasis added)[33]

> "The universe is seen as **a dynamic web** of interrelated events. None of the properties of any part of this web is fundamental; they all follow from the properties of the other parts, and **the *overall consistency* of their interrelations determines the structure of the entire web**." (emphasis added)[34]

> "[T]he subatomic world appears as *a web of relations* between the various parts of a *unified* whole." (emphasis added)[35]

That "the overall *consistency*" of interrelations "determines the structure of the entire web" is to be expected in this emerging faith of Oneness (and, yes, this science is an emerging *faith*). No overall consistency, no Oneness. And since Oneness, by its very nature, renders what people *believe* irrelevant, it is thus the overall consistency of what people *do*—specifically, *their relationships*—that is key to the entire web of Oneness. However, since the only relevant and *required* belief is a belief in *Oneness*, the overall consistency that *must* be reflected in these interrelations is of course an underlying belief in Oneness.

> "In a universe which is **an inseparable whole** and where **all forms are fluid and ever-changing**, there is **no room for any fixed fundamental entity**." (Fritjof Capra; emphasis added)[36]

In addition, Capra writes:

> "Relativity theory has made **the cosmic web** come alive, so to speak, by revealing its intrinsically dynamic character; by showing that **its *activity* is the very essence of its *being***." (emphasis added)[37]

> "... the ***being*** of matter **cannot be separated** from its ***activity***." (emphasis added)[38]

In other words, as is to be expected, "*being*" is about *verbs* not *nouns* in this "cosmic web" of Oneness. And since *doing* "is the very essence" of *being*, any difference between *doing* "God" and *being* "God" is thus neatly eliminated in this emerging faith/ New Quantum Spirituality in which "God" is "energy." It all becomes just a "cosmic dance of energy" in "the mysteries of *Being*."

> "... God is *whirling and swirling creation into being*. The missional thrust begins **in the very being of God**....
>
> "The impulse to create, to conceive, is what lies at the heart of the missional....
>
> "The universe was created by a God *in motion*, ... a God who is constantly creating, and a God who has left a creation still *unfinished*....
>
> "Even though the word itself is an adjective, *missional* is all about **verbs, not**

nouns …

"God lived in our midst and loved us and invited us to **'do God'** along with him." (Leonard Sweet; emphasis added, except to *missional*)[39]

"Missional … is living a life born **in the very being of God**. It is the body of the church **dancing to the tune of the Spirit**, …" (Leonard Sweet; emphasis added)[40]

"**God is the Spirit** of the universe, the consciousness **of the cosmos**: *its energy*, …" (Leonard Sweet; emphasis added)[41]

Neale Donald Walsch: "**Dancing with the energy of God**."
The seducing spirit calling itself "God": "That's a very good way of putting it. That's a wonderful metaphor." (emphasis added)[42]

"**At the subatomic level** the *interrelations* and *interactions* between the parts of the whole are more fundamental than the parts themselves.… **[T]here are no dancers, there is only the dance**." (Fritjof Capra; emphasis added)[43]

"**The self only exists at all inasmuch as it *participates* in the *being* of God**." (Leonard Sweet & Frank Viola; emphasis added)[44]

"The ultimate nudge [*Awakening … **to the God Who's Already There***] in life is helping others 'to be' and '**to arrive at *being***.' It's the ultimate art form: the artistry of *being*." (Leonard Sweet; emphasis added)[45]

"What we are in reality passing through is '**a religious initiation into the mysteries of *Being***,' …" (Alice Bailey; emphasis added)[46]

The seducing spirit calling itself "God": "*Doing* is a function of the body. **Being is a function of the soul**.… It is a state of beingness the soul is after, not a state of doingness."
Neale Donald Walsch: "**What is the soul seeking to be?**"
The seducing spirit calling itself "God": "**Me**.… Yes, Me. Your soul *is* Me, and it knows it. **What it is doing, is trying to *experience that***." (bold added)[47]

Basically, in this emerging faith/New Quantum Spirituality/New Age, *life* is a *process*—or *dance*—of *doing* and *being* "God." It is therefore without question that "there can be *no* final statement of theology"[48] of this "God" (and thus no final set of beliefs.) For starters, a "God" that is "in the very *substance* of <u>creation</u>" that "has left a *creation* still <u>unfinished</u>" is a "God" that is not "finished" with <u>itself</u>.

"**I am in a constant process of formation**.…

"**If you think of God as a process, or a being, that is 'finished,'** you have not correctly remembered what is so. **Here is a great secret: *God is never finished***.

"With anything.…

"**God is a process**." (the seducing spirit calling itself "God;" bold added)[49]

Moreover, since this "*God*"—a.k.a. "*energy*"—is "*interwoven* into the *fabric of all life*," *all* life is a dance of *doing* and *being* "*God*." Therefore *all life* becomes "*theology.*" And what better way to *eliminate* theology than to "reimagine" theology as *all life*? To make theology everything is to make theology nothing. This changes everything.

> "***Every living thing* has an architecture:** Architecture is ***theology* that takes material form**." (Leonard Sweet; emphasis added)[50]

> "**Matter is the energy of *Spirit***." (Leonard Sweet; emphasis added)[51]

> "**God is the energy**—the pure, raw energy—**which you call life**....
>
> "**Everything** you see in the heavens and the earth **is Me, being created**. The Process of **Creation is never over**. It is never complete. I am never 'done.' **This is another way of saying everything is forever changing**. Nothing stands still. Nothing—*nothing*—is without motion. Everything is **energy, in motion**....
>
> "The One Unchanging Truth is that **God is always changing**." (the seducing spirit calling itself "God;" bold added)[52]

> "*For I am the* LORD*, I change not;* ..." *(Malachi 3:6)*

> "*My son, **fear thou the* LORD *and the king: and meddle not with them that are given to change**: For their calamity shall rise suddenly; and who knoweth the ruin of them both?" (Proverbs 24:21-22)*

In this emerging faith of Oneness/panentheism, in which "Everything you see ... is Me, *being created*," creation's dance of *doing* and *being* "God" is inevitably brought full circle to a dance of *creating* "God." This is an integral part of "the mysteries of Being" and "secret of life" of an *immanent* "God."

> "**Whatever you are *being*, you are *creating*.**
>
> "The circle is complete ...
>
> "**This is the greatest secret of life**." (the seducing spirit calling itself "God;" bold added)[53]

Sweet writes:

> "**Jesus says, 'Go Do Me.' Go *be Jesus***." (emphasis added)[54]

> "The so-beautiful paradox of the MRI life is that **in *being* Jesus we *find* Jesus**." (emphasis added)[55]

> "**Jesus ... came to reveal the 'secret of life'** ... about **God's design** for how we humans should live our lives....
>
> "If God's hand is MRI-shaped—mission-shaped, relation-shaped, *incarnational*-shaped—then Jesus' followers are **shapesmiths *of the Spirit***." (emphasis added)[56]

> "The purpose of the church is to give form to, **to *put into form and shape*, the *energymatter* known as *Jesus Christ***." (emphasis added)[57]

Since "[w]hatever you are *being*, you are *creating*," it naturally follows that "in *being* Jesus we *find* Jesus" in this merging and emerging "Christian"/New Age "secret of life." And, of course, Sweet also writes that "[e]ach one of us is free to *become Jesus*."[58] *Jesus is God the Son*. So to be/become Jesus would be to be/become God. But it's all just a "cosmic dance of energy," right?

> "**The self only exists at all inasmuch as it *participates* in the *being* of God**." (Leonard Sweet & Frank Viola; emphasis added)[59]

> "Part of the secret to unlocking that magical phrase 'bless what there is for being' is to understand that what matters in life is not being good but being God's. One of the most difficult tasks in life is to know the difference between 'be good' and 'be God's.' It's a lot easier to 'go and do likewise' than to '**go and be likewise.**' But Jesus calls us to **a doing based on being**. Jesus is saying, '**Don't *act* like me. Be me!**'" (Leonard Sweet; bold added)[60]

It would have been more straightforward to omit the apostrophe in "being God's"/"be God's." But those in this emerging faith prefer to talk in circles for a reason. Again, *Jesus is God*. In truth, we are not now and never will be *Jesus* or *God* or *God* "*incarnate*" or participants in the *being* (either verb or noun) of *God*. To the contrary, today's dance of *doing and being "God"* is the "*make-it-up-as-you-go-along*" dance of those who would rather create/shape/form a "reimagined" "God" than believe and obey the true God. In other words, this dance is as follows (which goes along with "Whatever you are *being*, you are *creating*"):

> "**You are Me choosing to be Me**.
>
> "**You are Me, choosing to be What I Am**—and *choosing what I am going to be*.
>
> "All of you, collectively, are creating that. You are doing it on an individual basis, as each of you decides Who You Are, and experiences that, and you are doing it collectively, **as the co-creative collective being that you are**." (the seducing spirit calling itself "God;" emphasis added)[61]

> "**In this, and in all things, you are making it all up. That is, you are creating it on the spot. You are the Creator and the Created.**" (the seducing spirit calling itself "God;" emphasis added)[62]

In a nutshell, in this quantum dance of doing and being "God" everyone and everything are collectively making up the being of "God" (in more ways than one) which, in turn, becomes the "*creation*" of "*God*" (also in more ways than one). (With serpentine subtilty, the deceptive language in this emerging faith/New Quantum Spirituality goes *both ways* so that those in this emerging faith are both "*deceiving, and being deceived*.") And, by the way, in an emerging faith in which "*God* is the *energy* … you call life," life is thus a "cosmic dance of *energy*" that is *automatically* a "cosmic dance" of *doing* and *being* "*God*." This emerging faith thus basically comes down to one all-encompassing "make-it-up-as-you-go-along process."

> "Indeed, here is the grandest truth: **You are making *everything* up**.
>
> "**Life is The Process by which everything is being created. God is the**

energy ... you call life. By this awareness we come to a new truth.

"God is a Process....

"**God is not a person, place, or thing**. God is exactly what you have always thought—but not understood....

"You have always thought that God is the Supreme Being....

"**I am the *Supreme* Being. That is, the Supreme, comma, *being*....**

"I am the Creator, and **I am The Process *by which I am created*.**

"Everything you see in the heavens and the earth is **Me, *being created*....**

"When you look at a thing, you are **not** looking at a **static** 'something' that is 'standing there' in time and space. No! You are *witnessing an event*. Because **everything is moving, changing, evolving. *Everything*.**

"It was Buckminster Fuller who said, '**I seem to be a verb**.' *He was right*.

"**God is an *event*. You have called that event *life*.**" (the seducing spirit calling itself "God;" bold added)[63]

First, a "God" that is "not a person, place, or thing"—i.e., that is not a *noun*—is obviously not *a* "Being" that is to be *believed* in. Likewise, a "God" that is "a verb" is obviously not to be *believed* in but is to be *participated* in. And, of course, participation in this "God" is a participation in its creation (in more ways than one).

"Tomorrow's God does not require anyone to *believe* in God." (the seducing spirit calling itself "God;" emphasis added)[64]

"For **God is a work in progress**, ..." (the seducing spirit calling itself "God;" emphasis added)[65]

Second, a "Process" in which "[y]ou are making everything up" by just *living life*, not to mention in which "you are making it all up" by being "*the Creator* and the Created" (which are conveniently an "inseparable harmonious whole" in this "cosmic dance of energy"), does indeed open the door wide to *self*-regulating freedom.

"Opposed to the mechanistic conception of the world is the view of the *mystics* which may be epitomized by **the word 'organic'**, as it **regards all phenomena in the universe as integral parts of an inseparable harmonious whole**." (Fritjof Capra; emphasis added)[66]

"MRI [Missional, Relational, Incarnational] is an embrace of complexity theory. Your life and your community are living organisms: **That word *organism* means they are** by definition self-organizing, complex, adaptive, **self-regulating** systems. **An organic system makes it up as it goes along**." (Leonard Sweet; bold added)[67]

"[S]tructures are self-organizing, complex, adaptive systems where regulation ... exists to preserve the self-organizing, not to impose a grand plan or design but to assure a fair and level **playing field in which an *incarnational* outcome can emerge**. In epigenesis, the genes give a design for generating form and pattern, but they don't fit everything to the same pattern. Rather, they steer an organism into ergonomically optimal arrangements as an iterative, gradual, **make-it-up-as-you-**

go-along process." (Leonard Sweet; emphasis added)[68]

Obviously, a *self*-regulating system that wants to make it up as it goes along *must* include a "God" that will submit to this desired Self-Rule. And there is no "God" more submissive to this "make-it-up-as-you-go-along process" than this panentheistic "God" that is *itself* a "Process" of "making it all up." This "Process" is indeed a "playing field," one in which people can freely "play" at "reimagining" "God." In this "cosmic dance of energy" people can even seek to create/shape/form their "reimagined" "God" *literally*. After all, the term *incarnation* means "act of being *made flesh*."[69] And in the creative process of this emerging faith:

> "**When body, mind, and soul create together**, in harmony and in unity, **God is *made flesh*.**" (the seducing spirit calling itself "God;" emphasis added)[70]

The emerging faith/New Quantum Spirituality, with its submissive "*reimaginable*" "God" that gives everyone the "love and freedom" to *dictate* what *form* and *shape* (a.k.a. "energy pattern") it will take is quite the playing field.

> The seducing spirit calling itself "God": "And I tell you that Tomorrow's **God will change form** as each moment and **each individual** seeking to experience God **dictates**."
>
> Neale Donald Walsch: "Hold it. **You mean *we* get to decide who and what God is?**"
>
> The seducing spirit calling itself "God": "Why are you so surprised?" (bold added)[71]

> "All of your life you have been told that God created you. I come now to tell you this: **You are creating God**." (the seducing spirit calling itself "God;" emphasis added)[72]

> "**The soul conceives, the mind creates, the body experiences. The *circle* is complete**....
>
> "Conceive—create—experience. What you conceive you create, what you create you experience, what you experience you conceive." (the seducing spirit calling itself "God;" emphasis added)[73]

> "**This is the sacred rhythm of all life**. You do this not only by moving the energy around inside your body. You also do this by **moving around the larger energy inside the Body of God**....
>
> "The experience which I have described here, on the other hand, I am calling ***the Cosmic Wheel***, because there is *nothing of unworthiness, debt-repayment, punishment, or 'purification.'* The Cosmic Wheel simply describes **the ultimate reality**, or what you might call **the cosmology of the universe**.
>
> "It is **the cycle of life**, or what I sometimes term **The Process**. It is a picture phrase describing the **no-beginning-and-no-end** nature of things; **the continually connected path** to and from the all of everything, **on which the soul** joyfully **journeys** throughout eternity.
>
> "**It is the sacred rhythm of all life, by which you move the Energy of God**." (the seducing spirit calling itself "God;" emphasis added)[74]

This "cosmic dance of energy" of the emerging faith/New Quantum Spirituality is a dance of the circle ("Cosmic Wheel") of Oneness. And this "cosmic dance of energy" is a dance in which not only is this "reimagined" "God" "the energy—the pure, raw energy—which you call *life*,"[75] but "*Thought* is pure energy"[76] as well. (Again, it *all* comes down to only "*One Thing*.") Thus, moving this "Energy of God"—i.e., creating *changes* in "God"—is carried out by just *living life* as well as by just *thinking*. And, therefore, no matter what anyone ever chooses to *do* or *believe* in life it will never be "*wrong*" because this "God" conveniently moves and changes accordingly. This "spiritual journey" comes down to a dance of *doing and being and creating "God."* A dance of the *imagination* of cosmic proportions.

46

An imagination that is "God"

"Thought is pure energy." (the seducing spirit calling itself "God;" emphasis added)[1]

"**God is** the Spirit of the universe, the consciousness of the cosmos: **its energy**, its information, **its thought**." (Leonard Sweet; emphasis added)[2]

"**For my thoughts are not your thoughts, ... saith the LORD.**" (Isaiah 55:8)

"**God is the energy you call imagination.**" (the seducing spirit calling itself "God;" bold added)[3]

"... behold, **ye walk every one after the <u>imagination</u>** of his evil heart, **that they may <u>not</u> hearken unto <u>me</u>**." (Jeremiah 16:12)

Without question, an emerging faith/"spiritual journey" in which imagination is "God" changes everything. Instead of believing and obeying the "static" never-changing absolute truth of the true God and His Son Who *change for no one*, people can freely participate in the "dynamic" ever-changing dance of imagining/creating a "God" and/or "Jesus"/"Christ" in forms they are *willing* to accept. If nothing is ever "*wrong*" there is nothing to fear, and if *thought* is the "energy" of "*God*" there are certainly no *delusions*, right? Besides, how could there be *delusions* when in this "spiritual journey" of Oneness *false gods* and *false* "*Jesuses*"/"*Christs*" have been rendered *nonexistent* by giving *everyone* the *unconditional* "love and freedom" to *imagine and define* "God" and/or "Jesus"/"Christ" *however* they choose and to have this relationship *however* they choose on *whatever* "path" they choose? Think about it.

> "... Yea, **they have chosen their own ways**, and their soul delighteth in their abominations. **I also will choose their delusions, and will bring their fears upon them**; because when I called, none did answer; when I spake, they did not hear: but **they did evil before mine eyes, and chose that in which I delighted not**." (Isaiah 66:3-4)

> "Let the wicked forsake his way, and the unrighteous man his thoughts: and let him return unto the LORD, and he will have mercy upon him; and to our God, for he will abundantly pardon. **For my thoughts are not your thoughts, neither are your ways my ways, saith the LORD**." (Isaiah 55:7-8)

> "This I say therefore, and testify in the Lord, that ye henceforth walk not as other Gentiles walk, **in the vanity of their mind**, having the understanding darkened, **being alienated from <u>the life of God</u>** through the ignorance that is in them, because of the blindness of their heart." (Ephesians 4:17-18)

In the "spiritual journey" of the emerging faith (delusion) of Oneness/panentheism there is no such thing as "being alienated from *the life of God*." There is only "Being." That is, there is only "*One Being*" in which "everything in Life is really *One Thing*, Manifesting."[4] And this "One Thing," "the Energy of God," can be moved into whatever forms people are *willing* to accept, and even "*made flesh*" accordingly, through merely a dance of the *imagination*. But it shouldn't be surprising that this panentheistic/quantum "God" that is man's imagination is "made flesh" by the power of man's imagination. After all, an imagination that is "God" has the power "to create *anything*"—even man's very own "*God*."

> "**God *is* the energy you call imagination**." (the seducing spirit calling itself "God;" bold added)[5]

> "And **you can use your imagination to create *anything***." (the seducing spirit calling itself "God;" bold added)[6]

> "**You are creating God**." (the seducing spirit calling itself "God;" emphasis added)[7]

> "So change!...
>
> "**Allow your deepest truths to be <u>altered</u>**. Alter them yourself, for goodness' sake....
>
> "**Your new <u>idea</u> about *all of it* is** where the excitement is, **where <u>the creation</u> is**, where **God-in-<u>you</u>** is made manifest and becomes fully realized." (the seducing spirit calling itself "God;" bold & underline added)[8]

> "**The process of <u>creation</u> starts with <u>thought</u>**—an idea, conception, visualization....
>
> "**Thoughts are <u>ideas</u>** formed. **Ideas are <u>energies</u>** come together. **Energies are forces** released. **Forces are elements** existent. **Elements are particles of <u>God</u>, portions of All, the stuff of everything**." (the seducing spirit calling itself "God;" bold & underline added)[9]

"**It is the sacred rhythm of all life, by which you move the Energy of God**." (the seducing spirit calling itself "God;" emphasis added)[10]

"**If you move enough energy, you <u>create</u> <u>matter</u>**. Matter is energy conglomerated. Moved around. Shoved together. If you manipulate energy long enough in a certain way, you get matter. Every Master understands this law. It is the alchemy of the universe. **It is the secret of all life**.

"**Thought is pure energy**." (the seducing spirit calling itself "God;" emphasis added)[11]

"When body, mind, and soul create together, in harmony and in unity, **God is <u>made flesh</u>**." (the seducing spirit calling itself "God;" emphasis added)[12]

Likewise, Leonard Sweet writes:

"... **God is 'spirit' or 'energy.'**" (emphasis added)[13]

"***Matter* is the energy of *Spirit*. Ultimately, all that exists is spirit.**" (emphasis added)[14]

"**Thought** or consciousness are now part of the theories of **matter**....

"<u>***Ideas***</u> **of the mind** not only matter, ideas of the mind **move matter, even <u>become</u> <u>matter</u>**, ... every idea is 'psychokinetic'--it **materializes in some shape or form. The matter of faith is embodiment.**" (emphasis added)[15]

"Early Christians drew upon ***ideas***, phrases, metaphors, and customs of pagan cultures as 'seeds' of the divine Word that ***become* <u>*enfleshed*</u> in *Christ* ...**" (emphasis added)[16]

"**After energy <u>*becomes*</u> <u>*matter*</u>, the Word is <u>*made flesh*</u>**, space must be occupied, **and *incarnation* come to dwell among us.**" (emphasis added)[17]

"**The purpose** of the church is to give form to, **to *put* into *form* and *shape*, the energymatter known as *Jesus Christ***." (emphasis added)[18]

"... ***ideas*** ... ***become* <u>*enfleshed*</u> in *Christ* ...**" (emphasis added)[19]

And according to Alice Bailey:

"The first thing necessary for us to do is to consider somewhat the question of what a form really is. If we turn to a dictionary we will find the word defined as follows: 'The external shape or configuration of a body.'... To my mind, Plutarch conveys the idea of the manifestation of the subjective through the medium of the objective form in a much more illuminating way than does the dictionary. He says:

"'**An <u>*idea*</u>** is a being incorporeal, which has no subsistence by itself, but **gives figure and form unto shapeless matter, and becomes the cause of the manifestation**.'

"Here you have a most interesting sentence, and one of **real occult significance**." (emphasis added)[20]

What is most interesting is that this sentence of "real occult significance" is quite reminiscent of Sweet's teachings. And Bailey goes on to apply this occultly-significant sentence to the "manifestation" of "that vibrant centre of *energy*, and that great enfolding consciousness Whom we call *God*, or Force, or the *Logos*."[21]

No, "ideas" do *not* "become *enfleshed* in *Christ*." Not the *true* Christ anyway. And the *true* Christ and the *true* God and Word *made flesh* is Jesus Christ of Nazareth; *period*. But then, the "matter of faith" of this emerging faith is to materialize (or manifest) a new and <u>different</u> "Christ" (i.e., "Messiah"), as well as a new and <u>different</u> "God," "in some shape or form":

> "In every epoch, however, **the Word is *made flesh* *differently*. Energymatter is a dynamic process**, a time continuum that interacts with and occupies space. But *Logos* **materializes** in *Pathos* **in forms fundamental to, shapes revelatory of, the age**." (Leonard Sweet; emphasis added, except to *Logos* and *Pathos*)[22]

> "*Jesus* **is always an energy *event***." (Leonard Sweet; emphasis added)[23]

> "*In the beginning was the Word, and the Word was with God, and **the Word was God**.... And **the Word was made flesh**, and dwelt among us, (and we beheld his glory, the glory as of **the only begotten of the Father**,) full of grace and truth.... For the law was given by Moses, but grace and truth came by **Jesus Christ**.*" (John 1:1, 14, 17)

> "*And without controversy great is the mystery of godliness: **God was manifest in the flesh**, justified in the Spirit, seen of angels, preached unto the Gentiles, believed on in the world, received up into glory.*" (1 Timothy 3:16)

> "Just because ***Jesus* is <u>the same</u>** yesterday, today, and forever does not mean he does the same thing in the same way yesterday, today, and forever.... ***Energymatter*** **is dispersed through space-time in ways we have yet to comprehend**." (Leonard Sweet; emphasis added)[24]

> "**Space and energymatter have *coevolved*.**" (Leonard Sweet; emphasis added)[25]

> "**I am in a constant process of *formation*.** That process has been **called evolution**, and it is a process that never ends." (the seducing spirit calling itself "God;" emphasis added)[26]

> "Everything is energy, in motion....
>
> "When you look at a thing, you are **not** looking at a **static** 'something' that is 'standing there' in time and space. No! You are *witnessing an event*. Because **everything is moving, changing, evolving. *Everything***....
>
> "**God is an *event*.**" (the seducing spirit calling itself "God;" bold added)[27]

First, as pointed out earlier, a convenient justification for man's diverse "reimaginings" of God and the Lord Jesus Christ—i.e., for making up a *new* and *different* "God" and "Christ" ("Messiah")—can thus be that it is all merely the "evolution" of "the energymatter known as Jesus Christ" and of the "energy" known as "God." It can all "coevolve" together so that "the Word is made flesh *differently*" in "forms" and "shapes" "revelatory" of "the age;" that is, in forms and shapes revelatory of today's "*ideas*" ("*reimaginings*").

Second, as is to be expected in this emerging upside-down faith, "*differently*" is not seen as *differently* but, rather, "*the same.*" After all, the "*energy*" is still "*the same,*" right? Thus, a *different* "Jesus Christ"/"God" absurdly becomes just an "event" of rearranging the "energy" of "Jesus Christ"/"God" into a new "energy pattern." Never mind that this "energy" is all being moved around in a dance, or event, of the *imagination*. In Oneness/panentheism, thoughts, ideas, and imaginations are all "energies" of "the Energy of God," so *imagination* also becomes "*molecular.*" Naturally, people would see no idolatrous harm in creating a new "Jesus Christ"/"God" with the help of their "*molecular*" imagination. Rather, in this emerging faith the help of their *molecular* imagination is just the help of their *molecular* "Energy of God." And thus the creation of a new "Jesus Christ"/"God" is with the help of "*God.*" There's only one problem. This very helpful "God" that allows man to imagine and create both it and a new "Messiah" however man chooses is *already* a new "God" imagined and created by man. So man is spinning in circles to create a new "Messiah" and "God" with the help of man's created new "God." All man needs is to merely "tap into" its "energies." (And all because man isn't willing to simply believe and obey God and His Son!)

> "The challenge of the church in the twenty-first century is to become ... a seedbed in which *the texts* and traditions *of the faith recreate themselves in and through the body* until its **molecular** *imagination* is *awakened* by a living God.
>
> "Every believer, every body of Christ is called to become *the Third Testament*....
>
> "**The same** *cosmic* **dynamics and primordial energies that created** fire, land, wind, and sea **are at work today and continue to** *evolve*, **if only we develop the sensitivities to** *tap into them*." (Leonard Sweet; emphasis added)[28]
>
> "The point of having a God is to **use the essence and the energy that IS God**, and that is *life*, in a way that allows you to create your own experience, thereby **becoming as God is**: the creator." (Neale Donald Walsch; bold added)[29]

Contrary to the *many levels* of these false teachings, *man* cannot tap into or become as *God*. Rather, this emerging faith and its quantum dance of Oneness is actually a downward spiral into being "*as gods.*" And yet it is absurdly justified as *doing and being God*. As if that makes a difference! *Man* cannot do or be *the true God*. To put it another way, *man is not the true God*—and never will be. As used to be obvious, only the true God is the true God. And only the true God can do and be the true God. Man can only do and be man; period. For man to attempt to do and be God is to only be "*as gods.*" And all "gods" that have not "made the heavens and the earth"—even if these "gods" believe that they have the freedom and imagination power to make *God Himself* into a new and different "God"—will face the coming judgment of *the true God Himself*. (And, by the way, the *true* God made the heavens and the earth in six *days*; period. And He only took *that* long as an *example* for us. Believe it or not, we are to only work six *days* before we rest, not six *billion* years--e.g., see Genesis 1:1–2:3; Exodus 20:9-11; 31:15, 17.)

> "But the LORD is the true God, he is the living God, and an everlasting king: at his wrath the earth shall tremble, and the nations shall not be able to abide his indignation. Thus shall ye say unto them, The gods that have not made the heavens and

the earth, even they shall perish from the earth, and from under these heavens." (Jeremiah 10:10-11)

Obviously, the "God" of the emerging faith/New Quantum Spirituality of Oneness/panentheism that brings *all gods* together as just different forms/manifestations of *itself* is not *the true God*. So man's dance of doing and being this "God" is obviously not a dance of doing and being *the true God* by Whom these other *"gods ... shall perish."*

Amazingly enough, Scripture simply doesn't teach a dance of either doing and being or shaping and forming God. But this fact won't stop the emergence of this emerging "make-it-up-as-you-go-along" faith. Why would it? Especially since in this emerging faith "reimagining" God absurdly becomes *literally* "reimagining" God. That is, "reimagining" God becomes the "truth" about God by effecting literal changes in God by moving the "energy" of God into a *new* "reality" and "truth"—at least according to this emerging new way of thinking anyway. Man can thus *shape, form, and fashion* (not to mention *be*) *his own "God"* to his heart's content. What used to be (and still is) done with the *hands* is now being done with the *mind*. In desiring to be *"shapesmiths"* of God—i.e., in desiring the freedom to *dictate* what *form* God will take—people in the 21st century are *still* choosing "to *decide* who and what God is." But, of course, today's idol-making process is "scientific."

> *"Because that, when they knew God, they glorified him not as God, neither were thankful; but became vain in their imaginations, and their foolish heart was darkened. Professing themselves to be wise, they became fools." (Romans 1:21-22)*

The true God, Who does not bow the knee to *man's imaginations*, does not change; period. And He gives us *true understanding* through reading the words of His Word of truth.

> *"The entrance of thy words giveth light; it giveth understanding unto the simple." (Psalm 119:130)*

> *"Thy word is true from the beginning: and every one of thy righteous judgments endureth for ever." (Psalm 119:160)*

> *"Every word of God is pure: he is a shield unto them that put their trust in him. Add thou not unto his words, lest he reprove thee, and thou be found <u>a liar</u>." (Proverbs 30:5-6)*

In truth, man's "reimagined" changes to God—"scientific" or otherwise—are not *literal* but *fictitious*. Man is simply replacing the literal truth of God's Word with man's new fictitious "truth," all the while spinning in circles to defend man's new "truth" as both literal and not literal, fiction and truth. (In Oneness, no one is "a liar," so anyone and everyone can imagine and define God and His Son however they choose and decide for themselves whether they want to see these imaginings as literal or not literal, or fiction or truth.)

People can spin/dance in circles all they want, but "reimagined" changes to God will *never* be "the *truth* about *God*" because man's "reimagining" process will never effect even one *smidgeon* of *change* in the *true* God. And, therefore, man's "reimaginings"— which include The Shack—will never even be a *"better* understanding of God." Quite the contrary. "Reimagining" God is nothing but an attempt to imagine and create a *new* and *better "God"* that is then *whitewashed* as just a "new" and "better" "*understanding*" of God.

> *"Be not deceived; God is not mocked: for whatsoever a man soweth, that shall he also reap." (Galatians 6:7)*

> *"This evil people, which refuse to hear my words, which walk in the imagination of their heart, and walk after other gods, to serve them, and to worship them, shall even be as this girdle, which is good for nothing." (Jeremiah 13:10)*

Outside the "box" of God's Word of truth is outside the "box" of *God's* Word of *truth*. *The true God and false gods* and *truth and falsehood* and *right and wrong* are *not* just *different "patterns"* of the *same "energy."* Thus, it is without question that people in today's "make-it-up-as-you-go-along process" of conceiving, creating, shaping, and forming God and His Son into new and "improved" forms/manifestations/"energy patterns" that man is *willing* to accept are indeed choosing to *resist* the truth of <u>Who</u> God and His Son <u>are</u>. And regarding "[t]he day of *theology*" being "*over*," the seducing spirit world, which points out that people "are recognizing the dawn of *freedom*" and "realizing that every man should be free to worship God *in his own way*," of course sees this "*rejection of dogmas and doctrine*" as "*good and right and encouraging.*"[30]

> **"People need room to *move* and *choose* and *resist* airtight propositions that don't allow free breathing** (i.e., **freedom**). Jesus left space for people to *make their own* responses to him. He did not *dictate* to his disciples *what* they were to *believe* about him: '**Who do *you* say I am?**'" (Leonard Sweet; parentheses in the original; emphasis added)[31]

> **"Hold it. You mean *we* get to decide who and what God is?"** (Neale Donald Walsch; bold added)[32]

It is of the utmost absurdity, to say the least, that according to the emerging faith of Oneness *God* and *His Son* don't "dictate" to man what man is to believe about *God* and *His Son* but, rather, *man* gets to "dictate" to God and His Son what "form"/"shape" they will take according to who *man* decides they are! But, of course, this unconditional "love and freedom"—i.e., freedom from the truth of <u>Who</u> God and His Son <u>are</u>—is what more and more people today *want*. And, sadly, they are hell-bent on success. In the meantime, this emerging faith/new world religion/New Quantum Spirituality leaves them ample space for quite the playing field. But since all they are doing is moving "energy" around, there's nothing to fear in man dictating to God and His Son who man has decided they are, right?

> "**The church is *not* a set of propositions**, buildings, **or *beliefs*** …
>
> "We need to **learn to play** the spaces.… **All space is God's space**." (Leonard Sweet; last ellipsis dots in the original; emphasis added)[33]

> "***Incarnational energies*** are what make the restless intelligence of the Christian tradition **so eager to embrace the new, so open to change the old**, so free to be **creative** in its engagement with the world." (Leonard Sweet; emphasis added)[34]

> "In the Christian tradition resting and **play** begin the week rather than end it because they are the basis of all creative life. Without **play**, without repairs, without maintenance, we don't have **the creativity or energy to break out of the old patterns and see things in new and fresh ways**....
>
> "**Creativity that is revolutionary requires this violent, energy-sapping action of breaking away and breaking the rules**." (Leonard Sweet; emphasis added)[35]

> "'**Now, therefore, can we find *anew* the *power* to <u>name God</u> in a mystical-prophetic** way? That is theology's central postmodern question.'" (Leonard Sweet quoting "Priest/metaphysician/theologian" David W. Tracy)[36]

> "But with many of them God was not well pleased: for they were overthrown in the wilderness. Now these things were our examples, to the intent we should not lust after evil things, as they also lusted. **Neither be ye idolaters**, as were some of them; as it is written, The people sat down to eat and drink, and rose up to **play**." (1 Corinthians 10:5-7)

> "Thus saith the LORD of hosts, **Hearken not unto the words of the prophets that prophesy unto you**: they make you vain: **they speak a vision of their own heart, and not out of the mouth of the LORD**. They say still unto them that despise me, The LORD hath said, Ye shall have peace; and **they say unto every one that walketh after the imagination of his own heart, No evil shall come upon you**. For who hath stood in the counsel of the LORD, and hath perceived and heard his word? who hath marked his word, and heard it? Behold, a whirlwind of the LORD is gone forth in fury, even a grievous whirlwind: it shall fall grievously upon the head of the wicked. The anger of the LORD shall not return, until he have executed, and till he have performed the thoughts of his heart: in the latter days ye shall consider it perfectly. I have not sent these prophets, yet they ran: I have not spoken to them, yet they prophesied. **But if they had stood in my counsel, and had caused my people to hear my words, then they should have turned them from their evil way, and from the evil of their doings**." (Jeremiah 23:16-22)

Of course, Sweet also claims that "[t]he Bible is *not* a blueprint for action, nor a book of answers,"[37] and that we are to "*prophesy* our way forward into the future" and "live in the *incarnation*."[38] And, of course, when man's *ideas* "*become matter,*" man's *ideas* thus become "*prophetic.*" So it is not surprising that resisting *believing* and *obeying* God's Word of truth elicits no fear in the emerging faith/New Quantum Spirituality.

> "*Quantum spirituality* is always in flux, always aware of its own incompleteness.... For a *New Light* apologetic *there can be no final statement of theology* anymore [sic] than there can be any final 'laws of nature.' All life is *change* ... we must not foreclose our minds against the *truths* of God, even if they are *new*." (Leonard Sweet; emphasis added)[39]

> "An *incarnational* faith is what guarantees *generativity*, the possibility of every culture to 'know' things about God that have *never been 'known' before*." (Leonard Sweet; emphasis added)[40]

Generativity -- "the ability or *power* to generate or produce something."[41] To *generate* -- "*to bring into existence*; cause to be;" "to produce or *bring into being*; *create*."[42] To be *generative* -- "having the *power* of producing or *originating*."[43]

Absurdly, through *imagination* and *ideas*—i.e., *thoughts*—that are imagined to be *energy* that is literally *creative*, the emerging faith/New Quantum Spirituality is indeed attempting to bring its "reimagined" "God" of Oneness/panentheism "*into being*." An attempt to literally change God into a new and different "God." And, of course, this "God" is "never finished," so it is continually "made flesh"/"incarnating" *anew*, which then brings *new* "truths" into being that have never been known before. Nevertheless, since this "God" of Oneness/panentheism is not the *true* God but a *false* "God," its emerging new forms/manifestations/"truths" are not *truth* but *falsehood*. And to justify *falsehood* as something that has just "never been 'known' before" or that is "incarnational" is absurd. It is even more absurd to justify all this "generativity" as a mission to *put God and His Son into "form" and "shape."* Again, as if that makes a difference! A "shapesmith" is a "shapesmith." And a "shapesmith" is "[o]ne that undertakes to *improve the form of the body.*"[44]

Despite the process of man's emerging "make-it-up-as-you-go-along" faith, *God's* prophecy in His Word is from *God* Who *knows* the future. Likewise, God also knows *Who He is*, and it is this *truth* that His *names* are based upon. To the contrary, *man's* so-called "prophecy" is the attempt to *create* the future according to man's *ideas*. And in order to create the *future* man must also create the "*God*" of the future that man is looking to create. In other words, man must "name God" "*prophetically*"—i.e., "decide who and what God is"/"*choos[e]* what I am going to be" for man's desired future (which of course is a "new world" of Oneness). Man has quite a powerful imagination. But then, man always has wanted to be a shapesmith of God.

> "*Ye are my witnesses, saith the* LORD, *and my servant whom I have chosen: that ye may know and believe me, and understand that I am he:* **before me there was no God formed, neither shall there be after me.**" *(Isaiah 43:10)*

> "*And the residue thereof* **he maketh a god**, *even his graven image:* **he falleth down unto it, and worshippeth it, and prayeth unto it, and saith, Deliver me; for thou art my god**. *They have not known nor understood: for he hath shut their eyes, that they cannot see; and their hearts, that they cannot understand.* **And none considereth in his heart, neither is there knowledge nor understanding** *to say, I have burned part of it in the fire; yea, also I have baked bread upon the coals thereof; I have roasted flesh, and eaten it: and shall I make the residue thereof an abomination?* **shall I fall down to the stock of a tree?** *He feedeth on ashes:* **a deceived heart hath turned him aside, that he cannot deliver his soul, nor say, Is there not a lie in my right hand?**" *(Isaiah 44:17-20)*

> "*Who hath* **formed a god**, *or molten a graven image* **that is profitable for nothing**? *Behold, all his fellows shall be ashamed: and the workmen, they are of men: let them all be gathered together, let them stand up; yet they shall fear, and they shall be ashamed together.*" *(Isaiah 44:10-11)*

A god formed in the imagination is a *god* formed in the *imagination*.

> "**Study** *to show thyself approved unto* <u>God</u>, *a workman that needeth not to be ashamed, rightly dividing* **the word of <u>truth</u>**." *(2 Timothy 2:15)*

> ***"Casting down imaginations**, and every high thing that exalteth itself against <u>the knowledge</u> of <u>God</u>, and bringing into captivity every thought to the obedience of Christ."* (2 Corinthians 10:5)

Sadly, even in today's shifting Christianity more and more people are openly trading in the knowledge of God for the freedom to imagine and form God and His Son however they choose. They are indeed turning 2 Corinthians 10:5 upside down, and defiantly:

> Casting down the knowledge of God, and every scriptural truth that exalteth itself against the imaginations of man, ...

It is therefore not surprising that *"imaginations"* has been removed from 2 Corinthians 10:5 in new versions (again, *new* for *a reason*) in the circular, incremental process of changing more and more of the "old" truth of God's Word according to the "new" way of thinking. (Case in point, even *Sweet himself* has been chosen for man's never-ending process of <u>re</u>writing/<u>re</u>wording God's Word of truth, in yet another new version, a.k.a. "translation," of Thomas Nelson called "The Voice."[45] But more on this absurdity later.)

Basically, people today are choosing to risk everything on man's "reimaginings" of <u>Who</u> God and His Son <u>are</u>. In other words, they are trusting that man's imagination is "powerful" enough for today's "reimaginings" to become *literal changes* in <u>Who</u> God and His Son <u>are</u>. And they are essentially telling God that *"when the overflowing scourge shall pass through, it shall not come unto us: for we have made lies our refuge, and under falsehood have we hid ourselves"* (Isaiah 28:15b).

In reference to man's idol making, God's Word has to point out the obvious -- "the workman made it; therefore it is not God," and then goes on to warn, "For they have sown the wind, and they shall reap the whirlwind" (see Hosea 8:4-7). The workmen of the "God" of Oneness, who are indeed sowing the wind, are many and come from many religions/faiths/cultures. And even if they *"all be gathered together"* in this task of collectively forming and making up a "God" that can be imagined and defined however anyone chooses, they will still *"fear"* and *"be ashamed together"* when the *true* God and His Son are revealed from heaven. Again, a god formed in the imagination is a god formed in the imagination.

> *"... he maketh a god, ... he falleth down unto it, and worshippeth it, and prayeth unto it, and saith, Deliver me; for thou art my god.... a deceived heart hath turned him aside, that he cannot deliver his soul, nor say, Is there not a lie in my right hand?"* (Isaiah 44:17, 20)

47

Changing the "old" reality of the God of *judgment* into a new "reality" of a "God" of Oneness by simply *thinking* it "into being"

> **"You are One with everyone and everything in the Universe—including God."** (the seducing spirit calling itself "God;" emphasis added)[1]

> "**'We Are All One'** ... *is a precise description of* **the nature of Ultimate Reality**. When you understand this, you ... see **the relationship of all things** differently. You notice **the connectedness at a much higher level**." (the seducing spirit calling itself "God;" bold added)[2]

> "A **New Spirituality** truly is emerging upon the earth, and the idea of **Oneness is at its core**." (Neale Donald Walsch; emphasis added)[3]

> "**Unitary thinking, the highest level of understanding reality**, opens us up to a wider sensory realm and mystical dimension of the divine; it also heals the divisions that separate us from one another and life's *highest values*." (Leonard Sweet; emphasis added)[4]

> "... I also believe that our own spiritual traditions will have to undergo some *radical changes* in order to be in harmony with the *values* of the new paradigm.... **This kind of *new spirituality* is now being developed by many groups and movements, both within and outside the churches**....
>
> "We are embedded in the multiple alternative networks of what I have called the 'rising culture'—**a multitude of movements representing *different facets of***

***the same new vision of reality*, gradually coalescing** to form a powerful force of social transformation." (Fritjof Capra; emphasis added)[5]

Since there's clearly nothing "separative" or "divisive" about today's emerging "new spirituality" of Oneness that gives everyone the "love and freedom" to decide for themselves what is *the true God or false gods, truth or falsehood, right or wrong*, it is thus seen as the means to unifying the world into a harmonious whole. And it is radically changing and transforming today's Christianity along with the world. More and more people are shifting to this "spirituality"—i.e., emerging faith—because they also believe along with Capra that "the major problems of our time ... are *all* different facets of *one single crisis*," "a crisis of *perception*" derived from "an *outdated worldview*."[6] That is, from an "outdated worldview" of *non*-Oneness, or *dualism*. Sweet, for example, writes that "*all* dichotomized selves" and "*all* discursive dualisms," of which he says "one of the *worst* of which was 'sacred' and 'profane,'" are "*all disastrous separations* that *threaten our existence*."[7]

Seeking to leave *non*-Oneness and its "crisis of perception" behind, Capra describes the emerging "*new* spirituality"/"*new* paradigm"/"*new* vision of reality" as "a *holistic* worldview" that sees "the world as an *integrated whole* rather than a dissociated collection of parts."[8] He also describes it as "an *ecological* worldview" that "is rooted in a perception of *reality* that goes beyond the scientific framework to an awareness of *the oneness of all life*."[9] And, therefore, Capra points out that "[u]ltimately, such deep *ecological* awareness is *spiritual* awareness," and goes on to also give this explanation:

> "When the concept of **the human *spirit*** is understood as **the mode of consciousness in which the individual feels *connected to the cosmos* as a whole**, it becomes clear that **ecological awareness is *spiritual* in its deepest essence**, and it is then not surprising that the *new* vision of *reality* is in harmony with the visions of spiritual traditions....
>
> "The new physics is an integral part of **a *new worldview* that is now emerging in all the sciences and in society**." (emphasis added)[10]

This emerging "*new worldview*" is in fact the emerging "*new world religion*." Whether people call it a "paradigm," "worldview," "vision of reality," "science," "faith," "religion," "spirituality," "awakening," or "consciousness," etc., it *all* comes down to the same thing—*Oneness*. And not only is Oneness the complete *opposite* of God's Word of truth, it completely *defies* it. To say that this is a *radical transformation* as well as *revolution* is a tremendous understatement. But those who don't believe that the truth of God's Word is the truth of God don't see this revolution as against *God*. They just see this revolution, for instance, as "saving" the planet from "doom" by moving beyond "an outdated worldview," or "old" truth. Accordingly, Capra points out that this "*new* vision of *reality*" "will require a *new* philosophical and *religious* bias," specifically "of the oneness of all life," and writes that "the idea of the individual **being linked to the cosmos** is expressed in the Latin root of **the word religion, *religare* ('to bind strongly')** ..."[E, 11] Sounds familiar. And similar to Capra who writes of the "consciousness" of

---

E

Capra finishes this sentence with "... as well as in the Sanskrit *yoga*, which means union." Indeed. Yoga, *which cannot be separated from its religious purpose*, is specifically *designed* to bring *union* with

feeling "connected to the cosmos," Sweet likewise writes that "[t]ranscendent states of consciousness" are those "most connecting of the self to the cosmos."[12]

> "It is not religion and reason that go together, but **religion and relationship** that go together. Actually, **that's where the word *religion* comes from—*religare*—meaning 'to connect, to bind together.'** The future depends not on our ability to 'Come, let us reason together' but **'Come, let us relate together.'**" (Leonard Sweet; bold & underline added)[13]

> " ... **the *new world religion* ... The word 'religion' concerns *relationship*,** ..." (the seducing spirit calling itself Djwhal Khul; emphasis added)[14]

> "... '**having pervaded this entire Universe with a fragment of Himself**, He *remains*.' **God is *immanent*** in the forms of ***all* created things** ...

> "On the fact of God and of **man's *relation* to the divine ... the *new world religion* will be based.... of the fact of God Transcendent and of God *Immanent* within *every* form of life**.

> "**These are the foundational truths upon which the world religion** of the future **will rest**." (the seducing spirit calling itself Djwhal Khul; emphasis added, except to *remains*)[15]

> "Workers in the field of religion will formulate **the *universal* platform of the *new world religion*. It is a work of loving synthesis and will emphasize <u>the unity</u>** and the fellowship **<u>of the spirit</u>**." (the seducing spirit calling itself Djwhal Khul; emphasis added)[16]

> "Within the churches today there are men responding to **<u>the new spiritual idealism</u>**, to the *urgency* of the opportunity and to *the need for change*....

> "What is the solution of this intricate and difficult relationship throughout the world? **A *new* presentation of *truth*,** because God is not a fundamentalist ... These are *imperative* changes.

> "**Nothing can prevent the *new world religion* from eventually *emerging*.... It will be hindered by the fundamentalists**, the ***narrow*-minded** and the theologians in all the world religions, by those **who refuse to *let go* the *old* interpretations and methods, who love the *old* doctrines** ..." (the seducing spirit calling itself Djwhal Khul; emphasis added)[17]

Not surprisingly, Sweet, who is one of the anything but narrow-minded workers of this emerging faith/new world religion/new "spirituality," also writes:

> "Unfortunately, the church is still under the scientific spell of *old* teachings that science itself has long since repudiated." (emphasis added)[18]

"Brahman"—the Hindu god known as the "ultimate reality" in *everyone* and *everything*. In other words, yoga is *designed* to lead one into the "*consciousness*" of Oneness with *all that is*, and is doing so quite successfully. Again, meditation is *designed* to gradually remove "that which obscures the light" of Oneness. And *many* people have been seduced into practicing yoga, as well as many other forms of meditation, for "exercise," "health," and "stress management." There is *a reason* why the beliefs of people everywhere are *changing* . . .

Actually, today's shifting Christianity is under the "scientific" spell of new teachings of doctrines of devils that God's Word itself has long since repudiated. And, also not surprisingly, given his own "scientific" *mystical* beliefs in Oneness, Capra—a physicist, and one of the scientists that has "repudiated" the "old" teachings—likewise criticizes "Christian fundamentalists promoting medieval notions of reality."[19] The "medieval" reality being the Christian fundamentals of God's Word of *truth* that are the *opposite* of today's preferred "scientific" *fables*.

> *"I charge thee therefore before God, and the Lord Jesus Christ, who shall judge the quick and the dead at his appearing and his kingdom; preach the word; be instant in season, out of season; reprove, rebuke, exhort with all longsuffering and doctrine. For the time will come when they will not endure sound doctrine; but after their own lusts shall they heap to themselves teachers, having itching ears; and they shall turn away their ears from the truth, and shall be turned unto fables." (2 Timothy 4:1-4)*

In its epidemic of itching ears, today's shifting Christianity has heaped to itself teachers who have a gift in scratching, and this includes teachers in *"science falsely so called."*

> *"O Timothy, keep that which is committed to thy trust, avoiding profane and vain babblings, and oppositions of science falsely so called: Which some professing have erred concerning the faith. Grace be with thee. Amen." (1 Timothy 6:20-21)*

Yes, "Christian fundamentalists"—i.e., Christians who believe the *fundamentals* of God's Word of absolute truth—do indeed know that the true God is *separate* from His creation and is *not immanent* in everyone and everything. And it is *not* because of this so-called "*outdated* worldview" that the world is falling apart and facing "doom"! Rather, both the world and today's shifting Christianity are in a state of rebellion/anarchy/revolution *against God*. And God's absolute truth that *divides and separates Oneness* into opposites absurdly seen as "*outdated*"—such as *what is the true God and false gods, truth and falsehood, right and wrong*—is precisely what the world needs to be saved from its sin and wickedness. But people today are not *willing* to see it that way. To the contrary, people in both the world and today's shifting Christianity see the "overlay of power," "chain of command," and "final authority" of the true God and His Son as "ghastly." Consequently, they are understatedly facing a ghastly future that includes both apocalyptic and eternal "doom."

The Christian fundamentals of *God's* Word of *truth*, that is, the "medieval notion of reality" and "outdated worldview" of division/separation/dualism/*non*-Oneness that is absurdly believed to be behind "the major problems of our time" is indeed behind the biggest problem that man faces—the *soul "sort."* But since it is the "outdated" reality of the *non*-Oneness of the Christian fundamentals of *God's* Word of *truth* that is seen as the *problem*, all man has to do is simply "break free" from the fundamentals of God's Word of truth in order to "break free" from God's coming judgment of souls, right?

> *"And fear not them which kill the body, but are not able to kill the soul: but rather fear him which is able to destroy both soul and body in hell." (Matthew 10:28)*

> "[Y]ou do not have to fear God, **you merely have to be One with God**." (the seducing spirit calling itself "God;" emphasis added)[20]

> "**And all the world's souls can be set free. The New Spirituality is a *civil rights* movement for *the soul*,** freeing humanity at last from the oppression of its belief in a separate, angry, violent, and fearful God." (Neale Donald Walsch; emphasis added)[21]

> "**If we could break free from the** Greco-Roman **soul-sort** narrative [in which 'everyone will be sorted into either the destruction/damnation or the redemption/salvation bin'], **think of what could change**." (Brian McLaren; emphasis added)[22]

Sadly, the seducing spirit world doesn't have to work very hard to seduce people today. Even people in today's shifting Christianity aren't willing to believe the truth of God and are thus desperate for an *alternative*—i.e., for a new "truth" of a new "God" that is "*bigger*" than the truth of God so that they and the world can have the freedom to imagine and define "God" however they choose and to have this "relationship" however they choose on whatever religious "path" they choose. So it isn't surprising that this revolution and its emerging faith/religion/"paradigm"/"worldview"/"vision of reality"/ "science"/"spirituality"/"consciousness" of Oneness/panentheism comes down to a mission to "transcend" (bypass) the *soul "sort"*—i.e., the true God's *judgment*—so that "all the world's souls" in revolution against God "can be set free." This is, of course, only possible in a *universal salvation*, which is only possible if *man changes God*. Obviously, a God of *judgment* is not a God of *Oneness*, and a God of *Oneness* is essential to a universal salvation. Hence, in this pursuit of freedom from the fundamentals of God's Word of truth, the workmen are gathering together to create a new "God" and new future—a new world religion and new world—of Oneness.

McLaren, for example, writes of "a *better* vision of the future" in which "[w]e might say that in it, *the future is un-doomed* ... un-doomed from burning destruction and eternal conscious torment ['in hell']."[23] And, of course, he also writes:

> "[T]he Greco-Roman mind was habitually **dualistic**, in the sense that an enlightened or philosophic mind would always see **the world divided in two, the profane** physical world of matter, stuff, and change on the low side **and the sacred** metaphysical world of ideals, ideas, spirit, and changelessness on the high side." (emphasis added)[24]

> "**If we could break free** from the Greco-Roman *soul-sort* narrative, **think of what could** *change*.... **We would stop seeing *the line* that separates *good and evil* running between our religion and all others**....
>
> "Evangelism would *cease* to be a matter of *saving souls* from *a bad ending* ... It would no longer require *hellfire-and-brimstone scare tactics* ...
>
> "It would invite people into lifelong *spiritual formation* as disciples of Jesus, ... *whatever* the new disciple's *religious affiliation or lack thereof*....
>
> "... **calling people to *a way of life* in a *kingdom* (or *beautiful whole*) that transcends and includes *all* religions**." (parentheses in the original; emphasis added)[25]

> "... **God and the universe are *in relationship*....
>
> "Conventional eschatologies ... tend to argue about different arrangements or lengths of the lines in the Greco-Roman narrative. That's what makes **this new**

approach so different and difficult to label, because it **dispenses with the <u>linear</u> approach altogether**. We could borrow from Hans Küng and others and call it an *'improvisational eschatology.'* We could also call it *participatory*. **In a participatory eschatology, when we ask, 'What does the future hold?' the answer begins, 'That depends.** It depends on you and me. God holds out to us at every moment a brighter future; the issue is whether we are willing to receive it and **work with God to help create it. We are participating in the creation of what the future will be**.'" (bold & underline added)[26]

In other words, to eliminate those "disastrous separations" between the "sacred" and the "profane," this emerging faith is choosing to dispense with the linear truth of God's Word altogether in favor of an "improvisational" (or "make-it-up-as-you-go-along") "participatory" *new* "truth." And with a participatory "God" that brings everyone/everything into a quantum (i.e., panentheistic) dance of Oneness with itself in a *universal salvation/relationship*, man has the unconditional "love and freedom" to *not believe* the fundamentals of *God's* Word of *truth*. Since there is even emerging "proof" of all this Oneness in man's new science and New Quantum Spirituality, man can thus leave this "crisis of perception" behind and join the dance of Oneness of this emerging faith/"new spirituality"/"new worldview"/"new world religion"/"new vision of reality."

"[P]erhaps we could also say that we are **participating in the quest** or adventure **of God**: God is seeking, adventuring, questing to **create (with us) a universe that will become God's eternal dancing partner,** ... **The quest is a dance**, and the dance is in fact a holy, **cosmic**, unending romance **into which we all are invited**....

"As Gamaliel said, if our 'plan or undertaking is of human origin, it will fail.' But if our plan or undertaking is from God . . ." (Brian McLaren; last ellipsis dots & parentheses in the original; emphasis added)[27]

First, a cosmic dance/romance of Oneness that eliminates "dualistic" division between "the sacred" and "the profane" is anything but *holy*. In fact, this dance of Oneness *profanes* the *true* God.

*"... **they have put no difference between the holy and profane**, neither have they shown difference between the unclean and the clean, ... **and I am profaned among them**." (Ezekiel 22:26)*

So it is not surprising that McLaren writes:

"In my own experience as a lover and reader of the Bible, as **I am freed from the literalistic and dualistic straitjacket** ... I feel I can breathe a little freer ..." (Brian McLaren; emphasis added)[28]

"Perhaps when our conservative friends **ask those of us on this quest if we believe in the *inerrancy* of Scripture**, our reply should be: '**No**, I believe the Scripture is *better* than inerrant. I believe it's beautiful.'" (Brian McLaren; emphasis added)[29]

Second, a plan to dispense with the truth of God's Word will only be seen as "from *God*" if God's Word is not believed to be the truth of God. And a plan to create a *universal* salvation—a "beautiful whole" of "*all* religions"—that purposely breaks free from God's plan of salvation is no salvation at all. In other words, it will fail in saving souls. But man thinks that man knows more about God's plan of salvation than God does, so man just dispenses with it altogether . . .

> "For there is **one God**, and **one mediator** between God and men, the man Christ Jesus." (1 Timothy 2:5)

> "For God so loved the world, that he gave his only begotten Son, that whosoever believeth in him should not perish, but have everlasting life. For God sent not his Son into the world to condemn the world; but that the world through him might be saved. He that believeth on him is not condemned: but he that believeth not is condemned already, because he hath not believed in the name of the only begotten Son of God.... The Father loveth the Son, and hath given all things into his hand. He that believeth on the Son hath everlasting life: and **he that believeth not the Son shall not see life; but the wrath of God abideth on him**." (John 3:16-18, 35-36)

Again, obviously a God of *judgment* is not a God of Oneness, and a God of Oneness is *essential* to a *universal* salvation. So in order to create the new world and new future of a *universal* salvation/relationship of Oneness, man must also create a new "God" to go along with the new future of Oneness that man is looking to create. In other words, since God is not a God of Oneness, God Himself becomes a "disastrous separation." Hence the replacement of this "*outdated* worldview" and "*outdated*" God with the "*new* worldview"/"*new* world religion"/"*new* spirituality" and "*new* God" of Oneness/panentheism. It is this "God," which can be *imagined and defined however anyone chooses*, that offers a "brighter" and "creatable" future to a world that wants the unconditional "love and freedom" to believe and do whatever it wants with *no judgment*.

> "We must choose between Yesterday and Tomorrow.
>
> **"Humanity is being given an invitation to explore the wondrous possibilities of Tomorrow's God, and the world that this new God can create.**
>
> "It's not a new God at all, of course, only a new understanding of the present God, of the one God, of *The Only Thing That Is*." (Neale Donald Walsch; emphasis added)[30]

> "Tomorrow's God is unconditionally loving, **nonjudgmental**, noncondemning, and nonpunishing." (the seducing spirit calling itself "God;" emphasis added)[31]

> "Tomorrow's God will be understood to be **the very essence of freedom**, and since humans will understand themselves to **be One with Tomorrow's God**, they will also understand themselves to **be inherently free**." (the seducing spirit calling itself "God;" emphasis added)[32]

> "... **Your future is creatable. Create it as you want it**." (the seducing spirit calling itself "God;" emphasis added)[33]

And in this emerging faith/New Quantum Spirituality, imagining and creating a new "God" and new future—a new world religion and new world—of Oneness is, of course, all "scientific." In *A "Wonderful" Deception*, Warren B. Smith points out that:

"In *SoulTsunami*, Sweet states that **the 'new biology' and the 'new physics' hold the metaphysical key to the creation of this positive future**—this global civilization. He explains:

> "'Physics is increasingly becoming the study of matter so small (is it a wave? is it a particle?) as to become **the study of consciousness**. In other words, **physics is becoming metaphysics**.'
>
> "'The coming together of the *new* biology and the *new* physics is providing the basic metaphors for **this *new* global civilization** that esteems and encourages whole-brain experiences, full-life expectations, personalized expressions, and **a globalized consciousness**.'" (parentheses in the original; emphasis added)[34]

Sweet also writes that:

> "*SoulTsunami* is designed and dedicated not only to helping you predict, but to helping you intervene spiritually and socially to **invent and prevent the future**." (emphasis added)[35]

> "*Postmodern* Christians are spiritual interventionists. The **Postmodern Reformation** Church will **consciously intervene to help *design* this *new* world**. There are many futures out there. The future is not a 'single state,' but a scenario of possibilities. **There is a struggle between opposing visions of the future. It is not too late to choose which one we shall get.** The future is a function of our choices and creations." (emphasis added)[36]

> "*Postmodern* culture is an ***anti-Christian*** culture…. **This requires** not only a new ability to tell the story but also **a fresh way to *reframe* the story for 'a sinless society,'** a mission field where people don't see themselves as 'sinners.'…
>
> "It is time to live out of **the secret of life**, the secret of the cruciform life: **the double-helix divine *design*** for life and the church." (emphasis added)[37]

> "[I]t is time to **find *new* ways of being the church that are true to our *postmodern* context**. It is time for **a Postmodern Reformation**." (emphasis added)[38]

So the church is to be true to a "postmodern context" that is "*anti-Christian*"?! Actually, *we are to be true to God*. But, as previously addressed, this anti-Christian Reformation—i.e., Re-*formation*—"Church" is trying to re-*form* the Christian truth and faith of God's Word, and thus Christianity, into *a defragged "whole" with other religions/ faiths*. Thus, to help "design" this "*new* world" is to help "design" the "*new* world religion." That is, it is to help bring the whole world and its religion into an *interfaith "formation"* (i.e., into an interfaith "*spiritual*" formation), which is *everything but* true to God. But, of course, those who are caught up in this Re-*formation* of all *separateness* into *Oneness* don't see it that way. Sadly, this rapidly emerging faith/"new spirituality"/ "new worldview"/"new world religion"/Re-formation of Oneness is indeed the formation of a spiritual *web*. (And, yes, "spiritual formation," with its *mystical* "spiritual" "disciplines"/"exercises," is part of all this. Again, there is *a reason why beliefs are shifting to Oneness* . . .)

Despite the fact that this emerging faith/"new spirituality" of Oneness has invented a future universal/unconditional salvation for everyone in its "civil rights movement for the soul," it is precisely *because* people are not willing to see themselves as sinners in need of the Lord and Saviour Jesus Christ that the future consists of God's *non-*preventable judgment on the world. And to come together to "reframe"/re-"form"/ "*design*" God and His Son into a new "truth" and faith of *Oneness* that brings both the narrow way of <u>believing</u> in Jesus and the broad way of <u>not believing</u> in Jesus together as one in an all-encompassing "*nondualistic* double helix" "Möbius-strip" "*secret* of *life*" changes *nothing*.

> "*For I am the* LORD, *I change not;* ..." *(Malachi 3:6)*

The world is powerless to "prevent the future" of God's coming judgment. However, this future *is* changeable for all *individuals* who are willing to repent ("*repentance to the acknowledging of the truth*"--2 Timothy 2:25) and *believe* in the Lord Jesus Christ.

> "*I tell you, Nay: but, except ye repent, ye shall all likewise perish.*" *(Luke 13:3)*

> "*For God so loved the world, that he gave his only begotten Son, that <u>whosoever</u> believeth in him should not perish, but have everlasting life.*" *(John 3:16)*

> "*The Lord is not slack concerning his promise, as some men count slackness; but is longsuffering to us-ward, not willing that any should perish, but that all should come to repentance.*" *(2 Peter 3:9)*

The "*promise*" referred to here is of God's "*judgment*" (v. 7). And God's Word makes it clear that the day of His judgment has already been set. Despite the claims to the contrary, there is *no* "struggle between opposing visions of the future." Unlike man, God doesn't make it up as He goes along. Neither is God "*a man, that he should lie*" (Numbers 23:19). To the contrary, *God knows* the future and has recorded it in His Word to mercifully *warn us* of the consequences of unbelief. God also *knows* when people will no longer be willing to repent and believe in His Son. Sadly, that day is *clearly* approaching. If it doesn't speak to the lateness of the hour that today's *mission* of "love" and "freedom" is to help everyone "transcend" (bypass) *repentance* and *belief in Jesus*, then what does?!

Today's mission of *Oneness* is indeed changing *everything*. Although the world can freely make it up as it goes along, this is only for a season. When the set day of God's judgment arrives, then *God Himself* is going to change everything. There is an *absolute truth* whether people choose to believe it or not. God is not a "cosmic dance of energy." God is not a "cosmic dance" of doing and being and creating God. As people will find out soon enough, man's dance of the imagination is nothing more than *man's* dance of the *imagination*. To the contrary, God's Word of truth is *God's* Word of *truth*.

> "*I tell you, Nay: but, except ye repent, ye shall all likewise perish.*" *(Luke 13:5)*

> "*And the kings of the earth, and the great men, and the rich men, and the chief captains, and the mighty men, and every bondman, and every free man, hid themselves in the dens and in the rocks of the mountains; and said to the mountains and rocks, Fall on us, and hide us from the face of him that sitteth on the throne, and from the wrath of the Lamb: For the great day of his wrath is come; and who shall be able to stand?*" *(Revelation 6:15-17)*

Obviously, God and His Son are not in the "make-it-up-as-you-go-along process" of today's emerging faith and New Quantum Spirituality. But the seducing spirit world is, and it is adept at scratching itching ears—with serpentine craftiness of course.

> **"Yes, there is a One Great Truth; there is a Final Reality. But you will always get what you choose**, regardless of that reality—precisely because the reality is that you are a divine creature, **divinely creating your reality even as you are experiencing it**." (the seducing spirit calling itself "God;" emphasis added)[39]

> "The experience which I have described here, on the other hand, I am calling the Cosmic Wheel, because **there is *nothing* of** unworthiness, debt-repayment, **punishment**, or 'purification.' The Cosmic Wheel simply describes **the ultimate reality**, or what you might call **the cosmology of the universe**.
>
> "It is *the cycle of life*, or what I sometimes term The Process. It is a picture phrase describing *the no-beginning-and-no-end nature of things*; the *continually connected* path to and from *the all of everything*, **on which the soul joyfully journeys throughout eternity**.
>
> **"It is the sacred rhythm of all life, by which you move the Energy of God**." (the seducing spirit calling itself "God;" emphasis added)[40]

> "Have you ever watched children use a CD-ROM to play a computerized video game?...
>
> "Think of the Cosmic Wheel as that CD-ROM....
>
> "All the endings already exist, and which ending you experience depends on the choices you make....
>
> "As with the end of the game on the CD-ROM, **there is *more than one version [of the 'future']***.
>
> **"In one version, the Earth will be in upheaval. In another version, it won't**." (the seducing spirit calling itself "God;" emphasis added)[41]

And, of course, the seducing spirit world adds:

> "And when the game is over, whether you win, lose, or draw, the universe will say, 'Want to play again?'" (the seducing spirit calling itself "God")[42]

In this "game," it's all just "the sacred rhythm of all life, by which you move the Energy of God." And since this "game" of unbelief is just "play" that keeps moving the "energy" of "God" into new "patterns" that people *choose*, why wouldn't they be able to keep playing the game over and over whether they "win, lose, or draw"? Because there's this little matter of a soul "sort," i.e., the true God's judgment of souls . . .

> *"And as it is appointed unto men once to die, but after this the judgment." (Hebrews 9:27)*

Again, the only way to be saved from God's wrath and judgment is to *believe* in the *only* Mediator of the true God's covenant—God's Son, Jesus Christ of Nazareth. But, sadly, the world is *not willing* to *believe* and prefers to "play" at "reimagining" it all, hoping that its imaginative "play" is powerful enough to break free from God's coming wrath on a world that is *not willing* to *believe*. And "when the game is over, ... the universe will *[not]* say, 'Want to play again?'" First, it's not up to *"the universe."* Contrary to today's emerging faith/New Quantum Spirituality of Oneness/panentheism, the universe is not "God." There is no "God" in everyone and everything. And, second, the true God is infinitely more powerful than *everyone and everything in the entire universe put together*. To put it another way, *not even the entire universe/"cosmos" as a whole* has enough *power* to overcome *the true God*. And He said what He meant and meant what He said in His Word of truth.

It is worldwide *unrepentant unbelief*, not an "*outdated* worldview," that is the cause of the world's problems and its future judgment. But rather than repenting of their unbelief, more and more people are choosing instead to align their minds in the lie of Oneness. Conveniently for them, it is even absurdly imagined that this alignment of minds gives man the *mind power* to *change* the "old" God of judgment into a new "God" of Oneness. Thus, people everywhere who want a "bigger" and "better" "God" can all work together in this emerging "faith" to shape and form this new "God" of Oneness *collectively*. And since this alignment of minds is imagined to be an alignment of the "cosmic mind" and "consciousness"—i.e., "God"—in everyone and everything, it is this "cosmic mind"/"God" that even gives this work of the imagination its "power." Never mind that this work to create a new "God" of Oneness is with the help of man's created new "God" of Oneness. Being a shapesmith of "God" is now "scientific"— according to the emerging faith/New Quantum Spirituality anyway. So all those who are participating in the work to shape and re-form (or reform) the "old" God of *judgment* into a new "God" of *Oneness* are workmen who therefore have nothing to fear or be ashamed of, right?

> *"Who hath formed a god, or molten a graven image that is profitable for nothing? Behold, all his fellows shall be ashamed: and the workmen, they are of men: let them all be gathered together, let them stand up; yet they shall fear, and they shall be ashamed together." (Isaiah 44:10-11)*

> *"... the workman made it; therefore it is not God ..." (Hosea 8:6)*

> "It ['the mystical view'] regards **consciousness as the primary reality and ground of *all* being**. In its purest form consciousness, according to this view, is nonmaterial, formless, and *void of all content*; it is often described as 'pure consciousness,' '**ultimate reality**,' 'suchness,' and the like. **This manifestation of pure consciousness is associated with the Divine** in many spiritual traditions. It is said to be **the essence of the universe** and to manifest itself **in all things**; **all forms of matter and all living beings are seen as *patterns of divine consciousness***." (Fritjof Capra; emphasis added)[43]

> "**The ultimate reality of the universe appears to be consciousness**, out of which energymatter arises.... **God is** the Spirit of the universe, **the consciousness of the cosmos**: its energy, its information, its thought." (Leonard Sweet; emphasis added)[44]

> "Because **the systems view of mind is not limited to *individual* organisms** but can be extended to social and *ecological* systems, we may say that **groups of people, societies, and cultures** have **a *collective* mind**, and therefore also possess **a collective consciousness**.... As individuals **we *participate* in these**

collective mental patterns, are influenced by them, **and shape them** in turn. In addition the concepts of **a *planetary* mind and a *cosmic* mind** may be associated with **planetary and cosmic levels of consciousness**." (Fritjof Capra; emphasis added)[45]

"In the stratified order of nature, ***individual human minds are embedded in the larger minds*** of social and *ecological* systems, **and these are *integrated* into the *planetary* mental system—the mind of Gaia—which in turn must *participate* in some kind of *universal* or *cosmic* mind**. The conceptual framework of the new systems approach is in no way restricted by **associating this *cosmic mind* with the traditional idea of *God***." (Fritjof Capra; emphasis added)[46]

Thus, people "shape" "God," the "cosmic mind," with their own. This emerging faith/New Quantum Spirituality therefore makes it very easy to shape a new "God" by which the world can break free from the coming judgment of God. Just change the "collective mind," and poof! The collective has moved "the Energy of God" into a new "pattern." This "play" is simply a *mind* game (in more ways than one).

> "**Thought is pure energy**. Every thought you have, have ever had, and ever will have is **creative**....
>
> "All thoughts congeal; **all thoughts meet other thoughts**, criss-crossing in an incredible maze of energy, **forming an ever-changing pattern** of unspeakable beauty and unbelievable complexity....
>
> "You should now better understand how **people of *like* mind can work together to create a favored reality**." (the seducing spirit calling itself "God;" bold & underline added)[47]
>
> "This . . . *dance* that I've just described, this energy interaction I've explained, is occurring all the time—in and with *everything*....
>
> "**Every*one* and every*thing* on the planet—and in the universe—is emitting energy in every direction**. This energy mixes with all other energies, criss-crossing in patterns of complexity ...
>
> "This is the Matrix, of which I have spoken. **It is along this Matrix that you send signals to each other**—messages, meanings, healings, and other physical effects—**created** sometimes by individuals but **mostly by mass consciousness**....
>
> "**Like Thoughts attract Like Thoughts** along the Matrix—and when enough of these similar energies 'clump together,' so to speak, their vibrations become heavier, they slow down—and some become Matter.
>
> "**Thoughts *do* create physical form—and when many people are thinking the *same* thing**, there is a very high likelihood **their thoughts will form a Reality**." (the seducing spirit calling itself "God;" 1st ellipsis dots in the original; bold & underline added)[48]

After pointing out that Pierre Teilhard de Chardin "tried to integrate his scientific insights, *mystical* experiences, and theological doctrines into a coherent world view," Capra writes that "Teilhard also postulated *the manifestation of mind* in larger systems and wrote that in human evolution *the planet is covered with a web of ideas*, for which he coined the term '*mind-layer,*' or 'noosphere.'"[49] And, of course, Teilhard de Chardin is described by Sweet as "Twentieth-century Christianity's major voice."[50]

In this "web"/"mind-layer"/thought-"Matrix," *controlling what these "ideas" are* is clearly indispensable to shaping and forming and creating a new "*favored* reality." This inevitably turns the focus to what people *think*. And, without question, those in this emerging faith/New Quantum Spirituality/"new world religion"/"new world view" will want the "web" of "ideas" to be "ideas" consistent with *Oneness*.

> "**In the *new world view*, the universe is seen as a dynamic web** of interrelated events. None of the properties of any part of this web is fundamental; they all follow from the properties of the other parts, and **the overall consistency of their mutual interrelations determines the structure of the entire web**." (Fritjof Capra; emphasis added)[51]

> "**When the oneness of the totality of things is not recognised, then ignorance as well as *particularisation* arises**, and all phases of the ***defiled*** **mind** are thus developed ..." (Fritjof Capra quoting Ashvaghosha; emphasis added)[52]

Hence, perish the thought of any minds "defiled" by the *particular* truth of *God's Word* which puts an end to the mind games of Oneness. Of course, these *mind games* are more than just games—they're "scientific." In other words, they are also *mind science*. Or as the seducing spirit world teaches:

> "**You *think* it into being**." (the seducing spirit calling itself "God;" bold & underline added)[53]

Accordingly, in *Quantum Spirituality*, Leonard Sweet writes that "'*observer-participancy*' constitutes the creative *building material* of the *universe*."[54] That's quite a statement, "scientific" or otherwise! *Who's* the "Creator" in this dance of Oneness? He also writes that:

> "**Thought or consciousness are now part of the theories of matter**. Physicist David Bohm formulates the question this way: 'Whether **matter** is rather crude and mechanical or whether it gets more and more subtle and becomes **indistinguishable from** what people have called **mind**.' [sic]" (emphasis added)[55]

> "**The shape of our *physical* universe is dependent partly on *our* means of *perceiving* it**.... [T]he *New Light* apologetic's *essence* is its embodiment of an integrated, holistic, planetary spirituality ... When a multidimensional faith is lived synergistically and holistically, **a biodance takes place between the heavens and the earth, the Creator and the creation**." (emphasis added)[56]

> "Ideas of the mind not only matter, **ideas of the mind** move matter, **even become matter** ..." (emphasis added)[57]

> "**Quantum spirituality is** nothing more than your 'new account of everything old'--**your part of *the 'I Am'* that *we* are**." (emphasis added)[58]

> "The church does not have the option of standing safely by and watching these changes take place without taking part.... **The *universe*,** as ['Princeton physicist'

John] Wheeler puts it, **may 'in some strange sense be *'brought into being'* by the *participation* of those who participate.*'"* (emphasis added)[59]

In *The Tao of Physics* and *The Turning Point*, Fritjof Capra writes:

"John Wheeler sees this involvement of the observer as the most important feature of quantum theory and he has therefore suggested replacing the word 'observer' by the word 'participator'. In Wheeler's own words,

"... In some strange sense the universe is a participatory universe.

"The idea of '**participation instead of observation**' has been formulated in modern physics only recently, but it is an idea which **is well known to any student of mysticism**." (emphasis added)[60]

"The fact that all the properties of particles are determined by principles closely related to the methods of observation would mean that **the *basic structures* of the *material* world are determined, ultimately, by the way *we* look at this world**; that the observed **patterns of matter are** reflections of **patterns of mind**." (emphasis added)[61]

And Neale Donald Walsch, in *Conversations with "God"* and *Tomorrow's God*, writes:

"I 'got' ['at a very high metaphysical level'] that **all is energy**, and that **energy turns into 'matter'**—that is, physical 'stuff' and 'occurrences'—**according to how I thought about them**. I understood, then, that 'nothing matters' means that **nothing turns *into* matter except as *we* choose for it to**." (bold & underline added)[62]

"[P]hysicist John Wheeler has proposed a conception of the universe that he has called 'observer-participancy,' or **a closed-loop participatory universe** in which—as quantum physics would have it—nothing that is observed is unaffected by the observer. In other words, **the Creator and the Created are One**, *each creating the other*. Or, you ['God'] have often put it, **we** are 'God, Godding!'" (bold & underline added)[63]

*"**Which of you by taking thought can add one cubit unto his stature?**"* (Matthew 6:27)

Although formerly obvious that man can neither *do* God nor *be* God nor *create* God, *how* exactly does man merely *"think"* thoughts, ideas, and imaginations *into* *"being"/"matter"/"reality"/"truth"*? By "'*mind*-melding' with all of Life" which includes man's own inner "God," of course.

"Creation Education ... will always encourage humanity to seek the experience of reunification with All That Is. That means with God and with All Humans Everywhere. It means '***mind*-melding**' with all of Life in its many manifest forms. It means, **becoming One**." (the seducing spirit calling itself "God;" emphasis added)[64]

"**There is only One of Us**. You and I are One." (the seducing spirit calling itself

"God;" emphasis added)[65]

"Religions now have an opportunity to shift from 'There is only one God' to 'There is only One Thing at all.'...

"If **there is Only One Thing That Is**, then **everything and everyone must be part of that One Thing** ..." (Neale Donald Walsch; emphasis added)[66]

*"Elements are particles of **God**, portions of All, **the stuff of everything**."* (the seducing spirit calling itself "God;" emphasis added)[67]

"An incarnational God means that **God-stuff** is found **in the matter of the universe**." (Leonard Sweet; emphasis added)[68]

"**My Beingness is <u>in everything</u>**. *Everything.*" (the seducing spirit calling itself "God;" emphasis added)[69]

"**God *is* the energy**—the pure, raw energy—which you call life." (the seducing spirit calling itself "God;" emphasis added)[70]

"**God *is*** the Spirit of the universe ... **its energy**, its information, its thought." (Leonard Sweet; emphasis added)[71]

"God *is* the energy you call imagination. God *is* creation. God *is* first thought. And God *is* last experience. **And God <u>is everything</u> in between**." (the seducing spirit calling itself "God;" bold & underline added)[72]

Basically, when mind and matter are <u>all</u> the "energy" of "*God*," or the "cosmic mind," then the thoughts, ideas, and imaginations of man are the thoughts, ideas, and imaginations of "*God*." And it's no problem for "*God*" to think it all into "being"/ "matter"/"reality"/"truth," right? So just observe, participate, and create away. In this dance of the all-encompassing "*cosmic mind*":

"This is what your religions mean when they say that you were **created in the 'image and likeness of God.'**... It does mean that our *essence* is the same. *We are composed of the same stuff.* **We ARE the '*same stuff*'!** With all the same properties and abilities—**including the ability *to create physical reality* out of thin air**." (the seducing spirit calling itself "God;" bold & italics added)[73]

The same "stuff" is the same "stuff" whether people absurdly deny this emerging faith/New Quantum Spirituality is a faith of emerging *godhood* or not. To be made of the "stuff" of "God" is to be made of the "*stuff*" of "*God*." To be the "same stuff" as "God" is to be the "*same stuff*" as *God*. There are no two ways about it. Immanence is immanence. This "God" that is <u>in</u> everything is a "God" that <u>is</u> everything. Likewise, to "*think*" something "*into being*" is to do that which only *God* can do. But then, people today *want* to participate in *doing* and *being* "*God*." To *be* and *do* the new "God" of Oneness means freedom from having to *believe* and *obey* the "old" God of judgment— at least according to this emerging faith of Oneness/panentheism anyway.

"You are *already* a God. *You simply do not know it.*" (the seducing spirit calling itself "God")[74]

"[J]ust take my word for it—**you are a big creation machine, and <u>you</u> are turning out a new manifestation literally as fast as you can <u>think</u>**....

"Individual consciousness is powerful enough.... **And *mass* consciousness? Why, *that* is so powerful it can create events and circumstances of worldwide import and planetary consequences**." (the seducing spirit calling itself "God;" bold & underline added)[75]

Hence the aligning of minds. The more people there are of "*like mind*" the greater the likelihood that their thoughts/"energies" will all "connect" and "clump" together into a new "reality" (or "energy pattern"). In other words, in order to *think* "*into being*" a new "God" and new future—a new world religion and new world—of Oneness, people merely need to think Oneness. And since there is clearly more imagination/mind power in a *group/mass* "consciousness," the imagined "truth"/"reality" of this emerging faith of Oneness/panentheism *needs* more people to observe and participate in it in order to bring "into being" the emergence of this imagined "truth"/"reality."

Yet even if this emerging faith of Oneness/panentheism brings warm fuzzies to the whole world, the attempt to bring this *imagined* "truth" and "reality" "into being" as *truth* and *reality*—which includes its *universal* "*salvation*"—is a true and real exercise in futility. But, sadly, those in this emerging faith are still bound and determined to succeed. It's all about saving the world *from the truth of <u>Who</u> God <u>is</u>* so that "all the world's souls" in revolution against God "can be set free." And the seducing spirit world is more than willing to be of service in this journey of worldwide "spiritual" unbelief. This is, after all, its mission.

"... the god of this world hath **blinded <u>the</u> <u>minds</u>** of them **which believe not**, lest the light of the glorious gospel of Christ, who is the image of God, should shine unto them." (2 Corinthians 4:4)

48

The dance of aligning minds with the new "design"

In his 2010 book, *Nudge: Awakening Each Other to the God Who's Already There*, Sweet writes:

> "With Einstein's 1905 equation $E=mc^2$, we began the twentieth-century learning that matter and energy are essentially the same thing....
>
> "Wake up, church. Already we are post-Einstein. As we begin the twenty-first century, some are making the case for **mind and matter** being **essentially the same thing**—matter is just dense mind.[42] We now know that **mind affects matter**. We now know that mind affects matter **at a distance**. We now know our minds operate **beyond space and time**." (emphasis added)[1]

In his endnote #42 of this quote, Sweet writes:

> "Some philosophers have always argued this (Spinoza, Jung), but scientists are now getting into the hypothesis to prove it one way or the other. One evidence of this is **the GCP (Global Consciousness Project)**, which asks the question: What would it mean **to align minds in such a way that the impact ripples throughout the universe**?" (all parentheses in the original; emphasis added)[2]

Fittingly enough, in referring to its own system, the Global Consciousness Project website states:

> "**The heart of the system** is the server named '**noosphere**,' after Teilhard de

Chardin's idea of a global intelligence." (emphasis added)[3]

And in an abstract for this Project titled, "Interconnecting with everyone: Being in global consciousness," the website elaborates:

> "Just as the biosphere is composed of all the organisms on Earth and their interactions, Pierre Teilhard de Chardin postulated that **the noosphere** is composed of **all the interacting minds** on Earth. The word refers to **a *transhuman consciousness emerging from our interactions* to become a *guiding intelligence* for the earth**." (emphasis added)[4]

Again, Capra (who describes Teilhard de Chardin as a Western mystic/eminent scientist whose scientific/mystical/theological "world view" was "centered on the phenomenon of *evolution*"[5]) writes that "Teilhard ... wrote that in *human evolution* the planet is covered with *a web of ideas*, for which he coined the term '*mind-layer*,' or 'noosphere.'"[6] Capra then points out that Teilhard de Chardin's *own* "ideas ... are likely to contribute significantly to general recognition of *the harmony* between the views of *scientists and mystics*."[7] A scientist and mystic himself, Capra writes, "The parallels between science and mysticism are not confined to modern physics but can now be extended with equal justification to the new systems biology,"[8] and that "[a]mong Western mystics the one whose thought comes closest to that of the new systems biology is probably Pierre Teilhard de Chardin."[9] And, of course, it was Teilhard de Chardin who wrote, "What I am proposing to do is to narrow that gap between *pantheism* and Christianity."[10]

In his book *A "Wonderful" Deception*, Warren B. Smith points out that Teilhard de Chardin "who is frequently referred to as 'the father of the New Age movement,' believed that all of humanity is converging towards a universal New Age Christ in the future—an 'Omega Point' that will forever change and redefine mankind."[11] Smith also quotes the following from Teilhard de Chardin:

> "'**A general convergence of religions** upon **a universal Christ** who fundamentally satisfies them *all*: that seems to me the only possible conversion of the world, and **the only form in which a religion of the future can be conceived**.'
>
> "'I believe that **the Messiah whom we await**, whom we all without any doubt await, is the universal Christ; that is to say, **the Christ of *evolution***.'" (emphasis added)[12]

And Teilhard de Chardin is described by Sweet as "*Twentieth-century Christianity's major voice*"?[13] But then, Sweet's *own* teachings aren't much different, and now even Sweet himself is described as "[o]ne of the church's *most important* and provocative thinkers"![14] He even "serves as a consultant to many of America's denominational leaders and agencies."[15] The "web" of "ideas" being formed between those in the New Age and those in today's shifting Christianity certainly explains a lot. Without question, this aligning of minds is changing *everything*.

On its website, the Global Consciousness Project states the following:

> "What should we take away from this scientific evidence of interconnection?... One implication is that our *attention* matters in a way we have not imagined possible, such that cooperative intent can have real consequences....

"Knowing there is **a noosphere**, even if it is subtle and still developing, can motivate us to be more conscious of **the interconnections it implies. We are part of *a great being*,** ..." (emphasis added)[16]

And, of course, the inevitable:

"It is absolutely necessary to inspire world leaders with powerful *new* social and cultural *values* – the central *spiritual* intent of this forum – and to teach these *values* to every human being. We must have the power of numbers to *force* a movement toward wisdom and humanity....

"It is time for us to recognize and adopt a *Noospheric Ethical/Ecological Constitution* and in so doing lay the groundwork for the *transition* from biosphere *to* noosphere envisioned by Vernadsky and predicted by Teilhard." (emphasis added)[17]

In other words, people see it as time to go after what people *think*. And these latter two quotes are from a Paper written by the Director of the Global Consciousness Project, for the World Forum of *Spiritual* Culture, Kazakhstan, October 2010.

Incidentally, this Global Consciousness Project that is being conducted at Princeton University is also a Project of the Institute of Noetic Sciences,[18] which lists many New Age leaders in the Directory of its various Boards, Visionaries, and so forth. Neale Donald Walsch is even one of its Visionaries.[19] And according to the Institute's website, "'Noetic' comes from the Greek word nous, which means '*intuitive* mind' or '*inner knowing*.'"[20] It is therefore not surprising that this Institute encourages "open-minded explorations of consciousness through the meeting of *science* and *spirit*."[21] (The only "reality" that brings *science* and *spirit* together is the *immanence* of a *panentheistic/pantheistic* Oneness.) What is the Institute's purpose in bringing *science* and *spirit* together? To "help birth a *new worldview* that recognizes *our basic interconnectedness* and interdependence and promotes the flourishing of life in all its magnificent forms."[22] Not surprisingly, it, too, wants to create a "new story" of "Who We Are."

As previously mentioned, the Global Consciousness Project website refers to "the noosphere" as an emergence of "a guiding intelligence for the earth." Shortly thereafter, it then goes on to state that "[c]onsciousness has a *creative*, productive, *generative* role in the world" which gives us the "capability of changing the future" and thus "a capability and a responsibility for changing the world so that the future is *brighter*," which, naturally, "depends on coalescing into *a greater consciousness*," i.e., "*the power* of joining others."[23] Why does man want to create a "new story" of "Who We Are" by joining together and emerging as man's *own* "guiding intelligence" according to man's "inner knowing"/"intuitive mind"? Because *man* is not willing to *believe* and *obey* the absolute truth of the Word of God.

In the Institute of Noetic Sciences' October 2010 Issue of *Noetic Now* is an article titled, "Re-writing the Story of Who We Are." Under the heading "Getting Out of the Box," this article asks the question, "What are our greatest obstacles to assuming authorship and authority for creating a new story, a new worldview – and therefore a new world?" It then says that "our *brain*" is "one such 'obstacle,'" and, as is to be expected, gives the reason that "[o]nce its primary *set of beliefs* has been established, the brain finds it difficult to *integrate opposing ideas and beliefs*," a lack of integration that "has profound consequences for individuals and society." The article also says that "for those willing and able to consider a new story, the current challenges to and shifts in human consciousness promise exciting opportunities for personal and planetary change."[24]

One of those quoted in this article is Bruce Lipton—a cell biologist who "is regarded as one of the leading voices of the new biology" and "is an internationally recognized leader in bridging *science* and *spirit*."[25] It is therefore not surprising that this scientist participated in A Call to Conscious Evolution conference, August 2010, with renowned New Age leaders (a.k.a. "Evolutionary Leaders") such as Barbara Marx Hubbard, Marianne Williamson, Deepak Chopra, and others.[26] (Hubbard and Williamson are also among the New Age Visionaries of the Institute of Noetic Sciences[27] along with Walsch, and Chopra is on the Institute's International Advisory Board.[28]) Under the heading "Embracing Our Potential," the article "Re-writing the Story of Who We Are" says:

> "In his 2009 book, *Spontaneous Evolution: Our Positive Future (and a Way to Get There from Here)*, coauthored with Steve Bhaerman, Bruce Lipton writes that '... the critical mass of humanity involved with this evolution will change the world from the inside out. We are living positive future, practicing Heaven, and designing a bridge across which the whole of humanity will walk. . . . This is our love story, a universal love story for the entire Universe – you, me, everyone, and every living organism too.'" (parentheses & last ellipsis dots in the original)[29]

Of course, this "universal love story" of Oneness is all "*scientific*," right? If mystics become scientists and scientists become mystics doesn't mysticism become science? Hardly. It all just enters the category of "*science falsely so called*" (1 Timothy 6:20), in which mysticism and science are indeed merging in today's emerging faith/science of Oneness/panentheism.

In his 2002 book *Reinventing Jesus Christ*—which has now been republished as *False Christ Coming – Does Anybody Care?: What New Age leaders really have in store for America, the church, and the world* (2011)—Warren B. Smith writes:

> "Through the years ['futurist' and 'conscious evolutionist' and 'co-founding board member of the World Future Society' Barbara Marx] Hubbard has received voluminous information from her 'Christ.' In her 1993 book, *The Revelation: Our Crisis Is a Birth* (later renamed *The Revelation: A Message of Hope for the New Millennium*), **Hubbard and 'Christ' 'rewrite' the Bible's Book of Revelation**. In *The Revelation* Hubbard's 'Christ' provides specific instructions on how **a united humanity, purposefully *partnering with* God, can literally *re-create* the future**.... emphasizing that **a more 'positive' future can and will manifest when humanity — without exception — openly declares its 'oneness' with him and all creation**. This positive scenario and the means to attaining it is called **'the alternative to Armageddon.'**

> "Hubbard's 'Christ' describes how planet Earth is at an evolutionary crossroads. He states that the world is about to make an evolutionary leap that will take all creation to a new level. Those who **awaken to their own divinity, by *aligning* themselves as *one with* God and one with each other**, will evolve....

> "He describes, therefore, the necessity of **a 'selection process'** that **will select out resistant individuals** who 'choose' not to evolve. This 'selection process' is a 'purification' that will be accomplished through 'the shock of a fire.'...

> "**The 'selection process' results in the deaths of those who refuse to see themselves as *a part* of God**....

> "Barbara Marx Hubbard, politically well-connected and extremely influential, is a major figure in the emerging field of New Age/New Gospel/New Spirituality politics.

Her 'Campaign for a Positive Future' is still going strong. And her formal involvement with Marianne Williamson, Neale Donald Walsch and other New Age/New Gospel leaders ... represents a new kind of spiritual activism that is rapidly developing into a social and political movement." (parentheses in the original; emphasis added)[30]

The dance of this panentheistic Oneness/wholeness that seeks to "awaken" everyone to the "God"/"Christ"/"divinity" in everyone and everything is already so successful at aligning minds with this new "design" that when the "selection process" takes place under the Antichrist there won't be very many "resistant individuals" left who still know that *everyone and everything* are *not* "*a part* of God." That is, there won't be very many people who choose to believe *the truth* of <u>Who</u> God and His Son <u>are</u>. To the contrary, many will be (and already are) gladly and blindly participating in aligning their minds in this "evolutionary"/"quantum" leap *of faith* to the false "truth" and "reality" of Oneness with its false "God"/"Christ" in everyone and everything.

Direct quotes of Hubbard's "Christ," from *The Revelation*, are listed by Warren B. Smith in his book. The teachings of this *false* "Christ" include:

"You were born to **be me**. You were born to **be partners with God**."

"The church is the body of believers who are **conscious of being me**."

"I did not intend for you to deify me, but to **deify yourselves** as being at the same stage of evolution as I am."

"Your unfinished species is ready to evolve. The time has come on Earth for **this quantum change** to occur in many of you."

"Those who are not sufficiently educated to **align with the design**, experience God's purification process as long as necessary, until they **learn how to know God or the Intention of Creation *experientially*.**"

"The 'second death' is for those of you who cannot evolve by choice, due to some deeply seated error in your understanding of **the nature of reality**."

"There need be no greater punishment. There need be no threats. There is only choice. That is the purpose of freedom. Only those who choose to evolve, do. Henceforth, the choice is yours."

"**The alternative to Armageddon** is open to you. This is why we are writing this text."

"The end is near. The old play is almost over." (the seducing spirit calling itself "Christ" that channeled its teachings through Barbara Marx Hubbard; emphasis added)[31]

"And Jesus answering said unto them, ... I tell you, Nay: but, except ye repent, ye shall all likewise perish." (Luke 13:2, 3 & 5)

"Behold, I come as a thief. Blessed is he that watcheth, and keepeth his garments, lest he walk naked, and they see his shame. And he gathered them together into a

> *place called in the Hebrew tongue Armageddon." (Revelation 16:15-16)*
>
> *"And I saw heaven opened, and behold a white horse; and he that sat upon him was called Faithful and True, and in righteousness he doth judge and make war. His eyes were as a flame of fire, and on his head were many crowns ... and his name is called The Word of God. And the armies which were in heaven followed him upon white horses, clothed in fine linen, white and clean. And out of his mouth goeth a sharp sword, that with it he should smite the nations: and he shall rule them with a rod of iron: and he treadeth the winepress of the fierceness and wrath of Almighty God. And he hath on his vesture and on his thigh a name written, KING OF KINGS, AND LORD OF LORDS.... And I saw the beast, and the kings of the earth, and their armies, gathered together to make war against him that sat on the horse, and against his army." (Revelation 19:11-16, 20)*

The world can "align with the design" of a false "Christ" and "God" of *Oneness* all it wants, but this will *never* prevent the future *judgment* that the *true* Christ and God are going to execute on a world that remains *unrepentant of its unbelief*. In fact, so willfully is the world going to cling to its unbelief that it is even going to make war *against the Lord Jesus Christ, the KING OF KINGS, AND LORD OF LORDS!* Clearly, those who are unrepentant of their unbelief are bound and determined to succeed in this understatedly futile alignment of minds—not to mention of armies—that aims to *reform God* one way or the other.

Today's attempt to align minds—i.e., to get them *in formation* with each other—in *Oneness* in order to create its *new* "truth" of its *new* "reality" of its *new* "God," and thus its *new* "brighter" and "positive" future that is free from Armageddon and hell, inevitably changes everything (albeit only for a season). Absurdities notwithstanding, this new "favored reality" of Oneness is quite a tall order which requires the *"synergistic" power* of the *group/mass* "consciousness"—i.e., of the *"collective* mind"—in order to have *enough* imagination/mind power to collectively co-create it all. And therefore everyone must observe and participate *likemindedly* to bring "the design" of this new "reality" of Oneness "into being." This obviously requires trying to change and control what and how people *think*. Moreover, "as quantum physics would have it—nothing that is observed is unaffected by the observer,"[32] so if *everyone* does not participate in changing their *minds* and *perspective* then their *thoughts/minds* and *perspective* become *hindrances* that *negatively* affect this "scientific" creative process. In this emerging faith/New Quantum Spirituality/mind science, *"All That Is"* is *One* including *mind* and matter, so to change *minds* is to change *"All That Is."*

> *"Yet if you can remember this truth—***your perspective creates your thoughts, and your thoughts create everything*** ..."* (the seducing spirit calling itself "God;" emphasis added)[33]

Hence the changing of minds to a perspective of *Oneness*. Again, those in this emerging faith/New Quantum Spirituality just have to change the "collective mind," and poof! The collective has thus changed the "old" reality of the God of *judgment* into a new "reality" of a "God" of *Oneness*. Of course, even if those on this mission could manage to successfully change everyone's mind it would still be a *colossal failure* nonetheless. God says to man, *"I change not"* (Malachi 3:6), but man says to God, "I change You." This is a *delusion* to the nth *degree! There is not enough collective power in the entire universe/"cosmos" as a whole to effect one smidgeon of change to the true God.* Yet man believes that man can succeed in changing God. After all, man believes that man's science is always "true" and, therefore, since today's mind games are mind science this makes them "true," right? Just true mind games, with the help of "science falsely so called." And most helpful in these mind games is the seducing spirit world (which includes the fact that "the god of this world hath *blinded the minds* of them which *believe not*"--2 Corinthians 4:4).

> "**Thought is pure energy**....
>
> "All thoughts congeal; **all thoughts meet other thoughts**, criss-crossing in an incredible maze of energy, forming an ever-changing pattern of unspeakable beauty and unbelievable complexity.
>
> "**Like energy attracts like energy—forming** (to use simple words) **'clumps' of energy of like kind**. When enough similar 'clumps' criss-cross each other—run into each other—they *'stick to'* each other (to use another simple term). **It takes an incomprehensibly huge amount of similar energy 'sticking together,'** thusly, to form matter. But matter *will* form out of pure energy....
>
> "You should now better understand how **people of *like* mind can work together to create a favored reality**." (the seducing spirit calling itself "God;" all parentheses in the original; bold added)[34]
>
> "**You *think* it into being**." (the seducing spirit calling itself "God;" bold added)[35]

Again, absurdities notwithstanding, since *what* people *think* is key to aligning minds, and since people *think* about what they *observe*, the key to thinking the new "positive" and "brighter" future of today's "favored reality" of Oneness "into being" is getting people to *observe* the "God" of *Oneness*, i.e., the *panentheistic* "God" that is *in everyone and everything*. (By the way, the *true* God Who is *separate* from creation, rather than *one* with creation, is *invisible* and cannot be *observed*. And, no, people are not observing *God* by observing man's made-up "*ideas*" of what man's "reimagined" "God" is "up to" in the world!)

> "[T]here is no separation in God's World—that is, **nothing which is not God** ...
>
> "You cannot be separate from Me, for I Am All That Is....
>
> "You and I are One. We cannot be anything else if I Am What **I Am: All That Is**....
>
> "How could I separate Myself from Myself when My Self is All There Is, **and *there is nothing else***?" (the seducing spirit calling itself "God;" emphasis added)[36]
>
> "So go, now, and see each other as Who You Really Are.
>
> "**Observe. Observe. OBSERVE.**" (the seducing spirit calling itself "God;" bold added)[37]
>
> "'**We Are All One**' is more than a beautiful slogan. *It is a precise description of* **the nature of Ultimate Reality**. When you understand this, you ... see **the relationship of all things** differently. You notice **the connectedness** at a much higher level. Your awareness is expanded, your insight becomes very keen. You, quite literally, *see in*....

"A single sentence, uttered from your pulpits, lecterns, and rostrums, by your national congresses and your world summit leaders, could change everything.

"'Ours is not a better way, ours is merely another way.'

"This humble utterance could begin to **heal the divisions** between your religions, close the gap between your political parties, curb the conflicts between your nations.

"**With one *word* you could end them**.

"'Namasté.'

"**God in me honors God in you**.

"How simple. How beautiful. How wondrous, indeed.

"Yet how difficult, when one is caught up in the Illusion [of 'Superiority'], to **see God in every one and every thing**." (the seducing spirit calling itself "God;" bold added)[38]

Immediately preceding this quote the seducing spirit says, "There can be no such thing as Superiority when We Are All One. A thing cannot be superior to itself. *All things are One Thing, and there is nothing else.*"[39] And thus, since there is only "*One Thing*" and "*nothing else*," "heal" all divisions by seeing and honoring "*God*" in everyone and everything—the "Ultimate Reality" of *Oneness*. In other words, "observe" (pay attention to) everyone and everything *except* the absolute truth of God's Word which is *antithetical* to *Oneness*. So in this mission to see and honor "*God*" in everyone and everything it is not at all surprising that the focus is shifting from meaning to dancing and from God's Word to "signs." And, no, the dance of Oneness/panentheism is *not* the dance of the *Holy* Spirit.

"The art of **attention *repivots* the focus** of the church **from hermeneutics to semiotics**....

"Where hermeneutics is preoccupied with ***meaning***, semiotics (or *the art and science of **sign reading***) is preoccupied with ***dancing***. Semiotics is *the art and science of **paying attention***. A spiritual semiotics is paying attention to what the Holy Spirit is *up to* in our world today. **The future lies in those who can help others focus their attention and pay attention**." (Leonard Sweet; parentheses in the original; emphasis added)[40]

"**[P]aying attention changes your brain, your being, your future**. According to some scholars, **the root *lig* in the word *religion* means 'to pay attention.'** If so, from its very definition, religion helps us learn to pay attention **to people and to life**." (Leonard Sweet; bold added)[41]

"**In a state of semiotic awareness, *all of life* is bathed in beauty and sacredness**....

"Faith **widens** the imagination and lengthens the horizons. So why is church so **narrow** in its imagination, so short in its scope of thinking? Why is the body of Christ not bursting with creativity, but *a bastion of boredom?*...

"We are ... clueless as to **what the Spirit is up to** ..." (Leonard Sweet; emphasis added)[42]

"In fact, some sign readers are arguing that **our very survival as a species depends on our ability to 'read the signs.'**" (Leonard Sweet; emphasis added)[43]

"Faith is more than learning to live in the reality of God's invisible presence. Rather, faith is living in **the reality of God's *visible* presence**." (Leonard Sweet; bold added)[44]

"Faith is the gift of **reading the signs of the presence of God**....

"Signs of God's manifest presence **point me to Christ**." (Leonard Sweet; emphasis added)[45]

"Are you **finding Christ in** the **people** you meet? Are you **finding Christ in** the **things** you handle? Are you **finding Christ in** the **food you eat? Finding Christ in** the **voices** you hear? **Finding Christ in** the **smells** you breathe?" (Leonard Sweet; emphasis added)[46]

"The ideal of monastic holiness and in fact any tradition of holy living is precisely this: **an awareness** of the presence **of Christ *in all of life* and *in all things***." (Leonard Sweet; emphasis added)[47]

"Faith makes **a metanoized mulch of *all* dichotomized selves and heals *all* discursive dualisms** (one of the *worst* of which was 'sacred' and 'profane'), all disastrous **separations** that **threaten our existence**." (Leonard Sweet; parentheses in the original; emphasis added)[48]

"It is not religion and reason that go together, but **religion and relationship** that go together. Actually, that's where **the word *religion*** comes from—*religare*—meaning **'to connect, to bind together.' The future *depends*** not on our ability to 'Come, let us reason together' but **'Come, let us relate together.'**" (Leonard Sweet; bold added)[49]

This emerging faith of Oneness/panentheism that is not at all on the *narrow* way—and *purposely* so—is not at all what *God* is "up to." It is not *God's* purpose to clear out the narrow way that leads to life in order to bring a new panentheistic "God" of Oneness "into being" on the broad way that leads to destruction. And a "God" and "Christ" in everyone and everything are as broad and wide of a way as it gets. People would be far better served if they were readers (and *believers*) of *God's* Word of *truth* instead of "*sign* readers." But that would obviously defeat the purpose of aligning minds in order to *change* the truth of God's Word into a new "truth" of *Oneness*.

Believing the "medieval"/"outdated" *reality of opposites* such as *the true God and false gods, the true Christ and false "Christs," truth and falsehood, right and wrong* is the greatest *hindrance* to aligning minds in a *new* "reality" of *Oneness*. That is, there is nothing more *hindering* to today's desired dance of Oneness than the divisive *absolute truth* and *preeminent superiority* of <u>Who</u> the *true* God and the *true Person* of His Son, the Lord Jesus Christ, <u>are</u>. And thus this emerging faith pays attention to everyone and everything *except* the absolute truth of *God's* Word. The truth is simply too *narrow* to lead to today's desired all-encompassing new "reality" of Oneness. Hence the aligning of minds on the broad way to "*rethink*" it all.

"Enter ye in at the strait gate: for wide is the gate, and broad is the way, that leadeth to destruction, and many there be which go in thereat: Because strait is the gate, and narrow is the way, which leadeth unto life, and few there be that find it." (Matthew 7:13-14)

"Within the churches today there are men responding to **the *new spiritual idealism***, to the *urgency* of the opportunity and to *the need for change*....

"Nothing can prevent **the new world religion** from eventually emerging.... It **will be *hindered* by** the fundamentalists, **the *narrow*-minded** ..." (the seducing spirit calling itself Djwhal Khul; emphasis added)[50]

"The reality of the atomic physicist, like the reality of the Eastern mystic, ***transcends* the *narrow* framework of *opposite* concepts**....

"Faced with a reality which lies beyond opposite concepts, physicists and mystics have to adopt **a special way of thinking**, where **the mind is not *fixed*** in the ***rigid* framework** of classical logic, **but keeps *moving* and *changing* its viewpoint**.... In the words of Lama Govinda, 'The Eastern way of thinking rather consists in **a *circling*** round the object of contemplation ... a many-sided, i.e., multi-dimensional impression formed from the superimposition of single impressions **from *different* points of view**.'" (Fritjof Capra; last ellipsis dots in the original; emphasis added)[51]

In today's aligning of minds, no doubt *hindering thoughts* will indeed become a "*thought*-crime" (as well as a "*hate*" crime). After all, those who do not participate in dancing around the truth in a circle of Oneness in the new "special way of thinking" (or not thinking) that brings *all* the different opposites/"points of view" together in a new "reality" of Oneness are not participating in changing "All That Is." This hinders the world's ability to *think* Oneness and its universal "salvation" "*into being.*" In other words, this hinders the *emergence* of today's "new world religion." Moreover, in this emerging faith/new world religion/New Quantum Spirituality there is a reason why *its* "God is a work *in progress*"[52]—*no beliefs* necessary. *Beliefs* obviously require *thinking*, and unless this *thinking* is of *Oneness* it becomes a *hindrance*. So with this hindrance thus "transcended" (bypassed), people can just observe (pay attention to) and participate in the new "special way of thinking" (or not thinking) that dances around the truth *on purpose*.

So, how is this dance of aligning minds in the "favored reality" of this emerging faith—i.e., new world religion—of Oneness participated in?

- By learning to think, be, and do Oneness.
- By learning to replace *the meaning* of the truth with *dancing around* the truth.
- By learning to replace *the truth* with *storytelling*.
- By learning to "transcend" and "go beyond" *all opposites*.
- By learning to *see relationship* as preeminent in all things and as the ultimate "truth."
- By learning to not *believe*.
- By learning to *see* and *honor* and *relate to* the "God" that is/is in *everyone* and *everything*.
- By learning to "read the signs," "pay attention," and "observe and participate" in all Oneness.
- By learning to "think *connectness* rather than *correctness*."
- By learning to "*let go the narrow*."

In other words:

- By giving up *what is* truth and falsehood, right and wrong.
- By giving up *believing and obeying* God and His Son.
- By giving up holding to and standing fast in *the truth and faith* of *God's Word*.
- By giving up <u>Who</u> God and His Son <u>are</u>.

> "**We *must* resign from the proposition business** … and build up a relational theology in which '**Only Connect**' is the engine room of the *theological* enterprise …" (Leonard Sweet; emphasis added)[53]

> "Can we **give up TunnelVision for TogetherVision**? Can we turn away from the spotlights to turn on the searchlights and find the hidden and forgotten?
>
> "Where is God to be found?… '[I]n the next person you meet or not at all.'" (Leonard Sweet; emphasis added)[54]

All of humanity just has to get on board with bringing everyone and everything together as one. Then this panentheistic "theological enterprise" that is watching for its new "God" that is "hidden" in plain site *in everyone/everything* can run full throttle toward its future.

> *"Be ye not unequally yoked together with unbelievers: for what fellowship hath righteousness with unrighteousness? and what communion hath light with darkness? And what concord hath Christ with Belial? or what part hath he that believeth with an infidel? And what agreement hath the temple of God with idols?" (2 Corinthians 6:14-16)*

> *"And he said, I will hide my face from them, I will see what their end shall be: for they are a very froward generation, children in whom is no faith. They have moved me to jealousy with that which is not God; they have provoked me to anger with their vanities … O that they were wise, that they understood this, that they would consider their latter end!… And he shall say, Where are their gods, their rock in whom they trusted, … let them rise up and help you, and be your protection." (Deuteronomy 32:20-21, 29, 37-38)*

> *"Woe to the rebellious children, saith the LORD, that take counsel, but not of me; and that cover with a covering, but not of my spirit, that they may add sin to sin.… Now go, write it before them in a table, and note it in a book, that it may be for the time to come for ever and ever: That this is a rebellious people, lying children, children that will not hear the law of the LORD: Which say to the seers, See not; and to the prophets, Prophesy not unto us right things, speak unto us smooth things, prophesy deceits: Get you out of the way, turn aside out of the path, cause the Holy One of Israel to cease from before us." (Isaiah 30:1, 8-11)*

49

The "Parable of the Rock" and the "Big Bang"

Incredibly, in the emerging faith/science fiction of Oneness/panentheism the reason for "God's" *immanence* in the very substance of *everyone and everything* really is man's "*Big Bang*." And it is the exploding of this "God" into bits and pieces—i.e., into subatomic particles—that are immanent in the very substance of everyone and everything that is also the basis for this "God" being a verb that is a "dynamic," ever-changing, ever-moving, relative "Rock" that is "*Being.*" On the other hand, the true God (Who is only blasted to bits in the dreams of unbelieving man and especially of the soon-to-be-damned spirit world) has always been, and will always be, a noun that is a "static," never-changing, immoveable, absolute Rock Who is a̲ Being. The difference is eternal. Again, only the true God is the true God. And the pantheistic/panentheistic "God" of Oneness that is/is in everyone and everything is not the true God.

The following two quotes are from the seducing spirit world. The first one explodes "God." The second one, called "the Parable of the Rock," then glues these bits and pieces of its exploded "God" back together into its "Rock," which is only "the Rock of Ages" in its dreams to "be like the most High." The "Parable of the Rock," which is diabolically crafted through and through with the utmost of serpentine subtilty, epitomizes in a nutshell the emerging faith/New Quantum Spirituality of Oneness.

> "In the beginning, that which *Is* is all there was, and there was nothing else. Yet All That Is could not know itself—because **All That Is is all there was, and there was *nothing* else**....
>
> "This *energy*—this pure, unseen, unheard, unobserved, and therefore unknown-by-anyone-else energy—chose to experience Itself as the utter magnificence It was....

"It reasoned, quite correctly, ... that if It thus simply *divided* Itself into portions, each portion, being less than the whole, could look back on the rest of Itself and *see* magnificence.

"And **so All That Is divided Itself**—becoming, in one glorious moment, that which is *this*, and that which is *that*....

"... God made it possible for God to know Itself. **In the moment of this great explosion from within**, God created *relativity*—the greatest gift God ever gave to Itself. Thus, *relationship* is the greatest gift God ever gave to you ...

"From the No-Thing **thus sprang the Everything**—a spiritual event entirely consistent, incidentally, with what your scientists call **The Big Bang** theory....

"**In rendering the universe as a *divided version of Itself*, God produced, from pure energy, all that now exists—both seen and unseen**....

"*This is what your religions mean when they say that you were created in the 'image and likeness of God.'... It does mean that our essence is the same.* **We are composed of the same stuff. We ARE the 'same stuff'!**" (the seducing spirit calling itself "God;" bold added)[1]

"Consider **the Parable of the Rock**.

"Once there was **a Rock, filled with countless atoms, protons, neutrons, and subatomic particles of matter**. These particles were **racing around continually, in a pattern**, each particle going from 'here' to 'there,' and taking 'time' to do so, yet going so fast that the Rock itself seemed to move not at all. It just *was*. There it lay, drinking in the sun, soaking up the rain, and moving not at all.

"'What is this, inside of me, that is moving?' the Rock asked.

"'It is You,' said a Voice from Afar.

"'Me?' replied the Rock. 'Why, that is impossible. I am not moving at all. Anyone can *see* that.'

"'Yes, *from a distance*,' the Voice agreed. 'From way over *here* you *do* look as if you are solid, still, not moving. But when I come closer—when I look very closely at what is actually happening—I see that **everything that comprises What You Are is *moving*. It is moving at incredible speed through time and space in a particular pattern which *creates* You as the thing called 'Rock.'** And so, you are like magic! You are moving and *not moving* at the same time.'

"'But,' asked the Rock, **'which, then, is the illusion? The oneness, the stillness, of the Rock, or the separateness and the movement of Its parts?'**

"To which the Voice replied, 'Which, then, is the illusion? The oneness, the stillness, of **God**? Or the separateness and movement of **Its parts**?'

"**And I tell you this: Upon this Rock, I will build My church. For this is the Rock of Ages**. This is the eternal truth that leaves no stone unturned. I have explained it all for you here, in this little story. **This is The Cosmology**.

"Life is a series of minute, incredibly rapid movements. These movements do not affect at all the immobility and **the Beingness of Everything That Is**. Yet, just as with the atoms of the rock, **it is the movement which is creating the stillness**, right before your eyes.

"From this distance, **there is no separateness**. There cannot be, for **All That Is is All There Is, and there *is* nothing else**. I am the Unmoved Mover.

"From the limited perspective with which you view All That Is, you see yourself as separate and apart, not one unmovable being, but many, many beings, constantly in motion.

"Both observations are accurate. Both realities are 'real.'" (the seducing spirit calling itself "God;" bold added)[2]

First, it is actually *both* the "oneness"/"stillness" and the "separateness"/"movement" that are the illusion here (as is this whole "Parable"/emerging faith). The true God Who is *separate* from His Creation and an *immoveable* Being is the true Rock. Moreover, it is the *Oneness* that is the *movement* of the counterfeit "Rock"/"God" and "Its parts." It is also this *movement* of *Oneness* that brings "many, many beings" together as "one unmovable being"—i.e., as one glued-together "Rock." This "Parable" intertwines and redefines the nature of Oneness and separateness in the crafty attempt to bring both of these opposite "realities" together as one in the circle of Oneness. Nevertheless, *separateness* is the *true* reality. And "there is no separateness" in Oneness; *period*. It is *not* that there only *seems* to be no separateness *from a distance*! Separateness is separateness, at *any* distance. And *true* separateness is neither the "separateness" nor the "motion" of all the subatomic particles that comprise this false "God" of Oneness. Contrary to the absurdities of this emerging faith/New Quantum Spirituality of Oneness/panentheism, there is no "God" that is "the Beingness of Everything That Is." The *true* God is *not* the subatomic particles of His creation. Neither is He *in* them. God did not explode Himself.

Second, this moving "Rock" that consists of subatomic particles that are evermoving and ever-rearranging and thus ever-changing into new "energy patterns" is the "Rock" upon which *the seducing spirit world* is building *its* "church." And its counterfeit "church" of its counterfeit "Rock" is its interfaith "one Church" of its "new world religion," by which its "fullness of truth" will "be revealed":

> "The churches in the West need also to realize that basically **there is only one Church**, but it is *not* necessarily only the orthodox *Christian* institution. **God works in many ways, through many faiths and religious agencies**; this is one reason for the elimination of non-essential doctrines. By the emphasizing of the essential doctrines and **in their union will *the fullness of truth* be revealed. This, the new world religion will do** ..." (the seducing spirit calling itself Djwhal Khul; emphasis added)[3]

Sweet writes:

> "Can we **give up TunnelVision for TogetherVision**? Can we turn away from the spotlights to turn on the searchlights and find the hidden and forgotten?
>
> "Where is God to be found?... We are watching for the God who is to be found (as Gandhi said) 'in the next person you meet or not at all.'" (parentheses in the original; emphasis added)[4]

Ghandi (who taught E. Stanley Jones) was a self-proclaimed Hindu/Christian/Muslim/Buddhist/Jew[5] who also said:

- "There is only one God, but there are many paths to Him;"[6]
- "If all religions are one at source, we have to synthesize them;"[7]
- "Temples or mosques or churches...I make no distinction between these different abodes of God;"[8]

PART FIVE: THE CREATION 371

- "I would worship an idol even made of clay, if thereby my mind becomes lighter.... The stone is no God; but God resides in the stone;"[9] and
- "Live and let live or mutual forbearance and toleration is the Law of Life. That is the lesson I have learnt from the Quran, the Bible, the Zend Avesta and the Gita."[10]

Gandhi clearly relied on interfaith Oneness to teach him about "the Law of Life." This is not surprising. He is also said to have written that he believed "that *all life is in essence one* and that humans are working consciously or unconsciously towards the realisation of that identity."[11] Sadly, more and more people are indeed working towards this "identity." The Oneness of all life is today's preferred new "truth" and "reality."

> "It is one thesis of this book [*Nudge:* **Awakening** *Each Other* **to the God Who's Already There**] that if we only knew how to **sense God**, to **see, hear, smell, taste, touch the divine**, we could nudge the world with **the consciousness** that '**everything that lives is holy**' in some way." (Leonard Sweet; emphasis added)[12]

> "In this way we should **consciously discover our Lord in all things**. This requires much diligence, **demanding a total effort of our senses and power of mind**; then those who manage this are in *a right state*: **taking God equally in all things, they** *find* **God in equal measure in all**." (Leonard Sweet quoting Meister Eckhart; emphasis added)[13]

That is, they find what they have chosen to look for. And in this dance of aligning minds, those who are in this "right state" have chosen to see this *immanent* "God" of Oneness *in everyone/everything*. In other words: "*God in me honors God in you. How simple.... Yet how difficult, when one is caught up in the Illusion* [of 'Superiority'], *to see God in every one and every thing.*"[14] To put this another way, basically, in the so-called "Illusion" of *the superiority* of <u>truth</u> how difficult it is to see the Emperor's new clothes. (Lest anyone has forgotten this childhood story, the Emperor had no clothes.) Those in this emerging faith have donned the Emperor's same new wardrobe and are absurdly choosing to see and honor each other's new clothes, which does indeed demand "a *total effort*" of "power of mind." This new kind of "awareness" is precisely what is required to see and honor "God" in everyone and everything.

> "The more *attentive* you are, the more you **see Christ in** *every* **person and the sacramental nature of all of life**." (Leonard Sweet; emphasis added)[15]

> "Poet/critic Paul Mariani says **it is our lack of** *imagination* **that has closed us to an awareness of God** *in the world*." (Leonard Sweet; emphasis added)[16]

> "Faith is the gift of **reading the signs of the presence of God**." (Leonard Sweet; emphasis added)[17]

> "[F]aith is living in **the reality of God's** *visible* **presence**." (Leonard Sweet; bold added)[18]

> "*This I say therefore, and testify in the Lord, that ye henceforth walk not as other Gentiles walk, in* **the vanity of their mind**." (Ephesians 4:17)

Again, neither God nor His Son are in everyone and everything. There is an eternal difference between going into the world to "*see Christ* in every person" and going into the world to *teach and preach Christ* to every person. We are not saved by believing in our imagination.

> *"And he said unto them, Go ye into all the world, and* **preach the gospel to every creature**.*"* *(Mark 16:15)*

> *"Go ye therefore, and teach all nations, baptizing them in the name of the Father, and of the Son, and of the Holy Ghost:* **Teaching them to observe all things whatsoever I have commanded you** *..." (Matthew 28:19-20)*

> **"We were *not* put here to 'keep commandments' but to *conceive* beauty, truth, and goodness**." (Leonard Sweet; emphasis added)[19]

> "The passion for evangelism is nothing other than a passion for **reading the signs of what God is up to, connecting the God-dots**, signing up, and then laying down our lives on God's dotted lines." (Leonard Sweet; emphasis added)[20]

> "For nudge evangelism to work, we must bring together two things seldom seen together: evangelism and semiotics....
> "Semiotics ... is **the art of making connections, linking disparate dots**, ...
> "The Greek word for **signs** is *semeia* (from which we get the word **semiotics**). We are directed by Jesus to **learn how to read signs**, to read 'the handwriting on the wall.'...
> "Some things look easy until you try them (like juggling and jigsaws). Other things look hard until you try them (like semiotics)....
> **"We see what we choose to see**, ..." (Leonard Sweet; all parentheses in the original; emphasis added)[21]

> "Think of semiotics as a receiver. We live in an ocean of waves—radio, cell phone, wi-fi, infrared, cosmic.... These waves will continue to remain invisible unless there is a receiver that can channel them into forms we can hear and see....
> **"This book [*Nudge: Awakening Each Other to the God Who's Already There*] is your wireless card to pick up the signals of transcendence, the *immanent* transcendent**, that are out there but not being downloaded. Semiotics is the art of finding channels and making *connections*. Evangelism as semiotics is the art of **tuning our receivers to the 'I AM' channel** and setting the controls to receive and transmit transdimensional frequencies." (Leonard Sweet; emphasis added)[22]

> "Nudgers **listen for that background hum of *the Creator* built *into* the universe**.[34]" (Leonard Sweet; emphasis added)[23]

In his endnote #34 of this latter quote, Sweet writes:

> "According to some physicists, 1 percent of the static on a TV set tuned between stations is caused by microwave radiation that last interacted with matter at the time of the Big Bang 13.7 billion years ago."[24]

In other words, just listen for the hum of the shifting *sand* of *immanence*, i.e., the sand created from man's "Big Bang" having blasted the Rock. Accordingly, on the website for "Science and Nonduality (SAND)"—a collaborative partner with the Institute of Noetic Sciences,[25] and, yes, the acronym they chose really is SAND (this is one of those cases where "the handwriting [is] on the wall")—is the following quote:

> "Nonduality is the philosophical, spiritual, and scientific understanding of non-separation and fundamental *intrinsic oneness*.
>
> "For thousand [sic] of years, through deep inner inquiry, philosophers and sages have came [sic] to the realization that **there is only one substance** and we are therefore all part of it. **This substance can be called Awareness, Consciousness, Spirit, Advaita, Brahman, Tao, Nirvana or even God**. It is constant, ever present, unchangeable and is **the essence of all existence**.
>
> "In the last century Western scientists are arriving at the same conclusion: The universe does indeed comprise [sic] of **a single substance, presumably created during the Big Bang**, and all sense of being - consciousness - subsequently arises from it. This realization has ontological implications for humanity: fundamentally **we are individual expressions of a single entity, inextricably connected to one another**, we are all drops of the same ocean....
>
> "Our starting point is the statement '**we are all one**,' and this is meant not in some abstract sense but **at the deepest level of existence. Duality, or separation between the observer and the observed, is an illusion** that the Eastern *mystics* have long recognized and Western science has more recently come to understand through *quantum* mechanics." (emphasis added)[26]

And Sweet writes:

> "God is Pure Voice. In fact, scientists even contend that the background 'noise' of creation ('**The Big Bang**'?) is still out there. An **incarnational** God means that ***God-stuff* is found *in the matter* of the universe**." (parentheses in the original; emphasis added)[27]

> "Nudgers listen for that background hum of **the Creator built into the universe**." (Leonard Sweet; emphasis added)[28]

And as the seducing spirit world teaches:

> "*Elements are particles of God, portions of All, the stuff of everything.*" (the seducing spirit calling itself "God;" bold added)[29]

> "**In the moment of this great explosion from within**, God created <u>relativity</u>—the greatest gift God ever gave <u>to Itself</u>. Thus, <u>relationship</u> is the greatest gift God ever gave <u>to you</u> ...
>
> "From the No-Thing thus **sprang the Everything**—a spiritual event entirely consistent, incidentally, with what your scientists call **The Big Bang** theory....
>
> "**In rendering the universe as a *divided version of Itself*, God produced, from pure energy, all that now exists—both seen and unseen**." (the seducing spirit calling itself "God;" bold & underline added)[30]

When a "God" explodes itself into an infinite number of bits and pieces, these bits and pieces are *relative "truths"* that are *all* part of "the fullness of truth," or "the Totality of God." So in this *relativity*, "All the various truths form one Truth; ... your little bit of truth forms part of the group mosaic."[31] And, of course, with an exploded "God" that thereby gives *relativity* to itself, *relationship* thus becomes *universal* and *unconditional*. That is, *relationship* with "God" thus becomes a gift to everyone and everything automatically. After all, a little bit of "God" is in everyone and everything.

People in the emerging faith of Oneness/panentheism may think they are listening to *God's "Voice,"* but *the seducing spirit world*, not God, is the one that scratches itching ears that have turned away from the truth. And people are more than happy to believe in both a "Big Bang" and immanence—*fables* that give man his desired freedom from having to believe and obey the true God and His Word of absolute truth. According to the Word of God, those who do not believe the truth of either creation or of His past and coming global judgments *"willingly are ignorant"* (see 2 Peter 3:3-12). And, incidentally, God's coming judgment is one of fire in which *"the elements shall melt with fervent heat"* (v. 12). Contrary to the seducing spirit world's fables of immanence/Oneness, "*Elements are [not] particles of God.*" Not only did God not explode Himself, but *God is not going to melt* with fervent heat! But, of course, those who "willingly are ignorant" of the "medieval"/"outdated" reality of the truth of God's Word don't see it that way.

> "Thus saith the LORD of hosts, ... To whom shall I speak, and give warning, that they may hear? behold, their ear is uncircumcised, and they cannot hearken: behold, the word of the LORD is unto them a reproach; they have no delight in it." (Jeremiah 6:9-10)

> "And he said, I will hide my face from them, I will see what their end shall be: for they are a very froward generation, children in whom is no faith. **They have moved me to jealousy with that which is not God** ..." (Deuteronomy 32:20-21)

It is unbelievable, yet at the same time not surprising at all given today's massive shift to darkness, that Leonard Sweet has been chosen to contribute to a "Bible translation" that is to be published by Thomas Nelson. Given his teachings, it is a complete mockery of God and His Word that Sweet has been chosen *at all*, let alone to rewrite/reword the book of *Genesis*. As previously mentioned, this new version (*new for a reason*) is called *The Voice*. Sweet writes:

> "**God is Pure Voice**. In fact, scientists even contend that **the background 'noise' of creation ('The Big Bang'?)** is still out there. An incarnational God means that *God-stuff* is found *in* the *matter* of the universe." (parentheses in the original; emphasis added)[32]

> "Nudgers **listen for that background hum of the Creator built into the universe**....
> "**Voice** is the pleasure and privilege of the bodyless God.[40]" (emphasis added)[33]

And in his endnote #40 of this latter quote, Sweet writes:

> "Hence **the Bible translation**, *The Voice* (Nashville: Thomas Nelson, upcoming) of which **my contribution is the book of Genesis**." (parentheses in the original; bold added)[34]

It sends a very clear message as to what people think of God's Word when a "Scripture Project" (which will be addressed more later) has a person—"theologian" or otherwise—"translate" the book of Genesis who believes in *the fable* of evolution rather than *the truth* of Genesis. (Sweet repeatedly makes this clear, and *Quantum Spirituality* is a prime example.) And, despite the absurd claims to the contrary, neither "*The Big Bang*" nor *evolution* are "*creation*"!

Incidentally, Ken Ham, the founder of Answers in Genesis (an apologetics ministry that focuses on "the most-attacked book of the Bible"[35]), points out that although a "Big Bang" hasn't happened yet, one is *coming*. He says, "When people ask me if I believe in a 'Big Bang,' I answer: 'Sure—are you getting ready for it?'"[36] In the above-mentioned passage of 2 Peter chapter 3, verse 10 states:

> "But **the day of the Lord** will come as a thief in the night; in the which the heavens shall pass away **with a great noise**, and the elements shall melt with fervent heat, the earth also and the works that are therein shall be burned up."

Regarding this verse, Ken Ham says, "This is talking about the coming judgment by fire, when there will be a great noise. This is the real Big Bang—the final judgment on this Earth. *Are you ready* ...?"[37]

Moreover, Zephaniah 1:14 states:

> "**The great day of the LORD is near**, it is near, and hasteth greatly, **even the voice of the day of the LORD**: the mighty man shall cry there bitterly."

The "great *noise*" of this *future* "real Big Bang" is the "*voice*" of the true God's coming *judgment*. But, of course, those in today's emerging "faith"—i.e., revolution against God—are trying to *change* the "old" reality of the God of *judgment* into a new "reality" of a "God" of *Oneness*. So it isn't surprising that they are listening for a "Voice" that is the "noise" of a *past* "Big Bang"—a "reimagined" "Big Bang" of *Oneness* that just so happens to conveniently blast the God of *judgment* into *immanent* bits. But this is all "*scientific*," right?

> "O Timothy, keep that which is committed to thy trust, avoiding profane and vain babblings, and oppositions of **science falsely so called: Which some professing have erred concerning the faith**. Grace be with thee. Amen." (1 Timothy 6:20-21)

People today ascribe *inerrancy* to man's *science* rather than to God's inspired *Scripture* for a reason. They simply are not willing to accept the truth and reality of God's absolute truth. And, conveniently, the "truth" and "reality" of today's science gives people the freedom to rewrite/reword (i.e., "rethink") the truth of God's Word into a new and "improved" "Bible translation"—i.e., one that they are *willing* to accept.

Absurdly, Brian McLaren is also one of the "translators" for Thomas Nelson's *The Voice*. Never mind that according to this "translator" and *rewriter* of the truth of God's Word:

> "In my own experience as a lover and reader of the Bible, as **I am *freed* from the literalistic and dualistic straitjacket** ... I feel I can breathe a little freer ..." (Brian McLaren; emphasis added)[38]

> "Perhaps when our conservative friends **ask those of us on this quest if we believe in the *inerrancy* of Scripture**, our reply should be: '**No**, I believe the Scripture is *better* than inerrant.'" (Brian McLaren; emphasis added)[39]

> "If we believe that **the same God who created an *evolving* universe is revealed in an *evolving* Bible**, we can derive some fascinating insights from contemporary studies of genetics. Today's chickens, it turns out, still have the genetic information in their DNA that was used to produce long tails, scales, and teeth in their ancestors the dinosaurs.... We might say that *the Bible* similarly retains a record of *its own evolution* ..." (Brian McLaren; emphasis added)[40]

The only "reality" in which an "evolving *universe*" results in an "evolving *Bible*" is the "reality" of *Oneness/panentheism* in which "God," and thus the "truth" of "God," is *immanent in the universe* and therefore "evolving" right along with it. And, as is the whole point, in this case there *cannot* be absolute truth that must be *believed* because there would only be an *ever*-changing "truth" of an *ever*-changing "God." There's only one problem. The *non*-immanent, *never*-changing *true* God did *not* create "an *evolving* universe." Man's created new "God" of Oneness/panentheism did,[F] the "energies" of which man is tapping into in order to "evolve" the "old" truth of God and His Son into an all-encompassing testament/covenant/way to God that gives everyone the freedom to imagine and define God and His Son however they choose. Without question, an "*evolving*" "Bible"/"truth" frees man from the *never*-changing, absolute truth of God's inerrant inspired Scripture. And since this clearly saves the world *from the truth of Who God and His Son are*, man is thereby set free from the soul "sort," right?

> "*Be not deceived; God is not mocked: for whatsoever a man soweth, that shall he also reap.*" (Galatians 6:7)

> "*For our transgressions are multiplied before thee, and our sins testify against us: for our transgressions are with us; and as for our iniquities, we know them;* **in transgressing and lying against the LORD, and departing away from our God, speaking oppression and revolt, conceiving and uttering from the heart words of falsehood**.*" (Isaiah 59:12-13)

Again, it sends a very clear message to have people "*translate*" the truth of God's Word who *don't believe* the truth of God's Word. But no matter how many people try to change His truth—i.e., "translate" it into the new way of thinking—God promises to *preserve His words from this generation forever*. And God said what He meant and meant what He said in the *words* of His *inspired* Holy Scriptures. And, no, "*holy men of*

F

By the way, the universe is likewise not the "intelligent" design of an immanent "cosmic mind." Sadly, no the world is not being brought closer to believing in the *true* God through "Intelligent Design." Rather, "Intelligent Design" (ID) is leading the world into believing in *a* generic "intelligence" behind creation (a term now also deceptively applied to "*evolution*") that can be defined (or identified) however anyone chooses. This is the emerging faith of the generic "God" of Oneness. Moreover, this "God" of Oneness is also the "intelligence" (a.k.a. "cosmic mind"/"universal mind") that has "designed" the universe to be *panentheistic/pantheistic*. And, therefore, this design of Oneness gives people the freedom to *ID* "God" in everyone and everything. At any rate, a design of Oneness is not the design of the true God. The true God is not a generic "God"/"intelligence" that can be *ID'd* however people choose.

God" are not men that see *no difference* between *the holy and the profane*!

> "*Knowing this first, that no prophecy of the* **scripture** *is of any private interpretation. For the prophecy came* **not** *in old time* **by the will of man: but holy men of God spake as they were moved by the Holy Ghost.**" *(2 Peter 1:20-21)*

> "**Every word of God is pure**: *he is a shield unto them that put their trust in him.*" *(Proverbs 30:5)*

> "**The words of the LORD are pure words**: *as silver tried in a furnace of earth, purified seven times. Thou shalt keep them, O LORD,* **thou shalt preserve them from this generation for ever.**" *(Psalm 12:6-7)*

A key part of setting the world free from the "literalistic and dualistic straitjacket" of God's inerrant inspired Scripture—i.e., of God's *absolute truth*—is to lead people to *move beyond* the *words* of God's Word. And, thus, many people have been blindly moving into *the ditch* where, sadly, they have been falsely led to believe they can have a deeper relationship with God.

> "*Jesus said unto them, …* **He that is of God heareth God's words**: *ye therefore hear them not, because ye are not of God.*" *(John 8:42, 47)*

> "*… Can the blind lead the blind? shall they not both fall into the ditch?*" *(Luke 6:39)*

In *A Is for Abductive: The Language of the Emerging Church* by Leonard Sweet, Brian McLaren, and Jerry Haselmayer, is the following quote:

> "**V is for Voice** …
>
> "And **what postmoderns are listening for is less _words_ than the music of the spheres**, especially the heavenly spheres, but *sometimes the dances of demons.…*
>
> "Some things are too 'noisy'; other things have too much 'static.'…
>
> "**Voice is discovering the *intrinsic form*** through attentive listening **through the 'auditory _imagination_'** (T. S. Eliot) **and 'acoustic _ideas_'** (Thomas Mann)." (all parentheses in the original; emphasis added)[41]

> "*This evil people,* **which refuse to hear my _words_, which walk in the _imagination_ of their heart**, *and walk after* _other gods_, *to serve them, and to worship them, shall even be as this girdle, which is good for nothing.*" *(Jeremiah 13:10)*

> "*And the Father himself, which hath sent me, hath borne witness of me.* **Ye have neither heard his _voice_ at any time, nor seen his shape**. *And ye have not his word abiding in you: for whom he hath sent, him ye believe not.*" *(John 5:37-38)*

> "**Hold fast the _form_ of sound _words_**, *which thou hast heard of me, in faith and love which is in Christ Jesus.*" *(2 Timothy 1:13)*

> "*These words spake Jesus, and lifted up his eyes to heaven, and said, …* **For I have given unto them the _words_ which thou gavest me**; *… Sanctify them through thy truth:* **thy _word_ is truth.**" *(John 17:1, 8, 17)*

> "But this thing commanded I them, saying, **Obey my voice**, and I will be your God, and ye shall be my people: and walk ye in all the ways that I have commanded you, that it may be well unto you. **But they hearkened not, nor inclined their ear, but walked in the counsels and in the imagination of their evil heart, and went backward, and not forward**.... This is a nation that **obeyeth not the voice of the LORD their God**, nor receiveth correction: **truth is perished, and is cut off from their mouth**." (Jeremiah 7:23-24, 28)

The fact that Thomas Nelson is publishing a "Bible translation" (*The Voice*) that includes *Sweet, McLaren,* et al., in the never-ending mission to *rewrite* the truth of God's Word speaks volumes on *many levels*. But then, today's mission is not about getting people to believe and obey the truth. Quite the contrary. It is about getting people to *change their minds* to Oneness and its immanent, *interfaith* "God" that is *in everyone and everything*. In *Nudge: Awakening Each Other to the God Who's Already There*, Sweet writes:

> "**Christianity is not about 'Do you believe?' but 'Do you hear?'**...
>
> "Evangelism is **not getting people to believe this or that and they will be saved**. Evangelism is getting people to *hear* it for themselves." (emphasis added)[42]
>
> > "'We believe that **the divine presence is everywhere**. —*Rule of St. Benedict*, chapter 19'
>
> "When we fail to **shut up and listen**, we fall out of step with **the rhythm of God's presence**." (emphasis added)[43]
>
> "When we wake the church from its **dogmatic slumbers**, and point out that the *old* responses no longer get the *needed* reactions, we shouldn't expect flowers and hugs....
>
> "For nudgers, every **awakening** is a meeting—a call to **connection** with some one, some event, **some One**. Every awakening is a special **openness** to the strangeness of the world.... Can you **hear God sing in the world**, and the **different notes and beats** that go with **different cultures**? This is what semiotic nudges do ... help people, starting with ourselves, **wake well and hear the music of the spheres**." (last ellipsis dots in the original; emphasis added)[44]
>
> "... tuning our receivers to **the 'I AM' channel** and setting the controls to receive and transmit transdimensional **frequencies**." (emphasis added)[45]
>
> "If super-string physics is right (and the loop gravity school says it's not), then **the basic reality of the universe is vibration or sound**....
>
> "**String theory defines matter as 'vibrating strings of energy.'** That's it. What makes a turnip a turnip, and a carrot a carrot? A change in vibrations. Vibrations are what turn one vegetable into another. Why? Because matter is but vibrations, notes on God's violin. Anything that vibrates does so at speeds called frequencies, and **the frequencies of vibration create sound. When sounds are shaped together, that's called music**. Words like *vibration, frequency, sound,* and *music* are in some ways interchangeable. Oh, I forgot one term that should be added to that list: *matter*." (parentheses in the original; bold added)[46]

How fitting that in this emerging faith/New Quantum Spirituality the "music of the spheres" that is playing on the "channel" of its immanent "God" of *Oneness* comes from "*circular* 'strings'":

> "In microphysics, elementary matter or quanta are treated ... as **continuous stacks of strings *looping* out into space** with spaces between them." (Leonard Sweet; emphasis added)[47]

> "[E]nergy is the stuff of life. Fear itself is an energy, a vibration.
>
> "***Everything* is a vibration**. Quantum physics and **super-string theory**—and now the latest articulation of this, called M-theory—tell us that *everything in existence* is composed not of points, or '*dots*,' of energy, but of smaller-than-minuscule **circular 'strings' that vibrate constantly, at *differing* rates**. These strings have the ability to **interconnect, or intertwine, with each other, creating a 'superstring.'**" (Neale Donald Walsch; emphasis added)[48]

More like creating a super web. This sounds like the infinitely intertwined strips of the Möbius strip. Strips . . . strings . . . what's the difference? When infinitely intertwined, both are a super *web* which, incredibly, is what people in this emerging faith/New Quantum Spirituality *want*. Never mind that a web is created by spiders to catch their *prey*—which is fitting of "the cosmic web" of *Oneness* (as well as its web of infinitely intertwined *circles of Oneness* of *all opposites*). People don't think twice about a web because they have been desensitized to it all by *the worldwide web*—a web that is no doubt being *monitored* (to say the least) for its "*ideas*." (Incidentally, the worldwide web was created by and for the scientists of CERN's Large Hadron Collider,[49] which, as previously mentioned, is looking for "the God particle.") At any rate, whether people in this emerging faith/New Quantum Spirituality of Oneness/panentheism believe that it is *dots* of energy (or "*God dots*") or *circular strings* that constitute everything in existence, the end result is the same.

Again, *Oneness* was started by Satan in the Garden of Eden and does not lead to the true God. Even though it is perfectly clear in God's Word of truth that the true God is not a God of *Oneness* and is not *in everyone and everything*, people's ears today are positively itching for Oneness. So to easily change people's minds away from the truth of God and unto its fables of Oneness, all the seducing spirit world has to do is simply scratch itching ears. Sadly, there are many people who want *no difference* between the "sacred" and "profane"—i.e., who want *Oneness*—who are giving heed to this *diabolical* voice. But, of course, they don't hear it that way. Rather, in *Oneness*, where there is *no difference* between the holy and *profane*, it becomes the voice of "*God*" and sounds like "*music*" to their ears.

> "It is why I have said, play, play, *play* ... with all of life!
>
> "**Mix** what you call **the sacred with the sacrilegious** ...
>
> "**So go ahead! Mix what you call the profane and the profound**—*so that you can see* that there is *no difference*, and *experience All as One*....
>
> "When at last you see that there is no separation in God's World—that is, *nothing which is not God*—then, at last, will you let go of this invention of man which you have called *Satan*." (the seducing spirit calling itself "God;" emphasis added, except to *play*)[50]

> "Faith makes a metanoized *mulch* of <u>all</u> dichotomized selves and heals <u>all</u> dis-

cursive dualisms (**one of the *worst* of which was 'sacred' and 'profane'**), all ***disastrous* separations** that threaten our existence." (Leonard Sweet; parentheses in the original; emphasis added)[51]

"*... **they have put no difference between the holy and profane**, neither have they shown difference between the unclean and the clean, ... **and I am profaned among them**.*" *(Ezekiel 22:26)*

"For the time will come when they will not endure sound doctrine; but after their own lusts shall they heap to themselves teachers, having itching ears; and they shall turn away their ears from the truth, and shall be turned unto fables." (2 Timothy 4:3-4)

"Now the Spirit speaketh expressly, that in the latter times some shall depart from the faith, giving heed to seducing spirits, and doctrines of devils." (1 Timothy 4:1)

In the emerging faith of Oneness, <u>profaning God</u> becomes *irrelevant*. But this is to be expected given that this emerging "faith" is blasting God to immanent bits in order to *eliminate* all difference between the holy and profane. And as people change their minds to *Oneness*, they begin to "see" and "hear" it everywhere as their "consciousness"/ "awareness," i.e., their thinking, shifts accordingly. With the seducing spirit world's help, people even "awaken" to immanence and "know" this panentheistic Oneness experientially. So why would they see it as *profaning God*? Never mind that immanence/Oneness by its very nature of being *in everyone and everything* <u>automatically</u> profanes the true God.

In fact, since "reimagining" God as immanent *in all things* brings *all things* into Oneness with God, it is *the* <u>ultimate</u> *profaning of God*. But this emerging faith of Oneness/ panentheism doesn't even stop there. Since it then connects/defrags (glues) *all things* together *as "God,"* it is also *the* <u>ultimate</u> <u>idol</u>. And this all-encompassing "Totality" or "wholeness" of this new *profane "God" of Oneness is being formed and created to be a replacement of the "old" holy God of judgment*. But, as mentioned earlier, no matter what this emerging faith chooses to use for glue—from the "relationship" of New Age Oneness to taking truth from God's Word—this glued-together whole "God" of Oneness will never be anything more than a glued-together *counterfeit*. This gluing process can even be as "scientific" as "gluons" that "'glue' quarks together," and it will still be nothing more than a glued-together counterfeit.

"[I]n QCD ['quantum chromodynamics'] the strong interactions [between particles] are mediated by the exchange of **'gluons'** between coloured quarks. These are not real particles but some kind of quanta that **'glue' quarks together to form mesons and baryons**." (Fritjof Capra; emphasis added)[52]

The following is taken from an article of DISCOVER magazine titled, "The Glue That Holds the World Together":

"**Inside the proton lies the deep, unsettling truth: Stuff is made of nothing, or almost nothing, held together by glue, lots of glue**....

"Frank Wilczek ... helped develop this theory of the proton in 1973....

"A proton is made of three quarks, yes, but the quarks are infinitesimal ... imprisoned in flickering clouds of other particles—other quarks, ... and, above all, **gluons**, which **transmit the force that *binds* the quarks together**. Gluons are massless and evanescent, but **they carry most of the proton's energy**. That is why it is more accurate to say protons are made of gluons rather than quarks. **Protons are little blobs of glue**—but even that picture conveys something *too static* and *substantial*. All is *flux* and crackling energy inside a proton ... 'It's a very rich, *dynamic* structure,' says Wilczek....

"Quantum chromodynamics, or QCD, the theory that Wilczek [who 'lives in Einstein's old house' at Princeton] and his colleagues invented, is a type of quantum field theory ...

"In quantum chromodynamics ['the force that holds protons together'], quarks carry a new kind of charge, called color—which has nothing to do with ordinary color—and those charges generate a color field (hence the name chromodynamics). The quantum of the field, and the transmitter of the strong force, is the gluon....

"'It's only at the crudest level that a proton is made of three quarks,' Wilczek says. 'When you look close and get inside these clouds and start seeing **the basic structure**, you see that **it's mostly glue**.'

"Which makes all the more interesting the question of how the universe ever managed to design such a thing....

"[Wilczek says:] '**If you really study the equations, it gets almost mystical.**'" (parentheses in the original; emphasis added)[53]

Shortly after Capra's above quote on gluing "quarks together to form mesons and baryons," he comes back to "energy patterns" and the mind:

"To understand the essence of the new development it is necessary to clarify the meaning of quark structure within the context of S-matrix theory.... [T]he S-matrix approach, being *holistic* and thoroughly *dynamic*, sees particles as **interrelated energy patterns** in an ongoing universal process—as correlations, or **interconnections, between various parts of an inseparable cosmic web**. In such a framework, the term **'quark structure'** refers to the fact that **the transfer of *energy* and the flow of *information*** in this network of events proceed along well-defined lines, **producing the two-ness associated with mesons and the three-ness associated with baryons**.... [T]here are no distinct entities and **no basic building blocks**; there is **only a flow of energy** ...

"The question, then, is: **how do the specific quark patterns arise?**... [T]he quark structure appears as a manifestation of order and necessary consequence of **self-consistency** ...

"The clarification of the concept of order in a field of research where **patterns of matter and patterns of mind are increasingly being recognized as reflections of one another** promises thus to open fascinating frontiers of knowledge." (emphasis added)[54]

This "universal process" that has "no basic building blocks," just a colorful flow of "information" and "energy" that bring everyone/everything together as one, does not lead to the knowledge of the true God. No matter how many minds align, and no matter how many theories, "scientific" or otherwise, are conceived and believed, man's emerging tower of Oneness being built today will never reach unto heaven, even if it's "held together by glue, lots of glue."

> "And the whole earth was of one language, and of one speech. And it came to pass, **as they journeyed from the east**, that they found a plain in the land of Shinar; and they dwelt there. And they said one to another, Go to, let us make brick, and burn them thoroughly. And they had brick for stone, and slime had they for mortar. And they said, Go to, **let us build us a city and a tower, whose top may reach unto heaven; and let us make us a name**, lest we be scattered abroad upon the face of the whole earth. And the LORD came down to see the city and the tower, which the children of men builded. And the LORD said, **Behold, the people is one**, and they have all one language; and this they begin to do: and now nothing will be restrained from them, which they have imagined to do. Go to, let us go down, and there confound their language, that they may not understand one another's speech. So the LORD scattered them abroad from thence upon the face of all the earth: and they left off to build the city. Therefore is the name of it called Babel; because the LORD did there confound the language of all the earth: and from thence did the LORD scatter them abroad upon the face of all the earth." (Genesis 11:1-9)

> "For the wisdom of this world is foolishness with God. For it is written, He taketh the wise in their own craftiness." (1 Corinthians 3:19)

Today's Oneness, which is likewise a journey from the East, actually goes above and beyond the city and tower of Babel -- in thinking to *build* God. To "build" -- "to construct (esp. something complex) by assembling and joining *parts*;" "to mold, form, or create."[55] Yet the *true* God—Who did not explode Himself—has no parts. There are no bits and pieces of God that comprise "the Totality" of God. The true God is completely *separate* from creation and is complete and whole and total *in and of Himself*. The workmen who are gathering together to build a glued-together "Rock" of everyone and everything are not building *the true God*.

> "Who hath formed a god, or molten a graven image that is profitable for nothing? Behold, all his fellows shall be ashamed: and the workmen, they are of men: let them all be gathered together, let them stand up; yet they shall fear, and they shall be ashamed together.... he maketh a god, ... he falleth down unto it, and worshippeth it, and prayeth unto it, and saith, Deliver me; for thou art my god. They have not known nor understood: for he hath shut their eyes, that they cannot see; and their hearts, that they cannot understand. And none considereth in his heart, ... a deceived heart hath turned him aside, that he cannot deliver his soul, nor say, Is there not a lie in my right hand?" (Isaiah 44:10-11, 17-20)

50

The cosmic circle dance -- an "upward journey" of "evolving" back into "*God*"

"With Einstein's 1905 equation E=mc^2, we began the twentieth-century learning that **matter and energy are essentially *the same thing***." (Leonard Sweet; emphasis added)[1]

"***Matter* is the energy of *Spirit*. Ultimately, *all that exists is spirit***." (Leonard Sweet; emphasis added)[2]

"... ***God is 'spirit'*** or 'energy.'" (Leonard Sweet; emphasis added)[3]

So ultimately "*all that exists*" is "*God*"? Whether those in this merging and emerging "Christian"/*New Age* faith and New Quantum Spirituality of Oneness/panentheism straightforwardly admit it or not, this is indeed what this faith and its "God"—i.e., glued-together "Rock" of *everyone and everything*—boil down to.

"The realization that **you are One Being**—that **everything in Life is really One Thing, Manifesting**—can and will change your entire experience forever." (the seducing spirit calling itself "God;" emphasis added)[4]

"**God is the energy**—the pure, raw energy—which **you call life**." (the seducing spirit calling itself "God;" emphasis added)[5]

"God *is* the energy you call imagination. God *is* creation. God *is* first thought. And God *is* last experience. And **God is everything in between**." (the seducing spirit

383

calling itself "God;" bold added)[6]

"... there is no separation in God's World—that is, **nothing which is not God** ...

"You cannot be separate from Me, for **I Am All That Is**." (the seducing spirit calling itself "God;" emphasis added)[7]

And, again, the reason for this Oneness in which all that exists is "God" is that:

"In the beginning, that which *Is* is all there was, and there was nothing else....

"And so **All That Is divided Itself**—becoming, in one glorious moment, that which is *this*, and that which is *that*....

"**In the moment of this great explosion from within** ...

"From the No-Thing thus sprang the Everything—a spiritual event entirely consistent, incidentally, with what your scientists call **The Big Bang** theory....

"In rendering **the universe** as **a *divided version of Itself*, God** produced, from pure energy, all that now exists—both seen and unseen....

"*We are composed of the same stuff.* **We ARE the 'same stuff'!**" (the seducing spirit calling itself "God;" bold added)[8]

"***Elements* are *particles* of *God***, portions of All, **the stuff of everything**." (the seducing spirit calling itself "God;" emphasis added)[9]

Absurdities notwithstanding, the "God" of Oneness became "the Totality" of the universe by exploding *itself* into bits and pieces in a "Big Bang" from which "thus sprang the Everything" that has subsequently *"evolved" upward* into all that exists. As the saying goes—"from goo to you by way of the zoo." And in the larger *overall* picture of "evolution" this process is a *circle* in which all that exists is "evolving" back into "God."

"**Evolution is an upward journey**, not a downward spiral....

"Religions now have an opportunity to *shift from 'There is only one God' to 'There is only One Thing at all.'*...

"**If there is Only One Thing That Is, then *everything and everyone must be part of that One Thing*** ..." (Neale Donald Walsch; emphasis added)[10]

Basically, in this emerging faith/New Quantum Spirituality of Oneness/panentheism the process of gluing everyone/everything together as "the Totality of God" is simply the "evolutionary" process of rebuilding "God," or putting "God" *back together*. In other words, the whole "God" transformed itself into *bits and pieces (parts)* of "God" that then began "evolving" upward—and grouping together—in a process of *re*-forming back into a *whole* "God." Grouping by grouping—cell by cell, and "kingdom" by "kingdom"—the process of this "evolutionary" formation has progressed. Through the mineral, vegetable, and animal "kingdoms," and on up into the human "kingdom," this "evolution" of "All That Is" has been gradually working its way upward, bringing the bits and pieces (parts) of "God" back in *formation* as a defragged *whole* "God." And now that nations and *religions* (and, thus, *gods*) are being brought together in today's larger group formations in the human "kingdom," this process of putting all that exists back together as "God" is nearly complete. As Alice Bailey taught in her 1922 book, *The Consciousness Of The Atom*, which consists of a series of lectures she gave in New York regarding "the universality of the evolutionary process" and "the testimony of science as to the relation of matter and of consciousness"[11]:

> "We have earlier dealt with **the atom** *per se*, but have in no way considered **its building into form**, or into **that totality of forms which we call a kingdom in nature**. We have considered somewhat the essential nature of the atom, and its prime characteristic of intelligence, and have laid our emphasis upon **that out of which all the different forms as we know them are built—all forms in the mineral kingdom, in the vegetable kingdom, in the animal kingdom, and in the human kingdom**. In the sumtotal of all forms you have the totality of nature as generally understood.
>
> "Let us now extend our idea from the individual forms that go to the constitution of any of **these four kingdoms of nature**, and view them as **providing that still greater form which we call the kingdom itself**, and thus view that kingdom as a conscious unit, **forming a homogeneous whole**." (bold added)[12]

> "These ideas can be applied to **forms of government, forms of religions, and forms of scientific or philosophical thought**." (emphasis added)[13]

> "Again, **the whole trend of evolution is toward synthesis**. As we go down into matter, as we tend toward materialisation, we have heterogeneity; **as we work back towards spirit we shall tend towards unity**: so that in the religious world we can look for unity to make its appearance. There is, even now, a much greater spirit of tolerance abroad … but the time is rapidly approaching when **the great fundamental unity that underlies all the different religions**, and the fact that *each faith is a necessary part of one great whole*, **will be recognised by men everywhere**, and through this recognition we shall have the simplification of religion." (emphasis added)[14]

> "**What are the religions?**… **Simply the forms through which the great threefold central Life, Who *informs* our planet, seeks to express Himself**.… He expresses Himself **through the *totality* of the kingdoms of nature, and through the nations, races, religions, sciences, and philosophies**, in existence at this time." (emphasis added)[15]

> "[W]e shall have **the aggregate of *all* forms, of *all* groups**, and of all states of consciousness **blended, unified, and synthesised into a perfected whole**. This whole you may call *the solar system*, you may call it *nature*, or you may call it **God**. *Names* matter not.… I trust that we can prove that there is an intelligence underlying all; and that from separation will come union, produced **through *blending* and *merging* into *group formation***, and that **eventually from the many groups will be seen *emerging* the one perfect, fully conscious whole** …" (emphasis added)[16]

> "Thus we arrive finally at the concept that the solar system is but **the aggregate of all kingdoms and all forms**, and **the Body of a Being** Who is expressing Himself through it …" (emphasis added)[17]

> "This is **evolution, the process which unfolds *the life* within all units**, the *developing urge* which **eventually *merges all* units and *all* groups, until you have that *sumtotal of manifestation* which can be called Nature, or *God*, …

> This is **that Perfection which is *inherent* in matter itself, and the tendency which is latent in *the atom*, in man, and in *all that is***. This interpretation of the evolutionary process does not look upon it as the result of an *outside* Deity pouring His energy and wisdom upon a waiting world, but rather as something which is latent *within* that world itself, **that lies hidden at the heart of the atom** ..." (emphasis added)[18]

> "**[T]hrough every grade of form, spirit or life progresses, until** the path of return has been traversed and ***the point of origin achieved***. This is **the meaning of evolution** and **here lies the secret of *the cosmic incarnation***." (emphasis added)[19]

> "It has been said that all evolution proceeds from the homogenous, through heterogeneity, back again to homogeneity, and it has been pointed out that:
>
>> "'**Evolution is a continually accelerating march of *all the particles* of the universe** which leads them ... **from the material atom to that universal consciousness in which omnipotence and omniscience are realised**: in a word, **to the full realisation of the Absolute of God**.'
>
> "This proceeds from those minute diversifications which we call molecules and atoms up to their aggregate as they are built into forms; and continues on through the building of those forms into greater forms ..." (emphasis added)[20]

Step by step, layer upon layer, this emerging faith is the process of *connecting* and *blending* and *merging* everything into the formation of greater and greater forms until all that exists *emerges* as "the Totality of God," "the Absolute of God," in a "perfected whole." That is, until all that exists *emerges* as "God" -- "the point of origin." And this *emergence of a whole "God"* is a "latent" tendency to *godhood* lying "hidden" in the *atom*, a "*secret* of *the cosmic incarnation*" (i.e., of *immanence*). In other words, it is a "secret" dance of *subatomic divinity* (or *deity*). After all, in "the cosmic incarnation," "[*e*]*lements are particles of God*."

People can try to justify this false quantum "God" of Oneness/panentheism as the true God to their heart's content, but the true God is not *inherent (immanent)* in *creation*. The "*cosmic* incarnation" is not the "*incarnation*" of the true God. The universe/"cosmos" is not and never will be *God made flesh*. Rather, the *true Person* of the Lord Jesus Christ is; *period*. Contrary to this emerging faith, there is no cosmic circle dance that is a "*secret*" of "the cosmic incarnation" "that lies hidden at the heart of the atom." The "Trinity" will *never* be a "quaternity"!

> "***The secret of life*** is a *three-dimensional double helix*, which mirrors the threefold structure of the Trinity: the harmonious coming together and movement of two coordinating but conflicting strands in our lives—the missional and the relational, *which spin together to create the incarnational*....
>
> "**This is the 3-D dance of *the divine*,** which the church fathers **called 'perichoresis,' or 'circle dance,'** when they tried to explain the movement at the heart of the Trinity. **At the heart of the divine is a dance**, and ***the divine itself is a dance***. Motion. Movement. God created us to be dancing partners, to **join in the dance, *to make the Trinity <u>a quaternity</u>***, if you will, as we **dance to the tune of Jesus**." (Leonard Sweet; emphasis added)[21]

PART FIVE: THE CREATION 387

Before today's shifting Christianity began its pursuit of freedom from the "box" of God's Word of truth, it used to be obvious that *God* does not invite *man* to *join the Godhead*! God is not a *circle* dance of *Oneness*. Moreover, contrary to this emerging faith/New Quantum Spirituality of Oneness/panentheism, God is not *"energy."* Energy is a *creation* of God; it is *not God*. The "cosmic dance of *energy*" in which *everything*—including *"God"*—is "energy" in motion and movement is not the dance of the true God and His Son, the Lord Jesus Christ. The *"Trinity"* is not moving and changing and evolving into a *"quaternity." Man* is not moving and changing and evolving into *God*. And, by the way, unlike those in this emerging faith who have designs on becoming God, Jesus did not dance His way into "the Trinity." That is, He did not dance His way into *being God*. Jesus has *always* been in the Godhead.

Sweet, who wants "to make the *Trinity* a *quaternity*," describes "the church" as:

"... an alive spiritual organism **dancing to the rhythm of** sanctification (or what some call '**divinization**,' others 'christification,' still other [sic] 'celestification') ..." (parentheses in the original; emphasis added)[22]

Sweet also writes:

"*Matter* is the energy of *Spirit*." (emphasis added)[23]

"**Energy and matter** are *two expressions of the same higher order of reality*, with **the difference between them *only one of degree and pedigree***: The latter is *devolved* from the former." (emphasis added)[24]

"In a sense, the whole of creation may be said to be a *movement* between two involutions--**Spirit** in which all is involved and out of which all evolves or **devolves downward to the other pole of Matter**, **Matter** in which also all is involved and out of which all **evolves upward to the other pole of Spirit**." (Leonard Sweet quoting "Yogin/nationalist/poet" Sri Aurobindo [Sri Aurobindo is described by Barbara Marx Hubbard as "Teilhard de Chardin's Eastern counterpart," and both are listed by Hubbard as "teachers of conscious evolution"]; emphasis added)[25]

This cosmic circle dance of "evolving" upward into "God" is quite an imaginative testament/covenant/way to God! Never mind that believing in the Lord Jesus Christ—the only Christ (Messiah) and Mediator of *God's* testament/covenant—is the only *true* way to God.

"*For there is **one God**, and **one mediator** between God and men, **the man Christ Jesus**.*" (1 Timothy 2:5)

"*For God so loved the world, that he gave his <u>only</u> begotten Son, that whosoever **believeth** in him should not perish, but have everlasting life.*" (John 3:16)

"*And to **Jesus the mediator of the new covenant**, ... See that ye refuse not him that speaketh. For if they escaped not who refused him that spake on earth, much more shall not we escape, if we turn away from him that speaketh from heaven.*" (Hebrews 12:24-25)

"*And for this cause **he is the mediator of the new testament**, that by means of* death, for the redemption of the transgressions that were under the first testament, they which are called might receive the promise of eternal inheritance. For where a testament is, there must also of necessity be the death of the testator." (Hebrews 9:15-16)

"Something can be all new, yet nothing of the old be lost.... **The Third *Testament* is *everything new* about the old, old story. Or in Teilhard's more *mystical* phrasings, a 'descendent divine involution' combining with the 'ascendent cosmic evolution.'**" (Leonard Sweet; emphasis added)[26]

In her book *Towards A New Mysticism: Teilhard de Chardin and Eastern Religions*, Ursula King, "a founder of the Teilhard Center in London,"[27] writes:

"**Teilhard's view** of **the interrelationship between *religion and evolution*** is linked to the fundamental conviction that '**from the depths of Matter to the highest peak of the Spirit there is only *one evolution*'. Religions** have an indispensable role to play in furthering **man's *evolutionary* advance towards the spirit**." (emphasis added)[28]

Since "there is *Only One Thing That Is*" in this emerging faith, it is to be expected that "there is *only one evolution*." And this way, this *panentheistic/pantheistic* "God" can "evolve" right along with man and his chosen *religions*. Accordingly, King also writes that "[f]or Teilhard, a more sharply defined 'type' of God is found in *the 'universal Christ'* ..."[29] And Teilhard de Chardin wrote:

"**What I am proposing to do is to narrow that gap between *pantheism* and Christianity** by bringing out what one might call the Christian soul of pantheism or the pantheist aspect of Christianity." (emphasis added)[30]

"'**A general convergence of religions** upon **a universal Christ** who fundamentally satisfies them *all*: that seems to me the only possible conversion of the world, and **the only form in which a religion of the future can be conceived**.'" (emphasis added)[31]

"I believe that **the Messiah whom we await**, whom we all without any doubt await, is **the universal Christ**; that is to say, **the Christ of *evolution***." (emphasis added)[32]

A "God" of "evolution" . . . a "Christ" of "evolution" . . . it's all just a "secret" that lies "hidden" in the *atom*, right? A "secret" in which everyone can dance their way into "God" as their own "Messiah" ("Christ"). Hence, in this emerging "Christian"/New Age "secret," everyone can just dance around *believing* and *obeying* God and Christ by *being* and *doing* "God" and "Christ." But, of course, it is all absurdly justified as being and doing the *true* God and Christ. Again, as if that makes a difference! Sweet writes:

"**Quantum spirituality is** nothing more than your 'new account of everything old'--***your part of the 'I Am' that we* are**." (Leonard Sweet; emphasis added)[33]

"***Perichoresis*** is a composite Greek word that every Christian should know. It means **'move about' or 'dance around.'** The Cappadocian Fathers used it to define the communion of the Trinity as the 'Great Dance.' Father, Son, and Holy Spirit flow and frame their lives in a dance of perfect love, and **we are invited to add our moves to this dance of the divine**. A *perichoretic* relationship is one where we draw life and energy from this dance with the divine life. **Christians have a *perichoretic* relationship with Christ**. That relationship makes you more fully yourself than you could have ever been apart from Him....

"**[Y]our new self is the real 'you.' Christ has supplanted us!**" (Leonard Sweet & Frank Viola; bold added)[34]

"To '**Go Do Me**,' to '**doing God**' by doing good, I must be simultaneously seeing, following, and **being Christ**. I have no theology to impart, no biblical interpretation to argue, no agenda to accomplish. I only have *my* life." (Leonard Sweet; emphasis added)[35]

"Christ wants to become in your life and mine a verb, *not* a noun, and in part it is nudging [i.e., **Awakening Each Other to the God Who's Already There**] that **turns the word Christ from noun to verb**." (Leonard Sweet; emphasis added)[36]

"We are talking about **living in a unique Christ/you, 'I am' relationship**." (Leonard Sweet & Frank Viola; emphasis added)[37]

In *A "Wonderful" Deception* Warren B. Smith points out that Leonard Sweet (who admits that "[p]ostmodern culture is an *anti-Christian* culture"[38]) acknowledges New Age leader Matthew Fox as one of his "'personal role models' and 'heroes' of the 'true nature of the *postmodern* apologetic.'"[39] Smith writes that "[i]n *Quantum Spirituality*, Leonard Sweet not only hails Matthew Fox as one of his spiritual 'heroes,' but he also describes Pierre Teilhard de Chardin—as 'Twentieth-century Christianity's major voice.'"[40] Regarding Fox, who is indeed *anti-Christian*, Smith writes:

"Matthew Fox, like his mentor [Pierre Teilhard de] Chardin, taught that all creation is the 'Cosmic Christ'—therefore the Cosmic Christ is in *everyone* and *everything*. In his book *The Coming of the Cosmic Christ*, Fox writes:

"'... **We are all Cosmic Christs, 'other Christs.'** But what good is this if we do not know it?'

"'Divinity is found in all creatures. The divine name from Exodus 3:14, 'I Am who I Am,' is appropriated by **Jesus** who **shows us how to embrace *our own divinity*. The Cosmic Christ is the 'I am' in every creature**.'" (emphasis added)[41]

In other words, as Alice Bailey put it, "the cosmic Christ" is the "God" "immanent in the universe," and thus "the divinity which is in Him is in us also."[42] Hence, Bailey and the seducing spirit "Djwhal Khul" refer to "the Christed Jesus,"[43] and in this New Age terminology Jesus was "Christed" and everyone else can become "Christed," too.

"Many have been Christed, not just Jesus of Nazareth. **You can be Christed, too**." (the seducing spirit calling itself "God;" bold added)[44]

So regarding Sweet's above quote, would turning the word Christ "from noun to verb" be the verb "*Christed*," by any chance? Even though *Christ* (the *Messiah*) is a noun, a *Person—specifically* and *only* Jesus Christ of Nazareth—Sweet, of course, writes about "dancing to the rhythm of ... 'christification'":

> "... **dancing to the rhythm of sanctification** (or what some call '**divinization**,' others '**christification**,' still other [sic] '**celestification**') ..." (parentheses in the original; emphasis added)[45]

Sounds like "as above, so below." And, incidentally, "*divinize*" means "to make divine; *deify.*"[46] Again, so "just like Jesus," "[w]e, too, are to realize full *divinity*"? Or to put it another way, so just "make the Trinity *a quaternity* ... as we *dance to the tune of Jesus*"? To the contrary, a dance of "*divinization*" is *not* a "dance to the tune of *Jesus*"! Jesus -- "*whose goings forth have been from of old, from everlasting*" (Micah 5:2) -- always has been and always will be *eternally* God. Yet in "Panentheism - Perichoresis - Christology: Participatory Divinity," Mike Morrell writes:

> "... Jesus' divinity is one of those pesky spiritual themes that panentheism handles exceptionally well ...
>
> "If Rita Brock and Rebbecca Parker are to be believed (and I think their work speaks for itself), the earliest Christians had 'a high Christology *and* a high anthropology,' summed up in Athanasius' maxim '**God became man so that man might become God**.' (He meant you too, ladies) Panentheism says that Jesus is the 'uniquely' begotten son of God, not the 'only,' ... Jesus is glorious, divine, and there are certain unique and unrepeatable things Jesus does on our behalf, but overall, the earliest Christian spiritual thrust was one of **participatory divinity**. **We, too, are to realize full divinity** amidst (and *because of*) our full humanity – **just like Jesus**.
>
> "This might sound like 'New Age' quackery to the modern ear – but in ancient Christian faith, this was known as theosis or **divinization – participation in God via** the activity of God in **perichoresis** ... Through theosis, we are partakers of the divine nature – we become incorporated into the very life of **ever-flowing Godhead, a dance that goes on from eternity to eternity**. If the terminology makes you uncomfortable, think what we might mean by 'discipleship' or '**sanctification**' – only giving much more glory to God and to **a full-awakened humanity**.... [T]his is the gift of the Eastern church and the mystics." (all parentheses in the original; bold & underline added)[47]

First, as pointed out earlier, in May 2010 Mike Morrell interviewed Leonard Sweet and Frank Viola on their then upcoming new book, *Jesus Manifesto: Restoring the Supremacy and Sovereignty of Jesus Christ.*[48] Regarding this book Morrell writes:

> "To begin with, '**supremacy**' **is used in a mystical sense**, inspired by T. Austin Sparks. And **the divinity of Jesus championed by V&S [Viola & Sweet] is a *participatory* divinity**: We have become partakers of the divine nature through Christ. **It's a perichoretic divinity** ..." (bold & underline added)[49]

Restoring the Supremacy and Sovereignty of Jesus Christ is a very deceptive subtitle. Essentially, the supremacy and sovereignty of the *true Person* of Jesus Christ of Nazareth are being usurped and ascribed to *"another Jesus,"* one that those in this emerging faith of Oneness are *willing* to accept. Among other things, the "reimagined" "Jesus Christ" of this emerging faith is one whose very "being" and "divinity" is *participated in*, to the point that, as Sweet has put it, "[e]ach one of *us* is free to *become Jesus*."[50]

So *to whom*, exactly, are they "restoring" supremacy and sovereignty?

A dance of "*divinization*"—i.e., of *becoming God (or His Son)*—is a dance in which man wants God to share His divinity with man. In other words, it is a dance in which man absurdly wants *God* to *share being God* with *man*. (And with no less absurdity, this is likewise a dance in which man wants *Jesus, God's Son*, to *share being Christ—the Messiah*—with *man*.) But a *partnership* in which *both God and man* are *being God* (and *the Messiah*)—a partnership of *Oneness*—is just part and parcel of the "upward journey" of "evolving"/forming into "God," right?

> *"Thus saith the* LORD *the King of Israel, and his redeemer the* LORD *of hosts;* I *am the first, and* I *am the last; and beside* me *there is no God." (Isaiah 44:6; see also Revelation 22:13, 16)*

> *"Thus saith God the* LORD*, he that created the heavens, and stretched them out; he that spread forth the earth, and that which cometh out of it; he that giveth breath unto the people upon it, and spirit to them that walk therein: …* I *am the* LORD*: that is* my *name: and my glory will I not give to another, neither my praise to graven images." (Isaiah 42:5, 8)*

> *"For* I *am the* LORD *thy God, the Holy One of Israel, thy Saviour … understand that* I *am he: before me there was no God formed, neither shall there be after me." (Isaiah 43:3, 10)*

Man can choose to design a new "spirituality" out of "*science falsely so called*" if man wants to, but there is no cosmic circle dance of being *God* (or *the Messiah*). Despite today's false teachings and Scripture twistings, God's Word makes it clear that God only indwells those who *believe* in His Son, the Lord Jesus Christ. And, as addressed earlier, He indwells us as *in a* "*temple*" as a <u>separate</u> Being. As such, He lives <u>His</u> divine nature through us, thus making us "partakers of the divine nature" (2 Peter 1:4). But *we are not divine*. Nor do we ever *become divine*. *Divinity/deity* belongs to *God* and *God alone*. God shares being God with *no one!* Man can only share and participate in the *being* of "God" in the mind games (lies) of the emerging faith of Oneness/panentheism. Since this "God," and thus "divinity"/"deity," is in the very substance of everyone and everything, this *false* "God"—the *antithesis* of the *true* God—shares being "God" with *everyone and everything*. Hence, those in this emerging faith *share being a false* "*God*," which of course is "reimagined" as being the *true* God, . . . and the circle dance goes on and on.

Second, a dance of "becom[ing] God" is indeed the gift of the *mystics*, a gift they receive from the seducing spirit world in mystical "experiences" that "awaken" them— i.e., "open" their eyes—to Oneness. This gift of becoming "*God*"—or of "*divinization*"— is simply a perpetuation of the serpent's lie that "your eyes shall be opened, and ye shall be *as gods*" (Genesis 3:5).

No matter how many people fall for this lie and even absurdly see it as the truth of God, man is not *becoming* <u>God</u>. Neither is man *becoming* <u>Christ</u>. *Sanctification* is not a dance of "*divinization*" or "*christification*." *Man is not and never will be* "*part of the 'I Am.'*" *Man is not and never will be part of God*. No one becomes part of "*the Trinity*"— *no one* joins *the Godhead*! Rather, those in this emerging faith are "deceiving, and being deceived" (2 Timothy 3:13). They are "giving heed to *seducing* spirits, and doctrines of devils" (1 Timothy 4:1). There is an *eternal difference* between accepting the gift of *God* Who (contrary to Morrell's false teachings that "Jesus is the 'uniquely' begotten son of God, *not the* '<u>only</u>'") "*gave his* <u>only</u> *begotten Son*" so that we can have everlasting life and accepting the gift of the *mystics* who give the gift of "awakening" to a temporal life of Oneness with—and *even as*—a false "God." Awakening to this "secret" in which people can dance their way into this "God" however they choose as their own "Messiah" ("Christ") is the road to awakening someday in hell. And, no, this is *not* the "Path of *holiness*"—or of *sanctification*!

First, after writing that "the divinity which is in Him is in us also" and that "Christ" "has had boundless faith *in us*," Alice Bailey then flips holiness completely *upside down* (which those in this emerging faith *must* do in order to have *Oneness*):

> "… and His call goes out for us to **tread the Path of holiness**, and to **achieve that perfection** to which His life challenges us and for which He Himself tells us to work.…
>
> "**What is this holiness** to which He calls us, …? What is a holy man?
>
> "**Wholeness, unity, at-one-ment, completeness** - this is the hall mark of a perfect man.…
>
> "It means *listening for* and obeying the insistent demand of the soul for a nearer approach to God and **a fuller expression of divinity**; …
>
> "This is the doctrine of the At-one-ment; **God, immanent in the universe - the cosmic Christ**." (emphasis added)[51]

In other words, in this emerging faith that is as profane as it gets and that flips *everything* upside down, "holiness" is the (r)evolutionary—and "relational"—work of rebuilding the whole "God" of Oneness that is immanent (inherent)—incarnate—in *everyone and everything*.

> "**This is evolution**, the process which unfolds *the life within all* units, **the developing urge** which eventually *merges all* units and *all* groups, until you have that sumtotal of manifestation which can be called Nature, or God, … **This is that Perfection which is inherent** in matter itself, and the tendency which is latent in the atom, in man, and **in all that is**." (Alice Bailey; emphasis added)[52]
>
> "[T]hrough every grade of form, spirit or life progresses, until the path of return has been traversed and **the point of origin achieved**. This is **the meaning of evolution** and here lies **the secret of the cosmic incarnation**." (emphasis added)[53]
>
> "[W]e shall have the aggregate of all forms, of all groups, and of all states of consciousness **blended, unified, and synthesised into a perfected whole**.… you may call it **God**.… through blending and **merging into group formation**, and … eventually from the many groups will be seen **emerging the one perfect fully conscious whole** …" (Alice Bailey; emphasis added)[54]

Second, shortly after writing that a "*perichoretic* relationship is one where we draw life and energy from this *dance* with the *divine* life," Sweet and Viola not surprisingly write that "the Lord helps us *become* more '*rounded*' human beings—*not more straight*-edged, *straight*laced, *straight*-backed, *straight*-faced, *straight*jacketed human copies, but more '*rounded*,' more *complete* and *whole* humans."[55] This is very fitting of the emerging faith of Oneness and its upside-down "holiness" and "sanctification."

Sanctification (which, again, does *not* mean "*divinization*" or "*christification*") means to be <u>set apart</u> and *made holy*, which obviously has *nothing whatsoever* to do

PART FIVE: THE CREATION   393

with today's desired *circle* of relationship of *Oneness* with everyone and everything. In fact, to sanctify is *to separate*.[56] What *separates* us, thereby making us *holy*? Believing and obeying God's Word of truth (which is where we get the *true* Christian faith – not from ancient *mystics*.) The Lord Jesus Christ said, "*Sanctify them through thy truth: thy word is truth*" (John 17:17). But, sadly, those who prefer the (r)evolutionary dance of *Oneness* have basically "reimagined" every word of this verse, including Jesus Who said it. And for those who are not willing to believe and obey the specific truth of God's Word that *separates*, the "*whole*" "*truth*" of *Oneness* is conversely and conveniently "the Truth of Truths," "the fullness of truth," a "*group* mosaic," which is as *rounded* as it gets.

> "... **God works** in many ways, **through many faiths and religious agencies; in their *union* will the *fullness of truth* be revealed**." (the seducing spirit calling itself Djwhal Khul; emphasis added)[57]

> "**All the various truths form one Truth**; ... your little bit of truth forms part of **the group mosaic**." (the seducing spirit calling itself Djwhal Khul; emphasis added)[58]

> "The New Spirituality is ... a call to **expanded consciousness**....
>
> "This will create a revolution on your planet.... It will be **the Evolution Revolution**....
>
> "A revolution is a 'revolving.' It is **a coming full circle**.... **You are on a circle**, from the fullness of knowing to the emptiness of forgetfulness to the fullness of knowing again. **From Oneness to Separation to Oneness again**. From Total Consciousness to Unconsciousness to Total Consciousness again....
>
> "It is **the Truth of Truths**, the Wisdom of Wisdoms, the Nature of All Things, the Wonder of Life.
>
> "It IS Life, expressing AS Life, THROUGH Life, which process is circular and cyclical and circumferential. **It encompasses All and it encloses All and it includes All, because it IS All**....
>
> "All that will be asked of you is that you open your mind." (the seducing spirit calling itself "God;" bold added)[59]

In other words, just "open your mind" to *Oneness*. This "Evolution Revolution" is coming full circle *back into "God."*

> "Since God wished to Know Itself *experientially* as well as conceptually, God created a place **in the Kingdom** (or, if you will, **in Ultimate Reality**) where **all that God Is could be *experienced* as well as *known*.**
>
> "**God** did this by **dividing Itself up into a million ka-jillion different parts, or Aspects of Itself**, with each of the Parts created in different sizes and shapes, colors and textures, speeds and sounds, and levels of visibility and invisibility. **Then any Part of The Whole** (that is, any Individuated Aspect **of Divinity**) **could look back on The Whole from which It emerged and say, 'Oh, my God, how magnificent Thou art!' All it would take would be for that particular Aspect to have sufficient consciousness (self-awareness) to do so.**
>
> "And so, after dividing Itself up into a million ka-jillion individual parts, God merely had to imbue some of those parts with **sufficient consciousness to recognize (that is, re-cognize, or 'know again') Divinity** when it was looking right at It.

(Not all human beings have risen to that level of consciousness.) God put into place **a *system* by which Individuations of Itself *could* rise to such a level**, and that system was **called evolution**.

"This is **the *System of the Soul*.**" (Neale Donald Walsch; all parentheses in the original; bold & underline added)[60]

Since all that exists is *already* "the *same stuff*" as "*God*" all that is needed in this dance of "evolving" into "God" (or "divinization") is a shift in *thinking* (or "consciousness"). That is, everyone merely needs to "recognize" and "awaken" to and "remember" this "Reality"—this "secret"—of "Who We Really Are," or "Who We [Already] Are." Basically, everyone merely needs to participate in seeing and honoring *"God" in everyone and everything*. The "upward journey" of this "Evolution Revolution" (i.e., of this *circle* dance) is about *rebuilding* the "God" of Oneness, the *whole* "God"—with *no* duality, *no* separateness, *no* opposites—by connecting/joining/uniting/gluing all *its parts*.

> "May I pause here to remind you that **duality is only *a* stage on the evolutionary arc, leading eventually to the realization of unity**." (the seducing spirit calling itself Djwhal Khul; emphasis added)[61]

> "For instance, your penchant for, your insistence upon, comparisons, and your constant need to characterize something as '*better*' or '*worse*,' '*higher*' or '*lower*,' '*good*' or '*bad*' demonstrates how far into **duality** you have fallen; how deeply into **separatism** you have submerged....

> "The level of a society's advancement is reflected, inevitably, in the degree of its duality thinking. **Social evolution is demonstrated by *movement* towards *unity*, not separatism**." (the seducing spirit calling itself "God;" emphasis added)[62]

> "You are, have always been, and will always be, **a *divine* part of the *divine whole*, a member of the body**. That is why the act of **rejoining the whole**, of **returning to God**, is called *remembrance*. You actually choose **to re-member Who You Really Are**, or to join together with the various parts of you to experience **the all of you—which is to say, the All of Me**.

> "Your job on Earth, therefore, is not to *learn* (because you *already know*), but **to re-member Who You Are**. And to re-member who everyone else is. That is why a big part of your job is to remind others (that is, to **re-mind** them), so that they can re-member also.

> "All the wonderful spiritual teachers have been doing just that. **It is *your* sole purpose. That is to say, your *soul* purpose.**" (the seducing spirit calling itself "God;" all parentheses in the original; bold added)[63]

> "**The soul** is very clear that its **purpose is evolution**. That is its *sole* purpose—and its *soul* purpose." (the seducing spirit calling itself "God;" bold added)[64]

Hence, just "open your mind" and participate in the circle dance of aligning minds in this "evolutionary"/"quantum" leap *of faith* to *Oneness/panentheism* and see and honor "God" and "Christ" *in everyone and everything*. This way, the "old" truth and reality of God can "evolve" into a new "God" and new future—a new world religion and new world—of Oneness, and "all the world's souls can be set free."[65]

> "**The next phase ['of evolution'] is co-creative life, meaning life capable of consciously cooperating with the design of a harmonious new Earth and an operational new Heaven**, ...
>
> "All species capable of *participating* in the harmonizing phase on Earth will endure.
>
> "All human acts, intentions and desires that work toward **alignment with God's design**, love of all beings as self and love of <u>***self* as *Christ***</u> or <u>***co-creator***</u> will be selected for....
>
> "They will be **in perfect alignment with the evolutionary design**, the will of God....
>
> "There is a survival of the fittest. 'Fit' means able to know **God**, *not through some theology or institution, but as an experience of higher love, good, and wholeness*, **by *whatever* name it is called**.
>
> "If you are unable to know God, you are unable to align with the design. This self-centeredness makes one grow out of **alignment with the design of *the whole body***." (the seducing spirit calling itself "Christ;" emphasis added)[66]
>
> "This text is written to remind you of why you are here, to help you find others who are here for the same purpose, and to develop specific common strategies to ***achieve*** **the common design with which we are aligning—which is our understanding of the design of God**." (the seducing spirit calling itself "Christ;" emphasis added)[67]

Basically, if you are unable to know the whole "God" that is in *everyone* and *everything* that can be imagined and defined (i.e., *designed*) *however* man *chooses*, you are not aligning with the design of Oneness. Or to put it another way, if you believe and obey the absolute truth of God's Word, you are not participating in creating the "love and freedom" of "[o]urs is not a better way, ours is merely *another* way"[68] and are thus in the "*wrong*" state of judging between *truth and falsehood* and *right and wrong*. So what happens to those who choose to believe and obey God's Word rather than align their minds with the design of the false, whole new "God" of Oneness?

> "At the co-creative stage of evolution, one self-centered soul is like **a lethal cancer cell in a body**: deadly to itself and to **the whole**. The more complex and interrelated **an organism**, the more lethal a single cancer cell becomes." (the seducing spirit calling itself "Christ;" emphasis added)[69]
>
> "All entities have **the choice of aligning with the design, or of disintegrating**." (the seducing spirit calling itself "Christ;" emphasis added)[70]

In other words, believe and participate in Oneness, *or else*. Hindering minds hinder the whole process. Again, regarding the "selection process" of this false "Christ," Warren B. Smith writes:

> "He states that the world is about to make **an evolutionary leap** that will take all creation to a new level. **Those who awaken to their *own divinity*, by aligning themselves as *one with God* and one with each other, will evolve**....
>
> "He describes, therefore, the necessity of **a 'selection process'** that **will select out resistant individuals** who 'choose' not to evolve. This 'selection process' is a 'purification' that will be accomplished through 'the shock of a fire.'...

"The 'selection process' results in the deaths of those who refuse to see themselves as *a part* of God." (emphasis added)[71]

Even so, the *or else* that God gives us beats all others. We can fear God, or we can fear those who don't. Everyone has to make their choice. And regardless of whether people choose to be and do the new "God" of Oneness instead of believe and obey the "old" God of judgment, He said what He meant and meant what He said in His Word of *truth* that is *not* subject to *any* "reimaginings." But people today are bound and determined to change the unchangeable God. It is even absurdly imagined that man can change God in man's willful attempt to "become God" in the "evolutionary leap" to a "*God* consciousness" in which "*we* are Those In Charge"! Quite the opposite, in fact. This revolution *guarantees* God's judgment. Do people *really* think that *God* is going to bow the knee to *man*?? Do people *really* think that the *omnipotent God* is going to succumb to the "power" of *man's imagination*??

"Who is this that darkeneth counsel by words without knowledge? Gird up now thy loins like a man; for I will demand of thee, and answer thou me. Where wast thou when I laid the foundations of the earth? declare, if thou hast understanding." (Job 38:2-4)

"Hear now this, O foolish people, and without understanding; which have eyes, and see not; which have ears, and hear not: Fear ye not me? saith the LORD: will ye not tremble at my presence …? But this people hath a revolting and a rebellious heart; they are <u>revolted</u> and gone. Neither say they in their heart, Let us now fear the LORD our God …" (Jeremiah 5:21-24)

"[Y]ou do not have to fear God, you merely have to **be One with God**." (the seducing spirit calling itself "God;" emphasis added)[72]

"**And all the world's souls can be set free**. The New Spirituality is **a *civil rights* movement for the soul**, freeing humanity at last from the oppression of its belief in a separate, angry, violent, and fearful God." (Neale Donald Walsch; emphasis added)[73]

"Now comes a new revelation. Not from one teacher but from many, not from one voice but from a chorus. That chorus is singing **a different tune**. It's **the song of the soul**.

"4. The One Ruler's One Rule is **Self-Rule**.

"This is the antithesis of everything that the world's largest religions teach. **It's the thought that traditional religion says will be the cause of humanity's downfall. Wouldn't it be interesting if it turned out to be the thought that saved humanity?**

"There are those who say that putting oneself in **the role of self-ruler—that is, in the role of God**—is the worst insult to God. It's aggrandizement. It's ego run amok. It's the highest arrogance and the lowest blow. Human beings are *not* to attempt to rule themselves, but are to submit to *God's* rule.…

"Yet it is important for thinking people to ask, What if it *were* true?" (Neale Donald Walsch; bold added)[74]

"We are on the verge of the most extraordinary and exciting tomorrow. It is **a**

future undreamt of, precisely because it has *not* been dreamt of until now. It is the dreaming of it, quite literally the visioning of it in our minds, that will produce it. **Until now, not nearly enough people have held this vision to pull it into creation. Now, all of that is changing.**

"A huge shift is taking place all across the earth. It is a shift in the way we see ourselves, in the way we experience ourselves, in the way we express ourselves as sentient beings. **It is a movement away from our Old Thought that we must do as we have been told by Those In Charge, to a New Thought that *we* are Those In Charge.**

"This is the New Thought Movement, of which much has been written. This movement has been derided and ridiculed, made fun of and marginalized for years. **Now it is emerging as the next great evolutionary leap for humankind."** (Neale Donald Walsch; bold added)[75]

Today's "New Thought" that *"we* are Those In Charge" (or to put it another way, today's new way of thinking that gives up the "outdated" *rules*, or divisions between *truth and falsehood* and *right and wrong*) can only be "the thought that saved humanity" *from* the *true God*. But, sadly, this is what people in this emerging "faith," or revolution against God, *want*.

> *"... for, behold, ye walk every one after the imagination of his evil heart, that they may not hearken unto me."* (Jeremiah 16:12)

Since the "evolutionary leap" (or "quantum leap") is about mankind emerging as its *own* "*God* consciousness"—i.e., as its *own* "*guiding intelligence* for the earth"[76]—it is not surprising that in *The Consciousness of the Atom* Alice Bailey wrote:

> **"Everything is in a state of flux; the old order changeth, and a period of transition is in progress; the old forms**, in *every* department of thought, **are disintegrating**, but only in order that the life which gave them being may escape, and build for itself that which will be more satisfactory and adequate. **Take for instance, the old religious form of the Christian faith**.... I am not trying to prove that **the spirit of Christianity** is inadequate, ... I am only trying to point out that the form through which that spirit seeks to express itself has somewhat served its purpose, and **is proving a limitation**." (emphasis added)[77]

No doubt! The true *Holy* Spirit, Who is the Spirit of Christianity and Who is *not* immanent in everyone and everything, will indeed prove to be an *eternal* limitation to Oneness. And this will be so despite today's absurd and futile attempts to achieve the level of "*intelligence*" and "*consciousness*" of "*God*" by *grouping* everyone and everything including all *religions* and *gods*. This grouping, or aligning, that is bringing everyone and everything *in formation* as the whole "God" is not a march to "*omniscience*"! But it *is* greatly increasing everyone's knowledge of falsehood, which of course is "reimagined" as truth . . .

> "The idea might now be extended somewhat, and we might consider **that great Entity Who is the *informing* life of the planet**, and Who holds all the different kingdoms of nature within His consciousness. **May it not be possible that *His intelligence*, as it *informs* the *totality* of all groups and kingdoms, is *the goal for man***, the human atom?" (Alice Bailey; emphasis added)[78]

> "'**Evolution is a continually accelerating march** of all the particles of the universe which leads them ... **from the material atom to that universal consciousness** in which *omnipotence* and **omniscience** are realised: in a word, to the full realisation of **the Absolute of God**.'" (Alice Bailey; emphasis added)[79]

> "... **the consciousness of the great planetary Spirit**, which may perhaps be **best expressed in the term 'group consciousness.'**... Group consciousness, again, *will logically lead on* to that which we, for lack of a better term, might call **God consciousness**, though I deprecate the use of the word God because of the many quarrels it causes in the world ... When **the scientist**, for instance, speaks of **force**, or **energy**, and **the Christian** speaks of **God**, and **the Hindu** uses terms analogous to **the 'I am that I am,'** or **the Self**, they are all speaking of **one and the same** great life ..." (Alice Bailey; emphasis added)[80]

> "[A]fter merging his identity with the group—although never losing it—**the group itself has to be *blended* again with the consciousness of that great Identity Who is the synthesis of them *all***. Thus he [man] arrives at the final stage of intelligent appreciation of **divine unity**....
>
> "[T]he group consciousness itself will be merged in that of **the Aggregate of *all* groups**....
>
> "**What lies ahead for man? Simply the *expansion* of his *consciousness* to include the consciousness of the great life, or being, in whose body he is himself a cell**." (Alice Bailey; emphasis added)[81]

In other words, just *expand* your "consciousness"—or *thinking*—to go *outside* the "box" of God's Word of truth. This way, you can align your mind with the design of the all-encompassing *whole* "God" and thereby "transcend" the "limitation" of the <u>Holy</u> Spirit Who inspired the "narrow creeds" of *truth* and *falsehood* and *right* and *wrong*—an inspiration that <u>hinders</u> the whole process of <u>Oneness</u>. These "narrow creeds" that are to be *believed* and *obeyed* just aren't facilitative of Oneness and its emerging "*God* consciousness" that seeks to be *omniscient*, or all-<u>knowing</u>. That is, these "narrow creeds" of *what <u>is</u> truth and falsehood* and *right and wrong* are a hindrance to mankind's determined attempt to *become* its own "*God*" in this one big historical circle dance that goes all the way back to Genesis.

> "Thus, in summing up, we have four states of intelligent activity, which we might term consciousness, self-consciousness, group consciousness, and **God consciousness**....
>
> "[Robert] Browning expresses this idea of the gradual ***expansion* of the *consciousness*** of a human being into something greater and vaster in the following words:—
>
>> "'... **For *narrow creeds* of right and wrong, which *fade* ...**'" (Alice Bailey; emphasis added)[82]

> "As Browning has said: 'In man begins anew a tendency to God.' He is not a God yet, but **a God in the making**; ..." (Alice Bailey; emphasis added)[83]

"[A] God in the making"—a "tendency" that according to Bailey is "latent in the atom, in man, and in *all that is*."[84] But man's tendency to *godhood* is only a "God *consciousness,"* right?

> "The word **consciousness** comes from two Latin words: *con*, with; and *scio*, to know; and means literally '**that with which we know**.'" (Alice Bailey; bold added)[85]

> "**Yea, hath God said ...?** ... *your eyes shall be opened,* **and ye shall be as gods, knowing** *good and evil.*" *(Genesis 3:1b, 5)*

> "To be capable of being inspired means that a human mind has reached a stage in his evolution where he is **consciously** and positively **under the control of his** *own* **higher self, the God within. That inner** **ruler***,* **the real** *self,* can, by definite contact, control his physical brain, and enable the man to make decisions, and to understand the truth, apart from the *reasoning* faculty altogether; **this inner God** can enable the man to speak, to write, and to pass on the truth without the use of the lower mind. **Truth lies within ourselves**. When we can contact **our own inner God** all truth will be revealed to us. **We shall be Knowers**." (Alice Bailey; emphasis added)[86]

As a matter of fact this *is* only a "consciousness." And this "consciousness" is a *mind* game that has eternal consequences. In this mind game, rather than following those "narrow creeds of right and wrong" that are given to us by God in the Word of God, people can instead "know" whatever is "right" and "wrong" in their *own* eyes, thereby becoming their *own* god and ruler. So why would they see the need for *God* to be their God when they can be their own?

For starters, people aren't going to see the need to believe and obey God's Word when *everyone/everything* is "God's Information." This emerging faith/New Quantum Spirituality of Oneness/panentheism is diabolically convenient. When a "God" "*informs* the *totality* of all groups and kingdoms"—i.e., when the *totality* of the universe/"cosmos" is the "*information*" of "*God*"—people can find the information of "God" *wherever* they *choose* to look for it. No absolute *truth and falsehood* or *right and wrong*; just relative *information*. Nothing to *believe* and *obey* and *teach*; just *conversation* and *relationship*.

Thus, rather than know the information of *God's Word*, people can instead know the information of *everyone/everything* and *decide for themselves* what they are *willing* to believe. This way they can live by their own inner "knowing." Never mind that to be "God's Information"—"Information" lying "hidden at the heart of the atom" that is bringing all of life *in formation as the whole* "*God*"—is indeed the lie that "you are all *Gods in formation*," or "*ye shall be as gods*." The more subtle phrase "God's Information" is seemingly more justifiable in this cosmic circle dance of "evolving"/forming *into* "*God*." And, besides, in this emerging faith/New Quantum Spirituality "all that exists is *spirit*," so "*spirituality*" is "nothing more than *life itself*." So why would people see the need to repent of a "spirituality"—and a "*spiritual*" "*evolution*"—of all of life that is rendering them "*Gods in formation*"? Isn't it just *life*? Sweet writes:

> "**There is no spiritual life**. There is **only life**. **One life** where **the spiritual is not separate but the whole**." (emphasis added)[87]

> "Can you **let life become what it wants to become**, to content yourself with fumbling in the dark, and to play with life to paint a picture of transcendental beauty?" (emphasis added)[88]

"**God is** the Spirit of the universe, the consciousness of the cosmos: its energy, **its information**, its thought." (emphasis added)[89]

And the seducing spirit world writes:

"Spirituality … is universal. All people participate in it….

"This is because **'spirituality' is nothing more than life itself**, as it is….

"The only discussion left then is whether **life and God are the same things**. And I tell you, they are….

"Again I tell you, the words life and God are interchangeable. If the process you are observing is **the process of life in formation**, then it is as I have said to you before: **you are all Gods in formation**. That is, **you are God's Information**." (the seducing spirit calling itself "God;" bold added)[90]

Again, so why would people see the need for *God* to be their God when they can be their own? And why would they see the need for *salvation* when this emerging faith that gives everyone the "love and freedom" of Self-Rule offers them an *unconditional/ universal* salvation? Once again, according to the article "Re-writing the Story of Who We Are" in *Noetic Now* ("*Noetic*" meaning "*inner knowing*"[91]):

"In his 2009 book, *Spontaneous Evolution: Our Positive Future (and a Way to Get There from Here)*, coauthored with Steve Bhaerman, Bruce Lipton writes that '… the critical mass of humanity involved with **this evolution will change the world from the inside out. We are living positive future, practicing Heaven, and designing a bridge across which the whole of humanity will walk**. … This is our love story, a universal love story for the entire Universe – you, me, everyone, and every living organism too.'" (last ellipsis dots in the original)[92]

And according to the Global Consciousness Project website:

"… Pierre Teilhard de Chardin postulated that **the noosphere** is composed of all the interacting minds on Earth. The word refers to **a transhuman consciousness emerging** from our interactions **to become a guiding intelligence for the earth**.

"**Evolution** starts with particles that coalesce to become atoms and then molecules and eventually complicated molecules. These become life building blocks from which smaller and then larger animals emerge and eventually you have us, self-aware animals. While that has been quite a run, ***it's not over*. There is at least one more stage, in which we become a new organ of consciousness for the earth**, evolving into something analogous to the cerebral cortex in humans. We can, and to survive, I think **we must, engage in *conscious evolution* to decide what the future will be**.

"My favorite picture is that we are all already participants in a giant interaction, similar to that between the neurons in a brain…. I think we are participating already in something that is a higher level of consciousness and that for all we know, could even be conscious and self-aware already….

"So we have a capability and a responsibility for changing the world **so that the future is brighter**, and **it depends on coalescing into *a greater consciousness***." (emphasis added)[93]

A bridge of *universal* salvation ("across which the whole of humanity" in revolution against God intends to walk to "Heaven") *cannot exist* apart from a universal freedom of everyone following their own "inner knowing." To believe in a *universal salvation* is to believe in this *universal freedom*. And those who are aligning their minds in this universal freedom are those who are "coalescing"/"evolving" into—i.e., shifting to—a "*God* consciousness" in which "*narrow creeds ... fade.*" No matter how many workmen participate in "conscious evolution" and align their minds to build a bridge of universal salvation (not to mention a new "God" of Oneness), again, this work of universal Oneness will never reach unto heaven, even if it's "held together by glue, lots of glue."

To put it mildly, it boggles the mind that man actually believes in the "scientific" absurdities of evolution at all, let alone in its culmination—a "spiritual" formation of *a whole "God."* As also used to be obvious before the shift away from the truth of God's Word, the *true* God did not create *evolution*. Among other things, this would place *death before Adam* and thus *death before sin* which would make the truth and purpose of the true Gospel of Christ *a lie*--e.g., see Romans 5 and 1 Corinthians 15. But, of course, making the true Gospel of Christ a "lie" is *essential* to making the false "gospel" of Oneness "true." In other words, making the true Gospel of Christ *a "lie"* is *essential* to believing in the "God" of Oneness that is *in everyone and everything*. And it is *this* "God" that is working to "evolve" everyone and everything *back into "God."* It is not the *true* God that is evolving back into itself via the zoo. *God* did not create *evolution* any more than *evolution* creates *God*. But, sadly, when people are desperate for an alternative to the truth of the true God and His Son, they will obviously believe *anything*. They even see it as absurd to <u>not</u> believe that man has evolved upward from apes (or apelike "hominids"). People can believe evolutionary absurdities all they want, but apes (or *any* nonhuman creature for that matter) are *not* in the genealogy of *God's Son*.

> *"For that they hated knowledge, and did not choose the fear of the LORD: They would none of my counsel: they despised all my reproof. Therefore shall they eat of the fruit of their own way, and be filled with their own devices." (Proverbs 1:29-31)*

> *"But though we, or an angel from heaven, preach any other gospel unto you than that which we have preached unto you, let him be accursed. As we said before, so say I now again, If any man preach any other gospel unto you than that ye have received, let him be accursed. For do I now persuade men, or God? or do I seek to please men? for if I yet pleased men, I should not be the servant of Christ." (Galatians 1:8-10)*

Obviously, knowing and believing in the Lord Jesus Christ is completely irrelevant on a specially-designed bridge of *universal* salvation and Oneness. Rather, since this is a universal bridge that must therefore bridge *all polar opposites*, it just takes a "leap" of (r)evolutionary faith from one end of the line to the other—in a curved fashion of course. It is therefore fitting that Pierre Teilhard de Chardin wrote that "Evolution" is "a curve that all lines must follow."[94] With these (r)evolutionary "leaps" bridging *all opposites* in circles of Oneness, everyone has the "love and freedom" to simply "know" whatever they choose to "know" according to their own inner "knowing" of whatever they *decide for themselves* is true or false and right or wrong. After all, in this emerging faith/"God consciousness":

"Of course, no one seriously suggests that the Bible is to be taken literally." (Neale Donald Walsch)[95]

Sadly, not wanting to take God at His Word is the whole point of it *all*, and has been throughout man's history. Again, those who don't learn from history are bound to repeat it. And, absurdities notwithstanding, although the circle of "evolution" is coming full circle—basically, from "God" to apelike creatures to man and back to "God"—and is thus returning to its "point of origin," in truth, what is coming full circle here is simply the lie of "*ye shall be as gods*" complete with the "*knowing good and evil.*" This emerging faith of Oneness is returning to its true point of origin—man's *fall* in the Garden of Eden. It's all about wanting the freedom to *choose* rather than be told *what is* true or false and right or wrong. And, since uncertainty opens the door to freedom, all people have to do to feel *justified* in this desired freedom is *question* whether or not God actually said what He meant and meant what He said in His Word of truth . . .

> *"Yea, **hath God said ...?** ... Ye shall not surely die: For God doth know that in the day ye eat thereof, then your eyes shall be opened, and ye shall **be as gods, knowing good and evil**." (Genesis 3:1b, 4-5)*

"The New Spirituality is ... a call to **expanded consciousness**....

"It will be *the Evolution Revolution*....

"It is **a coming full circle**.... **You are on a circle, from the fullness of knowing** to the emptiness of forgetfulness **to the fullness of knowing again**. From Oneness to Separation to Oneness again....

"It encompasses All and it encloses All and it includes All, because it IS All....

"All that will be asked of you is that you **open your mind**." (the seducing spirit calling itself "God;" all emphases added, except caps)[96]

"[Robert] Browning expresses this idea of the gradual **expansion of the consciousness** ... in the following words:—

> "'... **For *narrow* creeds of right and wrong, which *fade*** ...'" (Alice Bailey; emphasis added)[97]

"'**Right' and 'wrong' are philosophical polarities** in a human value system **which have nothing to do with ultimate reality** ... values which keep shifting from time to time.

"**You are doing the *shifting*, *changing* your mind about these values as it suits you** (which rightly you should, **as *evolving* beings**) ... You keep changing your values, all the while proclaiming that it is unchanging values which you . . . well, *value*!

"The answer to the problems presented by this paradox is not to throw cold water on the sand in an attempt to make it concrete, but to **celebrate the shifting of the sand**. Celebrate its beauty while it holds itself in the shape of your castle, but then also **celebrate the new form and shape** it takes as the tide comes in." (the seducing spirit calling itself "God;" parentheses & 3rd ellipsis dots in the original; emphasis added, except to *value*)[98]

"So change! Yes, change! **Change your ideas of 'right' and 'wrong.'**...

"**Allow your deepest truths to be altered**.... **Your new idea of What Is So**

PART FIVE: THE CREATION 403

is where *evolution* accelerates. Your new idea of the Who, What, Where, When, How, and Why of it is where the mystery gets solved, the plot unravels, the story ends. **Then you can begin *a new story*, and a grander one.**" (the seducing spirit calling itself "God;" emphasis added)[99]

"[H]ell does not exist as this *place* you have fantasized, where you burn in some everlasting fire, or exist in some state of everlasting torment. What purpose could I have in that?...

"**[I]t is not My plan that you shall be separated from Me forever and ever.** Indeed, such a thing is **an impossibility**—for to achieve such an event, **not only would *you* have to deny Who You Are—I would have to as well**....

"I tell you this: ***You* are your own rule-maker**." (the seducing spirit calling itself "God;" bold added)[100]

So instead of believing and obeying *God's* Word of truth, just do what *you* want and "celebrate the shifting of the sand." This way, as the tide/floods come in you can "celebrate the new form and shape" that your castle/house takes as it is wiped out on the sand.

"And every one that heareth these sayings of mine, and doeth them not, shall be likened unto a foolish man, which built his house upon the sand: And the rain descended, and the floods came, and the winds blew, and beat upon that house; and it fell: and great was the <u>fall</u> of it." (Matthew 7:26-27)

Even Neale Donald Walsch knows that "putting oneself in the role of *self-ruler*" is to be "in the role of *God*."[101] But in this "civil rights movement for the soul"[102] that is setting everyone free from *what is* truth and falsehood, right and wrong, there is no "*fall*" right? Doesn't it all just become an "*evolutionary <u>leap</u>*" into a "God *consciousness*" in which the "narrow creeds of *right and wrong ... fade*" so that "*we* are Those In Charge"? Why would there be a <u>fall</u> in this "<u>upward</u> journey"?

"Our creation of a New Spirituality does not begin with us abandoning our faith tradition. This is not about rejecting religion. It is, in fact, about reinvigorating it, enlivening it, refreshing it....

"... Life Itself calls upon us to edge forward, *move forward*, push forward the limit of human understanding, to set the stage for the next great *quantum leap*, and to *never, ever fall back*.

"**Evolution is an *upward* journey, not a downward spiral**....

"**Religions now have an opportunity to *shift* ...**" (Neale Donald Walsch; emphasis added)[103]

So even those in today's Christianity can freely and fearlessly "*celebrate* the shifting of the sand" and "*celebrate* the *new* form and shape" that today's Christianity is taking (which is a new anti-Christian "Christianity") as the "tide" (or, rather, *spiritual tsunami*) of the emerging faith of Oneness comes in. After all, no one need fear *falling away* from the *right* faith—"*the faith which was once delivered unto the saints*" (Jude 1:3)—especially since in this emerging faith of Oneness "'[r]ight' and 'wrong' are *philosophical polarities ...* which have *nothing to do with* ultimate reality." Why do they "have nothing to do with *ultimate reality*"? Because polarities/opposites are a *line*, and in this emerging faith of *Oneness* "Ultimate Reality is actually a *circle*"—an *all-encompassing* "circle." And this all-encompassing "*circle*" is not only the "*Kingdom*" of "God"—it *is* "God."

> "Since God wished to Know Itself *experientially* as well as conceptually, God created a place in **the Kingdom** (or, if you will, in **Ultimate Reality**) where **all that God Is** could be *experienced* as well as *known*.
>
> "God did this by *dividing Itself up* into **a million ka-jillion different parts**, ... Then **any Part of The Whole** (that is, any Individuated Aspect of Divinity) **could look back on The Whole** from which It emerged **and say, 'Oh, my God, how magnificent Thou art!'**" (Neale Donald Walsch; all parentheses in the original; bold & underline added)[104]

> "You see, **the Ultimate Reality is actually a circle. One rounded whole. The energy of life travels in this circle**, through all eternity. It is the cycle of life. **In the beginning, God WAS this circle**, in place AS the circle, complete. **When God individuated Itself, it sent the individual Aspects of Divinity on a journey around the circle.** So fast did these **infinitesimal bits and pieces of God** travel that they seemed to be everywhere all the time. Like a tire spinning so fast that it seems like a solid circle not moving at all, so, too, the cycle of life replicated the Always Everywhere-ness of God by **seeming to create a solid** where there were **really moving parts**.
>
> "**By dividing itself up into a million ka-jillion such parts**, each part could look back upon The Whole and suddenly have **a context within which to consider the magnificence of The Whole—and thus, to *know* God.** Yet how could **each** of the Individuated Aspects also **know *Itself* as God**? That was the question! While each Individuation raced through the cycle of life, how would it know what it really was? **Seeing the rest of It, would it know that It WAS the rest of it, in singular part?**...
>
> "Ah, there's the twist. And so, in order to ensure this, **the Circle that is God twisted itself to form a figure 8**, reasoning that if at *one point* both sides of the circle could touch, then **the Totality of Being God** could at that point be known and experienced by every one of God's Individuations!!!
>
> "*Do you get it? Do you see it now???*
>
> "**Each Individuated Aspect of Divinity**, traveling on its journey through the endless cycle of life, may both know and experience Itself as **Who It Really Is** at any place on that cycle....
>
> "***This is what God is up to!***
>
> "God is doing this **through the reformation and the transformation of every aspect of Itself, *one aspect at a time*.**" (Neale Donald Walsch; bold added)[105]

It isn't the *true* God that is a circle dance of cosmic divinity/deity/godhood. This "secret of the cosmic incarnation" "that lies hidden at the heart of the atom" is the "secret" of the false immanent "God" of the merging and emerging "Christian"/New Age faith of Oneness. And this "God" gives everyone the universal freedom/"salvation" of the all-encompassing circle of Oneness because this "God" *is* the all-encompassing circle of Oneness. *No* duality. *No* separateness. *No* opposites. In other words, this "God" of Oneness is one cosmic circle dance of "Being God"—and, thus, of just simply "*Being*"— however one *chooses*, of course.

Since Oneness and its all-encompassing "God" bring *all* opposites together as one in a "cosmic web" of infinitely intertwined circles (strips) of *all* polar opposites in existence, a "reality" of Oneness is a "reality" of *infinite choices*. And a "reality" of infinite choices is obviously a "reality" of *Self-Rule*, which is a very real and true *revolution—against God*. This was the reason for man's fall in the Garden of Eden in the first place. Today, man is *still* unwilling to believe that God said what He meant and meant what He said. Nevertheless, God is *still* to be believed and obeyed. And even though people today believe that the "cosmic web" of Oneness (and its infinite choices) is "scientific," the many *lies* of Oneness are *not* in God's Word of *truth* for *a reason*.

> *"I have not written unto you because ye know not the truth, but because ye know it, and that **no lie is of the truth**." (1 John 2:21)*

> *"But evil men and seducers shall wax worse and worse, deceiving, and being deceived. But continue thou in the things which thou hast learned and hast been assured of, knowing of whom thou hast learned them; and that from a child thou hast known the holy scriptures, which are able to make thee wise unto salvation through faith which is in Christ Jesus. All scripture is given by inspiration of God, and is profitable for doctrine, for reproof, for correction, for instruction in righteousness." (2 Timothy 3:13-16)*

51

Creating Oneness --
"part dance; part sorcery, part science"

"C is for Connectivity …

"The experience of the self as a part of others—'We are all related'—is one of the most spiritual of experiences. **Everything is related**. Nothing exists in isolation.…

"***The threads of a spider's web are drawn out from within the spider's very being***. The threads in **the web's concentric circles are sticky**. The threads leading to the center are smooth.

"For *the way* to be made smooth to life's only true center—Jesus the Christ—**the circles of life must be gluey with connections**." (Leonard Sweet, Brian McLaren, & Jerry Haselmayer; emphasis added)[1]

It used to be obvious that a spider's web is "gluey" to catch and devour its *prey*: "Why Aren't Spider's Caught in Their Own Webs? A spider's web has two kinds of threads in it. The ones that make a spiral or circle pattern are sticky. The other threads are not. Those are the ones that the spider walks on. That is why he does not get caught."[2] Did you catch that? Since the spider spins the sticky/gluey circles to *catch its prey, it does not walk on the sticky/gluey circles* in order to avoid being *caught in the web*. And yet, sadly, people in this emerging faith *see these circles of the web as the way of life and are blindly flocking to these sticky/gluey circles on purpose. Easy prey*.

Fritjof Capra writes that "[i]n modern physics, the image of the universe" is "as one *indivisible, dynamic whole* whose parts are essentially *interrelated* and can be understood only as patterns of a *cosmic process*."[3] And in this "*indivisible, dynamic whole*," "the subatomic world appears as a *web* of *relations* between the various parts of a *unified* whole."[4] Essential to forming this *"web of relations"*—this *unification of parts*—is its *"activity"*:

> "Relativity theory has made **the cosmic web** come alive, so to speak, by revealing its intrinsically dynamic character; by showing that **its activity is the very essence of its being**." (Fritjof Capra; emphasis added)[5]

> "The universe is engaged in ceaseless *motion* and *activity*, in a continual *cosmic process* that the Chinese called Tao—**the Way**." (Fritjof Capra; emphasis added)[6]

And, of course, *"the Way"*—i.e., the *"activity"* of the *"cosmic web"*—is simply *moving* and *dancing* in *circles* in order to *unify* all opposites. Capra writes:

> "**The dynamic unity of polar opposites can be illustrated with** the simple example of a **circular** motion and its projection. Suppose you have a ball **going round a circle**. If this movement is projected on to a screen, it becomes an oscillation between *two extreme points*.... In any projection of that kind, **the circular movement will appear as an oscillation between two opposite points, but *in the movement itself* the opposites are *unified* and *transcended*.**" (emphasis added)[7]

> "The reality of the atomic *physicist*, like the reality of the Eastern *mystic*, **transcends the narrow framework of opposite concepts**....

> "Faced with a reality which lies beyond opposite concepts, physicists and mystics have to adopt **a special way of thinking**, where the mind is not fixed in the rigid framework of classical logic, but **keeps *moving* and changing its viewpoint**.... In the words of Lama Govinda, 'The Eastern way of thinking rather consists in a **circling round the object of contemplation** ... a many-sided, i.e., multi-dimensional impression formed from the superimposition of single impressions **from *different* points of view**.'" (last ellipsis dots in the original; emphasis added)[8]

Along with this *circular* thinking that purposely dances around the truth, this "special way of thinking" is simply *not* thinking. The two go hand in hand. This "spirituality" of Oneness is, after all, not about believing and obeying *God*, but about *self*.

> "It [*The Tao of Physics*] attempts to suggest that modern physics goes far beyond technology, that **the way**—or Tao—of physics can be a path with a heart, **a way to *spiritual* knowledge and *self*-realization**." (Fritjof Capra; emphasis added)[9]

> "A fool hath no delight in understanding, but that his heart may discover <u>itself</u>." (Proverbs 18:2)

> "Ever learning, and never able to come to the knowledge of <u>the truth</u>." (2 Timothy 3:7)

> "In the East ... it has always been considered as essential for attaining **enlightenment** to go **'beyond earthly opposites'** ..." (Fritjof Capra; emphasis added)[10]

> "The awareness that *all opposites* are polar, and thus a *unity*, is seen as one of *the highest aims of man* in the spiritual traditions of the East. 'Be in truth eternal,

beyond earthly opposites!' is Krishna's advice in the *Bhagavad Gita*, and the same advice is given to the followers of Buddhism....

"The whole of Buddhist teaching—and in fact the whole of Eastern mysticism—revolves about this absolute point of view which **is reached in the world of** *acintya*, or '*no-thought*', where **the unity of** *all* **opposites becomes a vivid experience.**" (Fritjof Capra; emphasis added, except to *acintya*)[11]

"The notion that all opposites are polar—that **light and dark, ... good and evil**, are **merely** *different* **aspects of** *the same* **phenomenon**—is one of the basic principles of **the Eastern** *way* **of life.**" (Fritjof Capra; emphasis added)[12]

"If the foundations be destroyed, what can the righteous do?" (Psalm 11:3)

"The wicked, through the pride of his countenance, will not seek after God: God is not in all his thoughts.... thy judgments are far above out of his sight ..." (Psalm 10:4-5)

"<u>Woe</u> unto them that call evil good, and good evil; that put darkness for light, and light for darkness; *that put bitter for sweet, and sweet for bitter! <u>Woe</u> unto them that are wise in their own eyes, and prudent in their own sight!"* (Isaiah 5:20-21)

Keep in mind that along with "Be in truth eternal, beyond earthly opposites!," also "summed up for us in the statement of Shri Krishna in *The Bhagavad Gita*: 'Having pervaded this whole Universe with a *fragment* of *Myself*, I remain'. God, greater than the created whole, yet God present also *in the part*."[13] And since the *defragging* of this *panentheistic* whole "God," as well as its whole "truth," is a defragging of *everyone* and *everything* including *all religions* and *all gods*, those who would participate in this circle dance certainly won't see any need to fear *destroyed foundations* or *woes*.

It is without question that *thinking* hinders the Oneness that comes from uniting *all opposites*—which includes *uniting the true God and false gods*. So it is not at all surprising that this unity must take place in the world of "*no-thought*." (And, again, this certainly explains a whole lot.) This "Way" to "spiritual knowledge" that is *hindered by thinking* is *not* "the way" of the true God and His Son. *Think* about it! This is the antithesis of God's Word of truth. Yes, *God's* Word is a Word of *words* that are to be *believed* and *obeyed*. And, obviously, both *believing* and *obeying* require *thinking*.

"**To** *free* **the human mind from words** and explanations is one of the main aims of Eastern mysticism.... **To** *transcend* **words** and explanations **means to** break the bonds of *karma* and **attain <u>liberation</u>**." (Fritjof Capra; emphasis added, except to *karma*)[14]

"Jesus said unto them, ... He that is of God heareth God's <u>words</u>: ye therefore hear them not, because ye are not of God." *(John 8:42, 47)*

To attain this "liberation" is to attain liberation *from God*. But, sadly, those who want freedom from the *words* of God really do want freedom from *God Himself*. People today want a *different* "God"—a new and "*better*" "God" that has *no expectations* for man. A "God" that wants *nothing* from man does not expect to be *believed* and *obeyed*. And, of course, a "God" that wants *nothing* from man gives all of mankind an *uncondi-*

tional, universal salvation. This way, everyone can just live life *however they choose.*

> "**God and Life are the same thing**.
>
> "You may call these things by two different names, but they are the same thing. God is what Life is, and Life is what God is. **God is the energy that you call Life, and Life is the energy that you call God.** It is all the same thing." (the seducing spirit calling itself "God;" bold added)[15]
>
> "**What does God want?**
>
> "Nothing.
>
> "**Absolutely nothing at all**." (Neale Donald Walsch; bold added)[16]
>
> "If in fact the words 'God' and 'life' are describing the same thing . . . well, we have some major, *major* theological implications here.
>
> "Do we need more evidence of the existence of life than life itself? No. And what does *life* want? Nothing. **Life simply is**." (Neale Donald Walsch; ellipsis dots in the original; bold added)[17]

Conveniently, life is just *all* part of "God's" "cosmic dance of *energy*"—a "cosmic dance" in which this "energy of life" travels *in a* "*circle.*" And, therefore, the *circular* journey of this "energy of life" becomes the *circular* journey of "*the Way*" of life.

> "You see, the **Ultimate Reality** is actually **a circle**. One rounded whole. **The energy of life travels in this circle**, through all eternity. It is the cycle of life. **In the beginning, God WAS this circle**, in place AS the circle, complete. When God individuated Itself, it sent the individual Aspects of Divinity on **a journey around the circle**." (Neale Donald Walsch; bold added)[18]

And in this journey in which *moving* and *dancing* in *circles* in order to *unify all opposites* is seen as "*the Way,*" not only is this a circle dance that is simply traveling the same circular path as "the energy of life," but this "energy of life" is even imagined to be "*Jesus.*" For example, in Thomas Nelson's aforementioned emerging "Bible translation" *The Voice* (in which Sweet and McLaren are contributors), its "reimagined" John 14:6 reads:

> "**I am** the path, the truth, and **the** *energy of* **life**. No one comes to the Father except through Me." (bold added)[19]

So no one comes to the Father except through "*the energy of life*"? This is conveniently *all-encompassing*. The "Jesus" of *The Voice* is the "path" to *which* "God"? No matter how many "Bible translators" "translate" otherwise, only the *true* Lord Jesus Christ is the way to the *true* God. A "*reimagined*" "*Jesus*" is only the way to a "*reimagined*" "*God.*" And in this case, "*the energy of life*" is just the way to "*the energy of life.*" And, yes, this is indeed the "way to … *self*-realization." In this merging and emerging "Christian"/New Age faith (i.e., New *Quantum* Spirituality), along with its "*Jesus*" being "the energy of life," its "*Father*" is "the energy of life" as well, which of course is a given with an all-encompassing "energy" that *is/is in everyone and everything*:

> "I tell you this: We are all the *same stuff*.

"**We are all the same energy**, coalesced, compressed in different ways to create different forms and different matter.

"Nothing 'matters' in and of itself. That is, nothing can *become matter* all by itself. Jesus said, 'Without the Father, I am nothing.' **The Father of all** is pure thought. This is **the energy of life**....

"There is only One of Us, and so, it is THAT WHICH YOU ARE." (the seducing spirit calling itself "God;" bold & underline added)[20]

The seducing spirit calling itself "God": "***God and Life are the same thing***.... **God is the energy that you call Life**, and Life is the energy that you call God. It is all the same thing. Life is God, *physicalized*."

Neale Donald Walsch: "**So, if we believe in Life, we believe in God, is that what you're saying?**"

The seducing spirit calling itself "God": "**Yes**." (bold added)[21]

So just believe in the "energy" of "*Life*" and *move* and *dance* in *circles* in order to unify everyone/everything in life. This way, you can participate in the "God" that is whirling and swirling the "cosmic web" into being. And since "its *activity* is the very essence of its *being*,"[22] this "cosmic web" of "God"/"Life"/Oneness becomes one "cosmic dance" of "unity, *expressing*."[23] No *duality*. No *separateness*. No *opposites*.

"... **a God and a World united, expressing as One**, projecting the glory of Life itself *into* life itself, and producing the possibility, at last, of **a New Way of Life for All Humanity**." (Neale Donald Walsch; bold added)[24]

"**It IS Life, expressing AS Life, THROUGH Life, which <u>process</u> is circular** and cyclical and circumferential. **It encompasses All** and it encloses All and it includes All, **because it IS All**." (the seducing spirit calling itself "God;" bold & underline added)[25]

But this circular "Way of Life" is just dancing to the tune/music/way of "*Jesus*," "*the energy of life*," right?

"**Jesus spent more time drawing *circles* to include people than in drawing lines** to keep people out." (Leonard Sweet; emphasis added)[26]

"We need to learn to **dance to the music of Jesus** once again." (Leonard Sweet; emphasis added)[27]

"**He ['Jesus'] is** the melody, the harmony, the rhythm, the tempo, and **the music behind *all* things**." (Leonard Sweet & Frank Viola; emphasis added)[28]

"Life isn't sacred and secular. ***There is only life***....

"You can't separate the secular and the sacred; **you can't polarize the sacred and the profane. The doctrine of the incarnation ... won't allow it**." (Leonard Sweet; emphasis added)[29]

"Jesus the dancers' master is, **A great skill at the dance is his, He turns to the right, he turns to the left,** All must follow his teaching deft." (Leonard Sweet quoting Catholic mystic and monk Bernard of Clairvaux; emphasis added)[30]

"In fact, **the incarnation brought *all* dualities together**, whether it be **the clean and the profane, the sacred and the secular**, or the '*out there*' and the '*in here*.'" (Leonard Sweet; emphasis added)[31]

This circular "Way" that is whirling and swirling the "cosmic web" into being is not a dance of the Lord Jesus Christ. The true *Person* of Jesus Christ is *God*, and God—whether Father, Son, or Holy Spirit—does not *ever* violate His own Word of truth.

"... they have put no difference between the holy and profane, neither have they shown difference between the unclean and the clean, ... and I am profaned among them." (Ezekiel 22:26)

"Therefore hearken unto me ye men of understanding: far be it from God, that he should do wickedness; and from the Almighty, that he should commit iniquity." (Job 34:10)

"Ponder the path of thy feet, and let all thy ways be established. **Turn not to the right hand nor to the left: remove thy foot from evil.**" (Proverbs 4:26-27)

"This is the 3-D dance of the divine, which the church fathers called '*perichoresis*,' or '**circle dance**,' ... At the heart of the divine is a dance, and **the divine itself is a dance. Motion. Movement. God created us to be dancing partners, to join in the dance,** to make the Trinity *a quaternity*, if you will, **as we dance to the tune of Jesus**." (Leonard Sweet; emphasis added)[32]

Which "God" wants man to be "dancing partners"?? *Obviously*, this is not "a dance" of the true God, and neither is it to "the tune" of His Son.

"**In Christ *all opposites* are** not so much reconciled as ***transcended*** in the Oneness of Twoness that becomes Threeness." (Leonard Sweet; emphasis added)[33]

"[T]heologian/evangelism professor William J. Abraham says it best: 'It is perfectly consistent to hold *both* that Jesus is the exclusive path to God *and* that people may **genuinely encounter God** outside the Christian church **without explicitly knowing about Jesus of Nazareth**.'" (Leonard Sweet; emphasis added)[34]

Despite today's determined dance to "transcend" *truth and falsehood, right and wrong*, Jesus of Nazareth *is* Jesus; *period*. And Jesus of Nazareth *is* Christ; *period*. This dance around the truth of the true *Person* of God's Son in order to "transcend" *all opposites* is neither "a dance" of nor to "the tune" of *Jesus of Nazareth*. But, of course, this is the whole point. Since Oneness *cannot* exist apart from dancing around the truth of the Lord Jesus Christ, Oneness is a dance to the tune of "*another Jesus*" that is an all-inclusive way to an all-inclusive "God." The dance of this broad "*way*" that moves and dances in circles around *the truth of Jesus Christ of Nazareth* is "*the way*" to destruction, not *life*. This is *not* "the way" of *Jesus*.

"Jesus saith unto him, I am the way, the truth, and the life: **no man cometh unto the Father, but by me.**" (John 14:6)

> *"Be it known unto you all, and to all the people of Israel, that by the name of **Jesus Christ of Nazareth**, whom ye crucified, whom God raised from the dead, ... This is the stone which was set at nought of you builders, which is become the head of the corner. **Neither is there salvation in any other: for there is none other name under heaven given among men, whereby we must be saved.**" (Acts 4:10-12)*

> *"Enter ye in at the strait gate: for wide is the gate, and **broad is the way, that leadeth to destruction**, and many there be which go in thereat: Because strait is the gate, and **narrow is the way, which leadeth unto life, and <u>few</u> there be that <u>find it</u>**." (Matthew 7:13-14)*

> *"... **a narrow place, where was <u>no way</u> to turn either to the right hand or to the left**." (Numbers 22:26)*

> *"And **thou shalt not go <u>aside</u> from any of the <u>words</u>** which I command thee this day, **to the right hand, or to the left, to go after <u>other gods</u> to serve them**." (Deuteronomy 28:14)*

And yet according to two of the writers of Thomas Nelson's new "Bible" *The Voice*:

> **"V is for Voice** ...
> "**And what postmoderns are listening for is less <u>words</u>** than the music of the spheres, especially the heavenly spheres, but **sometimes the <u>dances</u> of demons**." (Leonard Sweet, Brian McLaren, & Jerry Haselmayer; emphasis added)[35]

Indeed. For starters, the depths to which those in this emerging faith are willing to journey for Oneness is unbelievable. Yet they just turn around and absurdly tell us that "*you can't polarize the sacred and the profane*" because "[t]he doctrine of the *incarnation*" "*won't allow it.*"[36] In other words, the justification for the depths of their journey is the *blasphemy* of this emerging faith of Oneness/panentheism in which "*the incarnation goes all the way down, and the Spirit indwells <u>all</u> that exists.*"[37] But, of course, this *blasphemy* is "*scientific.*" So in this emerging faith/New Quantum Spirituality, <u>all</u> that exists blasphemously becomes just a different "*energy* pattern" of "*God*" in a "cosmic dance" of *quantum Oneness* that conveniently unites "*the sacred and the profane*"—"<u>all</u> *the way down.*"

This dance of Oneness is indeed a dance that *turns aside* to the right and to the left to the tune of—i.e., "*to go after*"—"*other gods,*" and this includes *Shiva*, the "King" of the dancing *devils*. And, by the way, Shiva is fittingly known as "*the Destroyer.*"

> "**Shiva is the Divine Dancer**, visualized in terms of **motion** and vibration, ...
>> "'The source of all **movement**, Shiva's dance,
>> Gives **rhythm** to **the universe**.
>> *He dances in <u>evil</u> places, In <u>sacred</u>*, ...
>> And woe to us if, blinded By illusions,
>> We detach ourselves From the dancing cosmos,
>> This universal **harmony**...'" (*The Ramagiri Journal*; last ellipsis dots in the original; emphasis added)[38]

> "**Through his dance, Shiva** sustains the manifold phenomena in the world, **unifying all things** by immersing them in his rhythm and making them **participate in the dance**—a magnificent image of the dynamic unity of the universe." (Fritjof Capra; emphasis added)[39]

> "**Faith** makes a metanoized mulch of <u>all</u> dichotomized <u>selves</u> and **heals all discursive dualisms (one of the worst of which was '<u>sacred</u>' and '<u>profane</u>')** …" (Leonard Sweet; parentheses in the original; emphasis added)[40]

> "At the heart of the divine is a dance, and **the divine itself is a dance. Motion. Movement**. God created us to be dancing partners, to **join in the dance**, to make the Trinity *a quaternity*, if you will, as we **dance to the tune of Jesus**." (Leonard Sweet; emphasis added)[41]

> "**He ['Jesus'] is** the melody, the **harmony**, the **rhythm**, the tempo, and the music behind *all* things." (Leonard Sweet & Frank Viola; emphasis added)[42]

No, this dance of Oneness is not to "the tune" of *God's Son*, Jesus Christ of Nazareth.

Sweet, of course, describes Pierre Teilhard de Chardin as "*Twentieth-century Christianity's* major voice."[43] And, along with wanting "to narrow that gap between pantheism and Christianity by bringing out what one might call the Christian soul of pantheism or the pantheist aspect of Christianity,"[44] Teilhard de Chardin wanted to make "*Christ*" more like "*Shiva*"! Ursula King writes:

> "**For Teilhard**, a more sharply defined *'type' of God* is found in **the 'universal Christ'** … This particular concept of God is seen as 'a privileged central *axis*' around which a *convergence of religions* might occur. Yet he also says that man's image of God is not complete; the human discovery of the Divine is an ongoing process. In this sense he speaks of a 'Christic nucleus' or what he calls in his diary 'Christ – the 'spearhead' of monotheism'. On the margin of the same diary entry one can read the addition **'Christ-Shiva'**. I have mentioned before that some months earlier he had noted down that **our understanding of Christ *must* somehow *integrate* those aspects of the Divine expressed by the Indian god Shiva**." [!] (emphasis added)[45]

This is "*Christianity's* major voice"?! And this "Faith" is in <u>whom</u>, exactly? If you take *the aspects of Shiva* and integrate them with a "*reimagined*" "*Christ*" . . .

Think about it! But this dancing "Faith" that "heals" the "'sacred' and 'profane'" is just being "*scientific*," right? After all, it is "the Dance of *Shiva*" that is "this cosmic dance of *energy*." And, of course, Fritjof Capra, a *physicist* who "had become very interested in Eastern mysticism,"[46] describes a mystical experience in which:

> "I was sitting by the ocean one late summer afternoon, watching the waves rolling in and feeling the rhythm of my breathing, when I suddenly became aware of **my whole environment** as being **engaged in a gigantic cosmic dance**. Being a physicist, I knew that **the sand, rocks, water, and air around me** were made of vibrating molecules and atoms, and that these consisted of particles which interacted with one another … As I sat on that beach my former experiences came to life; **I 'saw' cascades of energy coming down from outer space**, in which particles were created and destroyed in rhythmic pulses; **I 'saw' the atoms of**

the elements and those of my body participating in <u>this cosmic dance of energy</u>; I felt its rhythm and I 'heard' its sound, and at that moment **I *knew* that this was <u>the Dance of Shiva</u>**, the Lord of Dancers worshipped by the Hindus." (emphasis added, except italics to *knew*)[47]

First, some food for thought: Why would people in this emerging faith/New Quantum Spirituality see a problem with building their castle/house on the *sand* if they believe they are "scientifically" one with the sand—not to mention with the *water/floods* and the *air/winds*?? Thus, why would they fear a "*fall*" in this "scientific" Oneness, especially since this "cosmic dance of *energy*" is believed to be a "dance" of "secret" subatomic "divinity"/"deity"? Of course, the "secret" "deity" of this dance is *Shiva*. Yet regardless of which god/deity man chooses to see as this cosmic "dancer," the Lord Jesus Christ, Who is the Son of the *true* God, said: "*And every one that heareth these sayings of mine, and doeth them not, shall be likened unto a foolish man, which built his house upon the sand: And the rain descended, and the floods came, and the winds blew, and beat upon that house; and it fell: and great was the <u>fall</u> of it*" (Matthew 7:26-27).

Second, in addition to the quote that "He dances in <u>*evil*</u> places, In <u>*sacred*</u>," the article "The Great Lord Nataraja – the Hadron Collider; what do they have in common?" states:

> "**Shiva** ... is eternal and is also one who **offers *liberation* and *salvation***....
>
> "**Everything ... is Shiva**. What seems to be anything else is non-existent. **The God** of infinite who holds everything and lives **in everything** ..." (*The Ramagiri Journal*; last ellipsis dots in the original; emphasis added)[48]

Of course, CERN's Hadron Collider is racing protons around a *circle* in *opposite* directions to see if they can find "the *God* particle" in this energetic *unification/collision*. After all, this "God particle" is believed to be in everything. So how fitting that at CERN there is an *idol* ("statue") of the Hindu god Shiva in its form of Nataraja ("the Lord of Dance"/"King of Dancers"). It was donated by the Indian government in 2004 "to celebrate the research center's long association with India."[49] And in this same article on what the Hadron Collider and this Hindu god have in common is also the following:

> "**Nataraj, the dancing form of Lord Shiva**, is a symbolic synthesis of the most important aspects of **Hinduism**, and **the summary of the central tenets of this Vedic religion**. The term 'Nataraj' means 'King of Dancers' (Sanskrit nata = dance; raja = king).
>
> "**A special plaque next to the Shiva statue [at CERN] explains the significance** of the metaphor of *Shiva's* cosmic dance **with several quotations from top physicist Fritjof Capra's book – *The Tao of Physics*....**
>
> "'**... for the *modern physicists*, then, *Shiva's* dance is the dance of *subatomic* matter**. Hundreds of years ago, Indian artists created different forms of visual images of dancing Shiva in a beautiful series of bronzes. In our time, physicists have used the most advanced technology to portray the patterns of the cosmic dance. **The metaphor of the cosmic dance thus unifies ancient mythology, religious art and modern physics.**'" (parentheses in the original; emphasis added)[50]

How appropriate that physicist Fritjof Capra likened the work of today's physicists to that of "Indian artists" making idols. And this is indeed a "cosmic dance" that unifies modern physics with ancient *false gods* ("mythology") and *idols* ("religious art"). But this is all just "beautiful" "metaphor" and "symbolism," right? Sweet also writes of "the dance of *Shiva*," in *Quantum Spirituality*:

> **"The symbol for postmodern science** picked by Ilya Prigogine [a Nobel Prize-winning chemist and physicist] **is the dance of Shiva**. In the same way as the clock symbolized science in the seventeenth century and the thermal engine symbolized science in the nineteenth century, so dance--**the transforming dance of Shiva, *the dynamic principle in cosmology*--captures the essence of the contemporary scientific enterprise**. With a *flame* in one hand and a *musical drum* in another, **the dance of *Shiva*** entails both demonstration and reconstruction (as postmodern philosophers would put it), both denunciation and annunciation (in the words of liberation theologians), both night and day....
>
> **"The church has yet to learn to dance, much less find its way in the dark**." (all parentheses in the original; emphasis added)[51]

Actually, if today's shifting Christianity had found its *way* in the *light* it wouldn't be trying to find its *way* in the *dark*. And listening for "the dances of demons" is certainly not going to help it find its way!

> **"[W]hat postmoderns are listening for is less *words*** than the *music* of the spheres, ... **sometimes the dances of demons**." (Leonard Sweet, Brian McLaren, & Jerry Haselmayer; emphasis added)[52]

> "The entrance of **thy *words*** giveth **light**; it giveth understanding unto the simple." (Psalm 119:130)

> "... Can the blind lead the blind? shall they not both fall into the ditch?" (Luke 6:39)

> "To the law and to the testimony: if they speak not according to this *word*, it is because there is no *light* in them." (Isaiah 8:20)

> "They are of those that rebel against the light; they know not the ways thereof, nor abide in the paths thereof." (Job 24:13)

It also definitely speaks volumes about the dark times we live in that the symbol for *science* has gone from a clock to a thermal engine to the dance of *a false god*! But it is fitting, though, given the endless parallels between Shiva and the false "God" of today's emerging faith/New Quantum Spirituality. Capra—who said that he *"knew"* that "the Dance of *Shiva*, the Lord of Dancers worshipped by the Hindus" was the "cosmic dance of energy"—writes that "*Shiva*, the *Cosmic Dancer*, is perhaps the most perfect personification of *the dynamic universe*."[53] Make that of *this whole emerging faith of Oneness*. Case in point, Barbara Marx Hubbard's previously touched-on book, *The Revelation*, essentially an exposition of this emerging faith, was published by *Nataraj* Publishing. Moreover, this idol of Shiva in its form of *Nataraj/Nataraja* (the form displayed at CERN) is a depiction of Shiva dancing on a "demon" (or "dwarf") that symbolizes "ignorance"—which is naturally an ignorance of *Oneness*. In *The Tao of Physics*, in which Capra basically summarizes the emerging faith/New Quantum Spirituality of Oneness, he writes, for instance:

"**Shiva** is one of the oldest Indian gods who **can assume *many forms***." (emphasis added)[54]

"***Shiva's* dance**—in the words of Coomaraswamy—is **'the clearest image of the activity of *God* which any art or religion can boast of'**. As the god is a personification of *Brahman*, his activity is that of *Brahman's* **myriad manifestations** in the world. The dance of Shiva is the *dancing universe*; the ceaseless *flow* of *energy* going through **an *infinite* variety of patterns that melt into one another**." (emphasis added, except to *Brahman*)[55]

"The god is pictured as dancing on the body of *a demon*, the symbol of human *ignorance* which has to be conquered before **liberation** can be attained." (emphasis added)[56]

"The basis of Krishna's spiritual instruction, as of all Hinduism, is **the idea that the multitude of things and events around us are but *different manifestations* of *the same* ultimate reality**. This reality, called *Brahman*, is the unifying concept which gives Hinduism its essentially monistic character in spite of the worship of *numerous gods and goddesses*....

"***[A]ll these gods* are but reflections of the one ultimate reality** ..." (emphasis added, except to *Brahman*)[57]

"The general picture emerging from Hinduism is one of an **organic**, growing and rhythmically moving cosmos; of a universe in which **everything is *fluid and ever-changing*, all *static* forms** being *maya*, that is, **existing only as *illusory* concepts**." (emphasis added, except to *maya*)[58]

"The Eastern mystics tell us again and again that all things and events we perceive are **creations of the mind**, arising from a particular state of consciousness and dissolving again if this state is *transcended*. Hinduism holds that **all shapes and structures** around us are created by a mind under the spell of *maya*, and it regards our tendency **to attach deep significance to them as the basic human illusion**. Buddhists call this illusion *avidya*, or **ignorance**, and see it as the state of **a 'defiled' mind**. In the words of Ashvaghosha,

> "**When the oneness of the totality** of things **is not recognised**, then **ignorance** as well as ***particularisation*** arises, and all phases of **the defiled mind** are thus developed ..." (emphasis added, except to *maya* and *avidya*)[59]

"The basic recurring theme in Hindu mythology is the creation of the world by the self-sacrifice of God—'sacrifice' in the original sense of **'*making sacred'*—whereby God becomes the world which, in the end, *becomes* again God. This creative activity** of the Divine is called *lila*, **the play of God**, and the world is seen as the stage of the divine play." (emphasis added, except to *lila*)[60]

This desired *liberation* from man's "ignorance" of the "truth" of Oneness (i.e., from the so-called "illusion" of absolute truth) and thus from "*particularisation*" (i.e., from the *particular* truth of God's Word) *must* include freedom from *words*. As addressed earlier, in this emerging upside-down faith "that which obscures the light"—i.e., *darkness*—of Oneness is being "gradually removed."[61] And that which "obscures" the darkness is the *light*. So in order to see the *darkness* better to thus *unify and transcend all opposites* (which includes *Christ and Shiva*), those in this emerging faith of Oneness *must turn the light off*. Specifically, they *must* turn off the *particular* light of God's Word. And, therefore, they *must* remove ("transcend") its *words*. Again:

> "**The <u>entrance</u> of thy <u>words</u> giveth <u>light</u>; it giveth <u>understanding</u> unto the simple.**" *(Psalm 119:130)*

Obviously, the understanding that *God's* words give is *in no way, shape, or form* an "understanding of *Christ*" that seeks to "*integrate* those aspects of the Divine expressed by the Indian god *Shiva*"! But, sadly, nothing is obvious to those who are fearlessly looking in *the darkness* for God.

> "*The fear of the* LORD *is the beginning of wisdom: and* **the knowledge of the holy is understanding.**" *(Proverbs 9:10)*

> "... *Behold, the fear of the Lord, that is wisdom; and* **to depart from evil is understanding.**" *(Job 28:28)*

> "*By mercy and truth iniquity is purged: and* **by the fear of the** LORD **men depart from evil**.... **The highway of the upright is to depart from evil**: *he that keepeth his way preserveth his soul*.... **Understanding is a wellspring of life unto him that hath it: but the instruction of fools is folly**.... **There is a way that seemeth right unto a man, but the end thereof are the ways of death.**" *(Proverbs 16:6, 17, 22, 25)*

It is the entrance of *God's words* that give *light*. But to those who prefer Oneness, this light gives the *shunned* understanding of *what is truth and falsehood* and *what is right and wrong*. And even though *many* imagine otherwise, the broad way of darkness only leads to *destruction*. The narrow way of the *words* of God's Word aren't just *light*, they are *life*.

> "*It is the spirit that quickeneth; the flesh profiteth nothing:* **the <u>words</u> that I speak unto you**, *they are spirit, and* **they are <u>life</u>**. *But there are some of you that believe not.*" *(John 6:63-64)*

> "*Because strait is the gate, and* **<u>narrow</u> is the way, which leadeth unto <u>life</u>, and few there be that find it.**" *(Matthew 7:14)*

> "The reality of the atomic *physicist*, like the reality of the Eastern *mystic*, **transcends the <u>narrow</u>** framework of opposite concepts." (Fritjof Capra; emphasis added)[62]

> "To **transcend <u>words</u>** ... means to ... **attain <u>liberation</u>**." (Fritjof Capra; emphasis added)[63]

In reality, which is not Oneness, those in this emerging faith are transcending the narrow and *only* way that leads to life and are thus attaining liberation from eternal life. Again, the broad way of darkness only leads to *destruction*. And, along with everything else that this emerging faith of Oneness flips *upside down*, the true "demon" here is not "ignorance" of Oneness. Rather, the "demon"—i.e., *devil*—is actually *Shiva*, known as "*the Destroyer*" for good reason. Shiva is also typically adorned with *serpents* for good reason. But, again, this is all just "beautiful" "metaphor" and "symbolism," right? By the way, in its form of Nataraja, Shiva is dancing within *a circle* of *flames*. As an article titled, "Tandava — Shiva's Cosmic Dance" puts it:

> "On a universal scale, Shiva is the Cosmic Dancer …
>
> "**A *ring* of *flames* and *light*** (prabha-mandala) issues from and encompasses the god. This is said to signify the vital processes of the universe and its creatures, **nature's dance as *moved* by the dancing god within**. Simultaneously it is said to signify the energy of Wisdom, **the transcendental *light* of the *knowledge* of truth, dancing forth, from the personification *of the All***." (parentheses in the original; emphasis added)[64]

And what is "the dancing god within"? It is *vibrating* "divine" energy, or the *vibration/movement* of the "energy"/"God" in everyone and everything.

> "**Everything in life is energy**. Everything. **Everything in life is vibrating**. Everything. **Vibration is** the *movement* of *energy*. It is **The Essence, manifesting Itself in differing form** through the elegant process of *movement*." (Neale Donald Walsch; emphasis added)[65]

Although *many* people in the world are choosing to believe otherwise, *false gods* are not "beautiful." And that goes for this *false* "God" of Oneness—a panentheistic/quantum "God" that, to use their term, is "beautifully" described in the devil Shiva.

> "Shiva is **the Divine Dancer**, visualized in terms of **motion** and **vibration** …
>
> "To sum up, here's an excerpt from a beautiful poem by Ruth Peel:
>
>> "'The source of **all *movement***, Shiva's dance,
>> Gives rhythm to the universe.
>> **He dances in *evil* places, In *sacred*, …**'" (*The Ramagiri Journal*; emphasis added)[66]

There is *a reason* why Shiva *the Destroyer* dances in a "*ring* of *flames*"! The true God does not "dance" to the rhythm of man's *unbelief* and *disobedience*—a rhythm that has absurdly become the new "holiness" of today's emerging *upside-down* faith. The true God does not "dance" "in *evil* places, In *sacred*." But, sadly, as God's Word points out, "*it is abomination to fools to depart from evil*" (Proverbs 13:19). And, therefore, many see *false gods* as "*beautiful*" even though God's Word warns that they are *idols*—and not only so, but that they are representations of *devils*. Or should we say manifestations?

> "Take heed, brethren, lest there be in any of you an evil heart of unbelief, in **departing from the living God**." (Hebrews 3:12)

> "Take heed to yourselves, that your heart be not deceived, and ye turn aside, and serve **other gods**, and worship them." (Deuteronomy 11:16)

> "For **all the gods** of the nations **are idols**: but the LORD made the heavens." (Psalm 96:5)

*"For **all the gods** of the people **are idols**: but the LORD made the heavens." (1 Chronicles 16:26)*

Absurdly, in the emerging faith/New Quantum Spirituality of Oneness *all the gods* of the people/nations become just *different* "manifestations"/"forms"/"energy patterns" of *"God."* But despite this attempt to change reality, it isn't <u>God</u> that is represented in idols/false gods—and that goes for the *false god* (or *false "God"*) of this emerging faith as well.

*"They sacrificed **unto <u>devils</u>, <u>not to God</u>; to <u>gods</u>** whom they knew not, to new gods that came newly up, whom your fathers feared not. Of the Rock that begat thee thou art unmindful, and hast forgotten God that formed thee." (Deuteronomy 32:17-18)*

*"But were mingled among the heathen, and learned their works. And they served their idols: which were a snare unto them. Yea, **they sacrificed** their sons and their daughters **unto <u>devils</u>**, and shed innocent blood, even the blood of their sons and of their daughters, whom **they sacrificed unto the <u>idols</u>** of Canaan ..." (Psalm 106:35-38)*

*"And they shall no more offer their sacrifices unto **<u>devils</u>, after whom they have gone a whoring**...." (Leviticus 17:7)*

*"Take heed to thyself, lest thou make a covenant with the inhabitants of the land whither thou goest, lest it be for a snare in the midst of thee: But ye shall ... break <u>their images</u> ... For thou shalt worship no <u>other god</u>: for the LORD, whose name is Jealous, is a jealous God: Lest thou make a covenant with the inhabitants of the land, and **they go a whoring after their <u>gods</u>**, and do sacrifice unto their gods, and one call thee, and thou eat of his sacrifice." (Exodus 34:12-15)*

***"Wherefore, my dearly beloved, flee from idolatry.... What say I then? that the idol is any thing, or that which is offered in sacrifice to <u>idols</u> is any thing? But I say, that the things which the Gentiles sacrifice, they sacrifice to <u>devils</u>, and <u>not to God</u>: and I would not that ye should have fellowship with <u>devils</u>. Ye cannot drink the cup of the Lord, and the cup of <u>devils</u>: ye cannot be partakers of the Lord's table, and of the table of <u>devils</u>.** Do we provoke the Lord to jealousy? are we stronger than he?" (1 Corinthians 10:14, 19-22)*

In the light of God's Word, take another look at the following quote, keeping in mind that according to Sweet (who *himself* "is a frequent speaker at national and international conferences, state conventions, pastors' schools, retreats"[67]) this is "*Christianity's major voice*":

"For Teilhard, a more sharply defined *'type' of God* is found in **the 'universal Christ'** ... On the margin of the same diary entry one can read the addition **'Christ-Shiva'**. I have mentioned before that some months earlier he had noted down that **our understanding of Christ must somehow integrate those aspects of the Divine expressed by the Indian god Shiva**." (Ursula King; emphasis added)[68]

A "Christ" ("Messiah") with horns, so to speak, is <u>not</u> the Christ (Messiah) of

Christianity—at least not of <u>*true scriptural*</u> Christianity anyway!

> "**In Christ *all opposites* are** not so much reconciled as ***transcended*** in *the Oneness of Twoness that becomes Threeness*." (Leonard Sweet; emphasis added)[69]

In no way, shape, or form is the Oneness of all opposites—which includes *Christ and Shiva*—*the truth and faith of the <u>Lord Jesus</u> Christ*. And the Lord Jesus <u>*alone*</u> is Christ; *period*.

The many warnings in God's Word should be enough to motivate anyone in their right mind who does not want to have "fellowship with *devils*" to "flee" from participating in the dance of this emerging Oneness. But then, those in this emerging faith don't believe in the *literal existence* of *devils* as set forth in God's Word of truth. If they did, given that they believe in a "God" of Oneness that *is/is in everyone and everything*, then they would have to admit that they believe in a "God" that *is/is in devils*. And, sadly, rather than changing their minds about their beliefs in a *false* "*God,*" they are choosing instead to change their minds about the *literal* existence of *devils*. The bottom line is that people today want no *line*. They *want* a *different* "God"—this new and "*better*" "God" of *Oneness*. Hence the growing participation in the dance.

> "*In meekness instructing those that <u>oppose</u> themselves; if God peradventure will give them <u>repentance to the acknowledging of the truth</u>; and that they may recover themselves out of* **the snare of the <u>devil</u>**, *who are* **taken captive by him at his will**." (2 Timothy 2:25-26)

> "**Through *his* dance, *Shiva*** sustains the manifold phenomena in the world, **<u>*unifying all things*</u>** by immersing them in *his* rhythm **and making them participate in the dance** ..." (Fritjof Capra; emphasis added)[70]

> "**Now <u>the Spirit</u> speaketh expressly, that in the latter times some shall depart from <u>the faith</u>, giving heed to seducing spirits, and doctrines of <u>devils</u>**." (1 Timothy 4:1)

> "[T]he *incarnation* goes **all the way down**, and **the Spirit** indwells **<u>all that exists</u>**." [!] (Leonard Sweet; emphasis added)[71]

So "the Spirit" "goes *all the way down*" to indwell "*seducing spirits, and doctrines of devils*"?!? In just this one verse alone of God's Word, it is as obvious as it gets that the *Holy* Spirit is *not* in "<u>*all*</u> *that exists*" "*unifying <u>all</u> things*," and thus unifying "*the sacred and the profane*" "<u>*all*</u> *the way down*"! But then, people can believe this *doctrine of devils* if they want to . . .

> "[Y]ou *can't* **polarize the sacred** and **<u>*the profane*</u>**. The doctrine of **the *incarnation* ... won't allow it**." (Leonard Sweet; emphasis added)[72]

> "In fact, **the *incarnation* brought <u>*all*</u> *dualities* together** ..." (Leonard Sweet; emphasis added)[73]

> "... **I would not that ye should have fellowship with <u>devils</u>**." (1 Corinthians 10:20)

Of course, *dancing* with devils is fellowship, and it is everything but a "Way of Life" . . .

As is to be expected, the "movement" of "Shiva's dance" that brings the opposites of "evil" and "sacred" together in "universal harmony" is *circular* and has an "evolutionary" purpose. Included in the article "Tandava — Shiva's Cosmic Dance" is the following:

> "On a universal scale, **Shiva** is **the Cosmic Dancer**; in his *Dancing Manifestation* (nritya-murti) he embodies in himself and simultaneously **gives manifestation to Eternal Energy. The forces gathered and projected in his frantic, ever-enduring *gyration*, are the powers of the *evolution*,** maintenance, and dissolution of the world." (parentheses in the original; emphasis added)[74]

Gyration -- "circular or spiral motion; revolution;"[75] "[a] turning or whirling round."[76] To *gyrate* -- "to move in a circle or spiral, or around a fixed point; whirl;" "[t]o revolve around a fixed point or *axis*;" "curved or coiled into a circle."[77]

Whether people in the emerging faith of Oneness choose to see this circle dance as the motion/movement of Shiva or "God" or "Jesus" changes *nothing*. A lie is a lie, even if dressed up as the truth. The "forces"/"powers" behind this (r)evolution of the "cosmic dance" of Oneness are essentially the "vibrations" of an "energy" that is frantically whirling around the truth in a circular motion. All that is needed in this "Evolution Revolution" is for *everyone* to consciously "tune" in to these "vibrations" and participate. In other words, all that is needed to create Oneness is for everyone to align their minds and dance in circles whirling to the right and whirling to the left frantically trying to unify *truth and falsehood* and *right and wrong*. This way, as everyone then makes it up as they go along consciously dancing to the "tune" of or to the "vibrations" of "the dancing god within"—or the "God" in everyone and everything—the world will thus *realize* its own "*self*-regulating" inner "knowing" and thereby "evolve" into, or *become*, this "God." After all, according to this emerging faith/New Quantum Spirituality, "[v]ibrations are what turn one vegetable into another."

> "Man is beginning to **sense the *vibration* of that greater Life** within Whose body he is but as an atom, ..." (Alice Bailey; emphasis added)[78]

> "[T]he word '**evolution**' suggests **an unfolding *from within*** outwards ... It involves the conception of vibration, **and of response to *vibration*** ..." (Alice Bailey; emphasis added)[79]

> "We have seen that ***evolution***, whether it is **of matter**, of intelligence, of consciousness, **or of spirit**, consists in an ever-increasing power to *respond* to *vibration* ..." (Alice Bailey; emphasis added)[80]

Accordingly, Sweet writes in *Nudge: Awakening Each Other to the God Who's Already There*:

> "If super-string physics is right ... then **the basic reality of the universe is *vibration* or *sound*....**
>
> "String theory defines matter as 'vibrating strings of energy.' That's it. What makes a turnip a turnip, and a carrot a carrot? A *change* in vibrations. **Vibrations are what turn one vegetable into another**." (emphasis added)[81]

"British researcher Jill Purce took MacDiarmid's metaphor more literally in her argument that it was **the unique *mission* of humans to use *sound* to mediate the translation of spirit into matter, and matter into spirit**. 'If spirit can become matter through sound, then **_matter can become spirit_** again through sound.'" (emphasis added)[82]

It is the "*mission* of *humans* to use sound to *mediate* the translation of _spirit_ _into_ _matter_, and _matter_ _into_ _spirit_"?! This "God" that man is consciously trying to "evolve" back into—in order to participate in making it up (in more ways than one)—obviously bows the knee to man and his use of sound, or *vibration*. Sounds like man just needs one big "harmonic convergence" and poof!—the world becomes "God" in a new "reality" (i.e., a new age) of Oneness. Those in the New Age movement have been trying to do this for years. Of course, the likelihood of their success should increase now that a growing number of minds are aligning in this "scientific" emerging "reality." And one person (said to be a physics professor) writes:

"According to highly credible sources that *channel messages from the Spirit*, the next Harmonic Convergence should happen in the year 2012. **The Harmonic Convergence** is a cosmological and metaphysical event in which **the vibration level of the planet's energy is measured --spiritually--** and depending on the outcome of this measurement and if humans give permission for it, then 'the veil will be lifted' to allow **the global consciousness *move* onto the next evolutionary step**." (emphasis added)[83]

Whether those in this emerging faith have *enough* aligned minds yet in order to successfully bring the world full circle in Satan's lie of Oneness will be evident soon enough. In any case, it isn't surprising that in *Quantum Spirituality* Sweet writes:

"**The power of New Light** charisma comes ... from a dynamic persona of personalities, plays, and performances that is part poetry, **part dance; part sorcery, part science**." (emphasis added)[84]

Does Sweet know, by any chance, just how *accurate* that "part *sorcery*" is?
First, the article titled, "Tandava — Shiva's Cosmic Dance," begins:

"**Shiva** ... is Nataraja, **King of Dancers**.

"**Dancing is an ancient form of *magic*.** The dancer becomes amplified into a being endowed with supra-normal powers. His personality is transformed. *Like yoga*, **the dance induces** trance, ecstasy, the experience of *the divine*, **the realization** of one's own *secret nature*, and, finally, _mergence into the divine essence_....

"It has a cosmogonic function, in that it rouses dormant energies which them [sic] may shape the world." (emphasis added)[85]

Again, Sweet writes that "**the transforming dance of Shiva**, the dynamic principle in cosmology--*captures the essence of the contemporary scientific enterprise*."[86] (Think about that!) And shortly after he writes that this "dance of Shiva" is with "**a *flame* in one hand** and **a musical drum** in another," Sweet goes on to say that "[t]he church has yet to **learn to dance**, much less find its way in the dark."[87] Would that be a dance of *sorcery*, to help translate "matter *into spirit*"? Sweet, who wants to "**make the Trinity a quaternity**,"[88] writes about "**dancing to the rhythm of** … '**divinization**.'"[89] And regarding the *flame* and the *drum* that Shiva is holding, this article "Tandava — **Shiva's** Cosmic **Dance**," which states that "[d]ancing is an ancient form of *magic*" that "**induces**" man's "**mergence *into* the *divine essence***," also points out that:

> "The upper right hand … carries a little **drum**, shaped like an hour-glass, **for the beating of the rhythm. This connotes *Sound* … associated in India with Ether**, the first of the five elements. Ether is **the primary and most subtly *pervasive evolution of the universe***, all the other elements, Air, Fire, Water, and Earth. Together, therefore, Sound and Ether signify the first, truth-pregnant moment of creation, the productive energy of the Absolute, in its pristine, cosmogenetic strength.
>
> "The opposite hand, the upper left, … bears on its palm a tongue of **flame**. Fire is the element of **the destruction of the world**…. Here, then, in the balance of the hands, is illustrated a counterpoise of creation and destruction in **the play of the cosmic dance. Sound against flame**. And the field of the terrible interplay is the Dancing Ground of the Universe, brilliant and horrific with the dance of the god." (emphasis added)[90]

Any rhythm of sorcery/magic, let alone *Shiva's*—whose devilish "divinizing" beat induces this "evolutionary" "*mergence into the divine essence*," is not the "rhythm" of *the Lord Jesus Christ*! And it is *irrelevant* if people do not recognize *sorcery/magic* for what it is. *It is what it is* whether people see it that way or not. And it used to be obvious before *darkness* became today's preferred *new* "light" that *sorcery* gets its *power* from the kingdom of *darkness*. But people today are hell-bent on creating Oneness, and *darkness is essential* for everyone/everything to *merge into Oneness*, not to mention *into a whole* "*God.*" So, given that this emerging faith of Oneness is basically flipping Colossians 1:13 upside down and "delivering people *from* the power of God's dear Son, and translating them *into* the kingdom of darkness," it is not at all surprising that Shiva, the "King" of the dancing *devils*, is the "rhythm" behind Oneness.

Second, *during* God's coming judgment, one of the sins for which the world will *still* be *unwilling to repent* just so happens to be *sorcery*. And in the supposedly "irrelevant" words of God's Word, *sorcery* just so happens to be listed right along with *the worship of devils*:

> "And the rest of the men which were not killed by these plagues **yet repented not** of the works of their hands, **that they should not worship devils, and idols** of gold, and silver, and brass, and stone, and of wood: which neither can see, nor hear, nor walk: **Neither repented they** of their murders, nor **of their sorceries**, nor of their fornication, nor of their thefts." (Revelation 9:20-21)

> "And he said unto me, It is done. I am Alpha and Omega, the beginning and the end. I will give unto him that is athirst of the fountain of the water of life freely. He that overcometh shall inherit all things; and I will be his God, and he shall be my son. But the fearful, and **unbelieving**, and the abominable, and murderers, and whoremongers, and **sorcerers**, and **idolaters**, and all liars, **shall have their part in the lake which burneth with fire and brimstone**: which is the second death." (Revelation 21:6-8)

There is *nothing irrelevant* about *God's words of warning!*

Again, in the light of God's Word it is perfectly clear that it is *devils*, not God, that are represented in *idols/false gods*. And the ultimate *idol/false god* is the "God" of Oneness which brings all the gods throughout history together as this one "God" of Oneness. Whether people choose to imagine otherwise or not, to believe in this *false god* is, in reality, to not *believe* in the *true God*. And given that the *unbelieving*, etc., "*shall have their part in the lake which burneth with fire and brimstone*," obviously everyone and everything are *not* all "*part of God*" as today's emerging faith/New Quantum Spirituality of Oneness/panentheism would have everyone believe. There *is* a future of "doom" waiting for those who are rejecting the *words* of *truth* of God's Word.

But, sadly, those who want the freedom of Oneness aren't *willing* to see it that way. After all, the freedom of Oneness is a "New Way of Life for All Humanity."[91] And since this "*New Way*" is a *dance* of "*being*" in a "*cosmic web*" of *infinite circles of Oneness*, this is a dance of *infinite choices* in which there is *no "fundamental structure" to believe or obey*.

> "... Shiva reminds us that **the manifold forms** in the world are *maya*—**not fundamental, but illusory and ever-changing**—as he keeps creating and dissolving them in the ceaseless *flow* of his dance." (Fritjof Capra; emphasis added, except to *maya*)[92]

> "Woe unto him that saith to the wood, Awake; to the dumb stone, Arise, it shall teach! Behold, it is laid over with gold and silver, and there is no breath at all in the midst of it. But the LORD is in his holy temple: let all the earth keep silence before him." (Habakkuk 2:19-20)

> "Relativity theory has made **the cosmic web** come alive, so to speak, by revealing its **intrinsically dynamic** character; by showing that **its *activity* is the very essence of its *being***." (Fritjof Capra; emphasis added)[93]

> "Jesus answered and said unto them, This is the work of God, that ye believe on him whom he hath sent." (John 6:29)

> "Subatomic particles are not made of any material stuff; they are **patterns of energy**.... When we observe them, **we never see** any substance, nor **any fundamental structure**. What we observe are **dynamic patterns** continually changing into one another—**a continuous dance of energy**." (Fritjof Capra; emphasis added)[94]

> "My son, fear thou the LORD and the king: and meddle not with them that are given to change: For their calamity shall rise suddenly; and who knoweth the ruin of them both?" (Proverbs 24:21-22)

Those who want *no "fundamental structure" to believe or obey* (i.e., "rules") are just not *willing* to *see* this "scientific" dance as impending calamitous ruin (i.e., "doom"). Again, the activity of this "*cosmic web*" is a dynamic dance of *doing* and *being* and *creating "God."* So those in this emerging faith can thus "joyfully" "journey around the circle" of Oneness "throughout eternity" on its "continually connected path to and from the all of everything" in this "continuous dance of energy."

"**Imagine a life without fear of God and** without guilt over the tiniest infraction of what you imagine to be **God's Rules!**

"Imagine the freedom of soul and mind and body that would be experienced when you **understand at last that you really *are* One with God!**" (Neale Donald Walsch; bold added)[95]

"**God is the energy**—the pure, raw energy—**which you call life**....

"**Everything is energy, in *motion*.**" (the seducing spirit calling itself "God;" emphasis added)[96]

"You see, the **Ultimate Reality** is actually **a circle**.... It is the cycle of life. In the beginning, God WAS this circle, in place AS the circle, complete. **When God individuated Itself, it sent the individual Aspects of <u>Divinity</u> on a journey around the circle.**" (Neale Donald Walsch; bold & underline added)[97]

"It is the cycle of life, ... It is a picture phrase describing the *no-beginning-and-no-end* nature of things; **the continually connected path to and from <u>the all of everything</u>, on which the soul joyfully journeys throughout eternity**.

"It is **the *sacred rhythm*** of all life, **by which you *move* the Energy of God**." (the seducing spirit calling itself "God;" emphasis added)[98]

Since this "God" is "the *all of everything*," what's there to fear? Those who want to can thus fearlessly join the many who are flocking to the *sticky/gluey circles* of the "cosmic *web*" for their "New Way of Life." This "New Way of Life" of *sticky/gluey Oneness* is imagined to be a *universal "salvation."* So surely there's no way that those who are flocking to these *sticky/gluey circles* of the "cosmic *web*" of Oneness will learn the hard way that, like the spider's web, they are actually a *snare*, right? And thus surely there's no way that, rather than finding "*Life*," those who are ensnared in these *sticky/gluey circles* of Oneness will inevitably find that they, like the spider's prey, have become easy prey for the Adversary with his *spun* infinitely intertwined circular strings *wound tightly around them as a shroud*. Never mind that our Adversary is on a mission "seeking whom he may *devour*" (1 Peter 5:8). Warnings are spurned as a *fear*-based agenda. And flocking to the *sticky/gluey circles* of this "cosmic *web*" is seen as a "beautiful" "Way of *Life*" that simply *dances* to the music/rhythm of the panentheistic "God's" "vibrating strings of energy"—i.e., the "*circular 'strings'*" of "the energy of *life*." Again, *easy prey*.

"*The way of the wicked is as darkness: they know not at what they stumble.*" (Proverbs 4:19)

"*Enter not into the path of the wicked, and go not in the way of evil men. Avoid it, pass not by it, turn from it, and pass away.... Turn not to the right hand nor to the left: remove thy foot from evil.*" (Proverbs 4:14-15, 27)

And not just your foot, but your *eye* also.

"*The light of the body is the eye: therefore when thine eye is single, thy whole body also is full of light; but when thine eye is evil, thy body also is full of darkness. Take heed therefore that the light which is in thee be not darkness. If thy whole body therefore be full of light, having no part dark, the whole shall be full of light, ...*" (Luke 11:34-36)

Remember "the third eye"? According to the seducing spirit Djwhal Khul, this is the "inner eye" of "contemplation."[99] And Leonard Sweet writes:

> "Religion thinks in threes.... **It takes 'three eyes' to see God,** ... and **the eye of contemplation (by which we attain knowledge of the transcendent world**)." (Leonard Sweet; parentheses in the original; emphasis added)[100]

This is "sight" that is *not at all* given by the *true* God. Quite the contrary, "the third eye" just so happens to be "the eye of *Shiva*." And not only so, but it is brought to "life" by "*serpent force*." (Those who are participating in this circle dance who do not want to "*have fellowship with devils*" should rethink their move to Oneness—to say the very least!)

> "... **the 'eye of Shiva' which sees and knows all** ... **This third eye** is one of the objects **of *kundalinic* vivification** ... **and the beauties** of the higher, subtler planes ... **stand revealed**." (the seducing spirit calling itself Djwhal Khul; emphasis added)[101]

Paramahansa Yogananda, founder of Self-Realization Fellowship (and who "defined Self-realization as '*the knowing*—in body, mind, and soul—that we are one with the omnipresence of God; ... that we are just as much a part of Him now as we ever will be. All we have to do is improve our *knowing*"[102]), described "**kundalini**" as the "**serpent force (from Sanskrit** *kundala,* **'coiled')**"[103] ...

> "**And the serpent said** unto the woman, Ye shall not surely die: For God doth know that in the day ye eat thereof, **then your eyes shall be opened, and ye shall be as gods, knowing good and evil.**" (Genesis 3:4-5)

The seducing spirit calling itself Djwhal Khul refers to "**the third eye, or the 'Eye of Shiva,'**" which "has its position, as is already known, in the center of the forehead between the two physical eyes"—and "is not to be confounded with the pineal gland"—as "**the great organ of consciousness**" and "**the instrument of wisdom**."[104]

> "***The Eye of God. Shiva*** is ... the Destroyer, but at the same time the Final Absorber, the Whole and yet the part. This is the organ of the divine Will or Power, the Eye, **through whose directed gaze the power flows outward to its created Whole**." (the seducing spirit calling itself Djwhal Khul; bold added)[105]

Shortly after stating that "[t]he third eye manifests as a result of" "*vibratory* interaction," this seducing spirit also states:

> "**This is the eye of Shiva** ...
>
> "1. *It is the eye of vision*. By its means, **the spiritual man sees behind the forms of *all* aspects of divine expression**. He becomes **aware of the light of the world**, and contacts the soul **within *all* forms**. Just as the physical *eye* registers forms, so does the spiritual eye register the illumination within those forms which 'illumination' indicates a specific state of being. It opens up the world of radiance....
>
> "3. *It has a destructive aspect* and **the energy flowing through the third**

eye can have a disintegrating and destroying effect."

And about "this third work of the *soul*," this seducing spirit states here that it is "the destructive work of getting rid of the *old* forms, ... and of *breaking down the barriers and limitations* to true soul activity."[106]

> "**The great fabric of dogmas and doctrines**, as built up by the churchmen and theologians of the ages, **must inevitably disintegrate**, but only in order that the life within may escape, build for itself a *better* and more satisfactory means of expression, and thus measure up to **the mission** upon which it was sent." (Alice Bailey; emphasis added)[107]

> "... by surrendering himself to the life at the center and there holding himself poised and still, yet alert, **the light will break in and reveal to the disciple that which he needs to know**. He *learns* to express that *inclusive love* ... and **to *let go* the narrow** ... He welcomes then **all** visions, if they serve to lift and comfort his brothers; **he welcomes all truths**, if they are the agents of revelation to other minds; **he welcomes all dreams** if they can act as incentives to his fellow men. **He shares in them all**, yet retains his poised position at the center." (the seducing spirit calling itself Djwhal Khul; emphasis added)[108]

When *the Destroyer* illuminates his new *"light" of the world*—which obviously isn't Jesus Christ of Nazareth—this is meant to *eliminate the need to believe Jesus Christ's narrow words* that are *life*. In other words, this new *"light" of the world* is meant to *destroy*.

Regardless of who people imagine the panentheistic "God" of the emerging faith/ New Quantum Spirituality of Oneness to be, a "God" that is the *"energy"* in the subatomic particles of *everyone and everything* is thus an *intrinsic* and *inseparable* part of *everyone and everything*. This is indeed a *liberation* that renders believing and obeying God's Word of truth totally "irrelevant." This "way" to "*self-realization*" unarguably changes *everything*, especially since a "secret" dance of a *subatomic* "God" is automatically a dance of Oneness in which "the *distinction* between observer and observed breaks down completely." This, too, clearly serves to break down the "barriers and limitations" to being able to "see" or "observe" this new destructive "light" of the world "*within all forms*."

> "In *quantum* physics **the observer and the observed can no longer be separated**, but they can still be distinguished. *Mystics* in deep meditation arrive at a point where **the distinction between observer and observed breaks down completely**, where subject and object *fuse*." (Fritjof Capra; emphasis added)[109]

> "**Duality, or separation between the observer and the observed, is an illusion** that the Eastern *mystics* have long recognized and Western science has more recently come to understand through *quantum* mechanics." (Science and Nonduality--SAND; emphasis added)[110]

> "**In the beginning**, ... **All That Is** could not know itself—because All That Is is all there was, and there was *nothing else*....
>
> "**This *energy***—this pure, unseen, unheard, **unobserved, and therefore unknown-by-anyone-else energy**—chose to experience Itself as the utter mag-

nificence It was....

"It reasoned, quite correctly, ... that if It thus **simply divided Itself** into portions, **each portion**, being less than the whole, **could look back on the rest of Itself** and see magnificence....

"... **God made it possible for God to know Itself**." (the seducing spirit calling itself "God;" bold & underline added)[111]

"**Each** Individuated Aspect of Divinity, traveling on its journey through the endless cycle of life, **may both know and experience Itself as Who It Really Is** at any place on that cycle....

"*This is what God is up to!*" (Neale Donald Walsch; bold & underline added)[112]

This "secret" all-encompassing *circle dance* of *subatomic Oneness with "God"* conveniently blasts believing and obeying the absolute truth of God's Word into smithereens as it renders *duality* between the observer and the observed an *"illusion."* Again, a "God" that is the *"energy"* in the subatomic particles of *everyone and everything* is thus an *intrinsic* and *inseparable* part of *everyone and everything*. So those in this emerging "scientific" faith need merely believe in "the energy of life" and move and dance in *circles* in order to observe and thus connect (i.e., *re*-connect) this "God" *in everyone and everything*. Of course, since "In the beginning, God WAS this circle," when it "individuated Itself, it sent the individual Aspects of Divinity on a journey around the circle."[113] After all, how else is this "God" going to become *a connected/unified whole* again?

It is thus fitting that in the chapter titled, "A Piece of π," *The Shack*'s panentheistic "God"—"who is *the ground of all being*" that "dwells *in*, around, and through *all things*"[114]—refers to "the *quantum* stuff that is going on at a *subatomic* level where only I am the always-present *observer*."[115] And in the chapter titled, "**Verbs** and Other Freedoms," *The Shack*'s false "Jesus" says:

"Rather than a *pyramid* [i.e., 'a *hierarchy*'], I want to be the center of a *mobile*, where **everything in your life**—your friends, family, occupation, thoughts, activities—**is connected to me but *moves* with the wind**, in and out and back and forth, **in an incredible *dance* of being**." (emphasis added)[116]

To this *The Shack*'s false "Spirit" Sarayu[117] adds, "I am the wind."[118] A "dance of being" with "the ground of *all being*" is a dance of the all-encompassing circle of Oneness. This is indeed a life of *being windblown* by anything and everything. In fact, this is a life "tossed to and fro, and *carried about with every wind of doctrine*, by the sleight of men, and cunning craftiness, whereby they lie in wait to deceive" (Ephesians 4:14). But those in this emerging faith/journey don't see it that way. In *Oneness* there is nothing "*false* and *wrong*" so there is no *deception* to worry about—and certainly not from a *false god* that wants to blind the minds of man with its "light" of *Oneness*. This false "Spirit" subsequently says:

"Mackenzie, if you would allow me, I would like to give you a gift for this evening. **May I touch your eyes and heal them**, just for tonight?" (emphasis added)[119]

The result?:

"When Mack **opened his eyes** he had to immediately shield them from **a**

blinding light that overwhelmed him." (emphasis added)[120]

He then heard this false "Spirit" say:

"You will find it very difficult to look at me directly ... But as **your mind becomes accustomed to the changes**, it will be *easier*." (emphasis added)[121]

Of course it will! The minds of those in this emerging faith of Oneness will gradually become accustomed to the changes of the blinding *new* "light" of the *new* "gospel" of the *new* "God" of Oneness just as eyes become accustomed to *the dark*.

"... **the god of this world hath blinded** the **minds** of them which believe not, lest the light of the glorious gospel of Christ, who is the image of God, should shine unto them." (2 Corinthians 4:4)

"And no marvel; for **Satan himself is transformed into an angel of light**." (2 Corinthians 11:14)

"When, therefore, **sight** has been attained and **the light** streams forth, **revelation of the oneness of all life** is a simple and immediate occurrence ...

"[I]n these days many are attaining sight and light is pouring in." (the seducing spirit calling itself Djwhal Khul; emphasis added)[122]

"... then your **eyes** shall be **opened, and ye shall be as gods** ..." (Genesis 3:5)

"It is **this revelation of Deity** that **is the goal of the mystical endeavor** ... Through it, he later discovers his relation to the universe; he finds that **his physical body and his vital** *energies* **are part and parcel of Nature itself, which is, in fact, the outer garment of Deity** ... In fact, he arrives at God and discovers God as the central Fact. Knowing himself to be divine, he finds *the whole* is equally divine." (Alice Bailey; emphasis added)[123]

As is therefore to be expected, this "sight" and "light" of Oneness is given to *The Shack*'s character Mack after he allows Sarayu, the false "Spirit," to "heal" his eyes—the "healing" of course being this revelation of *Oneness* and its New *Quantum* Spirituality:

"He [Mack] was standing right where he had closed his eyes, but the shack was gone as well as the dock and shop. Instead he was outside, perched on the top of a small hill under a brilliant but moonless night sky. He could see that the stars were in **motion**, not hurriedly but smoothly and with precision, as if there were grand celestial conductors coordinating their **movements**.

"Occasionally, as if on cue, comets and meteor showers would tumble through the starry ranks, adding variation to **the flowing dance**. Then Mack saw some of the stars grow and change color as if they were turning nova or white dwarf. It was as if time itself had become **dynamic** and volatile, adding to the seeming *chaotic* but precisely managed heavenly display.

"He turned back to Sarayu, who still stood next to him. Although she was still difficult to look at directly, he could now make out symmetry and colors embedded within **patterns**, as if miniature diamonds, rubies, and sapphires of *all colors* had been sewn into **a garment of *light*, which moved *first* in *waves* and then scattered as *particulate***.

"'It is all so incredibly beautiful,' he whispered ..." (*The Shack*; emphasis added)[124]

This is "The Beautiful Side of Evil"—as Christian author Johanna Michaelsen titled her autobiography. The Angel of light is a master deceiver and is adept at blinding minds with *counterfeit* "beauty," "goodness," and "truth." And people today are easy prey since they are more than willing to trade the *objective words* of God's Word of truth for *subjective experiences*.[G] Sounding just like the descriptions of mystical experiences of Oneness, *The Shack's* character Mack goes on to describe seeing "everything" with this "light" and color: "Even in the darkness of the night everything had clarity and shone with halos of light in various hues and shades of color. The forest was itself afire with light and color ..."[125] He continues to describe his vision as one in which nature, animals, and he himself are "shining" with the "blaze"/"flames" of this "light" and color, a vision in which he "felt larger than life, as if he were able to be present wherever he looked."[126] He even adds:

> "In fact, he had never felt this well, this *whole*....
>
> "And then Mack saw **the lights. Single moving points emerging** from the forest, **converging** upon the meadow ...
>
> "They broke into the meadow, an army of children. There were no candles—they themselves were lights. And within **their *own* radiance**, each was dressed in distinctive garbs that Mack imagined represented **every tribe and tongue**.... These were **the children of the earth** ...
>
> "The children had now formed **a huge circle** within the meadow ..." (emphasis added)[127]

And Sarayu, the false "Spirit," tells him:

> "As you near them you will see that they have many **individual colors that have *merged* into white, which contains *all***. As they mature and grow to become **who they really are**, the colors they exhibit will become more distinctive, and unique hues and shades will *emerge*." (emphasis added)[128]

G

If people would just believe *Genesis 1:1*, they wouldn't be such easy prey for the lies of seducing spirits—lies that include lying *visions* and *experiences*. But it is this very first verse of God's Word that puts *everything* into perspective. The God Who created (not exploded, *created*; not evolved, *created*) has the right to expect His creation (not parts of God, *creation*; not co-creators, *creation*) to *believe* and *obey* its Creator. And thus, of course, choosing to believe *the very first verse* of God's Word would clearly defeat the whole *purpose* behind choosing to *not* believe it. The very first verse of God's Word puts an immediate end to the emerging faith/New *Quantum* Spirituality and thus to its convenient freedom from the absolute truth of God's Word. To say that this emerging faith isn't scriptural is a tremendous understatement. It can't even get in the door at the very first verse of God's Word! So it is not at all surprising that this emerging faith begins its many "reimaginings" with Genesis 1:1. It is as God's Word says, "*For this they <u>willingly</u> are <u>ignorant</u> of, that by the word of God the heavens were of old, and the earth standing out of the water and in the water: Whereby the world that then was, being overflowed with water, perished: But the heavens and the earth, which are now, by the same word are kept in store, reserved unto fire against the day of judgment and perdition of ungodly men*" (2 Peter 3:5-7).

PART FIVE: THE CREATION   431

Inevitably, in this revelation of Oneness *The Shack*'s character also finds that "light and color robed him completely; a clothing of purity that allowed him both freedom and propriety."¹²⁹ There's clearly no need to *believe* in Jesus Christ of Nazareth to be clothed in *this* "purity." Just "grow to become who [you] really are," and participate in the "dance of *being*" in this "beautiful" *all-encompassing* "energy"/circle/"God" of Oneness/wholeness. After all, this new "light" is the new "truth" that your "vital *energies* are part and parcel of Nature itself, which is, in fact, the outer garment of *Deity*."

> "So go, now, and **see each other as Who You Really Are**.
>
> "**Observe. Observe. OBSERVE.**" (the seducing spirit calling itself "God;" bold added)¹³⁰
>
> "All things are One Thing, and there is nothing else. 'We Are All One' is more than a beautiful slogan. *It is a precise description of the nature of Ultimate Reality*....
>
> "Yet how difficult, when one is caught up in the Illusion, to **see God in every one and every thing**." (the seducing spirit calling itself "God;" bold added)¹³¹

Actually, how difficult, when one is caught up in the illusion of *Oneness*, to judge between *truth and falsehood* and *right and wrong*.

> "*Judge not according to the appearance, but judge righteous judgment.*" (John 7:24)
>
> "*Run ye to and fro through the streets of Jerusalem, and* **see** *now, and know, and seek in the broad places thereof, if ye can find a man,* **if there be any that executeth judgment, that seeketh the truth**; *and I will pardon it. And* **though they say, The LORD liveth; surely they swear falsely. O LORD, are not thine eyes upon the truth?** *thou hast stricken them, but they have not grieved; thou hast consumed them,* **but they have refused to receive correction**: *they have made their faces harder than a rock;* **they have refused to return**. *Therefore I said, Surely these are poor; they are foolish:* **for they know not the way of the LORD, nor the judgment of their God**." (Jeremiah 5:1-4)

Since believers in the *true* God are to "walk by faith, not by sight" (2 Corinthians 5:7), what does the *true* God want us to observe? His *words*, which we are to *believe* and *obey*.

> "**Observe** and **hear** all these **words** which I command thee, that it may go well with thee, and with thy children after thee for ever, when thou doest that which is **good and right in the sight of the LORD thy God**.... What thing soever I command you, **observe to do it: thou shalt not add thereto, nor diminish from it**." (Deuteronomy 12:28, 32)
>
> "... O LORD God of heaven, the great and terrible God, that keepeth **covenant and mercy for them that love him and observe his commandments**." (Nehemiah 1:5)
>
> "**Chain of command? That sounds ghastly!**" (*The Shack*'s false "Jesus;" emphasis added)¹³²

"Submission is **not** about **authority** and it is **not obedience** ..." (*The Shack's* false "Jesus;" emphasis added)[133]

"[W]e have **no** concept of **final authority** among us, **only unity**. We are in **a circle of relationship, not a chain of command** ... What you're seeing here is relationship without any overlay of power.... Hierarchy would make no sense among us." (*The Shack's* false "Spirit;" bold added)[134]

"[W]e want you to **join us in our circle of relationship**." (*The Shack's* false "Jesus;" emphasis added)[135]

*"Ye shall **observe** to do therefore as the* LORD *your God hath **commanded** you: ye shall not turn aside to the right hand or to the left." (Deuteronomy 5:32)*

*"Go ye therefore, and teach all nations, baptizing them in the name of the Father, and of the Son, and of the Holy Ghost: Teaching them to **observe all things whatsoever I have commanded you**: and, lo, I am with you always, even unto the end of the world. Amen." (Matthew 28:19-20)*

As addressed earlier, people in the emerging "faith" of Oneness aren't even willing to observe the basic commandment of *believing* in *God's Son*. And, no, it isn't *love* to tell others that they don't have to *believe*.

"And this is his commandment, That we should believe on <u>the name of his Son Jesus Christ</u>, and love one another, as he gave us commandment." (1 John 3:23)

"Be it known unto you all, and to all the people of Israel, that by <u>the name of Jesus Christ of Nazareth</u>, whom ye crucified, whom God raised from the dead, ... Neither is there salvation in any other: for there is <u>none other name</u> under heaven given among men, whereby we must be saved." (Acts 4:10-12)

Any commandment whatsoever—but *especially* the one of *believing* in *Jesus Christ of Nazareth*—instantly sets forth *a division* between *truth and falsehood* and *right and wrong*. And where there is *division*, there is only an *either/or*—not a *both/and* dance of Oneness that turns to the right and turns to the left. Hence, since Oneness *cannot exist* where there is division, today's emerging faith *must* shift from observing God's Word of commanding, divisive truth to observing the "God" of Oneness.

The "God" of Oneness will "never command anyone to do anything." How could it? Besides, when everyone and everything are all <u>One</u> with "<u>God</u>," everyone and everything all <u>share being "God</u>." So the instant this "God" *commanded* anything, there would be no more *Oneness* between it and man. Thus, the instant the "God" of Oneness commanded *anything whatsoever*—or even <u>judged</u> between truth and falsehood and right and wrong in the first place—would be the instant of *its own undoing*. No Oneness, no "God" of Oneness. So never mind that this "God" of Oneness is *as blatantly false as it gets*, its *never-command-anyone-to-do-anything Oneness* "makes *no one wrong* for the way in which they are approaching the God of *their understanding*."[136] So who's to say that *other gods*, such as Krishna and Shiva, and all the other gods, are *false*? Who's to say that *idolatry* is *wrong*? In this dance of Oneness (i.e., in this *delusion* to beat *all delusions*), there's *no such thing* as "*false* and *wrong*." In Oneness:

"There is only One God. What God is this? Is it Adonai? Allah? Elohim? God? Hari? Jehovah? Krishna? Lord? Rama? Vishnu? Yahweh?

"*It's All of Them.*" (Neale Donald Walsch)[137]

And therefore:

"<u>Relinquish</u> the pride of mind which sees its way and its interpretations to be *correct* and *true*, and others' *false* and *wrong*." (the seducing spirit calling itself Djwhal Khul; emphasis added)[138]

But, not to worry. After all, the "humility" of these *sticky/gluey circles* is a dance of Oneness that is nothing more than just a "beautiful" "Way of *Life*" . . .

"**I never command *anyone* to do *anything*.**" (the seducing spirit calling itself "God;" emphasis added)[139]

"I have never set down a 'right' or 'wrong,' a 'do' or a 'don't.'" (the seducing spirit calling itself "God")[140]

"Understand that 'right' and 'wrong' are figments of your imagination …" (the seducing spirit calling itself "God")[141]

"**There is *nothing to fear* from God**, because **God wants nothing from you. Nothing.**…

"Tomorrow's God is **unconditionally** loving, **nonjudgmental**, noncondemning, and nonpunishing." (the seducing spirit calling itself "God;" emphasis added)[142]

So, naturally, *hell* is just a figment of the imagination, too, right? The Lord Jesus Christ, *the Creator of "all things"* (see John 1:3; Colossians 1:16; & Ephesians 3:9; but be forewarned that new *holey* versions have deleted the truth "*by Jesus Christ*" from Ephesians 3:9), *reiterated* His dire warnings about *hell*. And, yes, He said what He meant and meant what He said in His warnings that are being fearlessly dismissed by *many*.

"*… into hell, into the fire that never shall be quenched: Where their worm dieth not, and the fire is not quenched.*" (Mark 9:43-44)

"*… into hell, into the fire that never shall be quenched: Where their worm dieth not, and the fire is not quenched.*" (Mark 9:45-46)

"*… into hell fire: Where their worm dieth not, and the fire is not quenched.*" (Mark 9:47-48)

In light of these six verses alone, no wonder "scholars" who are turning away from believing the truth have tried to discredit the book of Mark! And, naturally, the "*best*" manuscripts (i.e., the ones conveniently full of holes) which are behind the *new* versions (again, *new for a reason*) are *missing* the Lord Jesus Christ's *reiteration* of these warnings. Hell is so serious and such a *terrible* place that the Lord Jesus Christ took the time to repeat His warnings. Just in these six verses, He refers to the fire as *unquenchable* five times, but up to four of these references have been deleted in too many new versions; He specifies *fire* six times, but up to five of these have been deleted; and He specifies *hell* three times, but up to all three of these have been changed or deleted in some new versions. But these *reiterations* of His were just a *fear-based agenda*, right? Well, as a matter of fact, the Lord Jesus Christ said, "I will *forewarn* you whom ye shall *fear: Fear him*, which after he hath killed hath power to cast into *hell*; yea, I say unto you, *Fear him*" (Luke 12:5). But, of course, *fear* is seen as "*negative*" because it takes all the "*fun*" out of today's *unbelief* and *disobedience* . . .

Sadly, people today really do want a *different* "God"—a new and "*better*" "God" that has *no expectations* for man and offers an *unconditional*, *universal* salvation. This way, everyone can just live life *however* they *choose*.

> "If we could **break free from the** Greco-Roman **soul-sort** narrative [**in which 'everyone will be sorted into either the destruction/damnation or the redemption/salvation bin'**], think of what could change.... We would **stop seeing the line that separates good and evil** running between our religion and <u>all</u> others....
>
> "Evangelism would *cease* to be a matter of *saving souls* from a bad ending ...
>
> "... **calling people to <u>a way of life</u> in a** kingdom (or **beautiful *whole*) that transcends and includes *all* religions**." (Brian McLaren; parentheses in the original; emphasis added)[143]

> "**W is for (The) Way** ...
>
> "The search for truth is a moral imperative. But Christian 'truth' is a person who invites us to *join him on* 'The Way.' Christianity is **a 'way of life.'** The Christian life is **more a *journey* than jelled <u>beliefs</u>**, more pilgrimage and practices **than propositions and principles**....
>
> "Way means journey ... and in the emerging culture, our journey is both personal and collective. **No other film expresses the beauty of pilgrimage and journey better than *The Wizard of Oz*.**" (Leonard Sweet, Brian McLaren, & Jerry Haselmayer; parentheses & last ellipsis dots in the original; emphasis added)[144]

How fitting. An emerging journey that includes a dance of "*sorcery*"/"*magic*" is unarguably "off to see the *wizard*." And just like on this movie's journey, those on the journey of today's emerging faith/New Quantum Spirituality of Oneness/panentheism are going to likewise discover that behind the "voice" they are hearing is not at all who they perceive it to be! But, like the wizard, this emerging faith is all just "A '*Wonderful*' Deception" (as Warren B. Smith warned in the title of his book). And, of course, even "*fictitious*" wizards are today's *heroes* because surely God's Word distinguishes between *sin* and "*fictitious*" sin, right? Only in the realm of *make-believe* which, sadly, is the realm that people today prefer. It gives them a *fictitious* sense of *freedom*. And, therefore, they don't see what the big deal is about being "off to see the wizard," whether in movies or otherwise.

> "*Regard not them that have familiar spirits*, **neither seek after wizards**, *to be defiled by them: I am the* LORD *your God.*" (Leviticus 19:31)

> "*And the soul that <u>turneth</u> after such as have familiar spirits, and after wizards, to go a whoring after them,* **I will even set my face against that soul** ..." (Leviticus 20:6)

> *"There shall not be found among you any one that maketh his son or his daughter to pass through the fire, or that useth divination, or an observer of times, or an enchanter, or a witch, or a charmer, or a consulter with familiar spirits, or a wizard, or a necromancer.* **For all that do these things are an abomination unto the LORD** *..."* (Deuteronomy 18:10-12)

Despite the dire warnings in God's Word, people today are still bound and determined not to see anything *wrong* with *wizards*. And if they don't see anything *wrong* with *wizards*, then why on earth would they see anything *wrong* with *sorcery*?! And thus even with *false gods*?? After all, it is *false gods* that dance "in *evil* places, In *sacred*"—a dance that gives people their desired "Way of Life" of *Oneness* in which there is no such thing as "*false* and *wrong*," not even that which God calls *abominations*. So never mind that this emerging journey is a journey with a false god. This is a journey of liberation and salvation for *everyone*—even *wizards, devils,* and *false gods*. Oneness is *Oneness*. And in Oneness, *everyone* and *everything* are *"One* with *God."*

> "Religions now have an opportunity to shift from 'There is only one God' to 'There is only One Thing at all.'...
> **"If there is Only One Thing That Is**, then ***everything and everyone*** **must be part of *that One Thing*** ..." (Neale Donald Walsch; emphasis added)[145]

So, to help participate in the process of making the new and "*better*" circular "God" whole again, simply "tune" in to the music/rhythm of the "vibrations" of its "circular 'strings'" (or "cosmic web") and you will be "tuning" in to its "energy of life" that is in everyone and everything. This way, not only can this circular "God" "know itself" as a connected/unified whole again—a "reality" that simply needs to be "observed"—but you can thus help "create" a whole new "reality" for everyone and everything.

> "Everything is connected to everything else. *Everything*. There is *nothing* that is 'disconnected' or 'dismembered.' We only *think* that there is....
> **"The All Of Everything** really is an enormous, larger than fathomable **matrix**. The matrix is **vibrating at differing frequencies** in different locations....
> "Words vibrate. Thoughts vibrate. Actions vibrate....
> **"The act of 'creation'** is simply the act of **tuning into the vibration** of that which already exists **in the All of Everything** ..." (Neale Donald Walsch; bold & underline added)[146]

> "You should now better understand how **people of *like* mind** can work together to **create a favored reality**." (the seducing spirit calling itself "God;" bold added)[147]

So "tune" in and you can *tune out* to God's Word and "awaken" to your own "intuition," or inner "knowing"—the "vibration" of "the dancing god within." And this way, as everyone makes it up as they go along, dancing to the rhythm of the "vibrations" of the "God" in everyone and everything—the world will thereby "know itself" to be "God" in one big (r)evolutionary "harmonic convergence." After all, "*[v]ibrations* are what turn one vegetable into another."

> "We can look, too, for ... **the <u>awakening</u> of the *intuition*.**" (Alice Bailey; empha-

sis added)[148]

"Man is beginning to **sense the *vibration* of that greater Life within Whose body he is but as an atom**, and he is commencing, in a small way, to **make a *conscious response* to that greater call**, and to <u>find</u> possible <u>channels</u> whereby he can understand that greater Life which he senses ..." (Alice Bailey; emphasis added)[149]

"This book [*Nudge:* **Awakening** *Each Other* **to the God Who's Already There**] is your wireless card to pick up the signals of transcendence, **the *immanent transcendent***, that are out there but not being downloaded. Semiotics is **the art of <u>finding</u> channels** and making *connections*. Evangelism as semiotics is **the art of <u>tuning</u> our receivers to the 'I AM' channel** and setting the controls to receive and transmit transdimensional frequencies." (Leonard Sweet; emphasis added)[150]

When discussing "the *threefold* manifestation of *Deity*, the *self*, the *not-self*, and *the relation* between," Alice Bailey then points out:

"**The self, <u>occultly</u>, hears and responds to vibration**, thus *realising Itself*." (emphasis added)[151]

She also elaborates:

"There is **a great *vibratory* sphere**, or plane, in the solar system, called in some **occult** books **the *intuitional* plane**; it is called in the Eastern literature the Buddhic plane, and **its symbol is *the air*.**" (emphasis added)[152]

By an amazing "coincidence," God's supposedly "*medieval*"/"*outdated*"/"*irrelevant*" Word warns that the devil is "the prince of the power of *the air*." So those who are "tuning" in to this "vibration" are indeed "tuning" in to "dances of *demons*."

> "Wherein in time past ye walked according to the course of this world, according to **the prince of the power of <u>the air</u>, the spirit that now worketh in the children of <u>disobedience</u>**." (Ephesians 2:2)

> "**Whoso despiseth <u>the word</u> shall be destroyed: but he that feareth the commandment shall be rewarded.**" (Proverbs 13:13)

> "Wherefore also it is contained in the scripture, Behold, I lay in Zion **a chief corner stone**, elect, precious: and he that believeth on him shall not be confounded. Unto you therefore which believe he is precious: but unto them which be disobedient, **the stone which the builders disallowed**, the same is made the head of the corner, and **a stone of stumbling, and a rock of offence, even to them which stumble at <u>the word</u>, being <u>disobedient</u>**: whereunto also they were appointed." (1 Peter 2:6-8)

> "**Therefore, my beloved brethren, be ye stedfast, <u>unmoveable</u>**, always abounding in the work of the Lord, forasmuch as ye know that your labour is not in vain in the Lord." (1 Corinthians 15:58)

No matter how many leaders of this emerging faith teach otherwise, we are not to learn to "pay attention," "hear," "read the signs," and "observe" and "participate" in this dance of Oneness—a dance of *unbelief* and *disobedience*. We are not to turn to the right and turn to the left to unify and transcend all opposites. We are not to "shut up and listen" and dance around the truth to "the music of the spheres," or the "vibration" of "the universe." In other words, we are not to turn the light off to look for "truth" in the *corner* of a dark *round* room. We are not to turn off the light of God's Word of truth for *any* reason, let alone to look for "truth" in the darkness of the <u>circle</u> of Oneness that has, by its very nature, "<u>disallowed</u>" the "<u>corner</u> stone."

So, are you heeding *the words of God's Word* or "*the dances of demons*"? Keep in mind that it is in her book *From Intellect to Intuition* that Alice Bailey wrote "[i]t is relatively *unimportant* what we mean in detail by that little word of three letters," i.e., "God"—and this is for the simple reason that the "meditation" of "mystics" leads to "these results":

> "**Union with God**, or At-one-ment with Divinity. God and man are at-one. **The Self and Not-Self are unified**." (Alice Bailey, *From Intellect to* **Intuition**; emphasis added)[153]

Those who are making this shift are indeed the *"true leader[s]" of this emerging faith*—a faith that is "part dance; part sorcery, part science" . . .

> "For the common sense to be the common good in the postmodern era, it must come to respect **the** *authority* **of** *intuitive* **modes of knowing**....
>
> "Modernity dismissed 'intuition' ... Postmodernity, on the other hand, thrives on **intuitional** *experience*, elevating its attributes to **the status of** *a true leader*: Someone 'gifted more than ordinary people with **a mystical quality--intuition--** which gives him 'inner conviction' ...'" (Leonard Sweet; emphasis added)[154]

> "... **the unition** *experience* **of the whole, of the self with all that is outside the self**, or of the experience **of God**, either from *within* or **in everything** *without*....
>
> "**Mysticism** begins in experience; it **ends in** *theology*." (Leonard Sweet; emphasis added)[155]

> "**M is for Mysticism** ...
>
> "Postmoderns are more likely to define **God as 'mystery that meaning** *alludes* **to.'** They carry within them a **mystical consciousness**. In their world, ... magic and mystery and miracle are everyday occurrences through nonconceptual thinking (**intuition**, aesthetic inclinations, spiritual enlightenment, emotions, images), through **mystical enlightenment**, through anomalous and peak experiences, and through soul journeys." (Leonard Sweet, Brian McLaren, & Jerry Haselmayer; parentheses in the original; emphasis added)[156]

> "Hence **the Bible translation,** *The Voice* (Nashville: Thomas Nelson, upcoming) of which my contribution is the book of Genesis." (Leonard Sweet; parentheses in the original; bold added)[157]

> "So, if you're interested, I think this new project *The Voice* **is going to really have a great effect in a lot of individual's lives and in a lot of churches**."

(Brian McLaren, whose contribution was to rewrite/reword the truth of Luke and Acts; bold added)[158]

That's an understatement if ever there was one—but a "great effect" in a *negative* sense. Provided, of course, that being led to neither *believe the true God* nor *obey His voice* is seen by people as *negative*. This is no longer a given now that today's mystical "experiences" are ending in *Oneness*—a "God"-in-everything "theology" and "way of life."

"**Prayer** is more than a form of synchronicity that transcends the space-time continuum, **a tuning in to the *rhythms* of God**, and **a getting in touch with the '*rhythm web*' that ties us together**. But it is at least that." (Leonard Sweet; emphasis added)[159]

"**V is for Voice** ...
"**And what postmoderns are *listening* for is less *words* than the music of the spheres**, especially the heavenly spheres, but **sometimes the *dances* of demons**....
"While ***rhythm* is the structuring principle of their lives**, postmoderns experience life in terms of sound levels. Some things are too 'noisy'; other things have too much 'static.'...
"The primacy of 'voice' beckons the church back to a more biblical [!] and more scientific framework....
"[I]n super-string physics the very building blocks of the universe are defined as '**vibrating *loops* of *energy***.'" (Leonard Sweet, Brian McLaren, & Jerry Haselmayer; emphasis added)[160]

"... **calling people to a *way of life* in a** kingdom (or **beautiful *whole***) that transcends and includes *all* religions." (Brian McLaren; parentheses in the original; emphasis added)[161]

No, it isn't the call and voice of *God* that those in this emerging Wordless faith are "listening for" and "tuning" in to.

*"And Moses brought forth the people out of the camp to meet with God ... And when the voice of the trumpet sounded long, and waxed louder and louder, Moses spake, **and God answered him by a voice.**... **And God spake all these words, saying, I am the Lord thy God, ... Thou shalt have no other gods before me. Thou shalt not make unto thee any graven image,** ... And all the people saw the thunderings, and the lightnings, and the noise of the trumpet, and the mountain smoking: and when the people saw it, they removed, and stood afar off." (Exodus 19:17, 19; 20:1-4, 18)*

*"And the sound of a trumpet, and **the voice of words; which voice they that heard entreated that the word should not be spoken to them any more**: (For they could not endure that which was commanded...."* (Hebrews 12:19-20)

"In my own experience as a lover and reader of the Bible, as **I am freed from the literalistic and dualistic straitjacket** ... I feel I can breathe a little freer ..." (Brian McLaren; emphasis added)[162]

Sadly, some things never change. "Some things are" still just "too 'noisy'" and "have too much 'static,'" right?

Despite the emerging faith of many who, sadly, don't know enough to *observe God's Word*, this "cosmic dance" of *Oneness* is not even remotely the "dance" of the true God and His Son, the Lord Jesus Christ. This *movement* is quite clearly and purposely a move *away from* the truth and *unto fables*, just as God's Word warns. But, even so, this is a *fearless* move. In this emerging faith, the warnings of God's Word fall on deaf ears. Why? Because in this emerging faith even <u>blasphemy</u> is "scientific," so why would anyone fear moving away from the truth of God's Word and unto *fables*?? They don't. And a growing number of people in today's shifting Christianity are seeming to barely give it a second thought.

In order for *Oneness* to even exist, people <u>must move</u> and dance around the truth of God's Word <u>on purpose</u>. No *circular motion*, no *unified opposites*. No *unified opposites*, no *Oneness*. And now that today's "scientific" fables of Oneness are providing the "proof" for this new blasphemous "reality," everyone can leave all *fears* behind and participate in aligning their minds in the global *movement* to create a new "God" and new future—a new world religion and new world—of Oneness. Of course, this call to Oneness is a call to see and honor *"God" in everyone and everything*. And, therefore, those who heed this call are indeed giving heed to "the dances of <u>demons</u>." But, naturally, those who are falling for this blasphemy of Oneness don't see it that way. Never mind that this emerging faith/New Quantum Spirituality of Oneness automatically renders *devils the same "energy"* as "God"! *No, this emerging faith of Oneness is not the call of <u>God</u>!*

As Sweet fearlessly writes in *Quantum Spirituality*, "[i]f the universe is a 'green dragon,' as *physicist/cosmologist* Brian Swimme would have it, New Lights are *the dragon's breath*" "*and breathing fire.*"[163] Indeed. This is quite obvious when comparing the teachings of this emerging faith to the teachings of God's Word. But the dragon behind this emerging "faith"—or "new world religion," "science," "paradigm," "worldview," "vision of reality," "Way," "dance," "play," "spirituality," "consciousness," "awakening," "enlightenment," "self-realization," "self-actualization," "evolutionary leap," "New Thought," etc.—isn't *green*. It's actually *red*, which fits the flames of hell that were created for it—and, yes, both the devil and the everlasting fire of hell have a literal existence. But thanks to "science falsely so called," man doesn't see it that way.

> *"And there appeared another wonder in heaven; and behold a great red dragon, ... And* **the great dragon** *was cast out, that old serpent, called the Devil, and Satan,* **which deceiveth the whole world***: he was cast out into the earth, and his angels were cast out with him." (Revelation 12:3, 9)*

> *"How art thou fallen from heaven, O Lucifer, son of the morning! how art thou cut down to the ground, which didst weaken the nations! For thou hast said in thine heart,* **I will ascend into heaven, ... I will be like the most High. Yet thou shalt be brought down to hell** *..." (Isaiah 14:12-15)*

> *"Then shall he say also unto them on the left hand, Depart from me, ye cursed,* **into everlasting fire, prepared for the devil and his angels** *... And these shall go away into everlasting punishment: but the righteous into life eternal." (Matthew 25:41, 46)*

Nevertheless, the dragon isn't the only one who still unrepentantly wants to "ascend into heaven" and "be like the most High."

In January 2010, physicist/cosmologist Brian Swimme (who wrote *The Universe Is a Green Dragon*) participated in an Online Teleseminar Series presented by *Integral Enlightenment* titled, "Awakening The Impulse To Evolve, The Birth of Evolutionary Spirituality."[164] After listing the 18 "most inspired visionary teachers" who participated, the website states:

> "**Join us on a Journey of Awakening . . .** Something big happened 13.7 billion years ago. Out of a tiny singularity, the entire Cosmos burst into existence. Now, at the dawn of the third millennium, something even bigger is happening. **The evolutionary impulse that gave birth to the Cosmos is waking up . . . as you**." (ellipsis dots in the original; emphasis added)[165]

The website also states: "Join us as we explore what it means to participate in the leading edge of evolution. Participation Is Free."[166] Actually, the cost of participating in this Journey of Awakening is *eternal*. But Oneness is a diabolical dance around the true and "*narrow*" meaning of the true Gospel of the true Christ that only a "*few*" are willing to believe (the events of which happened just about 2,000 years ago, thus making this the "dawn of the third *millennium*" since that eternally momentous event).

Sadly, many are being immersed in the "rhythm" of *the Destroyer* and are participating in his *broad way* "dance" and "play" that lead to *destruction*. Under the heading "Reinventing the World, Creating a New Cosmic Culture," the website for this Teleseminar Series also states that:

> "Brian Swimme will speak with us about **the need to *fundamentally re-imagine* our world, so that our internal view** of our lives and our planet **properly aligns** with the intelligent, *self-organizing, living Universe*....
>
> "Brian Swimme's primary field of research is the nature of the ***evolutionary dynamics*** of the Universe and the meaningful interpretation of **the human as *an emergent being*** within the Universe and Earth." (emphasis added)[167]

Also participating was Barbara Marx Hubbard, and under the heading "Impulse of Evolution, A Radical Path to the Future," this website states the following:

> "For over six decades Barbara Marx Hubbard has occupied a unique place in the field of **conscious evolution** (she coined the phrase) ... Her vitality draws upon **the timeless spiritual impulse *at the core* of our human *drive towards perfection*—the soul of evolution itself**. This 'Impulse of Evolution', **eternally unfolding within us all**, moves us toward ever deeper understanding and **greater participation in the processes of universal creation**. Join us as we explore with Barbara the vast co-creative movements of conscious evolution. *Tap into* your creative essence and expand your innate capacities for cosmic self-expression, self-development and *self-actualization*. **Become more *awake***, more aware and more responsible **co-creators of** our own fate and **the fate of the universe**....
>
> "Barbara Marx Hubbard is a pioneer in **positive options for the *future* of humanity**.... She has been instrumental in the creation of many future-oriented organizations, including the World Future Society, ... and the Association for **Global New Thought**....
>
> "She is also the producer of the award-winning DVD series ***Humanity Ascend-***

ing." (parentheses in the original; emphasis added)[168]

Sadly, rather than believe and obey God and His Son, too many people are choosing instead to "awaken" to today's preferred "reality" of *Oneness* in which humanity can bypass the soul "sort" and a negative future of "doom" in hell and simply "be like the most High" and "ascend into heaven." It therefore isn't surprising that, as reported by Discernment Ministries' Herescope, "[Mike] Morrell was a featured speaker, along with Emergent leader Brian McLaren at the New Age World Future Society Annual Conference held on July 26-28, 2008 in Washington, D.C."[169] As is pointed out in the quote about "Humanity Ascending," it is Barbara Marx Hubbard who was "instrumental in the creation of … the World Future Society." And at its Conference, Morrell and McLaren spoke on "The Future of the Religious Right," and the description of this talk includes the following:

> "[A] new progressive reality is challenging the monologue of the Religious Right, coming from such groups as Sojourners, Emergent Village and renewed mainline congregations. We'll explore … how younger evangelicals are increasingly **rejecting *doomsday* theology**, … **or a singular emphasis on *individual salvation*** … Three voices from the 'emergent church' will explore this capacity of *postmodern* Christianity to embrace and redefine tradition …
>
> "**Who should attend: Any *futurist* who feels that *everything must change* about religion** …" (emphasis added)[170]

Yes, everything is changing in today's merging and emerging "Christian"/New Age Oneness. And as Leonard Sweet openly admits, "*Postmodern* culture is an *anti-Christian* culture."[171] It is indeed. Hence its "conscious" "evolution" *away from* the Christian truth of God's Word—an "evolution" that has consciously journeyed so far outside the "box" of God's Word of truth that it has ascended into cosmic levels of apostasy.

This emerging faith that flips *everything upside down* is not a faith in which humanity is "*ascending*" into "*God*." Quite the opposite. Those in this emerging faith need to repent and believe in the true Person of God's Son before it's too late and they are literally "*brought down to hell*"—along with the master designer of Oneness, who is successfully aligning blinded minds in his new "light" of his new "gospel." A "gospel" in which humanity need merely "*ascend into heaven*" and "*be like the most High*." No, this false "gospel" of *Oneness* is not "*God's* Dream." And no matter how many minds align to "*think*" Oneness "*into being*," those who are co-creators of his emerging faith of Oneness are not "*living positive future, practicing Heaven*, and designing a bridge across which the whole of humanity will walk."[172]

> "And **no man hath ascended up to heaven**, but he that came down from heaven, even the Son of man which is in heaven…. For God so loved the world, that he gave his only begotten Son, that whosoever <u>believeth</u> in him should not <u>perish</u>, but have everlasting life." (John 3:13, 16)

Is your faith in *God's Gospel of Christ* or in *the devil's "gospel" of Oneness*? The first leads to *eternal life* and the second leads to *eternal hell*. But then, this is just one of those examples of "Christian fundamentalists promoting *medieval* notions of reality,"[173] right? After all, today's emerging "scientific" faith/New Quantum Spirituality of *Oneness* "reimagines" God as <u>in everyone/everything</u>, which of course includes <u>devils</u>. So what's there to fear? Only *eternal hell*.

This emerging faith that creates *Oneness* between *God* and "*all that exists*" is *blasphemy*. And *blasphemy* does not lead to *eternal life*. People can reject "doomsday theology" all they want, but *both hell and the devil have a literal existence*. And along with warning that "*hell*" is "*the fire that never shall be quenched*," God's Word warns that "*the Devil*" "*deceiveth the whole world*" (Mark 9:43-44; 45-46; Revelation 12:9). But then, those who are hell-bent on creating Oneness can choose not to heed God's warnings if they want to. After all, as Keith Green sang, the devil doesn't mind that no one believes in him anymore . . .

> "Oh my job keeps gettin' easier As time keeps slippin' away
> I can imitate the brightest light And make your night look just like day
> I put some truth in every lie To tickle itchin' ears
> You know I'm drawin' people Just like flies 'Cause they like what they hear
>
> "I'm gainin' power by the hour They're fallin' by the score
> You know it's gettin' very simple now Since no one believes in me anymore ...
>
> "You know they heard the truth But turned away And they followed me instead ...
>
> "Hey man you ain't no sinner No you've got the truth within
> And as your life slips by You'll believe the lie That you did it on your own
> But don't worry I'll be there to help you share Our dark eternal home ...
>
> "Well I used to have to sneak around But now they just open their doors
> No one's watchin' for my tricks Since no one Believes in me anymore ..."
> ("Satan's Boast")[174]

See Volume 2 . . .

. . . for the finale in which God alone is exalted. As stated in the Note to the Reader, Satan's emerging kingdom of his Antichrist, which is ready to burst forth in all its darkness in global opposition to God's coming Kingdom of His Son, will go down in bitter defeat taking far too many souls with it *in today's Christianity*. Is your soul going to be one of them?

(*Volume 2* can be ordered directly from Amazon, or read for free at http://www.inthenameofpurpose.org/ReimaginingGod.pdf.)

APPENDIX

The Majesty on High, the Everlasting True God in the Light of His Word

"Remember the former things of old: for I am God, and there is none else; I am God, and there is none like me." (Isaiah 46:9)

God Is . . .

- a God full of compassion
- a God of truth and without iniquity
- a refuge from the storm
- a shadow from the heat
- a shelter for us
- a shield unto them that put their trust in Him
- a strength to the needy in his distress
- a strong hold in the day of trouble
- a strong tower from the enemy
- a sure foundation
- a very present help in trouble
- able even to subdue all things unto Himself
- able to do exceeding abundantly above all that we ask or think
- able to keep that which we have committed unto Him
- able to keep us from falling, and to present us faultless before the presence of His glory with exceeding joy
- able to make all grace abound toward us, that we, always having all sufficiency in all things, may abound to every good work
- able to save them to the uttermost that come unto God by Jesus
- afflicted in all the affliction of His people
- Alpha and Omega, the beginning and the end, the first and the last
- before all things, and by Him all things consist
- clothed with majesty, strength, and honor
- exalted as head above all
- faithful and just to forgive us our sins and to cleanse us from all unrighteousness if we confess our sins
- faithful, Who shall stablish us and keep us from evil
- far above all principality, power, might, dominion, and every name that is named, not only in this world, but also in the one to come
- full of grace and truth
- glorious in holiness
- God, even from everlasting to everlasting
- good to all
- He that hears prayer
- He that opens and no man shuts, and shuts and no man opens
- He Who teaches man knowledge
- just in all that is brought upon us
- longsuffering
- love
- mighty in strength and wisdom
- mindful of us
- nigh unto all them that call upon Him in truth
- nigh unto them that are of a broken heart
- of great kindness
- of great power
- our deliverer
- our exceeding great reward
- our exceeding joy
- our fortress
- our hiding place
- our high tower
- our hope

- our life
- our peace
- our portion in the land of the living
- our refuge in the day of affliction and in times of trouble
- our song
- our strength in Whom we will trust
- our strong habitation whereunto we may continually resort
- perfect in knowledge
- precious
- ready to forgive
- right
- slow to anger
- strong Who executes His word
- the Almighty God
- the author and finisher of our faith
- the eternal God Who is our refuge, and underneath are the everlasting arms
- the everlasting God
- the Father of mercies
- the fountain of living waters
- the God of all comfort
- the God of Israel
- the health of our countenance
- the high and lofty one that inhabits eternity
- the King of all the earth
- the King of kings and Lord of lords
- the lifter up of our head
- the light of the world
- the LORD JEHOVAH in Whom is everlasting strength
- the LORD on high Who is mightier than the noise of many waters and the mighty waves of the sea
- the LORD Who goes before us, and will be with us
- the LORD that heals us
- the LORD Who exercises lovingkindness, judgment, and righteousness in the earth and delights in these things
- the LORD Who makes a way in the sea and a path in the mighty waters
- the Majesty on high
- the portion of our inheritance and of our cup
- the rock of our strength
- the Shepherd and Bishop of our souls
- the strength of our heart, and our portion for ever
- the strength of our life
- the strength of the righteous in the time of trouble
- the true God, the living God, and an everlasting King
- to be likened and made equal and compared to no one
- with us alway, even unto the end of the world
- with us to help us
- with us withersoever we go
- worthy to be praised

God Has . . .

- a multitude of tender mercies
- been our defense and refuge in the day of our trouble
- been our dwelling place in all generations
- blessed us with all spiritual blessings in heavenly places in Christ
- borne our griefs and carried our sorrows
- comprehended the dust of the earth in a measure, and weighed the mountains in scales
- delivered us from the power of darkness and has translated us into the kingdom of His dear Son
- gentleness
- given the Holy Spirit to them that obey Him
- given to us eternal life, and this life is in His Son
- given unto us all things that pertain unto life and godliness, through the knowledge of Him
- given us an understanding, that we may

- know Him that is true
- graven us upon the palms of His hands
- His way in the whirlwind and in the storm
- in His hand the soul of every living thing, and the breath of all mankind
- life in Himself
- loved us and has given us everlasting consolation and good hope through grace
- loved us with an everlasting love
- magnified His word above all His name
- measured the waters in the hollow of His hand
- no darkness in Him at all
- no pleasure in the death of him who dies
- not cast away His people
- not given us a spirit of fear, but of power, of love, and of a sound mind
- of old laid the foundation of the earth, and the heavens are the work of His hands
- removed our transgressions from us, as far as the east is from the west
- prepared His throne in the heavens, and His kingdom rules over all
- sent forth the Spirit of His Son into our hearts, crying, Abba, Father
- wrought all our works in us

God's . . .

- children shall have a place of refuge
- coming draws nigh
- compassions fail not
- counsels of old are faithfulness and truth
- delight is the prayer of the upright
- eye is upon them that fear Him, upon them that hope in His mercy to deliver their soul from death and to keep them alive in famine
- eyes are upon the righteous and His ears are open unto their cry and their prayers
- eyes run to and fro throughout the whole earth to show Himself strong in the behalf of them whose heart is perfect toward Him
- faithfulness reaches unto the clouds
- goodness and beauty are great
- grace is sufficient for us
- grace was exceeding abundant with faith and love which is in Christ Jesus
- greatness is unsearchable
- hand is upon all them for good that seek Him
- hand shall lead us
- is the greatness, the power, the glory, the victory, and the majesty
- judgments are upright
- kindness shall not depart from us
- kingdom is an everlasting kingdom
- lovingkindness is better than life
- mercy holds us up when our foot slips
- mercy toward them that fear Him is as great as the heaven is high above the earth
- peace passes all understanding and will keep our hearts and minds through Christ Jesus
- power works in us
- promises are exceeding great and precious
- right hand has spanned the heavens
- right hand shall hold us
- righteousness is an everlasting righteousness
- strength is made perfect in weakness
- tender mercies are over all His works
- thoughts unto us are more in number than the sand
- truth endures to all generations
- truth shall be our shield and buckler
- understanding is infinite
- voice is powerful and full of majesty
- way is perfect
- way is strength to the upright
- ways are everlasting
- ways are just, true, righteous, and right
- word is a lamp unto our feet and a light unto our path
- word is right
- word is true from the beginning
- word is truth

- word is settled in heaven for ever
- word shall stand for ever
- work is honorable, glorious, and perfect

God . . .

- begat us with the word of truth
- binds up the wounds of those broken in heart
- brings us out of the miry clay, and sets our feet upon a rock
- brought life and immortality to light through the gospel
- called us unto the fellowship of His Son Jesus Christ our Lord
- cannot be tempted with evil, and neither does He tempt anyone
- cares for us
- comforts those that are cast down
- comforts us in all our tribulation
- corrects, chastens, and rebukes those whom He loves
- crowns us with lovingkindness and tender mercies
- declares the end from the beginning and from ancient times the things that are not yet done
- declares things that are right
- directs our steps and paths and leads us by the way that we should go
- does according to His will in the army of heaven and among the inhabitants of the earth
- does great things which we cannot comprehend
- fails not
- faints not, neither is weary
- girds us with strength and makes our way perfect
- gives grace to the humble
- gives meat in due season
- gives power to the faint
- gives to all life, and breath, and all things
- gives us grace to help in time of need
- gives us the victory through our Lord Jesus

- works are great, marvelous, wondrous, holy, and all are done in truth

Christ
- gives wisdom to all men liberally who ask without upbraiding them
- heals the brokenhearted
- hears the cry of the afflicted
- hears the cry of the righteous and delivers them out of all their troubles
- hears the prayer of the righteous
- hears us when we seek Him and delivers us from all our fears
- in the midst of His people is mighty
- increases the strength of them that have no might
- keeps truth for ever
- keeps us by His power through faith unto salvation ready to be revealed in the last time
- knows how to deliver the godly out of temptations
- knows what things we have need of before we ask Him
- laid down His life for us
- lays up sound wisdom for the righteous
- leads us beside the still waters
- leads us in the paths of righteousness for His name's sake
- lifts up the meek and humble
- lifts us up above those that rise up against us
- lifts us up from the gates of death
- made the world and all things therein
- makes all things new
- makes known to us the ways of life
- makes the storm a calm so that the waves are still
- makes us to lie down in green pastures
- opens the eyes of the blind
- pities them that fear Him, as a father pities his children

- preserves all them that love Him
- purges every branch that bears fruit, that it may bring forth more fruit
- puts our tears in His book
- restores our soul
- rules by His power for ever
- rules the raging of the sea and when the waves arise, He stills them
- satisfies the longing soul and fills the hungry soul with goodness
- seals us with the Holy Spirit of promise after we believe
- shall sustain us when we cast our burden upon Him
- spake, and it was done; He commanded, and it stood fast
- stills the noise of the seas, the noise of their waves, and the tumult of the people
- takes pleasure in His people
- triumphed over the principalities and powers
- upholds all that fall
- upholds all things by the word of His power
- withdraws not His eyes from the righteous
- works all things after the counsel of His own will
- works all things together for good to them that love Him
- works in us both to will and to do of His good pleasure

God Will . . .

- abundantly pardon
- be a refuge for the oppressed
- be our everlasting light
- be with us in trouble, who have made the most High our habitation
- be with us when we pass through the waters
- bless His people with peace
- compass the righteous with favor as with a shield
- deliver the needy when he cries, the poor also, and him that hath no helper
- deliver us from every evil work
- draw nigh to us when we draw nigh to Him
- feed His flock like a shepherd and will cause them to lie down
- fulfill the desire of them that fear Him, and will hear their cry and will save them
- gather the lambs with His arm and carry them in His bosom
- give strength unto His people
- give us rest
- guide us with His counsel, and afterward receive us to glory
- have compassion according to the multitude of His mercies
- have mercy on us with everlasting kindness
- have mercy upon His afflicted
- hide them that fear Him and trust in Him in the secret of His presence
- hide us in His pavilion, in the secret of His tabernacle, in the time of trouble
- hold our right hand, saying, Fear not, I will help you
- instruct us and teach us in the way we shall go
- joy over His people with singing
- keep him in perfect peace whose mind is stayed on Him
- make us full of joy with His countenance
- make us perfect, stablish, strengthen, settle us
- neither slumber nor sleep
- never leave us nor forsake us
- not suffer His faithfulness to fail
- not suffer our foot to be moved
- not suffer the soul of the righteous to famish
- not suffer us to be tempted above that we are able, but will with the temptation also make a way to escape that we may be able to bear it

- perfect that which concerns us
- perform the good work He began in us until the day of Jesus Christ
- preserve our whole spirit and soul and body blameless unto the coming of our Lord Jesus Christ
- preserve us unto His heavenly kingdom
- revive us though we walk in the midst of trouble
- seek that which was lost
- set us in the way of His steps
- strengthen our heart
- strengthen that which was sick
- supply all our need according to His riches in glory by Christ Jesus
- swallow up death in victory
- take us up when our father and mother forsake us
- wipe away all tears from the eyes of His people

More About God

- all things were created by Him, and for Him
- at the LORD's right hand there are pleasures for evermore
- every good gift and every perfect gift is from the Father of lights
- for of Him and through Him and to Him are all things
- in God are hid all the treasures of wisdom and knowledge
- in God's hand there is power and might, so that none is able to withstand Him
- in the LORD's presence is fulness of joy
- it is impossible for Him to lie
- known unto God are all His works from the beginning of the world
- none can stay His hand
- nothing is too hard for Him
- O the depth of the riches both of the wisdom and knowledge of God!
- our times are in His hand
- safety is of the LORD
- the breath of the Almighty has given us life
- the heaven and heaven of heavens cannot contain Him
- the heaven and the heaven of heavens, the earth also with all that is therein are the LORD'S
- the inspiration of the Almighty gives man understanding
- the mercy of the LORD is from everlasting to everlasting upon them that fear Him
- the righteous, and the wise, and their works, are in the hand of God
- the throne of the Majesty is in the heavens
- the very hairs of our head are all numbered by God
- there has not failed one word of all His good promise
- there is no unrighteousness with God
- there is no wisdom nor understanding nor counsel against the LORD
- this God is our God for ever and ever, and will be our guide even unto death
- with Him is plenteous redemption
- with the Father of lights is no variableness, neither shadow of turning

"The LORD is high above all nations, and his glory above the heavens. Who is like unto the LORD our God, Who dwelleth on high, Who humbleth himself to behold the things that are in heaven and in the earth!" (Psalm 113:4-6)

ENDNOTES

(Website information was current at the time it was written.)

Part One: The Shift

3. "Sick of God and God's religion" (pages 23-24)
1. William P. Young, *The Shack: Where Tragedy Confronts Eternity* (Newbury Park, CA.: Windblown Media, 2007), p. 197. (Note: there is a slight variation of page numbers among the printings of *The Shack*.)
2. Ibid., p. 66.

4. "Man in the chambers of his imagery" (pages 25-27)
1. William Paul Young, "The Shack - update - Background #1," May 22, 2007, http://windrumors.com/2007/05/the-shack-update-background-1/.
2. William Paul Young, "Is the story of THE SHACK true...is Mack a 'real' person?," August 15, 2007, http://www.windrumors.com/30/is-the-story-of-the-shack-trueis-mack-a-real-person/.

5. "How great is that darkness!" (pages 28-30)
1. William P. Young, *The Shack: Where Tragedy Confronts Eternity*, pp. 99-100.
2. Ibid., p. 112.
3. For more information on the "peace" and "safety" of New Age Oneness, see "Are You 'Being Led Away with the Error of the Wicked' to the New Age Ark of Oneness?," by Tamara Hartzell, February 2008, posted online at http://www.inthenameofpurpose.org/arkofoneness.pdf.
4. Neale Donald Walsch, *What God Wants: A Compelling Answer to Humanity's Biggest Question* (New York, NY: Atria Books, 2005), p. 179.
5. Ibid., p. 172.
6. Ibid., p. 221.

7. The fear-based agenda of the "doctrine police" (pages 33-37)
1. William P. Young, *The Shack*, p. 203.
2. Ibid.

8. The faith that is set forth by God in His Word is the faith of God (pages 38-43)
1. William P. Young, *The Shack*, p. 182.
2. Ibid., pp. 225, 192.
3. Ibid., pp. 225, 181-182.
4. Ibid., pp. 181-182.
5. Ibid., p. 192; emphasis added.
6. Helena P. Blavatsky, "The New Cycle," *La Revue Theosophique* magazine, March 21, 1889, http://www.blavatsky.net/blavatsky/arts/NewCycle.htm. See also Helena P. Blavatsky, "To the Readers of 'Lucifer,'" *Lucifer* magazine, January 1888, http://www.blavatsky.net/blavatsky/arts/ToTheReadersOfLucifer.htm. For more information on this occult lie that "There is no Religion higher than Truth," see "Are You 'Being Led Away with the Error of the Wicked' to the New Age Ark of Oneness?," by Tamara Hartzell, http://www.inthenameofpurpose.org/arkofoneness.pdf.
7. William P. Young, *The Shack*, p. 112.

9. Faith in the truth is true faith (pages 44-46)
1. William P. Young, *The Shack*, p. 181.
2. Ibid., pp. 181-182.
3. Ibid., p. 99.
4. Ibid., p. 110.

10. Rock does not shift (pages 47-51)
1. William P. Young, *The Shack*, pp. 99-100.
2. Ibid., p. 66.
3. Ibid., p. 98.
4. Ibid., p. 204.

Part Two: The Circle

11. The heart and circle of the "relationship" (pages 55-58)
1. For more information see "Are You 'Being Led Away with the Error of the Wicked' to the New Age Ark of Oneness?," by Tamara Hartzell, http://www.inthenameofpurpose.org/arkofoneness.pdf.
2. William P. Young, *The Shack*, pp. 122, 146.
3. Ibid., p. 182.

12. The post-truth transformation of a Wordless "faith" (pages 59-62)
1. These subjects are addressed in detail in "Are You 'Being Led Away with the Error of the Wicked' to the New Age Ark of Oneness?," http://www.inthenameofpurpose.org/arkofoneness.pdf; and also in *In the Name of Purpose: Sacrificing Truth on the Altar of Unity* (Philadelphia, PA: Xlibris Corporation, 2007); both by Tamara Hartzell. [The latter is also posted online as a free e-book (© 2006) at http://www.inthenameofpurpose.org/inthename.pdf.]

13. Faith that comes by *the Word of God* vs. Faith that comes by *relationship* (pages 63-67)
1. William P. Young, *The Shack*, pp. 122, 146, 112.
2. Marcus J. Borg, *The God We Never Knew: Beyond Dogmatic Religion to a More Authentic Contemporary Faith* (New York, NY: HarperSanFrancisco, 1997), p. 12.
3. Ibid., p. 51.
4. Marcus Borg, "Character of God," sermon, March 16, 2003, Calvary Episcopal Church, http://www.explorefaith.org/homiliesLent/LentenHomily03.16.03.html.
5. Marcus Borg, "Faith: A Journey of Trust," originally delivered at Calvary Episcopal Church, http://www.explorefaith.org/faces/my_faith/borg/faith_by_marcus_borg.php?ht=.
6. Marcus Borg, "Meeting God Again," an interview with Borg by Liza Hetherington, http://www.gracecathedral.org/enrichment/interviews/int_19970601.shtml.

14. God's Word -- "a stumbling block in the way"! (pages 68-73)
1. Marcus Borg, "How We Imagine God Matters," http://www.beliefnet.com/Faiths/2000/03/How-We-Imagine-God-Matters.aspx?p=1.
2. Marcus J. Borg, *Reading the Bible Again for the First Time: Taking the Bible Seriously but Not Literally* (New York, NY: HarperOne, 2001), p. 23.
3. Marcus Borg, "I am uncomfortable with some of the doctrines professed in organized religion. Is believing certain creeds really what Christianity is all about?," http://www.explorefaith.org/faith/explore_christianity/questions_of_faith_and_doubt/is_believing_certain_creeds_really_what_christianity_is_all_about.php?ht=.
4. Marcus Borg, "Meeting God Again," an interview with Borg by Liza Hetherington, http://www.gracecathedral.org/enrichment/interviews/int_19970601.shtml.
5. Marcus Borg, "Faith, Not Belief," February 24, 2002, Calvary Episcopal Church, http://www.explorefaith.org/LentenHomily02.24.02.html.
6. Marcus J. Borg, *The God We Never Knew: Beyond Dogmatic Religion to a More Authentic Contemporary Faith*, p. 51.
7. Marcus J. Borg, *Reading the Bible Again for the First Time: Taking the Bible Seriously but Not Literally*, pp. 3-5.
8. Marcus Borg, "Meeting God Again," an interview with Borg by Liza Hetherington, http://www.gracecathedral.org/enrichment/interviews/int_19970601.shtml.
9. Marcus Borg, "I am uncomfortable with some of the doctrines professed in organized religion. Is believing certain creeds really what Christianity is all about?," http://www.explorefaith.org/faith/explore_christianity/questions_of_faith_and_doubt/is_believing_certain_creeds_really_what_christianity_is_all_about.php?ht=.
10. Marcus Borg, "How can Christians accept Christianity as the way to God and still give credence to the truth of other religions?," http://www.explorefaith.org/faith/explore_christianity/questions_of_faith_and_doubt/how_can_christians_give_credence_to_other_religions.php.

15. "Transforming theology" -- "God in the very substance of creation" (pages 74-78)
1. William P. Young, *The Shack*, p. 112.
2. Ibid., pp. 181-182.
3. Marcus Borg, "Faith: A Journey of Trust," originally delivered at Calvary Episcopal Church, http://www.explorefaith.org/faces/my_faith/borg/faith_by_marcus_borg.php?ht=.
4. Marcus J. Borg, *Reading the Bible Again for the First Time*, p. 83.

5. Leonard Sweet, *Quantum Spirituality: A Postmodern Apologetic* (Dayton, OH: Whaleprints for SpiritVenture Ministries, Inc., 1991, 1994), p. 125. Cited from *A "Wonderful" Deception: The Further New Age Implications of the Emerging Purpose Driven Movement*, by Warren B. Smith (Silverton, OR: Lighthouse Trails Publishing, 2009), pp. 113-114. [Note: Smith's book has since been republished by Mountain Stream Press under the same title (Magalia, CA: Mountain Stream Press, 2011).]
6. Ibid., (Sweet), p. 60.
7. Pierre Teilhard de Chardin, *Christianity and Evolution* (New York, NY: Harcourt Brace Jovanovich, Inc., 1971), p. 56. Cited from *A "Wonderful" Deception: The Further New Age Implications of the Emerging Purpose Driven Movement*, by Warren B. Smith, p. 114. The quote from Smith is: "The New Age implications of their [Rick Warren's and Leonard Sweet's] writings relate directly to the following statement made by Pierre Teilhard de Chardin: 'What I am proposing to do is to narrow that gap between pantheism and Christianity by bringing out what one might call the Christian soul of pantheism or the pantheist aspect of Christianity.'"
8. Leonard Sweet, *Quantum Spirituality: A Postmodern Apologetic*, p. 106; as quoted by Warren B. Smith in *A "Wonderful" Deception*, p. 111.
9. Warren B. Smith, *A "Wonderful" Deception*, p. 113.
10. Philip Clayton, Transforming Theology: Emergence for Emergents, Part One, March 13, 2009, "a conversation about emergence science and emergent church" between emergent leaders Philip Clayton and Tony Jones, transcribed from the video at Tony Jones' Blog, http://blog.beliefnet.com/tonyjones/science/2009/03/.
11. For more information see "Are You 'Being Led Away with the Error of the Wicked' to the New Age Ark of Oneness?," by Tamara Hartzell, http://www.inthenameofpurpose.org/arkofoneness.pdf.
12. "God," as quoted by Neale Donald Walsch, *Friendship with God: an uncommon dialogue* (New York, NY: The Berkley Publishing Group, 1999), p. 404.
13. Ibid., p. 375.
14. Ibid., p. 357.
15. Neale Donald Walsch, *What God Wants: A Compelling Answer to Humanity's Biggest Question*, p. 221.
16. Ibid., pp. 154-155.
17. Marcus Borg, "How can Christians accept Christianity as the way to God and still give credence to the truth of other religions?," http://www.explorefaith.org/faith/explore_christianity/questions_of_faith_and_doubt/how_can_christians_give_credence_to_other_religions.php.

16. The immanent "God" of Oneness, imagined and defined in *limitless* ways (pages 79-85)

1. Sue Monk Kidd, for one, would agree: "A Divine Feminine symbol ... begins to shift thousands of years of dualistic thinking, setting up a new mandate for the divinity of the earth and the holiness of the body.... Patriarchy has majored in divine transcendence, which means separateness from the material universe—being above, beyond, or apart from it. Divine immanence, on the other hand, is divinity here, near and now, inherent in the material stuff of life.... Restoring the feminine symbol of Deity means that divinity will no longer be *only* heavenly, other, out there, up there, beyond time and space, beyond body and death. It will also be right here, right now, in me, in the earth, in this river and this rock, in excrement and roses alike." Sue Monk Kidd, *The Dance of the Dissident Daughter: A Woman's Journey from Christian Tradition to the Sacred Feminine* (New York, NY: HarperCollins Publishers Inc., 1996), p. 160; underline added.

   Sue Monk Kidd is a former "conservative Southern Baptist Sunday school teacher" who changed after "introduced to the writings of [contemplative] Thomas Merton." See "Our Father in Heaven or Our Mother the Earth?," Lighthouse Trails Research Blog, August 5, 2009, http://www.lighthousetrailsresearch.com/blog/?p=1105&zoom_highlight=sue+monk+kidd. For more information on Kidd, see also "From Southern Baptist to Goddess Worship: Sue Monk Kidd," by David Cloud, July 15, 2008, Way of Life Literature, http://www.wayoflife.org/database/suemonkkidd.html; and Ray Yungen's book *A Time of Departing: How Ancient Mystical Practices are Uniting Christians with the World's Religions*, Second Edition, (Silverton, OR: Lighthouse Trails Publishing Company, 2002, 2006), pp. 134-137. Thanks to Ray Yungen for finding this quote—see "A Global Religion - Is God in Graffiti?" by Ray Yungen, http://www.crossroad.to/Quotes/spirituality/lighthousetrails/yungen-graffiti.htm.
2. "God," as quoted by Neale Donald Walsch, *Friendship with God: an uncommon dialogue*, pp. 375, 357.
3. "God," as quoted by Neale Donald Walsch, *Conversations with God: an uncommon dialogue, Book 1*, (New York, NY: G. P. Putnam's Sons, 1996), p. 152.
4. Ibid., p. 61.
5. Neale Donald Walsch's Humanity's Team website, http://humanitysteam.org/content/view/13/27/. Cited from "Are You 'Being Led Away with the Error of the Wicked' to the New Age Ark of Oneness?," by Tamara Hartzell, http://www.inthenameofpurpose.org/arkofoneness.pdf, p. 12.
6. Neale Donald Walsch, *What God Wants*, p. 144.

7. "God," as quoted by Neale Donald Walsch, *Tomorrow's God: Our Greatest Spiritual Challenge* (New York, NY: Atria Books, 2004), p. 28.
8. Neale Donald Walsch, and "God," as quoted by Walsch, ibid., p. 26.
9. "God," as quoted by Neale Donald Walsch, ibid., pp. 29-30.
10. Neale Donald Walsch, *What God Wants*, pp. 154-156.
11. Ibid., p. 167.
12. Ibid., p. 209.
13. Ibid., p. 172.

Part Three: The Lie
17. "When we can contact our own inner God all truth will be revealed to us" (pages 89-92)
1. Marcus Borg, "How can I know the truth about Christianity if I question the Bible's status as the literal Word of God?," http://www.explorefaith.org/faith/explore_christianity/questions_of_faith_and_doubt/how_can_i_k now_the_truth_about_christianity_if_i_question_the_bibles_status_as_the_literal_word_of_god.php.
2. Marcus J. Borg, *The God We Never Knew*, p. 5.
3. Alice Bailey and Djwhal Khul, *The Rays and the Initiations*, Part I - Fourteen Rules for Group Initiation, Rule Fourteen, (Caux, Switzerland: Netnews Association and/or its suppliers, 2002), Lucis Trust, 1960 [see http://web.archive.org/web/20050726004029/http://laluni.helloyou.ws/netnews/bk/toc.html], http://www.netnews.org -- http://web.archive.org/web/20060213230403/laluni.helloyou.ws/netnews/bk/rays/rays1111.html.
4. Alice Bailey, *From Intellect to Intuition*, Chapter Three - The Nature of the Soul, (Caux, Switzerland: Netnews Association and/or its suppliers, 2002), Lucis Trust, 1932 [see http://web.archive.org/web/20050726 004029/http://laluni.helloyou.ws/netnews/bk/toc.html], http://www.netnews.org -- http://web.archive.org/web/20070327142259/laluni.helloyou.ws/netnews/bk/intellect/inte1017.html.
5. Ibid., Chapter Eight - The Universality of Meditation, http://web.archive.org/web/20070327142351/laluni.helloyou.ws/netnews/bk/intellect/inte1055.html.
6. Ibid., http://web.archive.org/web/20070324100220/laluni.helloyou.ws/netnews/bk/intellect/inte1061.html.
7. Marcus Borg, "Mystical Experiences of God," January 5, 2007, The Washington Post and Newsweek, On Faith, http://newsweek.washingtonpost.com/onfaith/panelists/marcus_borg/2007/01/mystical_religious_experiences.html.
8. Alice Bailey and Djwhal Khul, *The Rays and the Initiations*, Part I - Fourteen Rules for Group Initiation, Rule Fourteen, http://web.archive.org/web/20060210231040/laluni.helloyou.ws/netnews/bk/rays/rays1110.html.
9. Alice Bailey, *From Bethlehem to Calvary*, Chapter Seven - Our Immediate Goal, The Founding of the Kingdom, (Caux, Switzerland: Netnews Association and/or its suppliers, 2002), Lucis Trust, 1937 [see http://web.archive.org/web/20050726004029/http://laluni.helloyou.ws/netnews/bk/toc.html], http://www.netnews.org -- http://web.archive.org/web/20060209132541/http://laluni.helloyou.ws/netnews/bk/bethlehem/beth1079.html.
10. Alice A. Bailey, *The Consciousness Of The Atom* (New York, NY: Lucis Publishing Company, 1961), First Printing 1922, Ninth Printing 1974, p. 136.

18. *"Ye shall not surely die"* (pages 93-101)
1. Marcus J. Borg, *Reading the Bible Again for the First Time*, p. 214.
2. Ibid., p. 218.
3. "God," as quoted by Neale Donald Walsch, *Conversations with God: an uncommon dialogue, Book 3* (Charlottesville, VA: Hampton Roads Publishing Company, Inc., 1998), pp. 56-57.
4. Ibid., p. 366.
5. "God," as quoted by Neale Donald Walsch, *The New Revelations: A Conversation with God* (New York, NY: Atria Books, 2002), p. 132.
6. Alice Bailey, *From Bethlehem to Calvary*, Chapter Seven - Our Immediate Goal, The Founding of the Kingdom, http://web.archive.org/web/20070213074428/laluni.helloyou.ws/netnews/bk/bethlehem/beth1082.html.
7. Marcus J. Borg, *Reading the Bible Again for the First Time*, p. 23.
8. Marcus Borg, "Character of God," sermon, March 16, 2003, Calvary Episcopal Church, http://www.explorefaith.org/homiliesLent/LentenHomily03.16.03.html.
9. Marcus J. Borg, *Reading the Bible Again for the First Time*, p. 299.
10. "God," as quoted by Neale Donald Walsch, *Tomorrow's God: Our Greatest Spiritual Challenge*, p. 22.
11. "God," as quoted by Neale Donald Walsch, *Conversations with God: an uncommon dialogue, Book 1*, p. 197.
12. "God," as quoted by Neale Donald Walsch, *Tomorrow's God*, p. 32.

13. Ibid., pp. 29-30.
14. Neale Donald Walsch, *What God Wants*, p. 179.
15. Ibid., p. 221.
16. Alice Bailey and Djwhal Khul, *A Treatise on White Magic*, Rule Ten - The Present Age and the Future, (Caux, Switzerland: Netnews Association and/or its suppliers, 2002), Lucis Trust, 1934 [see http://web.archive.org/web/20050726004029/http://laluni.helloyou.ws/netnews/bk/toc.html], http://www.netnews.org -- http://web.archive.org/web/20050505135414/http://laluni.helloyou.ws/netnews/bk/magic/magi1139.html.
17. Alice Bailey, *From Intellect to Intuition*, Chapter Eight - The Universality of Meditation, http://web.archive.org/web/20070327142351/laluni.helloyou.ws/netnews/bk/intellect/inte1055.html.
18. "God," as quoted by Neale Donald Walsch, *Conversations with God: an uncommon dialogue*, Book 3, p. 57.
19. William P. Young, *The Shack*, p. 204; emphasis added.
20. Ibid., p. 112; emphasis added.
21. Ibid., p. 225.
22. Ibid., p. 192.
23. Ibid.
24. Ibid., p. 120.
25. Ibid., pp. 122, 146.
26. Ibid., p. 99.
27. Ibid., p. 98.

19. "The way of Jesus is a universal way ... not a set of beliefs about Jesus" (pages 102-108)
1. Marcus J. Borg, *Reading the Bible Again for the First Time*, p. 218.
2. Ibid., pp. 215-217.
3. Ibid., pp. 299-300.
4. Ibid., p. 24.
5. Ibid., pp. 3-5.
6. Neale Donald Walsch, *What God Wants*, p. 221; emphasis added.
7. "God," as quoted by Neale Donald Walsch, *Friendship with God*, p. 375.
8. Alice Bailey and Djwhal Khul, *Esoteric Psychology II*, Chapter I - The Egoic Ray, The Seven Laws of Soul or Group Life, (Caux, Switzerland: Netnews Association and/or its suppliers, 2002), Lucis Trust, 1942 [see http://web.archive.org/web/20050726004029/http://laluni.helloyou.ws/netnews/bk/toc.html], http://www.netnews.org -- http://web.archive.org/web/20051123134656/http://laluni.helloyou.ws/netnews/bk/psychology2/psyc2040.html.
9. Marcus J. Borg, *Reading the Bible Again for the First Time*, p. 26.
10. Marcus Borg, "Faith, Not Belief," February 24, 2002, Calvary Episcopal Church, http://www.explorefaith.org/LentenHomily02.24.02.html.

20. The "participatory divinity" of "the Jesus way" (pages 109-115)
1. Gary Dorsey, "Tie that Binds 'Emergent' Church," September 1, 2004, *The Atlanta Journal-Constitution*, posted on Mike Morrell's Blog at http://zoecarnate.wordpress.com/tie-that-binds-emergent-church/.
2. William P. Young, *The Shack*, p. 112.
3. Ibid., p. 181.
4. Ibid., p. 182; emphasis added.
5. Mike Morrell, "Panentheism & Interspirituality - What's Jesus Got to do With It?," June 25, 2009, http://zoecarnate.wordpress.com/2009/06/25/panentheism-interspirituality-whats-jesus-got-to-do-with-it/; also posted online at http://www.theooze.com/blog/2006/04/panentheism-interspirituality-whats.html.
6. Marcus J. Borg, *Reading the Bible Again for the First Time*, p. 218.
7. Neale Donald Walsch, *What God Wants*, p. 206.
8. Ibid., pp. 154-155.
9. Marcus Borg, "How can Christians accept Christianity as the way to God and still give credence to the truth of other religions?," http://www.explorefaith.org/faith/explore_christianity/questions_of_faith_and_doubt/how_can_christians_give_credence_to_other_religions.php.
10. Marcus Borg, "Character of God," sermon, March 16, 2003, Calvary Episcopal Church, http://www.explorefaith.org/homiliesLent/LentenHomily03.16.03.html.
11. "God," as quoted by Neale Donald Walsch, *Friendship with God*, p. 357.
12. For more information on the nature of this "Cosmic Christ" and how "it" is entering today's shifting Christianity, see *A "Wonderful" Deception*, by Warren B. Smith, especially chapters 10 and 11.
13. Alice Bailey, *From Bethlehem to Calvary*, Chapter Two - The First Initiation, The Birth at Bethlehem, http://web.archive.org/web/20070219003449/http://laluni.helloyou.ws/netnews/bk/bethlehem/beth1025.html.

14. Ibid., Chapter Seven - Our Immediate Goal, The Founding of the Kingdom, http://web.archive.org/web/20070213074428/laluni.helloyou.ws/netnews/bk/bethlehem/beth1082.html.
15. Ibid., Chapter Two - The First Initiation, The Birth at Bethlehem, http://web.archive.org/web/20070218064534/http://laluni.helloyou.ws/netnews/bk/bethlehem/beth1022.html.
16. Mike Morrell, "Panentheism - Perichoresis - Christology: Participatory Divinity," June 30, 2009, http://zoecarnate.wordpress.com/2009/06/30/panentheism-perichoresis-christology-participatory-divinity/.
17. Alice Bailey and Djwhal Khul, *The Rays and the Initiations*, Part I - Fourteen Rules for Group Initiation, http://web.archive.org/web/20070218153043/http://laluni.helloyou.ws/netnews/bk/rays/rays1111.html.
18. "God," as quoted by Neale Donald Walsch, *Tomorrow's God*, pp. 162-163.
19. Ibid., p. 11.
20. Alice Bailey, *From Bethlehem to Calvary*, Chapter Seven - Our Immediate Goal, The Founding of the Kingdom, http://web.archive.org/web/20070213074428/laluni.helloyou.ws/netnews/bk/bethlehem/beth1082.html.
21. Ibid., http://web.archive.org/web/20070216005818/laluni.helloyou.ws/netnews/bk/bethlehem/beth1079.html.
22. Mike Morrell, "Panentheism - Perichoresis - Christology: Participatory Divinity," June 30, 2009, http://zoecarnate.wordpress.com/2009/06/30/panentheism-perichoresis-christology-participatory-divinity/.

21. "Chain of command? That sounds ghastly!" -- "We want you to join us in our circle of relationship" (pages 116-123)

1. William P. Young, *The Shack*, pp. 225, 192; emphasis added.
2. Ibid., pp. 145-146.
3. Ibid., p. 122.
4. Ibid.
5. Ibid., pp. 122-123.
6. Neale Donald Walsch, *What God Wants*, pp. 209-210.
7. Ibid., pp. 103-104.
8. Ibid., p. 179.
9. "God," as quoted by Neale Donald Walsch, *Conversations with God, Book 1*, p. 95.
10. Ibid., p. 41.
11. Ibid., p. 135.
12. Neale Donald Walsch, *What God Wants*, p. 167.
13. "God," as quoted by Neale Donald Walsch, *Friendship with God*, pp. 185-186.
14. "God," as quoted by Neale Donald Walsch, *Conversations with God, Book 3*, p. 366.
15. William P. Young, *The Shack*, p. 122.
16. Ibid., p. 145.
17. Ibid., p. 124.

Part Four: The Transformation
22. "What if we were to think connectness rather than correctness?" (pages 127-129)

1. Leonard Sweet, *So Beautiful: Divine Design for Life and the Church* (Colorado Springs, CO: David C. Cook, 2009), back cover.
2. "God Sent a Person, Not a Proposition," "A Conversation with Len Sweet," by Tamara Cissna, *George Fox Journal*, Fall 2005, Volume 1, Number 3, http://www.georgefox.edu/journalonline/fall05/emerging.html (also posted on Leonard Sweet's website at http://www.leonardsweet.com/article_details.php?id=49). Prefacing this interview of Sweet is the statement: "Calling on his understanding of postmodern ideals and his years as a mentor to pastors, he shares his insights into The Emerging Church." Leonard Sweet is "Visiting Distinguished Professor" at George Fox University and "Lead Mentor" at George Fox Evangelical Seminary—see Faculty & Staff, http://www.georgefox.edu/seminary/programs/dmin/sfs/fac_staff.html. (Incidentally, this Seminary focuses on "spiritual formation;" see http://www.georgefox.edu/seminary/about/index.html).
3. About, http://leonardsweet.com/about.php; and Sermons.com, Leonard Sweet, http://www.sermons.com/leonardSweet.asp. See also News Release, "Christian Author/Futurist Leonard Sweet Speaking in Meridian," October 7, 2003, http://blogs.georgefox.edu/newsreleases/?p=2353.
4. Ibid., (About and News Release).
5. Leonard Sweet, *So Beautiful: Divine Design for Life and the Church*, p. 139.
6. Ibid., pp. 110-111.

23. "MRI theology is the only theology worth bothering with" (pages 130-137)

1. Leonard Sweet, *So Beautiful*, p. 18.

2. Ibid., p. 47.
3. Ibid., p. 27.
4. Ibid.
5. Ibid., p. 31.
6. Ibid., p. 27.
7. Ibid., p. 31.
8. Ibid., p. 124.
9. Ibid., p. 37.
10. Ibid., p. 65.
11. Ibid., p. 129.
12. Ibid., pp. 59-60.
13. Ibid., p. 217.
14. Ibid., p. 214.
15. Ibid., p. 114.
16. Ibid., p. 106.
17. Leonard Sweet, *Quantum Spirituality*, p. 125. Cited from *A "Wonderful" Deception*, by Warren B. Smith, p. 104; ellipsis dots in the original.
18. Leonard Sweet, *So Beautiful*, p. 139.
19. Ibid., p. 122.
20. Ibid., p. 110.
21. Ibid., p. 111.
22. Ibid., p. 129.
23. Marcus Borg, "Faith, Not Belief," February 24, 2002, Calvary Episcopal Church, http://www.explorefaith.org/LentenHomily02.24.02.html.
24. Leonard Sweet, *So Beautiful*, p. 114.
25. Ibid., p. 110.
26. Ibid., p. 128.
27. Marcus Borg, "Faith, Not Belief," February 24, 2002, Calvary Episcopal Church, http://www.explorefaith.org/LentenHomily02.24.02.html.
28. Leonard Sweet, *So Beautiful*, p. 114.
29. Ibid., p. 126.
30. Ibid., p. 117.
31. Ibid., p. 139.
32. Ibid., p. 110.
33. Ibid., p. 122.
34. Ibid., p. 111.
35. Ibid., back cover.
36. Sermons.com, Leonard Sweet, http://www.sermons.com/leonardSweet.asp; and About, http://leonardsweet.com/about.php.
37. Ibid., (About).
38. Ibid.; and also Sermons.com, Leonard Sweet, http://www.sermons.com/leonardSweet.asp.
39. About, http://leonardsweet.com/about.php.
40. "God Sent a Person, Not a Proposition," "A Conversation with Len Sweet," by Tamara Cissna, *George Fox Journal*, Fall 2005, Volume 1, Number 3, http://www.georgefox.edu/journalonline/fall05/emerging.html (also posted on Leonard Sweet's website at http://www.leonardsweet.com/article_details.php?id=49).
41. For examples, see *A "Wonderful" Deception*, by Warren B. Smith, chapters 10 and 11. The fact that Rick Warren and Leonard Sweet are compatible coworkers is not surprising given that they share similar beliefs. A very telling example is the anti-scriptural book *Growing Spiritual Redwoods* which they both highly endorsed (for more information on this book, see chapter 22 of *In the Name of Purpose*, by Tamara Hartzell, which is also posted online at http://www.inthenameofpurpose.org/inthename.pdf). Also, Leonard Sweet's book *SoulTsunami* prominently featured Rick Warren's endorsement on its front cover. [See William M. Easum and Thomas G. Bandy, *Growing Spiritual Redwoods* (Nashville, Tennessee: Abingdon Press, 1997), back cover; and Leonard Sweet, *SoulTsunami: Sink or Swim in New Millennium Culture* (Grand Rapids, MI: Zondervan, 1999).]
42. About, http://leonardsweet.com/about.php. See also News Release, "Christian Author/Futurist Leonard Sweet Speaking in Meridian," October 7, 2003, http://blogs.georgefox.edu/newsreleases/?p=2353; and Sermons.com, Leonard Sweet, http://www.sermons.com/leonardSweet.asp.
43. Ibid., (Sermons.com).

24. "Christians aren't people who follow Christianity" (pages 138-145)

1. Marcus Borg, "Faith, Not Belief," February 24, 2002, Calvary Episcopal Church, http://www.explorefaith.org/LentenHomily02.24.02.html
2. Leonard Sweet, *So Beautiful*, p. 99.
3. Marcus Borg, "Faith, Not Belief," February 24, 2002, Calvary Episcopal Church, http://www.explorefaith.org/LentenHomily02.24.02.html.
4. Leonard Sweet, *So Beautiful*, p. 101.
5. Gerard W. Hughes, *God in All Things* (London: Hodder & Stoughton, 2003), p. 19. Cited from *So Beautiful*, by Leonard Sweet, p. 270.
6. Leonard Sweet, *So Beautiful*, p. 111.
7. Leonard Sweet, *Quantum Spirituality*, p. 125.
8. Ibid., p. 63.
9. Ibid., p. 125.
10. Ibid., p. 124.
11. Leonard Sweet, *So Beautiful*, p. 184.
12. Leonard Sweet, *Quantum Spirituality*, p. 121.
13. Leonard Sweet, *So Beautiful*, p. 152.
14. Ibid., p. 64.
15. Ibid., p. 128.
16. Ibid., p. 126.
17. Ibid., p. 111.
18. Alice Bailey, *From Bethlehem to Calvary*, Chapter Two - The First Initiation, The Birth at Bethlehem, http://web.archive.org/web/20070219003449/http://laluni.helloyou.ws/netnews/bk/bethlehem/beth1025.html.
19. Leonard Sweet, *Quantum Spirituality*, pp. 124-125.
20. Alice Bailey and Djwhal Khul, *The Rays and the Initiations*, Part I - Fourteen Rules for Group Initiation, http://web.archive.org/web/20070218153043/http://laluni.helloyou.ws/netnews/bk/rays/rays1111.html.
21. Alice Bailey, *From Bethlehem to Calvary*, Chapter Two - The First Initiation, The Birth at Bethlehem, http://web.archive.org/web/20070218064534/http://laluni.helloyou.ws/netnews/bk/bethlehem/beth1022.html.
22. Leonard Sweet, *Quantum Spirituality*, p. 278.
23. Warren B. Smith, *A "Wonderful" Deception*, p. 123.
24. Ibid., pp. 128-129; and Smith's quotes of Spangler are from *Reimagination of the World: A Critique of the New Age, Science, and Popular Culture*, by David Spangler and William Irwin Thompson, (Santa Fe, NM: Bear & Company Publishing, 1991), pp. 139-140.
25. Leonard Sweet, *Quantum Spirituality*, p. 312. Cited from *A "Wonderful" Deception*, by Warren B. Smith, p. 123.
26. Ibid., (Sweet), p. 63.
27. Ibid., p. 65.
28. Ibid., p. 121.
29. Ibid., p. 134.
30. Ibid., p. 122.
31. Ibid., p. 101.

25. "Ideas, phrases, metaphors, and customs of pagan cultures" are "'seeds' of the divine Word that become enfleshed in Christ"?! (pages 146-149)

1. Online Etymology Dictionary, "incarnate," http://www.etymonline.com/index.php?term=incarnate.
2. Ibid., "incarnation," http://www.etymonline.com/index.php?term=incarnation.
3. Leonard Sweet, *Quantum Spirituality*, p. 101.
4. Leonard Sweet, *So Beautiful*, pp. 165-167.

26. "The word 'religion' concerns relationship" (pages 150-155)

1. Leonard Sweet, *Quantum Spirituality*, p. 125. Cited from *A "Wonderful" Deception*, by Warren B. Smith, p. 104; ellipsis dots in the original.
2. Marcus J. Borg, *The God We Never Knew*, p. 51.
3. Leonard Sweet, *So Beautiful*, p. 110.
4. Marcus J. Borg, *Reading the Bible Again for the First Time*, p. 18.
5. Ibid., p. 31.
6. Marcus Borg, "How can Christians accept Christianity as the way to God and still give credence to the truth of other religions?," http://www.explorefaith.org/faith/explore_christianity/questions_of_faith_and_doubt/how_can_christians_give_credence_to_other_religions.php.
7. Leonard Sweet, *So Beautiful*, p. 128.

8. Leonard Sweet, *Quantum Spirituality*, p. 130.
9. Marcus Borg, "Character of God," sermon, March 16, 2003, Calvary Episcopal Church, http://www.explorefaith.org/homiliesLent/LentenHomily03.16.03.html.
10. Leonard Sweet, *Quantum Spirituality*, p. 274.
11. Marcus J. Borg, *Reading the Bible Again for the First Time*, p. 218.
12. Leonard Sweet, *So Beautiful*, p. 104.
13. Online Etymology Dictionary, "religion," http://www.etymonline.com/index.php?l=r&p=9.
14. Alice Bailey and Djwhal Khul, *The Reappearance of the Christ*, Chapter IV - The Work of the Christ Today and in the Future, (Caux, Switzerland: Netnews Association and/or its suppliers, 2002), Lucis Trust, 1948 [see http://web.archive.org/web/20050726004029/http://laluni.helloyou.ws/netnews/bk/toc.html], http://www.netnews.org -- http://web.archive.org/web/20070220093122/http://laluni.helloyou.ws/netnews/bk/reappearance/reap1025.html.
15. Ibid., Chapter VI - The New World Religion, http://web.archive.org/web/20070218152806/laluni.helloyou.ws/netnews/bk/reappearance/reap1043.html.
16. Ibid., http://web.archive.org/web/20070218120732/laluni.helloyou.ws/netnews/bk/reappearance/reap1042.html.
17. Leonard Sweet, *So Beautiful*, p. 104.
18. Leonard Sweet, *Quantum Spirituality*, p. 125.
19. Ibid., p. 124.
20. Leonard Sweet, *So Beautiful*, p. 184.
21. Ibid., p. 122.
22. Ibid., pp. 166-167; emphasis added.
23. Ibid., p. 155.
24. Ibid., p. 99.
25. Ibid., p. 37; ellipsis dots in the original.
26. Ibid., p. 158.
27. Alice Bailey and Djwhal Khul, *A Treatise on White Magic*, Rule Ten - The Present Age and the Future, http://web.archive.org/web/20050505135414/http://laluni.helloyou.ws/netnews/bk/magic/magi1139.html.

27. "The world waits to hear your message for its salvation. That message is your life, lived." (pages 156-162)
1. Leonard Sweet, *So Beautiful*, p. 59.
2. Ibid., p. 217.
3. Ibid., p. 273.
4. Ibid., p. 59.
5. Ibid., p. 95.
6. Ibid., p. 129.
7. Ibid., p. 91.
8. Ibid., p. 152.
9. Ibid., p. 111.
10. Ibid., p. 101.
11. Ibid., p. 74.
12. "God," as quoted by Neale Donald Walsch, *The New Revelations: A Conversation with God*, p. 157. Cited from *Deceived on Purpose: The New Age Implications of the Purpose-Driven Church*, Second Edition, by Warren (B.) Smith, (Magalia, CA: Mountain Stream Press, 2004), p. 62.
13. "God," as quoted by Neale Donald Walsch, *Communion with God* (New York, NY: Berkley Books, 2000), p. 211.
14. Leonard Sweet, *So Beautiful*, p. 37.
15. Ibid., p. 59.

28. For God so loved ... culture? (pages 163-166)
1. Leonard Sweet, *So Beautiful*, p. 180.
2. Ibid., p. 139.
3. Ibid., p. 99.
4. Ibid., p. 171.

29. "There is no neat line of demarcation between the things of the world and the things of the Spirit" (pages 167-174)
1. Pierre Teilhard de Chardin, *Christianity and Evolution*, pp. 219-220. Cited from *A "Wonderful" Deception*, by Warren B. Smith, p. 119; brackets & ellipsis dots in the original.

2. Leonard Sweet, *Quantum Spirituality*, p. 106. Cited from ibid., (Smith), p. 119.
3. Leonard Sweet, *So Beautiful*, p. 139.
4. Ibid., p. 46.
5. Ibid., p. 99.
6. Ibid., p. 115.
7. Ibid., p. 64.
8. William P. Young, *The Shack*, pp. 122-123.
9. Leonard Sweet, *So Beautiful*, p. 152.
10. Ibid., p. 111.
11. Ibid., p. 139.
12. Ibid., p. 155.
13. Ibid., pp. 166-167.
14. Ibid., p. 61.
15. Ibid., p. 64.
16. Ibid., p. 152.
17. Ibid.
18. Leonard Sweet, *Quantum Spirituality*, pp. 59-60.
19. Leonard Sweet, *So Beautiful*, p. 25.
20. "God," as quoted by Neale Donald Walsch, *Friendship with God*, p. 377.
21. Ibid., p. 264.
22. "God," as quoted by Neale Donald Walsch, *Tomorrow's God*, p. 236.
23. Neale Donald Walsch, *What God Wants*, pp. 209-210.
24. "God," as quoted by Neale Donald Walsch, *Conversations with God, Book 3*, p. 326.
25. Leonard Sweet, *Quantum Spirituality*, pp. 28-29.
26. Leonard Sweet, *So Beautiful*, p. 46.
27. Ibid., pp. 44-45.
28. Ibid., p. 64.
29. Neale Donald Walsch's Humanity's Team website, http://humanitysteam.org/content/view/13/27/. Cited from "Are You 'Being Led Away with the Error of the Wicked' to the New Age Ark of Oneness?," by Tamara Hartzell, http://www.inthenameofpurpose.org/arkofoneness.pdf, p. 12.
30. Leonard Sweet, *Quantum Spirituality*, p. 60; parentheses in the original; emphasis added.
31. Pierre Teilhard de Chardin, *Christianity and Evolution*, p. 56. Cited from *A "Wonderful" Deception*, by Warren B. Smith, p. 114.
32. Leonard Sweet, *So Beautiful*, p. 95.
33. Leonard Sweet, *Quantum Spirituality*, pp. 25-26.

30. "The Bible is *not* a blueprint for action, nor a book of answers" (pages 175-181)

1. Marcus J. Borg, *Reading the Bible Again for the First Time*, pp. 3-5.
2. Leonard Sweet, *So Beautiful*, p. 43.
3. Ibid., p. 215.
4. Ibid., p. 123.
5. Ibid., pp. 203-204.
6. Ibid., p. 165.
7. Ibid., p. 71; quoting Antonio Machado.
8. Leonard Sweet, *Quantum Spirituality*, pp. 273-274.
9. Leonard Sweet, *So Beautiful*, p. 129.
10. "God," as quoted by Neale Donald Walsch, *Friendship with God*, p. 264.
11. "God" as quoted by Neale Donald Walsch, *Tomorrow's God*, p. 36.
12. Neale Donald Walsch, *What God Wants*, p. 172.
13. Ibid., p. 103.
14. Ibid., p. 179.
15. Leonard Sweet, *Quantum Spirituality*, p. 273.
16. Leonard Sweet, *So Beautiful*, p. 134.
17. Ibid., p. 123.
18. Ibid., p. 165.
19. Ibid., p. 116.
20. "God," as quoted by Neale Donald Walsch, *Tomorrow's God*, pp. 199-200.
21. Ibid., pp. 11-12.
22. Ibid., pp. 56-57.
23. Neale Donald Walsch, *What God Wants*, p. 209.

24. "God," as quoted by Neale Donald Walsch, *Friendship with God*, p. 264.
25. "God," as quoted by Neale Donald Walsch, *Conversations with God, Book 3*, pp. 90-91.

Part Five: The Creation
31. Let there be "more light"? (pages 185-188)
1. Leonard Sweet, *So Beautiful*, p. 123.
2. Leonard Sweet, *Quantum Spirituality*, p. 252.
3. Ibid., p. 259.
4. Ibid., p. 249.
5. Leonard Sweet, *So Beautiful*, p. 46.
6. Ibid., p. 152.
7. Neale Donald Walsch, *What God Wants*, pp. 209-210.
8. Leonard Sweet, *Quantum Spirituality*, p. 255.
9. Leonard Sweet, *So Beautiful*, pp. 57-58.
10. Ibid., p. 111.
11. "God," as quoted by Neale Donald Walsch, *Conversations with God, Book 3*, p. 341.
12. Ibid., p. 90.
13. "God," as quoted by Neale Donald Walsch, *Tomorrow's God*, pp. 11-12.
14. Leonard Sweet, *So Beautiful*, p. 64.
15. Ibid., p. 165.

32. The mission of creating "the Third Testament" as "part of *the 'I Am' that we* are" (pages 189-195)
1. Leonard Sweet, *Quantum Spirituality*, pp. 255-257.
2. Leonard Sweet, *So Beautiful*, p. 139.
3. Ibid., p. 111.
4. Leonard Sweet, *Quantum Spirituality*, pp. 273-274.
5. Leonard Sweet, *So Beautiful*, p. 43.
6. Leonard Sweet, *Quantum Spirituality*, p. 259.
7. Leonard Sweet, *So Beautiful*, p. 58.
8. Ibid., p. 111.
9. Ibid., p. 37.
10. Leonard Sweet, *Quantum Spirituality*, pp. 255-256.
11. Ibid., p. 133.
12. Ibid., pp. 296-297.
13. Ibid., pp. 260-261.
14. Leonard Sweet, *So Beautiful*, p. 59.
15. "God," as quoted by Neale Donald Walsch, *Friendship with God*, p. 23. Cited from *Reinventing Jesus Christ: The New Gospel*, by Warren (B.) Smith, (Ravenna, OH: Conscience Press, 2002), p. 23. [Note: Smith's book has been republished as *False Christ Coming – Does Anybody Care?: What New Age leaders really have in store for America, the church, and the world* (Magalia, CA: Mountain Stream Press, 2011), and this quote is on p. 41.]
16. "God," as quoted by Neale Donald Walsch, *Conversations with God, Book 3*, pp. 56-57.
17. Ibid., p. 50.
18. "God," as quoted by Neale Donald Walsch, *Conversations with God, Book 1*, p. 28.
19. Ibid., pp. 75-76.
20. "God," as quoted by Neale Donald Walsch, *Conversations with God, Book 3*, p. 341.
21. "God," as quoted by Neale Donald Walsch, *Tomorrow's God*, pp. 138-139.
22. "God," as quoted by Neale Donald Walsch, *Conversations with God, Book 1*, p. 61.
23. "God," as quoted by Neale Donald Walsch, *Tomorrow's God*, p. 145.
24. Ibid., p. 342.
25. Leonard Sweet, *So Beautiful*, pp. 57-60.
26. Ibid., p. 114.
27. "God," as quoted by Neale Donald Walsch, *The New Revelations*, p. 157. Cited from *Deceived on Purpose: The New Age Implications of the Purpose-Driven Church*, by Warren (B.) Smith, p. 62.
28. "God," as quoted by Neale Donald Walsch, *Tomorrow's God*, p. 208.
29. Leonard Sweet, *Quantum Spirituality*, p. 256.
30. "God," as quoted by Neale Donald Walsch, *Friendship with God*, pp. 394-395.
31. Leonard Sweet, *Quantum Spirituality*, pp. 260-261.

32. Leonard Sweet, *So Beautiful*, p. 27.
33. "God," as quoted by Neale Donald Walsch, *The New Revelations*, p. 11.

33. "It is through creative intuition that postmoderns continue the work of *divine* creation" (pages 196-204)
1. Leonard Sweet, *Quantum Spirituality*, p. 297.
2. Alice A. Bailey, *The Consciousness Of The Atom*, p. 136.
3. Alice Bailey, *From Intellect to Intuition*, Chapter Five - Stages in Meditation, http://web.archive.org/web/20070331183610/laluni.helloyou.ws/netnews/bk/intellect/inte1029.html.
4. Marcus Borg, "How can I know the truth about Christianity if I question the Bible's status as the literal Word of God?," http://www.explorefaith.org/faith/explore_christianity/questions_of_faith_and_doubt/how_can_i_know_the_truth_about_christianity_if_i_question_the_bibles_status_as_the_literal_word_of_god.php.
5. Leonard Sweet, *Quantum Spirituality*, pp. 296-297.
6. Ibid., p. 76.
7. Alice Bailey, *From Intellect to Intuition*, Chapter Four - The Objectives in Meditation, http://web.archive.org/web/20060209202950/laluni.helloyou.ws/netnews/bk/intellect/inte1024.html.
8. Ibid., Chapter Eight - The Universality of Meditation, http://web.archive.org/web/20070327142351/laluni.helloyou.ws/netnews/bk/intellect/inte1055.html.
9. Leonard Sweet, *Quantum Spirituality*, p. 76.
10. Marcus Borg, "Mystical Experiences of God," January 5, 2007, The Washington Post and Newsweek, On Faith, http://newsweek.washingtonpost.com/onfaith/panelists/marcus_borg/2007/01/mystical_religious_experiences.html.
11. Leonard Sweet, *So Beautiful*, p. 64.
12. Leonard Sweet, *Quantum Spirituality*, p. 70.
13. Ibid., pp. 294-295.
14. "God," as quoted by Neale Donald Walsch, *Conversations with God, Book 3*, p. 50.
15. Alice Bailey and Djwhal Khul, *The Rays and the Initiations*, Part I - Fourteen Rules for Group Initiation, http://web.archive.org/web/20070218153043/http://laluni.helloyou.ws/netnews/bk/rays/rays1111.html.
16. Leonard Sweet, *Quantum Spirituality*, pp. 69-70.
17. Alice Bailey and Djwhal Khul, *The Rays and the Initiations*, Part I - Fourteen Rules for Group Initiation, http://web.archive.org/web/20070218153043/http://laluni.helloyou.ws/netnews/bk/rays/rays1111.html.
18. Leonard Sweet, *Quantum Spirituality*, p. 278.
19. Leonard Sweet, *So Beautiful*, p. 126.
20. Leonard Sweet, *Quantum Spirituality*, pp. 73-74.
21. "God," as quoted by Neale Donald Walsch, *Conversations with God, Book 1*, p. 8.
22. Leonard Sweet, *Quantum Spirituality*, p. 300.
23. Ibid., p. 69.
24. Ibid., p. 114.
25. Ibid., pp. 298-299.
26. Ibid., pp. 253-254.
27. Alice Bailey and Djwhal Khul, *A Treatise on Cosmic Fire*, Section Two - Thought Elementals and Fire Elementals, (Caux, Switzerland: Netnews Association and/or its suppliers, 2002), Lucis Trust, 1925 [see http://web.archive.org/web/20050726004029/http://laluni.helloyou.ws/netnews/bk/toc.html], http://www.netnews.org -- http://web.archive.org/web/20051123102546/laluni.helloyou.ws/netnews/bk/fire/fire1380.html.
28. Alice Bailey, *From Intellect to Intuition*, Chapter VI - Stages in Meditation, III. The Stage of Contemplation, http://web.archive.org/web/20060225030720/http://laluni.helloyou.ws/netnews/bk/intellect/inte1042.html.
29. Leonard Sweet, *Quantum Spirituality*, p. 250.
30. Ibid., p. 252.
31. Ibid., pp. 130-131.
32. "God," as quoted by Neale Donald Walsch, *Tomorrow's God*, p. 208.
33. Leonard Sweet, *So Beautiful*, p. 73.
34. Ibid., p. 111.
35. Alice Bailey and Djwhal Khul, *Esoteric Psychology II*, Chapter II - The Ray of Personality, The Coordination of the Personality, http://web.archive.org/web/20060105121243/http://laluni.helloyou.ws/netnews/bk/psychology2/psyc2149.html.
36. Alice Bailey and Djwhal Khul, *The Rays and the Initiations*, Part I - Fourteen Rules for Group Initiation, Rule Fourteen, http://web.archive.org/web/20060210231040/laluni.helloyou.ws/netnews/bk/rays/rays1110.html.
37. Alice Bailey, *From Intellect to Intuition*, Chapter Four - The Objectives in Meditation, http://web.archive.org/web/20060209202950/laluni.helloyou.ws/netnews/bk/intellect/inte1024.html.

38. Alice Bailey and Djwhal Khul, *Esoteric Psychology II*, Chapter II - The Ray of Personality, The Coordination of the Personality, http://web.archive.org/web/20060105121243/http://laluni.helloyou.ws/netnews/bk/psychology2/psyc2149.html.

34. "*No person or living thing in the universe stands outside of the community of God*" (pages 205-209)
1. "God," as quoted by Neale Donald Walsch, *Communion with God*, p. 90.
2. Leonard Sweet, *Quantum Spirituality*, p. 130.
3. "God," as quoted by Neale Donald Walsch, *Tomorrow's God*, pp. 28-30.
4. Neale Donald Walsch, *What God Wants*, p. 206.
5. "God," as quoted by Neale Donald Walsch, *Tomorrow's God*, p. 235.
6. Leonard Sweet, *Quantum Spirituality*, pp. 130-131.
7. Alice Bailey and Djwhal Khul, *The Labors of Hercules*, Labor IX, The Spirit of Truth, (Caux, Switzerland: Netnews Association and/or its suppliers, 2002), Lucis Trust, 1974 [see http://web.archive.org/web/20050726004029/http://laluni.helloyou.ws/netnews/bk/toc.html], http://www.netnews.org -- http://web.archive.org/web/20070324030138/laluni.helloyou.ws/netnews/bk/hercules/herc1049.html.
8. Alice Bailey and Djwhal Khul, *A Treatise on White Magic*, Rule Ten - The New Group of World Servers, http://web.archive.org/web/20070218221047/http://laluni.helloyou.ws/netnews/bk/magic/magi1172.html.
9. Ibid., The Present Age and the Future, http://web.archive.org/web/20070218152715/http://laluni.helloyou.ws/netnews/bk/magic/magi1139.html.
10. "God," as quoted by Neale Donald Walsch, *Tomorrow's God*, p. 357.
11. Leonard Sweet, *Quantum Spirituality*, pp. 114-115.
12. Leonard Sweet, *So Beautiful*, p. 37.
13. Ibid., p. 184.
14. Leonard Sweet, *Quantum Spirituality*, p. 125.
15. Alice Bailey, *From Intellect to Intuition*, Chapter Eight - The Universality of Meditation, http://web.archive.org/web/20070327142351/laluni.helloyou.ws/netnews/bk/intellect/inte1055.html.
16. Alice Bailey and Djwhal Khul, *The Reappearance of the Christ*, Chapter VI - The New World Religion, http://web.archive.org/web/20070218120732/laluni.helloyou.ws/netnews/bk/reappearance/reap1042.html.
17. "God," as quoted by Neale Donald Walsch, *The New Revelations*, p. 282. Cited from *Deceived on Purpose*, by Warren (B.) Smith, p. 65.

35. "*Relinquish the pride of mind which sees its way ... to be correct and true*" (pages 210-217)
1. "God," as quoted by Neale Donald Walsch, *Communion with God*, pp. 90-91.
2. Leonard Sweet, *Quantum Spirituality*, pp. 294-295.
3. Ibid., p. 114.
4. Alice Bailey and Djwhal Khul, *Esoteric Psychology II*, Chapter I - The Egoic Ray, The Seven Laws of Soul or Group Life, http://web.archive.org/web/20070219003559/http://laluni.helloyou.ws/netnews/bk/psychology2/psyc2040.html.
5. Leonard Sweet, *So Beautiful*, p. 139.
6. Ibid., pp. 110-111.
7. Leonard Sweet, *Quantum Spirituality*, pp. 130-131.
8. Ibid., p. 158.
9. Ibid., p. 104.
10. Ibid., pp. 116-117.
11. Leonard Sweet, *Quantum Spirituality*, p. 130.
12. Leonard Sweet, *So Beautiful*, p. 128.
13. Marcus Borg, "Faith, Not Belief," February 24, 2002, Calvary Episcopal Church, http://www.explorefaith.org/LentenHomily02.24.02.html.
14. Leonard Sweet, *Quantum Spirituality*, pp. 255-257, 260-261; emphasis added.
15. Leonard Sweet, *So Beautiful*, p. 134.
16. Ibid., p. 110.
17. Ibid., p. 129.
18. Ibid., p. 122.
19. Leonard Sweet, *Quantum Spirituality*, pp. 294-295.
20. Ibid., pp. 273-274.
21. Leonard Sweet, *So Beautiful*, p. 128.
22. Leonard Sweet, *Quantum Spirituality*, pp. 65, 121; emphasis added.
23. Leonard Sweet, *So Beautiful*, p. 106; emphasis added.
24. Ibid., p. 114; emphasis added.

25. Ibid., p. 217; emphasis added.
26. Ibid., p. 172.
27. Ibid., p. 37.
28. Marcus Borg, "I am uncomfortable with some of the doctrines professed in organized religion. Is believing certain creeds really what Christianity is all about?," http://www.explorefaith.org/faith/explore_christianity/questions_of_faith_and_doubt/is_believing_certain_creeds_really_what_christianity_is_all_about.php?ht=.
29. Marcus Borg, "How can Christians accept Christianity as the way to God and still give credence to the truth of other religions?," http://www.explorefaith.org/faith/explore_christianity/questions_of_faith_and_doubt/how_can_christians_give_credence_to_other_religions.php.

36. "The *Gospel* According to" anything and everyone? (pages 218-223)
1. "God," as quoted by Neale Donald Walsch, *Tomorrow's God*, p. 208.
2. Leonard Sweet, *So Beautiful*, p. 287; quoting Lamin O. Sanneh, *Whose Religion Is Christianity?* (Grand Rapids, MI: Eerdmans, 2003), p. 106.
3. Leonard Sweet, *Quantum Spirituality*, p. 51.
4. Leonard Sweet, *So Beautiful*, p. 37.
5. Leonard Sweet, *Quantum Spirituality*, pp. 130-131.
6. Leonard Sweet, *So Beautiful*, pp. 165-167.
7. Ibid., p. 158.
8. Leonard Sweet, *Quantum Spirituality*, pp. 255-256.
9. Ibid., p. 163.
10. Leonard Sweet, *So Beautiful*, p. 139.
11. Sermons.com, Leonard Sweet, http://www.sermons.com/leonardSweet.asp; emphasis added.
12. Leonard Sweet, *Quantum Spirituality*, p. 101.
13. Leonard Sweet, *So Beautiful*, pp. 166-167.
14. Leonard Sweet, *Quantum Spirituality*, pp. 121-123.
15. Ibid., p. 274.
16. Ibid., p. 65.
17. Ibid., pp. 255-256.
18. Ibid., pp. 114-115.
19. Leonard Sweet, *So Beautiful*, p. 155.
20. Ibid., p. 165.
21. Leonard Sweet, *Quantum Spirituality*, p. 124.
22. Ibid., p. 142.
23. Leonard Sweet, *So Beautiful*, p. 204.
24. Ibid., p. 114.
25. "God," as quoted by Neale Donald Walsch, *Tomorrow's God*, p. 208.

37. Dialoguing to the consensus/connectness/Oneness of today's new "truth" (pages 224-233)
1. Leonard Sweet, *So Beautiful*, p. 111.
2. Leonard Sweet, *Quantum Spirituality*, pp. 294-295.
3. "God," as quoted by Neale Donald Walsch, *Tomorrow's God*, pp. 11-12.
4. Neale Donald Walsch, *What God Wants*, p. 221.
5. Leonard Sweet, *So Beautiful*, p. 99.
6. Ibid., pp. 116-117.
7. William P. Young, *The Shack*, p. 124.
8. Marcus Borg, "Faith, Not Belief," February 24, 2002, Calvary Episcopal Church, http://www.explorefaith.org/LentenHomily02.24.02.html.
9. Leonard Sweet, *So Beautiful*, p. 101.
10. Gerard W. Hughes, *God in All Things*, p. 19. Cited from *So Beautiful*, by Leonard Sweet, p. 270; emphasis added.
11. "God," as quoted by Neale Donald Walsch, *Tomorrow's God*, p. 328.
12. Ibid., p. 343.
13. Leonard Sweet, *So Beautiful*, p. 111.
14. "God," as quoted by Neale Donald Walsch, *Conversations with God, Book 3*, p. 326.
15. "God," as quoted by Neale Donald Walsch, *Tomorrow's God*, pp. 11-12.
16. Ibid., pp. 235-236.
17. Leonard Sweet, *Quantum Spirituality*, pp. 28-29.
18. Ibid., pp. 273-274.
19. Ibid., pp. 293-295.

20. Marcus Borg, "How can Christians accept Christianity as the way to God and still give credence to the truth of other religions?," http://www.explorefaith.org/faith/explore_christianity/questions_of_faith_and_doubt/how_can_christians_give_credence_to_other_religions.php.
21. "God," as quoted by Neale Donald Walsch, *Tomorrow's God*, p. 218.
22. Dictionary.com, "curve," http://dictionary.reference.com/browse/curve; emphasis added.
23. Ibid.; emphasis added.
24. Ibid.
25. *American Dictionary of the English Language*, Noah Webster 1828 (San Francisco, CA: Foundation for American Christian Education, 1967 & 1995), "deceive."
26. Answers.com, "curve ball," http://www.answers.com/topic/curveball.
27. Leonard Sweet, *Quantum Spirituality*, pp. 293-295.
28. For more information see Dean Gotcher's website, The Institution for Authority Research, http://www.authorityresearch.com/.
29. Answers.com, "curve ball," http://www.answers.com/topic/curveball.
30. Dictionary.com, "curve," http://dictionary.reference.com/browse/curve.
31. *American Dictionary of the English Language*, Noah Webster 1828, "deceive;" emphasis added.
32. Dictionary.com, "deceive," http://dictionary.reference.com/browse/deceive; emphasis added.
33. Leonard Sweet, *So Beautiful*, p. 139.
34. Answers.com, "curve ball," http://www.answers.com/topic/curveball.
35. Dictionary.com, "spin," http://dictionary.reference.com/browse/spin; emphasis added.

38. "Transcending current beliefs is not an outright rejection of them; it is an 'adding to' them" (pages 234-240)
1. Leonard Sweet, *So Beautiful*, p. 165; emphasis added.
2. Ibid., p. 139.
3. Leonard Sweet, *Quantum Spirituality*, p. 259.
4. Ibid., p. 249.
5. Ibid., p. 258.
6. "God," as quoted by Neale Donald Walsch, *The New Revelations*, pp. 8-9.
7. Leonard Sweet, *Quantum Spirituality*, pp. 260-261.
8. Ibid., p. 133.
9. Ibid., p. 261; emphasis added.
10. Leonard Sweet, *So Beautiful*, p. 111.
11. Ibid., p. 134.
12. Ibid., p. 158.
13. Leonard Sweet, *Quantum Spirituality*, p. 259.
14. Leonard Sweet, *So Beautiful*, p. 204.
15. Ibid., p. 114.
16. Ibid., pp. 128-129.
17. Leonard Sweet, *Quantum Spirituality*, p. 256.
18. Online Etymology Dictionary, "stretch (v.)," http://www.etymonline.com/index.php?l=s&p=46; emphasis added.
19. For more on this, see "Are You 'Being Led Away with the Error of the Wicked' to the New Age Ark of Oneness?," by Tamara Hartzell, http://www.inthenameofpurpose.org/arkofoneness.pdf.

39. Breaking free from the soul "sort" in the "kingdom" that "transcends and includes all religions" (pages 241-254)
1. Marcus Borg, "How can Christians accept Christianity as the way to God and still give credence to the truth of other religions?," http://www.explorefaith.org/faith/explore_christianity/questions_of_faith_and_doubt/how_can_christians_give_credence_to_other_religions.php.
2. "God," as quoted by Neale Donald Walsch, *Conversations with God, Book 3*, p. 326.
3. Marcus J. Borg, *Reading the Bible Again for the First Time*, p. 218.
4. Mike Morrell, "Panentheism & Interspirituality - What's Jesus Got to do With It?," June 25, 2009, http://zoecarnate.wordpress.com/2009/06/25/panentheism-interspirituality-whats-jesus-got-to-do-with-it/; also posted online at http://www.theooze.com/blog/2006/04/panentheism-interspirituality-whats.html; bold added.
5. Leonard Sweet, *Quantum Spirituality*, p. 274.
6. "God," as quoted by Neale Donald Walsch, *Tomorrow's God*, p. 22.
7. "God," as quoted by Neale Donald Walsch, *Conversations with God, Book 1*, p. 8.
8. Marcus J. Borg, *Reading the Bible Again for the First Time*, p. 299.
9. Neale Donald Walsch, *What God Wants*, p. 209.

10. Leonard Sweet, *Quantum Spirituality*, p. 13.
11. "God," as quoted by Neale Donald Walsch, *Friendship with God*, p. 375.
12. Leonard Sweet, *Quantum Spirituality*, p. 114.
13. Alice Bailey, *From Bethlehem to Calvary*, Chapter Five - The Fourth Initiation, The Crucifixion, http://web.archive.org/web/20070218152756/http://laluni.helloyou.ws/netnews/bk/bethlehem/beth1064.html.
14. Alice Bailey and Djwhal Khul, *The Rays and the Initiations*, Part I - Fourteen Rules for Group Initiation, Rule Fourteen, http://web.archive.org/web/20060213230403/laluni.helloyou.ws/netnews/bk/rays/rays1111.html.
15. Leonard Sweet, *So Beautiful*, p. 107.
16. Ibid., pp. 22-23.
17. Leonard Sweet, *Quantum Spirituality*, p. 121; emphasis added.
18. Ibid., p. 101; emphasis added.
19. *American Dictionary of the English Language*, Noah Webster 1828, "shapesmith;" emphasis added.
20. Ibid., "shaping."
21. Academics, http://www.leonardsweet.com/academics.php.
22. "Celebrating Dr. E. Stanley Jones," 01/27/06, by Jerome Smith, Director of Communications, The Foundation for Evangelism, http://foundationforevangelism.org/news_and_press/news/article/Celebrating_Dr_E_Stanley_Jones/browse/13/?tx_ttnews%5BbackPid%5D=76&cHash=778786f7c5; emphasis added.
23. Ibid.; emphasis added.
24. E. Stanley Jones, *The Christ of the Indian Road* (Lucknow, India: Lucknow Publishing House, 1925), p. 151.
25. Ibid., p. 33.
26. Ibid., p. 134.
27. Ibid., p. 144.
28. Ibid., p. 42.
29. Ibid., p. 179.
30. Ibid., pp. 101-103.
31. Ibid., pp. 181-182.
32. Ibid., pp. 170-171.
33. "Ashram, the Unbreakable Fellowship," 03/30/06, by Jerome Smith, Director of Communications, The Foundation for Evangelism, http://foundationforevangelism.org/news_and_press/news/article/Ashram_the_Unbreakable_Fellowship/browse/13/?tx_ttnews%5BbackPid%5D=76&cHash=d0a63909ab.
34. "E. Stanley Jones, Missionary Extraordinary," United Christian Ashrams, http://www.christianashram.org/Pages2/ESJones2.html.
35. Leonard Sweet, Brian D. McLaren, and Jerry Haselmayer, *A Is for Abductive: The Language of the Emerging Church*, "Preface by Leonard Sweet," p. 10; emphasis added.
36. Ibid., "Preface by Brian McLaren," p. 13.
37. Brian D. McLaren, *Everything Must Change: Jesus, Global Crises, and a Revolution of Hope* (Nashville, TN: Thomas Nelson, 2007), p. 154, and its endnote on p. 316, #10; emphasis added.
38. Brian D. McLaren, *A New Kind of Christianity: Ten Questions That Are Transforming the Faith* (New York, NY: HarperCollins Publishers, 2010), p. 99.
39. Ibid., pp. 38-39.
40. Ibid., p. 195.
41. Ibid., pp. 215-216.
42. Ibid., p. 139.
43. Ibid., p. 272, #6.
44. Leonard Sweet, *So Beautiful*, p. 119.
45. "God," as quoted by Neale Donald Walsch, *Conversations with God, Book 3*, pp. 56-57.
46. Ibid., p. 366.
47. "God," as quoted by Neale Donald Walsch, *The New Revelations*, p. 132.
48. Neale Donald Walsch, *What God Wants*, p. 209.
49. Ibid., p. 211.
50. Alice Bailey, *From Bethlehem to Calvary*, Chapter Five - The Fourth Initiation, The Crucifixion, http://web.archive.org/web/20070219003459/http://laluni.helloyou.ws/netnews/bk/bethlehem/beth1063.html.
51. Ibid., Chapter Seven - Our Immediate Goal, The Founding of the Kingdom, http://web.archive.org/web/20070213074428/laluni.helloyou.ws/netnews/bk/bethlehem/beth1082.html.
52. Ibid., Chapter Five - The Fourth Initiation, The Crucifixion, http://web.archive.org/web/20070218152756/http://laluni.helloyou.ws/netnews/bk/bethlehem/beth1064.html.
53. Alice Bailey and Djwhal Khul, *Problems of Humanity*, Chapter V - The Problem of the Churches, (Caux, Switzerland: Netnews Association and/or its suppliers, 2002), Lucis Trust, 1947 [see http://web.archive.org/web/20050726004029/http://laluni.helloyou.ws/netnews/bk/toc.html], http://www.netnews.org -- http://web.archive.org/web/20070218153113/http://laluni.helloyou.ws/netnews/bk/problems/prob1055.html.

40. The significance of a "Third Testament" (pages 255-267)
1. Leonard Sweet, *Quantum Spirituality*, pp. 260-261.
2. Leonard Sweet, *So Beautiful*, pp. 57-59.
3. Ibid., p. 165.
4. "God," as quoted by Neale Donald Walsch, *Conversations with God, Book 3*, p. 345.
5. Brian D. McLaren, *A New Kind of Christianity: Ten Questions That Are Transforming the Faith*, p. 273, #5.
6. Ibid., p. 99.
7. "God," as quoted by Neale Donald Walsch, *Conversations with God, Book 3*, p. 90.
8. Leonard Sweet, *Quantum Spirituality*, p. 252.
9. Ibid., p. 253.
10. Ibid., p. 255.
11. *American Dictionary of the English Language*, Noah Webster 1828, "establish."
12. Mike Morrell, "Panentheism - Perichoresis - Christology: Participatory Divinity," June 30, 2009, http://zoecarnate.wordpress.com/2009/06/30/panentheism-perichoresis-christology-participatory-divinity/.
13. Leonard Sweet, *So Beautiful*, p. 217.
14. "God," as quoted by Neale Donald Walsch, *The New Revelations*, p. 157. Cited from *Deceived on Purpose*, by Warren (B.) Smith, p. 62.
15. Leonard Sweet, *So Beautiful*, p. 114.
16. Ibid., p. 37.
17. Leonard Sweet, *Quantum Spirituality*, pp. 260-261.
18. Leonard Sweet, *So Beautiful*, p. 59.
19. Leonard Sweet, *Quantum Spirituality*, p. 256.
20. Ibid., p. 125.
21. Leonard Sweet, *So Beautiful*, pp. 116-117.
22. Leonard Sweet, *Nudge: Awakening Each Other to the God Who's Already There* (Colorado Springs, CO: David C. Cook, 2010), p. 55.
23. Leonard Sweet, *So Beautiful*, p. 114.
24. Pierre Teilhard de Chardin, *Christianity and Evolution*, pp. 219-220. Cited from *A "Wonderful" Deception*, by Warren B. Smith, p. 119; ellipsis dots in the original.
25. Leonard Sweet, *Quantum Spirituality*, p. 274.
26. Leonard Sweet, *So Beautiful*, pp. 45-46.
27. Ibid., p. 134.
28. Ibid., p. 111.
29. William M. Easum and Thomas G. Bandy, *Growing Spiritual Redwoods*, p. 39; emphasis added. Cited from *In the Name of Purpose*, by Tamara Hartzell, pp. 303-304. This book is reviewed in detail in chapter 22 of *In the Name of Purpose* (see http://www.inthenameofpurpose.org/inthename.pdf, which, as noted earlier, has different page numbers than the print version that is cited in these endnotes.) Citation information for footnote C: Endorsements cited from *In the Name of Purpose*, pp. 299-300; emphasis added to both.

41. An "*anti-Christian*" "double helix, Möbius-strip culture of both-and's" is "*the secret of life*"? (pages 268-285)
1. Leonard Sweet, *So Beautiful*, p. 20.
2. Leonard Sweet, *Quantum Spirituality*, pp. 28-29.
3. Ibid., p. 274.
4. Leonard Sweet, *So Beautiful*, pp. 44-46.
5. Mike Morrell, "Frank Viola & Leonard Sweet on 'Jesus Manifesto,'" a May interview, posted June 1, 2010, http://zoecarnate.wordpress.com/2010/06/01/frank-viola-leonard-sweet-on-a-jesus-manifesto/; emphasis added.
6. Leonard Sweet, *Quantum Spirituality*, p. 297; emphasis added.
7. Ibid., pp. 296-297.
8. Ibid., p. 76.
9. Ibid., p. 125.
10. Leonard Sweet, *So Beautiful*, p. 20.
11. Ibid., p. 44.
12. Leonard Sweet, *Nudge*, p. 157.
13. Ibid., p. 55.
14. Leonard Sweet, *Quantum Spirituality*, p. 31.
15. Leonard Sweet, *So Beautiful*, pp. 45-47.
16. Leonard Sweet, *Quantum Spirituality*, p. 255.
17. Leonard Sweet, *So Beautiful*, p. 20.

18. Ibid., p. 37.
19. Leonard Sweet, *Quantum Spirituality*, pp. 114-115.
20. Leonard Sweet and Frank Viola, *Jesus Manifesto: Restoring the Supremacy and Sovereignty of Jesus Christ* (Nashville, TN: Thomas Nelson, 2010), pp. 147-148.
21. Leonard Sweet, *Quantum Spirituality*, p. 130.
22. Leonard Sweet, *So Beautiful*, pp. 44-45.
23. Answers.com, "helix," http://www.answers.com/topic/helix; emphasis added.
24. Ibid.
25. Ibid.
26. Leonard Sweet, *So Beautiful*, p. 204.
27. Ibid.
28. "The Gospel of Thomas," The Nag Hammadi Library, The Gnostic Society Library, Translated by Thomas O. Lambdin, http://www.gnosis.org/naghamm/gthlamb.html.
29. Leonard Sweet, *Quantum Spirituality*, p. 274.
30. Leonard Sweet, *So Beautiful*, p. 46.
31. Warren (B.) Smith, *Deceived on Purpose*, p. 32; quoting from *As Above, So Below: Paths to Spiritual Renewal in Daily Life*, by Ronald S. Miller and the Editors of *New Age Journal*, (Los Angeles, CA: Jeremy P. Tarcher, Inc., 1992), p. xi.
32. "Exposing the QUANTUM LIE: God is *NOT* in everything!," DVD #2, Warren B. Smith, "The Big Picture/A Wonderful Deception." This lecture series was filmed and produced at Twin City Fellowship in St. Louis Park, MN, (Silverton, OR: Lighthouse Trails Publishing, 2009). The DVD set is available at http://www.lighthousetrails.com/; and, specifically, http://lighthousetrails.com/mm5/merchant.mvc?Screen=PROD&Store_Code=LTP&Product_Code=QL&Category_Code=DVD.
33. Leonard Sweet, *Nudge*, p. 31.
34. Ibid., p. 28.
35. Ibid., p. 67.
36. Ibid., pp. 71-72.
37. Ibid., p. 40.
38. Alice A. Bailey, *The Consciousness Of The Atom*, p. 136.
39. Alice Bailey, *From Bethlehem to Calvary*, Chapter Seven - Our Immediate Goal, The Founding of the Kingdom, http://web.archive.org/web/20070213074428/laluni.helloyou.ws/netnews/bk/bethlehem/beth1082.html.
40. Leonard Sweet and Frank Viola, *Jesus Manifesto: Restoring the Supremacy and Sovereignty of Jesus Christ*, p. 176.
41. Leonard Sweet, *Nudge*, p. 40.
42. Ibid., p. 30.
43. Ibid., p. 120.
44. Ibid., pp. 76-77.
45. Ibid., p. 55.
46. Ibid., p. 103.
47. Ibid., p. 67.
48. Ibid., pp. 134-135.
49. Ibid., p. 56.
50. Ibid., p. 45.
51. Ibid., p. 93.
52. Ibid., p. 55; emphasis added.
53. Neale Donald Walsch, and "God," as quoted by Walsch, *The New Revelations*, pp. 27-28.
54. Leonard Sweet, *Quantum Spirituality*, pp. 59-60.
55. "The Mobius Strip," Mobius Products and Services, http://www.mobiusproductsandservices.com/tms.html. [Note: the last part of the 3rd paragraph of this quote has since been changed. But it is still posted on Sensitive Planet, "Yoga Jewelry-Mobius Yantra," http://www.sensitiveplanet.com/category.jhtm?cid=124.]
56. Leonard Sweet, *Quantum Spirituality*, p. 274.
57. Leonard Sweet, *So Beautiful*, p. 64.
58. Leonard Sweet and Frank Viola, *Jesus Manifesto*, pp. 57-58.
59. Leonard Sweet, *Nudge*, p. 157; emphasis added.
60. *American Dictionary of the English Language*, Noah Webster 1828, "universal;" emphasis added.
61. Online Etymology Dictionary, "universe," http://www.etymonline.com/index.php?term=universe.
62. Leonard Sweet and Frank Viola, *Jesus Manifesto*, p. 22.
63. Leonard Sweet, *Nudge*, pp. 226-227.
64. Ibid., pp. 76-77.

65. Ibid., p. 228.
66. Leonard Sweet, *So Beautiful*, p. 123.
67. Leonard Sweet, LEADERSHIP ART #6, "seeing through scopes: VISION," transcribed from the video posted on YouTube at http://www.youtube.com/watch?v=ha2w1NnNv1U&feature=related.
68. Leonard Sweet, *So Beautiful*, pp. 44-47.
69. Leonard Sweet, LEADERSHIP ART #9, "valuing the crew: COLLABORATION AND TEAMWORK," transcribed from the video posted on YouTube at http://www.youtube.com/watch?v=plehK49DqBI&feature=related.
70. Leonard Sweet, *So Beautiful*, pp. 22-23.
71. Leonard Sweet and Frank Viola, *Jesus Manifesto*, p. 57.
72. Leonard Sweet, *Quantum Spirituality*, p. 274.
73. Leonard Sweet, *Nudge*, p. 56.
74. For more on "God's Dream" see Warren B. Smith's book *A "Wonderful" Deception*, especially the section "'God's Dream' and Metaphysics" on p. 155, and chapter 8 titled, "'God's Dream': A Deceptive Scheme?"
75. Leonard Sweet, *Nudge*, p. 67.
76. Leonard Sweet, *So Beautiful*, p. 107.
77. Leonard Sweet, LEADERSHIP ART #6, "seeing through scopes: VISION," transcribed from the video posted on YouTube at http://www.youtube.com/watch?v=ha2w1NnNv1U&feature=related.
78. Leonard Sweet, *So Beautiful*, p. 135.
79. Ibid., p. 167.
80. Leonard Sweet, *Nudge*, p. 56.
81. Ibid., p. 76.
82. Leonard Sweet, *Quantum Spirituality*, p. 70.

42. "The Oneness of Twoness that becomes Threeness" -- the *tertium quid*, or Laodicean third way (pages 286-290)
1. Leonard Sweet, *Quantum Spirituality*, p. 31.
2. Leonard Sweet, *So Beautiful*, pp. 45-47.
3. Leonard Sweet, *Quantum Spirituality*, p. 255.
4. John Kissick, *Art: Context and Criticism*, Second Edition, (Boston, MA: The McGraw-Hill Companies, Inc., 1996, 1993), p. 28.
5. Ibid.
6. Leonard Sweet, *Quantum Spirituality*, p. 274.
7. Leonard Sweet, *So Beautiful*, p. 119.
8. Answers.com, "tertium quid," http://www.answers.com/topic/tertium-quid.
9. Ibid., "Apollinarianism," http://www.answers.com/topic/apollinarianism; parentheses in the original.
10. Ibid.

43. Connecting the dots of the immanent "God" and "Christ" (pages 291-307)
1. Alice Bailey and Djwhal Khul, *The Labors of Hercules*, Labor IX, The Spirit of Truth, http://web.archive.org/web/20070324030138/laluni.helloyou.ws/netnews/bk/hercules/herc1049.html.
2. Leonard Sweet, *Quantum Spirituality*, p. 114.
3. "God," as quoted by Neale Donald Walsch, *Tomorrow's God*, p. 235.
4. Leonard Sweet, *So Beautiful*, p. 222.
5. Ibid., p. 224.
6. Leonard Sweet, *Nudge*, p. 157.
7. "God," as quoted by Neale Donald Walsch, *Conversations with God, Book 3*, p. 50.
8. Sue Monk Kidd, *The Dance of the Dissident Daughter: A Woman's Journey from Christian Tradition to the Sacred Feminine*, p. 160. (For more information on Kidd, see endnote #1 of chapter 16, "The immanent 'God' of Oneness, imagined and defined in *limitless* ways," in Part Two.)
9. Leonard Sweet, *Quantum Spirituality*, pp. 59-60.
10. Leonard Sweet, *Nudge*, pp. 54-55.
11. Ibid., pp. 133-134.
12. Leonard Sweet, *Quantum Spirituality*, pp. 124-125.
13. "God," as quoted by Neale Donald Walsch, *Tomorrow's God*, p. 357.
14. Ibid., p. 235; and p. 234 for bracketed information.
15. Neale Donald Walsch, *What God Wants*, p. 206.
16. Leonard Sweet, *Quantum Spirituality*, pp. 130-132.
17. Leonard Sweet, *So Beautiful*, p. 222.
18. Leonard Sweet, *Quantum Spirituality*, p. 236.

19. Ibid., p. 130.
20. Leonard Sweet, *So Beautiful*, p. 291, #94; quoting Lamin O. Sanneh, *Whose Religion Is Christianity?*, pp. 10-11.
21. Neale Donald Walsch, Conversations with God Weekly Bulletin, April 14, 2006, #188, http://www.cwg.org/bulletins/bulletin_188/bulletin_188.html.
22. "What Is the Proper Response to Hatred and Violence?" by Neale Donald Walsch, an essay in *From the Ashes: A Call to Action—The Spiritual Challenge*, Beliefnet Editors, (USA: Rodale Inc., 2001), pp. 19-21. Cited from *In the Name of Purpose*, by Tamara Hartzell, p. 233.
23. Leonard Sweet, *So Beautiful*, p. 193.
24. Ibid., p. 196.
25. Alice Bailey and Djwhal Khul, *The Externalization of the Hierarchy*, Section II - The General World Picture, (Caux, Switzerland: Netnews Association and/or its suppliers, 2002), Lucis Trust, 1957 [see http://web.archive.org/web/20050726004029/http://laluni.helloyou.ws/netnews/bk/toc.html], http://www.netnews.org -- http://web.archive.org/web/20070218040026/http://laluni.helloyou.ws/netnews/bk/externalisation/exte1040.html.
26. Alice Bailey and Djwhal Khul, *The Reappearance of the Christ*, Chapter VI - The New World Religion, http://web.archive.org/web/20070218152816/http://laluni.helloyou.ws/netnews/bk/reappearance/reap1046.html.
27. Alice Bailey, *From Intellect to Intuition*, Chapter Eight - The Universality of Meditation, http://web.archive.org/web/20070327142351/laluni.helloyou.ws/netnews/bk/intellect/inte1055.html.
28. Alice Bailey and Djwhal Khul, *Problems of Humanity*, Chapter V - The Problem of the Churches, http://web.archive.org/web/20070218040238/http://laluni.helloyou.ws/netnews/bk/problems/prob1062.html.
29. H. P. Blavatsky, "To the Readers of 'Lucifer,'" *Lucifer* magazine, January 1888, http://www.blavatsky.net/blavatsky/arts/ToTheReadersOfLucifer.htm.
30. H. P. Blavatsky, "What Is Truth?," *Lucifer* magazine, February 1888, http://www.blavatsky.net/blavatsky/arts/WhatIsTruth.htm.
31. Alice Bailey and Djwhal Khul, *The Reappearance of the Christ*, Chapter IV - The Work of the Christ Today and in the Future, http://web.archive.org/web/20060722012639/http://laluni.helloyou.ws/netnews/bk/reappearance/reap1019.html.
32. Brian D. McLaren, *A New Kind of Christianity*, pp. 215-216.
33. Leonard Sweet and Frank Viola, *Jesus Manifesto*, pp. 89-91.
34. Leonard Sweet, *So Beautiful*, p. 43.
35. Leonard Sweet and Frank Viola, *Jesus Manifesto*, p. 116.
36. Leonard Sweet, *Quantum Spirituality*, p. 274.
37. William P. Young, *The Shack*, p. 182; emphasis added.
38. Pastor Kendall Adams' interview of William Paul Young aired on KAYP, March 6, 2009. Transcribed from the audio interview, part 4 of 5, available online at http://www.youtube.com/watch?v=IqnvsxYvwlA&feature=related. The interview is also archived at http://rock-life.com/KAYP.html in an mp3 file format. [For more information on the interview, see pastor Adams' Blog, http://alwaysreformingtoscripture.blogspot.com/2009/03/shack-inspection.html. Also see, "Shack Author Rejects Biblical Substitutionary Atonement," by John Lanagan, March 19, 2009, http://www.crossroad.to/Quotes/spirituality/lighthousetrails/09/3-shack-atonement.htm.]
39. Ibid., (interview).
40. William P. Young, *The Shack*, p. 112; emphasis added.
41. Ibid., p. 101; emphasis added.
42. Neale Donald Walsch, and "God," as quoted by Walsch, *Friendship with God*, pp. 357-359.
43. Leonard Sweet and Frank Viola, *Jesus Manifesto*, p. 94.
44. Leonard Sweet, *So Beautiful*, pp. 139-140.
45. Leonard Sweet and Frank Viola, *Jesus Manifesto*, pp. 138-139.
46. Leonard Sweet, *So Beautiful*, p. 249.
47. Ibid., p. 129.
48. Marcus J. Borg, *The God We Never Knew*, pp. 19-20.
49. Leonard Sweet, *So Beautiful*, p. 20.
50. Leonard Sweet, *Quantum Spirituality*, pp. 28-29.
51. "God," as quoted by Neale Donald Walsch, *Tomorrow's God*, p. 236.
52. Ibid., p. 235; emphasis added.
53. Leonard Sweet, *So Beautiful*, pp. 22-23.
54. Leonard Sweet and Frank Viola, *Jesus Manifesto*, pp. 57-58.
55. Ibid., p. 22.
56. Leonard Sweet, *Quantum Spirituality*, p. 274.

57. Leonard Sweet, *AquaChurch 2.0: Piloting Your Church in Today's Fluid Culture*, Second Edition 2008, (Colorado Springs, CO: David C. Cook, 1999), p. 47.
58. Leonard Sweet and Frank Viola, *Jesus Manifesto*, p. 67.
59. Leonard Sweet, *Quantum Spirituality*, p. 274.
60. H. P. Blavatsky, "What Is Truth?," *Lucifer* magazine, February 1888, http://www.blavatsky.net/blavatsky/arts/WhatIsTruth.htm.
61. Leonard Sweet, *So Beautiful*, pp. 166-167.
62. Alice Bailey and Djwhal Khul, *The Reappearance of the Christ*, Chapter III - World Expectancy, http://web.archive.org/web/20060504193959/http://laluni.helloyou.ws/netnews/bk/reappearance/reap1018.html.
63. H. P. Blavatsky, "What Is Truth?," *Lucifer* magazine, February 1888, http://www.blavatsky.net/blavatsky/arts/WhatIsTruth.htm.

44. A "'*loyalty test*' to following Jesus" is "to open ourselves up and stop clinging to our precious preconceptions"? (pages 308-317)
1. Leonard Sweet, *So Beautiful*, p. 224.
2. Ibid., p. 167.
3. Ibid., p. 165.
4. Ibid., p. 221.
5. Ibid., p. 158.
6. Ibid., p. 221; quoting Marvin Minsky.
7. Leonard Sweet, *Quantum Spirituality*, p. 274.
8. Leonard Sweet, *So Beautiful*, p. 168.
9. Ibid., p. 194.
10. Ibid., p. 163.
11. Ibid., p. 222.
12. Ibid., p. 111; emphasis added.
13. Ibid., p. 221; quoting Marvin Minsky.
14. Alice Bailey and Djwhal Khul, *The Reappearance of the Christ*, Chapter III - World Expectancy, http://web.archive.org/web/20060504193959/http://laluni.helloyou.ws/netnews/bk/reappearance/reap1018.html.
15. Leonard Sweet, *So Beautiful*, p. 221.
16. Ibid., pp. 220-221; emphasis added.
17. Ibid., pp. 221-222.
18. Leonard Sweet, *Quantum Spirituality*, pp. 130-131.
19. Leonard Sweet, *So Beautiful*, p. 165.
20. Ibid., p. 194.
21. Ibid., p. 222.
22. *American Dictionary of the English Language*, Noah Webster 1828, "deceive;" emphasis added.
23. Leonard Sweet, *So Beautiful*, p. 119.
24. Leonard Sweet and Frank Viola, *Jesus Manifesto*, p. 61.
25. Leonard Sweet, *So Beautiful*, p. 119.
26. Ibid., p. 140.
27. Leonard Sweet, *Nudge*, p. 231.
28. Ibid., pp. 230-231.
29. About, http://leonardsweet.com/about.php.
30. Leonard Sweet, *So Beautiful*, p. 83.

45. "The day of theology is over" -- doing and being and creating "God" in a quantum dance of Oneness (pages 318-330)
1. Leonard Sweet, *Quantum Spirituality*, p. 125. Cited from *A "Wonderful" Deception*, by Warren B. Smith, p. 104; ellipsis dots in the original.
2. "God," as quoted by Neale Donald Walsch, *Tomorrow's God*, p. 343.
3. Ibid., p. 196.
4. Ibid., p. 261.
5. Alice Bailey and Djwhal Khul, *Problems of Humanity*, Chapter V - The Problem of the Churches, http://web.archive.org/web/20070218120906/http://laluni.helloyou.ws/netnews/bk/problems/prob1052.html.
6. Neale Donald Walsch, and "God," as quoted by Walsch, *Tomorrow's God*, p. 26.
7. For example, see "Large Hadron Collider Enables Hunt For 'God' Particle To Complete 'Theory of Everything,'" University of Washington, *ScienceDaily*, May 29, 2008, http://www.sciencedaily.com/releases/2008/05/080527200600.htm; "Large Hadron Collider fired up in 'God particle' hunt," CNN, September 10, 2008, http://www.cnn.com/2008/TECH/09/10/lhc.collider/index.html; "Countdown to man's Big Bang

begins," Mark Prigg, Science Correspondent, London Evening Standard, September 9, 2008, http://www.thisislondon.co.uk/standard/article-23552722-countdown-to-mans-big-bang-begins.do; "Hawking bets CERN mega-machine won't find 'God's Particle,'" Breitbart, September 9, 2008, http://www.breitbart.com/article.php?id=080909150154.yzfml9cn&show_article=1; and CBS News "60 Minutes," "The Collider," which aired on September 28, 2008 (archived at http://www.cbsnews.com/video/watch/?id=4484053n).

8. "God," as quoted by Neale Donald Walsch, *Tomorrow's God*, p. 24.
9. Leonard Sweet, *Quantum Spirituality*, p. 65.
10. "God," as quoted by Neale Donald Walsch, *Conversations with God, Book 3*, p. 344.
11. William P. Young, *The Shack*, p. 112.
12. Warren B. Smith, *A "Wonderful" Deception*, pp. 167-169; quoting Fritjof Capra, *The Tao of Physics: An Exploration of the Parallels between Modern Physics and Eastern Mysticism* (Boston, MA: Shambhala Publications, Inc., 1999), pp. 11, 323, 341.
13. Neale Donald Walsch, *What God Wants*, p. 209.
14. Fritjof Capra, *The Turning Point: Science, Society, and the Rising Culture*, Bantam Edition, 1983, (New York, NY: Bantam Books, 1982), p. 78.
15. Fritjof Capra, *The Tao of Physics: An Exploration of the Parallels between Modern Physics and Eastern Mysticism*, Third Edition, Updated, (Boston, MA: Shambhala Publications, Inc., 1975, 1983, 1991), pp. 130-131.
16. Ibid., p. 303.
17. Alice Bailey and Djwhal Khul, *The Rays and the Initiations*, Part I - Fourteen Rules for Group Initiation, http://web.archive.org/web/20070218153043/http://laluni.helloyou.ws/netnews/bk/rays/rays1111.html.
18. Alice Bailey, *From Bethlehem to Calvary*, Chapter Seven - Our Immediate Goal, The Founding of the Kingdom, http://web.archive.org/web/20070216005818/http://laluni.helloyou.ws/netnews/bk/bethlehem/beth1079.html.
19. Alice Bailey, *From Intellect to Intuition*, Chapter Eight - The Universality of Meditation, http://web.archive.org/web/20070327142351/laluni.helloyou.ws/netnews/bk/intellect/inte1055.html.
20. Ibid., Chapter Three - The Nature of the Soul, http://web.archive.org/web/20070327142259/laluni.helloyou.ws/netnews/bk/intellect/inte1017.html.
21. "God," as quoted by Neale Donald Walsch, *Communion with God*, p. 164.
22. "God," as quoted by Neale Donald Walsch, *Conversations with God, Book 3*, p. 344.
23. "God," as quoted by Neale Donald Walsch, *Conversations with God: an uncommon dialogue, Book 2* (Charlottesville, VA: Hampton Roads Publishing Company, Inc., 1997), p. 173.
24. "God," as quoted by Neale Donald Walsch, *Tomorrow's God*, p. 317.
25. Fritjof Capra, *The Tao of Physics: An Exploration of the Parallels between Modern Physics and Eastern Mysticism*, p. 130.
26. Fritjof Capra, *The Turning Point*, pp. 80-81.
27. Ibid., p. 90; emphasis added.
28. Ibid., p. 340.
29. Ibid., p. 91; emphasis added.
30. Ibid., p. 90; emphasis added.
31. Fritjof Capra, *The Tao of Physics*, pp. 23-24.
32. Fritjof Capra, *The Turning Point*, p. 94.
33. Ibid., p. 92.
34. Ibid., p. 93.
35. Fritjof Capra, *The Tao of Physics*, p. 159.
36. Ibid., p. 291.
37. Fritjof Capra, *The Turning Point*, p. 92.
38. Ibid., p. 87.
39. Leonard Sweet, *So Beautiful*, pp. 57-60.
40. Ibid., p. 27.
41. Leonard Sweet, *Quantum Spirituality*, p. 63.
42. Neale Donald Walsch, and "God," as quoted by Walsch, *Friendship with God*, p. 21.
43. Fritjof Capra, *The Turning Point*, p. 92.
44. Leonard Sweet and Frank Viola, *Jesus Manifesto*, p. 102.
45. Leonard Sweet, *Nudge*, p. 136.
46. Alice Bailey, *From Bethlehem to Calvary*, Chapter Seven - Our Immediate Goal, The Founding of the Kingdom, http://web.archive.org/web/20070216005818/http://laluni.helloyou.ws/netnews/bk/bethlehem/beth1079.html.
47. Neale Donald Walsch, and "God," as quoted by Walsch, *Conversations with God, Book 1*, p. 170.
48. Leonard Sweet, *Quantum Spirituality*, p. 252.

49. "God," as quoted by Neale Donald Walsch, *Communion with God*, p. 105.
50. Leonard Sweet, *So Beautiful*, p. 194.
51. Leonard Sweet, *Quantum Spirituality*, p. 59.
52. "God," as quoted by Neale Donald Walsch, *Conversations with God, Book 3*, pp. 344-345.
53. Ibid., p. 17.
54. Leonard Sweet, *So Beautiful*, p. 60.
55. Ibid., p. 217.
56. Ibid., pp. 22-23.
57. Leonard Sweet, *Quantum Spirituality*, p. 121.
58. Leonard Sweet, *So Beautiful*, p. 114; emphasis added
59. Leonard Sweet and Frank Viola, *Jesus Manifesto*, p. 102.
60. Leonard Sweet, *Nudge*, p. 135.
61. "God," as quoted by Neale Donald Walsch, *Conversations with God, Book 3*, p. 51.
62. "God," as quoted by Neale Donald Walsch, *Tomorrow's God*, p. 139.
63. "God," as quoted by Neale Donald Walsch, *Conversations with God, Book 3*, pp. 344-345.
64. "God," as quoted by Neale Donald Walsch, *Tomorrow's God*, p. 22.
65. "God," as quoted by Neale Donald Walsch, *Conversations with God, Book 3*, p. 349.
66. Fritjof Capra, *The Tao of Physics*, p. 304.
67. Leonard Sweet, *So Beautiful*, p. 43.
68. Ibid., pp. 203-204.
69. Online Etymology Dictionary, "incarnation," http://www.etymonline.com/index.php?term=incarnation.
70. "God," as quoted by Neale Donald Walsch, *Conversations with God, Book 1*, p. 175.
71. Neale Donald Walsch, and "God," as quoted by Walsch, *Tomorrow's God*, p. 26.
72. "God," as quoted by Neale Donald Walsch, *Conversations with God, Book 3*, p. 256. Cited from *Reinventing Jesus Christ: The New Gospel*, by Warren (B.) Smith, p. 22. [In *False Christ Coming – Does Anybody Care?: What New Age leaders really have in store for America, the church, and the world*, it is p. 38.]
73. "God," as quoted by Neale Donald Walsch, *Conversations with God, Book 1*, p. 196.
74. "God," as quoted by Neale Donald Walsch, *Conversations with God, Book 3*, pp. 54-55.
75. Ibid., p. 344.
76. "God," as quoted by Neale Donald Walsch, *Conversations with God, Book 1*, p. 54.

46. An imagination that is "God" (pages 331-340)
1. "God," as quoted by Neale Donald Walsch, *Conversations with God, Book 1*, p. 54.
2. Leonard Sweet, *Quantum Spirituality*, p. 63.
3. "God," as quoted by Neale Donald Walsch, *Conversations with God, Book 1*, p. 198.
4. "God," as quoted by Neale Donald Walsch, *Tomorrow's God*, p. 317; emphasis added.
5. "God," as quoted by Neale Donald Walsch, *Conversations with God, Book 1*, p. 198.
6. "God," as quoted by Neale Donald Walsch, *Conversations with God, Book 3*, p. 361.
7. Ibid., p. 256.
8. Ibid., p. 90.
9. "God," as quoted by Neale Donald Walsch, *Conversations with God, Book 1*, p. 74.
10. "God," as quoted by Neale Donald Walsch, *Conversations with God, Book 3*, p. 55.
11. "God," as quoted by Neale Donald Walsch, *Conversations with God, Book 1*, p. 54.
12. Ibid., p. 175.
13. Leonard Sweet, *Quantum Spirituality*, p. 65.
14. Ibid., pp. 59-60.
15. Ibid., pp. 62-63.
16. Leonard Sweet, *So Beautiful*, p. 166.
17. Leonard Sweet, *Quantum Spirituality*, p. 167.
18. Ibid., p. 121.
19. Leonard Sweet, *So Beautiful*, p. 166.
20. Alice A. Bailey, *The Consciousness Of The Atom*, pp. 54-55.
21. Ibid., pp. 55-56; emphasis added.
22. Leonard Sweet, *Quantum Spirituality*, p. 101.
23. Ibid., p. 71.
24. Ibid., p. 255.
25. Ibid., p. 167.
26. "God," as quoted by Neale Donald Walsch, *Communion with God*, p. 105.
27. "God," as quoted by Neale Donald Walsch, *Conversations with God, Book 3*, p. 345.
28. Leonard Sweet, *Quantum Spirituality*, pp. 256-257.

29. Neale Donald Walsch, *What God Wants*, p. 187.
30. Alice Bailey and Djwhal Khul, *Problems of Humanity*, Chapter V - The Problem of the Churches, http://web.archive.org/web/20070218120906/http://laluni.helloyou.ws/netnews/bk/problems/prob1052.html; emphasis added.
31. Leonard Sweet, *So Beautiful*, p. 134.
32. Neale Donald Walsch, and "God," as quoted by Walsch, *Tomorrow's God*, p. 26.
33. Leonard Sweet, *So Beautiful*, p. 140.
34. Ibid., p. 165.
35. Leonard Sweet, *Quantum Spirituality*, p. 188.
36. Ibid., p. 76; quoting David W. Tracy.
37. Leonard Sweet, *So Beautiful*, p. 123.
38. Ibid., p. 182; emphasis added.
39. Leonard Sweet, *Quantum Spirituality*, p. 252.
40. Leonard Sweet, *So Beautiful*, p. 165.
41. Dictionary.com, "generativity," http://dictionary.reference.com/browse/generativity; emphasis added.
42. Ibid., "generate," http://dictionary.reference.com/browse/generate; emphasis added.
43. *Webster's New World Dictionary of the American Language*, Second College Edition, (New York, NY: Simon & Schuster, Inc., 1970, 1984), "generative."
44. *American Dictionary of the English Language*, Noah Webster 1828, "shapesmith;" emphasis added.
45. Leonard Sweet, *Nudge*, p. 305, #40.

47. Changing the "old" reality of the God of *judgment* into a new "reality" of a "God" of *Oneness* by simply *thinking* it "into being" (pages 341-356)
1. "God," as quoted by Neale Donald Walsch, *Tomorrow's God*, p. 311.
2. "God," as quoted by Neale Donald Walsch, *Communion with God*, p. 90.
3. Neale Donald Walsch, *What God Wants*, p. 209.
4. Leonard Sweet; *Quantum Spirituality*, pp. 294-295.
5. Fritjof Capra, *The Tao of Physics*, pp. 340-341.
6. Ibid., p. 325; emphasis added.
7. Leonard Sweet, *Quantum Spirituality*, p. 70; emphasis added.
8. Fritjof Capra, *The Tao of Physics*, p. 325; emphasis added.
9. Ibid., pp. 325-326; emphasis added.
10. Ibid., p. 326.
11. Fritjof Capra, *The Turning Point*, pp. 411-412; emphasis added.
12. Leonard Sweet, *Quantum Spirituality*, p. 234; emphasis added.
13. Leonard Sweet, *So Beautiful*, p. 104.
14. Alice Bailey and Djwhal Khul, *The Reappearance of the Christ*, Chapter IV - The Work of the Christ Today and in the Future, http://web.archive.org/web/20070402084438/http://laluni.helloyou.ws/netnews/bk/reappearance/reap1025.html.
15. Ibid., Chapter VI - The New World Religion, http://web.archive.org/web/20070218152806/http://laluni.helloyou.ws/netnews/bk/reappearance/reap1043.html.
16. Ibid., http://web.archive.org/web/20070218152816/http://laluni.helloyou.ws/netnews/bk/reappearance/reap1046.html.
17. Alice Bailey and Djwhal Khul, *Problems of Humanity*, Chapter V - The Problem of the Churches, http://web.archive.org/web/20070218153113/http://laluni.helloyou.ws/netnews/bk/problems/prob1055.html.
18. Leonard Sweet, *Quantum Spirituality*, p. 4.
19. Fritjof Capra, *The Turning Point*, p. 418.
20. "God," as quoted by Neale Donald Walsch, *Tomorrow's God*, p. 216.
21. Neale Donald Walsch, *What God Wants*, p. 209.
22. Brian D. McLaren, *A New Kind of Christianity*, p. 215; and p. 195 for bracketed information.
23. Ibid., p. 195; emphasis added.
24. Ibid., pp. 38-39.
25. Ibid., pp. 215-216.
26. Ibid., p. 196.
27. Ibid., p. 241.
28. Ibid., p. 99.
29. Ibid., p. 272, #6.
30. Neale Donald Walsch, *What God Wants*, p. 211.
31. "God," as quoted by Neale Donald Walsch, *Tomorrow's God*, p. 196.
32. Ibid., p. 261.

33. "God" as quoted by Neale Donald Walsch, *Conversations with God: an uncommon dialogue, Book 2*, p. 235. Cited from *Reinventing Jesus Christ*, by Warren (B.) Smith, p. 22; ellipsis dots in the original. [In *False Christ Coming – Does Anybody Care?*, it is p. 38.]
34. Warren B. Smith, *A "Wonderful" Deception*, pp. 180-181; quoting Leonard Sweet, *SoulTsunami: Sink or Swim in New Millennium Culture*, pp. 109, 121.
35. Leonard Sweet, *SoulTsunami: Sink or Swim in New Millennium Culture*, p. 55. Cited from *A "Wonderful" Deception*, by Warren B. Smith, p. 179.
36. Ibid. Cited from ibid., (Smith), p. 180.
37. Leonard Sweet, *So Beautiful*, p. 20.
38. Leonard Sweet, *SoulTsunami*, p. 17. Cited from *A "Wonderful" Deception*, by Warren B. Smith, p. 131.
39. "God," as quoted by Neale Donald Walsch, *Conversations with God, Book 3*, p. 76.
40. Ibid., pp. 54-55.
41. Ibid., pp. 107-108.
42. Ibid., p. 108.
43. Fritjof Capra, *The Turning Point*, p. 297.
44. Leonard Sweet, *Quantum Spirituality*, p. 63.
45. Fritjof Capra, *The Turning Point*, p. 296.
46. Ibid., p. 292.
47. "God," as quoted by Neale Donald Walsch, *Conversations with God, Book 1*, pp. 54-55.
48. "God," as quoted by Neale Donald Walsch, *Conversations with God, Book 2*, pp. 87-88.
49. Fritjof Capra, *The Turning Point*, p. 304; emphasis added.
50. Leonard Sweet, *Quantum Spirituality*, p. 106.
51. Fritjof Capra, *The Tao of Physics*, p. 286.
52. Ibid., p. 277; quoting Ashvaghosha.
53. "God," as quoted by Neale Donald Walsch, *Conversations with God, Book 1*, p. 52.
54. Leonard Sweet, *Quantum Spirituality*, p. 80; emphasis added.
55. Ibid., pp. 62-63.
56. Ibid., p. 10.
57. Ibid., p. 63.
58. Ibid., p. 261.
59. Ibid., p. 26.
60. Fritjof Capra, *The Tao of Physics*, p. 141.
61. Fritjof Capra, *The Turning Point*, p. 93.
62. Neale Donald Walsch, *Conversations with God, Book 3*, pp. 351-352.
63. Neale Donald Walsch, *Tomorrow's God*, pp. 24-25.
64. "God," as quoted by Neale Donald Walsch, ibid., p. 317.
65. "God," as quoted by Neale Donald Walsch, *Friendship with God*, p. 23. Cited from *A "Wonderful" Deception*, by Warren B. Smith, p. 158.
66. Neale Donald Walsch, *What God Wants*, p. 114.
67. "God," as quoted by Neale Donald Walsch, *Conversations with God, Book 1*, p. 74.
68. Leonard Sweet, *Nudge*, p. 157.
69. "God," as quoted by Neale Donald Walsch, *Conversations with God, Book 3*, p. 50.
70. Ibid., pp. 344-345.
71. Leonard Sweet, *Quantum Spirituality*, p. 63.
72. "God," as quoted by Neale Donald Walsch, *Conversations with God, Book 1*, p. 198.
73. Ibid., p. 26.
74. Ibid., p. 202.
75. Ibid., p. 35.

48. The dance of aligning minds with the new "design" (pages 357-367)
1. Leonard Sweet, *Nudge*, p. 154.
2. Ibid., p. 306, #42.
3. "Global Consciousness Project: Brief Overview," http://noosphere.princeton.edu/abstract.html.
4. "Theory and Speculations," in the abstract titled, "Interconnecting with everyone: Being in global consciousness," Global Consciousness Project, http://noosphere.princeton.edu/speculations.html.
5. Fritjof Capra, *The Turning Point*, pp. 303-304; emphasis added.
6. Ibid., p. 304; emphasis added.
7. Ibid.; emphasis added.
8. Ibid., pp. 302-303.
9. Ibid., pp. 303-304.

10. Pierre Teilhard de Chardin, *Christianity and Evolution*, p. 56. Cited from *A "Wonderful" Deception*, by Warren B. Smith, p. 114; emphasis added.
11. Warren B. Smith, *A "Wonderful" Deception*, pp. 110-111.
12. Pierre Teilhard de Chardin, *Christianity and Evolution*, pp. 130, 95. Cited from ibid., p. 119.
13. Leonard Sweet, *Quantum Spirituality*, p. 106; emphasis added.
14. Sermons.com, Leonard Sweet, http://www.sermons.com/leonardSweet.asp; emphasis added.
15. About, http://leonardsweet.com/about.php. See also News Release, "Christian Author/Futurist Leonard Sweet Speaking in Meridian," October 7, 2003, http://blogs.georgefox.edu/newsreleases/?p=2353.
16. "Scientific Evidence for the Existence of a True Noosphere: Foundation for a Noo-Constitution," Paper for the World Forum of Spiritual Culture, Section 5, The Noo-Constitution, Astana, Kazakhstan, October 18-20, 2010, Roger Nelson, Director, Global Consciousness Project, Princeton Engineering Anomalies Research (PEAR) lab at Princeton University, http://noosphere.princeton.edu/papers/pdf/noosphere.forum.4.pdf, p. 13.
17. Ibid., pp. 14-16.
18. Ibid., p. 16; see also Projects, Currently Active, Global Consciousness Project, Institute of Noetic Sciences, http://www.noetic.org/research/project/global-consciousness-project/.
19. IONS Directory, Visionaries, Institute of Noetic Sciences, http://www.noetic.org/directory/group/visionaries/; and IONS Directory Profile, http://www.noetic.org/directory/person/neale-donald-walsch/.
20. IONS Overview, Institute of Noetic Sciences, http://www.noetic.org/about/overview/; emphasis added.
21. Our Vision, Institute of Noetic Sciences, http://www.noetic.org/about/vision/; emphasis added.
22. Ibid.; emphasis added.
23. "Theory and Speculations," in the abstract titled, "Interconnecting with everyone: Being in global consciousness," Global Consciousness Project, http://noosphere.princeton.edu/speculations.html; emphasis added.
24. "Re-writing the Story of Who We Are" by Lisa Reagan, *Noetic Now*, Issue Three, October 2010, Institute of Noetic Sciences, http://www.noetic.org/noetic/issue-three-october/re-writing-the-story-of-who-we-are/; emphasis added.
25. Bruce H. Lipton, PhD, Biography, http://www.brucelipton.com/about-bruce; emphasis added.
26. A Call to Conscious Evolution: Our Moment of Choice, August 31, 2010, UCLA, http://www.brucelipton.com/files/ellaeventflyer.pdf. For more information on Barbara Marx Hubbard, Marianne Williamson, Neale Donald Walsch, and other New Age leaders, see *False Christ Coming – Does Anybody Care?*, by Warren B. Smith.
27. IONS Directory, Visionaries, Institute of Noetic Sciences, http://www.noetic.org/directory/group/visionaries/; and IONS Directory Profile, http://www.noetic.org/directory/person/barbara-marx-hubbard/ and http://www.noetic.org/directory/person/marianne-williamson/.
28. IONS Directory, International Advisory Board, Institute of Noetic Sciences, http://www.noetic.org/directory/group/international-advisory-board/; and IONS Directory Profile, http://www.noetic.org/directory/person/deepak-chopra/.
29. "Re-writing the Story of Who We Are" by Lisa Reagan, *Noetic Now*, Issue Three, October 2010, Institute of Noetic Sciences, http://www.noetic.org/noetic/issue-three-october/re-writing-the-story-of-who-we-are/.
30. Warren B. Smith, *False Christ Coming – Does Anybody Care?*, pp. 27-29; and pp. 25, 27 for bracketed information. [In *Reinventing Jesus Christ*, it is pp. 15-16; and pp. 14, 15 for bracketed information.]
31. "Christ," as quoted by Barbara Marx Hubbard, *The Revelation: A Message of Hope for the New Millennium* (Novato, CA: Nataraj Publishing, 1995), pp. 148, 102, 231, 65, 255, 267, 195, 264, 195. Cited from ibid., (*Reinventing Jesus Christ*), pp. 17-19. [In *False Christ Coming – Does Anybody Care?*, it is pp. 31-34; however, it did not include the last sentence in the 7th quote listed here.]
32. Neale Donald Walsch, *Tomorrow's God*, p. 24.
33. "God," as quoted by Neale Donald Walsch, *Conversations with God, Book 3*, p. 67.
34. "God," as quoted by Neale Donald Walsch, *Conversations with God, Book 1*, pp. 54-56.
35. Ibid., p. 52.
36. "God," as quoted by Neale Donald Walsch, *Conversations with God, Book 3*, pp. 56-57.
37. Ibid., p. 349.
38. "God," as quoted by Neale Donald Walsch, *Communion with God*, pp. 90-91.
39. Ibid., p. 90.
40. Leonard Sweet, *Nudge*, pp. 275-276.
41. Ibid., pp. 50-51.
42. Ibid., pp. 47-48.
43. Ibid., p. 46.
44. Ibid., p. 93.
45. Ibid., p. 58.
46. Ibid., p. 134.

47. Ibid., p. 67.
48. Leonard Sweet, *Quantum Spirituality*, p. 70.
49. Leonard Sweet, *So Beautiful*, p. 104.
50. Alice Bailey and Djwhal Khul, *Problems of Humanity*, Chapter V - The Problem of the Churches, http://web.archive.org/web/20070218153113/http://laluni.helloyou.ws/netnews/bk/problems/prob1055.html.
51. Fritjof Capra, *The Tao of Physics*, pp. 154-155.
52. "God," as quoted by Neale Donald Walsch, *Conversations with God, Book 3*, p. 349; emphasis added.
53. Leonard Sweet, *So Beautiful*, p. 99.
54. Leonard Sweet, *Nudge*, p. 214.

49. The "Parable of the Rock" and the "Big Bang" (pages 368-382)
1. "God," as quoted by Neale Donald Walsch, *Conversations with God, Book 1*, pp. 22-26.
2. "God," as quoted by Neale Donald Walsch, *Conversations with God, Book 3*, pp. 63-64.
3. Alice Bailey and Djwhal Khul, *The Reappearance of the Christ*, Chapter VI - The New World Religion, http://web.archive.org/web/20070218152816/http://laluni.helloyou.ws/netnews/bk/reappearance/reap1046.html.
4. Leonard Sweet, *Nudge*, p. 214.
5. Beliefnet, "Inspirational Quotes from Mahatma Gandhi," "The Wisdom of Gandhi," http://www.beliefnet.com/Faiths/Hinduism/2009/07/Gandhi-Quotes.aspx.
6. *The Encyclopedia of Gandhian Thoughts*, by Anand T. Hingorani & Ganga A. Hingorani, "Religions," http://www.mkgandhi.org/encyclopedia/r.htm.
7. Ibid.
8. Ibid., "Temples," http://www.mkgandhi.org/encyclopedia/t.htm; ellipsis dots in the original.
9. Ibid., "Idol Worship," http://www.mkgandhi.org/encyclopedia/i.htm.
10. Ibid., "Toleration," http://www.mkgandhi.org/encyclopedia/t.htm.
11. "Why we value Gandhi?," A Hindu Perspective, Vijay Mehta, The Gandhi Foundation, "A talk given at the 2005 Annual Multi-Faith Service (Kingsley Hall, London)," http://www.arcuk.org/pages/why_we_value_gandhi.htm.
12. Leonard Sweet, *Nudge*, p. 130.
13. Ibid., p. 299, #80; see also p. 116; quoting Meister Eckhart.
14. "God," as quoted by Neale Donald Walsch, *Communion with God*, p. 91; emphasis added.
15. Leonard Sweet, *Nudge*, p. 60.
16. Ibid., p. 56.
17. Ibid., p. 58.
18. Ibid., p. 93.
19. Leonard Sweet, *So Beautiful*, p. 111.
20. Ibid., p. 23.
21. Leonard Sweet, *Nudge*, pp. 41-42.
22. Ibid., pp. 44-45.
23. Ibid., p. 152.
24. Ibid., p. 305, #34.
25. About, Nonduality, Science and Nonduality (SAND), http://scienceandnonduality.com/nonduality.shtml; and About, Partners, Institute of Noetic Sciences, http://www.noetic.org/about/partners/.
26. Ibid., (SAND).
27. Leonard Sweet, *Nudge*, p. 157.
28. Ibid., p. 152.
29. "God," as quoted by Neale Donald Walsch, *Conversations with God, Book 1*, p. 74.
30. Ibid., pp. 24-25.
31. Alice Bailey and Djwhal Khul, *The Labors of Hercules*, Labor IX, The Spirit of Truth, http://web.archive.org/web/20070324030138/laluni.helloyou.ws/netnews/bk/hercules/herc1049.html.
32. Leonard Sweet, *Nudge*, p. 157.
33. Ibid., pp. 152-153.
34. Ibid., p. 305, #40.
35. About Answers in Genesis, http://www.answersingenesis.org/about.
36. Ken Ham, Answers in Genesis, February 1999 Newsletter, Didyaknow?, http://www.answersingenesis.org/docs/3951.asp.
37. Ibid.; emphasis added.
38. Brian D. McLaren, *A New Kind of Christianity*, p. 99.
39. Ibid., p. 272, #6.
40. Ibid., p. 273, #5.

41. Leonard Sweet, Brian D. McLaren, and Jerry Haselmayer, *A Is for Abductive: The Language of the Emerging Church*, pp. 299-300.
42. Leonard Sweet, *Nudge*, p. 145.
43. Ibid., p. 113.
44. Ibid., p. 117.
45. Ibid., p. 45.
46. Ibid., pp. 154-156.
47. Leonard Sweet, *Quantum Spirituality*, p. 110.
48. Neale Donald Walsch, *What God Wants*, p. 202.
49. CBS News "60 Minutes" correspondent Steve Kroft asked CERN's chief spokesman James Gillies, "Can you give me an example of something that was created here for research purposes and changed the world?" Gillies answered, "Well the best known one is the worldwide web." Kroft then explains that it was "invented in these corridors to help scientists do research" and "given to the world for free" "because CERN has been required to share its scientific discoveries." Transcribed from CBS News "60 Minutes," "The Collider," which aired on September 28, 2008.
50. "God," as quoted by Neale Donald Walsch, *Conversations with God, Book 3*, p. 56.
51. Leonard Sweet, *Quantum Spirituality*, p. 70.
52. Fritjof Capra, *The Tao of Physics*, p. 315.
53. "The Glue That Holds the World Together," by Robert Kunzig, *DISCOVER* magazine, July 2000 issue, http://discovermagazine.com/2000/jul/featgluons.
54. Fritjof Capra, *The Tao of Physics*, pp. 317-319.
55. Dictionary.com, "build," http://dictionary.reference.com/browse/build; parentheses in the original; emphasis added.

50. The cosmic circle dance -- an "upward journey" of "evolving" back into "God" (pages 383-405)

1. Leonard Sweet, *Nudge*, p. 154.
2. Leonard Sweet, *Quantum Spirituality*, pp. 59-60.
3. Ibid., p. 65.
4. "God," as quoted by Neale Donald Walsch, *Tomorrow's God*, p. 317.
5. "God," as quoted by Neale Donald Walsch, *Conversations with God, Book 3*, pp. 344-345.
6. "God," as quoted by Neale Donald Walsch, *Conversations with God, Book 1*, p. 198.
7. "God," as quoted by Neale Donald Walsch, *Conversations with God, Book 3*, pp. 56-57.
8. "God," as quoted by Neale Donald Walsch, *Conversations with God, Book 1*, pp. 24-26.
9. Ibid., p. 74.
10. Neale Donald Walsch, *What God Wants*, p. 114.
11. Alice A. Bailey, *The Consciousness Of The Atom*, p. 5.
12. Ibid., p. 58.
13. Ibid., p. 65.
14. Ibid., p. 133.
15. Ibid., p. 73.
16. Ibid., pp. 26-27.
17. Ibid., p. 61.
18. Ibid., pp. 21-22.
19. Ibid., p. 62.
20. Ibid., p. 53.
21. Leonard Sweet, *So Beautiful*, p. 49.
22. Leonard Sweet, *Quantum Spirituality*, p. 162.
23. Ibid., p. 59.
24. Ibid., pp. 61-62.
25. Ibid., p. 64; quoting Sri Aurobindo. [Note: the added descriptions here by Barbara Marx Hubbard were taken from her book *The Revelation: A Message of Hope for the New Millennium*, Second Edition, (Mill Valley, CA: Nataraj Publishing, 1995), pp. 339, 349.]
26. Ibid., (Sweet), p. 259.
27. Ursula King, *Towards A New Mysticism: Teilhard de Chardin and Eastern Religions* (New York, NY: The Seabury Press, 1980), back cover.
28. Ibid., p. 182.
29. Ibid., p. 181; emphasis added.
30. Pierre Teilhard de Chardin, *Christianity and Evolution*, p. 56. Cited from *A "Wonderful" Deception*, by Warren B. Smith, p. 114.
31. Ibid., p. 130. Cited from ibid., (Smith), p. 119.

32. Ibid., p. 95. Cited from ibid., (Smith).
33. Leonard Sweet, *Quantum Spirituality*, p. 261.
34. Leonard Sweet and Frank Viola, *Jesus Manifesto*, pp. 96-97.
35. Leonard Sweet, *So Beautiful*, p. 59.
36. Leonard Sweet, *Nudge*, p. 66.
37. Leonard Sweet and Frank Viola, *Jesus Manifesto*, p. 95.
38. Leonard Sweet, *So Beautiful*, p. 20; emphasis added.
39. Warren B. Smith, *A "Wonderful" Deception*, pp. 106-107; quoting from Leonard Sweet's "Acknowledgments" in *Quantum Spirituality*; emphasis added.
40. Ibid., (Smith), p. 111.
41. Ibid.; quoting Matthew Fox, *The Coming of the Cosmic Christ: The Healing of Mother Earth and the Birth of a Global Renaissance* (San Francisco, CA: Harper & Row Publishers, 1988), pp. 137, 154.
42. Alice Bailey, *From Bethlehem to Calvary*, Chapter Two - The First Initiation, The Birth at Bethlehem, http://web.archive.org/web/20070219003449/laluni.helloyou.ws/netnews/bk/bethlehem/beth1025.html.
43. Alice Bailey and Djwhal Khul, *The Labors of Hercules*, Labor X, Prologue, http://web.archive.org/web/20070117072904/laluni.helloyou.ws/netnews/bk/hercules/herc1052.html.
44. "God" as quoted by Neale Donald Walsch, *Conversations with God, Book 2*, p. 22. Cited from *False Christ Coming – Does Anybody Care?*, by Warren B. Smith, p. 41.
45. Leonard Sweet, *Quantum Spirituality*, p. 162.
46. Dictionary.com, "divinize," http://dictionary.reference.com/browse/divinize.
47. Mike Morrell, "Panentheism - Perichoresis - Christology: Participatory Divinity," June 30, 2009, http://zoecarnate.wordpress.com/2009/06/30/panentheism-perichoresis-christology-participatory-divinity/.
48. Mike Morrell, "Frank Viola & Leonard Sweet on 'Jesus Manifesto,' a May interview, posted June 1, 2010, http://zoecarnate.wordpress.com/2010/06/01/frank-viola-leonard-sweet-on-a-jesus-manifesto/.
49. Mike Morrell, "'I Don't Want to be Part of Any Jesus Revolution Without a Perichoretic Dance' – Why We Need Both Jesus Manifestoes," June 2, 2010, http://zoecarnate.wordpress.com/2010/06/02/i-don't-want-to-be-part-of-any-jesus-revolution-without-a-perichoretic-dance-why-we-need-both-jesus-manifestoes/.
50. Leonard Sweet, *So Beautiful*, p. 114.
51. Alice Bailey, *From Bethlehem to Calvary*, Chapter Two - The First Initiation, The Birth at Bethlehem, http://web.archive.org/web/20070219003449/laluni.helloyou.ws/netnews/bk/bethlehem/beth1025.html.
52. Alice A. Bailey, *The Consciousness Of The Atom*, p. 21.
53. Ibid., p. 62.
54. Ibid., pp. 26-27.
55. Leonard Sweet and Frank Viola, *Jesus Manifesto*, pp. 96-97; emphasis added.
56. *American Dictionary of the English Language*, Noah Webster 1828, "sanctify;" see also "sanctification," and "sanctified."
57. Alice Bailey and Djwhal Khul, *Problems of Humanity*, Chapter V - The Problem of the Churches, http://web.archive.org/web/20070218040238/http://laluni.helloyou.ws/netnews/bk/problems/prob1062.html.
58. Alice Bailey and Djwhal Khul, *The Labors of Hercules*, Labor IX, The Spirit of Truth, http://web.archive.org/web/20070324030138/laluni.helloyou.ws/netnews/bk/hercules/herc1049.html.
59. "God," as quoted by Neale Donald Walsch, *Tomorrow's God*, pp. 56-58.
60. Neale Donald Walsch, *When Everything Changes, Change Everything: In a Time of Turmoil, a Pathway to Peace* (Charlottesville, VA: Hampton Roads Publishing Company, Inc., 2009), p. 194.
61. Alice Bailey and Djwhal Khul, *A Treatise on White Magic*, Rule Fifteen - The Negation of the Great Illusion, http://web.archive.org/web/20070314194202/laluni.helloyou.ws/netnews/bk/magic/magi1254.html.
62. "God," as quoted by Neale Donald Walsch, *Conversations with God, Book 3*, p. 260.
63. "God," as quoted by Neale Donald Walsch, *Conversations with God, Book 1*, p. 28.
64. Ibid., p. 82.
65. Neale Donald Walsch, *What God Wants*, p. 209.
66. "Christ," as quoted by Barbara Marx Hubbard, *The Revelation: A Message of Hope for the New Millennium*, pp. 253-254.
67. Ibid., p. 256.
68. "God," as quoted by Neale Donald Walsch, *The New Revelations*, p. 282.
69. "Christ," as quoted by Barbara Marx Hubbard, *The Revelation*, p. 255.
70. Ibid., p. 254.
71. Warren B. Smith, *False Christ Coming – Does Anybody Care?*, pp. 27-28.
72. "God," as quoted by Neale Donald Walsch, *Tomorrow's God*, p. 216.
73. Neale Donald Walsch, *What God Wants*, p. 209.
74. Ibid., pp. 103-104.

75. Neale Donald Walsch, *Happier than God: Turn Ordinary Life into an Extraordinary Experience* (Charlottesville, VA: Hampton Roads Publishing Company, Inc., 2008), p. 241.
76. "Theory and Speculations," in the abstract titled, "Interconnecting with everyone: Being in global consciousness," Global Consciousness Project, http://noosphere.princeton.edu/speculations.html; emphasis added.
77. Alice A. Bailey, *The Consciousness Of The Atom*, p. 65.
78. Ibid., p. 70.
79. Ibid., p. 53.
80. Ibid., pp. 145-146.
81. Ibid., pp. 89-90.
82. Ibid., pp. 92-93.
83. Ibid., p. 103.
84. Ibid., p. 21.
85. Ibid., p. 99.
86. Ibid., pp. 135-136.
87. Leonard Sweet, *So Beautiful*, p. 25.
88. Ibid., p. 215.
89. Leonard Sweet, *Quantum Spirituality*, p. 63.
90. "God," as quoted by Neale Donald Walsch, *Friendship with God*, pp. 377-378.
91. IONS Overview, Institute of Noetic Sciences, http://www.noetic.org/about/overview/; emphasis added.
92. "Re-writing the Story of Who We Are" by Lisa Reagan, *Noetic Now*, Issue Three, October 2010, Institute of Noetic Sciences, http://www.noetic.org/noetic/issue-three-october/re-writing-the-story-of-who-we-are/.
93. "Theory and Speculations," in the abstract titled, "Interconnecting with everyone: Being in global consciousness," Global Consciousness Project, http://noosphere.princeton.edu/speculations.html.
94. Pierre Teilhard de Chardin, *The Phenomenon of Man*, English translation by Bernard Wall, (New York, NY: Harper & Row Publishers Inc., 1959), Perennial, 2002, HarperCollins Publishers Inc., p. 219.
95. Neale Donald Walsch, *What God Wants*, p. 179.
96. "God," as quoted by Neale Donald Walsch, *Tomorrow's God*, pp. 56-58.
97. Alice A. Bailey, *The Consciousness Of The Atom*, p. 93.
98. "God," as quoted by Neale Donald Walsch, *Conversations with God, Book 3*, pp. 145-146.
99. Ibid., p. 90.
100. "God," as quoted by Neale Donald Walsch, *Conversations with God, Book 1*, pp. 40-41.
101. Neale Donald Walsch, *What God Wants*, p. 103; emphasis added.
102. Ibid., p. 209.
103. Ibid., pp. 113-114.
104. Neale Donald Walsch, *When Everything Changes, Change Everything: In a Time of Turmoil, a Pathway to Peace*, p. 194.
105. Ibid., pp. 197-198.

51. Creating Oneness -- "part dance; part sorcery, part science" (pages 406-442)
1. Leonard Sweet, Brian D. McLaren, and Jerry Haselmayer, *A Is for Abductive*, pp. 72, 74.
2. *Insect World*, A Child's First Library of Learning, (Alexandria, VA: Time-Life Books, 1988), p. 71.
3. Fritjof Capra, *The Turning Point*, p. 92; emphasis added.
4. Fritjof Capra, *The Tao of Physics*, p. 159; emphasis added.
5. Fritjof Capra, *The Turning Point*, p. 92.
6. Ibid., p. 37.
7. Fritjof Capra, *The Tao of Physics*, pp. 146-147.
8. Ibid., pp. 154-155.
9. Ibid., p. 25.
10. Ibid., p. 114.
11. Ibid., pp. 145-146.
12. Ibid., p. 146.
13. Alice Bailey and Djwhal Khul, *The Reappearance of the Christ*, Chapter VI - The New World Religion, http://web.archive.org/web/20070218120732/laluni.helloyou.ws/netnews/bk/reappearance/reap1042.html; emphasis added.
14. Fritjof Capra, *The Tao of Physics*, p. 291.
15. Neale Donald Walsch, and "God," as quoted by Walsch, *The New Revelations*, p. 27.
16. Neale Donald Walsch, *What God Wants*, p. 87.
17. Ibid., p. 100.
18. Neale Donald Walsch, *When Everything Changes, Change Everything*, p. 197.

19. "The Book of John," *The Voice New Testament*, http://www.hearthevoice.com/pdf/Book_of_John.pdf. (The link to this download says, "Experience The Voice *Translation*" -- "The Gospel of John, The Voice Revealed," http://www.hearthevoice.com/.)
20. "God," as quoted by Neale Donald Walsch, *Conversations with God, Book 3*, pp. 180-181.
21. Neale Donald Walsch, and "God," as quoted by Walsch, *The New Revelations*, pp. 27-28.
22. Fritjof Capra, *The Turning Point*, p. 92; emphasis added.
23. "God," as quoted by Neale Donald Walsch, *Friendship with God*, p. 264; emphasis added.
24. Neale Donald Walsch, *What God Wants*, p. 210.
25. "God," as quoted by Neale Donald Walsch, *Tomorrow's God*, p. 57.
26. Leonard Sweet, *So Beautiful*, p. 249.
27. Ibid., p. 119.
28. Leonard Sweet and Frank Viola, *Jesus Manifesto*, p. 16.
29. Leonard Sweet, *Nudge*, pp. 76-77.
30. Leonard Sweet, *Quantum Spirituality*, p. 90; quoting St. Bernard of Clairvaux.
31. Leonard Sweet, *So Beautiful*, p. 64.
32. Ibid., p. 49.
33. Ibid., p. 46.
34. Leonard Sweet, *Quantum Spirituality*, p. 274.
35. Leonard Sweet, Brian D. McLaren, and Jerry Haselmayer, *A Is for Abductive*, pp. 299-300.
36. Leonard Sweet, *Nudge*, pp. 76-77; emphasis added.
37. Ibid., p. 55; emphasis added.
38. "The Great Lord Nataraja – the Hadron Collider; what do they have in common?," by Jai Sita Ram, September 29, 2008, *The Ramagiri Journal*, http://journal.ramagiri.in/archives/164#more-164.
39. Fritjof Capra, *The Tao of Physics*, p. 191.
40. Leonard Sweet, *Quantum Spirituality*, p. 70.
41. Leonard Sweet, *So Beautiful*, p. 49.
42. Leonard Sweet and Frank Viola, *Jesus Manifesto*, p. 16.
43. Leonard Sweet, *Quantum Spirituality*, p. 106; emphasis added.
44. Pierre Teilhard de Chardin, *Christianity and Evolution*, p. 56. Cited from *A "Wonderful" Deception*, by Warren B. Smith, p. 114.
45. Ursula King, *Towards A New Mysticism: Teilhard de Chardin and Eastern Religions*, p. 181.
46. Fritjof Capra, *The Tao of Physics*, p. 11.
47. Ibid.
48. "The Great Lord Nataraja – the Hadron Collider; what do they have in common?," by Jai Sita Ram, September 29, 2008, *The Ramagiri Journal*, http://journal.ramagiri.in/archives/164#more-164.
49. "Shiva's Cosmic Dance at CERN," http://www.fritjofcapra.net/shiva.html.
50. "The Great Lord Nataraja – the Hadron Collider; what do they have in common?," by Jai Sita Ram, September 29, 2008, *The Ramagiri Journal*, http://journal.ramagiri.in/archives/164#more-164. [Note: this quote from the plaque is on p. 245 of Fritjof Capra's book *The Tao of Physics*.]
51. Leonard Sweet, *Quantum Spirituality*, p. 86.
52. Leonard Sweet, Brian D. McLaren, and Jerry Haselmayer, *A Is for Abductive*, p. 300.
53. Fritjof Capra, *The Tao of Physics*, p. 191; emphasis added.
54. Ibid., pp. 89-90.
55. Ibid., p. 244.
56. Ibid.
57. Ibid., p. 87.
58. Ibid., p. 191.
59. Ibid., p. 277.
60. Ibid., p. 87.
61. Alice Bailey, *From Intellect to Intuition*, Chapter Four - The Objectives in Meditation, http://web.archive.org/web/20060209202950/laluni.helloyou.ws/netnews/bk/intellect/inte1024.html.
62. Fritjof Capra, *The Tao of Physics*, p. 154.
63. Ibid., p. 291.
64. "Tandava — Shiva's Cosmic Dance," by Atanu Dey, (said to be from Heinrich Zimmer's book, *Philosophies of India*), http://www.deeshaa.org/tandava-shivas-cosmic-dance/.
65. Neale Donald Walsch, *Happier than God: Turn Ordinary Life into an Extraordinary Experience*, pp. 159-160.
66. "The Great Lord Nataraja – the Hadron Collider; what do they have in common?," by Jai Sita Ram, September 29, 2008, *The Ramagiri Journal*, http://journal.ramagiri.in/archives/164#more-164.
67. About, http://leonardsweet.com/about.php.

68. Ursula King, *Towards A New Mysticism*, p. 181.
69. Leonard Sweet, *So Beautiful*, p. 46.
70. Fritjof Capra, *The Tao of Physics*, p. 191.
71. Leonard Sweet, *Nudge*, p. 55.
72. Ibid., pp. 76-77.
73. Leonard Sweet, *So Beautiful*, p. 64.
74. "Tandava—Shiva's Cosmic Dance," by Atanu Dey, http://www.deeshaa.org/tandava-shivas-cosmic-dance/.
75. Dictionary.com, "gyration," http://dictionary.reference.com/browse/gyration.
76. *American Dictionary of the English Language*, Noah Webster 1828, "gyration."
77. Dictionary.com, "gyrate," http://dictionary.reference.com/browse/gyrate; emphasis added.
78. Alice A. Bailey, *The Consciousness Of The Atom*, pp. 109-110.
79. Ibid., p. 20.
80. Ibid., pp. 23-24.
81. Leonard Sweet, *Nudge*, pp. 154-155.
82. Ibid., p. 158.
83. About Metaphysics, "The Next Harmonic Convergence in 2012," Ulysses Castillo, Physics Professor, April 14, 2005, http://aboutmetaphysics.blogspot.com/2005/04/next-harmonic-convergence-in-2012.html.
84. Leonard Sweet, *Quantum Spirituality*, p. 49.
85. "Tandava—Shiva's Cosmic Dance," by Atanu Dey, http://www.deeshaa.org/tandava-shivas-cosmic-dance/.
86. Leonard Sweet, *Quantum Spirituality*, p. 85; emphasis added.
87. Ibid.; emphasis added.
88. Leonard Sweet, *So Beautiful*, p. 49; emphasis added.
89. Leonard Sweet, *Quantum Spirituality*, p. 162; emphasis added.
90. "Tandava—Shiva's Cosmic Dance," by Atanu Dey, http://www.deeshaa.org/tandava-shivas-cosmic-dance/.
91. Neale Donald Walsch, *What God Wants*, p. 210.
92. Fritjof Capra, *The Tao of Physics*, pp. 242-243.
93. Fritjof Capra, *The Turning Point*, p. 92.
94. Fritjof Capra, *The Tao of Physics*, p. 329.
95. Neale Donald Walsch, *What God Wants*, p. 172.
96. "God," as quoted by Neale Donald Walsch, *Conversations with God, Book 3*, pp. 344-345.
97. Neale Donald Walsch, *When Everything Changes, Change Everything*, p. 197.
98. "God," as quoted by Neale Donald Walsch, *Conversations with God, Book 3*, p. 55.
99. Alice Bailey and Djwhal Khul, *A Treatise on Cosmic Fire*, Section Two - Thought Elementals and Fire Elementals, http://web.archive.org/web/20051123102546/laluni.helloyou.ws/netnews/bk/fire/fire1380.html.
100. Leonard Sweet, *Quantum Spirituality*, pp. 253-254.
101. Alice Bailey and Djwhal Khul, *A Treatise on Cosmic Fire*, Section Two - Thought Elementals and Fire Elementals, http://web.archive.org/web/20070323182943/laluni.helloyou.ws/netnews/bk/fire/fire1337.html.
102. Glossary, Self-Realization Fellowship, http://www.yogananda.com.au/g/g_self-realization.html.
103. "Kundalini Awakening," Paramahansa Yogananda, Self-Realization Fellowship, http://www.yogananda.com.au/sc14_kundalini1.html; parentheses in the original; bold added.
104. Alice Bailey and Djwhal Khul, *A Treatise on Cosmic Fire*, Section Two - Thought Elementals and Fire Elementals, http://web.archive.org/web/20060213193716/laluni.helloyou.ws/netnews/bk/fire/fire1381.html; emphasis added.
105. Alice Bailey and Djwhal Khul, *Discipleship in the New Age II*, Teachings on Initiation - Part II, http://web.archive.org/web/20060206233929/laluni.helloyou.ws/netnews/bk/discipleship2/disc2085.html.
106. Alice Bailey and Djwhal Khul, *A Treatise on White Magic*, Rule Six - The Work of the Eye, http://web.archive.org/web/20060209210344/laluni.helloyou.ws/netnews/bk/magic/magi1090.html; emphasis added, except italics to *It is the eye of vision* and *It has a destructive aspect*.
107. Alice A. Bailey, *The Consciousness Of The Atom*, p. 66.
108. Alice Bailey and Djwhal Khul, *Esoteric Psychology II*, Chapter II - The Ray of Personality, The Coordination of the Personality, http://web.archive.org/web/20070218120604/http://laluni.helloyou.ws/netnews/bk/psychology2/psyc2149.html.
109. Fritjof Capra, *The Tao of Physics*, p. 331.
110. About, Nonduality, Science and Nonduality (SAND), http://scienceandnonduality.com/nonduality.shtml.
111. "God," as quoted by Neale Donald Walsch, *Conversations with God, Book 1*, pp. 22-24.
112. Neale Donald Walsch, *When Everything Changes, Change Everything*, p. 198.
113. Ibid., p. 197.
114. William P. Young, *The Shack*, p. 112; emphasis added.
115. Ibid., p. 95; emphasis added.
116. Ibid., p. 207.

117. Appropriately enough, the name "Sarayu" just so happens to be from *India*. This *Sanskrit* word means "air, wind,"[a] and is also said to mean "moving fast."[b] A very fitting choice for this *false* "Spirit."

   [a] *Monier Williams Sanskrit-English Dictionary*, p. 1182, "Sarayu," page posted online at http://www.sanskrit-lexicon.uni-koeln.de/cgi-bin/monier/serveimg.pl?file=/scans/MWScan/MWScanjpg/mw1182-sayoni.jpg. This online page is a link from the search results for "sarayu" at http://www.sanskrit-lexicon.uni-koeln.de/monier/indexcaller.php. [Note: this search must be in lower case for the term results to come up.]

   [b] See Behind the Name, http://www.behindthename.com/bb/fact/7327 and Babynology, http://www.babynology.com/meaning-sarayu-f55.html.

118. William P. Young, *The Shack*, p. 207.
119. Ibid.
120. Ibid., p. 209.
121. Ibid.
122. Alice Bailey and Djwhal Khul, *The Rays and the Initiations*, Part I - Fourteen Rules for Group Initiation, Rule Fourteen, http://web.archive.org/web/20060213230403/laluni.helloyou.ws/netnews/bk/rays/rays1111.html.
123. Alice Bailey, *From Intellect to Intuition*, Chapter Three - The Nature of the Soul, http://web.archive.org/web/20070327142259/laluni.helloyou.ws/netnews/bk/intellect/inte1017.html.
124. William P. Young, *The Shack*, pp. 209-210.
125. Ibid., p. 210.
126. Ibid.
127. Ibid., p. 211.
128. Ibid., pp. 212-213.
129. Ibid., p. 211.
130. "God," as quoted by Neale Donald Walsch, *Conversations with God, Book 3*, p. 349.
131. "God," as quoted by Neale Donald Walsch, *Communion with God*, pp. 90-91.
132. William P. Young, *The Shack*, p. 122.
133. Ibid., p. 145.
134. Ibid., p. 122.
135. Ibid., p. 146.
136. Neale Donald Walsch, *What God Wants*, p. 221; emphasis added.
137. Ibid., p. 206.
138. Alice Bailey and Djwhal Khul, *Esoteric Psychology II*, Chapter I - The Egoic Ray, The Seven Laws of Soul or Group Life, http://web.archive.org/web/20070219003559/http://laluni.helloyou.ws/netnews/bk/psychology2/psyc2040.html.
139. "God," as quoted by Neale Donald Walsch, *Friendship with God*, p. 24.
140. "God," as quoted by Neale Donald Walsch, *Conversations with God, Book 1*, p. 39.
141. "God," as quoted by Neale Donald Walsch, *Conversations with God, Book 3*, p. 146.
142. "God," as quoted by Neale Donald Walsch, *Tomorrow's God*, p. 196.
143. Brian D. McLaren, *A New Kind of Christianity*, pp. 215-216; and p. 195 for bracketed information.
144. Leonard Sweet, Brian D. McLaren, and Jerry Haselmayer, *A Is for Abductive*, pp. 303, 306.
145. Neale Donald Walsch, *What God Wants*, p. 114.
146. Neale Donald Walsch, *Happier than God*, p. 160.
147. "God," as quoted by Neale Donald Walsch, *Conversations with God, Book 1*, p. 55.
148. Alice A. Bailey, *The Consciousness Of The Atom*, p. 134.
149. Ibid., pp. 109-110.
150. Leonard Sweet, *Nudge*, p. 45.
151. Alice A. Bailey, *The Consciousness Of The Atom*, p. 107.
152. Ibid., pp. 131-132.
153. Alice Bailey, *From Intellect to Intuition*, Chapter Eight - The Universality of Meditation, http://web.archive.org/web/20070327142351/laluni.helloyou.ws/netnews/bk/intellect/inte1055.html.
154. Leonard Sweet, *Quantum Spirituality*, pp. 296-297.
155. Ibid., p. 76.
156. Leonard Sweet, Brian D. McLaren, and Jerry Haselmayer, *A Is for Abductive*, pp. 201-202.
157. Leonard Sweet, *Nudge*, p. 305, #40.
158. Brian McLaren on *The Voice*, transcribed from the video posted on YouTube at http://www.youtube.com/watch?v=deeWA_UBg2A&feature=related.
159. Leonard Sweet, *Quantum Spirituality*, p. 239.
160. Leonard Sweet, Brian D. McLaren, and Jerry Haselmayer, *A Is for Abductive*, pp. 299-300.
161. Brian D. McLaren, *A New Kind of Christianity*, p. 216.
162. Ibid., p. 99.

163. Leonard Sweet, *Quantum Spirituality*, p. 80; emphasis added.
164. Integral Enlightenment Presents Awakening The Impulse To Evolve, The Birth of Evolutionary Spirituality, http://evolutionaryspirituality.com/. See also Calendar, Center for the Story of the Universe, http://www.brianswimme.org/calendar/index.asp.
165. Ibid., (http://evolutionaryspirituality.com/).
166. Ibid.
167. Integral Enlightenment Presents Awakening The Impulse To Evolve, The Birth of Evolutionary Spirituality, "Reinventing the World, Creating a New Cosmic Culture," A Free Online Teleseminar Featuring Brian Swimme, http://evolutionaryspirituality.com/people/brian-swimme.php.
168. Integral Enlightenment Presents Awakening The Impulse To Evolve, The Birth of Evolutionary Spirituality, "Impulse of Evolution, A Radical Path to the Future," A Free Online Teleseminar Featuring Barbara Marx Hubbard, http://evolutionaryspirituality.com/people/barbara-marx-hubbard.php.
169. "The Great Confluence, The Emergent New Apostolic Reformation Flowing into the New Age," June 5, 2010, Herescope, http://herescope.blogspot.com/2010/06/great-confluence.html.
170. WorldFuture 2008, "Seeing the Future Through New Eyes," The Annual Conference of the World Future Society, July 26-28, 2008, Washington, D.C., Preliminary Program, http://www.wfs.org/March-April08/WF2008_preliminary.pdf, p. 23. See also "Brian McLaren to speak at World Future Society," March 24, 2008, Herescope, http://herescope.blogspot.com/2008_03_01_archive.html.
171. Leonard Sweet, *So Beautiful*, p. 20; emphasis added.
172. Cell biologist Bruce Lipton, as quoted from his book *Spontaneous Evolution: Our Positive Future (and a Way to Get There from Here)*, in the article "Re-writing the Story of Who We Are" by Lisa Reagan, *Noetic Now*, Issue Three, October 2010, Institute of Noetic Sciences, http://www.noetic.org/noetic/issue-three-october/re-writing-the-story-of-who-we-are/; emphasis added.
173. Fritjof Capra, *The Turning Point*, p. 418; emphasis added.
174. "No One Believes In Me Anymore (Satan's Boast)," Keith and Melody Green, © 1977, April Music, Inc.

BIBLIOGRAPHY

Ardagh, Arjuna. *Awakening into Oneness: The Power of Blessing in the Evolution of Consciousness.* Boulder, CO: Sounds True, Inc., 2007, 2009.

Ardagh, Arjuna. *The Translucent Revolution: How People Just Like You Are WAKING UP and CHANGING the World.* Novato, CA: New World Library, 2005.

Bailey, Alice A. *The Consciousness Of The Atom.* New York, NY: Lucis Publishing Company, 1961. First Printing 1922, Ninth Printing 1974.

Beliefnet editors. *From the Ashes: A Call to Action—The Spiritual Challenge.* USA: Rodale Inc., 2001.

Bell, Rob. *Love Wins: A Book About Heaven, Hell, and the Fate of Every Person Who Ever Lived.* New York, NY: HarperOne, 2011.

Bell, Rob. *Velvet Elvis: Repainting the Christian Faith.* Grand Rapids, MI: Zondervan, 2005.

Borg, Marcus J. *Reading the Bible Again for the First Time: Taking the Bible Seriously but Not Literally.* New York, NY: HarperOne, 2001.

Borg, Marcus J. *The God We Never Knew: Beyond Dogmatic Religion to a More Authentic Contemporary Faith.* New York, NY: HarperSanFrancisco, 1997.

Braden, Gregg. *Fractal Time: The Secret of 2012 and a New World Age.* Carlsbad, CA: Hay House, Inc., 2009.

Capra, Fritjof, David Steindl-Rast, and Thomas Matus. *Belonging to the Universe: Explorations on the Frontiers of Science and Spirituality.* New York, NY: HarperCollins Publishers, 1991.

Capra, Fritjof. *The Tao of Physics: An Exploration of the Parallels between Modern Physics and Eastern Mysticism.* Third Edition, Updated. Boston, MA: Shambhala Publications, Inc., 1975, 1983, 1991.

Capra, Fritjof. *The Turning Point: Science, Society, and the Rising Culture.* Bantam Edition, 1983. New York, NY: Bantam Books, 1982.

Chevalier, Jean, and Alain Gheerbrant. Trans. John Buchanan-Brown. *The Penguin Dictionary of Symbols.* London, England: Penguin Books, 1996. First published in France 1969.

Claiborne, Shane. *The Irresistible Revolution: Living as an Ordinary Radical.* Grand Rapids, MI: Zondervan, 2006.

Douglas, J. D., and Merrill C. Tenney, editors. Revised by Moisés Silva. *Zondervan Illustrated Bible Dictionary.* Grand Rapids, MI: Zondervan, 1987, 2011.

Dowd, Michael. *Thank God for Evolution: How the Marriage of Science and Religion Will Transform Your Life and Our World.* New York, NY: Penguin Group, 2007.

Easum, William M., and Thomas G. Bandy. *Growing Spiritual Redwoods.* Nashville, TN: Abingdon Press, 1997.

Ferguson, Marilyn. *Aquarius Now: Radical Common Sense and Reclaiming Our Personal Sovereignty.* Boston, MA: Red Wheel/Weiser, LLC, 2005.

Ferguson, Marilyn. *The Aquarian Conspiracy: Personal and Social Transformation in the 1980s.* Los Angeles, CA: J. P. Tarcher, Inc., 1980.

Foster, Richard J. *Celebration of Discipline: The Path to Spiritual Growth*. New York, NY: HarperCollins Publishers, 1978, 1988, 1998.

Foster, Richard J. *Sanctuary of the Soul: Journey into Meditative Prayer*. Downers Grove, IL: InterVarsity Press, 2011.

Fox, Matthew. *The Coming of the Cosmic Christ: The Healing of Mother Earth and the Birth of a Global Renaissance*. San Francisco, CA: Harper & Row Publishers, 1988.

Hartzell, Tamara. *In the Name of Purpose: Sacrificing Truth on the Altar of Unity*. Philadelphia, PA: Xlibris Corporation, 2007. [Note: this book is also posted online as a free e-book, 2006, <http://www.inthenameofpurpose.org/inthename.pdf>.]

Horn, Thomas, and Chuck Missler, et al. *God's Ghostbusters: Vampires? Ghosts? Aliens? Werewolves? Creatures of the Night Beware!* Crane, MO: Defender, 2011.

Hubbard, Barbara Marx. *Birth 2012 and Beyond: Humanity's Great Shift to the Age of Conscious Evolution*. Shift Books, 2012.

Hubbard, Barbara Marx. *The Revelation: A Message of Hope for the New Millennium*. Second Edition. Mill Valley, CA: Nataraj Publishing, 1995.

Jones, E. Stanley. *The Christ of the Indian Road*. Lucknow, India: Lucknow Publishing House, 1925.

Kidd, Sue Monk. *The Dance of the Dissident Daughter: A Woman's Journey from Christian Tradition to the Sacred Feminine*. New York, NY: HarperCollins Publishers Inc., 1996.

King, Ursula. *Towards A New Mysticism: Teilhard de Chardin and Eastern Religions*. New York, NY: The Seabury Press, 1980.

Kissick, John. *Art: Context and Criticism*. Second Edition. Boston, MA: The McGraw-Hill Companies, Inc., 1996, 1993.

McLaren, Brian D. *A New Kind of Christianity: Ten Questions That Are Transforming the Faith*. New York, NY: HarperCollins Publishers, 2010.

McLaren, Brian D. *Everything Must Change: Jesus, Global Crises, and a Revolution of Hope*. Nashville, TN: Thomas Nelson, 2007.

McLaren, Brian D. *Why Did Jesus, Moses, the Buddha, and Mohammed Cross the Road?: Christian Identity in a Multi-faith World*. New York, NY: Jericho Books, 2012.

Missler, Chuck. *Cosmic Codes: Hidden Messages From the Edge of Eternity*. Coeur d' Alene, ID: Koinonia House, 1999, 2004.

Peck, M. Scott. *The Different Drum: Community Making and Peace*. New York, NY: Simon & Schuster, Inc.: 1987.

Peck, M. Scott. *The Road Less Traveled*. New York, NY: Simon & Schuster, Inc.: 1978.

Perlmutter, M.D., F.A.C.N., David, and Alberto Villoldo, Ph.D. *Power Up Your Brain: The Neuroscience of Enlightenment*. New York, NY: Hay House, Inc., 2011.

Smith, Warren B. *A "Wonderful" Deception: The Further New Age Implications of the Emerging Purpose Driven Movement*. Magalia, CA: Mountain Stream Press, 2011.

Smith, Warren (B). *Deceived on Purpose: The New Age Implications of the Purpose-Driven Church*. Second Edition. Magalia, CA: Mountain Stream Press, 2004.

Smith, Warren B. *False Christ Coming – Does Anybody Care?: What New Age leaders really have in store for America, the church, and the world*. Magalia, CA: Mountain Stream Press, 2011.

Smith, Warren (B). *Reinventing Jesus Christ: The New Gospel*. Ravenna, OH: Conscience Press, 2002.

Strong, LL.D., S.T.D., James. *The New Strong's Exhaustive Concordance of the Bible*. Nashville, TN: Thomas Nelson Publishers, 1990.

Sweet, Leonard, and Frank Viola. *Jesus Manifesto: Restoring the Supremacy and Sovereignty of Jesus Christ*. Nashville, TN: Thomas Nelson, 2010.

Sweet, Leonard, and Lori Wagner. *The Seraph Seal*. Nashville, TN: Thomas Nelson, 2011.

Sweet, Leonard. *AquaChurch 2.0: Piloting Your Church in Today's Fluid Culture*. Second Edition, 2008. Colorado Springs, CO: David C. Cook, 1999.

Sweet, Leonard, Brian D. McLaren, and Jerry Haselmayer. *A Is for Abductive: The Language of the Emerging Church*. Grand Rapids, MI: Zondervan, 2003.

Sweet, Leonard. *I Am a Follower: The Way, Truth, and Life of Following Jesus*. Nashville, TN: Thomas Nelson, 2012.

Sweet, Leonard. *Nudge: Awakening Each Other to the God Who's Already There*. Colorado Springs, CO: David C. Cook, 2010.

Sweet, Leonard. *Quantum Spirituality: A Postmodern Apologetic*. Dayton, OH: Whaleprints for SpiritVenture Ministries, Inc., 1991, 1994.

Sweet, Leonard. *So Beautiful: Divine Design for Life and the Church*. Colorado Springs, CO: David C. Cook, 2009.

Sweet, Leonard. *SoulTsunami: Sink or Swim in New Millennium Culture*. Grand Rapids, MI: Zondervan, 1999.

Teilhard de Chardin, Pierre. *The Future of Man*, English trans. by HarperCollins. First Image Books Edition. New York, NY: DoubleDay, 1959, 1964.

Teilhard de Chardin, Pierre. *The Phenomenon of Man*. English trans. by Bernard Wall. New York, NY: Harper & Row Publishers Inc., 1959. Perennial, 2002, HarperCollins Publishers Inc.

The Voice New Testament. Nashville, TN: Thomas Nelson, 2008.

Walsch, Neale Donald. *Communion with God*. New York, NY: Berkley Books, 2000.

Walsch, Neale Donald. *Conversations with God: an uncommon dialogue, Book 1*. New York, NY: G. P. Putnam's Sons, 1996.

Walsch, Neale Donald. *Conversations with God: an uncommon dialogue, Book 2*. Charlottesville, VA: Hampton Roads Publishing Company, Inc., 1997.

Walsch, Neale Donald. *Conversations with God: an uncommon dialogue, Book 3*. Charlottesville, VA: Hampton Roads Publishing Company, Inc., 1998.

Walsch, Neale Donald. *Friendship with God: an uncommon dialogue*. New York, NY: The Berkley Publishing Group, 1999.

Walsch, Neale Donald. *Happier than God: Turn Ordinary Life into an Extraordinary Experience*. Charlottesville, VA: Hampton Roads Publishing Company, Inc., 2008.

Walsch, Neale Donald. *The Mother of Invention: The Legacy of Barbara Marx Hubbard and the Future of YOU*. Carlsbad, CA: Hay House, Inc., 2011.

Walsch, Neale Donald. *The New Revelations: A Conversation with God*. New York, NY: Atria Books, 2002.

Walsch, Neale Donald. *Tomorrow's God: Our Greatest Spiritual Challenge.* New York, NY: Atria Books, 2004.

Walsch, Neale Donald. *What God Wants: A Compelling Answer to Humanity's Biggest Question.* New York, NY: Atria Books, 2005.

Walsch, Neale Donald. *When Everything Changes, Change Everything: In a Time of Turmoil, a Pathway to Peace.* Charlottesville, VA: Hampton Roads Publishing Company, Inc., 2009.

Warren, Rick. *The Purpose Driven Life: What on Earth Am I Here For?* Grand Rapids, MI: Zondervan, 2002.

Webster, Noah. *American Dictionary of the English Language.* 1828. San Francisco, CA: Foundation for American Christian Education, 1967 & 1995.

Webster's New World Dictionary of the American Language. Second College Edition. New York, NY: Simon & Schuster, Inc., 1970, 1984.

Young, Sarah. *Jesus Calling: Enjoying Peace in His Presence.* Nashville, TN: Thomas Nelson, Inc., 2004.

Young, William P. *The Shack: Where Tragedy Confronts Eternity.* Newbury Park, CA: Windblown Media, 2007.

Young, Wm Paul. *Cross Roads.* Great Britain: Hodder & Stoughton Ltd, 2012. Published in association with FaithWords, New York, NY.

Yungen, Ray. *A Time of Departing: How Ancient Mystical Practices are Uniting Christians with the World's Religions.* Second Edition. Silverton, OR: Lighthouse Trails Publishing Company, 2002, 2006.

Books online:

Bailey, Alice, and Djwhal Khul. *A Treatise on Cosmic Fire.* Lucis Trust, 1925. Caux, Switzerland: Netnews Association and/or its suppliers, 2002. Courtesy of Netnews Association, <http://www.netnews.org>. Archived at <http://web.archive.org/web/20050726004029/http://laluni.helloyou.ws/netnews/bk/toc.html>.

Bailey, Alice, and Djwhal Khul. *A Treatise on White Magic.* Lucis Trust, 1934. Caux, Switzerland: Netnews Association and/or its suppliers, 2002. Courtesy of Netnews Association, <http://www.netnews.org>. Archived at <http://web.archive.org/web/20050726004029/http://laluni.helloyou.ws/netnews/bk/toc.html>.

Bailey, Alice, and Djwhal Khul. *Discipleship in the New Age.* Volume I. Lucis Trust, 1944. Caux, Switzerland: Netnews Association and/or its suppliers, 2002. Courtesy of Netnews Association, <http://www.netnews.org>. Archived at <http://web.archive.org/web/20050726004029/http://laluni.helloyou.ws/netnews/bk/toc.html>.

Bailey, Alice, and Djwhal Khul. *Discipleship in the New Age.* Volume II. Lucis Trust, 1955. Caux, Switzerland: Netnews Association and/or its suppliers, 2002. Courtesy of Netnews Association, <http://www.netnews.org>. Archived at <http://web.archive.org/web/20050726004029/http://laluni.helloyou.ws/netnews/bk/toc.html>.

Bailey, Alice, and Djwhal Khul. *Education in the New Age.* Lucis Trust, 1954. Caux, Switzerland: Netnews Association and/or its suppliers, 2002. Courtesy of Netnews Association, <http://www.netnews.org>. Archived at <http://web.archive.org/web/20050726004029/http://laluni.helloyou.ws/netnews/bk/toc.html>.

Bailey, Alice, and Djwhal Khul. *Esoteric Healing.* Lucis Trust, 1953. Caux, Switzerland: Netnews Association and/or its suppliers, 2002. Courtesy of Netnews Association, <http://www.netnews.org>. Archived at <http://web.archive.org/web/20050726004029/http://laluni.helloyou.ws/netnews/bk/toc.html>.

Bailey, Alice, and Djwhal Khul. *Esoteric Psychology II.* Lucis Trust, 1942. Caux, Switzerland: Netnews Association and/or its suppliers, 2002. Courtesy of Netnews Association, <http://www.netnews.org>. Archived at <http://web.archive.org/web/20050726004029/http://laluni.helloyou.ws/netnews/bk/toc.html>.

Bailey, Alice, and Djwhal Khul. *Glamor - A World Problem.* Lucis Trust, 1950. Caux, Switzerland: Netnews Association and/or its suppliers, 2002. Courtesy of Netnews Association, <http://www.netnews.org>. Archived at <http://web.archive.org/web/20050726004029/http://laluni.helloyou.ws/netnews/bk/toc.html>.

Bailey, Alice, and Djwhal Khul. *Initiation, Human and Solar.* Glossary S-Z. Lucis Trust, 1922. Caux, Switzerland: Netnews Association and/or its suppliers, 2002. Courtesy of Netnews Association, <http://www.netnews.org>. Archived at <http://web.archive.org/web/20050726004029/http://laluni.helloyou.ws/netnews/bk/toc.html>.

Bailey, Alice, and Djwhal Khul. *Letters on Occult Meditation.* Lucis Trust, 1922. Caux, Switzerland: Netnews Association and/or its suppliers, 2002. Courtesy of Netnews Association, <http://www.netnews.org>. Archived at <http://web.archive.org/web/20050726004029/http://laluni.helloyou.ws/netnews/bk/toc.html>.

Bailey, Alice, and Djwhal Khul. *Problems of Humanity.* Lucis Trust, 1947. Caux, Switzerland: Netnews Association and/or its suppliers, 2002. Courtesy of Netnews Association, <http://www.netnews.org>. Archived at <http://web.archive.org/web/20050726004029/http://laluni.helloyou.ws/netnews/bk/toc.html>.

Bailey, Alice, and Djwhal Khul. *Telepathy and the Etheric Vehicle.* Lucis Trust, 1950. Caux, Switzerland: Netnews Association and/or its suppliers, 2002. Courtesy of Netnews Association, <http://www.netnews.org>. Archived at <http://web.archive.org/web/20050726004029/http://laluni.helloyou.ws/netnews/bk/toc.html>.

Bailey, Alice, and Djwhal Khul. *The Externalization of the Hierarchy.* Lucis Trust, 1957. Caux, Switzerland: Netnews Association and/or its suppliers, 2002. Courtesy of Netnews Association, <http://www.netnews.org>. Archived at <http://web.archive.org/web/20050726004029/http://laluni.helloyou.ws/netnews/bk/toc.html>.

Bailey, Alice, and Djwhal Khul. *The Labors of Hercules.* Lucis Trust, 1974. Caux, Switzerland: Netnews Association and/or its suppliers, 2002. Courtesy of Netnews Association, <http://www.netnews.org>. Archived at <http://web.archive.org/web/20050726004029/http://laluni.helloyou.ws/netnews/bk/toc.html>.

Bailey, Alice, and Djwhal Khul. *The Rays and the Initiations.* Lucis Trust, 1960. Caux, Switzerland: Netnews Association and/or its suppliers, 2002. Courtesy of Netnews Association, <http://www.netnews.org>. Archived at <http://web.archive.org/web/20050726004029/http://laluni.helloyou.ws/netnews/bk/toc.html>.

Bailey, Alice, and Djwhal Khul. *The Reappearance of the Christ.* Lucis Trust, 1948. Caux, Switzerland: Netnews Association and/or its suppliers, 2002. Courtesy of Netnews Association, <http://www.netnews.org>. Archived at <http://web.archive.org/web/20050726004029/http://laluni.helloyou.ws/netnews/bk/toc.html>.

Bailey, Alice, and Djwhal Khul. *The Yoga Sutras of Patanjali*. Lucis Trust, 1927. Caux, Switzerland: Netnews Association and/or its suppliers, 2002. Courtesy of Netnews Association, <http://www.netnews.org>. Archived at <http://web.archive.org/web/20050726004029/http://laluni.helloyou.ws/netnews/bk/toc.html>.

Bailey, Alice. *From Bethlehem to Calvary*. Lucis Trust, 1937. Caux, Switzerland: Netnews Association and/or its suppliers, 2002. Courtesy of Netnews Association, <http://www.netnews.org>. Archived at <http://web.archive.org/web/20050726004029/http://laluni.helloyou.ws/netnews/bk/toc.html>.

Bailey, Alice. *From Intellect to Intuition*. Lucis Trust, 1932. Caux, Switzerland: Netnews Association and/or its suppliers, 2002. Courtesy of Netnews Association, <http://www.netnews.org>. Archived at <http://web.archive.org/web/20050726004029/http://laluni.helloyou.ws/netnews/bk/toc.html>.

Bailey, Alice. *The Soul and its Mechanism*. Lucis Trust, 1930. Caux, Switzerland: Netnews Association and/or its suppliers, 2002. Courtesy of Netnews Association, <http://www.netnews.org>. Archived at <http://web.archive.org/web/20050726004029/http://laluni.helloyou.ws/netnews/bk/toc.html>.

Bailey, Alice. *The Unfinished Autobiography*. Lucis Trust, 1951. Caux, Switzerland: Netnews Association and/or its suppliers, 2002. Courtesy of Netnews Association, <http://www.netnews.org>. Archived at <http://web.archive.org/web/20050726004029/http://laluni.helloyou.ws/netnews/bk/toc.html>.

Blavatsky, Helena P. *The Secret Doctrine: The Synthesis of Science, Religion, and Philosophy*. Volumes I & II. London: The Theosophical Publishing Company, Limited, 1888. Courtesy of Theosophy Library Online, <http://theosophy.org/Blavatsky/Secret%20Doctrine/SD-I/SD Volume I.htm> & <http://theosophy.org/Blavatsky/Secret%20Doctrine/SD-II/SDVolume 2.htm>.

Schucman, Helen. *A Course in Miracles*. Foundation for Inner Peace, 1976. Courtesy of Circle of Atonement, <http://www.circleofa.org/a-course-in-miracles/>.

Three Initiates, *The Kybalion: Hermetic Philosophy*. Chicago, IL: Yogi Publication Society, 1912, 1940. Courtesy of The Kybalion Resource Page, <http://www.kybalion.org/>.

Made in the USA
Lexington, KY
15 September 2018